Applications of Computer Vision, 2nd Edition

Applications of Computer Vision, 2nd Edition

Guest Editor

Eva Cernadas

Basel • Beijing • Wuhan • Barcelona • Belgrade • Novi Sad • Cluj • Manchester

Guest Editor
Eva Cernadas
CiTIUS (Singular Research
Center on Intelligent
Technologies)
University of Santiago de
Compostela
Santiago de Compostela
Spain

Editorial Office
MDPI AG
Grosspeteranlage 5
4052 Basel, Switzerland

This is a reprint of the Special Issue, published open access by the journal *Electronics* (ISSN 2079-9292), freely accessible at: https://www.mdpi.com/journal/electronics/special_issues/EE3574H9IH.

For citation purposes, cite each article independently as indicated on the article page online and as indicated below:

Lastname, A.A.; Lastname, B.B. Article Title. *Journal Name* **Year**, *Volume Number*, Page Range.

ISBN 978-3-7258-3867-7 (Hbk)
ISBN 978-3-7258-3868-4 (PDF)
https://doi.org/10.3390/books978-3-7258-3868-4

© 2025 by the authors. Articles in this book are Open Access and distributed under the Creative Commons Attribution (CC BY) license. The book as a whole is distributed by MDPI under the terms and conditions of the Creative Commons Attribution-NonCommercial-NoDerivs (CC BY-NC-ND) license (https://creativecommons.org/licenses/by-nc-nd/4.0/).

Contents

About the Editor vii

Preface ix

Eva Cernadas
Applications of Computer Vision, 2nd Edition
Reprinted from: *Electronics* 2024, *13*, 3779, https://doi.org/10.3390/electronics13183779 1

Jie Qin, Weihua Yu, Xiaoxi Feng, Zuqiang Meng and Chaohong Tan
A UAV Aerial Image Target Detection Algorithm Based on YOLOv7 Improved Model
Reprinted from: *Electronics* 2024, *13*, 3277, https://doi.org/10.3390/electronics13163277 11

Ke Wang, Hao Zhou, Hao Wu and Guowu Yuan
RN-YOLO: A Small Target Detection Model for Aerial Remote-Sensing Images
Reprinted from: *Electronics* 2024, *13*, 2383, https://doi.org/10.3390/electronics13122383 26

Yueming Huang, Chenrui Ma, Hao Zhou, Hao Wu and Guowu Yuan
Dense Object Detection Based on De-Homogenized Queries
Reprinted from: *Electronics* 2024, *13*, 2312, https://doi.org/10.3390/electronics13122312 41

Minling Zhu and En Kong
Multi-Scale Fusion Uncrewed Aerial Vehicle Detection Based on RT-DETR
Reprinted from: *Electronics* 2024, *13*, 1489, https://doi.org/10.3390/electronics13081489 59

Guang Zeng, Zhizhou Wu, Lipeng Xu and Yunyi Liang
Efficient Vision Transformer YOLOv5 for Accurate and Fast Traffic Sign Detection
Reprinted from: *Electronics* 2024, *13*, 880, https://doi.org/10.3390/electronics13050880 79

Junying Gan, Heng Luo, Junling Xiong, Xiaoshan Xie, Huicong Li and Jianqiang Liu
Facial Beauty Prediction Combined with Multi-Task Learning of Adaptive Sharing Policy and
Attentional Feature Fusion
Reprinted from: *Electronics* 2023, *13*, 179, https://doi.org/10.3390/electronics13010179 100

Zhihe Wu, Zhi Jin and Xiying Li
Two-Stage Progressive Learning for Vehicle Re-Identification in Variable Illumination
Conditions
Reprinted from: *Electronics* 2023, *12*, 4950, https://doi.org/10.3390/electronics12244950 117

Yongqiang Chen, Weifeng Liu and Chenglin Wen
DBENet: Dual-Branch Brightness Enhancement Fusion Network for Low-Light Image
Enhancement
Reprinted from: *Electronics* 2023, *12*, 3907, https://doi.org/10.3390/electronics12183907 134

Zhimin Yu, Fang Wan, Guangbo Lei, Ying Xiong, Li Xu, Zhiwei Ye, et al.
RSLC-Deeplab: A Ground Object Classification Method for High-Resolution Remote Sensing
Images
Reprinted from: *Electronics* 2023, *12*, 3653, https://doi.org/10.3390/electronics12173653 148

Ning Gan, Fang Wan, Guangbo Lei, Li Xu, Chengzhi Xu, Ying Xiong and Wen Zhou
YOLO-CID: Improved YOLOv7 for X-ray Contraband Image Detection
Reprinted from: *Electronics* 2023, *12*, 3636, https://doi.org/10.3390/electronics12173636 164

Jiaqi Liu, Kwok Tai Chui and Lap-Kei Lee
Enhancing the Accuracy of an Image Classification Model Using Cross-Modality Transfer Learning
Reprinted from: *Electronics* **2023**, *12*, 3316, https://doi.org/10.3390/electronics12153316 . . . . . **182**

Jiajia Liu, Jiapeng Zhang, Zhongli Ma, Hangtian Zhang and Shun Zhang
Three-Dimensional Measurement of Full Profile of Steel Rail Cross-Section Based on Line-Structured Light
Reprinted from: *Electronics* **2023**, *12*, 3194, https://doi.org/10.3390/electronics12143194 . . . . . **208**

Jiajia Liu, Shun Zhang, Zhongli Ma, Yuehan Zeng and Xueyin Liu
A Workpiece-Dense Scene Object Detection Method Based on Improved YOLOv5
Reprinted from: *Electronics* **2023**, *12*, 2966, https://doi.org/10.3390/electronics12132966 . . . . . **224**

Yiming Li, Lixin He, Min Zhang, Zhi Cheng, Wangwei Liu and Zijun Wu
Improving the Performance of the Single Shot Multibox Detector for Steel Surface Defects with Context Fusion and Feature Refinement
Reprinted from: *Electronics* **2023**, *12*, 2440, https://doi.org/10.3390/electronics12112440 . . . . . **241**

Qi Hu, Lin Li, Jin Duan, Meiling Gao, Gaotian Liu, Zhiyuan Wang and Dandan Huang
Object Detection Algorithm of UAV Aerial Photography Image Based on Anchor-Free Algorithms
Reprinted from: *Electronics* **2023**, *12*, 1339, https://doi.org/10.3390/electronics12061339 . . . . . **259**

Lei Shao, Han Wu, Chao Li and Ji Li
A Vehicle Recognition Model Based on Improved YOLOv5
Reprinted from: *Electronics* **2023**, *12*, 1323, https://doi.org/10.3390/electronics12061323 . . . . . **273**

Nan Xiang, Zehao Gong, Yi Xu and Lili Xiong
Material-Aware Path Aggregation Network and Shape Decoupled SIoU for X-ray Contraband Detection
Reprinted from: *Electronics* **2023**, *12*, 1179, https://doi.org/10.3390/electronics12051179 . . . . . **287**

Rongjun Chen, Weijie Li, Kailin Lan, Jinghui Xiao, Leijun Wang and Xu Lu
Fast Adaptive Binarization of QR Code Images for Automatic Sorting in Logistics Systems
Reprinted from: *Electronics* **2023**, *12*, 286, https://doi.org/10.3390/electronics12020286 . . . . . **304**

Andrew Sumsion, Shad Torrie, Dah-Jye Lee and Zheng Sun
Surveying Racial Bias in Facial Recognition: Balancing Datasets and Algorithmic Enhancements
Reprinted from: *Electronics* **2024**, *13*, 2317, https://doi.org/10.3390/electronics13122317 . . . . . **319**

About the Editor

Eva Cernadas

Eva Cernadas is a Professor of Artificial Intelligence (AI) at the University of Santiago de Compostela (USC), a Senior Researcher at the Singular Research Center of Intelligent Technology (CiTIUS) at the USC, and a member of CIFEX (Interdisciplinary Center for Feminist Research and Gender Studies) at the USC. Her scientific career in computer vision and artificial intelligence started 28 years ago, when she received her PhD from the USC in 1997. Her present research activity focuses on the development of new image analysis and machine learning algorithms and their application in the fields of food technology, marine resource management, or medicine, participating in the development of several publicly available software in these fields. For example, MarblingPredictor is to predict the marbling of dry-cured ham slices; CystAnalyser for the automatic detection and quantification of cysts in polycystic kidney and liver disease and other cystic disorders from histological images; STERapp to help in marine resource management, estimating fish fecundity from histological images of gonads; PDApp to estimate the third molar eruption potential from the panoramic radiological images of adolescents/teenagers patients; BreastAnalyser to help breast cancer studies from the automatic quantification of immunohistochemical images of breast tissue; or OralImmunoAnalyser to help in the study of oral cancer, quantifying immunohistochemical images of mouth tissue.

She received an award from the USC in 2021 for introducing a gender perspective into the teaching of machine learning in higher education. She also participates in the creation of educational materials for schools using a gender equality perspective and conducts workshops in non-university education centers. She has been invited to different forums to reflect on gender biases in artificial intelligence.

Preface

Computer vision (CV) is a topic within artificial intelligence intended for the processing of image or video data. CV aims to perceive, observe, and understand the physical world as humans do. While the advances and new applications of computer vision in recent years have been significant, computer vision faces several scientific and technological challenges related to the semantic understanding of context from image or video analysis, as well as the trade-off between computational time requirements and data quality and size. The semantic understanding of images and videos is especially relevant to automating critical tasks such as autonomous drivers or other applications in which humans are at risk. The contributions cover these challenges, aiming to move one step ahead in the automation of different tedious human tasks.

Eva Cernadas
Guest Editor

Editorial

Applications of Computer Vision, 2nd Edition

Eva Cernadas

CiTIUS (Singular Research Center on Intelligent Technologies), University of Santiago de Compostela, 15782 Santiago de Compostela, Spain; eva.cernadas@usc.es

Citation: Cernadas, E. Applications of Computer Vision, 2nd Edition. *Electronics* **2024**, *13*, 3779. https://doi.org/10.3390/electronics13183779

Received: 14 September 2024
Accepted: 19 September 2024
Published: 23 September 2024

Copyright: © 2024 by the author. Licensee MDPI, Basel, Switzerland. This article is an open access article distributed under the terms and conditions of the Creative Commons Attribution (CC BY) license (https://creativecommons.org/licenses/by/4.0/).

1. Introduction to the Applications of Computer Vision

Computer vision (CV) is a broad term mainly used to refer to processing image and video data. CV aims to enable machines to perceive, observe, and understand the physical world as if they have human eyes. While this area of knowledge began to develop during the 1970s and 1980s, the last three decades have been characterized by the field maturing. This progress can be seen in the increasing number of software and hardware products on the market, the significant growth of active applications, and the rise in recent scientific publications on this research area. The first applications of computer vision were in the field of medical imaging and the processing of remote sensing data. Hence, the scientific journals *IEEE Transaction on Medical Imaging* and *IEEE Transactions on Geoscience and Remote Sensing* were created by the Institute of Electrical and Electronics Engineers (IEEE) association in 1982 and 1980, respectively, to manage the engineering aspects for medical imaging and satellite data.

Remote sensing (RS) images are obtained using remote sensing technology such as airplanes and satellites under long-distance conditions. The detection of targets in RS images is very important in military applications, urban planning, resource exploration, agriculture, and other fields. CV techniques like content-based image retrieval techniques [1], semantic segmentation [2], scene classification [3], nonsupervised learning [4], and transfer learning [4], among others, have been applied to RS images. One specific application is cropland field identification, which is a key element of precision agriculture [5].

Common imaging techniques like X-ray radiographs, computed tomography (CT), and/or magnetic resonance imaging (MRI) have revolutionized the field of diagnostic medicine, providing non-destructive procedures for examining the interior of our bodies. Due to overlaps between anatomical structures, interpreting medical images is very challenging, even for experienced radiologists. The clinical interest in understanding these medical images explains the interest in developing computer algorithms that can aid experts in their clinical tasks. Across 40 years, the intersection of CV techniques and medical imaging has provided many clinical solutions. Common CV tasks like feature detection, recognition, segmentation, and three-dimensional modeling have been developed for processing different types of medical images and solving specific clinical problems. Some examples are chest radiograph analysis [6]; dental imaging (panoramic X-rays and other imaging modalities), to aid dental experts in diagnosing various dental disorders [7]; brain MRI modalities, for identifying distinct features that characterize autism spectrum disorder [8]; skin lesion analysis from RGB images to diagnosis skin cancer [9]; diagnosing glaucoma by analyzing retinal imaging data [10]; and detecting lung and colorectal cancer using CT imaging [11,12]. Recent advances in robotics now permit the acquisition of more medical images that can help clinicians make diagnoses or guide surgeons, in which the source and detector are positioned by robots with greater precision and accuracy [13,14]. Although X-ray imaging technology has been used in clinical tasks for decades, it has recently been extended to industrial production and security applications, where it can detect anomalies or defects inside products non-destructively and identify prohibited objects inside baggage without opening it [15].

Machine vision systems make use of different processing stages like image preprocessing, target image or video segmentation, feature extraction and selection, object recognition, classification, and 3D modeling, among others. These different types of tasks have typically involved different types of algorithms, with the classical CV techniques using explicitly programmed algorithms to solve specific tasks [16,17]. In recent years, deep learning (DL) models have yielded a new generation of CV methods [18] based on multi-layered neural networks such as convolutional neural networks and transformers, endowing computers with the ability to learn without them being explicitly programmed. The most popular architectures for computer vision are convolutional neural networks (CNNs) [19], which have become the standard DL-based approches for many recognition tasks due to their ability to learn high-level features in their convolutional layers; generative adversarial networks (GANs) [20], which learn from a given training set to generate new data; recurrent neural networks (RNNs), which have the capability to process temporal information and sequential data; different versions of YOLO (You Only Look Once) for object detection [21,22]; and transformers [23], which are primarily based on self-attention mechanisms [24]. These have all found applications in numerous fields, such as medicine [8,25–28], image generation [29], and remote sensing [2,4], among others. In conclusion, several algorithms have emerged over time, each with its own set of advantages and disadvantages. While DL models have good learnability, they often require a substantial number of real labels for training, provide poor interpretability due to their black-box structure, and require intensive computational resources or specific hardware.

As previously mentioned, the medical and remote sensing fields have used CV techniques for the automation of different tasks extensively. Nevertheless, recent advances in the image acquisition technology available, mainly due to research in optics and digital sensing, as well as increasing computer power, have unleashed new opportunities to apply CV techniques to new types of images, like microscopy imaging [30] or unmanned aerial vehicle (UAV) acquisitions [31]. UAVs are flying robots either remotely controlled by somebody or navigated autonomously using a computer system on board the vehicle or on the ground. They are able to acquire images in complex applications due to their small size, low cost, and high mobility. UAV systems enable the acquisition of real-time environmental data for developing CV applications such as vehicle detection [32] and digital precision agriculture [33–35], with the latter involving a variety of tasks, such as weed, crop pest, and disease detection, in order to apply the right practice at the right place, the right time, and the right quantity. Thus, UAVs are versatile, with the capacity for different kinds of sensors to be boarded onto them [36]. In capturing both the spatial and spectral features of an object's surface, hyperspectral images are also used for agricultural tasks like disease detection, weed, and stress detection; crop monitoring; applying nutrients; soil mineralogy studies; yield estimation; and sorting applications [37,38].

Microscopy imaging has a prominent role in modern biology for the visualization of tissues, cells, proteins, and macromolecular structures at all resolutions. Indeed, biopsy diagnosis is the gold standard for cancer diagnosis in pathology. Machine vision has recently been employed in the biomedical field to detect, measure, and recognize cells and patterns in histopathology images or for target tracking and 3D reconstruction [28,39]. These biomedical applications can be grouped together on the basis of the tissue or organ analyzed—for example, renal pathology [40,41], computational cytology [42], breast cancer [43], oral cancer [44], and intestine pathology [45], among others. However, microscopy imaging has also found applications to pollen identification [46,47], microorganism recognition [48], and estimating the fecundity of fish based on histological images of their gonads [49,50].

CV techniques have also played an important role in the product life cycle across the entire industrial manufacturing process, including product design, modeling and simulation, planning and scheduling, the production process, inspection and quality control, assembly, transportation, and disassembly [51,52]. Equally, they have been applied to a myriad of domains: car parking lot management, detecting the positions of parking spaces [53] or used in autonomous driving [54]; the mushroom industry, for the identification of poisonous mushrooms, plucking cultivated mushrooms covered by the soil, and mechanized grading of mushrooms [55]; continuous monitoring of beehives [56] and beehive products such as honeybee pollen [57]; marine ecosystems, in monitoring fish habitats using underwater videos or images [58] or estimating the fecundity of fish from histological images of their gonads [50,59]; crop disease monitoring [35,60,61]; the identification of insects from digital images [62]; food quality assessments [63,64], covering potatoes [65], fruit damage [66], and dry-cured ham [67,68]; automation within the chicken farming industry [69]; and plant identification [70].

All of these computer vision applications involve the integration of the following elements:

1. **Support for data recording**: Microscopes; UAVs; satellites; robots; MRI, X-ray, and CT devices; and others.
2. **Type of input data**: 2D images, videos, or other information, dependent on the high-performance sensors used to perceive the given scenario, which could be RGB cameras; multispectral, hyperspectral, thermal, and infrared sensors; synthetic-aperture radar (SAR) cameras; Light Detection and Ranging or Laser Imaging Detection and Ranging (LiDAR) sensors; or other cameras [71].
3. **Machine vision-related aim of the application**: Feature detection or recognition, image segmentation, image classification, 3D modeling or reconstruction, object tracking, defect detection, object counting or measurements from images, and visual inspection, among others. The evaluation methodology used in CV techniques is dependent on the aims and application in question.
4. **Type of processing**: CV methods can be roughly divided into three categories: non-learning-based methods, learning-based methods, and hybrid methods. The first types of methods are usually known as the classical methods, and these rely on unsupervised, manually designed feature extractors or statistical models, in which the output is calculated from direct processing of the input data. Currently, the second types are methods based on deep learning, in which previous training with ground-truth data is needed to compute the output. Hybrid strategies normally combine the extraction of features from the input data with a subsequent machine learning stage.
5. **Experimental testing**: Using publicly available datasets or private data.

Despite the abundance of works and reviews published in this domain in recent years, many challenges are still open questions. From a computational point of view, future work should focus on designing more efficient algorithms that can operate in real time or run on low-capacity devices such as UAVs. As mentioned, some machine vision techniques require a substantial amount of ground-truth labeled data for training. Transfer learning or unsupervised annotation algorithms have been proposed to alleviate the need for labeled data, addressing domain shift or directly labeling the data, but there is still room for further research on this aspect. At the same time, a considerable number of the studies in the literature on CV only use private data or use public datasets with different experimental setups, complicating comparison between algorithms. So, new data must be made public in order for the field to mature.

For CV applications in which the decision-making involved affects people, there is substantial evidence that AI-based systems take on race-, ethnicity-, culture-, age-, and gender-based biases, among others, that disadvantage minority populations. Gender bias typically intersects with other biases [72], and Natural Language Processing (NLP) and facial analysis and recognition are research fields that feel greater effects of gender bias—for example, gender bias in commercial facial recognition systems [73,74] or the social impact of image generation models [75]. Machine vision systems perpetuated or intensified social inequalities in recent applications of developing systems that integrated NLP and CV [76,77], with biases introduced by both. Biases can be introduced into CV systems in many different ways: the ground-truth labeling of the data, the selection of the data included for training, the algorithm design, and evaluation of the prediction quality, among other design decisions. Gender biases can be imbued into CV systems unintentionally due to our cultural experience or gender stereotypes. Therefore, CV system developers should be aware of gender bias in their future work. Equally, some of the images and videos used in CV research are obtained without the explicit consent of the people photographed. Hence, recently, the IEEE announced that it will no longer allow the use of the Lena image in its publications. Furthermore, in some CV applications, such as emotional computing, people's right to privacy and intimacy should be socially debated [78].

2. Overview of This Special Issue

This Special Issue called for scientific articles related to the computer vision applications previously covered, and after a double-blind review process, nineteen articles were published. This section provides a brief overview of each contribution in order to encourage further exploration on the part of the reader.

The first contribution, entitled "A UAV Aerial Image Target Detection Algorithm Based on YOLOv7 Improved Model", proposes an enhanced YOLOv7 model for detecting small targets in UAV images. Experiments were carried out on the UAV aerial photo dataset VisDrone2019 and compared with the YOLOv7 model.

The second contribution, entitled "RN-YOLO: A Small Target Detection Model for Aerial Remote-Sensing Images", applies a new YOLO model based on YOLOv8, called RN-YOLO, to detecting small targets in RS images. These experiments were conducted on the TGRS-HRRSD and RSOD datasets and compared with the YOLOv8 model.

The third contribution, entitled "Dense Object Detection Based on De-Homogenized Queries", establishes a new method for dense object detection in images and videos. Experiments were run on the CrowdHuman dataset and compared with other state-of-the-art (SOTA) methods.

The fourth contribution, entitled "Multi-Scale Fusion Uncrewed Aerial Vehicle Detection Based on RT-DETR", covers an enhanced model of a real-time detection transformer (RT-DETR), a real-time end-to-end object detection model for detecting drones in images. Two available UAV datasets were used for the experiments.

The fifth contribution, entitled "Efficient Vision Transformer YOLOv5 for Accurate and Fast Traffic Sign Detection", details a new model for detecting traffic signs, which is a vital task in autonomous driving systems. It achieved faster and more accurate results than the YOLOv5 model. Experiments were conducted on the 3L-TT100K traffic sign dataset.

The sixth contribution, entitled "Facial Beauty Prediction Combined with Multi-Task Learning of Adaptive Sharing Policy and Attentional Feature Fusion", presents a strategy for improving facial attractiveness assessments, involving experimental testing on the LSAFBD and SCUT-FBP5500 databases.

The seventh contribution, entitled "Two-Stage Progressive Learning for Vehicle Re-Identification in Variable Illumination Condition", elucidates a TSPL framework for recognizing vehicles in images acquired by surveillance cameras with varying viewpoints, levels of illumination, and resolutions. A private large-scale dataset (VERI-DAN) and the Vehicle-1M dataset were used for the experiments, and the framework proposed was compared with other SOTA methods.

Inspired by the separation of luminance and chrominance information in the YCbCr color space, the eighth contribution, entitled "DBENet: Dual-Branch Brightness Enhancement Fusion Network for Low-Light Image Enhancement", describes a new model for enhancing RGB images with low light, minimizing brightness, color distortion, and noise pollution in the enhanced images. The experiments in this paper made use of multiple publicly available low-light image datasets, and the results were evaluated against those of classical algorithms.

The ninth contribution, entitled "RSLC-Deeplab: A Ground Object Classification Method for High-Resolution Remote Sensing Images", suggests a semantic segmentation network for accurately segmenting remote sensing images. Experiments conducted using the WHDLD dataset demonstrated its outperformance of the PSP-NET, U-NET, MACU-NET, and DeeplabV3+ networks.

The tenth contribution, entitled "YOLO-CID: Improved YOLOv7 for X-ray Contraband Image Detection", augments the YOLOv7 method for contraband image detection in X-ray inspection systems in order to detect small objects under occlusion or low contrast. Its results on the PIDray public dataset were an improvement upon the results of the YOLOv7 algorithm.

The eleventh contribution, entitled "Enhancing the Accuracy of an Image Classification Model Using Cross-Modality Transfer Learning", proposes a cross-modality transfer learning approach to shifting the knowledge when the source and target domains are different, specifically from the text domain to the image domain.

The twelfth contribution, entitled "Three-Dimensional Measurement of Full Profile of Steel Rail Cross-Section Based on Line-Structured Light", solves the industrial problem of improving railway operation safety by proposing a method for three-dimensional measurement of the cross-sectional profiles of steel rails based on binocular line-structured light. Private data were used in this paper.

The thirteenth contribution, entitled "A Workpiece-Dense Scene Object Detection Method Based on Improved YOLOv5", optimizes the YOLOv5 method for detecting workpieces in dense images of industrial production lines, using a self-built artifact dataset to compare the results with the original method.

The fourteenth contribution, entitled "Improving the Performance of the Single Shot Multibox Detector for Steel Surface Defects with Context Fusion and Feature Refinement", devises a method for improving the ability to identify steel surface defects. Experiments were run on the public NEU-DET dataset and compared with other SOTA methods (Faster R-CNN, RetinaNet, and different YOLO methods).

The fifteenth contribution, entitled "Object Detection Algorithm of UAV Aerial Photography Image Based on Anchor-Free Algorithms", constructs an algorithm for anchor-free target detection in UAV aerial photography images. In experiments performed on the VisDrone dataset, it outperformed the fully convolutional one-stage object detection algorithm.

The sixteenth contribution, entitled "A Vehicle Recognition Model Based on Improved YOLOv5", in order to increase vehicle driving safety, validated the results of an improved YOLOv5s algorithm for vehicle identification and detection on a self-built dataset against the results of the YOLOv5 method.

The seventeenth contribution, entitled "Material-Aware Path Aggregation Network and Shape Decoupled SIoU for X-ray Contraband Detection", outlines a method, based on variants of the YOLO model, for detecting and classifying contraband in X-ray baggage images. They evaluated the method proposed on the public X-ray contraband SIXray and OPIXray datasets and conducted a comparison of the results with those of other SOTA X-ray baggage inspection detection methods.

The eighteenth contribution, entitled "Fast Adaptive Binarization of QR Code Images for Automatic Sorting in Logistics Systems", presents an adaptive binarization method for reading unevenly illuminated QR codes in automatic sorting in logistics systems. The image quality, recognition rate, and computation speed of the proposed method was tested against other SOTA methods on different examples.

The nineteenth contribution, entitled "Surveying Racial Bias in Facial Recognition: Balancing Datasets and Algorithmic Enhancements", is a review on facial recognition systems that involve specific racial categories, discussing balanced facial recognition datasets, addressing and analyzing the racial bias of the methods, and exploring the interrelation of racial and gender bias.

Funding: This article received no external funding.

Acknowledgments: The Guest Editor of this Special Issue sincerely thanks all the scientists who submitted their research articles, the reviewers who assisted in evaluating these manuscripts, and both the Editorial Board Members and the Editors of Electronics for their overall support. Financial support from the Xunta de Galicia and the European Union (European Regional Development Fund—ERDF), Project ED431G-2019/04, is also acknowledged.

Conflicts of Interest: The author declares no conflicts of interest.

List of Contributions

1. Qin, J.; Yu, W.; Feng, X.; Meng, Z.; Tan, C. A UAV Aerial Image Target Detection Algorithm Based on YOLOv7 Improved Model. *Electronics* **2024**, *13*, 3277. https://doi.org/10.3390/electronics13163277.
2. Wang, K.; Zhou, H.; Wu, H.; Yuan, G. RN-YOLO: A Small Target Detection Model for Aerial Remote-Sensing Images. *Electronics* **2024**, *13*, 2383. https://doi.org/10.3390/electronics13122383.
3. Huang, Y.; Ma, C.; Zhou, H.; Wu, H.; Yuan, G. Dense Object Detection Based on De-Homogenized Queries. *Electronics* **2024**, *13*, 2312. https://doi.org/10.3390/electronics13122312.
4. Zhu, M.; Kong, E. Multi-Scale Fusion Uncrewed Aerial Vehicle Detection Based on RT-DETR. *Electronics* **2024**, *13*, 1489. https://doi.org/10.3390/electronics13081489.
5. Zeng, G.; Wu, Z.; Xu, L.; Liang, Y. Efficient Vision Transformer YOLOv5 for Accurate and Fast Traffic Sign Detection. *Electronics* **2024**, *13*, 880. https://doi.org/10.3390/electronics13050880.
6. Gan, J.; Luo, H.; Xiong, J.; Xie, X.; Li, H.; Liu, J. Facial Beauty Prediction Combined with Multi-Task Learning of Adaptive Sharing Policy and Attentional Feature Fusion. *Electronics* **2024**, *13*, 179. https://doi.org/10.3390/electronics13010179.
7. Wu, Z.; Jin, Z.; Li, X. Two-Stage Progressive Learning for Vehicle Re-Identification in Variable Illumination Conditions. *Electronics* **2024**, *13*, 4950. https://doi.org/10.3390/electronics12244950.
8. Chen, Y.; Wen, C.; Liu, W.; He, W. DBENet: Dual-Branch Brightness Enhancement Fusion Network for Low-Light Image Enhancement. *Electronics* **2024**, *13*, 3907. https://doi.org/10.3390/electronics12183907.
9. Yu, Z.; Wan, F.; Lei, G.; Xiong, Y.; Xu, L.; Ye, Z.; Liu, W.; Zhou, W.; Xu, C. RSLC-Deeplab: A Ground Object Classification Method for High-Resolution Remote Sensing Images. *Electronics* **2024**, *13*, 3653. https://doi.org/10.3390/electronics12173653.
10. Gan, N.; Wan, F.; Lei, G.; Xu, L.; Xu, C.; Xiong, Y.; Zhou, W. YOLO-CID: Improved YOLOv7 for X-ray Contraband Image Detection. *Electronics* **2024**, *13*, 3636. https://doi.org/10.3390/electronics12173636.
11. Liu, J.; Chui, K.T.; Lee, L.K. Enhancing the Accuracy of an Image Classification Model Using Cross-Modality Transfer Learning. *Electronics* **2024**, *13*, 3316. https://doi.org/10.3390/electronics12153316.
12. Liu, J.; Zhang, J.; Ma, Z.; Zhang, H.; Zhang, S. Three-Dimensional Measurement of Full Profile of Steel Rail Cross-Section Based on Line-Structured Light. *Electronics* **2024**, *13*, 3194. https://doi.org/10.3390/electronics12143194.
13. Liu, J.; Zhang, S.; Ma, Z.; Zeng, Y.; Liu, X. A Workpiece-Dense Scene Object Detection Method Based on Improved YOLOv5. *Electronics* **2024**, *13*, 2966. https://doi.org/10.3390/electronics12132966.
14. Li, Y.; He, L.; Zhang, M.; Cheng, Z.; Liu, W.; Wu, Z. Improving the Performance of the Single Shot Multibox Detector for Steel Surface Defects with Context Fusion and Feature Refinement. *Electronics* **2024**, *13*, 2440. https://doi.org/10.3390/electronics12112440.
15. Hu, Q.; Li, L.; Duan, J.; Gao, M.; Liu, G.; Wang, Z.; Huang, D. Object Detection Algorithm of UAV Aerial Photography Image Based on Anchor-Free Algorithms. *Electronics* **2024**, *13*, 1339. https://doi.org/10.3390/electronics12061339.
16. Shao, L.; Wu, H.; Li, C.; Li, J. A Vehicle Recognition Model Based on Improved YOLOv5. *Electronics* **2024**, *13*, 1323. https://doi.org/10.3390/electronics12061323.

17. Xiang, N.; Gong, Z.; Xu, Y.; Xiong, L. Material-Aware Path Aggregation Network and Shape Decoupled SIoU for X-ray Contraband Detection. *Electronics* **2024**, *13*, 1179. https://doi.org/10.3390/electronics12051179.
18. Chen, R.; Li, W.; Lan, K.; Xiao, J.; Wang, L.; Lu, X. Fast Adaptive Binarization of QR Code Images for Automatic Sorting in Logistics Systems. *Electronics* **2024**, *13*, 286. https://doi.org/10.3390/electronics12020286.
19. Sumsion, A.; Torrie, S.; Lee, D.J.; Sun, Z. Surveying Racial Bias in Facial Recognition: Balancing Datasets and Algorithmic Enhancements. *Electronics* **2024**, *13*, 2317. https://doi.org/10.3390/electronics13122317.

References

1. Zhou, W.; Guan, H.; Li, Z.; Shao, Z.; Delavar, M.R. Remote Sensing Image Retrieval in the Past Decade: Achievements, Challenges, and Future Directions. *IEEE J. Sel. Top. Appl. Earth Obs. Remote Sens.* **2023**, *16*, 1447–1473. [CrossRef]
2. Huang, L.; Jiang, B.; Lv, S.; Liu, Y.; Fu, Y. Deep-Learning-Based Semantic Segmentation of Remote Sensing Images: A Survey. *IEEE J. Sel. Top. Appl. Earth Obs. Remote Sens.* **2024**, *17*, 8370–8396. [CrossRef]
3. Tan, X.; Xi, B.; Li, J.; Zheng, T.; Li, Y.; Xue, C.; Chanussot, J. Review of Zero-Shot Remote Sensing Image Scene Classification. *IEEE J. Sel. Top. Appl. Earth Obs. Remote Sens.* **2024**, *17*, 11274–11289. [CrossRef]
4. Ma, Y.; Chen, S.; Ermon, S.; Lobell, D.B. Transfer learning in environmental remote sensing. *Remote Sens. Environ.* **2024**, *301*, 113924. [CrossRef]
5. Xu, F.; Yao, X.; Zhang, K.; Yang, H.; Feng, Q.; Li, Y.; Yan, S.; Gao, B.; Li, S.; Yang, J.; et al. Deep learning in cropland field identification: A review. *Comput. Electron. Agric.* **2024**, *222*, 109042. [CrossRef]
6. Van Ginneken, B.; Ter Haar Romeny, B.; Viergever, M. Computer-aided diagnosis in chest radiography: A survey. *IEEE Trans. Med. Imaging* **2001**, *20*, 1228–1241. [CrossRef]
7. Priya, J.; Raja, S.K.S.; Kiruthika, S.U. State-of-art technologies, challenges, and emerging trends of computer vision in dental images. *Comput. Biol. Med.* **2024**, *178*, 108800. [CrossRef]
8. Alharthi, A.G.; Alzahrani, S.M. Do it the transformer way: A comprehensive review of brain and vision transformers for autism spectrum disorder diagnosis and classification. *Comput. Biol. Med.* **2023**, *167*, 107667. [CrossRef]
9. Hasan, M.K.; Ahamad, M.A.; Yap, C.H.; Yang, G. A survey, review, and future trends of skin lesion segmentation and classification. *Comput. Biol. Med.* **2023**, *155*, 106624. [CrossRef]
10. Ashtari-Majlan, M.; Dehshibi, M.M.; Masip, D. Glaucoma diagnosis in the era of deep learning: A survey. *Expert Syst. Appl.* **2024**, *256*, 124888. [CrossRef]
11. Porto-Álvarez, J.; Barnes, G.T.; Villanueva, A.; García-Figueiras, R.; Baleato-González, S.; Huelga Zapico, E.; Souto-Bayarri, M. Digital Medical X-ray Imaging, CAD in Lung Cancer and Radiomics in Colorectal Cancer: Past, Present and Future. *Appl. Sci.* **2023**, *13*, 2218. [CrossRef]
12. González-Castro, V.; Cernadas, E.; Huelga, E.; Fernández-Delgado, M.; Porto, J.; Antunez, J.R.; Souto-Bayarri, M. CT Radiomics in Colorectal Cancer: Detection of KRAS Mutation Using Texture Analysis and Machine Learning. *Appl. Sci.* **2020**, *10*, 6214. [CrossRef]
13. Salcudean, S.E.; Moradi, H.; Black, D.G.; Navab, N. Robot-Assisted Medical Imaging: A Review. *Proc. IEEE* **2022**, *110*, 951–967. [CrossRef]
14. Schmidt, A.; Mohareri, O.; DiMaio, S.; Yip, M.C.; Salcudean, S.E. Tracking and mapping in medical computer vision: A review. *Med. Image Anal.* **2024**, *94*, 103131. [CrossRef] [PubMed]
15. Rafiei, M.; Raitoharju, J.; Iosifidis, A. Computer Vision on X-Ray Data in Industrial Production and Security Applications: A Comprehensive Survey. *IEEE Access* **2023**, *11*, 2445–2477. [CrossRef]
16. González, R.C.; Woods, R.E.R.E. *Digital Image Processing*, 4th ed.; Pearson: New York, NY, USA, 2018.
17. Sonka, M.; Hlavac, V.; Boyle, R. *Image Processing, Analysis and Machine Vision*, 3rd ed.; PWS: Pacific Grove, CA, USA, 2008.
18. Hassaballah, M.; Awad, A.I. *Deep Learning in Computer Vision: Principles and Applications*, First Issued in Paperback 2021 ed.; Digital Imaging and Computer Vision Series; CRC Press, Taylor & Francis Group: Boca Raton, FL, USA, 2021.
19. LeCun, Y.; Bengio, Y.; Hinton, G. Deep learning. *Nature* **2015**, *444*, 436–444. [CrossRef]
20. Goodfellow, I.J.; Pouget-Abadie, J.; Mirza, M.; Xu, B.; Warde-Farley, D.; Ozair, S.; Courville, A.; Bengio, Y. Generative Adversarial Networks. *arXiv* **2014**, arXiv:stat.ML/1406.2661.
21. Zou, Z.; Chen, K.; Shi, Z.; Guo, Y.; Ye, J. Object Detection in 20 Years: A Survey. *Proc. IEEE* **2023**, *111*, 257–276. [CrossRef]
22. Chaudhari, S.; Malkan, N.; Momin, A.; Bonde, M. Yolo Real Time Object Detection. *Int. J. Comput. Trends Technol.* **2020**, *68*, 70–76. [CrossRef]
23. Han, K.; Wang, Y.; Chen, H.; Chen, X.; Guo, J.; Liu, Z.; Tang, Y.; Xiao, A.; Xu, C.; Xu, Y.; et al. A Survey on Vision Transformer. *IEEE Trans. Pattern Anal. Mach. Intell.* **2023**, *45*, 87–110. [CrossRef]
24. Gonçalves, T.; Rio-Torto, I.; Teixeira, L.F.; Cardoso, J.S. A Survey on Attention Mechanisms for Medical Applications: Are we Moving Toward Better Algorithms? *IEEE Access* **2022**, *10*, 98909–98935. [CrossRef]

25. Papanastasiou, G.; Dikaios, N.; Huang, J.; Wang, C.; Yang, G. Is Attention all You Need in Medical Image Analysis? A Review. *IEEE J. Biomed. Health Inform.* **2024**, *28*, 1398–1411. [CrossRef] [PubMed]
26. Azad, R.; Kazerouni, A.; Heidari, M.; Aghdam, E.K.; Molaei, A.; Jia, Y.; Jose, A.; Roy, R.; Merhof, D. Advances in medical image analysis with vision Transformers: A comprehensive review. *Med. Image Anal.* **2024**, *91*, 103000. [CrossRef] [PubMed]
27. Shamshad, F.; Khan, S.; Zamir, S.W.; Khan, M.H.; Hayat, M.; Khan, F.S.; Fu, H. Transformers in medical imaging: A survey. *Med. Image Anal.* **2023**, *88*, 102802. [CrossRef] [PubMed]
28. Hu, W.; Li, X.; Li, C.; Li, R.; Jiang, T.; Sun, H.; Huang, X.; Grzegorzek, M.; Li, X. A state-of-the-art survey of artificial neural networks for Whole-slide Image analysis: From popular Convolutional Neural Networks to potential visual transformers. *Comput. Biol. Med.* **2023**, *161*, 107034. [CrossRef] [PubMed]
29. Dubey, S.R.; Singh, S.K. Transformer-based Generative Adversarial Networks in Computer Vision: A Comprehensive Survey. *IEEE Trans. Artif. Intell.* **2024**, 1–16. [CrossRef]
30. Kervrann, C.; Acton, S.T.; Olivo-Marin, J.C.; Sorzano, C.; Unser, M. Introduction to the Issue on Advanced Signal Processing in Microscopy and Cell Imaging. *IEEE J. Sel. Top. Signal Process.* **2016**, *10*, 3–5. [CrossRef]
31. Han, Y.; Liu, H.; Wang, Y.; Liu, C. A Comprehensive Review for Typical Applications Based Upon Unmanned Aerial Vehicle Platform. *IEEE J. Sel. Top. Appl. Earth Obs. Remote Sens.* **2022**, *15*, 9654–9666. [CrossRef]
32. Bouguettaya, A.; Zarzour, H.; Kechida, A.; Taberkit, A.M. Vehicle Detection From UAV Imagery With Deep Learning: A Review. *IEEE Trans. Neural Networks Learn. Syst.* **2022**, *33*, 6047–6067. [CrossRef]
33. Phang, S.K.; Chiang, T.H.A.; Happonen, A.; Chang, M.M.L. From Satellite to UAV-Based Remote Sensing: A Review on Precision Agriculture. *IEEE Access* **2023**, *11*, 127057–127076. [CrossRef]
34. Toscano, F.; Fiorentino, C.; Capece, N.; Erra, U.; Travascia, D.; Scopa, A.; Drosos, M.; D'Antonio, P. Unmanned Aerial Vehicle for Precision Agriculture: A Review. *IEEE Access* **2024**, *12*, 69188–69205. [CrossRef]
35. Joshi, P.; Sandhu, K.S.; Singh Dhillon, G.; Chen, J.; Bohara, K. Detection and monitoring wheat diseases using unmanned aerial vehicles (UAVs). *Comput. Electron. Agric.* **2024**, *224*, 109158. [CrossRef]
36. López, Y.A.; García-Fernández, M.; Álvarez-Narciandi, G.; Andrés, F.L.H. Unmanned Aerial Vehicle-Based Ground-Penetrating Radar Systems: A review. *IEEE Geosci. Remote Sens. Mag.* **2022**, *10*, 66–86. [CrossRef]
37. Ram, B.G.; Oduor, P.; Igathinathane, C.; Howatt, K.; Sun, X. A systematic review of hyperspectral imaging in precision agriculture: Analysis of its current state and future prospects. *Comput. Electron. Agric.* **2024**, *222*, 109037. [CrossRef]
38. Shuai, L.; Li, Z.; Chen, Z.; Luo, D.; Mu, J. A research review on deep learning combined with hyperspectral Imaging in multiscale agricultural sensing. *Comput. Electron. Agric.* **2024**, *217*, 108577. [CrossRef]
39. He, W.; Liu, T.; Han, Y.; Ming, W.; Du, J.; Liu, Y.; Yang, Y.; Wang, L.; Jiang, Z.; Wang, Y.; et al. A review: The detection of cancer cells in histopathology based on machine vision. *Comput. Biol. Med.* **2022**, *146*, 105636. [CrossRef]
40. Cordido, A.; Cernadas, E.; Fernández-Delgado, M.; García-González, M.A. CystAnalyser: A new software tool for the automatic detection and quantification of cysts in Polycystic Kidney and Liver Disease, and other cystic disorders. *PLoS Comput. Biol.* **2020**, *16*, e1008337. [CrossRef]
41. Deng, R.; Yang, H.; Jha, A.; Lu, Y.; Chu, P.; Fogo, A.B.; Huo, Y. Map3D: Registration-Based Multi-Object Tracking on 3D Serial Whole Slide Images. *IEEE Trans. Med. Imaging* **2021**, *40*, 1924–1933. [CrossRef]
42. Jiang, H.; Zhou, Y.; Lin, Y.; Chan, R.C.; Liu, J.; Chen, H. Deep learning for computational cytology: A survey. *Med. Image Anal.* **2023**, *84*, 102691. [CrossRef]
43. Rodríguez-Candela Mateos, M.; Azmat, M.; Santiago-Freijanes, P.; Galán-Moya, E.M.; Fernández-Delgado, M.; Aponte, R.B.; Mosquera, J.; Acea, B.; Cernadas, E.; Mayán, M.D. Software BreastAnalyser for the semi-automatic analysis of breast cancer immunohistochemical images. *Sci. Rep.* **2024**, *14*, 2995. [CrossRef]
44. Al-Tarawneh, Z.A.; Pena-Cristóbal, M.; Cernadas, E.; Suarez-Peñaranda, J.M.; Fernández-Delgado, M.; Mbaidin, A.; Gallas-Torreira, M.; Gándara-Vila, P. OralImmunoAnalyser: A software tool for immunohistochemical assessment of oral leukoplakia using image segmentation and classification models. *Front. Artif. Intell.* **2024**, *7*, 1324410. [CrossRef] [PubMed]
45. Jing, Y.; Li, C.; Du, T.; Jiang, T.; Sun, H.; Yang, J.; Shi, L.; Gao, M.; Grzegorzek, M.; Li, X. A comprehensive survey of intestine histopathological image analysis using machine vision approaches. *Comput. Biol. Med.* **2023**, *165*, 107388. [CrossRef] [PubMed]
46. Rodríguez-Damián, M.; Cernadas, E.; Formella, A.; Fernández-Delgado, M.; Sa-Otero, P.D. Automatic detection and classification of grains of pollen based on shape and texture. *IEEE Trans. Syst. Man Cybern. Part C* **2006**, *36*, 531–542. [CrossRef]
47. Li, J.; Cheng, W.; Xu, X.; Zhao, L.; Liu, S.; Gao, Z.; Ye, C.; You, H. How to identify pollen like a palynologist: A prior knowledge-guided deep feature learning for real-world pollen classification. *Expert Syst. Appl.* **2024**, *237*, 121392. [CrossRef]
48. Kulwa, F.; Li, C.; Zhao, X.; Cai, B.; Xu, N.; Qi, S.; Chen, S.; Teng, Y. A State-of-the-Art Survey for Microorganism Image Segmentation Methods and Future Potential. *IEEE Access* **2019**, *7*, 100243–100269. [CrossRef]
49. Mbaidin, A.; Cernadas, E.; Al-Tarawneh, Z.A.; Fernández-Delgado, M.; Domínguez-Petit, R.; Rábade-Uberos, S.; Hassanat, A. MSCF: Multi-Scale Canny Filter to Recognize Cells in Microscopic Images. *Sustainability* **2023**, *15*, 13693. [CrossRef]
50. Mbaidin, A.; Rábade-Uberos, S.; Dominguez-Petit, R.; Villaverde, A.; Gónzalez-Rufino, M.E.; Formella, A.; Fernández-Delgado, M.; Cernadas, E. STERapp: Semiautomatic Software for Stereological Analysis. Application in the Estimation of Fish Fecundity. *Electronics* **2021**, *10*, 1432. [CrossRef]
51. Zhou, L.; Zhang, L.; Konz, N. Computer Vision Techniques in Manufacturing. *IEEE Trans. Syst. Man, Cybern. Syst.* **2023**, *53*, 105–117. [CrossRef]

52. Ahmad, H.M.; Rahimi, A. Deep learning methods for object detection in smart manufacturing: A survey. *J. Manuf. Syst.* **2022**, *64*, 181–196. [CrossRef]
53. de Almeida, P.R.L.; Alves, J.H.; Parpinelli, R.S.; Barddal, J.P. A systematic review on computer vision-based parking lot management applied on public datasets. *Expert Syst. Appl.* **2022**, *198*, 116731. [CrossRef]
54. Zhao, J.; Zhao, W.; Deng, B.; Wang, Z.; Zhang, F.; Zheng, W.; Cao, W.; Nan, J.; Lian, Y.; Burke, A.F. Autonomous driving system: A comprehensive survey. *Expert Syst. Appl.* **2024**, *242*, 122836. [CrossRef]
55. Yin, H.; Yi, W.; Hu, D. Computer vision and machine learning applied in the mushroom industry: A critical review. *Comput. Electron. Agric.* **2022**, *198*, 107015. [CrossRef]
56. Bilik, S.; Zemcik, T.; Kratochvila, L.; Ricanek, D.; Richter, M.; Zambanini, S.; Horak, K. Machine learning and computer vision techniques in continuous beehive monitoring applications: A survey. *Comput. Electron. Agric.* **2024**, *217*, 108560. [CrossRef]
57. Carrión, P.; Cernadas, E.; Gálvez, J.F.; Damián, M.; de Sá-Otero, P. Classification of honeybee pollen using a multiscale texture filtering scheme. *Mach. Vis. Appl.* **2014**, *15*, 186–193. [CrossRef]
58. Saleh, A.; Sheaves, M.; Jerry, D.; Rahimi Azghadi, M. Applications of deep learning in fish habitat monitoring: A tutorial and survey. *Expert Syst. Appl.* **2024**, *238*, 121841. [CrossRef]
59. González-Rufino, E.; Carrión, P.; Cernadas, E.; Fernández-Delgado, M.; Domínguez-Petit, R. Exhaustive comparison of colour texture features and classification methods to discriminate cells categories in histological images of fish ovary. *Pattern Recognit.* **2013**, *46*, 2391–2407. [CrossRef]
60. Ariza-Sentís, M.; Vélez, S.; Martínez-Peña, R.; Baja, H.; Valente, J. Object detection and tracking in Precision Farming: A systematic review. *Comput. Electron. Agric.* **2024**, *219*, 108757. [CrossRef]
61. Kumar, D.; Kukreja, V. Image segmentation, classification, and recognition methods for wheat diseases: Two Decades' systematic literature review. *Comput. Electron. Agric.* **2024**, *221*, 109005. [CrossRef]
62. De Cesaro Júnior, T.; Rieder, R. Automatic identification of insects from digital images: A survey. *Comput. Electron. Agric.* **2020**, *178*, 105784. [CrossRef]
63. Meenu, M.; Kurade, C.; Neelapu, B.C.; Kalra, S.; Ramaswamy, H.S.; Yu, Y. A concise review on food quality assessment using digital image processing. *Trends Food Sci. Technol.* **2021**, *118*, 106–124. [CrossRef]
64. Pu, H.; Yu, J.; Sun, D.-W.; Wei, Q.; Wang, Z. Feature construction methods for processing and analysing spectral images and their applications in food quality inspection. *Trends Food Sci. Technol.* **2023**, *138*, 726–737. [CrossRef]
65. Sanchez, P.D.C.; Hashim, N.; Shamsudin, R.; Mohd Nor, M.Z. Applications of imaging and spectroscopy techniques for non-destructive quality evaluation of potatoes and sweet potatoes: A review. *Trends Food Sci. Technol.* **2020**, *96*, 208–221. [CrossRef]
66. Mahanti, N.K.; Pandiselvam, R.; Kothakota, A.; Ishwarya S., P.; Chakraborty, S.K.; Kumar, M.; Cozzolino, D. Emerging non-destructive imaging techniques for fruit damage detection: Image processing and analysis. *Trends Food Sci. Technol.* **2022**, *120*, 418–438. [CrossRef]
67. Ávila, M.; Durán, M.; Antequera, T.; Caballero, D.; Palacios-Pérez, T.; Cernadas, E.; Fernández-Delgado, M. Magnetic Resonance Imaging, texture analysis and regression techniques to non-destructively predict the quality characteristics of meat pieces. *Eng. Appl. Artif. Intell.* **2019**, *82*, 110–125. [CrossRef]
68. Cernadas, E.; Fernández-Delgado, M.; Fulladosa, E.; Muñoz, I. Automatic marbling prediction of sliced dry-cured ham using image segmentation, texture analysis and regression. *Expert Syst. Appl.* **2022**, *206*, 117765. [CrossRef]
69. Yang, D.; Cui, D.; Ying, Y. Development and trends of chicken farming robots in chicken farming tasks: A review. *Comput. Electron. Agric.* **2024**, *221*, 108916. [CrossRef]
70. Akhtar, M.S.; Zafar, Z.; Nawaz, R.; Fraz, M.M. Unlocking plant secrets: A systematic review of 3D imaging in plant phenotyping techniques. *Comput. Electron. Agric.* **2024**, *222*, 109033. [CrossRef]
71. Gallego, G.; Delbrück, T.; Orchard, G.; Bartolozzi, C.; Taba, B.; Censi, A.; Leutenegger, S.; Davison, A.J.; Conradt, J.; Daniilidis, K.; et al. Event-Based Vision: A Survey. *IEEE Trans. Pattern Anal. Mach. Intell.* **2022**, *44*, 154–180. [CrossRef]
72. Shrestha, S.; Das, S. Exploring gender biases in ML and AI academic research through systematic literature review. *Front. Artif. Intel.* **2022**, *5*, 976838. [CrossRef]
73. Schwemmer, C.; Knight, C.; Bello-Pardo, E.D.; Oklobdzija, S.; Schoonvelde, M.; Lockhart, J.W. Diagnosing Gender Bias in Image Recognition Systems. *Socius* **2020**, *6*, 2378023120967171. [CrossRef] [PubMed]
74. Khalil, A.; Ahmed, S.G.; Khattak, A.M.; Al-Qirim, N. Investigating Bias in Facial Analysis Systems: A Systematic Review. *IEEE Access* **2020**, *8*, 130751–130761. [CrossRef]
75. Katirai, A.; Garcia, N.; Ide, K.; Nakashima, Y.; Kishimoto, A. Situating the social issues of image generation models in the model life cycle: A sociotechnical approach. *AI Ethics* **2024**. [CrossRef]
76. Reale-Nosei, G.; Amador-Domínguez, E.; Serrano, E. From vision to text: A comprehensive review of natural image captioning in medical diagnosis and radiology report generation. *Med. Image Anal.* **2024**, *97*, 103264. [CrossRef] [PubMed]

77. Nam, W.; Jang, B. A survey on multimodal bidirectional machine learning translation of image and natural language processing. *Expert Syst. Appl.* **2024**, *235*, 121168. [CrossRef]
78. Crawford, K. *The Atlas of AI*; Yale University Press: New Haven, CT, USA, 2021.

Disclaimer/Publisher's Note: The statements, opinions and data contained in all publications are solely those of the individual author(s) and contributor(s) and not of MDPI and/or the editor(s). MDPI and/or the editor(s) disclaim responsibility for any injury to people or property resulting from any ideas, methods, instructions or products referred to in the content.

Article

A UAV Aerial Image Target Detection Algorithm Based on YOLOv7 Improved Model

Jie Qin [1], Weihua Yu [1], Xiaoxi Feng [2], Zuqiang Meng [1,3,*] and Chaohong Tan [3]

1. School of Computer Science and Electronic Engineering, Guangxi University, Nanning 530004, China; 2107210102@st.gxu.edu.cn (J.Q.); 2102010127@st.gxu.edu.cn (W.Y.)
2. School of Electrical Engineering, Guangxi University, Nanning 530004, China
3. Guangxi Key Laboratory of Digital Infrastructure, Guangxi Zhuang Autonomous Region Information Center, Nanning 530201, China
* Correspondence: zqmeng@gxu.edu.cn

Abstract: To address the challenges of multi-scale objects, dense distributions, occlusions, and numerous small targets in UAV image detection, we present CMS-YOLOv7, a real-time target detection method based on an enhanced YOLOv7 model. Firstly, the detection layer P2 for small targets was added to YOLOv7 to enhance the detection ability of small and medium-sized targets, and the deep detection head P5 was taken out to mitigate the influence of excessive downsampling on small target images. The anchor frame was calculated by the K-means++ method. Using the concept of Inner-IoU, the Inner-MPDIoU loss function was constructed to control the range of the auxiliary border and improve detection performance. Furthermore, the CARAFE module was introduced to replace traditional upsampling methods, offering improved integration of semantic information during the image upsampling process and enhancing feature mapping accuracy. Simultaneously, during the feature extraction stage, a non-strided convolutional SPD-Conv module was constructed using space-to-depth techniques. This module replaced certain convolutional operations to minimize the loss of fine-grained information and improve the model's ability to extract features from small targets. Experiments on the UAV aerial photo dataset VisDrone2019 demonstrated that compared with the baseline YOLOv7 object detection algorithm, CMS-YOLOv7 achieved an improvement of 3.5% mAP@0.5, 3.0% mAP@0.5:0.95, and the number of parameters decreased by 18.54 M. The ability of small target detection was significantly enhanced.

Keywords: UAV; small target detection; YOLOv7

1. Introduction

In today's rapidly advancing technological landscape, UAV technology has also progressed swiftly. Unmanned aerial vehicles (UAVs) are now widely utilized across various fields, including military, agriculture, emergency rescue, and geological surveys, owing to their unique advantages. This has made UAV technology a prominent focus in modern science and technology [1–3]. Target detection, an important research area in computer vision [4], includes identifying and locating objects within images or videos. Traditional target detection algorithms often fall short in effectively extracting features for accurate detection. However, with advancements in deep learning technology [5], the performance of target detection algorithms has significantly improved, enabling UAVs to perform target detection in complex scenes [6].

There are four factors that cause various problems in UAV applications when performing target detection. First, UAVs typically shoot from an overhead perspective, resulting in a too-singular angle for feature extraction, which may affect the detection algorithm's ability to identify and locate targets [7,8]. Second, UAVs may encounter complex background environments during detection, including season, weather, target occlusion, lighting, and similarly shaped objects, increasing the complexity of small target detection [9]. Third, during inspection or surveillance, targets often exhibit characteristics of small targets, with fewer pixels and relatively simple features. This can lead to targets being easily overlooked or misdetected during detection. Fourth, UAV target detection often needs to be performed in real-time with high accuracy requirements.

At present, UAV target detection methods are usually used in specific scenarios, typically suitable for scenes where the background and target image sizes are similar and uniform, such as maritime targets and agriculture. Therefore, in multi-class targets with complex backgrounds, detection performance is reduced, and feature loss occurs at different scales, increasing the risk of missed detections. UAVs frequently detect numerous small objects with limited detail, which can make them difficult to distinguish from the background or from other similar objects. This challenge arises because the limited resolution and fine detail in the images can cause these small objects to blend in with their surroundings or be easily misidentified.

To reply to these challenges, this paper introduces an enhanced model, CMS-YOLOv7, which builds upon the YOLOv7 framework. The proposed algorithm was tested using the VisDrone2019 dataset [10] and aims to advance UAV applications in small target detection by improving both precision and efficiency. This study accomplished the following:

(1) The small target detection layer (P2) was added, and the deep detection layer (P5) was eliminated. At the same time, the K-means++ method [11] was used to compute the anchor frame after operation. This enhanced the performance of the model in detecting small targets and reduced the possibility of false detection or missed detection.
(2) The Inner-MPDIoU loss function was constructed using the idea of Inner-IoU [12], replacing the CIoU [13], to improve the detection capability of small target objects in complicated surroundings.
(3) Introducing the CARAFE module [14] as a replacement for traditional upsampling methods allowed for a larger field of view, effectively aggregating contextual information to enhance the acquisition of target feature information.
(4) A new convolution module, SPD-Conv [15], was introduced to improve computational efficiency, enhance the model's performance and generalization ability, reduce information loss, and strengthen the feature extraction capability for small target objects.

2. Related Work
2.1. Common Target Detection Algorithms

Traditional target detection techniques are based on manually designed feature extractors [16,17]. While these methods offer the advantage of requiring fewer algorithm parameters for specific detection tasks, facilitating their integration into various small platforms, they also have notable drawbacks. Specifically, designing different feature extractors for diverse target detection needs limits the algorithm's adaptability. Despite their accuracy, these traditional methods often suffer from the problems of too-complex computation, a slow speed of processing tasks, insufficient adaptability, and reduced robustness.

Deep learning-based target detection frameworks are primarily classified in two ways—anchor-based and anchor-free methods—depending on their approach to defining ground truth. Within the anchor-based category, there are two primary types: multi-stage and single-stage methods. Multi-stage approaches, including R-CNN [18], Fast R-CNN [19], and Faster R-CNN [20], begin by generating region proposals and then apply convolutional neural networks to categorize objects and perform boundary box regression. These techniques are designed to improve detection accuracy and speed while addressing issues such as class imbalance. Conversely, single-stage methods, for example, the YOLO series [21–28], SSD [29], and RetinaNet [30], integrate feature extraction, classification, and localization into a single process, which leads to faster detection times. Although these single-stage detectors might have slightly lower accuracy compared with multi-stage methods, they significantly reduce computational requirements and are thus more suitable for real-time applications. However, despite the advancements offered by these deep learning techniques, their direct application to UAV aerial image detection may still present challenges.

2.2. YOLO Architectures Suitable for Aerial Imagery

YOLO series algorithms have gained widespread recognition in academia and industry for their excellent detection efficiency and accuracy in target detection. Among them, YOLOv5 [25] and YOLOv7 [27] are currently two of the most widely adopted models. YOLOv5 enhances real-time target detection tasks through advanced deep learning techniques, boasting improvements over its predecessor, YOLOv4 [24], in model architecture, training strategies, and overall performance. YOLOv5 integrates the CSP (Cross Stage Partial) network architecture, which significantly mitigates redundant computations and improves overall computational efficiency. Despite its advancements, YOLOv5 still faces difficulties in detecting small and densely packed objects and grappling with occlusions and pose variations. To overcome these challenges and boost the performance of real-time object detectors, YOLOv7 introduces a novel training scheme known as the Trainable Bag of Freebies (TBoF). This innovative approach has markedly enhanced the accuracy and generalization capabilities of various object detection models.

Extensive research has made numerous advancements to improve YOLO models, specifically for UAV target detection. Researchers have introduced multiple modifications and improvements to optimize these models for the unique challenges associated with aerial surveillance and detection tasks. Zhu et al. [31] proposed TPH-YOLOv5, a modification of YOLOv5 that substitutes the conventional prediction heads with Transformer Prediction Heads. This adaptation improves the model's capacity to handle complex scene variations. Qin et al. [32] developed the MCA-YOLOv7 algorithm, an improvement on the YOLOv7 model, by optimizing the Feature Pyramid Network (FPN) structure, incorporating attention mechanisms, and enhancing context aggregation blocks to better detect small targets. Wu et al. [33] amended the spatial pyramid pooling framework by integrating and cascading manifold pooling layers, which enhances the network's capacity for feature learning. Liu et al. [34] proposed EdgeYOLO, which features a lightweight decoupled head for target detection, achieving faster inference speeds and higher accuracy. Similarly, Zhao et al. [35] introduced the MS-YOLOv7 model, which leverages the Swin Transformer and attention mechanisms to improve the feature extraction capabilities of the network's neck, strengthening detection precision.

These studies have successfully enhanced UAV target detection performance to a certain extent. However, in practical UAV applications, target objects still face issues, such as complex and variable backgrounds, small sizes, and mutual occlusion, leading to missed and false detections. Constructing a more efficient target detection algorithm remains a significant challenge.

2.3. YOLOv7 Network Structure

YOLOv7 [27] represents a sophisticated single-stage target detection model known for its exceptional balance between speed and precision. Its advanced architecture ensures versatility and effectiveness across various application contexts. YOLOv7 offers different network configurations by adjusting width and depth parameters to address varying complexity and performance needs. Each configuration provides a tailored solution for diverse target detection tasks. The architecture of YOLOv7 is organized into three fundamental components: Backbone, Neck, and Head.

The Backbone network performs feature extraction; it consists of two main components: ELAN and MP. The ELAN module captures more contextual information by expanding the convolutional layer's receptive field, enhancing the network's learning ability. The MP module enhances feature extraction capability through multi-path convolution and receptive field expansion. The use of these two modules allows the backbone network to efficiently extract and represent image features while maintaining high computational efficiency.

To optimally merge feature information across multiple scales, the Neck network employs both the Feature Pyramid Network (FPN) architecture and the SPP-PANet design. The SPPCSPC structure, which combines Spatial Pyramid Pooling (SPP) with Cross Stage Partial Connections (CSPC), effectively enhances the network to extract and use the feature information.

In the Head part, the Rep structure is used to flexibly regulate the number of image channels in the output features. Then, through 1 × 1 convolution operations, the network can accurately predict object confidence, class, and anchor box position.

3. Method

3.1. CMS-YOLOv7

In aerial small target detection, while YOLOv7 demonstrates impressive performance due to its advanced network architecture, it faces challenges in extracting fine features from small targets due to the limited pixel information available. Additionally, the restricted receptive field of the model may impede its ability to capture comprehensive contextual information, complicating detection in complex environments. To solve these problems, we propose an enhanced model based on the YOLOv7 architecture named CMS-YOLOv7, specifically designed for UAV aerial image target detection tasks. The network architecture is depicted in Figure 1.

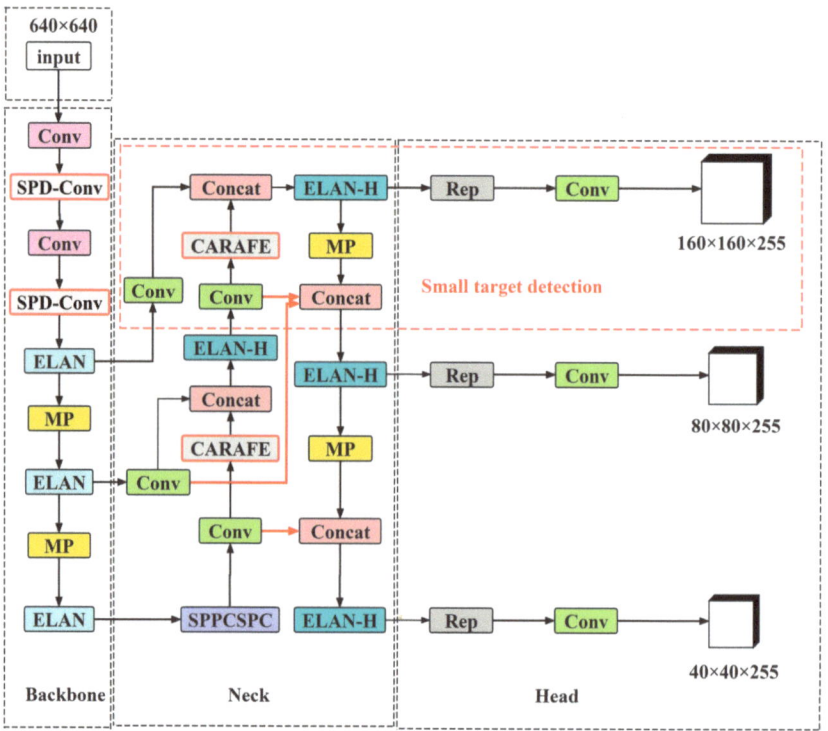

Figure 1. Network architecture of CMS-YOLOv7.

In this model, a small target detection layer is introduced while the deep detection layer is removed, allowing for better extraction of target pixel information and improved accuracy in detecting small targets. To enhance both regression and classification performance, we propose the Inner-MPDIoU loss function and incorporate an auxiliary bounding box for faster and more effective regression results. To overcome the limitations of traditional upsampling methods and improve target feature retrieval, we replace them with the

CARAFE module. Furthermore, the integration of the SPD-Conv module enhances the network's ability to obtain image features and minimize information loss, leading to improved detection of small objects in images.

3.2. Small Target Detection Layer

In UAV images characterized by complex backgrounds, detecting ground objects can be particularly challenging due to factors such as their small size, dense environments, and occlusion. To address these issues, we integrated an additional detection head into the baseline YOLOv7 framework, thereby enhancing its capability to more effectively identify small objects within UAV imagery.

The benchmark YOLOv7 network effectively detects objects of different scales from large to small using three different scale feature maps (80 × 80 × 255, 40 × 40 × 255, and 20 × 20 × 255). By adding a small target detection layer P2 (160 × 160 × 255), more small object feature information can be obtained from the shallow feature map, significantly enhancing the network's ability to capture medium and small object features. By directly feeding the feature map obtained from this layer into the prediction module, the accuracy of medium and small target detection is effectively improved, and the possibility of detecting errors and detecting omissions is significantly reduced, enhancing the network's adaptability to target scales and detection robustness.

Downsampling in deep feature maps often leads to a significant loss of information for small objects, making it difficult to capture their features effectively in the deep detection layer and potentially impacting final predictions during feature fusion. To address this issue, we introduce the P2 small target detection layer and remove the P5 deep detection layer. While adding the P2 detection head increases the network's parameter count, removing the P5 head reduces the large number of parameters, achieving a balanced adjustment in the overall parameter count.

However, eliminating the P5 detection head may also result in a partial loss of semantic information. Therefore, we further optimized the connectivity channels in the neck network to preserve more semantic information and strengthen the fusion of features.

Since YOLOv7 is an anchor-based target detection algorithm, its performance is sensitive to the sizes of anchor boxes. To optimize the size of anchor boxes, we used the K-means++ method [11]. Table 1 displays the optimized anchor box dimensions tailored for the VisDrone2019 dataset, configured for an image resolution of 640 × 640 pixels.

Table 1. Anchor box size setting.

Detection Layer	Feature Map Size	Anchor Frame Setting
P2	160 × 160	[3, 4, 4, 8, 7, 6]
P3	80 × 80	[7, 12, 14, 8, 11, 17]
P4	40 × 40	[27, 15, 21, 28, 48, 38]

3.3. Inner-MPDIoU

In YOLOv7, the CIoU loss function [13] is employed to enhance the accuracy of bounding box alignment evaluation. Unlike the traditional IoU loss, CIoU provides a more nuanced assessment by incorporating the overlap area, the distance between box centers, and the difference in aspect ratios. This detailed evaluation improves the precision of the predicted bounding boxes. The calculation formula of CIoU is provided in Equation (1).

$$L_{CIoU} = 1 - \text{IoU} + \frac{\rho(b, b^{gt})}{c^2} + \alpha v \quad (1)$$

where $\text{IoU} = \frac{|B \cap B^{gt}|}{|B \cup B^{gt}|}$ indicates the extent of overlap between the predicted box and the truth box, $v = \frac{4}{\pi^2} \left(\arcsin \frac{w^{gt}}{h^{gt}} - \arcsin \frac{w^{gt}}{h} \right)^2$ is used to represent the aspect ratio, and

$\alpha = \frac{v}{(1-\text{IoU})+v}$ represents the balancing parameter. b^{gt} and b represent the calculation results of the truth box and the predicted box, respectively. The Euclidean distance between the center points of the prediction box and the truth box is denoted by $\rho(b, b^{gt})$. $L_{IoU} = 1 - \text{IoU}$ is defined as the loss corresponding to IoU.

Many IoU-based Bounding Box Regression (BBR) loss functions aim to enhance convergence speed by incorporating additional loss terms, yet they frequently overlook the intrinsic limitations of IoU loss. Inner-IoU [12] addresses these limitations by integrating an auxiliary bounding box loss and applying a scaling factor to adjust the auxiliary bounding box size. This approach refines the bounding box regression process and improves detection accuracy. The detailed formulas are provided in Equations (2)–(6):

$$b_l = x_c - \frac{w \times ratio}{2}, b_r = x_c + \frac{w \times ratio}{2} \quad (2)$$

$$b_t = y_c - \frac{h \times ratio}{2}, b_b = y_c + \frac{h \times ratio}{2} \quad (3)$$

$$inter = (\min(b_r^{gt}, b_r) - \max(b_l^{gt}, b_l)) \times (\min(b_b^{gt}, b_b) - \max(b_t^{gt}, b_t)) \quad (4)$$

$$union = (w^{gt} \times h^{gt}) \times (ratio)^2 + (w \times h) \times (ratio)^2 - inter \quad (5)$$

$$\text{IoU}^{inner} = \frac{inter}{union} \quad (6)$$

where $ratio \in [0.5, 1.5]$, and when $ratio = 1$, Inner-IoU can be considered identical to ordinary IoU. When $ratio > 1$, the auxiliary bounding box is larger than the actual bounding box, promoting the regression of low IoU, which is beneficial for detecting small objects in the image. When $ratio < 1$, the auxiliary bounding box is smaller than the actual bounding box, accelerating the convergence of high IoU samples, which is beneficial for detecting large objects in the image.

MPDIoU [36] is an advanced evaluation criterion designed to improve the precision of object detection tasks. Unlike traditional IoU, which measures the overlap between predicted and truth bounding boxes, MPDIoU integrates probabilistic information to provide a more nuanced assessment of localization accuracy. This metric helps address challenges related to precise object boundary delineation and enhances the evaluation of detection models, particularly in complex scenarios where traditional IoU may fall short.

$$d_1^2 = (x_1^{prd} - x_1^{gt})^2 + (y_1^{prd} - y_1^{gt})^2 \quad (7)$$

$$d_2^2 = (x_2^{prd} - x_2^{gt})^2 + (y_2^{prd} - y_2^{gt})^2 \quad (8)$$

$$\text{MPDIoU} = \text{IoU} - \frac{d_1^2}{w^2 + h^2} - \frac{d_2^2}{w^2 + h^2} \quad (9)$$

$$L_{MPDIoU} = 1 - \text{MPDIoU} \quad (10)$$

The distance between the upper left and lower right corners of the predicted and truth boxes is symbolized by d_1^2 and d_2^2. Building on the concept of Inner-IoU, MPDIoU is enhanced by employing a scale factor to generate auxiliary boxes of varying scales for loss calculation. This adjustment results in faster and more effective regression outcomes. The Inner-MPDIoU calculation formula is shown in Equation (11).

$$L_{Inner-MPDIoU} = L_{MPDIoU} + \text{IoU} - \text{IoU}^{inner} \quad (11)$$

3.4. CARAFE

Upsampling is a crucial operation in convolutional neural networks (CNNs) primarily used in the feature fusion stage to improve feature resolution. This process increases the size of feature maps, allowing for finer detail representation in images. In deep learning and computer vision, various methods for upsampling exist, including interpolation techniques like nearest-neighbor, bilinear, and trilinear interpolation. YOLOv7 uses nearest-neighbor interpolation for upsampling, which relies only on adjacent pixels and does not fully utilize the semantic information within the feature map.

CARAFE, introduced by Wang et al. [14], represents a lightweight and resource-efficient image upsampling technique designed to overcome the limitations of traditional nearest-neighbor interpolation methods, particularly in handling small targets where feature degradation often occurs. CARAFE enhances feature reconstruction by leveraging larger receptive fields to incorporate a richer context of feature information, thus improving the accuracy of upsampled images.

In this study, we integrated the CARAFE module into the neck region of our network, replacing the previous upsampling component. The CARAFE module is composed of two main parts: the upsampling prediction module and the feature reassembly module, as depicted in Figure 2.

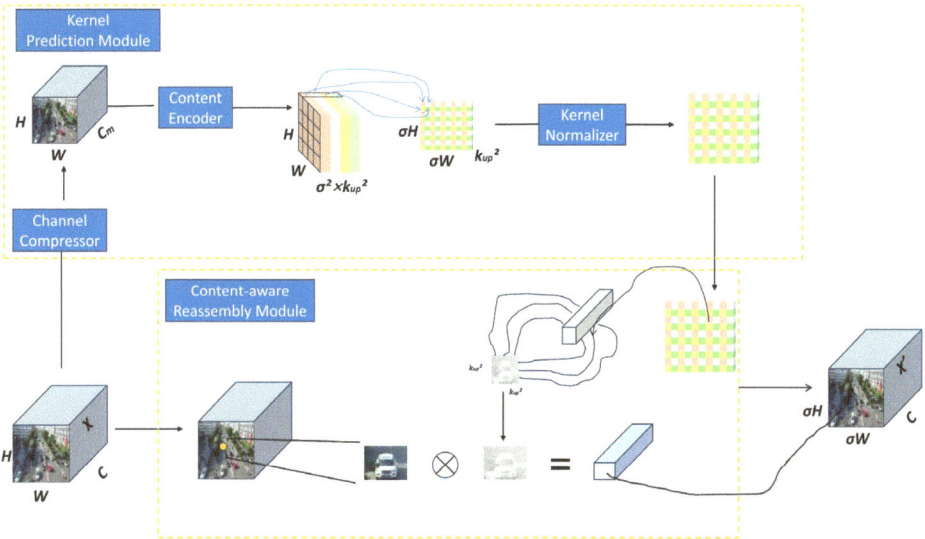

Figure 2. Structure of CARAFE.

In the upsampling prediction module, the process begins with input images of size $H \times W \times C$. With an upsampling factor of σ, a 1×1 convolutional layer first reduces the number of image channels. Next, a convolution kernel of size $k_{up} \times k_{up}$ performs convolution operations, expanding the channel count to channels $\sigma^2 \times k_{up}^2$ for content encoding. To finalize the process, output normalization is applied to optimize the parameter count, ensuring efficient model performance. Next, the feature reassembly module takes these features after processing and integrates them through an element-wise multiplication operation. This is performed between the prediction reassembly kernel and the corresponding areas of the original feature map. This operation effectively reconstructs the upsampling output, leveraging the preserved information from the original features. By carefully reassembling and enhancing these features, the module achieves a high-quality upsampling result that maintains fidelity and detail from the initial input.

3.5. SPD-Conv

In the domains of target detection and image classification, convolutional neural networks (CNNs) have demonstrated exceptional performance and set new benchmarks. However, for small target detection tasks, especially when these small objects overlap, occlude, or are very small and blurry in the image, traditional CNN architectures often face challenges. These scenarios require the network to capture and retain fine-grained image information, but current designs often struggle to handle these details, leading to a decline in feature learning ability and significantly affecting model performance. To tackle this challenge, the paper presents a novel convolutional neural network architecture, SPD-Conv [15], integrated into the backbone network. The SPD-Conv structure is depicted in Figure 3.

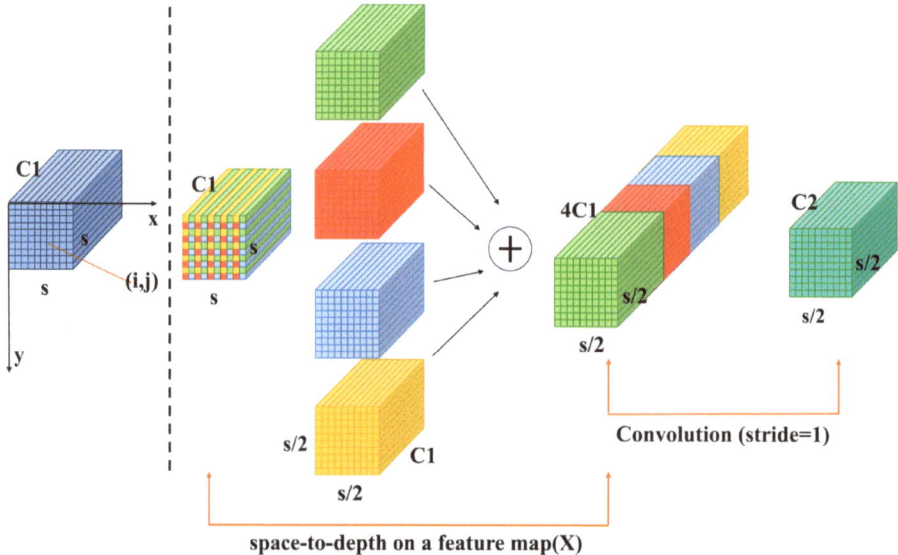

Figure 3. Structure of SPD-Conv.

The SPD-Conv architecture introduces an innovative approach to convolutional neural networks by incorporating two key components: the SPD (space-to-depth) layer and a non-strided convolutional layer. The SPD module ensures that all information within the channel dimension is fully preserved during the downsampling process, avoiding any information loss. A non-strided convolutional layer is added after each SPD module. This convolutional layer reduces the number of channels by learning parameters, minimizing non-discriminative information loss. This design is particularly advantageous for low-resolution and small target detection tasks. It works by segmenting the original feature map into multiple sub-feature maps, each downsampled at different scales. Then, the sub-feature maps are connected by the channel dimension, and a feature map with reduced scale but enhanced information richness. When the method is applied to the backbone, more feature information in the image is preserved through the feature connection of multiple sub-feature graphs. In the same downsampling process, the computational efficiency of the model is improved, the model performance and generalization are significantly enhanced, and the information loss is minimized.

4. Experiments
4.1. Dataset

To assess the ability of CMS-YOLOv7, we used the VisDrone2019 dataset [10], which was compiled by the AISKYEYE team at Tianjin University's Machine Learning and Data Mining Laboratory. This dataset comprises 6471 training images, 548 validation images, and 1610 testing images, all captured from a drone's perspective. It includes ten kinds of objects: pedestrians, people, bicycles, cars, vans, trucks, tricycles, awning-tricycles, buses, and motors. The images feature numerous small to medium-sized objects, some of which overlap, and cover diverse scenes such as highways and intersections under various weather conditions, like sunny, rainy, cloudy, and nighttime conditions. These characteristics pose significant challenges for target detection. The VisDrone2019 dataset is shown in Figure 4.

Figure 4. Partial image of the VisDrone2019 dataset.

4.2. Parameter Settings

The experiments were performed on a Windows 11 system featuring an Intel® Core™ i7-13700F CPU, an RTX 4090 24 GB GPU, CUDA 11.1, and Python 3.8, with PyTorch 1.13.0 as the deep learning framework. The training configuration included a batch size of 8 and 300 epochs and input image dimensions of 640 × 640 pixels. All other parameters were configured to the default settings of YOLOv7.

4.3. Evaluation Metrics

Four metrics are used in this paper to evaluate the performance of the target detection algorithm: mAP@0.5, mAP@0.5:0.95, Parameters, GFLOPs, and FPS.

In the context of object detection evaluations, mAP@0.5 refers to the mean average precision (mAP) computed using a fixed IoU threshold of 0.5. This metric assesses the accuracy of the model's predictions by calculating how well the predicted bounding boxes overlap with the truth boxes when this overlap is at least 50%.

By contrast, mAP@0.5:0.95 offers a more detailed performance assessment by averaging mAP values over a range of IoU thresholds from 0.5 to 0.95, with 0.05 increments. This broader evaluation captures the model's performance across various levels of localization accuracy, providing a more comprehensive picture of its robustness and effectiveness in different detection scenarios. By incorporating multiple IoU thresholds, mAP@0.5:0.95 reflects how well the model performs under varying degrees of overlap, thus offering a more nuanced understanding of its overall detection capabilities.

Precision (P) is used to measure the percentage of the predicted positive samples that actually turn out to be positive. Essentially, it represents the number of samples that were predicted to be positive that were actually positive. The formula for calculating Precision is detailed in Equation (12).

$$\text{Precision} = \frac{TP}{TP + FP} \quad (12)$$

Recall (R) is used to indicate the percentage of actual positive samples that are correctly predicted to be positive examples. In other words, it indicates how many of all the true positive examples are correctly predicted as positive. The detailed formula for calculating Recall is provided in Equation (13).

$$\text{Recall} = \frac{TP}{TP + FN} \tag{13}$$

mAP is an integral metric for assessing the performance of object detection models across a range of classes. It is calculated as the weighted average of the average precision (AP) scores for each individual class within the dataset. The specific formula of mAP is detailed in Equation (14).

$$\text{mAP} = \frac{\sum_{n=1}^{\infty} \int_0^1 P(R) dR}{N} \tag{14}$$

Additionally, GFLOPs serve as a metric for evaluating the computational complexity of a model, reflecting the volume of arithmetic operations required during inference. FPS is employed to express the inference speed of the model when it actually performs the detection task. The parameters can measure the size of the model.

4.4. Ablation Experiments

In order to further evaluate the effectiveness of the CMS-YOLOv7 model, ablation studies were performed using the VisDrone2019 dataset.

4.4.1. Comparison with Baseline Model

The validation set of the VisDrone2019 dataset was used to assess the performance of each component introduced. To effectively demonstrate changes in algorithm performance, we measured metrics such as mAP@0.5, mAP@0.5:0.95, number of parameters, GFLOPs, and FPS. All experiments were conducted under uniform conditions with consistent parameters to ensure accuracy.

Table 2 outlines the progressive introduction of several key improvement strategies relative to the baseline YOLOv7. This detailed the development process of the CMS-YOLOv7 on the VisDrone2019 dataset and analyzed the resulting performance changes. The introduction of these strategies led to a significant enhancement in the model's detection performance.

Table 2. Experimental results on the VisDrone2019 dataset.

Add P2	Remove P5 with Optimized Neck	Inner-MPDIoU	CARAFESPD-Conv	mAP@0.5	mAP@0.5:0.95	Params (M)	GFLOPs	FPS
				48.8%	27.7%	36.53	103.3	119
✓				50.0%	29.5%	37.08	117.1	96
✓	✓			50.3%	29.7%	17.71	116.9	102
✓	✓	✓		50.7%	29.9%	17.71	116.9	104
✓	✓	✓	✓	51.1%	30.2%	17.84	117.9	88
✓	✓	✓	✓	**52.3%**	**30.7%**	17.99	**166.0**	73

Initially, the addition of the P2 detection head resulted in notable improvements in performance metrics, with mAP@0.5 and mAP@0.5:0.95 increasing by 1.2% and 1.8%, respectively. Subsequently, removing the P5 detection head and optimizing the connectivity channels in the neck network led to further gains, with mAP@0.5 and mAP@0.5:0.95 increasing by an additional 0.3% and 0.2%. These modifications significantly enhanced the model's capability to detect small objects, while resulting in an 18.82 M drop in parameters and a small increase in GFLOPs compared with baseline YOLOv7.

Next, the Inner-MPDIoU loss function was adopted in place of the original CIoU loss function. This improvement strategy resulted in a successful increase of 0.4% in mAP@0.5 and 0.2% in mAP@0.5:0.95, without requiring any additional parameters or GFLOPs.

Following this, the use of the CARAFE module instead of traditional upsampling methods slightly increased both parameter count and GFLOPs. This adjustment led to enhancements of 0.4% in mAP@0.5 and 0.3% in mAP@0.5:0.95.

Finally, optimizing the network's backbone with SPD-Conv was introduced to enhance the detection of small objects. This addition led to a notable improvement in performance, with mAP@0.5 and mAP@0.5:0.95 increasing by 1.2% and 0.5%, respectively. Although this improvement made the parameters increase slightly and generated some additional computational overhead, the impact on the detection performance and real-time ability of the model was still small.

Overall, these four improvements resulted in a 3.5% increase in mAP@0.5 and a 3.0% increase in mAP@0.5:0.95 for the model while reducing the parameter count by 18.54 M, achieving a degree of lightweight model optimization.

4.4.2. Determining Parameters in Inner-MPDIoU

In Inner-IoU, the scaling factor *ratio* is used to adjust the size of the auxiliary bounding box during loss calculation. Increasing *ratio* enlarges the auxiliary bounding box, which helps the model better capture feature information for small and medium-sized targets, thereby enhancing detection accuracy. To assess the effectiveness of this approach, an empirical study was conducted to examine how varying *ratio* affects the performance of the target detection algorithm.

Firstly, the P2 detection head was introduced into the YOLOv7 network, the P5 detection head was removed, and the neck connection channels were adjusted. Then, on the basis of this, Inner-MPDIoU was introduced, and the network's *ratio* value was adjusted to adapt to the changes in feature map size brought by the previous improvements. This adjustment ensured that the model could fully utilize the feature information of small and medium-sized targets extracted by the previous improvements, further enhancing the accuracy of target detection.

Table 3 indicates variations when adjusting within the range of $ratio \in [1.30, 1.45]$, affecting both mAP@0.5 and mAP@0.5:0.95. The optimal performance improvement was observed at $ratio = 1.33$. Therefore, for subsequent experiments, Inner-MPDIoU was set to 1.33.

Table 3. Effect of ratio values on experimental results.

Ratio	mAP@0.5	mAP@0.5:0.95
1.30	50.6%	29.8%
1.33	**50.7%**	**29.9%**
1.35	50.7%	29.8%
1.37	50.6%	29.7%
1.40	50.5%	29.7%
1.41	50.5%	29.6%
1.45	50.3%	29.5%

4.5. Detection Results Visualization

From the detailed analysis of the experimental data, it is evident that the CMS-YOLOv7 model significantly outperforms the baseline YOLOv7 on the VisDrone2019 dataset. To illustrate the performance differences between the two models in target detection, we present predictions on three representative images. These examples offer an intuitive comparison of their relative effectiveness.

Figure 5 presents the prediction results categorized into three groups—(a), (b), and (c)—for comparative analysis. In each group, the left image shows the detection outcomes from the baseline YOLOv7 model, while the right image depicts the results from the CMS-YOLOv7 model.

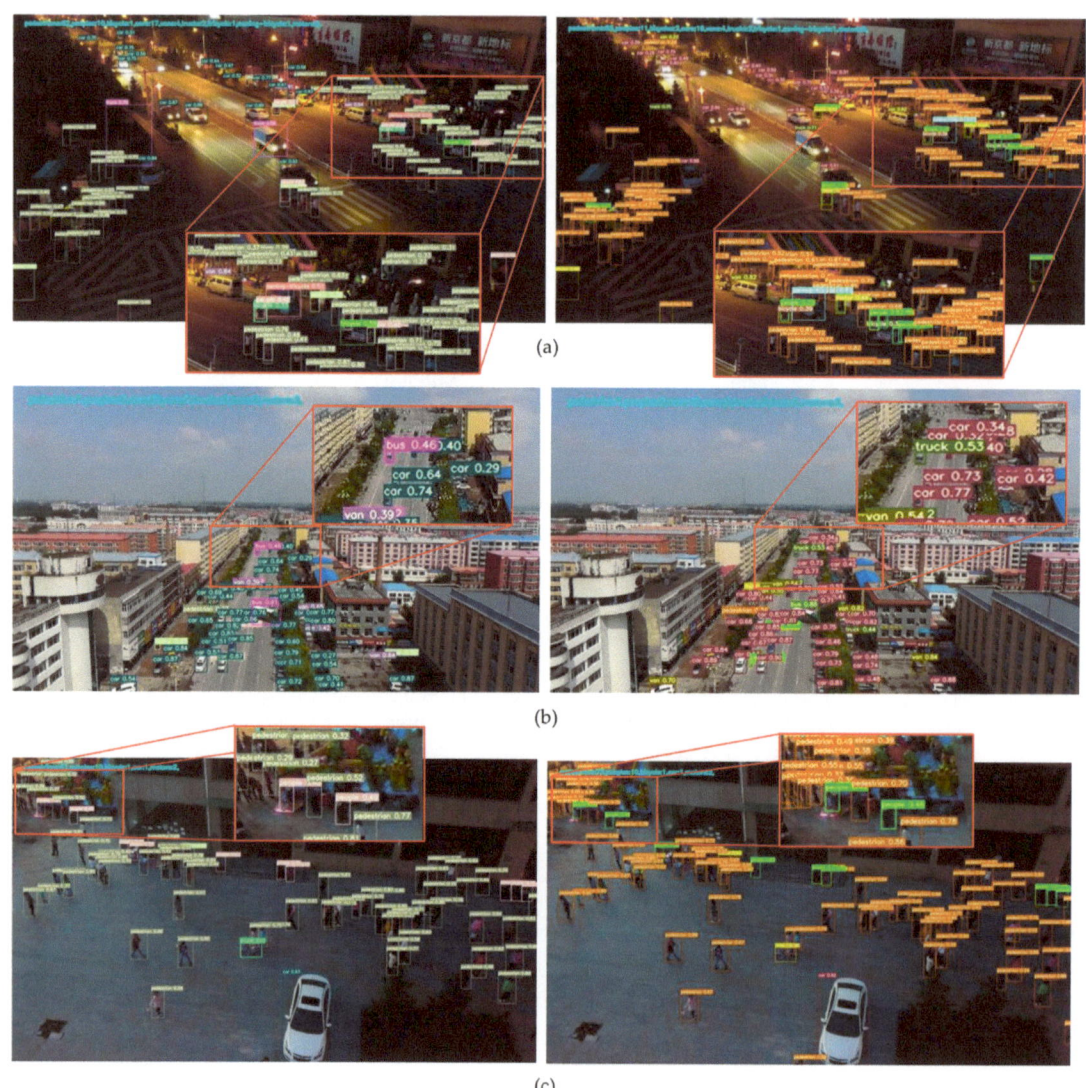

Figure 5. Comparative analysis of baseline YOLOv7 and CMS-YOLOv7 on VisDrone2019 dataset.

In group (a) images, the YOLOv7 baseline model detected 72 pedestrians, 10 individuals, 1 bicycle, 17 cars, 4 vans, 2 trucks, 1 tricycle, 1 tricycle with awning, and 5 motorcycles. By contrast, the CMS-YOLOv7 model detected 85 pedestrians, 11 individuals, 2 bicycles, 19 cars, 4 vans, 2 trucks, 1 tricycle, 1 tricycle with awning, and 6 motorcycles.

In group (b) images, the baseline YOLOv7 model detected 1 pedestrian, 2 individuals, 39 cars, 7 trucks, 2 buses, 2 motorcycles, and 3 other vehicles. The CMS-YOLOv7 model detected 1 pedestrian, 2 individuals, 43 cars, 9 trucks, 3 buses, 2 motorcycles, and 3 other vehicles.

In group (c) images, the baseline YOLOv7 model detected 61 pedestrians, 10 individuals, 1 bicycle, 1 car, and 2 motorcycles. The CMS-YOLOv7 model detected 73 pedestrians, 10 individuals, 1 bicycle, 1 car, and 2 motorcycles.

The position marked in the red box in the figure shows more intuitively that CMS-YOLOv7 can detect more small targets.

In summary, the CMS-YOLOv7 model exhibited markedly superior detection performance compared with the baseline YOLOv7 on the VisDrone2019 dataset. The CMS-YOLOv7 model not only detected a greater number of targets but also demonstrated enhanced accuracy and improved capability in detecting small objects. These experimental results strongly support the application of the CMS-YOLOv7 model for tasks such as drone target detection.

4.6. Comparison with Other Algorithms

To thoroughly assess the performance of the CMS-YOLOv7 model for target detection, a comparative analysis was performed against several established models, including YOLOv4, YOLOv5l, TPH-YOLOv5 [31], YOLOv6m, YOLOv7, and YOLOv8. Comprehensive experiments were conducted on the VisDrone2019 dataset, focusing on key evaluation metrics such as mAP@0.5 and mAP@0.5:0.95 to gauge detection accuracy across various IoU thresholds. This comparative evaluation facilitates a nuanced understanding of the CMS-YOLOv7 model's effectiveness in target detection, with the detailed results summarized in Table 4.

Table 4. Comparison between different models.

Model	mAP@0.5	mAP@0.5:0.95
YOLOv4	47.5%	26.1%
YOLOv5l	39.8%	22.9%
TPH-YOLOv5	46.4%	27.6%
YOLOv6m	31.9%	21.8%
YOLOv7	48.8%	27.7%
YOLOv8	45.5%	27.8%
CMS-YOLOv7	**52.3%**	**30.7%**

The experimental findings reveal that the CMS-YOLOv7 model exhibits outstanding performance on the VisDrone2019 dataset. It shows notable improvements in both mAP@0.5 and mAP@0.5:0.95, highlighting its effectiveness and superiority in target detection tasks. Given that the VisDrone2019 dataset closely mirrors real-world scenarios in drone target detection, these results underscore the practicality and effectiveness of CMS-YOLOv7 for real-world applications.

5. Conclusions

Addressing prevalent challenges in UAV image object detection such as multi-scale objects, dense distributions, occlusions, and the high prevalence of small targets, this paper introduces the CMS-YOLOv7 algorithm. This novel approach enhances detection performance by incorporating a specialized small target detection layer (P2), eliminating the deep detection layer (P5), and adjusting the neck connection channels, thereby significantly improving the detection of small objects in aerial imagery. Introducing Inner-MPDIoU to replace CIoU accelerated the bounding box regression process by incorporating auxiliary bounding boxes for loss calculation, thereby enhancing learning capabilities for small target samples in complex backgrounds. Substituting the CARAFE module for traditional upsampling modules effectively aggregates contextual information, improving feature acquisition capabilities. Finally, integrating SPD-Conv into the backbone architecture mitigated information loss in images and bolsters the model's capacity to extract features from small targets, thereby enhancing overall detection performance. The experimental results demonstrate that CMS-YOLOv7 achieves significantly higher accuracy in object detection compared with other advanced algorithm models, particularly excelling in detecting small targets.

In addition, CMS-YOLOv7 shows excellent detection performance, significantly reduces the model parameters, and realizes the light weight of the model. At the same time, GFLOPs is added to enhance the computational power of the model and improve the detection performance. In a word, the model meets the requirements of UAV image detection accuracy and real-time detection.

Author Contributions: Conceptualization, J.Q.; methodology, J.Q.; software, J.Q. and W.Y.; validation, J.Q. and W.Y.; formal analysis, J.Q. and X.F.; investigation, J.Q. and X.F.; resources, J.Q.; data curation, J.Q.; writing—original draft preparation, J.Q., W.Y. and X.F.; writing—review and editing, J.Q., W.Y. and X.F.; visualization, J.Q.; supervision, Z.M. and C.T.; project administration, Z.M. and C.T.; funding acquisition, Z.M. and C.T. All authors have read and agreed to the published version of the manuscript.

Funding: This research was funded by the National Natural Science Foundation of China (under Grant No. 62266004), supported by the Open Project Program of Guangxi Key Laboratory of Digital Infrastructure (under Grant No. GXDINBC202401) and the National Training Program of Innovation and Entrepreneurship for Undergraduates (under Grant No. 202310593066).

Data Availability Statement: Data set: https://github.com/VisDrone (accessed on 23 July 2024).

Conflicts of Interest: The authors declare no conflicts of interest.

References

1. Fan, B.; Li, Y.; Zhang, R.; Fu, Q. Review on the technological development and application of UAV systems. *Chin. J. Electron.* **2020**, *29*, 199–207. [CrossRef]
2. Do-Duy, T.; Nguyen, L.D.; Duong, T.Q.; Khosravirad, S.R.; Claussen, H. Joint optimisation of real-time deployment and resource allocation for UAV-aided disaster emergency communications. *IEEE J. Sel. Areas Commun.* **2021**, *39*, 3411–3424. [CrossRef]
3. Villarreal, C.A.; Garzón, C.G.; Mora, J.P.; Rojas, J.D.; Ríos, C.A. Workflow for capturing information and characterizing difficult-to-access geological outcrops using unmanned aerial vehicle-based digital photogrammetric data. *J. Ind. Inf. Integr.* **2022**, *26*, 100292. [CrossRef]
4. Zhao, Z.-Q.; Zheng, P.; Xu, S.-T.; Wu, X. Object detection with deep learning: A review. *IEEE Trans. Neural Netw. Learn. Syst.* **2019**, *30*, 3212–3232. [CrossRef] [PubMed]
5. LeCun, Y.; Bengio, Y.; Hinton, G. Deep learning. *Nature* **2015**, *521*, 436–444. [CrossRef] [PubMed]
6. Wu, X.; Li, W.; Hong, D.; Tao, R.; Du, Q. Deep learning for unmanned aerial vehicle-based object detection and tracking: A survey. *IEEE Geosci. Remote Sens. Mag.* **2021**, *10*, 91–124. [CrossRef]
7. Zou, Z.; Chen, K.; Shi, Z.; Guo, Y.; Ye, J. Object detection in 20 years: A survey. *Proc. IEEE* **2023**, *111*, 257–276. [CrossRef]
8. Zhu, P.; Wen, L.; Du, D.; Bian, X.; Fan, H.; Hu, Q.; Ling, H. Detection and tracking meet drones challenge. *IEEE Trans. Pattern Anal. Mach. Intell.* **2021**, *44*, 7380–7399. [CrossRef] [PubMed]
9. Oksuz, K.; Cam, B.C.; Kalkan, S.; Akbas, E. Imbalance problems in object detection: A review. *IEEE Trans. Pattern Anal. Mach. Intell.* **2020**, *43*, 3388–3415. [CrossRef] [PubMed]
10. Du, D.; Zhu, P.; Wen, L.; Bian, X.; Lin, H.; Hu, Q.; Peng, T.; Zheng, J.; Wang, X.; Zhang, Y. VisDrone-DET2019: The vision meets drone object detection in image challenge results. In Proceedings of the IEEE/CVF International Conference on Computer Vision Workshops, Seoul, Republic of Korea, 27–28 October 2019.
11. Arthur, D.; Vassilvitskii, S. *k-Means++: The Advantages of Careful Seeding*; Stanford: Stanford, CA, USA, 2006.
12. Zhang, H.; Xu, C.; Zhang, S. Inner-IoU: More effective intersection over union loss with auxiliary bounding box. *arXiv* **2023**, arXiv:2311.02877.
13. Zheng, Z.; Wang, P.; Ren, D.; Liu, W.; Ye, R.; Hu, Q.; Zuo, W. Enhancing geometric factors in model learning and inference for object detection and instance segmentation. *IEEE Trans. Cybern.* **2021**, *52*, 8574–8586. [CrossRef] [PubMed]
14. Wang, J.; Chen, K.; Xu, R.; Liu, Z.; Loy, C.C.; Lin, D. Carafe: Content-aware reassembly of features. In Proceedings of the IEEE/CVF International Conference on Computer Vision, Seoul, Republic of Korea, 27–28 October 2019; pp. 3007–3016.
15. Sunkara, R.; Luo, T. No more strided convolutions or pooling: A new CNN building block for low-resolution images and small objects. In Proceedings of the Joint European Conference on Machine Learning and Knowledge Discovery in Databases, Grenoble, France, 19–23 September 2022; pp. 443–459.
16. Lowe, D.G. Distinctive image features from scale-invariant keypoints. *Int. J. Comput. Vis.* **2004**, *60*, 91–110. [CrossRef]
17. Dalal, N.; Triggs, B. Histograms of oriented gradients for human detection. In Proceedings of the 2005 IEEE Computer Society Conference on Computer Vision and Pattern Recognition (CVPR'05), San Diego, CA, USA, 20–25 June 2005; pp. 886–893.

18. Girshick, R.; Donahue, J.; Darrell, T.; Malik, J. Rich feature hierarchies for accurate object detection and semantic segmentation. In Proceedings of the IEEE Conference on Computer Vision and Pattern Recognition, Columbus, OH, USA, 23–28 June 2014; pp. 580–587.
19. Girshick, R. Fast r-cnn. In Proceedings of the IEEE International Conference on Computer Vision, Las Condes, Chile, 11–18 December 2015; pp. 1440–1448.
20. Ren, S.; He, K.; Girshick, R.; Sun, J. Faster r-cnn: Towards real-time object detection with region proposal networks. *Adv. Neural Inf. Process. Syst.* **2015**, *28*, 91–99. [CrossRef] [PubMed]
21. Redmon, J.; Divvala, S.; Girshick, R.; Farhadi, A. You only look once: Unified, real-time object detection. In Proceedings of the IEEE Conference on Computer Vision and Pattern Recognition, Las Vegas, NV, USA, 27–30 June 2016; pp. 779–788.
22. Redmon, J.; Farhadi, A. YOLO9000: Better, faster, stronger. In Proceedings of the IEEE Conference on Computer Vision and Pattern Recognition, Honolulu, HI, USA, 21–26 July 2017; pp. 7263–7271.
23. Redmon, J.; Farhadi, A. Yolov3: An incremental improvement. *arXiv* **2018**, arXiv:1804.02767.
24. Bochkovskiy, A.; Wang, C.-Y.; Liao, H.-Y.M. Yolov4: Optimal speed and accuracy of object detection. *arXiv* **2020**, arXiv:2004.10934.
25. Ultralytics: Yolov5. [EB/OL]. Available online: https://github.com/ultralytics/yolov5 (accessed on 23 July 2024).
26. Li, C.; Li, L.; Jiang, H.; Weng, K.; Geng, Y.; Li, L.; Ke, Z.; Li, Q.; Cheng, M.; Nie, W. YOLOv6: A single-stage object detection framework for industrial applications. *arXiv* **2022**, arXiv:2209.02976.
27. Wang, C.-Y.; Bochkovskiy, A.; Liao, H.-Y.M. YOLOv7: Trainable bag-of-freebies sets new state-of-the-art for real-time object detectors. In Proceedings of the IEEE/CVF Conference on Computer Vision and Pattern Recognition, Vancouver, BC, Canada, 17–24 June 2023; pp. 7464–7475.
28. Wang, C.; Yeh, I.; Liao, H. YOLOv9: Learning what you want to learn using programmable gradient information. *arXiv* **2024**, arXiv:2402.13616.
29. Liu, W.; Anguelov, D.; Erhan, D.; Szegedy, C.; Reed, S.; Fu, C.-Y.; Berg, A.C. Ssd: Single shot multibox detector. In Proceedings of the Computer Vision–ECCV 2016: 14th European Conference, Amsterdam, The Netherlands, 11–14 October 2016; pp. 21–37, Proceedings, Part I 14.
30. Lin, T.-Y.; Goyal, P.; Girshick, R.; He, K.; Dollár, P. Focal loss for dense object detection. In Proceedings of the IEEE International Conference on Computer Vision, Venice, Italy, 22–29 October 2017; pp. 2980–2988.
31. Zhu, X.; Lyu, S.; Wang, X.; Zhao, Q. TPH-YOLOv5: Improved YOLOv5 based on transformer prediction head for object detection on drone-captured scenarios. In Proceedings of the IEEE/CVF International Conference on Computer Vision, Montreal, BC, Canada, 11–17 October 2021; pp. 2778–2788.
32. Qin, Z.; Chen, D.; Wang, H. MCA-YOLOv7: An Improved UAV Target Detection Algorithm Based on YOLOv7. *IEEE Access* **2024**, *12*, 42642–42650. [CrossRef]
33. Wu, H.; Hua, Y.; Zou, H.; Ke, G. A lightweight network for vehicle detection based on embedded system. *J. Supercomput.* **2022**, *78*, 18209–18224. [CrossRef]
34. Liu, S.; Zha, J.; Sun, J.; Li, Z.; Wang, G. EdgeYOLO: An edge-real-time object detector. In Proceedings of the 2023 42nd Chinese Control Conference (CCC), Tianjin, China, 24–26 July 2023; pp. 7507–7512.
35. Zhao, L.; Zhu, M. MS-YOLOv7: YOLOv7 based on multi-scale for object detection on UAV aerial photography. *Drones* **2023**, *7*, 188. [CrossRef]
36. Siliang, M.; Yong, X. MPDIoU: A loss for efficient and accurate bounding box regression. *arXiv* **2023**, arXiv:2307.07662.

Disclaimer/Publisher's Note: The statements, opinions and data contained in all publications are solely those of the individual author(s) and contributor(s) and not of MDPI and/or the editor(s). MDPI and/or the editor(s) disclaim responsibility for any injury to people or property resulting from any ideas, methods, instructions or products referred to in the content.

Article

RN-YOLO: A Small Target Detection Model for Aerial Remote-Sensing Images

Ke Wang, Hao Zhou, Hao Wu and Guowu Yuan *

School of Information Science and Engineering, Yunnan University, Kunming 650504, China; 20211120029@mail.ynu.edu.cn (K.W.); zhouhao@ynu.edu.cn (H.Z.); haowu_sise@ynu.edu.cn (H.W.)
* Correspondence: gwyuan@ynu.edu.cn

Abstract: Accurately detecting targets in remote-sensing images is crucial for the military, urban planning, and resource exploration. There are some challenges in extracting detailed features from remote-sensing images, such as complex backgrounds, large-scale variations, and numerous small targets. This paper proposes a remote-sensing target detection model called RN-YOLO (YOLO with RepGhost and NAM), which integrates RepGhost and a normalization-based attention module (NAM) based on YOLOv8. Firstly, NAM is added to the feature extraction network to enhance the capture capabilities for small targets by recalibrating receptive fields and strengthening information flow. Secondly, an efficient RepGhost_C2f structure is employed in the feature fusion network to replace the C2f module, effectively reducing the parameters. Lastly, the WIoU (Wise Intersection over Union) loss function is adopted to mitigate issues such as significant variations in target sizes and difficulty locating small targets, effectively improving the localization accuracy of small targets. The experimental results demonstrate that compared to the YOLOv8s model, the RN-YOLO model reduces the parameter count by 13.9%. Moreover, on the DOTAv1.5, TGRS-HRRSD, and RSOD datasets, the detection accuracy (mAP@.5:.95) of the RN-YOLO model improves by 3.6%, 1.2%, and 2%, respectively, compared to the YOLOv8s model, showcasing its outstanding performance and enhanced capability in detecting small targets.

Keywords: target detection; remote sensing; YOLOv8; attention mechanism; lightweight convolution

Citation: Wang, K.; Zhou, H.; Wu, H.; Yuan, G. RN-YOLO: A Small Target Detection Model for Aerial Remote-Sensing Images. *Electronics* **2024**, *13*, 2383. https://doi.org/10.3390/electronics13122383

Academic Editor: Eva Cernadas

Received: 15 May 2024
Revised: 7 June 2024
Accepted: 13 June 2024
Published: 18 June 2024

Copyright: © 2024 by the authors. Licensee MDPI, Basel, Switzerland. This article is an open access article distributed under the terms and conditions of the Creative Commons Attribution (CC BY) license (https:// creativecommons.org/licenses/by/ 4.0/).

1. Introduction

Target detection in aerial remote-sensing images aims to identify and determine the position and type of specific objects contained in the remote-sensing images. With the rapid development of drone and satellite technologies, it has been widely applied in both military and civilian sectors, playing a crucial role in various aspects, such as environmental monitoring [1], urban planning [2], agricultural management [3], and disaster response [4]. As depicted in Figure 1, aerial remote-sensing images have many features, such as overhead imaging, significant changes in object size, and many small targets. These features pose a major challenge to aerial remote-sensing image detection.

In target detection for remote-sensing images, traditional approaches often rely on specific feature selection [5] and hand-designed algorithms [6]. While these methods have yielded some success in specific scenarios, they need help to adapt to the complexities and variations inherent in remote sensing. Deep learning has provided a novel solution to these challenges in recent years. The target detection model is categorized into two main types: two-stage and one-stage. Two-stage detection involves generating candidate regions within the image, which are fed into a convolutional neural network (CNN) for target identification and localization through classification and regression. Representative algorithms in this category include R-CNN [7], Fast R-CNN [8], and Faster R-CNN [9]. On the other hand, single-stage detection directly computes the coordinates and category probabilities of target objects from the image features extracted using CNN, such as the algorithms in SSD [10,11] and the YOLO series [12–15]. Notably, while two-stage detection algorithms necessitate sequential steps for region proposal and subsequent classification and regression, they tend to be slower than their single-stage counterparts. Moreover, with the introduction of the YOLO family of algorithms, single-stage detection methods have significantly enhanced detection accuracy while maintaining high-speed performance.

 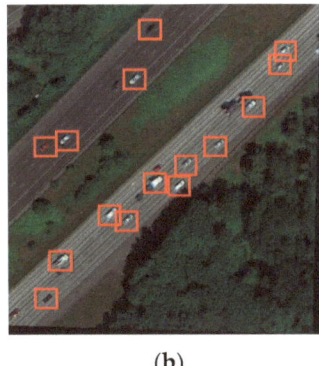

(a)   (b)

Figure 1. Remote-sensing image, red frames represent the identification box. (**a**) Large difference in target size; (**b**) Numerous small targets.

Many researchers have made notable progress in refining YOLO models specifically for detecting targets in remote-sensing images in recent years. Zhu et al. [16] proposed TPH-YOLOv5, which integrates the transformer module to enhance the feature extraction capability of the model but increases the number of parameters and the computational complexity. Yang et al. [17] introduced RS-YOLOX, leveraging the ECA attention mechanism and ASFF feature extraction algorithm to boost small targets' detection accuracy effectively. Yet, there remains room for improvement in terms of lightweighting. Yu et al. [18] leveraged the centralized feature pyramid (CFP) and the hybrid attention ACmix but encountered suboptimal enhancement accuracy and instances of missed detection. Liu et al. [19] combined hybrid extended convolution with a self-designed residual network, bolstering feature extraction for targets of varying sizes. However, their model's scope could have been broadened to localizing and classifying aircraft on the DOTA dataset, constraining its generalization capability. Wang et al. [20] introduced a feature processing module in YOLOv8 to integrate the superficial features and deep features.. Still, the target sizes in the experimental dataset are more similar, and there is a certain degree of misdetection for targets with a large span of size and missed detection.

From the collective efforts of the researchers above, it becomes evident that despite the widespread adoption of YOLO models in remote-sensing target detection, significant opportunities for enhancement persist. Thus, this paper introduces the RN-YOLO (RepGhost NAM YOLO) model, building upon the foundation of improved YOLOv8, and achieves commendable detection results across the DOTAv1.5, TGRS-HRRSD, and RSOD datasets. The main contributions of this study include the following:

(1) Tackling the difficulty of detecting small targets and extracting detailed features within limitations is achieved by integrating NAM [21] between the feature extraction and fusion networks. NAM optimally preserves small target features through its lightweight design and enhances detection accuracy by adjusting the weight contribution factor.
(2) The RepGhost module [22] is introduced within the feature fusion network, creating RepGhost_C2f. This innovation effectively tackles the issue of inadequate detection capacity for targets spanning a wide range of sizes while significantly reducing model parameters.

(3) The WIoU loss function [23] replaces the CIoU in the original model, enhancing detectors' overall performance by assigning different weights to the targets with various sizes and alleviating the challenge of localizing small targets.

2. Related Works

2.1. Machine Learning in Remote-Sensing Images

With the continuous evolution of machine-learning technology, feature-based classifiers have emerged as promising tools in remote-sensing target detection. Compared to traditional approaches, these methods offer enhanced capability to handle intricate data relationships, thereby improving detection robustness. Through meticulously crafted features, these classifiers proficiently identify, classify, and localize targets. Support Vector Machine (SVM) [24] stands out as a formidable classifier, partitioning data into distinct classes by identifying optimal hyperplanes. Meanwhile, Random Forest (RF) [25] employs an ensemble learning approach, constructing multiple decision trees and aggregating their outputs through voting, ensuring high accuracy and resilience. On the other hand, AdaBoost [26] iteratively enhances the classification performance by training a sequence of weak classifiers and combining their outputs with appropriate weights.

These machine learning-based methodologies provide a robust framework for remote-sensing target detection, facilitating accurate identification and localization of targets within vast remote-sensing datasets. However, one limitation persists: the reliance on manual feature engineering, which is intricate and laborious. This constraint hampers scalability for target detection in extensive remote-sensing datasets and impedes real-time applicability in remote-sensing image target detection.

2.2. Reinforcement Learning in Remote-Sensing Images

Reinforcement learning-based models typically involve the design of an intelligent agent capable of interacting with its environment and learning optimal action strategies based on feedback. In the context of target detection in remote-sensing images, the environment typically comprises the dataset of remote-sensing images containing the targets to be identified. Following each action within this environment, the intelligent agent receives a portion of the image and a corresponding reward. Subsequently, the model selects its following action based on its learned strategy, such as zooming in on a specific image region or shifting focus to another part of the image to pinpoint a particular detection target.

DQN [27] optimizes decision-making in target detection tasks by learning a value function that guides action selection. However, DQN utilized in target detection often demands many samples and much training time, consuming significant computational resources. Actor–Critic [28] integrates a policy gradient and a value function, allowing for updates to both during the learning process, thereby enhancing stability. Nevertheless, Actor–Critic methods typically necessitate well-designed reward functions and state representations, which is usually tricky in remote-sensing image target detection.

2.3. YOLOv8 Model

Thus far, deep learning-based remote-sensing image target detection remains widely utilized, with YOLO emerging as a frontrunner due to its faster speed and higher accuracy. YOLOv8 has swiftly become the prevailing model in target detection, leveraging its robust generalization capabilities and enhanced accuracy. The network architecture of YOLOv8 [29] comprises two key components: the backbone and the head part, with the latter encompassing feature fusion and target detection. Breaking away from previous iterations, YOLOv8 opts for the C2f module over the C3 module, enhancing the flow of gradient information while still upholding its lightweight design. Additionally, YOLOv8 shifts from an anchor-based approach to an anchor-free mode, eliminating the necessity for predefined bounding boxes and providing a more adaptable solution space. Finally, YOLOv8 employs distribution focal loss, facilitating a quicker focus near the target and expediting convergence.

3. Methods

3.1. Overall Architecture

YOLOv8 has demonstrated significant success in various domains, owing to its robust generalization and heightened accuracy. In addressing challenges such as wide-ranging object sizes, numerous small targets, and limited network feature extraction in remote-sensing images, this paper endeavors to enhance YOLOv8 for remote-sensing image detection. Initially, the NAM module is introduced after the C2f module within the backbone to bolster the learning of crucial image features. This paper adopts three NAM modules, aiming to subject the outputs of varying size dimensions in the backbone to comprehensive feature learning. Furthermore, after conducting comparative experiments on both the backbone and the head, this paper opts to substitute the C2f module connected to the detection head in the head segment with RepGhost_C2f. This modification amplifies feature fusion, enhances model detection accuracy, and streamlines the network model's parameter count. Lastly, the CIoU loss function is supplanted with WIoU in the detection head to further refine small targets' localization. The enhanced model structure, depicted in Figure 2, incorporates improvements across three key areas: the backbone, head, and detection head, with the subsequent Sections 3.2–3.4 elaborating on the respective ideas and methodologies for enhancement.

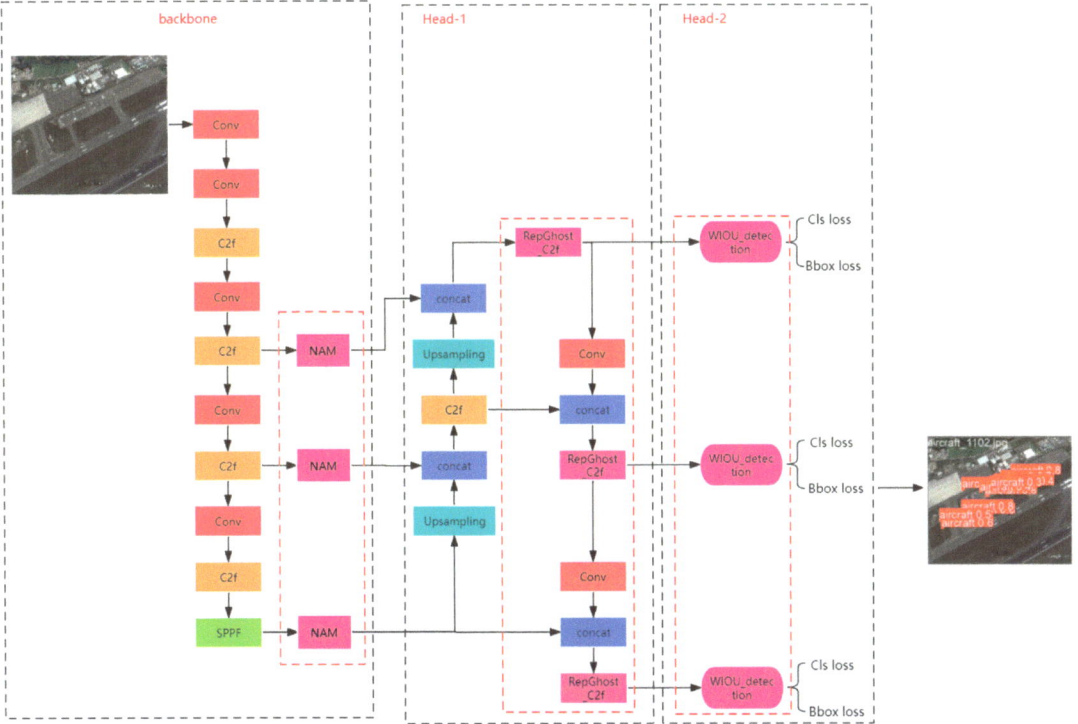

Figure 2. RN-YOLO model structure for remote-sensing image detection, red dotted boxes represent additional or modified parts of the model and the final arrow points to the eventual output of the model.

3.2. Normalization-Based Attention Module (NAM)

The attention mechanism directs the network towards vital information within the image, identifying critical features while filtering out non-essential ones. Therefore, incorporating such a mechanism into target detection can effectively retain the detailed features, bolster the model's memory, and ultimately elevate the detection accuracy. This paper uses the normalization-based attention module (NAM), which improves the convolutional block attention module (CBAM).

CBAM represents a noteworthy attention mechanism model with versatile applications. It generates two sets of weights for each channel by employing global average pooling and global maximum pooling. These weights then undergo a series of transformations, including feedforward neural network processing with shared parameters, element-wise summation, and softmax activation, yielding final channel-specific weights.

In contrast, NAM alters this intermediate process, as shown in Figure 3. Initially, the individual channels undergo batch-wise normalization, and a scaling factor $\lambda_i (i \leq C)$ in normalization is introduced. Since this scaling factor is learnable, the standard deviation W_i of the scaling factor is used to represent the importance of each channel, as shown in Equation (1), obviating the cumbersome parameters associated with fully connected and convolutional layers.

$$W_i = \frac{\lambda_i}{\sum_{j=1}^{C} \lambda_j} \quad (1)$$

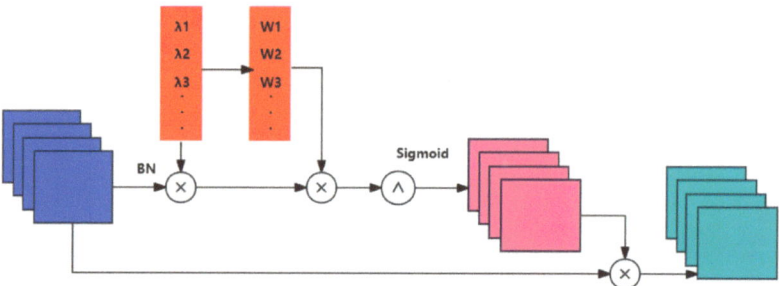

Figure 3. Normalization-based attention module structure diagram.

Subsequently, the channel weights are multiplied with each pixel point and activated by the softmax function, akin to CBAM. Finally, the probabilities at the positions of each pixel point are used as weights and multiplied with each pixel point to enable filtering of the features represented by each channel. The NAM module ensures feature integrity by reducing rather than deleting, and it also highlights specific features to capture details about small targets. The subsequent experimental results can verify that NAM can enhance the extraction of crucial information and lay a solid foundation for subsequent feature fusion.

3.3. RepGhost_C2f

In addition to enhancing the backbone's feature extraction using NAM, this paper further optimizes the C2f module in the head and proposes RepGhost_C2f. The RepGhost module can achieve a simultaneous reduction in hardware computation and the model's parameters, as demonstrated by experiments showcasing its robustness.

Given that numerous similar feature maps are generated during convolution operations, GhostNet addresses this redundancy by employing inexpensive linear operations to derive additional feature maps from a subset of the original ones, as depicted in Figure 4a. Building upon GhostNet, RepGhost further refines this process by substituting concat operations with addition operations, as illustrated in Figure 4b. RepGhost enhances the feature fusion efficiency and reduces the computational overhead at the hardware level. Moreover, RepGhost enhances the model parameter efficiency by repositioning the ReLU activation function after the addition operation, ensuring that only genuinely influential features undergo nonlinear transformation. Additionally, by halving the channels in the middle of RepGhost compared to GhostNet, the model significantly reduces parameters when traversing through the SE attention mechanism or the depth-divisible convolution module, thereby reducing the parameter and computational load.

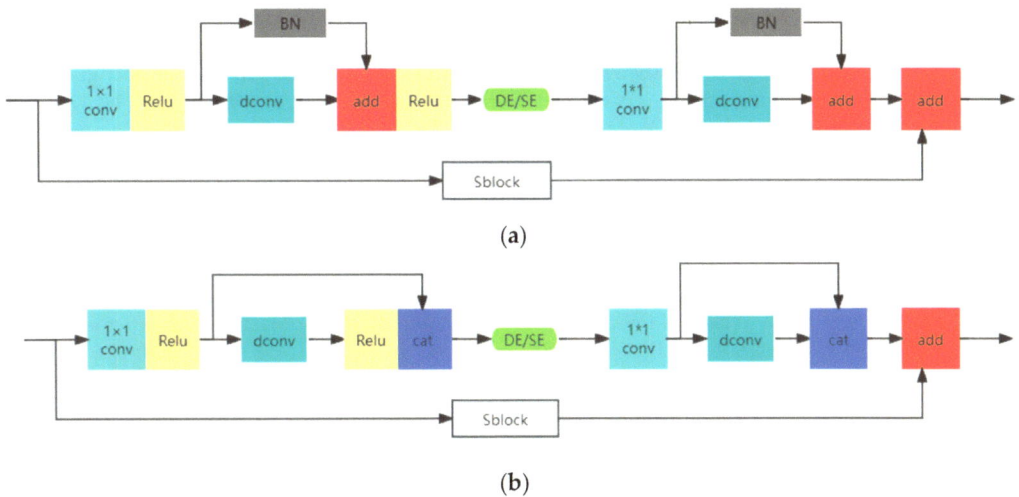

Figure 4. GhostNet and RepGhost structure. (**a**) GhostNet structure; (**b**) RepGhost structure.

C2f stands out as the pivotal module within YOLOv8, offering lightweight characteristics and the capability to amalgamate intricate abstract information from the deep network with detailed information from the shallow network, thereby enhancing target detection accuracy. This paper replaces the core bottleneck module in C2f with RepGhost to construct the new RepGhost_C2f module, as depicted in Figure 5. This modification amplifies the network's feature extraction and fusion capabilities and further reduces the network's parameter and computational load. Thus, it accomplishes a dual enhancement in both performance and efficiency.

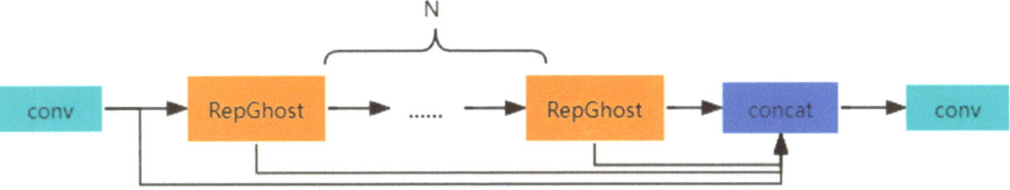

Figure 5. RepGhost_C2f structure.

3.4. WioU (Wise Intersection over Union)

Choosing an appropriate loss function is crucial for accurately localizing the target object and giving its coordinate position. IoU-based functions for calculating the bounding box loss constantly develop and appear as SIoU, EIoU, and GIoU. In YOLOv8, the CIoU (Complete Intersection over Union) loss function is employed to quantify the disparity between the predicted and ground truth boxes, as depicted in Equations (2)–(4).

$$L_{CIoU} = 1 - IoU + \frac{\rho(b, b^{gt})}{H^2 + W^2} + \alpha v \quad (2)$$

$$v = \frac{4}{\pi} \left(\arctan \frac{w^{gt}}{h^{gt}} - \arctan \frac{w}{h} \right)^2 \quad (3)$$

$$\alpha = \frac{v}{(1 - IoU) + v} \quad (4)$$

where *IoU* represents the intersection over union ratio between the ground truth bounding box and the predicted bounding box. b and b^{gt} signify the center coordinates of the two bounding boxes, and $\rho(b, b^{gt})$ denotes the Euclidean distance between the center coordinates. αv indicates the aspect ratio similarity of the real frame and the bounding box. In the last two supplementary formulas, w^{gt} and h^{gt} state the side length of the target bounding box, w and h state the side length of the predicted bounding box, and H and W mean the length of the outer sides of the two bounding boxes together.

However, the CIoU loss function solely considers the width and height factors and lacks discrimination between large and small targets. The size of targets in remote-sensing images varies greatly. Consequently, it employs the same computational approach for any bounding box, which may not adequately distinguish between different target sizes. Therefore, we introduce the WIoU loss function to sufficiently reduce the loss of easily fitted large targets while prioritizing the loss associated with small targets.

Wise-IoU (WIoU) employs a combinatorial approach to calculate the loss function, illustrated in Figure 6. First, as shown in Equation (5), WIoU adopts a multiplicative approach to consider the width and height, effectively reducing the loss associated with large targets in high quality.

$$L_{WIoUv1} = exp\left(\frac{(x_a - y_a)^2 + (x_b - y_b)^2}{H^2 + W^2}\right)(1 - IoU) \quad (5)$$

where (x_a, x_b) and (y_a, y_b) means the center coordinate of the predicted bounding box and the ground truth bounding box, and H and W mean the length of the outer sides of the two bounding boxes together. IoU represents the intersection over union ratio between the ground truth bounding box and the predicted bounding box.

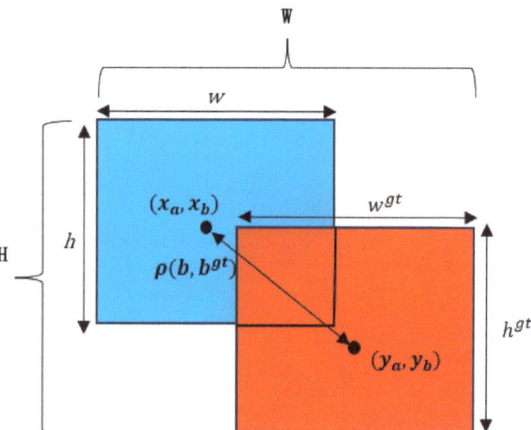

Figure 6. The important symbols of WIoU and CIoU representation diagram.

Referring to focal loss, a monotone focusing mechanism L_{WIoUv2} for cross-entropy is designed, which effectively reduces the contribution of simple examples to the loss value. This enables the model to focus on difficult examples and improve the classification performance.

$$L_{WIoUv2} = \left(\frac{L^*_{IoU}}{\overline{L_{IoU}}}\right)^{\gamma} L_{WIoUv1} \quad (6)$$

where L^*_{IoU} is a dynamic gradient gain, $\overline{L_{IoU}}$ is a momentum average value that slows convergence in the latter stages of training by normalizing the loss function, and γ is the dynamic update normalization factor.

Finally, to counterbalance the detrimental gradients produced by low-quality targets and prioritize the detection of abundant small targets, WIoU uses β to construct non-monotonic focusing coefficients, as depicted in Equations (7) and (8), where α and δ are hyper-parameters. This ensures that high-quality large and low-quality small targets receive a low loss value.

$$L_{WIoUv3} = \frac{\beta}{\delta\alpha^{\beta-\delta}} L_{WIoUv1} \qquad (7)$$

where

$$\beta = \frac{L_{IoU}^*}{L_{IoU}} \qquad (8)$$

4. Experiments

4.1. Experimental Datasets and Their Preprocessing

The RN-YOLO model is tested and evaluated using three aerial remote-sensing image datasets: DOTAv1.5 [30], TGRS-HRRSD [31], and RSOD [32]. Primarily, DOTAv1.5 serves as the main dataset for this experiment, facilitating exhaustive comparisons and ablation experiments. To ensure the model's generalization, experimental validations and comparisons are conducted on the TGRS and RSOD datasets respectively.

DOTAv1.5, provided by the China Resources Satellite Data and Application Center (CRSDAC), encompasses 2806 super-large images spanning 16 categories and containing 403,318 instances. Due to its extensive coverage, this dataset is widely utilized across various research domains. However, given the impractical size of the images—up to 20,000 × 20,000 pixels—they are unsuitable for direct model training. Hence, before experimentation, we resized the images to 640 × 640. Subsequently, we used a variety of techniques and pairwise combinations to enhance the dataset, including horizontal and vertical flipping images, enhancing the brightness, adding Gaussian noise, and injecting perceptual noise, as illustrated in Figure 7. The final dataset comprises 25,114 images, divided into training, validation, and testing sets in a 6:2:2 ratio.

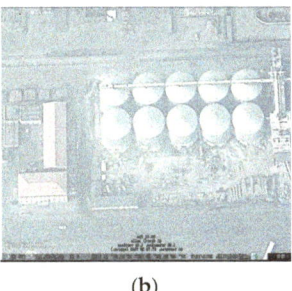

(a)   (b)   (c)

Figure 7. Sample image dataset enhancement. (**a**) Original image; (**b**) Image with horizontal flip and pretzel noise; (**c**) Image with vertical flip and brightness boost.

Similarly, TGRS-HRRSD offers a sizable, high-resolution dataset. For our experiments, we focused solely on comparison and validation tests, selecting images with dimensions under 1000 × 1000, totaling 5406 images with 400 images per category. We partitioned this dataset into training, validation, and testing sets following the same 6:2:2 ratio.

RSOD consists of 976 images spread across four categories, primarily sized at 1000 × 1000. We applied identical image augmentation techniques to ensure dataset balance, resulting in 1916 augmented images, with approximately 400 images per category.

Additionally, to visualize the distribution of object sizes in the image, we count the percentage of each abscissa and divide the horizontal coordinate every 0.5%, as shown in Figure 8. The figures clearly demonstrate that the majority of objects occupy less than 3% of the total area, with those in DOTAv1.5 typically accounting for less than 1%, which will validate the performance of our model in small object detection.

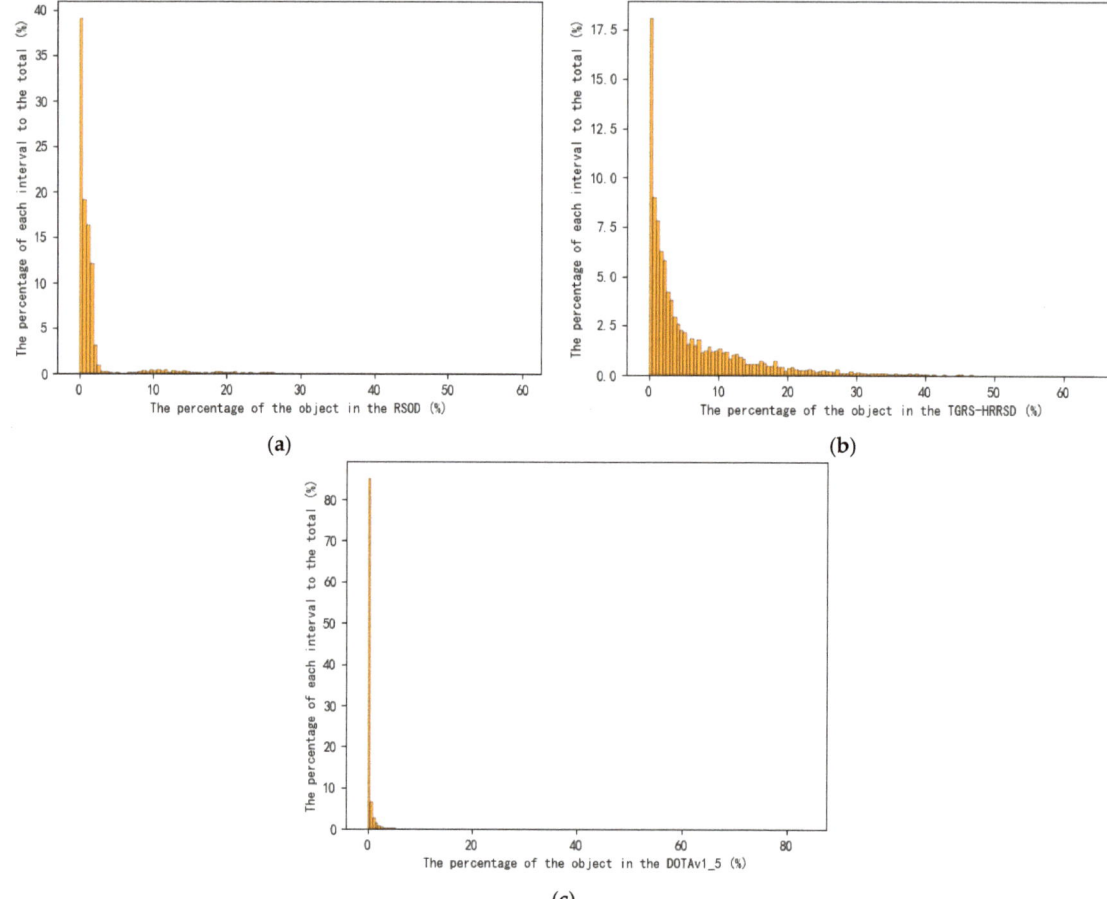

Figure 8. The percentage of each object in three datasets bar chart. (**a**) Bar chart with the percentage of each object in RSOD; (**b**) Bar chart with the percentage of each object in TGRS-HRRSD; (**c**) Bar chart with the percentage of each object in DOTAv1_5.

4.2. Experimental Environment and Training Setting

This study's experimental hardware is Intel Xeon Platinum 8352V, with 120G memory and NVIDIA GeForce RTX4090 GPU. The experimental software environment is Python 3.8, pythoch2.0.0, cuda11.8, and ubuntu22.04.1. In addition, the version of the ultralytics package for YOLOv8 relied on was 8.0.212. In the experiment, we set the warm epochs to 3 and the learning rate in this section to 0.1, and we put the learning rate to 0.01 in the initial section and gradually changed it to 0.0001. The batch size is 16 to adapt the model and avoid memory explosion. Furthermore, we adopt a cross-entropy loss function for classification and distribution focal loss for bounding box regression. We also modified the CIoU to WIoU, proving that it leads to a better performance.

4.3. Experimental Comparison and Analysis

In remote-sensing target detection, achieving a balance between model precision and speed is often paramount. To comprehensively evaluate model performance, this paper assesses accuracy using metrics such as P (Precision), R (Recall), mAP@50, and mAP@.5:.95. Additionally, the number of parameters (Parameters) in the model is considered to evaluate the operational efficiency. This holistic approach provides a thorough and detailed assessment of both precision and efficiency, offering valuable insights into the model's applicability. By considering these metrics collectively, a more accurate evaluation of the model's performance is attained, thus facilitating informed decisions for further enhancement and optimization. Definitions of these evaluation metrics can be found in the literature [17].

4.3.1. Comparative Experiments for Attention Module

To assess NAM's efficacy, we conducted experiments incorporating various other commonly employed attention modules for comparison. For instance, CBAM [33] uses a sequential application of channel attention followed by spatial attention, exemplifying a typical hybrid attention mechanism. Context aggregation [34] fuses pixel relationships at multiple scales and in different spaces, thus weighting them separately. Shuffle attention [35] spatially divides the data and assigns attention weights separately for channel-wise information exchange.

To ensure comparability across experimental results, all attention mechanisms in this paper are positioned after C2f modules, which connect the backbone and head. Following training and testing on DOTAv1.5, the results are summarized in Table 1. Based on mAP@.5:.95, it is evident that the model augmented with the NAM module exhibits a superior detection performance, boasting a 1.3% enhancement over the YOLOv8 benchmark model. Notably, the NAM module utilizes the fewest parameters, with virtually no additional parameters added. This underscores the efficacy of the NAM module in achieving significant improvement while maintaining parameter stability.

Table 1. Comparison of the effectiveness of different attention mechanisms.

Methods	P (%)	R (%)	Paras (M)	mAP@50 (%)	mAP @.5:.95 (%)
Yolov8	85.0	81.6	11.13	86.2	60.2
+NAM	86.3	82.3	11.13	86.7	61.5
+CBAM	85.2	82.3	11.48	86.7	60.8
+ContextAggregation	86.9	82.0	11.82	86.9	61.3
+ShuffleAttention	87.2	82.6	11.13	87.2	61.2

Furthermore, comparison experiments were carried out on the RSOD and TGRS-HRRSD datasets, as outlined in Table 2. The findings demonstrate that the model integrating the NAM consistently surpasses YOLOv8 across all three datasets, yielding enhancements of 1.2%, 0.8%, and 1.3% on RSOD, TGRS-HRRSD, and DOTAv1.5, respectively. This underscores the substantial influence of the NAM module in improving the detection accuracy across diverse datasets.

Table 2. Performance of NAM attention mechanisms on three aerial remote-sensing datasets.

Methods	RSOD			TGRS-HRRSD			DOTAv1_5		
	P (%)	R (%)	mAP@.5:.95 (%)	P (%)	R (%)	mAP@.5:.95 (%)	P (%)	R (%)	mAP@.5:.95 (%)
Yolov8	95.1	94.5	78.5	91.2	87.1	67.9	82.0	81.6	60.2
+NAM	95.4	95.7	79.7	91.6	87.2	68.7	86.3	82.3	61.5

4.3.2. Comparative Experiments for Lightweight Convolution

YOLOv8 utilizes C2f modules in both the backbone and the head section. The improved C2f module in this paper can enhance model performance while maintaining generalization. This paper conducted comparative experiments on the RSOD and DOTAv1.5 datasets to ascertain the impact of integrating improved C2f modules. This paper replaced all C2f modules in the backbone and the head section to ensure the consistency of the experiments. Furthermore, two lightweight modules, Scconv [36] and RepGhost, are employed for comparison purposes, and the results are presented in Table 3. It is observed that although both lightweight modules can decrease the number of parameters, the lightweight module is more effective in the head part. At the same time, its application in the backbone may result in a decreased detection performance. Therefore, we decided to improve and replace the C2f modules connected to the detector head to achieve an optimal detection performance. The comparison with YOLOv8 reveals that the lightweight module reduces the number of model parameters, and the RepGhost module demonstrates a superior performance on RSOD and DOTAv1.5, improving by 1.0% and 2.1%, respectively. Consequently, the RepGhost module was selected in this paper to enhance C2f, enabling simultaneous enhancement of the model parameters and performance.

Table 3. Comparative experiments for lightweight modules used in different parts.

Position	Methods	P (M)	RSOD mAP@50 (%)	mAP@.5:.95 (%)	Paras (M)	DOTAv1.5 mAP@50 (%)	mAP@.5:.95 (%)
None	YOLOv8	11.13	99.1	78.5	11.13	86.2	60.2
backbone	+Scconv	10.36	97.3	77.7	10.36	84.9	58.6
backbone	+RepGhost	9.59	97.5	78.2	9.59	86.6	60.4
head	+Scconv	10.51	98.0	79.4	10.51	86.7	60.9
head	+RepGhost	9.50	97.5	79.5	9.76	87.0	62.3

Table 4 shows the experimental results conducted on TGRS-HRRSD. Table 4 indicates a significant reduction in the model's parameter and a considerable improvement in performance following the integration of RepGhost. This underscores the strong generalization capability of RepGhost_C2f, prompting us to replace the C2f modules connecting the head with the detection head with RepGhost_C2f modules.

Table 4. Performance comparison for RepGhost_C2f on different datasets.

Methods	RSOD P (%)	R (%)	mAP@.5:.95 (%)	TGRS-HRRSD P (%)	R (%)	mAP@.5:.95 (%)	DOTAv1_5 P (%)	R (%)	mAP@.5:.95 (%)
YOLOv8	95.1	94.5	78.5	91.2	87.1	67.9	85.0	81.6	60.2
+RepGhost	95.8	95.9	79.5	91.1	88.0	68.4	88.1	82.4	62.3

4.3.3. Comparative Experiments for Loss Function

YOLOv8 uses the CIoU loss function but only considers the width and height without distinguishing between high and normal-quality targets. To address this limitation, WIoU and GIoU were employed as replacements for the CIoU loss function in this study, and the resulting experimental outcomes are summarized in Table 5. The tables show that the WIoU achieves improvements of 0.9%, 0.6%, and 1.8% over the original YOLOv8 model across the three datasets, respectively, with WIoU exhibiting further enhancement over GIoU.

Table 5. Performance comparison for three loss functions on different datasets.

Methods	RSOD mAP@50 (%)	mAP@.5:.95 (%)	TGRS-HRRSD mAP@50 (%)	mAP@.5:.95 (%)	DOTAv1_5 mAP@50 (%)	mAP@.5:.95 (%)
YOLOv8	99.1	78.5	91.6	67.9	86.2	60.2
+WIoUv3	98.4	79.4	91.9	68.5	87.6	62.0
+GIoU	98.8	78.5	92.0	68.3	86.4	60.5

4.3.4. Ablation Study

We systematically integrated the enhancements above into the original YOLOv8 model and evaluated its performance on the cropped and augmented DOTAv1.5 dataset. The results are presented in Table 6. The accuracy mAP@.5:.95 of RN-YOLO is improved by 3.6% after modifying YOLOv8. Moreover, the parameter is reduced by 13.9%.

Table 6. Ablation experiments.

Model	RepGhost	WIoUv3	NAM	P (%)	R (%)	Paras (M)	mAP@50 (%)	mAP@.5:.95 (%)
Yolov8				85.0	81.6	11.13	86.2	60.2
Yolov8	√			88.1	82.4	9.76	87.0	62.3 (+2.1)
Yolov8	√	√		87.3	83.8	9.77	87.8	62.8 (+0.5)
Yolov8	√	√	√	87.9	84.9	9.77	87.8	63.8 (+1.0)

4.3.5. Comparative Experiments with Other Models

To thoroughly assess our proposed model's target detection accuracy and generalization capability, we conducted a comprehensive comparative analysis across three datasets, employing state-of-the-art target detection algorithms for remote sensing as benchmarks. The summarized results are presented in Table 7. It is clear from the table that our proposed model consistently surpasses existing algorithms across all three aerial image datasets, demonstrating a superior detection accuracy. Additionally, our model boasts a significantly lower parameter than YOLOv8.

Table 7. Comparative experimental results with other models.

Dataset	Evaluation Metrics	Improved Faster R-CNN	YOLO X	YOLO v5	YOLO v7	YOLO v8	RN-YOLO (Ours)
DOTA-v1.5	mAP@50 (%)	72.5	84.2	87.3	85.7	86.2	87.8
	mAP@.5:.95 (%)	50.3	59.9	58.9	58.5	60.2	63.8
	Param (M)	60.40	8.94	7.05	36.56	11.13	9.77
TGRS-HRRSD	mAP@50 (%)	74.3	77.4	91.7	92.0	91.6	92.5
	mAP@.5:.95 (%)	53.2	58.9	66.3	67.5	67.9	69.1
	Param (M)	60.42	8.94	7.04	36.54	11.13	9.77
RSOD	mAP@50 (%)	80.8	92.1	97.9	98.5	99.1	98.0
	mAP@.5:.95 (%)	62.1	70.9	73.5	76.6	78.5	80.5
	Param (M)	60.42	8.94	7.02	36.4	11.13	9.77

Finally, we comprehensively compared the YOLO series models and RN-YOLO on the TGRS-HRRSD dataset. Table 8 presents the prediction accuracies for each category. Our model demonstrates an absolute accuracy advantage in the majority of categories.

Table 8. Accuracy comparison for each categories in the TGRS-HRRSD dataset.

Categories	YOLOv5 (%)	YOLOv7 (%)	YOLOv8 (%)	RN-YOLO (Ours) (%)
ship	66.7	72.4	65.2	61.2
bridge	35.3	40.6	43.5	50.1
ground_track	74.5	79.9	77.5	81.1
storage_tank	84.2	84.1	85.4	88.3
basketball_court	67.9	71.9	69.0	63.9
tennis_court	87.5	87.7	88.2	89.2
airplane	86.2	87.6	85.5	83.5
baseball_diamond	63.4	63.1	65.8	70.3
harbor	73.9	71.3	80.6	82.8
vehicle	74.6	71.9	73.7	72.9
crossroad	53.5	52.7	54.9	58.1
T_junction	45.1	44.3	43.3	42.6
parking_lot	48.1	49.4	49.6	55.2

4.4. Visualization Experiments

To showcase the improved detection performance of the RN-YOLO model, we conducted visualization experiments on representative scenes from the three datasets, as illustrated in Figure 9. The comparison images on the top row show the detection results obtained using YOLOv8, while the bottom row demonstrates the enhanced detection performance achieved by RN-YOLO. The comparison indicates that YOLOv8 still struggles with significant leakage detection issues when detecting small targets. Conversely, RN-YOLO exhibits a remarkable capability in detecting small targets, even amidst large image size spans and many small targets. Moreover, the comparison images selected encompass various datasets: the first from the DOTA dataset, the second from the RSOD dataset, and the third from the TGRS-HRRSD dataset. This highlights the effectiveness of RN-YOLO in detecting small targets and its robust generalization across diverse datasets.

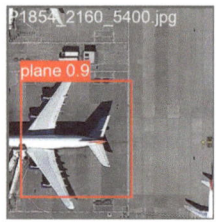 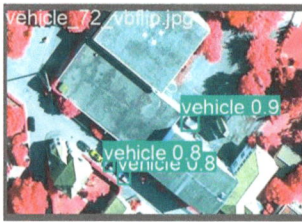 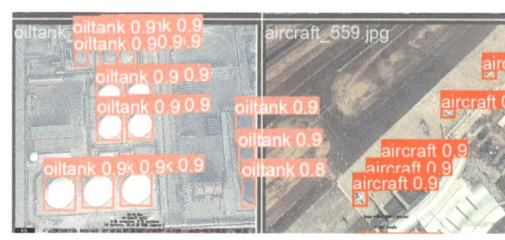

(a)

(b)

Figure 9. Detection comparison for YOLOv8 and RN-YOLO. (**a**) Detection results using YOLOv8; (**b**) Detection results using RN-YOLO.

5. Discussion

In remote-sensing image detection, there are problems with large target size spans and many small targets. The existing models cannot extract detailed features, leading to missing and false detection. This paper improves the feature extraction network, feature fusion network, and location loss function of YOLOv8 and proposes RN-YOLO. RN-YOLO improves the target detection accuracy while reducing the parameters. Firstly, we integrate NAM into the feature extraction network to filter features. NAM can prioritize key features and suppress insignificant features. Secondly, we introduce RepGhost_C2f in the feature fusion network. RepGhost_C2f can boost the object detection accuracy while substantially reducing the parameters. Lastly, we refine the localization loss function WIoU to mitigate difficulties in localizing small targets and enhance the object detection accuracy. The experimental results demonstrate that our model effectively enhances mAP@.5:.95 by 3.6%, 1.2%, and 2% on the DOTAv1.5, TGRS, and RSOD datasets, respectively, compared to YOLOv8, while reducing the parameters by 13.9%, showcasing strong generalization. This study underscores the effectiveness of lightweight convolution, attention mechanisms, and appropriate loss functions in improving target detection algorithms, offering novel methods and insights in remote-sensing target detection.

Future research will focus on optimizing the network structure and extensively exploring attention mechanisms to enhance the network detection accuracy further while maintaining a lower number of parameters. Additionally, we aim to refine the loss function to ensure a robust performance when encountering tilted bounding boxes. Lastly, leveraging the reasoning capabilities of multimodal macro models on detected images provides a pathway for reflecting on and enhancing detection results.

Author Contributions: Conceptualization, K.W. and G.Y.; methodology, K.W. and G.Y.; software, K.W.; validation, K.W.; data curation, H.W.; writing—original draft preparation, K.W.; writing—review and editing, H.Z. and G.Y.; supervision, G.Y.; funding acquisition, H.Z. All authors have read and agreed to the published version of the manuscript.

Funding: This research was financially supported by the Key R&D Projects of Yunnan Province (Grant No. 202202AD080004) and the Natural Science Foundation of China (Grant No. 62061049, 12263008).

Data Availability Statement: All the original datasets mentioned in this paper are accessible. DOTAv1.5 can be obtained from https://captain-whu.github.io/DOAI2019/dataset.html (accessed on 20 April 2023), TGRS-HRRSD can be acquired from https://github.com/CrazyStoneonRoad/TGRS-HRRSD-Dataset (accessed on 20 April 2023), and RSOD can be downloaded from https://github.com/RSIA-LIESMARS-WHU/RSOD-Dataset- (accessed on 20 April 2023).

Conflicts of Interest: The authors declare there is no conflict of interest.

References

1. Melesse, M.; Weng, Q.; Thenkabail, P.S.; Senay, G.B. Remote sensing sensors and applications in environmental resources mapping and modelling. *Sensors* **2007**, *7*, 3209–3241. [CrossRef] [PubMed]
2. Gakhar, S.; Tiwari, K.C. Spectral–spatial urban target detection for hyperspectral remote sensing data using artificial neural network. *Egypt. J. Remote Sens. Space Sci.* **2021**, *24*, 173–180. [CrossRef]
3. Yang, C. Remote sensing and precision agriculture technologies for crop disease detection and management with a practical application example. *Engineering* **2020**, *6*, 528–532. [CrossRef]
4. Koshimura, S.; Moya, L.; Mas, E.; Bai, Y. Tsunami damage detection with remote sensing: A review. *Geosciences* **2020**, *10*, 177. [CrossRef]
5. Bi, Y.; Bai, X.; Jin, T.; Guo, S. Multiple feature analysis for infrared small target detection. *IEEE Geosci. Remote Sens. Lett.* **2017**, *14*, 1333–1337. [CrossRef]
6. Zhou, P.; Cheng, G.; Liu, Z.; Bu, S.; Hu, X. Weakly supervised target detection in remote sensing images based on transferred deep features and negative bootstrapping. *Multidimens. Syst. Signal Process.* **2016**, *27*, 925–944. [CrossRef]
7. Girshick, R.; Donahue, J.; Darrell, T.; Malik, J. Rich feature hierarchies for accurate object detection and semantic segmentation. In Proceedings of the IEEE Conference on Computer Vision and Pattern Recognition, Columbus, OH, USA, 23–28 June 2014; pp. 580–587. [CrossRef]
8. Girshick, R. Fast r-cnn. In Proceedings of the IEEE International Conference on Computer Vision, Santiago, Chile, 7–13 December 2015; pp. 1440–1448. [CrossRef]
9. Ren, S.; He, K.; Girshick, R.; Sun, J. Faster r-cnn: Towards real-time object detection with region proposal networks. In Proceedings of the Advances in Neural Information Processing Systems, Montreal, QC, Canada, 7–12 December 2015; Volume 28. [CrossRef]
10. Liu, W.; Anguelov, D.; Erhan, D.; Szegedy, C.; Reed, S.; Fu, C.Y.; Berg, A.C. Ssd: Single shot multibox detector. In Proceedings of the 14th European Conference of Computer Vision (ECCV 2016), Amsterdam, The Netherlands, 11–14 October 2016; Volume 14, pp. 21–37, Part I. [CrossRef]
11. Li, Z.; Yang, L.; Zhou, F. FSSD: Feature fusion single shot multibox detector. *arXiv* **2017**, arXiv:1712.00960. [CrossRef]
12. Redmon, J.; Farhadi, A. Yolov3: An incremental improvement. *arXiv* **2018**, arXiv:1804.02767. [CrossRef]
13. Redmon, J.; Divvala, S.; Girshick, R.; Farhadi, A. You only look once: Unified, real-time object detection. In Proceedings of the IEEE Conference on Computer Vision and Pattern Recognition, Las Vegas, NV, USA, 27–30 June 2016; pp. 779–788. [CrossRef]
14. Ge, Z.; Liu, S.; Wang, F.; Li, Z.; Sun, J. Yolox: Exceeding yolo series in 2021. *arXiv* **2021**, arXiv:2107.08430. [CrossRef]
15. Wang, C.Y.; Bochkovskiy, A.; Liao, H.Y.M. YOLOv7: Trainable bag-of-freebies sets new state-of-the-art for real-time object detectors. In Proceedings of the IEEE/CVF Conference on Computer Vision and Pattern Recognition, Vancouver, BC, Canada, 17–24 June 2023; pp. 7464–7475. [CrossRef]
16. Zhu, X.; Lyu, S.; Wang, X.; Zhao, Q. TPH-YOLOv5: Improved YOLOv5 based on transformer prediction head for object detection on drone-captured scenarios. In Proceedings of the IEEE/CVF International Conference on Computer Vision, Montreal, BC, Canada, 11–17 October 2021; pp. 2778–2788. [CrossRef]
17. Yang, L.; Yuan, G.; Zhou, H.; Liu, H.; Chen, J.; Wu, H. RS-Yolox: A high-precision detector for object detection in satellite remote sensing images. *Appl. Sci.* **2022**, *12*, 8707. [CrossRef]
18. Yu, J.; Liu, S.; Xu, T. Research on YOLOv7 remote sensing small target detection algorithm incorporating attention mechanism. *J. Comput. Eng. Appl.* **2023**, *59*, 167. (In Chinese) [CrossRef]
19. Liu, Z.; Gao, Y.; Du, Q.; Chen, M.; Lv, W. YOLO-extract: Improved YOLOv5 for aircraft object detection in remote sensing images. *IEEE Access* **2023**, *11*, 1742–1751. [CrossRef]

20. Wang, G.; Chen, Y.; An, P.; Hong, H.; Hu, J.; Huang, T. UAV-YOLOv8: A small-object-detection model based on improved YOLOv8 for UAV aerial pho-tography scenarios. *Sensors* **2023**, *23*, 7190. [CrossRef]
21. Liu, Y.; Shao, Z.; Hoffmann, Y.N. NAM: Normalization-based attention module. *arXiv* **2021**, arXiv:2111.12419. [CrossRef]
22. Chen, C.; Guo, Z.; Zeng, H.; Xiong, P.; Dong, J. Repghost: A hardware-efficient ghost module via re-parameterization. *arXiv* **2022**, arXiv:2211.06088. [CrossRef]
23. Tong, Z.; Chen, Y.; Xu, Z.; Yu, R. Wise-IoU: Bounding box regression loss with dynamic focusing mechanism. *arXiv* **2023**, arXiv:2301.10051. [CrossRef]
24. Vedaldi, A.; Gulshan, V.; Varma, M.; Zisserman, A. Multiple kernels for object detection. In Proceedings of the 2009 IEEE 12th International Conference on Computer Vision, Kyoto, Japan, 27 September–4 October 2009; pp. 606–613. [CrossRef]
25. Ranzato, M.A.; Boureau, Y.L.; Cun, Y. Sparse feature learning for deep belief networks. In Proceedings of the Advances in Neural Information Processing Systems, Vancouver, BC, Canada, 3–6 December 2007; Volume 20. [CrossRef]
26. Viola, P.; Jones, M. Rapid object detection using a boosted cascade of simple features. In Proceedings of the 2001 IEEE Computer Society Conference on Computer Vision and Pattern Recognition, Kauai, HI, USA, 8–14 December 2001; Volume 1, p. I. [CrossRef]
27. Mnih, V.; Kavukcuoglu, K.; Silver, D.; Rusu, A.A.; Veness, J.; Bellemare, M.G.; Graves, A.; Riedmiller, M.; Fidjeland, A.K.; Ostrovski, G.; et al. Human-level control through deep reinforcement learning. *Nature* **2015**, *518*, 529–533. [CrossRef] [PubMed]
28. Lillicrap, T.P.; Hunt, J.J.; Pritzel, A.; Heess, N.; Erez, T.; Tassa, Y.; Silver, D.; Wierstra, D. Continuous control with deep reinforcement learning. *arXiv* **2015**, arXiv:1509.02971. [CrossRef]
29. Terven, J.; Cordova-Esparza, D.-M.; Romero-González, J.-A. A comprehensive review of YOLO: From YOLOv1 to YOLOv8 and beyond. *Mach. Learn. Knowl. Extr.* **2023**, *5*, 1680–1716. [CrossRef]
30. Xia, G.S.; Bai, X.; Ding, J.; Zhu, Z.; Belongie, S.; Luo, J.; Datcu, M.; Pelillo, M.; Zhang, L. DOTA: A large-scale dataset for object detection in aerial images. In Proceedings of the IEEE Conference on Computer Vision and Pattern Recognition, Salt Lake City, UT, USA, 18–23 June 2018; pp. 3974–3983. [CrossRef]
31. Zhang, Y.; Yuan, Y.; Feng, Y.; Lu, X. Hierarchical and robust convolutional neural network for very high-resolution remote sensing object detection. *IEEE Trans. Geosci. Remote Sens.* **2019**, *57*, 5535–5548. [CrossRef]
32. Long, Y.; Gong, Y.; Xiao, Z.; Liu, Q. Accurate object localization in remote sensing images based on convolutional neural networks. *IEEE Trans. Geosci. Remote Sens.* **2017**, *55*, 2486–2498. [CrossRef]
33. Woo, S.; Park, J.; Lee, J.Y.; Kweon, I.S. Cbam: Convolutional block attention module. In Proceedings of the European Conference on Computer Vision (ECCV), Munich, Germany, 8–14 September 2018; pp. 3–19. [CrossRef]
34. Gao, P.; Lu, J.; Li, H.; Mottaghi, R.; Kembhavi, A. Container: Context aggregation network. *arXiv* **2021**, arXiv:2106.01401. [CrossRef]
35. Zhang, Q.L.; Yang, Y.B. Sa-net: Shuffle attention for deep convolutional neural networks. In Proceedings of the IEEE International Conference on Acoustics, Speech and Signal Processing (ICASSP 2021), Toronto, ON, Canada, 6–11 June 2021; pp. 2235–2239. [CrossRef]
36. Li, J.; Wen, Y.; He, L. Scconv: Spatial and channel reconstruction convolution for feature redundancy. In Proceedings of the IEEE/CVF Conference on Computer Vision and Pattern Recognition, Vancouver, BC, Canada, 17–24 June 2023; pp. 6153–6162. [CrossRef]

Disclaimer/Publisher's Note: The statements, opinions and data contained in all publications are solely those of the individual author(s) and contributor(s) and not of MDPI and/or the editor(s). MDPI and/or the editor(s) disclaim responsibility for any injury to people or property resulting from any ideas, methods, instructions or products referred to in the content.

Article

Dense Object Detection Based on De-Homogenized Queries

Yueming Huang [1], Chenrui Ma [2], Hao Zhou [1], Hao Wu [1] and Guowu Yuan [1,*]

[1] School of Information Science and Engineering, Yunnan University, Kunming 650504, China; huangyueming@mail.ynu.edu.cn (Y.H.); zhouhao@ynu.edu.cn (H.Z.); haowu_sise@ynu.edu.cn (H.W.)
[2] School of Computer Science and Engineering, Central South University, Changsha 410083, China; 8208210320@csu.edu.cn
* Correspondence: gwyuan@ynu.edu.cn

Abstract: Dense object detection is widely used in automatic driving, video surveillance, and other fields. This paper focuses on the challenging task of dense object detection. Currently, detection methods based on greedy algorithms, such as non-maximum suppression (NMS), often produce many repetitive predictions or missed detections in dense scenarios, which is a common problem faced by NMS-based algorithms. Through the end-to-end DETR (DEtection TRansformer), as a type of detector that can incorporate the post-processing de-duplication capability of NMS, etc., into the network, we found that homogeneous queries in the query-based detector lead to a reduction in the de-duplication capability of the network and the learning efficiency of the encoder, resulting in duplicate prediction and missed detection problems. To solve this problem, we propose learnable differentiated encoding to de-homogenize the queries, and at the same time, queries can communicate with each other via differentiated encoding information, replacing the previous self-attention among the queries. In addition, we used joint loss on the output of the encoder that considered both location and confidence prediction to give a higher-quality initialization for queries. Without cumbersome decoder stacking and guaranteeing accuracy, our proposed end-to-end detection framework was more concise and reduced the number of parameters by about 8% compared to deformable DETR. Our method achieved excellent results on the challenging CrowdHuman dataset with 93.6% average precision (AP), 39.2% MR^{-2}, and 84.3% JI. The performance overperformed previous SOTA methods, such as Iter-E2EDet (Progressive End-to-End Object Detection) and MIP (One proposal, Multiple predictions). In addition, our method is more robust in various scenarios with different densities.

Keywords: object detection; dense detection; DETR; transformer

Citation: Huang, Y.; Ma, C.; Zhou, H.; Wu, H.; Yuan, G. Dense Object Detection Based on De-Homogenized Queries. *Electronics* **2024**, *13*, 2312. https://doi.org/10.3390/electronics13122312

Academic Editor: Eva Cernadas

Received: 16 May 2024
Revised: 9 June 2024
Accepted: 11 June 2024
Published: 13 June 2024

Copyright: © 2024 by the authors. Licensee MDPI, Basel, Switzerland. This article is an open access article distributed under the terms and conditions of the Creative Commons Attribution (CC BY) license (https://creativecommons.org/licenses/by/4.0/).

1. Introduction

Dense object detection is an essential task in computer vision, aiming at accurately detecting and locating multiple mutually occluded objects from an image or video. There is a trade-off in the design of dense object detection algorithms. On the one hand, the detector has to integrate the coded information and regress each target as much as possible to avoid miss detection. On the other hand, while pursuing a higher recall, it is important to prevent causing duplicate predictions, i.e., multiple predictions corresponding to the same GT (Ground Truth). This trade-off is fundamental in dense detection tasks.

Among the current detection methods, there are two main ways to solve the problem of missed detection and repeated prediction as follows: (1) box-level post-processing de-duplication strategy; (2) matching the strategy of candidate boxes to the set of GTs during the training process, i.e., to determine which candidate anchor or query should predict which GT, and which one should not. They correspond to detection algorithms based on anchors and post-processing and end-to-end detection algorithms based on queries.

In the widely used anchor-based detection algorithms [1–4], training is conducted using manually set dense anchors for many-to-one matching with GTs. Each anchor predicts the nearest IoU distance to itself in the neighborhood, as shown in Figure 1a. The many-to-one matching training strategy and the absence of additional penalties for repeated predictions in these methods make the network inherently incapable of de-duplication. This results in multiple neighboring anchors regressing to the same GT during the prediction, so additional post-processing methods, such as non-maximum suppression (NMS), are required to remove duplicate predictions. However, this greedy algorithm-based box-level method, NMS, which sets a fixed IoU threshold for removing highly overlapping predictions and adjusts IoU suppression thresholds to balance the contradiction between repeated prediction and missed detection, is still unable to solve the contradiction in different dense scenarios. In the subsequent improvement algorithms, SoftNMS [5] mitigates this contradiction by setting the soft threshold for box suppression, and adaptive NMS [6] adaptively changes the threshold for suppression. However, box-level NMS and other greedy-based post-processing methods still perform poorly in dense scenes.

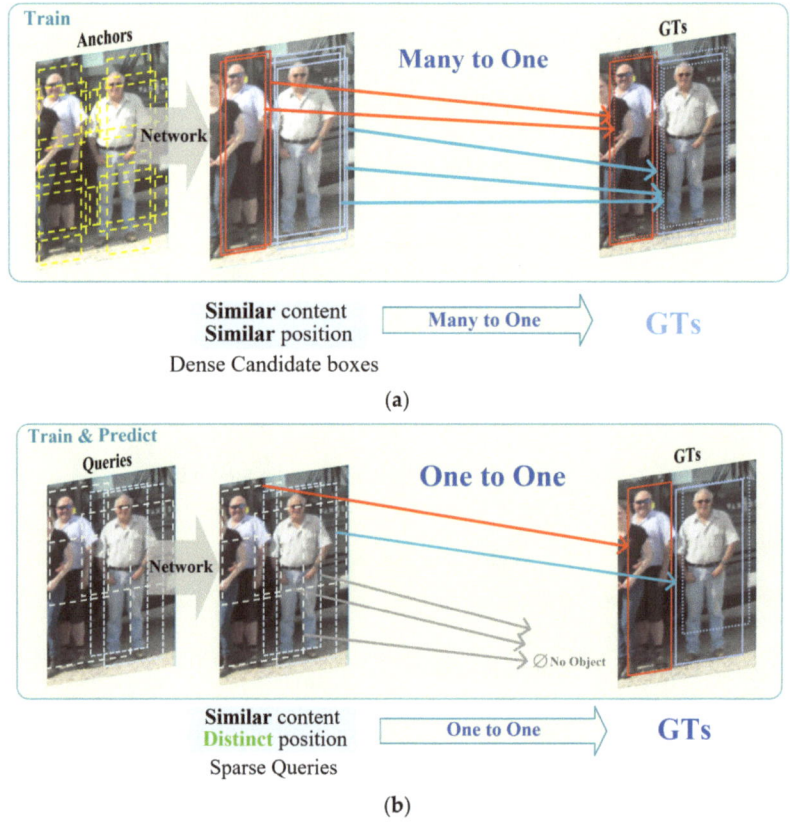

Figure 1. Current mainstream detection frameworks, different coloured arrows are matched with the same coloured GTs. (**a**) Anchor-based detector; (**b**) query-based detector.

In the end-to-end query-based detection algorithm [7,8], as shown in Figure 1b, a global one-to-one matching algorithm based on bipartite graph matching is used to replace the previous many-to-one greedy matching algorithms in training, and a learnable sparse query is used to replace the manually set dense anchors. During the training process, each query learns to focus on objects of different regions and shapes according to statistical laws and performs global scale segmentation matching on the set of GTs (the queries that should predict which GTs should and should not be used). During training, the network learns the one-to-one matching of queries for GTs, and there is a loss penalty for repeated predictions during training, so the model learns the de-duplication capability inside the network through query location segmentation without additional post-processing de-duplication such as NMS.

However, in query-based detection algorithms, queries with similar locations focus on similar encoding information, and queries with similar content tend to make repeated predictions after the same regression and classification headers, which means that such a problem is worse in dense scenes. In addition, since similar queries do not have enough differentiated information for the network to learn the ability of duplicate removal in training, similar queries bring unstable backpropagation during the training, which reduces the learning efficiency of the encoder in crowded scenarios.

1.1. Solving the Query Homogenization Problem

Query homogeneity is mainly the result of two reasons: content homogeneity and location homogeneity. For location homogenization, DN-DETR, and DINO-DETR [9,10] improve the convergence speed by limiting the distance of query fine-tuning in the training phase so that the matching division between GT and the query becomes more stable. In the work of DDQ [11], good results were achieved by adding non-maximal suppression (NMS) to the initialized query process to filter the initialized positions and suppress the queries with similar positions. However, due to the high density of GTs in dense scenarios, the location similarity is very high, so the differentiation of query locations can only alleviate the repetitive prediction in dense scenarios. Secondly, the computational cost of non-maximal suppression (NMS) is too high, and the experiments in RT-DETR [12] demonstrate the high time cost of NMS.

In this paper, we address this problem by differentiating the content of the query. When query locations are close, the encoded content is homogeneous due to similar attentional scopes. Therefore, we designed a learnable differentiated encoding for each query to break the strong correlation between the content of the query and its location. In this way, even if the predicted locations of the queries are close to each other, the model can adopt different learning strategies with differentiated information. This can significantly improve the de-duplication ability of the decoder and the encoder. As shown in Figure 2, the colors of the query prediction boxes represent their content differences; we aim to propose a detection framework based on content differentiation. Meanwhile, in generating differential encoding, the query can exchange differential information with the surrounding prediction, replacing the self-attention among the queries in the original decoder and simplifying the network structure.

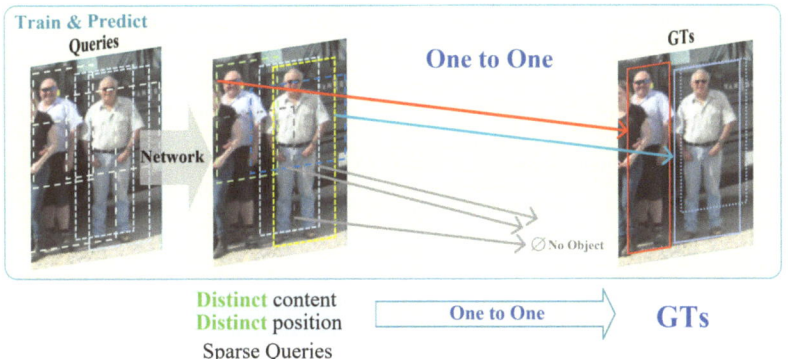

Figure 2. Our detection framework based on differentiated query. Different colored arrows are matched with the same colored GTs, and different colored boxes represent differences in the encoded content of the queries.

1.2. Alligned Decoder

In DETR-like detectors, the encoder generates feature maps for the decoder to query, allowing for layer-by-layer fine-tuning to achieve more precise predictions. However, the structural differences between the encoder and decoder lead to disparities in their encoding and decoding methodologies. Much work has been conducted to improve the end-to-end detector by aligning the design of encoders and decoders, enabling the more effective integration of information during cross-attention and enhancing model efficiency. For example, DAB-DETR [13] and conditional DETR [14] add the same positional coding in the decoder as in the encoder to align the coding and decoding methods, which reduces the information discrepancy caused by the difference between the encoder and the decoder methods and obtains an improvement in accuracy. Inspired by these papers, we designed the decoder as a structure aligned with the encoder, eliminating the self-attention among the queries in the decoder. At the same time, using the asymmetric difference aggregation (ADA) mechanism in the difference encoding process can be a good substitute for the communication between queries. Without decreasing the detection efficiency and accuracy of the model, the method in this paper can reduce the number of parameters by about 8%.

1.3. Query Initialization Considering Both Position and Confidence

In a two-stage DETR-like detection model, the query is usually initialized using the encoder's output confidence score Top-K algorithm. Due to the separate setting of confidence and location loss functions, there is a mismatch between the confidence score and IoU when selecting the initialized query, i.e., there are candidate predictions with high IoU but low confidence, resulting in them being filtered out by the Top-k algorithm. For this reason, this paper proposes using the joint loss of confidence and GIoU to supervise the training of the encoder output and to optimize the mismatch between the confidence and IoU to initialize the query more efficiently and achieve better detection results with fewer queries.

1.4. Our Contribution

In this paper, we address the problem of homogeneous queries in query-based detectors by proposing learnable differential encoding to add to the query, which increases the de-duplication capability in the network while improving the learning efficiency of the encoder and decoder; secondly, we used a higher-quality initialization of the query by taking into account both the positional and confidence losses; and finally, we optimized the structure of the decoder to reduce the number of model parameters without significantly affecting the model accuracy. With the proposed differential query learning strategy, the method in this paper outperformed the recent SOTA methods of Iter-E2EDet (Progressive End-to-End Object Detection) [15], MIP (One proposal, Multiple predictions) [16], and AD-DETR (Asymmetrical Decoupled Detection Transformer) [17], while the parameters were reduced by about 8% with fewer decoders.

2. Analysis of Similar and Differentiated Queries

This section mainly discusses how similar queries in query-based detectors can lead to repeated predictions and training inefficiency in dense scenarios. Queries with similar locations focus on similar encoded feature information, which results in content-similar queries, and they are more inclined to make similar duplicate predictions when passing through the same fully connected classification and regression heads.

In Figure 3, we statistically represent the query content's similarity and relative IoU distance in deformable-DETR. The vertical coordinate is the cosine similarity between the queries, and the horizontal coordinate is the IoU distance between the queries. The encoded content and location of the queries are strongly correlated. The closer the IoU distance between queries, the greater the probability that they have high content similarity.

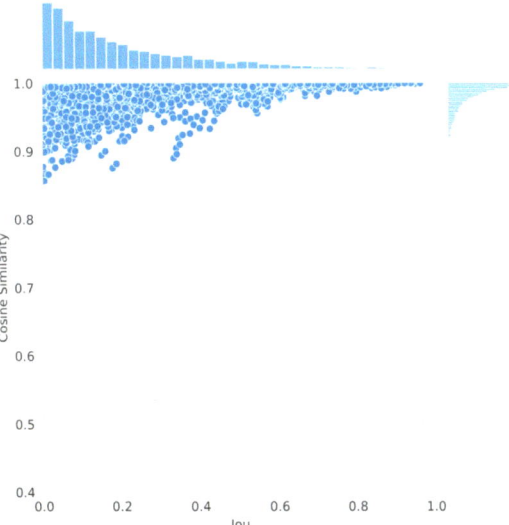

Figure 3. Statistics of IoU distance and cosine similarity among queries.

Homogeneous queries can lead to duplicate prediction problems. We explain this with an intuitive example, assuming that the two queries are very close to each other at the initialization time; for the sake of generality, we adopt the binary cross-entropy loss as the classification loss and the cross-entropy loss L for a single query can be expressed as follows:

$$L = -[y \cdot \log(p) + (1-y) \cdot \log(1-p)] \tag{1}$$

where y denotes the one-hot classification label corresponding to the GT and p denotes the confidence score.

In the case of two queries, if one query q_1 matches the target GT and the other query q_2 does not match the object, according to Equation (1), the total loss of the two queries is the following:

$$L_{1,2} = L_1 + L_2 = -[\log(p_1) + \log(1-p_2)] \tag{2}$$

Assuming that the two queries are very close to each other at their initialization, due to the strong correlation between the content similarity and the relative IoU distance, in the extreme case where we assume that the two queries are the same, their confidence scores have $p_1 = p_2 = p$, in which case the total loss in Equation (2) is the following:

$$L_{1,2} = -[\log(p) + \log(1-p)] \tag{3}$$

The gradient of the loss with respect to the confidence level is as follows:

$$\frac{\partial L}{\partial p} = \frac{1}{1-p} - \frac{1}{p} \tag{4}$$

It can be seen that when the confidence score is $p > 0.5$, the gradient is positive, the loss decreases with the decrease in confidence, and the network reduces the confidence of both predictions; when $p < 0.5$, the loss decreases with the increase in confidence, so the network increases the confidence of both predictions during training. Eventually, when $p = 0.5$, the network reaches the equilibrium point of backward gradient propagation, at which there is no updated gradient for both queries, and the local optimum point of the loss function is reached. That is, in this case, the network prefers to keep the two low-confidence predictions instead of a de-duplication strategy that increases the confidence of one prediction to eliminate the other. As queries become dense and similar, more similar queries may correspond to a GT, generating duplicate predictions.

Homogeneous queries also bring unstable backpropagation during the training, which reduces the learning efficiency of the encoder. As in Figure 4, we assume that there are two queries that are close to the target GT, and in the two-part graph matching algorithm, query q_1, which matches GT produces a gradient update matrix M_1 that increases the confidence score of q_1, while query q_2 that matches no object produces a gradient update matrix M_2 that decreases the confidence score of q_2.

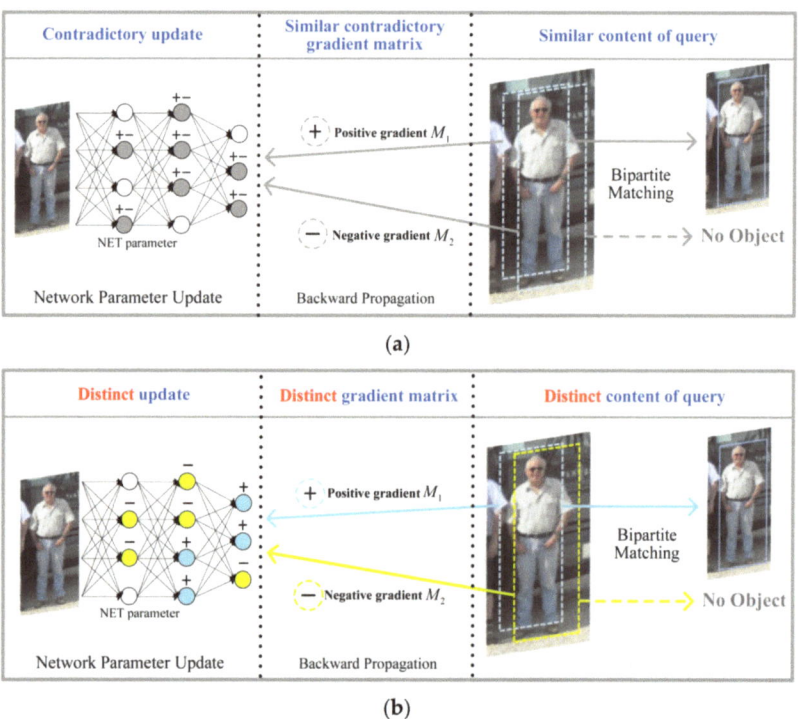

Figure 4. Network updates for different queries in training, and different colored boxes represent differences in the encoded content of the queries. (**a**) Detection methods based on homogeneous queries; (**b**) our proposed detection method based on de-homogenized queries.

As shown in Figure 4a, when the contents of two queries q_1 and q_2 are very similar, the resulting updated matrix M_1 and M_2 has similar absolute values but opposite sign directions. In the extreme case, when $q_1 = q_2$, the updated matrices M_1 and M_2 have the same absolute value but an opposite sign, that is $M_1 = -M_2$. Such contradictory updates make it difficult for the network's encoder to learn efficiently in dense scenarios, and the repeated predictions are difficult to be penalized by the back-propagation gradient in training.

As shown in Figure 4b, after adding differential coding to q_1 and q_2, even when their positions are almost coincident, the gradient update matrices M_1 and M_2 generated by the backpropagation of different symbol directions are significantly different from each other in absolute value. Such differentiated updates allow the encoder to learn more efficiently, and this model can learn the de-duplication strategy better through the differentiated information.

3. Our Method

The general framework proposed in this paper is shown in Figure 5, where the image is first passed through a feature extractor (including a backbone network and a stacked encoder) to obtain multi-scale feature maps, and then a fixed number of queries are initialized using our proposed GIoU-aware query selector, which is input to the subsequent decoder, and output location predictions through the first layer of the decoder with auxiliary prediction heads aligned to the encoder. Positional prediction is output through the first layer of the decoder aligned with auxiliary prediction heads. Then, the De-Homo Coding Generator (DCG) generates differentiated codes, which are added to the original query to form a differentiated query, which is then passed to the subsequent decoder to obtain the final confidence prediction.

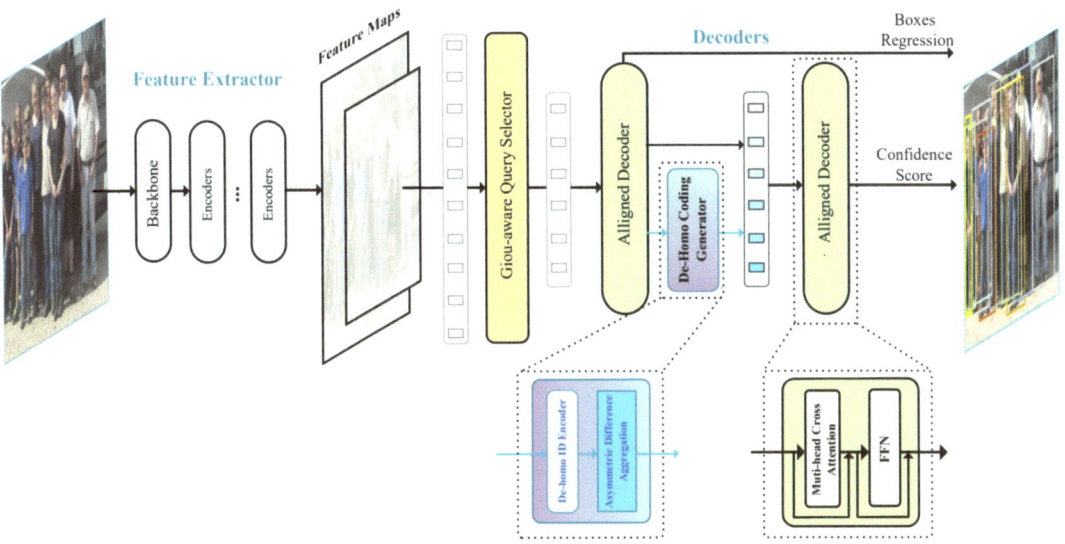

Figure 5. Overall framework of our proposed detector.

3.1. De-Homo Coding Generator

As mentioned above, homogeneous queries make it difficult for the network to learn effective de-duplication strategies. In this paper, we design a DCG (De-Homo Coding Generator) module to generate differentiated coded information to add to the query, which enables the network to learn the de-duplication ability through the differentiated information.

The DCG module, as illustrated in Figure 6, operates in two stages. In the first stage, a De-Homo ID Encoder generates a unique De-Homo ID for each query to learn the distinctions among them. The De-Homo ID for the ith query, e_i^{id}, is calculated as follows:

$$e_i^{id} = LN(\mathcal{H}(q_i)) \qquad (5)$$

where $\mathcal{H}(\cdot)$ encodes the query using two fully connected layers and an activation function. LN represents layer normalization, which normalizes the encoded De-Homo ID for subsequent difference computation.

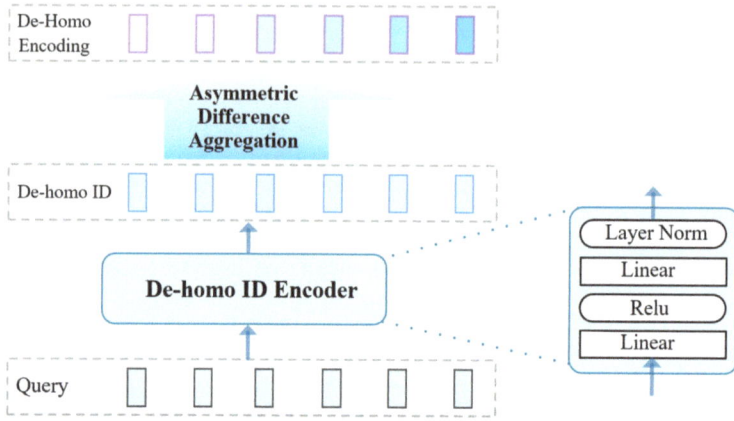

Figure 6. Structure of the DCG (De-Homo Coding Generator) module.

In the second stage, each query integrates the difference information from the De-Homo IDs of surrounding queries through an asymmetric difference fusion mechanism, producing differentiation encoding for de-duplication. This fusion mechanism also facilitates information exchange between queries, serving as an alternative to self-attention among them. For the ith query, the differentiation encoding q_i^{DE} is given as follows:

$$q_i^{DE} = ADA\left(e^{id}\right) = Maxpooling\left(\left\{\left(e_i^{id} - e_j^{id}\right) \cdot \mathbb{I}(c_j > c_i) \middle| IoU(b_j, b_i) < 0.5, c_j > C_{low}\right\}\right) \quad (6)$$

where c_i and b_i represent the confidence and positional predictions of the ith query, respectively. $\mathbb{I}$ is an indicator function that is 1 when $c_j > c_i$ and is 0 otherwise. The minimum threshold for confidence attention C_{low} is set to avoid the computational complexity increase due to a large number of low-confidence predictions.

The asymmetric relationship based on confidence can further reinforce differentiated information, allowing each query to integrate the information of predictions with higher confidence scores from their surrounding. In traditional self-attention mechanisms among queries, where $q_j = W^T \sum_{i=1}^{N} k_i W q_i$, the focus is only on information that improves recall without considering the differentiation from surrounding predictions to avoid redundancy. Our paper introduces the asymmetric difference aggregation (ADA) mechanism, which is a function that processes the difference of encoded content between queries $q_i - q_j$ to encode differentiated information.

The de-homogenized query is obtained by adding q_i^{DE} to the original query, where $q_i^{De-Homo} = q_i + ffn(q_i^{DE})$. Here, ffn represents a fully connected feedforward network consisting of two linear layers and an activation layer. $q_i^{De-Homo}$ is then fed into subsequent decoders to generate confidence predictions, addressing the issue of the network's difficulty in learning deduplication capabilities due to homogenized queries.

3.2. GIoU-Aware Query Selector

For the past two-stage query-based detectors [9,10,13,18], most algorithms use the Top-K algorithm with confidence scores to filter the queries from the encoder's predictions for initialization. However, the quality of the query's initialization is determined by the combination of the position and the confidence level, which results in the initialized query with a high IoU but a low confidence level being filtered out or a prediction with a low IoU but a high confidence level being selected, leading to the degradation of the quality of the query's initialization.

To solve this problem, we used a combined quality score that considered both confidence and location for query initialization. At the same time, the GIoU [19] can better reflect the overlap between prediction boxes based on IoU, so we use GIoU to indicate the quality of location prediction. We finally used Top-K based on the combined scores of GIoU and the Classification score to filter for query initialization. Meanwhile, we still used bipartite graph matching for a one-to-one mapping between predicted and real boxes.

We propose supervising the training of the encoder's output using GIoU-aware's combined predictive quality loss, which is as follows:

$$\mathcal{L}(\hat{y}, y) = \mathcal{L}_{box}\left(\hat{b}, b\right) + \mathcal{FL}_{giou-cls}(\hat{c}, c, Giou) \tag{7}$$

where $\hat{y}$ and y denote the prediction and GT, $\hat{y}$ consists of the position prediction $\hat{b}$ and the category prediction $\hat{c}$, y also corresponds to the position label b and the category label c of the GT. We incorporate the idea of focal loss [20] to consider the loss that can focus more on hard samples, and our proposed GIoU-aware loss is as follows:

$$\mathcal{FL}_{giou-cls}(\hat{c}, c, Giou) = \begin{cases} -Giou \cdot \omega \cdot \log(\hat{p}) \text{ if } c = 1 \\ -\omega \log(1 - \hat{p}) \text{ if } c = 0. \end{cases} \tag{8}$$

where ω is modulating weight, which is similar to the idea of focal loss, and is used to determine the attention degree of difficult and easy samples, where the expression is as follows:

$$\omega = (\hat{p} \cdot Giou + (1 - \hat{p})(1 - Giou))^{\gamma} \tag{9}$$

where $\gamma > 0$ is an adjustable factor. For simple samples where the predicted value is already very close to the true value, ω tends to zero, and for hard-to-predict samples, ω is given a higher weight.

In our test, we used the joint score Top-k for query initialization, which considers both location and confidence, to avoid the filtering out of low confidence and high IoU predictions caused by only confident scores so that we could achieve higher quality query initialization and higher accuracy with fewer queries. As shown in Figure 7, the predicted scores after using GQS have a better correlation with the IoU, resulting in higher IoU predictions when using the score Top-k algorithm, which corresponds to a better initialization quality. In the decoder loss design, in order to maintain the convergence of the model loss function, we still used the original discrete-label classification loss for supervised learning to obtain the final predictions.

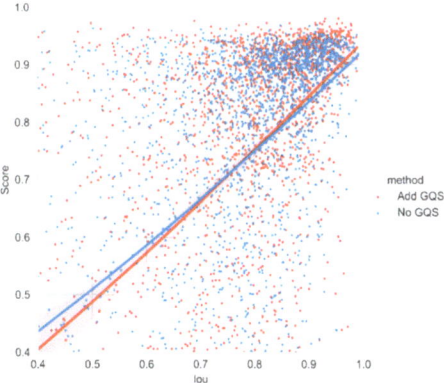

Figure 7. Statistics of score and IoU scores in initialized queries. The red line is the regression curve after the use of the GQS, and the blue line is without it.

3.3. Alligned Decoder

Many previous works attempted to reduce the differences between encoding and decoding methods by aligning the encoder and decoder so the model could integrate the information more efficiently in the cross-attention mechanism. Since the difference fusion mechanism in our proposed DEG was also available to perform information fusion among queries, we eliminated the self-attention module between the queries and used a decoder aligned with the encoder. While maintaining the original method's accuracy, we reduced the number of parameters by about 8%. With the addition of differential coding, both the encoder and decoder results improved because of the more stable one-to-one mapping relationship obtained in training. We also found that using only the first few layers of the trained decoder in the prediction stage reduced the number of parameters and maintained a relatively high accuracy.

4. Experiment and Analysis

We focus on the experimental validation of our approach through a benchmark test dataset, CrowdHuman [21], and compare it with SOTA's anchor-based detection method and query-based end-to-end detection method. We also performed ablation experiments for our proposed components and tested their robustness in scenarios with different densities.

4.1. Experiment Dataset

The CrowdHuman dataset contains 15k training images and 4.4k validation images, with an average of about 23 mutually occluded targets per image. We used the AP, MR^{-2} and JI as metrics as follows:

- Average precision (AP): Expressed by the area enclosed by the precision–recall curve and coordinates. In object detection, AP is often used to reflect precision and recall, and a larger AP indicates better detection performance.
- MR^{-2}: The average missing detection rate is calculated on the logarithmic scale of the false detection rate for each image. This metric is often used in pedestrian detection because it reflects the false and missed detection, and a smaller MR^{-2} indicates better detection performance.
- Jaccard index (JI): The index mainly evaluates the degree of overlap between the predicted set and the GTs. It reflects the overall distribution similarity between the prediction boxes set and the actual GTs, and a higher JI indicates better detection performance.

4.2. Experiment Details

We used the standard ResNet-50 [22], pre-trained on ImageNet [23], as the backbone for deformable DETR [18] and ran 50 epochs for training. We trained our model with the AdamW optimizer, where the momentum was set to 0.9 and the weight decay to 0.0001. The model's learning rate was 0.0002, and the learning rate of the backbone network was 0.00002. The batch size was 8, the number of attention headers was set to 8, and 4 RTX 3090 GPUs were used for training.

The end-to-end detector DETR [7], deformable DETR [18], Iter-E2Edet [15], etc., employed in our experiments used the default 6-layer encoder and 6-layer decoder; our method was implemented using only the 6-layer encoder and 3-layer decoder, and other hyper-parameter settings are kept the same as deformable DETR.

4.3. Comparative Experiments with Other Advanced Detectors

Table 1 shows a comparison of the results of our method on the CrowdHuman validation set with those of several SOTA methods, including anchor-based detectors [3,4,6,16,20,24–26] and query-based detectors [7,8,15,18,27,28]. It can be seen that the traditional anchor-based methods perform poorly in dense and high occlusion scenarios because they need to be de-duplicated by greedy algorithms such as NMS. In contrast, end-to-end detection methods learn the de-weighting inside the network and perform better overall. However, query-based methods usually need to continuously increase the number of queries to adapt to performance in dense scenarios, and most of the methods need to fine-tune the results hierarchically by stacking the decoder structure to improve the detection effect.

Table 1. Comparative experimental results on the CrowdHuman validation set.

Method	#Queries	AP ↑	MR^{-2} ↓	JI ↑	Params
Anchor-based detectors					
RetinaNet [20]	-	85.3	55.1	73.7	
ATSS [24]	-	87.0	55.1	75.9	
ATSS [24] + MIP [16]	-	88.7	51.6	77.0	
Faster R-CNN [3]	-	85.0	50.4	-	
Cascade R-CNN [4]		86.0	44.1	-	
FPN [25] + Adaptive-NMS [6]		84.7	47.7		
FPN [25] + Soft-NMS [5]		88.2	42.9	79.8	
FPN [25] + MIP [16]		90.7	41.4	82.3	
PBM [26]	-	89.3	43.3	-	
Query-based detectors					
DETR [7]	100	75.9	73.2	74.4	
PED [27]	1000	91.6	43.7	83.3	
Sparse-RCNN [8]	500	90.7	44.7	81.4	
D-DETR (one-stage) [18]	500	89.1	50.0		37.7 M
	1000	91.3	43.8	83.3	37.7 M
D-DETR (two-stage) [18]	500	92.6	43.1	82.9	37.7 M
	1000	92.8	43.2	83.0	37.7 M
UniHCP (direct eval) [28]		90.0	46.6	82.2	109.1 M
UniHCP (finetune) [28]		92.5	41.6	85.8	109.1 M
Iter-E2EDet [15]	500	91.2	42.6	84.0	38.0 M
	1000	92.1	41.5	84.0	38.0 M
Ours(6-3) *	500	93.6	39.2	84.3	34.6 M
Ours(6-3(2)) *	500	93.5	39.3	84.1	33.7 M

* The numbers in parentheses after the method name indicate the number of layers of the encoder and decoder used for training and testing. X-Y (Z) indicates the X-layer encoder and Y-layer decoder for training and the Z-layer decoder for testing. If no special instruction exists, other methods are 6-6 (6) by default.

Comparing these methods, using fewer queries, our method achieved higher accuracy and lower miss detection rates. Our method reduced about 3.9% and improved AP by 1% compared to the benchmark method of two-stage deformable DETR using six decoders, while our model reduced the number of parameters by about 8% in the parameter scale. UniHCP [28] was first trained across tasks on 33 datasets with about 109.1 million parameters, which were then fine-tuned on the Crowdhuman dataset. Our method still outperformed them in AP and MR^{-2} metrics, using only about 32% of the parameters.

4.4. Ablation Experiment

To test the effectiveness of the different components in our proposed method, we performed ablation experiments on Crowdhuman. As in Table 2, in the first row of the table, we used six decoders of deformable-DETR (ResNet50 as the backbone network) as the benchmark method for comparison, and three decoders were used by default in our method. Our proposed De-Homo Coding Generator (DCG) significantly improved the detector's performance, with the leakage rate MR^{-2} reduced from the original 43.2% to 40.2%. After using the GIoU-aware query selector, GQS, the miss prediction was further reduced because of the improved initialization efficiency of the query.

Table 2. Ablation experiments on CrowdHuman validation set.

DCG	AD	GQS	AP ↑	MR^{-2} ↓	JI ↑	Params(M)
			92.8	43.2	83.0	37.7
✓			93.3	40.2	83.8	35.4
✓	✓		93.5	40.0	84.0	34.6
✓	✓	✓	93.6	39.2	84.3	34.6

DCG—De-Homo Coding Generator. AD—aligned decoder. GQS—GIoU query selector.

At the same time, our method did not need a redundant layer fine-tuning structure and obtained high accuracy at the early stage of the decoder, as shown in Figures 8 and 9. We tested the AP and MR^{-2} of the prediction results in our method and the benchmark method deformable DETR for different stages of the decoder. In the second decoder block, our model achieved an accuracy of 93.5% for AP and 39.3% for MR^{-2}, which basically guaranteed accuracy while reducing the number of parameters. Comparing the outputs of the encoder and the first decoder, our method significantly reduced the information gap between the decoder and the encoder.

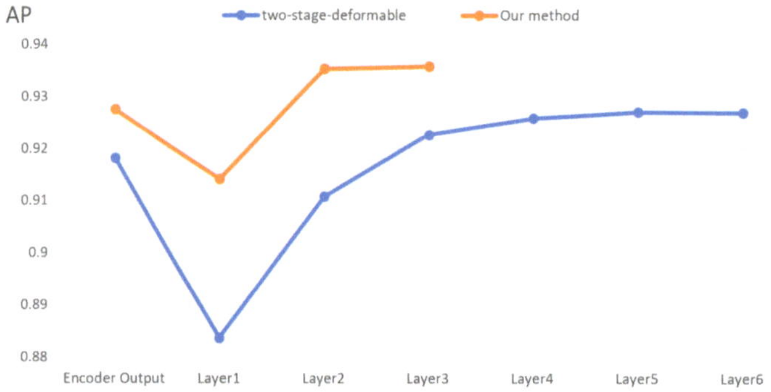

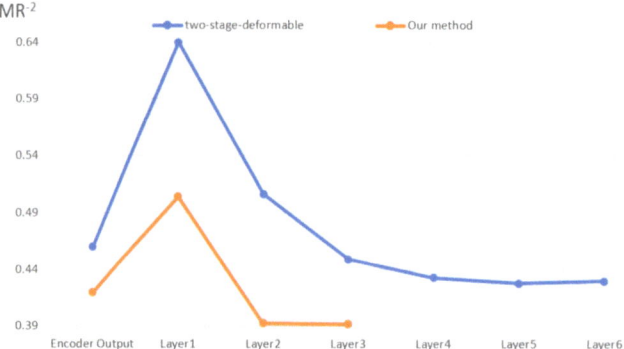

Figure 8. AP of detection results for each stage of the decoder.

Figure 9. MR^{-2} of detection results for each stage of the decoder.

It can also be seen that when the encoder's structure is exactly the same, its performance improves significantly due to the distinctive gradient update brought about by the differentiated query.

4.5. Hyperparameter Analysis

Table 3 compares the model's performance on the CrowdHuman validation set when different decoders are assigned before and after the differential coding generator DCG. The results are better when more decoders are used after differential coding.

Table 3. Performance of the model when different numbers of decoders are used before and after the DCG.

Decoders (before)	Decoders (after)	AP ↑	MR^{-2} ↓	JI ↑	Params (M)
1	1	93.3	40.1	84.1	33.7
2	1	93.4	40.3	84.2	34.4
1	2	93.6	39.2	84.3	34.6
1	2(1)[1]	93.5	39.3	84.1	33.7

[1] Here, 2(1) means that 2 decoders are used for training, but only 1 decoder is used for testing.

At the same time, we compared the impact of using different queries, as shown in Table 4; our method improved the benchmark method when using various queries. Figure 10 shows the performance trend of the model with different numbers of queries, and it is clear that our method can perform better with fewer queries. Performance degradation tends to be slower when the number of queries becomes smaller.

Table 4. Performance of the model with different numbers of queries in the Crowdhuman validation set.

#Queries	Our Method		Deformable DETR	
	AP ↑	MR^{-2} ↓	AP ↑	MR^{-2} ↓
100	88.93	39.87	87.59	47.56
200	92.53	39.24	91.40	44.35
300	93.26	39.21	92.23	43.44
500	93.58	39.20	92.61	43.10
1000	93.75	39.20	92.77	43.19
2000	93.77	39.21	92.79	43.25

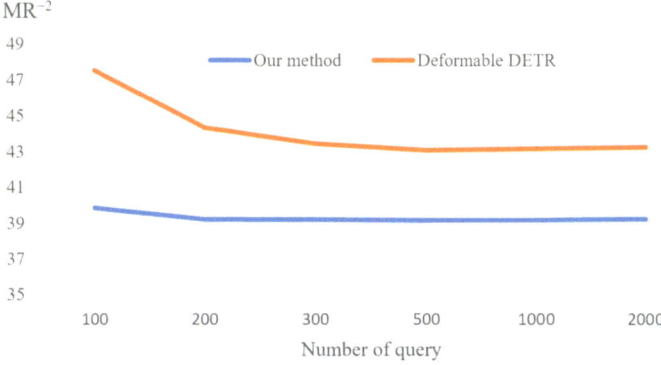

Figure 10. Comparison of model performance when using different numbers of queries. Comparative analysis of differentiated queries.

To compare the effect of our method on query differentiation, as shown in Figure 11, we computed the IOU distances and the cosine similarities between the queries with positive predictive confidence in the deformable DETR and our method, respectively. Our method can significantly reduce query homogeneity and break the strong correlation between query location and the encoded content.

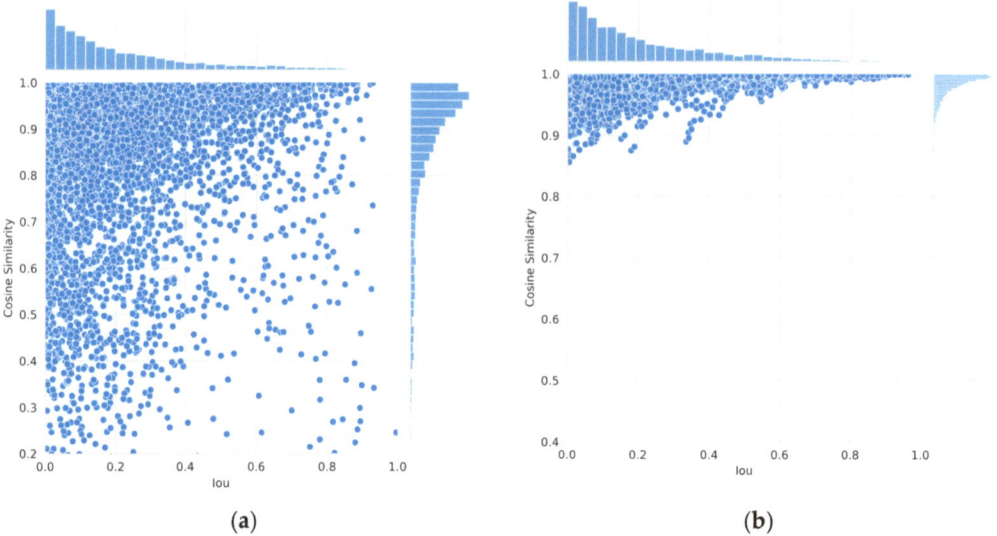

Figure 11. Cosine similarity of query at different IoU distances (**a**) before de-homogenization, (**b**) after de-homogenization.

4.6. Analysis of Detection Results

We analyzed the detection results of our method and the benchmark method two-stage deformable-DETR in detail. We also made false positive (FP) and true positive (TP) statistics at different confidence scores in the detection results of the CrowdHuman validation set. The statistical results are shown in Figure 12, with the matching IOU threshold set to 0.8. Our method significantly improved the TP at each confidence level while largely suppressing the FP of repeated predictions.

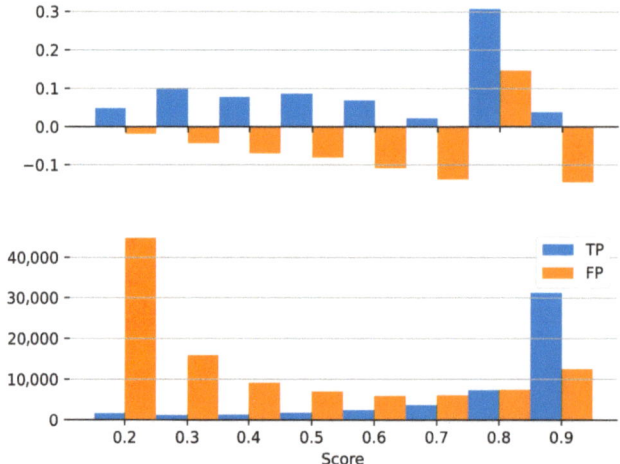

Figure 12. Comparing the relative improvement of our detection results in different confidence scores.

To verify the generalization performance and robustness of our method in scenarios with different densities, we statistically measured the changes in TP and FP between our method and the benchmark method in scenarios with different densities, as shown in Figure 13; when we set the matching IOU threshold to 0.5, our method significantly increased the TP and inhibited the repeated prediction of FP in various scenarios with different densities. When the IOU threshold was set to 0.8, as shown in Figure 14, the improvement of our method over the benchmark method was even more significant. Our method can regress the target location more accurately and simultaneously reduce the FP of repeated prediction and false detection.

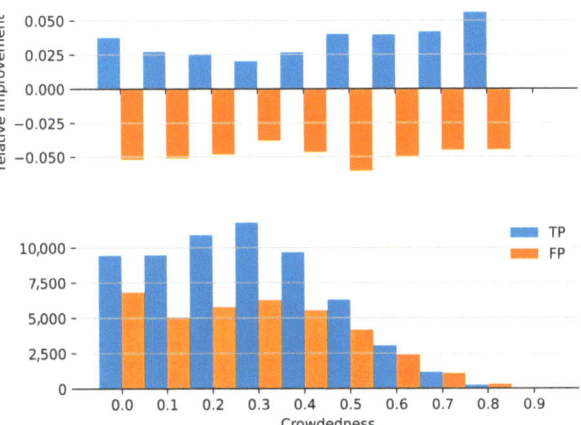

Figure 13. The relative improvement of our method over deformable DETR in different dense scenarios (the matching IoU threshold is 0.5).

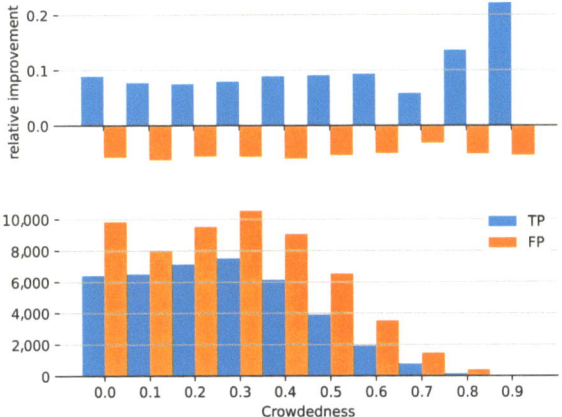

Figure 14. The relative improvement of our method over deformable DETR in different dense scenarios (the matching IoU threshold is 0.8).

4.7. Comparison of Actual Test Result Images

As shown in Figure 15, we compared the detection effect of two-stage deformable DETR with that of our method and found that our method still performed well in dense and heavily occluded scenes.

Figure 15. Comparison of the actual detection results for (**a**) the two-stage deformable DETR (**b**) and our method.

5. Discussion

In this paper, we propose a differentiated query strategy, which significantly increases the de-duplication capability of the query-based detection model and improves the learning efficiency of the encoder in dense scenarios; at the same time, we optimize the initialization of the query and the structure of the decoder, which reduces the number of parameters in the model while improving the accuracy of the end-to-end detector. Compared with the current SOTA detection methods, this method achieves higher accuracy while keeping the number of parameters lower, and its robustness in different dense scenes is experimentally verified. Nevertheless, our proposed DCG (De-Homo Coding Generator) module leads to a higher time complexity in the inference phase, especially in dense scenarios, because of the computation of IoU among dense queries. In addition, to avoid excessive time complexity, we limited the computational scope of the De-Homo Coding and the depth of the network for the coding methods. Our approach still has potential for improvement in complex and dense scenarios. Also, the initialization of the query using encoder features incurs an extra high computational complexity in inference. Future work will further optimize the model based on this to enhance its robustness in more complex scenarios and further optimize the computational complexity of the model.

Author Contributions: Conceptualization, Y.H. and G.Y.; methodology, Y.H. and G.Y.; software, Y.H. and C.M.; validation, Y.H. and C.M.; data curation, H.W.; writing—original draft preparation, Y.H. and G.Y.; writing—review and editing, H.Z. and G.Y.; visualization, H.W.; supervision, H.Z. and G.Y.; funding acquisition, H.Z. All authors have read and agreed to the published version of the manuscript.

Funding: This research was funded by the Natural Science Foundation of China (grant no. 62162065, 62061049, 12263008), the Department of Science and Technology of Yunnan Province–Yunnan University Joint Special Project for Double-Class Construction (grant no. 202201BF070001-005).

Data Availability Statement: The CrowdHuman dataset is available at http://www.crowdhuman.org (accessed on 1 June 2023). Our codes can be opened at https://github.com/YuemingMrdream/DH_DETR_paper(accessed on 12 June 2024).

Conflicts of Interest: The authors declare no conflicts of interest.

References

1. Redmon, J.; Divvala, S.; Girshick, R.; Farhadi, A. You only look once: Unified, real-time object detection. In Proceedings of the IEEE Conference on Computer Vision and Pattern Recognition, Las Vegas, NV, USA, 27–30 June 2016; pp. 779–788.
2. Wang, C.-Y.; Bochkovskiy, A.; Liao, H.-Y.M. YOLOv7: Trainable bag-of-freebies sets new state-of-the-art for real-time object detectors. In Proceedings of the IEEE/CVF Conference on Computer Vision and Pattern Recognition, Vancouver, BC, Canada, 17–24 June 2023; pp. 7464–7475.
3. Ren, S.; He, K.; Girshick, R.B.; Sun, J. Faster R-CNN: Towards Real-Time Object Detection with Region Proposal Networks. In Proceedings of the Advances in Neural Information Processing Systems (NIPS), Montreal, QC, Canada, 4–9 December 2017; pp. 91–99.
4. Cai, Z.; Vasconcelos, N. Cascade r-cnn: Delving into high quality object detection. In Proceedings of the IEEE Conference on Computer Vision and Pattern Recognition, Salt Lake City, UT, USA, 18–23 June 2018; pp. 6154–6162.
5. Bodla, N.; Singh, B.; Chellappa, R.; Davis, L.S. Soft-NMS—Improving Object Detection with One Line of Code. In Proceedings of the IEEE International Conference on Computer Vision (ICCV), Venice, Italy, 22–29 October 2017; pp. 5562–5570.
6. Liu, S.; Huang, D.; Wang, Y. Adaptive nms: Refining pedestrian detection in a crowd. In Proceedings of the IEEE/CVF Conference on Computer Vision and Pattern Recognition, Long Beach, CA, USA, 15–20 June 2019; pp. 6459–6468.
7. Carion, N.; Massa, F.; Synnaeve, G.; Usunier, N.; Kirillov, A.; Zagoruyko, S. End-to-End Object Detection with Transformers. In Proceedings of the European Conference on Computer Vision (ECCV), Glasgow, UK, 23–28 August 2020; pp. 213–229.
8. Sun, P.; Zhang, R.; Jiang, Y.; Kong, T.; Xu, C.; Zhan, W.; Tomizuka, M.; Li, L.; Yuan, Z.; Wang, C.; et al. Sparse R-CNN: End-to-End Object Detection With Learnable Proposals. In Proceedings of the IEEE Conference on Computer Vision and Pattern Recognition (CVPR), Nashville, TN, USA, 20–25 June 2021; pp. 14454–14463.
9. Li, F.; Zhang, H.; Liu, S.; Guo, J.; Ni, L.M.; Zhang, L. DN-DETR: Accelerate DETR Training by Introducing Query DeNoising. In Proceedings of the IEEE/CVF Conference on Computer Vision and Pattern Recognition (CVPR), New Orleans, LA, USA, 20–25 June 2021; pp. 13609–13617.
10. Zhang, H.; Li, F.; Liu, S.; Zhang, L.; Su, H.; Zhu, J.; Ni, L.M.; Shum, H. DINO: DETR with Improved DeNoising Anchor Boxes for End-to-End Object Detection. *arXiv* **2022**, arXiv:2203.03605.
11. Zhang, S.; Wang, X.; Wang, J.; Pang, J.; Chen, K. What Are Expected Queries in End-to-End Object Detection? *arXiv* **2022**, arXiv:2206.01232.
12. Lv, W.; Xu, S.; Zhao, Y.; Wang, G.; Wei, J.; Cui, C.; Du, Y.; Dang, Q.; Liu, Y. DETRs Beat YOLOs on Real-time Object Detection. *arXiv* **2023**, arXiv:2304.08069. [CrossRef]
13. Liu, S.; Li, F.; Zhang, H.; Yang, X.; Qi, X.; Su, H.; Zhu, J.; Zhang, L. DAB-DETR: Dynamic Anchor Boxes are Better Queries for DETR. In Proceedings of the Tenth International Conference on Learning Representations(ICLR), Virtual, 25–29 April 2022.
14. Meng, D.; Chen, X.; Fan, Z.; Zeng, G.; Li, H.; Yuan, Y.; Sun, L.; Wang, J. Conditional detr for fast training convergence. In Proceedings of the IEEE/CVF International Conference on Computer Vision, Montreal, QC, Canada, 10–17 October 2021; pp. 3651–3660.
15. Zheng, A.; Zhang, Y.; Zhang, X.; Qi, X.; Sun, J. Progressive End-to-End Object Detection in Crowded Scenes. In Proceedings of the IEEE/CVF Conference on Computer Vision and Pattern Recognition (CVPR), New Orleans, LA, USA, 18–24 June 2022; pp. 847–856.
16. Chu, X.; Zheng, A.; Zhang, X.; Sun, J. Detection in Crowded Scenes: One Proposal, Multiple Predictions. In Proceedings of the IEEE/CVF Conference on Computer Vision and Pattern Recognition (CVPR), Seattle, WA, USA, 13–19 June 2020; pp. 12211–12220.
17. Huang, Y.; Yuan, G. AD-DETR: DETR with asymmetrical relation and decoupled attention in crowded scenes. *Math. Biosci. Eng.* **2023**, *20*, 14158–14179. [CrossRef] [PubMed]
18. Zhu, X.; Su, W.; Lu, L.; Li, B.; Wang, X.; Dai, J. Deformable DETR: Deformable Transformers for End-to-End Object Detection. In Proceedings of the International Conference on Learning Representations, Virtual, 3–7 May 2021.
19. Rezatofighi, H.; Tsoi, N.; Gwak, J.; Sadeghian, A.; Reid, I.; Savarese, S. Generalized Intersection over Union: A Metric and A Loss for Bounding Box Regression. *arXiv* **2019**, arXiv:1902.09630. [CrossRef]
20. Lin, T.; Goyal, P.; Girshick, R.B.; He, K.; Dollr, P. Focal Loss for Dense Object Detection. In Proceedings of the IEEE International Conference on Computer Vision (ICCV), Venice, Italy, 22–29 October 2017; pp. 2999–3007.
21. Shao, S.; Zhao, Z.; Li, B.; Xiao, T.; Yu, G.; Zhang, X.; Sun, J. CrowdHuman: A Benchmark for Detecting Human in a Crowd. *arXiv* **2018**, arXiv:1805.00123.

22. Russakovsky, O.; Deng, J.; Su, H.; Krause, J.; Satheesh, S.; Ma, S.; Huang, Z.; Karpathy, A.; Khosla, A.; Bernstein, M.S.; et al. ImageNet Large Scale Visual Recognition Challenge. *Int. J. Comput. Vis.* **2015**, *115*, 211–252. [CrossRef]
23. He, K.; Zhang, X.; Ren, S.; Sun, J. Deep residual learning for image recognition. In Proceedings of the IEEE Conference on Computer Vision and Pattern Recognition (CVPR), Las Vegas, NV, USA, 27–30 June 2016; pp. 770–778.
24. Zhang, S.; Chi, C.; Yao, Y.; Lei, Z.; Li, S.Z. Bridging the gap between anchor-based and anchor-free detection via adaptive training sample selection. In Proceedings of the IEEE/CVF conference on computer vision and pattern recognition, Seattle, WA, USA, 13–19 June 2020; pp. 9759–9768.
25. Lin, T.; Dollr, P.; Girshick, R.B.; He, K.; Hariharan, B.; Belongie, S.J. Feature Pyramid Networks for Object Detection. In Proceedings of the IEEE Conference on Computer Vision and Pattern Recognition (CVPR), Honolulu, HI, USA, 21–26 July 2017; pp. 936–944.
26. Huang, X.; Ge, Z.; Jie, Z.; Yoshie, O. NMS by Representative Region: Towards Crowded Pedestrian Detection by Proposal Pairing. In Proceedings of the IEEE/CVF Conference on Computer Vision and Pattern Recognition (CVPR), Seattle, WA, USA, 13–19 June 2020; pp. 10747–10756.
27. Dollr, P.; Wojek, C.; Schiele, B.; Perona, P. Pedestrian Detection: An Evaluation of the State of the Art. *IEEE Trans. Pattern Anal. Mach. Intell.* **2012**, *34*, 743–761. [CrossRef] [PubMed]
28. Ci, Y.; Wang, Y.; Chen, M.; Tang, S.; Bai, L.; Zhu, F.; Zhao, R.; Yu, F.; Qi, D.; Ouyang, W. Unihcp: A unified model for human-centric perceptions. In Proceedings of the IEEE/CVF Conference on Computer Vision and Pattern Recognition, Vancouver, BC, Canada, 17–24 June 2023; pp. 17840–17852.

Disclaimer/Publisher's Note: The statements, opinions and data contained in all publications are solely those of the individual author(s) and contributor(s) and not of MDPI and/or the editor(s). MDPI and/or the editor(s) disclaim responsibility for any injury to people or property resulting from any ideas, methods, instructions or products referred to in the content.

Article

Multi-Scale Fusion Uncrewed Aerial Vehicle Detection Based on RT-DETR

Minling Zhu * and En Kong

Computer School, Beijing Information Science and Technology University, Beijing 100101, China; kongen@bistu.edu.cn
* Correspondence: zhuminling@bistu.edu.cn

Abstract: With the rapid development of science and technology, uncrewed aerial vehicle (UAV) technology has shown a wide range of application prospects in various fields. The accuracy and real-time performance of UAV target detection play a vital role in ensuring safety and improving the work efficiency of UAVs. Aimed at the challenges faced by the current UAV detection field, this paper proposes the Gathering Cascaded Dilated DETR (GCD-DETR) model, which aims to improve the accuracy and efficiency of UAV target detection. The main innovations of this paper are as follows: (1) The Dilated Re-param Block is creatively applied to the dilatation-wise Residual module, which uses the large kernel convolution and the parallel small kernel convolution together and fuses the feature maps generated by multi-scale perception, greatly improving the feature extraction ability, thereby improving the accuracy of UAV detection. (2) The Gather-and-Distribute mechanism is introduced to effectively enhance the ability of multi-scale feature fusion so that the model can make full use of the feature information extracted from the backbone network and further improve the detection performance. (3) The Cascaded Group Attention mechanism is innovatively introduced, which not only saves the computational cost but also improves the diversity of attention by dividing the attention head in different ways, thus enhancing the ability of the model to process complex scenes. In order to verify the effectiveness of the proposed model, this paper conducts experiments on multiple UAV datasets of complex scenes. The experimental results show that the accuracy of the improved RT-DETR model proposed in this paper on the two UAV datasets reaches 0.956 and 0.978, respectively, which is 2% and 1.1% higher than that of the original RT-DETR model. At the same time, the FPS of the model is also improved by 10 frames per second, which achieves an effective balance between accuracy and speed.

Keywords: UAV detection; DETR; attention mechanism; multi-scale fusion

1. Introduction

With the development of uncrewed aerial vehicle (UAV) technology and its wide application, how to effectively monitor and control the flight of UAVs has become an important topic. The flight of UAVs may affect airspace security, civil aviation, military, government, public facilities, personal privacy, etc. And it may even be used for illegal or malicious purposes [1]. In military terms, UAV detection can help the military find and lock the enemy's UAV or other targets [2] for accurate attack or interception. It can also help the military protect its own UAV from being found or interfered with by the enemy and improve the effectiveness and security of surveillance [3]. In areas such as airports, drone detection can help airports prevent drones from entering no-fly areas and causing flight delays or hazards. UAV detection can also help the airport to monitor and manage UAV activities around the airport and maintain the order and safety of the airspace [4]. In areas with high confidentiality, such as government agencies or military bases, UAV detection can help government agencies prevent UAV snooping or threats to important people or occasions and protect the interests and security of the country [5]. Therefore,

UAV detection is a key technology that can help us find, locate, track, and manage UAVs to protect the interests and security of society and the country [6].

Traditional UAV detection methods mainly include methods based on radar, acoustic waves, electromagnetic, optical, infrared, and other sensors, but they all have some shortcomings. For example, the disadvantage of radar is that it is easily affected by electromagnetic interference or reflection, and the disadvantage of an acoustic wave is that it has a small detection range and is easily affected by environmental noise or wind speed [7]. The disadvantage of electromagnetic interference or reflection is that its detection range is limited by signal strength and frequency, and it is vulnerable to encryption or spoofing [8]. The disadvantage of infrared is that its detection is affected by ambient temperature and humidity, and it requires complex temperature calibration and analysis [9]. Therefore, optical image-based detection methods can be used, and UAV detection methods using image detection have many advantages that make them highly favored in various application scenarios. For example, it can automate the monitoring process of the UAV and also achieve accurate target detection and positioning in complex environments. Image-based detection methods can be adjusted and optimized according to different environments and weather conditions to ensure that UAVs can be effectively detected in various complex environments [10]. This adaptability makes the image detection system widely applicable in diverse application scenarios.

By using advanced object detection algorithms, we will be able to detect and identify various types of UAVs more accurately, including small UAVs and high-speed vehicles. This will not only help improve public safety but also promote the sustainable development and application of UAV technology. UAV detection can help regulators detect and respond to potential UAV threats in time to protect people's lives and property. In the field of commercial applications, it can provide UAV operators with more reliable monitoring and management solutions to help them better plan flight paths and avoid collisions and unexpected events between UAVs.

With the continuous development of machine learning and computer vision algorithms, image-based detection techniques are constantly improving. Object detection models such as Faster R-CNN [11], You Only Look Once (YOLO) family [12], SSD [13], Mask R-CNN [14], RetinaNet [15], and EfficientDet [16] have been widely used and studied in various object detection. However, these object detection models are rarely used in UAV detection, which has only been commonly used in the last two years and is still limited by factors such as data scarcity, complex environments, diversity of target categories, computational resource requirements, and legal and privacy issues. UAV detection involves various UAV morphologies, complex environmental conditions, and challenges such as data acquisition and privacy protection. More research and resource investment are needed to realize its wide application in practice.

In recent years, some works have been applied to UAV detection. The Facebook AI research team proposed Detection Transformer (DETR) in 2020 [17]. The model uses the Transformer architecture for object detection and realizes object detection and recognition in an end-to-end manner without the use of traditional techniques such as prior boxes and non-maximum suppression. The proposed DETR model has attracted extensive attention and achieved remarkable results in the field of object detection. In 2023, Tushar Sangam et al. improved DETR and Dogfight [18] and applied them to UAV detection. They proposed a simple and effective improved DETR framework TransVisDrone [19], providing an end-to-end solution with higher computational efficiency. The CSPDarkNet-53 network is used to learn the spatial features related to the target. Then, the VideoSwin model is used to understand the spatio-temporal dependencies of the UAV motion to improve the detection ability of the UAV in challenging scenes.

At present, there is a lot of work on designing efficient DETR-based models that are applied to other object detection tasks. However, the high computational cost of these schemes limits the practical application of DETR, which cannot make full use of its advantages, such as non-maximum suppression (NMS). In 2023, Wenyu Lv proposed the real-time detection transformer (RT-DETR) [20], a real-time end-to-end object detector. In particular, they designed an efficient hybrid encoder to process multi-scale features efficiently by decoupling intra-scale interactions and cross-scale fusion. RT-DETR outperforms comparably sized state-of-the-art YOLO detectors in both speed and accuracy. At the same time, Xinyu Liu et al. [21] proposed a new Attention mechanism called Cascaded Group Attention to solve the problems of computational efficiency and attention diversity in vision transformers. By providing different input data segmentation for each attention head, the Cascaded Group Attention reduces computational redundancy and improves attention diversity. Haoran Wei et al. proposed the DWRSeg network [22] in 2023 to address the efficiency of capturing multi-scale context information in real-time semantic segmentation. They designed the dilatation-wise Residual module, which employs a well-designed two-step feature extraction method aimed at capturing multi-scale information efficiently. The module effectively obtains multi-scale context information through region residualization and semantic residualization. Chengcheng Wang et al. [23] improved feature fusion by globally integrating features from different levels using convolution and self-attention operations. They injected global information into features at various levels, thereby enhancing information fusion capability. We are inspired by these works to propose the Gathering Cascaded Dilated DETR (GCD-DETR) model for UAV detection, and we primarily make the following contributions:

(1) First, we propose the DWR-DRB Module, which applies Dilated Re-param Block in the Dilatation-Wise Residual module, uses large kernel convolution with parallel small kernel convolution, and fuses multi-scale perceptual wild generated feature maps. The feature extraction ability is greatly improved.

(2) Secondly, Cascaded Group Attention (CGA) and the Gather-and-Distribute Mechanism (GD) are applied to the RT-DETR model. The model provides complete feature segmentation to each detection head, and the attention calculation is explicitly decomposed to each detection head. Moreover, multi-scale fusion is carried out to save the computational cost and improve the attention to the target feature region.

(3) We design new real-time Transformer models that strike a good balance between efficiency and accuracy. The model has shown good detection ability in a variety of comparative experiments.

The remainder of this paper is organized as follows: In Section 2, we will first review the current state of the art in UAV detection technology to provide a deeper understanding of the background and motivation of the research. In Section 3, we present the details of our proposed novel UAV detection method, including the details of the adopted GCT-DETR model and the modules in it. In Section 4, we will present and analyze the experimental results to verify the effectiveness of our model. Finally, we summarize and discuss the results of this study and suggest future research directions and improvements in Section 5.

2. Related Work
2.1. Drone Detection

UAV dataset has challenges such as high-altitude perspective, low resolution, motion blur, illumination change, and occlusion. Therefore, there are few existing public and recognized datasets that are faced with the problems of insufficient data volume and low data quality. In recent years, deep learning has been widely used in the field of UAV detection, but it uses non-uniform data sets. Therefore, there is still a lot of room for the development of UAV detection, and it is necessary to gradually improve the quality of various environmental datasets and use more efficient and accurate models.

In 2020, Ulzhalgas et al. embarked on the UAV detection challenge by dissecting it into two distinctive subtasks: moving object detection and object classification. Their approach was innovative as it leveraged background subtraction for moving object detection while relying on the robust feature extraction capabilities of convolutional neural networks (CNNs) for object classification [24]. This division of labor ensured a comprehensive and efficient method for identifying UAVs amidst complex visual backgrounds.

Aamish Sharjeel introduced a groundbreaking UAV detection methodology in 2021, merging Continuous Outlier Representation with Online Low-rank Approximation (COROLA) alongside CNNs. The brilliance of this approach lay in COROLA's adeptness at pinpointing small moving objects within scenes, complemented by CNNs' prowess in accurately classifying UAVs across diverse and intricate backgrounds [25]. This amalgamation not only fortified the detection system's resilience but also significantly elevated its efficacy. In the same year, Muhammad et al. proposed "Dogfight" [18], a novel approach diverging from conventional region proposal-based methods. Instead, they adopted a two-stage segmentation technique grounded on spatio-temporal attention cues. Their method intricately incorporated pyramid pooling to capture detailed contextual information within convolutional feature maps, followed by pixel and channel-level attention mechanisms to precisely localize UAVs. This sophisticated strategy underscored a paradigm shift in UAV detection methodologies, prioritizing accuracy and adaptability. Yaowen Lv et al. introduced a novel detection paradigm in 2022, intertwining background difference analysis with the lightweight SAG-YOLOv5s network. By exploiting background difference, their method effectively isolated potential UAV targets within high-resolution images while concurrently minimizing computational overhead by eliminating extraneous background elements [26]. This innovative fusion of techniques showcased a leap forward in optimizing detection efficiency while conserving computational resources. Yuliang Zhao's 2023 proposal, the information enhancement model TGC-YOLOv5, marked a significant advancement in UAV detection methodologies. By integrating Transformer encoder modules and Global Attention Mechanisms (GAMs) into YOLOv5, the model exhibited a twofold increase in detection accuracy. This augmentation facilitated enhanced focus on the regions of interest while mitigating information diffusion across layers, thus enhancing the model's overall effectiveness [27]. Jun-Hwa Kim's 2023 contribution revolutionized UAV detection by integrating multi-scale image fusion layers and P2 layers into the YOLO-V8 medium model. This integration aimed at bolstering the model's adaptability to diverse UAV scales, thereby fortifying its robustness in detection scenarios [28]. This strategic enhancement underscored a concerted effort towards ensuring comprehensive and accurate UAV detection across varying environmental conditions. Qianqing Cheng's 2023 innovation, the CA-PANet multi-scale attention module, heralded a breakthrough in feature fusion for UAV detection. Leveraging improved MobileViT as a feature extraction network, the introduction of coordinate attention within PANet facilitated enhanced fusion of low-dimensional and high-dimensional features. This not only enriched location information capture but also significantly augmented detection accuracy, highlighting a pivotal advancement in UAV detection methodologies [29].

2.2. Detection Transformer

Conditional DETR makes an innovative improvement to solve the problem of slow convergence speed of DETR. In particular, this method increases the number of queries from 100 to 300 and optimizes the classification loss by adopting Focal loss to improve the performance of the model. The key contribution of conditional DETR is the proposal of the conditional attention mechanism. By decoupling content attention and location attention, they implement a redesign of self-attention and cross-attention inputs. The original method is to add query and query_pos and input them into the linear layer of the attention structure. At the same time, Conditional DETR modifies it so that query and query_pos go through different linear layers, respectively, and then aggregate the results, thereby improving the effect of the attention mechanism of the model [30]. Deformable DETR proposes Multi-scale Deformable Attention (MSDA) to replace Self-attention in the Encoder and Cross-attention in the Decoder. The model of DETR multi-scale feature detection is designed, which not only gives DETR the advantage of multi-scale but also reduces the amount of calculation. In addition, it also proposes the idea of a two-stage DETR, which uses the encoder output features to initialize the decoder query and its corresponding position [31]. Sparse DETR offers an effective encoder token sparsification method for end-to-end object detectors, by which the attention complexity in the encoder is reduced. This efficiency allows Deformable DETR to stack more encoder layers, thus improving performance with the same amount of computation [32]. The end-to-end object detection algorithm DETR does not require hand-crafted post-processing (NMS), but it requires longer training to converge. It is found that one-to-one label matching makes DETR lack supervision signal in the training process (because the number of positive object Queries is small), so it needs to extend the training time to achieve good results.

Group DETR provides a new label assignment strategy for the DETR family of algorithms: group-wise One-to-Many label assignment. The algorithm cleverly decouples the "one-to-many allocation" problem into the "one-to-one allocation of multiple groups" problem. It accelerates the convergence of DETR series algorithms, removes redundant predictions while ensuring the support of multiple positive queries, and realizes end-to-end detection [33]. In 2023, Decoupled DETR proposes the Task-aware Query Generation Module: this module is responsible for initializing queries to match different visual regions, thus providing more suitable features for classification and localization tasks. They also propose a Disentangled Feature Learning Process: in this process, the classification and localization tasks are spatially separated, allowing task-aware queries to be matched to different visual regions. It solves the problem of space misalignment encountered in traditional DETR training [34].

3. Proposed Methods

Figure 1 shows the network structure of GCD-DETR designed in this paper. In the backbone part, we first propose the Dilation-wise Residual and Dilated Re-param Block (DWR-DRB) module for feature extraction, which can reduce the difficulty of extracting multi-scale context information and is an efficient multi-scale feature extraction method. Next, we introduce the Cascaded Group Attention module (CGA). Cascaded Group Attention assigns different weights to the feature maps based on the relevance of different positions in the input image. It can help the model better understand the features in the image, thus improving the detection performance. In the Neck part, we use a novel information interaction and fusion Mechanism: Gather-and-Distribute mechanism (GD). The mechanism obtains global information by fusing features at different levels globally and injects global information into features at different levels to achieve efficient information interaction and fusion. It improves the detection ability of the model for objects of different sizes.

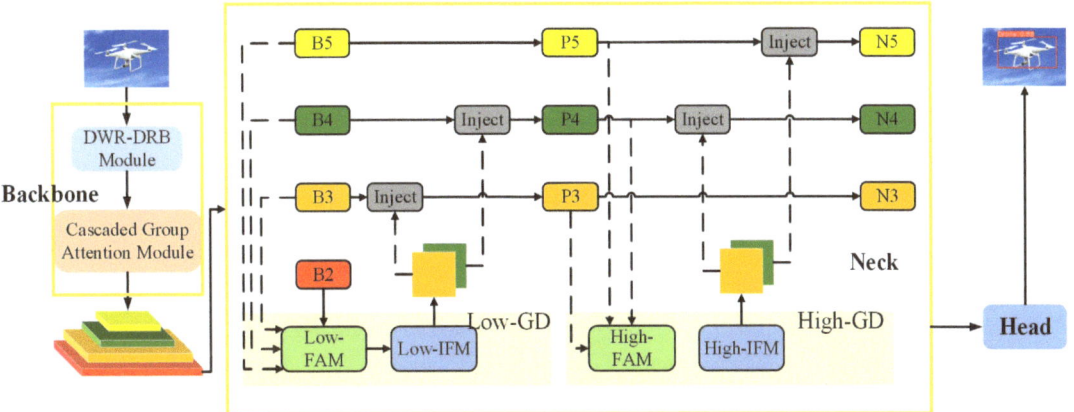

Figure 1. The network structure of GCD-DETR.

3.1. Dilation-Wise Residual and Dilated Re-Param Block Module

In this section, we propose the Dilation-wise Residual and Dilated Re-param Block (DWR-DRB). We incorporate the Dilated Re-param Block into the dilatation-wise Residual module and utilize a combination of large kernel convolutions and parallel small kernel convolutions. Furthermore, we fuse multi-scale receptive field-generated feature maps, thereby significantly enhancing the feature extraction capability.

3.1.1. Dilated Re-Param Block

In convolutional neural networks (CNNs), combining large kernel convolutions with parallel small kernel convolutions helps capture features at various scales. Their outputs are summed after two respective batch normalization (BN) layers [35]. The structural re-parameterization method [36] can be employed to integrate BN layers with convolutional layers, and after training, they can be merged effectively to incorporate small kernel convolutions into large kernel convolutions for inference.

The main idea of Dilated Re-param Block (DRB) structure is to use the combination of large kernel convolution and dilated convolution to improve the performance of convolutional neural network. By using large kernel convolutions and multiple dilated convolutional layers in parallel, the "Dilated Re-param Block" structure is able to capture both local fine features and widely distributed sparse features. This combination enables the model to perceive the structural information of the input data more comprehensively. The whole module is converted into a single non-dilated convolutional layer in the inference phase. This step consists of converting each dilated convolutional layer into an equivalent non-dilated convolutional layer and merging their output feature maps. The performance of the structure can be flexibly controlled by adjusting the large kernel size K, the dilation rate r, and the small kernel size k, as shown in Figure 2, $K = 9$, $r = (1, 2, 3, 4)$, and $k = (5, 5, 3, 3)$ [37].

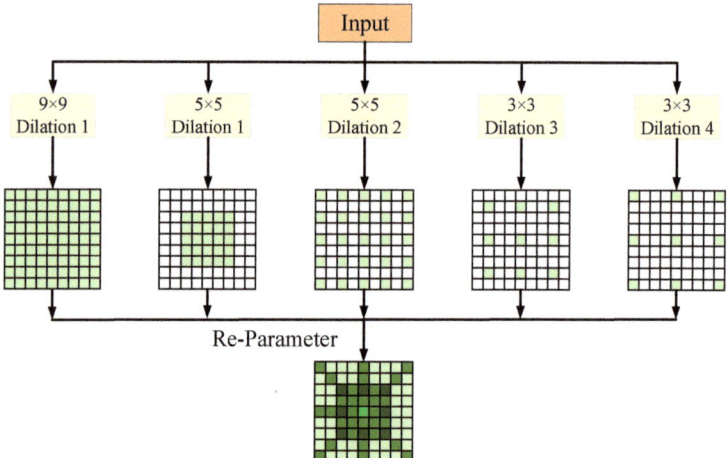

Figure 2. Dilated Re-param Block.

3.1.2. Dilation-Wise Residual and Dilated Re-Param Block Module

In this section, we introduce the Dilation-wise Residual and Dilated Re-param Block (DWR-DRB) module, designed to efficiently acquire multi-scale context information, as illustrated in Figure 3. This module effectively extracts and fuses feature maps generated from multiple receptive fields through a two-step multi-scale context information acquisition method within the dilation-wise Residual (DWR) [22] in combination with the previously mentioned Dilated Re-param Block.

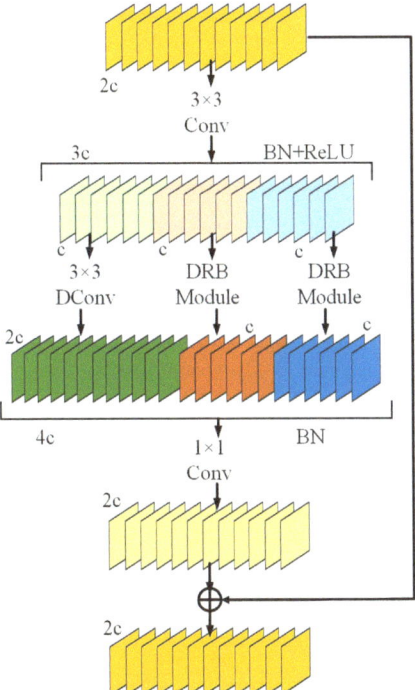

Figure 3. DWR-DRB module.

In particular, the first step involves generating region residual features from input features through a regular 3 × 3 convolution combined with batch normalization (BN) and ReLU activation. The second step employs multi-rate depth-wise deformable convolution (DConv) and Dilated Re-param Block (DRB) modules to perform morphological filtering on region features of different sizes, referred to as semantic residualization. This method not only extracts multi-scale contextual information but also refines features and effectively controls redundant receptive fields through the generation of region residual features and reverse matching of receptive fields. Consequently, the model maintains simplicity while dealing with complex semantic information and achieves significant improvements in feature representation and model performance. Furthermore, aggregating multiple output feature maps, employing batch normalization, and merging feature maps using pointwise convolution enhance the model's perception of multi-scale information, thereby improving feature representation and performance.

3.2. Cascaded Group Attention

Cascaded Group Attention is based on the concept of group attention, dividing the image into multiple groups or regions and focusing on features within each group. Unlike traditional global attention mechanisms, Cascaded Group Attention achieves more intricate feature focus by cascading multiple layers of attention.

In Cascaded Group Attention, the input image is first divided into groups, where each group may contain specific semantic information or adjacent pixels in space. Subsequently, a local attention mechanism is applied to each group, allowing the network to concentrate more on the features within each group. This progressive focusing process enables the network to refine feature representation at multiple levels, thereby enhancing the model's perceptual ability and accuracy in feature representation [21]. This attention mechanism can be described as follows:

$$\widetilde{X}_{ij} = Attn(X_{ij}W_{ij}^Q, X_{ij}W_{ij}^K, X_{ij}W_{ij}^V) \quad (1)$$

$$\widetilde{X}_{i+1} = Concat[\widetilde{X}_{ij}]_{j=1:h}W_i^P \quad (2)$$

For the j-th attention head, it computes self-attention on the j-th split X_{ij} of the input feature X_i. The input feature X_i is divided into h different splits, with each split corresponding to one attention head. This partitioning is achieved by projection layers $W_{ij}^Q, W_{ij}^K, W_{ij}^V$, which split the input feature X_i into different subspaces. The purpose of splitting the input features into different subspaces is to compute the self-attention on each subspace. W_i^P is the linear layer. These projection layers map the input feature into different subspaces, enabling self-attention computation in each subspace.

During the computation of the attention map for each head, a cascaded approach is employed, where the output of each head is added to the subsequent heads' inputs. This cascading method facilitates gradual improvement in feature representation, enabling the model to better capture the structure and relationships within the data, as shown in Figure 4. This entails aggregating the output of each attention head with that of the following heads, enabling the iterative enhancement of feature representation:

$$X'_{ij} = X_{ij} + \widetilde{X}_{i(j-1)}, \quad 1 < j \leq h \quad (3)$$

the output X'_{ij} of each head is the addition of its input split X_{ij} and the output $X_{i(j-1)}$ of the previous head $(j-1)$, calculated by Equation (2). $X_{i(j-1)}$ replaces X_{ij} as the new input feature for computing self-attention in the j-th head. Additionally, after Q projection, there is a flag indicating the inclusion of an interaction layer, enabling the self-attention mechanism to simultaneously capture both local and global features.

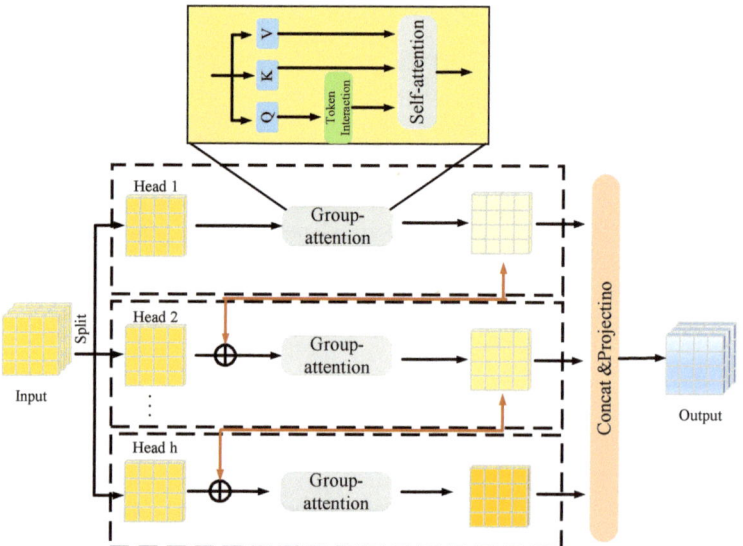

Figure 4. Cascaded Group Attention module.

The introduction of the Cascaded Group Attention module allows the model to effectively focus on specific regions or features, thereby enhancing feature representation. By iteratively refining feature representation at multiple levels, this module improves the model's perceptual ability and accuracy. Additionally, its adaptability to various datasets and scenarios further highlights its versatility and effectiveness in enhancing feature understanding and interpretation.

3.3. Gather-and-Distribute Mechanism

When detecting UAV targets, targets of different sizes are often generated due to the distance between them. In order to improve the detection ability of these targets, we use the low-stage gather-and-distribute branch (Low-GD) and the high-stage gather-and-distribute branch (High-GD) [23]. The core idea of this method is to use different feature extraction and fusion strategies for different sizes of objects to better adapt to various sizes of target objects. Two key modules are included in both branch networks: feature alignment module (FAM) and information injection module (IFM), as shown in Figures 5 and 6. These modules are designed to efficiently extract and fuse feature maps from the backbone network in order to better capture various size features of the target object. The inputs of these two branch networks are the feature maps B2, B3, B4, and B5 output by the backbone network, where $B_i \in R^{N \times C_{Bi} \times R_{Bi}}$. Here, the batch size is denoted by N, the channel by C, and the feature map size by $R = H \times W$, where H and W denote the height and width of the feature map, respectively. And the dimensions of $R_{B2}, R_{B3}, R_{B4}, R_{B5}$ are $R, \frac{1}{2}R, \frac{1}{4}R$, and $\frac{1}{8}R$, respectively.

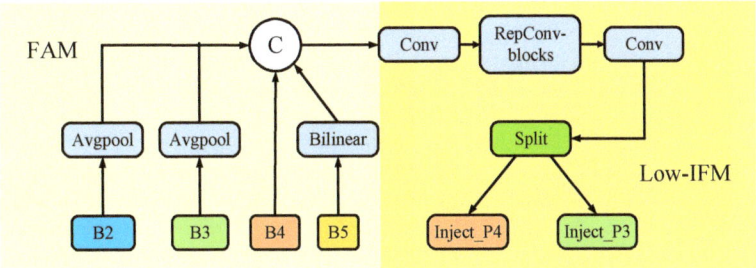

Figure 5. Low-stage gather-and-distribute branch.

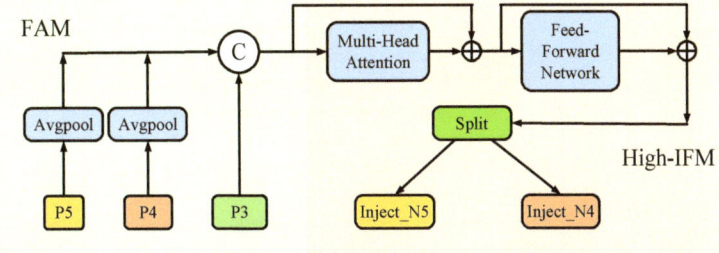

Figure 6. High-stage gather-and-distribute branch.

3.3.1. Feature Alignment Module

The main function of FAM module is to align the feature maps of different levels to a uniform size and then merge these feature maps by the concatenation operation on the channel. This reduces information loss and enhances the ability of the model to detect objects of different sizes without significantly increasing the latency.

In particular, the FAM module will first adjust the input feature maps to the same spatial resolution by average pooling operation, and then concatenate them in the channel dimension. In this process, the feature map is resized to the smallest feature size within the group in order to control the computation latency while preserving low-level information. As shown in Figure 5, if the feature maps of B2, B3, B4, and B5 correspond to different dimensions, the FAM module will unify them to the dimensions of B4 and then concatenate them on the channel. In Figure 6, the input feature maps are P3, P4, and P5, and the FAM module will unify them to the dimensions of P3. There are several benefits to resizing the feature map to the dimensions of B4. Firstly, B4 provides a balance point where it is neither the largest feature map (as in B2) nor the smallest feature map (as in B5), which means that it is able to preserve sufficient details while avoiding the computational stress caused by processing overly large feature maps. Secondly, feature alignment using B4 as a benchmark can better preserve the information of medium-size objects, which is especially important for object detection, as it ensures that the model can effectively detect objects of various sizes. Finally, selecting B4 as the benchmark for alignment can simplify the process of information fusion. By resizing all feature maps to the size of B4, the concatenation can be performed directly on the channel, which reduces the average pooling operation, which helps to reduce the latency and makes the model more suitable for real-time application scenarios. Therefore, B4 is chosen as the benchmark for feature alignment in order to find a compromise between preserving critical information and controlling computational cost to improve the performance and efficiency of the model.

3.3.2. Information Fusion Module

The Information Fusion Module (IFM) is designed to improve the ability of multi-scale feature fusion. As shown in Figure 5, first, the low-stage IFM (Low-IFM) receives the aligned feature maps from the FAM module. These feature maps have been unified in spatial resolution for further processing. The aligned feature map goes through a multi-layer Rep-Block structure, which is a combination of a series of convolutional layers and activation functions to extract and enhance feature information. The feature maps processed by Rep-Block will be split into two parts in the channel dimension, which can provide more specialized information for feature maps at different scales. The segmented feature maps are regarded as global information, and they will be used to inject features at different levels to achieve effective information interaction and fusion. IFM is designed to reduce information loss and enhance the model's ability to detect objects of different sizes without significantly increasing latency. This mechanism obtains global information by fusing features at different levels globally and injects global information into features at different levels to achieve efficient information interaction and fusion. The advantage of this procedure is that it allows the model to make better use of the features extracted from backbone and can be easily integrated into existing similar network structures. Through its design, IFM improves the overall performance of the model, making it more accurate and efficient when dealing with objects of different sizes.

The High-stage Information Fusion Module (High-IFM) is designed to improve the accuracy of object detection while maintaining low latency. As shown in Figure 6, High-FAM first receives feature maps from different layers of the network and aligns them to a uniform spatial resolution. This step is carried out by FAM, which ensures that the feature maps have the same dimensions before the subsequent fusion. The aligned feature maps are then passed to High-IFM, where transformer modules are used for processing. Each transformer module consists of a multi-head attention module and a feedforward network module. These operations allow the model to combine features at a higher level, which are typically more abstract but contain more semantic information. These modules work together to capture long-distance dependencies between features. The High-IFM processed feature maps are channel-simplified by the Conv 1×1 operation, which helps to reduce the computational complexity and maintain the efficiency of the model.

Feature segmentation and fusion: The reduced feature map is segmented in the channel dimension and fused with the horizontal features of the current stage. This step ensures that the features of different levels can be effectively combined, thus improving the model's ability to detect objects of different sizes.

3.3.3. Information Injection Module

To effectively utilize global information in images and inject it into different levels of feature representations, we employ the information injection module for information fusion, as illustrated in Figure 7.

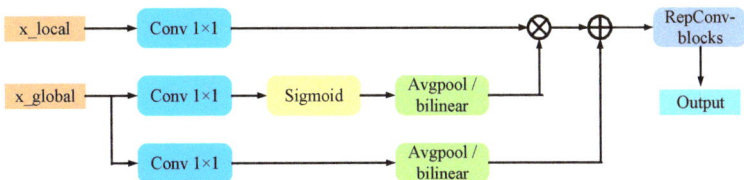

Figure 7. Information injection module.

The information injection module is responsible for injecting global information into different levels of features to enhance the ability of the model to detect objects. The information injection module first receives global information from the Information Fusion Module, which contains features fused from different levels of the network. The module uses the attention mechanism to weight the received global information. This step highlights the key information by calculating the importance of each feature while suppressing the unimportant information. The weighted global information is subsequently injected into the local features at the current level. This process is accomplished by specific operations such as addition or concatenation, which enables the effective combination of global information with local features. By injecting global information, local features are enhanced, allowing the model to better understand and recognize objects in the image. Finally, the information injection module outputs feature representations that fuse global and local information, and these features will be used in subsequent object detection layers.

4. Experiments

4.1. Datasets and Implementation Details

We utilized two UAV datasets in our experiments. We first utilized the Rotor UAV dataset proposed by DASMEHDIXTR et al., which consists of 1360 images of drones. All images are labeled with the class "drone" and include various complex backgrounds and drone models. We randomly selected 1000 images as the training set, 200 images as the validation set, and 160 images as the test set. The dataset we used can be found at https://www.kaggle.com/datasets/dasmehdixtr/drone-dataset-uav/data (accessed on 1 February 2024).

We also utilized an open-source, available military UAV dataset on Roborflow. This dataset comprises multiple environments, including sky, city, countryside, and coastline. It encompasses UAV images captured under different weather conditions and at various times, covering a wide range of UAV use scenarios. The dataset can be found at https://universe.roboflow.com/military-drone/dronemil-u8fqk (accessed on 7 February 2024). It consists of 5238 training images, 1345 validation images, and 678 test images.

For training and evaluation, we conducted numerous experiments using these two UAV datasets. The model architecture was implemented using PyTorch 1.11.0 and Timm 0.5.4. The model was trained from scratch for 200 epochs on 2 Nvidia V100 GPUs using the AdamW optimizer and cosine learning rate scheduler. The size of all the image is 640 × 640. We used a batch size of 16. The input images were resized and randomly cropped to a size of 640 × 640. The initial learning rate is 1×10^{-4}, and the weight decay is 2.5×10^{-2}.

4.2. Comparision Results

4.2.1. Comparison with Prior Works

To evaluate the performance of our UAV detection model, we conducted a series of comparative experiments. Firstly, we compared the number of parameters and Floating

Point Operations Per Second (FLOPs) across various models to evaluate their efficiency. Subsequently, we evaluated the models using metrics such as Recall, AP@50, and AP@50:95. Recall measures the proportion of correctly detected objects among all labeled objects. AP@50 represents the Mean Average Precision for each class when the Intersection over Union (IOU) threshold is set to 0.5. AP@50:95 calculates the average AP over different IOU thresholds ranging from 0.5 to 0.95 with a step size of 0.05.

Our model was compared against several established models, including different versions of YOLOv7 [12], YOLOv8, RT-DETR [20], and the latest Gold-YOLO [23]. The comparison results on Rotor UAV dataset are presented in Table 1.

Table 1. Comparative experiments with prior works on Rotor UAV dataset.

Model	Input Size	Backbone	Neck	Layers	Parameters	GFLOPs	Recall	AP@50	AP@50:95
YOLOv7 [12]	640	CBS + ELAN	SPPSCP + E-ELAN	415	37,196,556	105.1	0.814	0.858	0.476
YOLOv7x [12]	640	CBS + ELAN	SPPSCP + E-ELAN	467	70,815,092	188.9	0.837	0.883	0.53
YOLOv7-w6 [12]	1280	CBS + ELAN	SPPSCP + E-ELAN	477	80,944,472	102.4	0.824	0.924	0.57
YOLOv7-d6 [12]	1280	CBS + ELAN	SPPSCP + E-ELAN	733	152,886,360	198.3	0.878	0.934	0.588
YOLOv8s	640	C2F + SPPF	C2F	168	11,125,971	28.4	0.878	0.941	0.626
YOLOv8m	640	C2F + SPPF	C2F	295	25,856,899	79.1	0.864	0.948	0.631
YOLOv8n	640	C2F + SPPF	C2F	225	3,157,200	8.9	0.90	0.949	0.626
Gold-YOLO-s [23]	640	Efficient-Rep	Gather-and-Distribute	/	21.5M	46.0	0.670	0.928	0.582
Gold-YOLO-m [23]	640	Efficient-Rep	Gather-and-Distribute	/	41.3M	87.5	0.693	0.934	0.604
Gold-YOLO-n [23]	640	Efficient-Rep	Gather-and-Distribute	/	5.6M	12.1	0.671	0.919	0.580
RT-DETR-r18 [20]	640	ResNet 18	AIFI + CCFM	299	19,873,044	56.9	0.941	0.936	0.621
RT-DETR-r34 [20]	640	ResNet 34	AIFI + CCFM	387	31,106,233	88.8	0.896	0.933	0.602
RT-DETR-r50 [20]	640	ResNet 50	AIFI + CCFM	629	42,782,275	134.4	0.878	0.905	0.581
GCD-DETR (Ours)	640	DWR-DRB + CGB	Gather-and-Distribute	494	23,262,488	61.0	0.93	0.956	0.624

We list the network structures used in the backbone and neck parts of all models. The backbone of Yolov7 uses CBS (Conv + BN + SiLU) and ELAN modules, which are composed of multiple CBS modules. The neck part is mainly composed of information fusion module SPPCSP and ELAN module. The backbone and neck of YOLOv8 are mainly composed of C2f (CSPLayer2Conv) module and SPPF (Spatial Pyramid Pooling Fast). C2f has more skip connections and additional split operations. Gold-YOLO is mainly composed of Efficient Repblock and Gather-and-Distribute (GD). The GD mechanism significantly enhances the information fusion ability of the neck part and improves the detection ability of the model for objects of different sizes. RT-DETR is mainly composed of Attention-based Intro-scale Feature Interaction (AIFI) module and the CNN based Cross-scale Feature-fusion Module (CCFM).

The backbone of our model mainly consists of the Dilation-wise Residual and Dilated Re-param Block Module (DWR-DRB) module and Cascaded Group Attention (CGB) module, and the neck is mainly composed of GD mechanism. Despite variations in the parameters of these aforementioned methods, the accuracy of the largest model from each of these methods is consistently lower than that of our proposed GCD-DETR model.

On the rotor UAV dataset, our model achieves a 2% higher AP@50 compared to the highest accuracies of RT-DETR prior to improvement and a 1% higher accuracy than YOLOv8n. On the military UAV dataset, as shown in Table 2, our model exhibits a 1% higher AP@50 than YOLOv8s and a 0.5% higher AP@50 than Gold-YOLO -s. These results demonstrate that our model can achieve high accuracy with a parameter count similar to other models. Our model showcases its lightweight nature by achieving higher accuracy while having significantly fewer GFLOPs compared to YOLOv7-d6. It indicates that our model can achieve precision while being lightweight and can be more easily deployed on UAV equipment. The effectiveness of our model can be attributed to the multi-dimensional feature extraction of the DWR-DRB module and the Gather-and-Distribute mechanism, which efficiently combines features from different maps. Additionally, the skip connection helps reduce computational requirements, further contributing to high precision with minimal computation.

Table 2. Comparative experiments with prior works on military UAV dataset.

Model	Input Size	Year	Layers	Parameters	GFLOPs	Recall	AP@50	AP@50:95
YOLOv7 [12]	640	2022	415	37,196,556	105.1	0.914	0.955	0.624
YOLOv7x [12]	640	2022	467	70,815,092	188.9	0.919	0.958	0.631
YOLOv7-w6 [12]	1280	2022	477	80,944,472	102.4	0.92	0.954	0.633
YOLOv7-d6 [12]	1280	2022	733	152,886,360	198.3	0.922	0.964	0.657
YOLOv8s	640	2023	168	11,125,971	28.4	0.934	0.968	0.687
YOLOv8m	640	2023	295	25,856,899	79.1	0.946	0.959	0.658
YOLOv8n	640	2023	225	3,157,200	8.9	0.957	0.962	0.676
Gold-YOLO-s [23]	640	2023	/	21.5M	46.0	0.897	0.973	0.680
Gold-YOLO-m [23]	640	2023	/	41.3M	87.5	0.944	0.953	0.636
Gold-YOLO-n [23]	640	2023	/	5.6M	12.1	0.950	0.958	0.675
RT-DETR-r18 [20]	640	2023	299	19,873,044	56.9	0.954	0.953	0.692
RT-DETR-r34 [20]	640	2023	387	31,106,233	88.8	0.925	0.977	0.639
RT-DETR-r50 [20]	640	2023	629	42,782,275	134.4	0.927	0.967	0.657
GCD-DETR (Ours)	640	/	494	23,262,488	61.0	0.966	0.978	0.711

The DWR-DRB module has significant advantages in dealing with multi-scale information. Through deep-separated dilated convolution and a two-step residual feature extraction method, it can effectively extract the features of small objects and perform well in real-time semantic segmentation tasks. This allows the DWR-DRB module to outperform traditional backbone networks such as Gold-YOLO and RT-DETR in terms of accuracy and efficiency, especially in scenarios where large amounts of detail and dynamic range need to be processed. In addition, the design of the DWR-DRB module also considers the optimization of computing resources so that it can maintain high performance even in resource-constrained environments. The advantage of the DWR-DRB module and the CGB module is its advanced multi-scale feature extraction ability, especially for small object detection and real-time semantic segmentation tasks, which provides more accurate feature extraction than YOLOv7 and YOLOv8 through deep separation dilated convolution and refined receptive field design, thereby improving the overall network performance.

4.2.2. Comparison of Evaluation Metrics

We conducted a comparison between the training process curves of the original RT-DETR and our model in the military UAV detection task. Throughout the training process, we recorded the precision and recall values of each model on the training set, as well as AP@0.5 and AP@0.5:0.95. We plotted corresponding curves to observe their training progress in Figure 8.

Our model demonstrates superior performance in terms of precision. The precision curve of our model maintains a high level of stability during training and converges to a high precision level. Conversely, while the precision curve for the original RT-DETR starts with an increasing pattern, it experiences considerable fluctuations during training, ultimately settling at a precision slightly inferior to that of our model.

Regarding recall, our model also surpasses the original RT-DETR. The recall curve of our model exhibits early-stage growth, maintains a stable upward trend throughout training, and finally converges to a high level. However, the recall curve of the original RT-DETR demonstrates a slower growth rate and noticeable fluctuations in the later stages of training. Overall, our model showcases higher precision and recall during training, along with better stability and faster convergence speed.

In addition, we compare the AP@0.5 and AP@0.5:0.95 curves between our model and the original RT-DETR for object detection. These metrics evaluate the detection accuracy and robustness of the models at different confidence thresholds. In terms of AP@0.5, our model outperforms the original RT-DETR at lower confidence thresholds. The curve shows a faster upward trend and eventually reaches a relatively high average precision. Conversely, the AP@0.5 curve of the original RT-DETR exhibits slower growth, and the detection performance at lower confidence thresholds is slightly lower than that of our model.

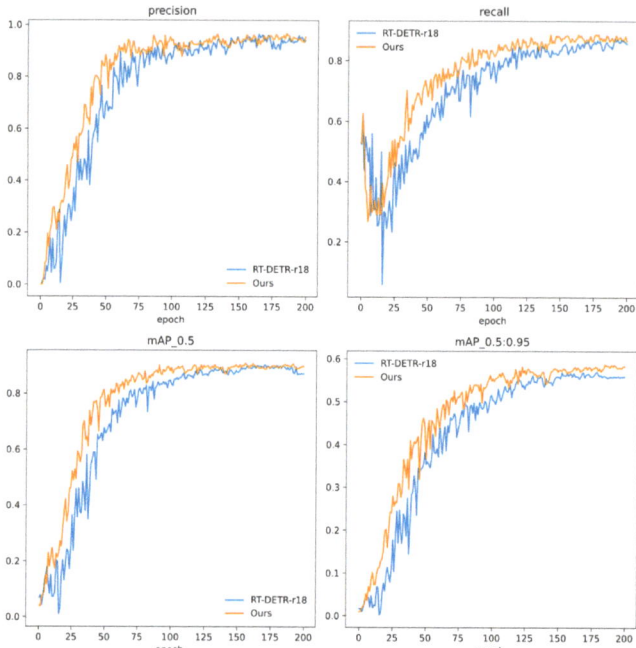

Figure 8. Comparison of evaluation metrics between GCD-DETR and RT-DETR-r18.

When considering the AP@0.5:0.95 curve, the performance gap between our model and the original DETR becomes more evident at higher confidence thresholds. Our model's curves maintain high stability and exhibit high average accuracy across a range of confidence thresholds from 0.5 to 0.95. However, the AP@0.5:0.95 curve of the original RT-DETR performs poorly at high confidence thresholds, with significantly lower average accuracy compared to our model. Therefore, in a comprehensive sense, our model demonstrates better detection performance not only at low confidence thresholds but also at high confidence thresholds, showcasing better overall robustness. Overall, our model demonstrates superior precision, recall, and detection accuracy during training when compared to the original RT-DETR.

4.2.3. Comparison of Detection

We conducted a comparison of the images detected by the original RT-DETR-r18 model and our model. Figure 9a illustrates that the RT-DETR-r18 model fails to detect multiple targets, while Figure 9b demonstrates that our GCD-DETR successfully detects all targets. This discrepancy may arise from the fact that when neighboring targets are in close proximity, the larger target can obstruct the detection of the smaller target, resulting in missed detections. However, our model overcomes this limitation by incorporating an attention module and performing multi-scale feature fusion. As a result, our model accurately identifies objects of various sizes, hence achieving the detection of all objects in the given scenario.

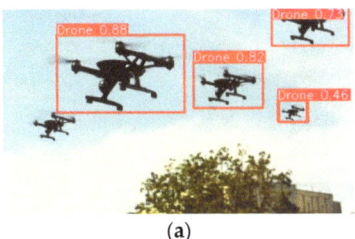 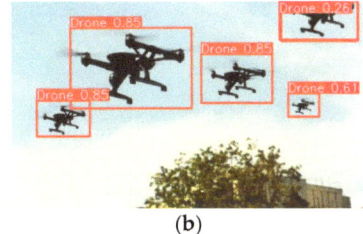

(a) (b)

Figure 9. Comparison of detection results between RT-DETR-r18 and GCD-DETR: (**a**) RT-DETR-r18 and (**b**) GCD-DETR.

4.2.4. Comparison of Heatmap

The heatmap is a visualization technique utilized in object detection to display the intensity distribution of objects detected by a model in an input image. Heatmaps are commonly employed to indicate the location and confidence of the detected target, with brighter areas representing higher confidence in the detection. In Figure 10, we compare the heatmaps generated by the RT-DETR-r18 model and our proposed model.

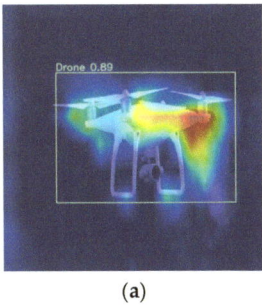 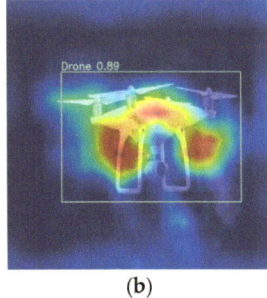

(a) (b)

Figure 10. Comparison results of heat map visualization: (**a**) RT-DETR-r18 and (**b**) GCD-DETR.

The first heatmap corresponds to the RT-DETR-r18 model, revealing that the deeper regions of intensity are concentrated only in a specific area of the UAV, while other regions show lower levels of focus. Conversely, the second heatmap corresponds to our model, where darker-colored areas are concentrated on the body and support parts of the UAV, encompassing almost the entire UAV. Additionally, a high level of attention is observed towards the overall structure of the UAV in our model's heatmap, indicating a more confident detection of the UAV target. These findings demonstrate the effectiveness of our model in detecting UAVs compared to the RT-DETR-r18 model.

4.3. Training Metrics

During the training process of object detection models, loss functions are the key indicators used to assess the accuracy of model predictions and guide model optimization. The Generalized Intersection over Union Loss (giou_loss) is a metric for evaluating the localization accuracy of object detection models. It measures not only the overlap between the predicted and actual bounding boxes but also includes a penalty term that considers the area of the smallest enclosing box containing both bounding boxes. The lower the giou_loss, the more accurate the model is at localizing targets. Classification Loss (cls_loss) is used to measure the model's performance in recognizing and classifying targets. It calculates the difference between the model's predicted output and the actual target values. In object detection, this often involves classification problems, and the lower the Classification Loss, the more accurate the model is at classification tasks. The l1 loss is a method for measuring the difference between predicted values and actual values. It works by calculating the average absolute difference between them. This method performs well when dealing with outlier data because it does not allow individual extreme values to overly influence the overall loss. The lower the l1_loss, the better the model's performance.

Figure 11 shows the changes in the various metrics of our model during the training process. We note that the GCD-DETR model not only exhibits smooth performance across all evaluation indicators but also consistency. The steady decline in giou_loss indicates a continuous improvement in the model's accuracy in target localization. The reduction in Classification Loss reflects an enhanced ability of the model to distinguish between different categories of targets. The gradual decline in the l1_loss demonstrates a better balance between precision and recall. These smooth curves of the indicators show that the model exhibits stability and reliability during training, with no overfitting or underfitting issues. Additionally, our model performs exceptionally well in AP@0.5 and AP@0.5:0.95, meaning it maintains high-level performance in object detection tasks of varying difficulty levels. These results indicate that the GCD-DETR model excels not only in single tasks but also has strong adaptability and robustness when dealing with diverse and complex object detection scenarios.

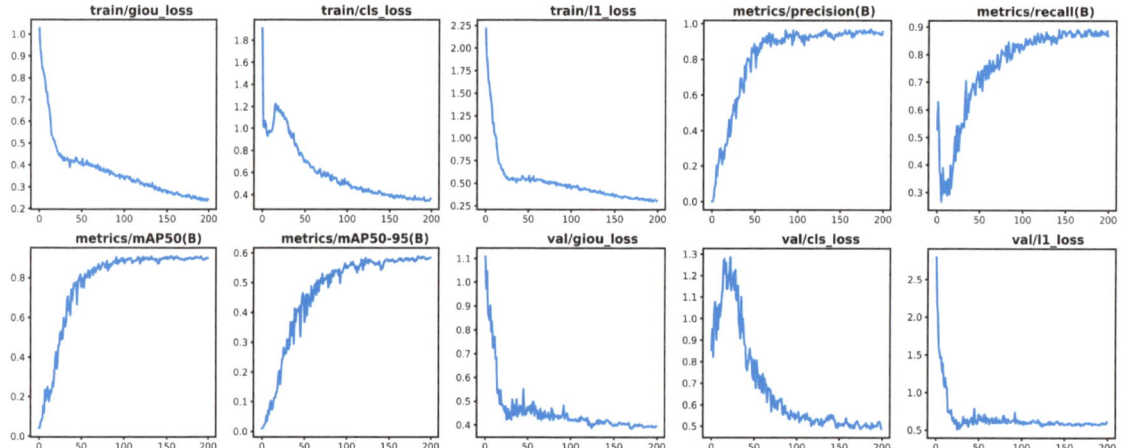

Figure 11. Training metrics over 200 epochs.

4.4. Ablation Results

In this section, we remove important design elements in our designed model for ablation experiments. To amplify the difference and reduce the training time, all models are trained 200 epochs.

First, we just use the original RT-DETR model for testing; then, we add our Cascaded Group Attention (CGA), Dilation-wise Residual and Dilated Re-param Block Module (DWR-DRB), and Gather-and-Distribute Mechanism (GD) in turn. The results are shown in Table 3. It is shown that after adding Cascaded Group Attention, AP@50 improved by 1.3%, and the FPS reached 52.5 frames per second with almost no increase in GFLOPs. It shows that Cascaded Group Attention reduces the amount of computation with almost no increase in cost, and the AP@50 is improved by 1% when only adding the DWR-DRB module. In the case of adding only Gather-and-Distribute mechanism, the AP@50 is improved by 1.2%. With all modules added, our final model improves the AP@50 by 3% over the original RT-DETR-r18 model and achieves 41.9 frames per second at almost no additional computational cost, which is about 10 frames per second higher than RT-DETR-r18. It shows that our model improves the inference speed while improving the accuracy and can be better applied to UAV detection.

Table 3. Ablation experiments.

RT-DETR	DWR-DRB	CGA	GD	Layers	Parameters	GFLOPs	Recall	AP@50	AP@50:95	FPS
✓				299	19,873,044	56.9	0.941	0.937	0.621	31.7
✓		✓		330	19,703,192	57.0	0.94	0.95	0.629	52.5
✓	✓			328	21,048,084	57.9	0.953	0.947	0.625	29.8
✓			✓	434	22,257,300	59.9	0.92	0.949	0.624	27.9
✓		✓	✓	463	23,432,340	60.9	0.899	0.952	0.635	25.0
✓	✓	✓	✓	494	23,262,488	61.0	0.93	0.956	0.624	41.9

4.5. Detection Results

We have used our model to detect UAV pictures with different scenes and sizes, and the detection results are shown in Figure 12. Figure 12a shows that in the dusk scene, our model can also accurately identify when there is less light and the UAV is dark. Figure 12b shows that the sky color of the background and the color of the UAV are both white, indicating that our model can still achieve accurate recognition when the color of the UAV is similar to the sky background. In Figure 12c, it can be seen that the target UAV is very small, and its color is almost integrated into the background sky. However, our model can still recognize it, indicating that our model also has a good effect on detecting small targets. Figure 12d is a picture of the UAV at a close distance, and the UAV takes up a large portion of the picture, indicating that when using the UAV to detect the UAV, the recognition of a nearby target can achieve a high accuracy rate. Figure 12e,f shows UAV detection under a complex background. It can be seen that in the complex background, the UAV is easier to integrate with the environment, and at the same time, it is more difficult to detect, but our model can still achieve a high accuracy rate, indicating the effectiveness of our model in the face of complex background detection. Figure 13 shows the detection results of more complex scenes, which can be seen in the woods or on the road. Our model can detect drones even when there are occlusions or complex backgrounds.

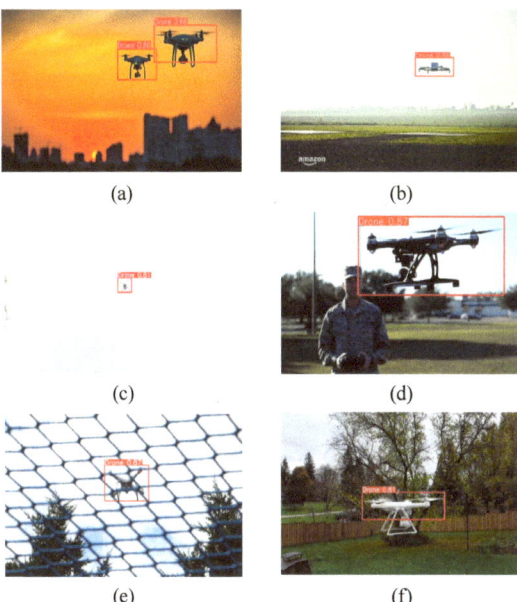

Figure 12. Detection results on rotor UAV dataset.(**a**) drones at dusk (**b**)drone is similar in color to the sky (**c**) small target drone (**d**) large target drone (**e**) drone in complex background (**f**) drone in a forest scene.

Figure 13. Detection results on military UAV dataset.

5. Conclusions

The appearance of uncrewed aerial vehicles in images or videos is diverse and variable, with their scale, angle, appearance, and other characteristics changing based on distance and viewpoint. This variability greatly increases the complexity and challenges of UAV detection algorithms. In complex backgrounds like the sky, trees, or buildings, UAV detection algorithms must possess excellent object detection capability to exclude interference information. Moreover, UAVs may also face occlusion from other objects, further complicating detection.

Additionally, UAVs differ in morphology and appearance due to varying models, manufacturers, and purposes. It requires detection algorithms to have strong adaptability and accurately identify UAVs in different situations. Real-time detection and tracking of UAVs are often required in applications like military surveillance and border monitoring. As a result, detection algorithms must exhibit efficient computing performance and fast response speeds. However, obtaining a representative UAV image dataset is challenging due to the diverse operating environments and the substantial workload associated with data collection and annotation.

To address these challenges, this paper proposes an improved transformer model called GCD-DETR and conducts extensive experiments on two public datasets. The GCD-DETR model introduces the DWR-DRB module, leveraging the Cascaded Group Attention and Gather-and-Distribute mechanism to strike a balance between efficiency and accuracy. In particular, the DWR-DRB module enhances adaptability to changes in UAV morphology and appearance via a two-step multi-scale context information acquisition method. Cascaded Group Attention assists the model in focusing on UAV targets and eliminating interference information in complex backgrounds. The Gather-and-Distribute mechanism further enhances detection accuracy through global information interaction and fusion. The experimental results demonstrate significant performance improvements in the GCD-DETR model in UAV detection tasks, particularly when dealing with complex backgrounds and occlusions. The successful application of this model offers substantial support for the intelligent development of UAVs, especially in areas such as military surveillance and border monitoring.

However, practical applications of UAV detection technology still face limitations and challenges, including computing resource constraints and real-time requirements. Future research aims to improve the robustness and efficiency of UAV detection technology to address even more complex and variable application scenarios. Additionally, with the continuous development and popularization of UAV technology, the application of UAV detection technology will witness further expansion and development opportunities.

Author Contributions: Methodology, M.Z. and E.K.; Formal analysis, E.K. All authors have read and agreed to the published version of the manuscript.

Funding: This research was funded by National Natural Science Foundation of China (No. 62076028), Subject Research of Beijing Information Science and Technology University (No. 5027023400), Qiyuan Innovation Foundation and sub-themes: (S20210201067) (No. 9072323404).

Data Availability Statement: Data are contained within the article.

Conflicts of Interest: The authors declare no conflict of interest.

References

1. Kaleem, Z.; Rehmani, M.H. Amateur drone monitoring: State-of-the-art architectures key enabling technologies and future research directions. *IEEE Wirel. Commun.* **2018**, *25*, 150–159. [CrossRef]
2. Rossiter, A. Military technology and revolutions in warfare: Priming the drone debate. *Def. Secur. Anal.* **2023**, *39*, 253–255. [CrossRef]
3. Emimi, M.; Khaleel, M.; Alkrash, A. The current opportunities and challenges in drone technology. *Int. J. Electr. Eng. Sustain.* **2023**, *1*, 74–89.
4. McFarland, M. Airports Scramble to Handle Drone Incidents. Available online: https://edition.cnn.com/2019/03/05/tech/airports-drones/index.html (accessed on 5 March 2019).
5. Raivi, A.M.; Huda, S.A.; Alam, M.M.; Moh, S. Drone Routing for Drone-Based Delivery Systems: A Review of Trajectory Planning, Charging, and Security. *Sensors* **2023**, *23*, 1463. [CrossRef] [PubMed]
6. Taha, B.; Shoufan, A. Machine learning-based drone detection and classification: State-of-the-art in research. *IEEE Access* **2019**, *7*, 138669–138682. [CrossRef]
7. Ahmad, B.I.; Harman, S.; Godsill, S. A Bayesian track management scheme for improved multi-target tracking and classification in drone surveillance radar. *IET Radar Sonar Navig.* **2024**, *18*, 137–146. [CrossRef]
8. Zhang, H.; Li, T.; Li, Y.; Li, J.; Dobre, O.A.; Wen, Z. RF-based drone classification under complex electromagnetic environments using deep learning. *IEEE Sens. J.* **2023**, *23*, 6099–6108. [CrossRef]
9. Han, Z.; Zhang, C.; Feng, H.; Yue, M.; Quan, K. PFFNET: A Fast Progressive Feature Fusion Network for Detecting Drones in Infrared Images. *Drones* **2023**, *7*, 424. [CrossRef]
10. Valaboju, R.; Harshitha, C.; Kallam, A.R.; Babu, B.S. Drone Detection and Classification using Computer Vision. In Proceedings of the 2023 7th International Conference on Trends in Electronics and Informatics (ICOEI), Tirunelveli, India, 11–13 April 2023; IEEE: Piscataway, NJ, USA, 2023; pp. 1320–1328.
11. Girshick, R. Fast r-cnn. In Proceedings of the IEEE International Conference on Computer Vision, Santiago, Chile, 11–18 December 2015; pp. 1440–1448.
12. Wang, C.Y.; Bochkovskiy, A.; Liao, H.Y. YOLOv7: Trainable bag-of-freebies sets new state-of-the-art for real-time object detectors. In Proceedings of the IEEE/CVF Conference on Computer Vision and Pattern Recognition, Vancouver, BC, Canada, 17–24 June 2023; pp. 7464–7475.
13. Liu, W.; Anguelov, D.; Erhan, D.; Szegedy, C.; Reed, S.; Fu, C.Y.; Berg, A.C. Ssd: Single shot multibox detector. In Proceedings of the Computer Vision–ECCV 2016: 14th European Conference, Amsterdam, The Netherlands, 11–14 October 2016; Proceedings, Part I 14. Springer International Publishing: Berlin/Heidelberg, Germany, 2016; pp. 21–37.
14. He, K.; Gkioxari, G.; Dollár, P.; Girshick, R. Mask R-CNN. In Proceedings of the 2017 IEEE International Conference on Computer Vision (ICCV), Venice, Italy, 22–29 October 2017; pp. 2980–2988.
15. Lin, T.Y.; Goyal, P.; Girshick, R.; He, K.; Dollár, P. Focal loss for dense object detection. In Proceedings of the IEEE International Conference on Computer Vision, Venice, Italy, 22–29 October 2017; pp. 2980–2988.
16. Tan, M.; Pang, R.; Le, Q.V. Efficientdet: Scalable and efficient object detection. In Proceedings of the IEEE/CVF Conference on Computer Vision and Pattern Recognition, Seattle, WA, USA, 14–19 June 2020; pp. 10781–10790.
17. Carion, N.; Massa, F.; Synnaeve, G.; Usunier, N.; Kirillov, A.; Zagoruyko, S. End-to-end object detection with transformers. In Proceedings of the European Conference on Computer Vision, Glasgow, UK, 23–28 August 2020; Springer International Publishing: Cham, Switzerland, 2020; pp. 213–229.
18. Ashraf, M.W.; Sultani, W.; Shah, M. Dogfight: Detecting dronesfrom drones videos. In Proceedings of the IEEE/CVF Conference on Computer Vision and Pattern Recognition (CVPR), Nashville, TN, USA, 20–25 June 2021; pp. 7067–7076.
19. Sangam, T.; Dave, I.R.; Sultani, W.; Shah, M. Transvisdrone: Spatio-temporal transformer for vision-based drone-to-drone detection in aerial videos. In Proceedings of the 2023 IEEE International Conference on Robotics and Automation (ICRA), London, UK, 29 May–2 June 2023; IEEE: Piscataway, NJ, USA, 2023; pp. 6006–6013.
20. Lv, W.; Xu, S.; Zhao, Y.; Wang, G.; Wei, J.; Cui, C.; Du, Y.; Dang, Q.; Liu, Y. Detrs beat yolos on real-time object detection. *arXiv* **2023**, arXiv:2304.08269.
21. Liu, X.; Peng, H.; Zheng, N.; Yang, Y.; Hu, H.; Yuan, Y. EfficientViT: Memory Efficient Vision Transformer with Cascaded Group Attention. In Proceedings of the IEEE/CVF Conference on Computer Vision and Pattern Recognition, Vancouver, BC, Canada, 17–24 June 2023.

22. Wei, H.; Liu, X.; Xu, S.; Dai, Z.; Dai, Y.; Xu, X. DWRSeg: Rethinking Efficient Acquisition of Multi-scale Contextual Information for Real-time Semantic Segmentation. *arXiv* **2022**, arXiv:2212.01173.
23. Wang, C.; He, W.; Nie, Y.; Guo, J.; Liu, C.; Wang, Y.; Han, K. Gold-YOLO: Efficient object detector via gather-and-distribute mechanism. In Proceedings of the 37th Conference on Neural Information Processing Systems, Virtual, 10–16 December 2024; Volume 36.
24. Seidaliyeva, U.; Akhmetov, D.; Ilipbayeva, L.; Matson, E.T. Real-time and accurate drone detection in a video with a static background. *Sensors* **2020**, *20*, 3856. [CrossRef] [PubMed]
25. Sharjeel, A.; Naqvi, S.A.Z.; Ahsan, M. Real time drone detection by moving camera using COROLA and CNN algorithm. *J. Chin. Inst. Eng.* **2021**, *44*, 128–137. [CrossRef]
26. Lv, Y.; Ai, Z.; Chen, M.; Gong, X.; Wang, Y.; Lu, Z. High-Resolution Drone Detection Based on Background Difference and SAG-YOLOv5s. *Sensors* **2022**, *22*, 5825. [CrossRef] [PubMed]
27. Zhao, Y.; Ju, Z.; Sun, T.; Dong, F.; Li, J.; Yang, R.; Fu, Q.; Lian, C.; Shan, P. TGC-YOLOv5: An Enhanced YOLOv5 Drone Detection Model Based on Transformer, GAM & CA Attention Mechanism. *Drones* **2023**, *7*, 446. [CrossRef]
28. Kim, J.H.; Kim, N.; Won, C.S. High-Speed Drone Detection Based On Yolo-V8. In Proceedings of the ICASSP 2023–2023 IEEE International Conference on Acoustics, Speech and Signal Processing (ICASSP), Rhodes Island, Greece, 4–10 June 2023; IEEE: Piscataway, NJ, USA, 2023; pp. 1–2.
29. Cheng, Q.; Li, X.; Zhu, B.; Shi, Y.; Xie, B. Drone detection method based on MobileViT and CA-PANet. *Electronics* **2023**, *12*, 223. [CrossRef]
30. Meng, D.; Chen, X.; Fan, Z.; Zeng, G.; Li, H.; Yuan, Y.; Sun, L.; Wang, J. Conditional detr for fast training convergence. In Proceedings of the IEEE/CVF International Conference on Computer Vision, Montreal, BC, Canada, 11–17 October 2021; pp. 3651–3660.
31. Zhu, X.; Su, W.; Lu, L.; Li, B.; Wang, X.; Dai, J. Deformable detr: Deformable transformers for end-to-end object detection. *arXiv* **2020**, arXiv:2010.04159.
32. Roh, B.; Shin, J.; Shin, W.; Kim, S. Sparse detr: Efficient end-to-end object detection with learnable sparsity. *arXiv* **2021**, arXiv:2111.14330.
33. Chen, Q.; Chen, X.; Wang, J.; Zhang, S.; Yao, K.; Feng, H.; Han, J.; Ding, E.; Zeng, G.; Wang, J. Group detr: Fast detr training with group-wise one-to-many assignment. In Proceedings of the IEEE/CVF International Conference on Computer Vision, Paris, France, 2–6 October 2023; pp. 6633–6642.
34. Zhang, M.; Song, G.; Liu, Y.; Li, H. Decoupled detr: Spatially disentangling localization and classification for improved end-to-end object detection. In Proceedings of the IEEE/CVF International Conference on Computer Vision, Paris, France, 2–6 October 2023; pp. 6601–6610.
35. Ding, X.; Zhang, X.; Han, J.; Ding, G. Scaling up your kernels to 31x31: Revisiting large kernel design in cnns. In Proceedings of the IEEE/CVF Conference on Computer Vision and Pattern Recognition, New Orleans, LA, USA, 19–20 June 2022; pp. 11963–11975.
36. Ding, X.; Zhang, X.; Ma, N.; Han, J.; Ding, G.; Sun, J. Repvgg: Making vgg-style convnets great again. In Proceedings of the IEEE/CVF Conference on Computer Vision and Pattern Recognition, Nashville, TN, USA, 20–25 June 2021; pp. 13733–13742.
37. Ding, X.; Zhang, Y.; Ge, Y.; Zhao, S.; Song, L.; Yue, X.; Shan, Y. Unireplknet: A universal perception large-kernel convnet for audio, video, point cloud, time-series and image recognition. *arXiv* **2023**, arXiv:2311.15599.

Disclaimer/Publisher's Note: The statements, opinions and data contained in all publications are solely those of the individual author(s) and contributor(s) and not of MDPI and/or the editor(s). MDPI and/or the editor(s) disclaim responsibility for any injury to people or property resulting from any ideas, methods, instructions or products referred to in the content.

Article

Efficient Vision Transformer YOLOv5 for Accurate and Fast Traffic Sign Detection

Guang Zeng [1], Zhizhou Wu [2,3,4,*], Lipeng Xu [1] and Yunyi Liang [5]

[1] School of Intelligent Manufacturing Modern Industry, Xinjiang University, Urumqi 830017, China; 107552103823@stu.xju.edu.cn (G.Z.); 107552103972@stu.xju.edu.cn (L.X.)
[2] School of Traffic and Transportation Engineering, Xinjiang University, Urumqi 830017, China
[3] College of Transportation Engineering, Tongji University, Shanghai 201804, China
[4] Xinjiang Key Laboratory for Green Construction and Smart Traffic Control of Transportation Infrastructure, Xinjiang University, Urumqi 830017, China
[5] Department of Mobility Systems Engineering, Technical University of Munich, 80333 Munich, Germany; yunyi.liang@tum.de
* Correspondence: wuzhizhou@tongji.edu.cn

Abstract: Accurate and fast detection of traffic sign information is vital for autonomous driving systems. However, the YOLOv5 algorithm faces challenges with low accuracy and slow detection when it is used for traffic sign detection. To address these shortcomings, this paper introduces an accurate and fast traffic sign detection algorithm–YOLOv5-Efficient Vision TransFormer(EfficientViT)). The algorithm focuses on improving both the accuracy and speed of the model by replacing the CSPDarknet backbone of the YOLOv5(s) model with the EfficientViT network. Additionally, the algorithm incorporates the Convolutional Block Attention Module(CBAM) attention mechanism to enhance feature layer information extraction and boost the accuracy of the detection algorithm. To mitigate the adverse effects of low-quality labels on gradient generation and enhance the competitiveness of high-quality anchor frames, a superior gradient gain allocation strategy is employed. Furthermore, the strategy introduces the Wise-IoU (WIoU), a dynamic non-monotonic focusing mechanism for bounding box loss, to further enhance the accuracy and speed of the object detection algorithm. The algorithm's effectiveness is validated through experiments conducted on the 3L-TT100K traffic sign dataset, showcasing a mean average precision (mAP) of 94.1% in traffic sign detection. This mAP surpasses the performance of the YOLOv5(s) algorithm by 4.76% and outperforms the baseline algorithm. Additionally, the algorithm achieves a detection speed of 62.50 frames per second, which is much better than the baseline algorithm.

Keywords: traffic sign detection; attention mechanism; wise-IoU; YOLOv5; efficient vision transformer

1. Introduction

A crucial component of autonomous driving is the accurate and fast detection of traffic signs [1]. The recognition of traffic signs is a deep learning-based procedure where the detection algorithm learns from labeled signage data to extract important information about the signage. The causes of 94% of these incidents, including human mistake and inattentive driving, can be eliminated with autonomous vehicles [2]. Traffic accidents caused by self-driving cars that are traveling too fast and lack information from signage for decision-making judgement can be avoided by accurate and fast object detection algorithms that capture signage information.

Deep learning-based traffic sign detection algorithms, shape-based traffic sign detection algorithms, and color-based traffic sign detection algorithms are the three basic types of traffic sign detection algorithms [3,4]. For instance, one technique uses color features to separate traffic signs by assessing color variances between the signs and the surrounding environment and defining color thresholds [5]. However, weather and lighting changes might affect color-based techniques. Yakimov et al. use the Hough transform technique to identify traffic signs based on their distinct shapes. However, when signs are partially hidden, this shape-based strategy is useless [6]. Balali et al. present a fusion strategy that uses both color and form features in order to overcome the shortcomings of the aforementioned methods. In comparison to applying each characteristic independently, the combination of these factors improves detection performance [7]. However, multi-feature fusion-based traffic sign recognition algorithms run into issues like the inability to recognize connected traffic signs and subpar real-time performance.

Driven by the advancements in deep learning detection algorithms, traffic sign detection algorithms have emerged as a powerful tool for extracting meaningful semantic information from images using convolutional neural networks. These algorithms leverage various detection frameworks to extract precise location and category information of traffic signs. Broadly speaking, deep learning traffic sign detection algorithms can be categorized into two types: two-stage region proposal (Two-Stage) and single-stage regression algorithm (One-Stage) [8,9]. Two-stage algorithms, such as R-CNN, Fast R-CNN, and Faster R-CNN, typically exhibit higher detection accuracy but slower speed [10–12]. Conversely, single-stage algorithms, including SSD [13], RetinaNet [14], and YOLO series [15–17], treat localization and classification as a regression problem, enabling end-to-end detection with faster processing but comparatively lower detection accuracy.

With the growth of migration learning, it has become popular to integrate a transformer model into the field of vision in order to address the issues of low detection accuracy and slow detection speed of existing detection algorithms [18]. The Vision Transformer (ViT) proposal demonstrates the value of the transformer paradigm in the realm of vision [19]. The ViT model resolves the issue that convolutional networks are unable to extract information about the global feature layer order and content, considerably enhancing the precision of detection algorithms. A unique lightweight multi-scale attention technique is used in the semantic segmentation model called the Efficient Vision Transformer (EfficientViT) [20]. The issue of the ViT model's big parameters and slow speed is resolved by the EfficientViT, which also enhances the detection algorithm's accuracy and speed in real time.

The mian contribution of this study is summarized as follows: (1) An EfficientViT network is designed as the backbone of YOLOv5 to improve the accuracy and speed of traffic sign detection. (2) The feature pyramid component's incorporation of the CBAM attention mechanism, which enables the feature map to self-correct, suppresses irrelevant noise input and improves detection accuracy. (3) Making use of the WIoU (Wise IoU) bounding box loss function, which prioritizes crucial image features, mutes pointless regional replies and enhances the detection network's overall performance.

The rest of the paper is structured as follows: The EffcientVit network's fundamental structure, the attention mechanism, and information on the bounding box loss function are all introduced in Section 2. The experimental design and the experimental structure assessment index are introduced in Section 3. The experimental results and analysis are presented in Section 4. Finally, the conclusion is given in Section 5.

2. The YOLOv5-EfficinetViT Traffic Sign Detection Algorithm's General Framework

Four primary components make up the YOLOv5(s) algorithm: input, backbone network (Backbone), neck, and head. The Focus, Conv, CSP, and SPPF networks make up the majority of the backbone network. The Focus structure separates the input image into 16 identically sized blocks, then joins the blocks to create four identical images for additional processing. The CSP network divides the input into two sections, stacking the remaining blocks in the first and performing extra operations in the second. The 5×5 MaxPool layers are successively applied to the input by the SPPF structure, which then sums the computed values from each layer. The output is then generated using a Conv+BN+Relu structure. Figure 1 shows how YOLOv5(s) is structured.

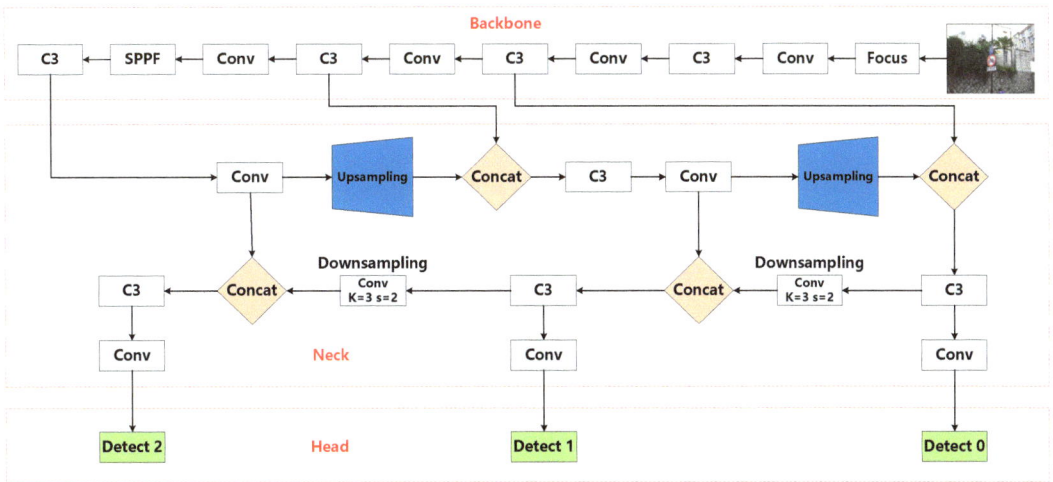

Figure 1. YOLOv5(s) object detection model structure.

The YOLOv5-EfficientViT traffic sign detection algorithm presented in this paper is shown in Figure 2. The algorithm adds three crucial parts for a better performance. First off, a more effective extraction of traffic sign features is made possible by the EfficientViT network, which takes the place of the original YOLOv5 backbone CSPDarkNet network. Second, the CBAM attention mechanism improves the FPN structure by adding more refined characteristics and a stronger emphasis on non-noise information. Last but not least, the algorithm integrates the dynamic non-monotonic focusing mechanism known as the Wise IoU module to address the complementing balance between better and worse quality samples in the CIoU bounding frame loss function.

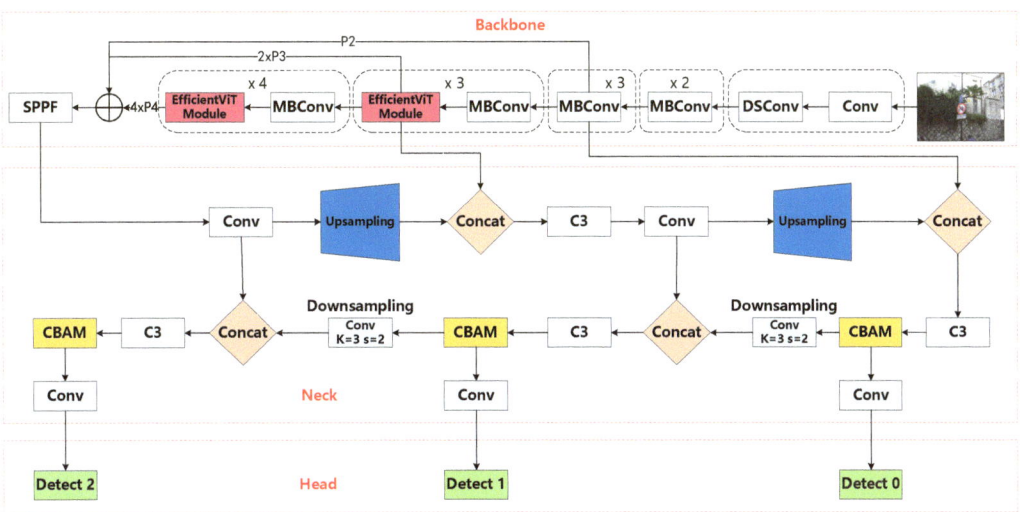

Figure 2. YOLOv5 -EfficientViT (Ours) object detection model structure.

2.1. EfficientViT Backbone

The Vision TransFormer (ViT) architecture serves as the foundation for the image categorization model known as EfficientViT. The DSConv structure, MBConv structure, and EfficientViT module structure are only a few of the structures that this model comprises. The full structure of EfficientViT is shown in Figure 3.

The model first inputs the image and uses a convolution layer (Conv) to perform feature extraction and dimensionality reduction procedures. The output is placed via a depthwise separable convolution (DSConv) structure to boost performance and efficiency. The point-by-point convolution convolves the depthwise convolution output with a 1×1 convolution kernel to produce the final output feature map, whereas the depthwise convolution just conducts convolutions within each channel. This strategy maintains computational economy while improving the model's performance.

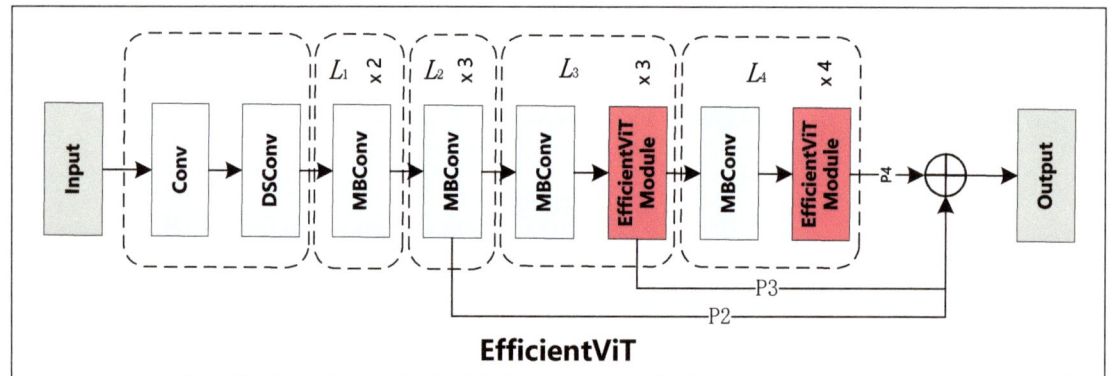

Figure 3. EfficientViT general structure.

The MBConv network processes the DSConv output twice, using the L1 layer and the L2 layer for feature extraction to obtain the P2 feature layer. The lightweight Inverted Residual Bottleneck (MBConv) architecture that serves as the foundation of the MBConv network starts with a 1×1 convolution. The SE (squeeze-and-excitation) module is also incorporated into the MBConv module to increase the relevance of features and improve the model's overall performance. For a graphic illustration of the MBConv structure, please see Figure 4.

Two MBConv modules are incorporated into the EfficientViT model to create a P2 feature layer. The L3 EfficientViT module structure and one MBConv module are then applied to this P2 feature layer to produce the P3 feature layer. The input image and its features go through dimensionality leveling using a linear layer inside the EfficientViT module structure. Three containers $(Q/K/V)$ with an equal distribution of the data are used for three parallel operations. In the first operation, feature representation and information fusion are immediately implemented using the global attention mechanism with ReLU activation. In order to handle data about graph structure, the second operation first performs a deep convolution operation using a 3×3 kernel. The output is then activated by ReLU and sent into the global attention mechanism. The third step, which processes data about graph structure, includes a deep convolution operation with a 5×5 kernel, followed by graph convolution. The output is then inputted with ReLU activation into the global attention mechanism. The three parallel processes' outputs are merged and stitched together, and the finished product is then run through a linear layer. Finally, the output's dimensional representation is recovered by using the MBConv structure. Figure 5's representation of the EfficientViT module structure shows a network of self-attentive mechanisms.

The input to the Relu-based global attention is $x \in \mathbb{R}^{N \times f}$, and the generalized self-attention mechanism is formulated as follows:

$$O_i = \sum_{j=1}^{N} \frac{Sim(Q_i, K_i)}{\sum_{j=1}^{N} Sim(Q_i, K_i)} V_j \tag{1}$$

where $Q = xW_Q, K = xW_K, V = xW_V$, and $W_Q/W_K/W_V \in \mathbb{R}^{f \times d}$ is the linear projection matrix, and O_i denotes the ith row of matrix $Sim(.,.)$, which is the similarity function. When using the similarity function $Sim(Q,K) = exp(\frac{QK^T}{\sqrt{d}})$, Equation (1) is the original self-attention mechanism.

$$Sim(Q,K) = ReLU(Q)ReLU(K)^T \tag{2}$$

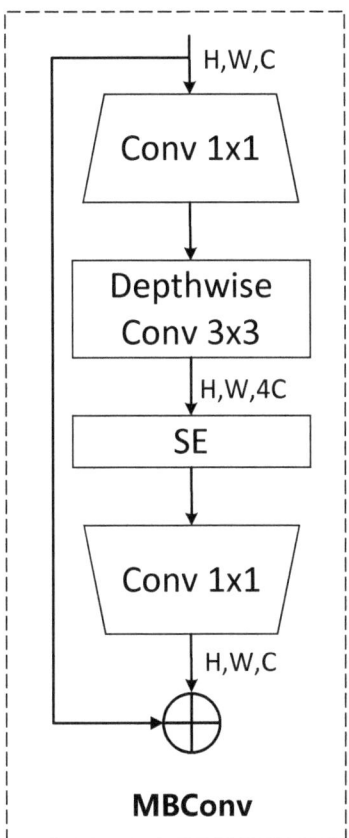

Figure 4. MBConv structure.

With $Sim(Q,K) = ReLU(Q)ReLU(K)^T$, Equation (1) can be rewritten as follows:

$$Q_i = \sum_{j=1}^{N} \frac{ReLU(Q_i) ReLU(K_j)^T}{\sum_{j=1}^{N} ReLU(Q_i) ReLU(K_j)^T} V_j = \frac{\sum_{j=1}^{N} \left(ReLU(Q_i) ReLU(K_j)^T\right) V_j}{ReLU(Q_i) \sum_{j=1}^{N} ReLU(K_j)^T} \tag{3}$$

The L4 EfficientViT module structure processes the P3 special layer after it has been input into an MBConv module, resulting in the derivation of the P4 feature layer. The P4 broad dimension is extended using a multiplication factor of 4, whereas the P3 wide dimension is expanded using a factor of 2. The P2, P3, and P4 feature layers are additionally concatenated, and the resulting cumulative outputs are then fed into L5 MBConv modules for convolutional processing, producing the final output feature layer.

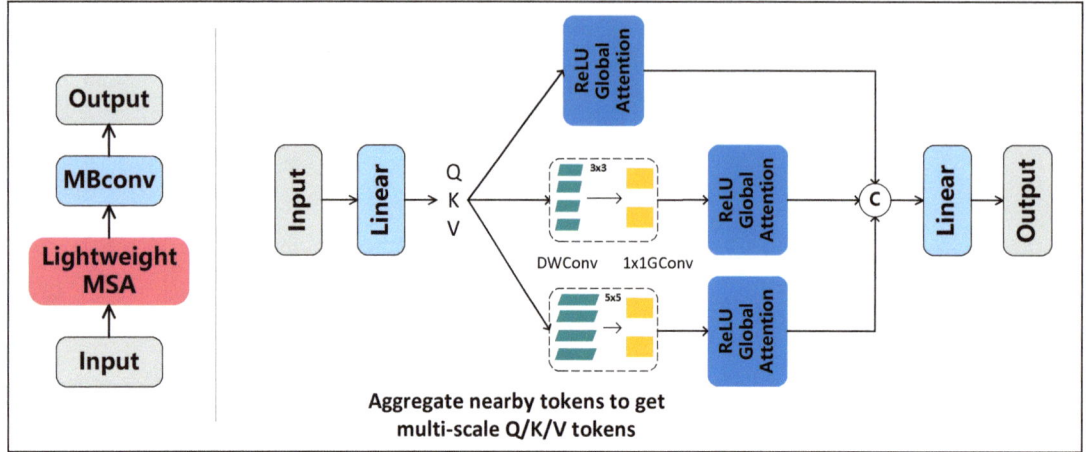

Figure 5. EfficientViT module structure.

2.2. Attention Mechanism

The Attention Mechanism is a frequently used deep learning technique that improves the model's capacity to focus on incoming data and to selectively highlight important information. By learning weights that only emphasize particular portions of the input throughout the aggregation process, it simulates human attention.

2.2.1. CBAM Attention Mechanism

The Channel Attention Module and the Spatial Attention Module are the two sub-modules that make up the CBAM (Convolutional Block Attention Module) attention mechanism [21]. To capture various degrees of feature representation, these sub-modules carry out attentional operations on several dimensions, namely the channel dimension and the spatial dimension, respectively.

The purpose of the Channel Attention Module is to record the relationships between the feature maps in the channel dimension. This is accomplished by using fully connected layers and global average pooling to learn channel weights, allowing the module to selectively enhance or suppress particular channels within the feature maps. This attention mechanism focuses the model's attention on important channel information, leading to the extraction of representations that are more thorough and feature-rich.

The goal of the spatial attention module is to comprehend the spatial importance of the feature map. This is carried out by applying a number of operations to the feature graph, including maximum pooling, average pooling, convolution layers, and activation functions, to create a spatial attention graph. The features at different positions within the feature map are then given weights using this graph. As a result, the model may analyze characteristics at many locations while concentrating on important spatial information. Figure 6 provides a diagram of the procedure.

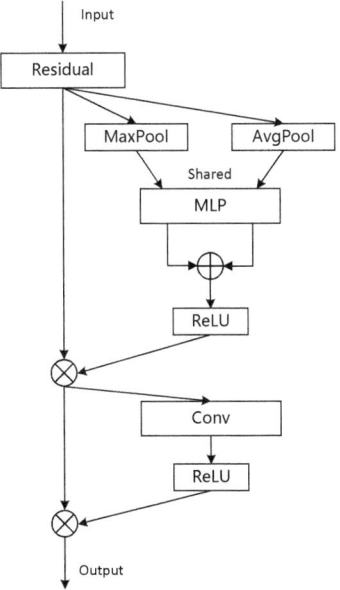

Figure 6. CBAM attention mechanism.

2.2.2. CA Attention Mechanisms

The feature map's channels can be selectively enhanced or suppressed using the coordinate attention mechanism (CA). It makes it easier to extract richer and more important characteristics by learning channel weights [22]. In order to allow the model to prioritize important channel information during feature processing, CA primarily operates on the channel dimension of the feature map. For a visual illustration, see Figure 7.

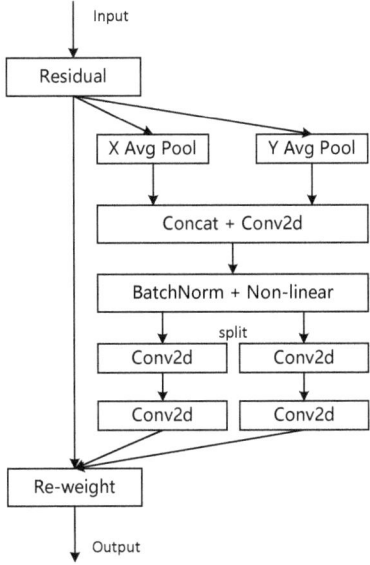

Figure 7. CA attention mechanism.

2.3. IoU Loss

In many object detection tasks, the Intersection over Union (IoU) loss function is used, as shown in Figure 8 below [23]. The overlap between the anticipated bounding box and the actual labeling of the model output is measured by this loss function. The anticipated bounding box and the ground truth box's common area is indicated by the intersection, while their combined area is shown by the union. By minimizing the IoU loss function during training, the model modifies the location and dimensions of the predicted bounding box with the goal of getting it to resemble the ground truth box as much as possible. The model may better capture the shape and location of the item by optimizing the IoU loss function, which raises the object detection accuracy.

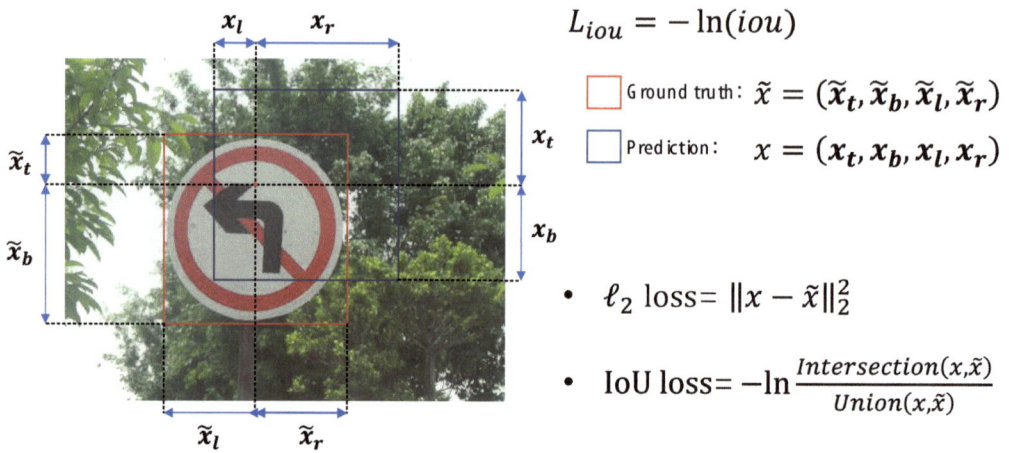

Figure 8. IoU Loss.

2.3.1. EIoU Loss Function

The non-negativity, symmetry, triangle inequality, and scale insensitivity of the *IoU* loss function are all positive qualities. The loss value is 0 because it is unable to accurately gauge the distance between two boxes that do not intersect. A disadvantage of the *IoU* loss function is its delayed convergence.

The GIoU loss function is proposed as an improvement over the *IoU* loss function, which suffers from the limitation of always yielding a value of 0 when there is no intersection between two boxes [24]. Let A and B represent any two boxes and C represent the smallest box that encloses both A and B. The IoU is calculated as $|A \cap B|/|A \cup B|$. The GIoU loss function becomes valid when $|A \cap B| = 0$. In such cases, the GIoU loss aims to increase the area of the bounding box to ensure overlap with the object box, contrary to the intuition of reducing the spatial location difference. When $|A \cap B| > 0$, the area of $|C - A \cup B|$ is always a decimal or zero (this term is zero when A contains B, and vice versa). Consequently, the GIoU loss degenerates to the *IoU* loss in this scenario. As a result, the convergence rate of the GIoU loss remains slow.

$$L_{GIoU} = 1 - IoU + \frac{|C - (A \cup B)|}{|C|} \quad (4)$$

The CIoU loss function takes into account three crucial geometric elements: overlap area, center distance, and aspect ratio [25]. In this context, B represents the prediction frame, B^{gt} denotes the object frame, and b and b^{gt} represent the centroids of B and B^{gt}, respectively. The Euclidean distance between b and b^{gt} is denoted as $\rho(\cdot) = \|b - b_{gt}\|^2$. Additionally, c represents the diagonal of the smallest box that covers both boxes. The aspect ratio difference is measured by $v = \frac{4}{\pi^2}(\arctan\frac{w^{gt}}{h^{gt}} - \arctan\frac{w}{h})^2$, and α is computed as $\alpha = \frac{v}{(1-IoU)+v}$.

The CIOU loss function is defined as follows:

$$L_{CIoU} = 1 - IoU + \frac{\rho^2(\mathbf{b}, \mathbf{b}^{gt})}{c^2} + \alpha v \tag{5}$$

The EIoU (Efficient *IoU*) introduces improvements to the CIoU (Complete *IoU*) loss by addressing the aspect ratio inconsistency issue. It replaces the aspect ratio-related component of the CIoU loss with separate consistency losses for length and width. This modification results in the EIoU loss, which provides a more reasonable and accurate representation [26]. The definitions of the EIoU loss are as follows:

$$L_{EIoU} = L_{IoU} + L_{dis} + L_{asp} \tag{6}$$

$$L_{EIoU} = 1 - IoU + \frac{\rho^2(\mathbf{b}, \mathbf{b}^{gt})}{(w^c)^2 + (h^c)^2} + \frac{\rho^2(w, w^{gt})}{(w^c)^2} + \frac{\rho^2(h, h^{gt})}{(h^c)^2} \tag{7}$$

The loss function is divided into three parts: IOU loss L_{IoU}, distance loss L_{dis}, and direction loss L_{asp}. In this context, hw and hc represent the width and height of the minimum enclosing frame that covers the two boxes. Additionally, the EIOU loss is introduced to directly minimize the disparity between the object and anchor boxes' width and height. This approach leads to faster convergence and improved localization.

2.3.2. SIoU Loss Function

The SIoU (SCYLLA-IoU) loss function incorporates traditional metrics such as distance, shape, and IoU to calculate the penalty for mismatches between the true value in the image and the model's bounding box [27]. This addition significantly improves the training process by causing the prediction frame to converge quickly towards the nearest axis, allowing subsequent methods to rely on only one coordinate (X or Y) for regression. In essence, the introduction of angular penalty effectively reduces the overall degrees of freedom. The SIoU loss function comprises four cost functions: angle, distance, shape, and IoU. The angular cost function allows the model to make predictions in the X and Y axes first, and during convergence, attempts are made to minimize the value of α in $\tan\alpha = \frac{Y}{X}$; the value of β in $\tan\beta = \frac{X}{Y}$ is minimized when $\alpha \leq \frac{\pi}{4}$. The distance cost function is defined taking into account the angular cost defined above. When $\alpha \to 0$, the contribution of the distance cost is greatly reduced. Conversely, when $\alpha \to \frac{\pi}{4}$, the contribution of the distance cost is greater. The shape cost function is defined as

$$\Omega = \sum_{t=w,h}(1 - e^{-\omega_t})^\theta \tag{8}$$

$$\omega_w = \frac{|w - w^{gt}|}{\max(w, w^{gt})}, \omega_h = \frac{|h - h^{gt}|}{\max(h, h^{gt})} \tag{9}$$

and the value of θ defines the shape cost, and its value is unique for each data set. θ controls the attention value required for the shape cost. If $\theta = 1$, this will immediately optimize the shape and thus affect the free motion of the shape.

2.3.3. Wise IoU Loss Function

A problem of including low-quality data in the training dataset is that geometric measurements, such as distance and aspect ratio, might amplify the penalty applied to such samples, causing the model's generalization performance to degrade. To solve this problem, an efficient loss function should reduce the penalty imposed by geometric metrics in cases when the anchor frame and the object frame strongly overlap. The model can acquire improved generalization skills by minimizing interference during training. A two-layer distance attention mechanism loss function based on the distance metric is introduced in this context by WIoU [28]. The dynamic non-monotonic focusing mechanism uses "outliers" as an alternative to IoU for quality assessment of anchor frames and provides a judicious gradient gain assignment strategy. This strategy reduces the competitiveness of high-quality anchor frames while reducing the harmful gradients generated by low-quality examples. This allows the WIoU to focus on anchor frames of average quality, improving the detection accuracy of the detector.

- $\mathcal{R}_{WIoU} \in [1, e)$; this will significantly amplify the $\mathcal{L}_{IoU}$ of the common mass anchor frame.
- $\mathcal{L}_{IoU} \in [0, 1]$; this will significantly reduce the $\mathcal{R}_{WIoU}$ of high quality anchor frames and significantly reduce their focus on the center distance when the anchor frame is well overlapped with the object frame.

$$\mathcal{L}_{WIoUv1} = \mathcal{R}_{WIoU} \mathcal{L}_{IoU} \quad (10)$$

$$\mathcal{R}_{WIoU} = exp\left(\frac{(x - x_{gt})^2 - (y - y_{gt})^2}{(W_g^2 - H_g^2)^*}\right) \quad (11)$$

In the above equation, W_g, H_g are the length and width of the minimum outer bounding box of the prediction and real boxes. In order to prevent $\mathcal{R}_{WIoU}$ from generating gradients that impede convergence, W_g, H_g are separated from the computational graph (the superscript * indicates this operation). Because it effectively eliminates the factors that hinder convergence, no new variables are introduced, such as the horizontal to vertical ratio, so the convergence efficiency of the model is improved.

3. Experimental Design

3.1. Experimental Dataset

Six wide-angle DSLR cameras with large pixel counts were used to create the TT100K traffic signs dataset [29], and various lighting and weather conditions were present at each shooting location. The dataset's final size is 2048 × 2048, with the original image's resolution being 8192 × 2048. The panorama was then divided into four pieces. There are more thorough categories of traffic signs in the TT100K dataset, which has 221 distinct categories overall and 128 tagged categories. This study randomly chooses 9050 photos with traffic signs from the TT100K dataset and reclassifies the categories because the number of categories in the dataset is seriously unequal. This study uses the CCTSDB dataset categorization standard to divide the dataset into three categories: required directional signs, prohibitory signs, and warning signs. Table 1 lists the numbers for each category under the designation 3L-TT100K. The 3L-TT100K with dimensions 2048 × 2048 is used as a model to accelerate model training and verify the model's capacity to detect the target. The size of the 3L-TT100K dataset is shrunk to 640 × 640 from 2048 × 2048.

Table 1. 3L-TT100K dataset.

Classification	Quantity (pcs)
prohibitory	16,745
mandatory	4539
warning	1241

3.2. Evaluation Metrics

For assessing the consistency of test outcomes, the model assessment metrics utilized in this article use fixed IoU and confidence levels. The determination of precision and recall for the prediction outcomes allows for the measurement of the model's object detection and object categorization capabilities. Additionally, by varying the confidence thresholds, precision–recall curves (P-R curves) can be created, providing a visual depiction of the model's detection efficiency. Based on the true labels, the detection results are divided into four groups when the precision and recall metrics are computed: true positive (TP), true negative (TN), false positive (FP), and false negative (FN).

By evaluating the ratio of correctly predicted samples to all predicted samples in the detection results, precision is a statistic that assesses a model's capacity to categorize an object. It is calculated as follows to indicate the ratio of successfully detected samples to all detected samples:

$$Precision = \frac{TP}{TP + FP} \quad (12)$$

Recall is a metric that gauges how well the model can identify the object. It is derived by dividing the number of real samples overall in the detection results by the proportion of samples that were correctly predicted. In other words, it symbolizes the proportion of successfully recognized samples to all true samples, offering information on the model's detection abilities. It is calculated as follows:

$$Recall = \frac{TP}{TP + FN} \quad (13)$$

Recall is a metric that gauges how well the model can identify the object. It is derived by dividing the number of real samples overall in the detection results by the proportion of samples that were correctly predicted. In other words, it symbolizes the proportion of successfully recognized samples to all true samples, offering information on the model's detection abilities. It is calculated as follows:

The average precision (AP) value derived by averaging the precision values along the precision–recall (PR) curve is represented by this term. It is computed by integrating the PR curve's area under the curve.

$$AP = \int_0^1 p(r)dr \quad (14)$$

An essential evaluation statistic for object detection systems is the mean average precision (mAP). It provides a thorough evaluation of the model's performance and is calculated as the average of the average precision (AP) values. To evaluate object detection algorithms, the speed and accuracy (mAP) metrics are frequently used, providing a fair knowledge of their capabilities. A more advanced object detection model for the particular dataset under consideration is indicated by a higher mAP value.

Furthermore, the quantity of sent frames per second (FPS) is used to gauge how quickly the algorithm detects motion. This statistic is a crucial gauge of how well the algorithm works in real-time detection.

4. Analysis of Experimental Results

4.1. Experimental Environment

The experiment was carried out in a Linux environment using the Ubuntu 20.04 operating system. The experimental device has an NVIDIA RTX3090 GPU with 24 GB of video RAM, Pytorch 1.11.0, Python 3.8, and CUDA 11.3 loaded to assist the experiment.

4.2. Experimental Setup

The network structure of both YOLOv5s and YOLOv5l models are shown in Figure 1, and the resultant frameworks of the two models are the same, with the YOLOv5l model having a parameter count that is about seven times larger than that of YOLOv5s by controlling the number of C3 modules. When the algorithm is trained, the parameters are tuned using both manual and genetic algorithms to prove that the algorithm in this paper is the optimal model. In the manual tuning experiment, the parameter optimiser, batch size, and learning rate (lr) were tuned. optimizerSGD, Adam, and AdamW were tuned in the middle of the three; the batch size was tuned between 32 and 64; and lr was tuned between 0.01 and 0.001, respectively. In the genetic algorithm (GA) evolutionary iteration of lr, a mutation technique with a probability of 80% and a variance of 004 was used to generate new offspring based on the best parent in the previous generations.The YOLOv5-EfficientViT algorithm migrated the weights of the EfficientViT network of ImageNet, and the model was trained for a total of 500 rounds. The results of parameter tuning are shown in Table 2; different optimizers have a greater impact on the model, and the optimal optimizer is SGD. The batch size also has a certain impact on the model, and the smaller the batch-size, the better the results. The size of the learning rate affects the convergence speed of the model, and the optimal learning rate corresponding to different optimizers is also the optimal learning rate for different optimizers.

Table 2. Algorithm tuning test table.

Optimizer	Batch-Size	Learning Rate	mAp@0.5%
SGD	32	0.01	94.0%
SGD	64	0.01	93.9%
SGD	32	0.001	89.1%
Adam	32	0.01	84.1%
Adam	64	0.01	80.8%
Adam	32	0.001	92.5%
AdamW	32	0.01	93.2%
AdamW	64	0.01	92.9%
AdamW	32	0.001	92.0%
GA(SGD)	32	0.0136	94.1%

4.3. Algorithm Detection Performance Comparison Analysis

4.3.1. Algorithm P-R Curve Comparison

To assess the detection performance of the algorithm, we conducted tests comparing YOLOv5-EfficientViT with YOLOv5(s), YOLOv5(l), YOLOv4-tiny, YOLOv7, and YOLOv8. These three categories were used to validate the five methods on the TT100K dataset, and Table 3 shows the experimental outcomes. Additionally, we produced P-R curves to graphically display the algorithm's effectiveness on this dataset. In Figure 9, below, these curves are shown.

The self-attention mechanism from the transformer is used by the YOLOv5-EfficientViT method to improve the analysis and processing of global characteristics in images. This algorithm outperforms other widely used detection techniques in terms of recall rates for the detection of the three item classes indicated in Table 3. In addition, it achieves significant accuracy gains over YOLOv4-tiny, YOLOv7, and YOLOv8.

Table 3. Comparison table of P-R curves of algorithms.

Algorithm	Parameters	Prohibitory	Mandatory	Warning
YOLOv5(s)	P	95.87%	94.64%	93.00%
	R	80.08%	79.85%	73.23%
YOLOv5(l)	P	96.05%	96.25%	95.54%
	R	86.43%	87.01%	84.25%
YOLOv4-tiny	P	76.72%	75.27%	81.73%
	R	61.52%	65.35%	66.93%
YOLOv7	P	89.4%	91.7%	67.6%
	R	68.7%	67.6%	73.3%
YOLOv8	P	92.8%	92.9%	87.4%
	R	84.9%	84.9%	89.4%
YOLOv5-EfficientViT(Ours)	P	93.50%	93.70%	88.10%
	R	88.3%	90.6%	90.4%

The P-R curve in Figure 9a indicates that the current approach outperforms two widely used object identification algorithms, YOLOv4-tiny, YOLOv7, and YOLOv8, in terms of detecting prohibitory category objects. This conclusion is supported by the rest of Figure 9. Furthermore, the P-R curves shown in Figure 9b,c unmistakably show that the current approach outperforms the YOLOv7 object detection algorithm in terms of recognizing mandatory class and warning items. Notably, the 3L-TT100K dataset consistently performs better than the other five object detection algorithms for all three classes of objects when the precision is 0.9.

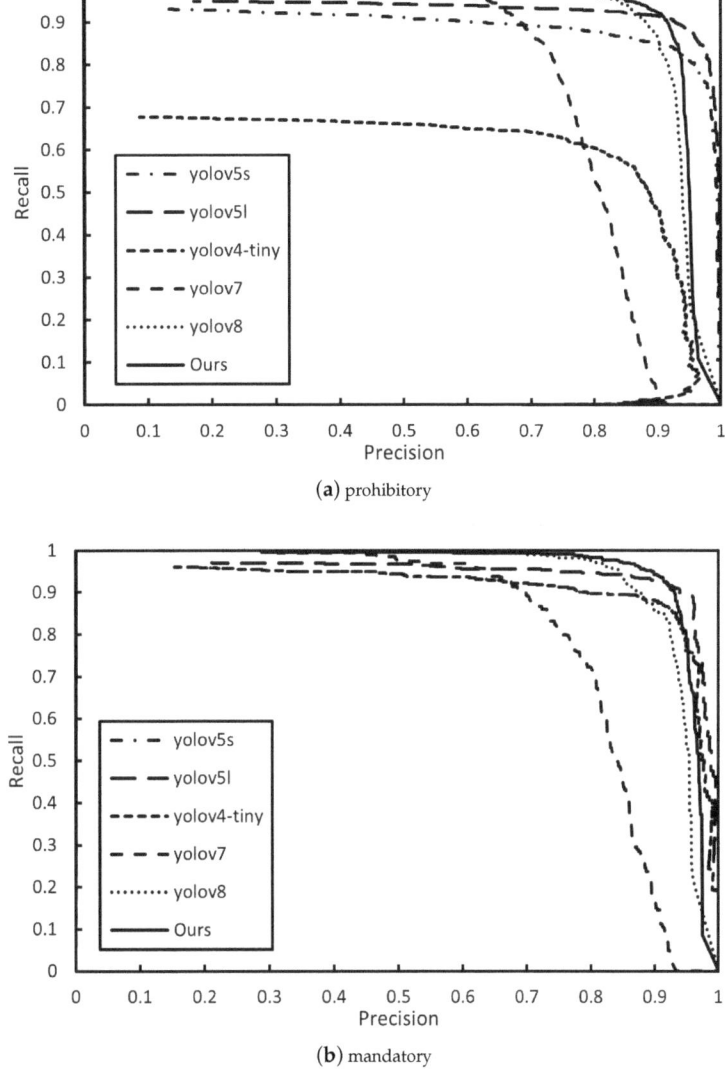

Figure 9. *Cont.*

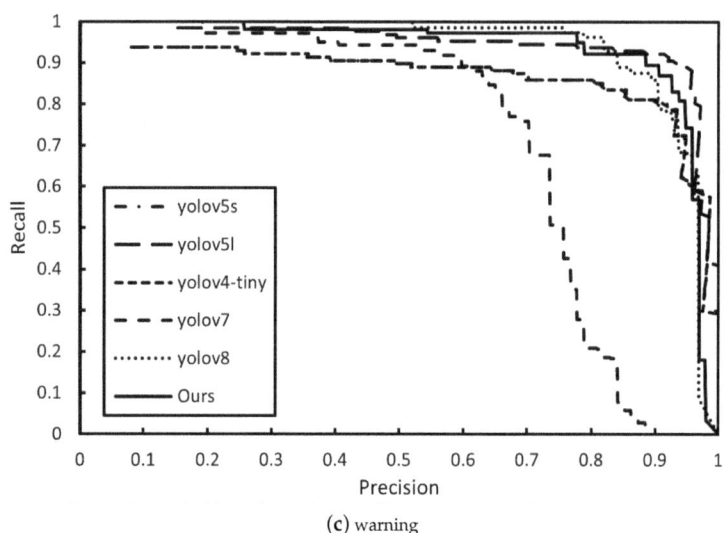

(c) warning

Figure 9. P-R curve comparison. (**a**) is the Prohibitory traffic sign P-R curve; (**b**) is the Mandatory traffic sign P-R curve; (**c**) is the Warning traffic sign P-R curve.

4.3.2. Comparative Analysis of Algorithm in Real-Time

A comparison and study of frames per second (FPS) between the algorithm described in this research and the YOLOv5(s), YOLOv5(l), YOLOv4-tiny, YOLOv7, and YOLOv8 algorithms are completed to verify the real-time performance of the approach. Table 4 presents the outcomes. The fastest of these algorithms, YOLOv4-tiny, processes 122.06 images per second, while YOLOv5(l) processes 39.30 images per second. The processing rate of the algorithm used in this study is 62.50 images per second, which is slightly slower than the YOLOv7 and YOLOv8 object detection algorithms. The approach presented in this study accelerates feature map extraction and provides noticeably faster image processing speeds than both the YOLOv5(s) and YOLOv5(l) algorithms by substituting the YOLOv5 backbone with the EfficientViT network. The technique described in this research ensures that the required image processing speed for real-time detection while maintaining a balance between detection accuracy and real-time performance when compared to several standard object detection algorithms. Considering the lack of such a high-performance hardware equipment configuration in the test in the application scenario, the algorithm in this paper was verified in the test on the 2080 ti, which can process 57.80 pictures per second and can meet the requirements of real-time detection, with good applicability.

Table 4. Algorithm inference speed comparison.

Algorithm	FPS (frame/s)
YOLOv5(s)	44.47
YOLOv5(l)	39.30
YOLOv4-tiny	122.06
YOLOv7	64.52
YOLOv8	65.70
YOLOv5-EfficientViT(Ours)	62.50

4.3.3. Comparative Analysis of Algorithmic Ablation Experiments

A number of comparative ablation experiments were carried out in order to better understand the internal network structure of the YOLOv5-EfficientViT algorithm and gauge the effect of modules with various architectures on its detection performance. The backbone network replacement, the insertion of attention mechanisms at various locations, and the replacement of the IoU loss function were the three main focuses of the ablation experiment design. Four network architectures were used for the backbone replacement: Mobilenetv3, EfficientFormerv2, Efficient Model (EMO), and EfficientViT. We investigated the impact of backbone model size on detection performance using the Mobilenetv3 network, a lightweight network that has gained popularity recently, and the latter three models, which are Vision Transformer models with improved detection performance.

The results of the ablation experiment are shown in Table 5, which contrasts the backbone replacements for the YOLOv5 model with the Mobilenetv3 network (which achieved the fastest processing speed of 85.47 FPS for images) and the EfficientFormerv2 (l) network (which produced the best detection performance with a mAP of 94.4%). The YOLOv5-EfficientViT backbone was created by replacing the YOLOv5 backbone with the EfficientViT (b1) network after taking into account both detection accuracy (mAP) and speed (FPS) measures in comparison with YOLOv5. (From here on, EfficientViT will always refer to the EfficientViT (b1) model).

An attention mechanism is introduced to improve attention to the input and selectively focus on important information during feature extraction. As shown in Figure 10a–d, we chose the CA attention network and the CBAM attention network for this study and included them in the model. As shown in Table 5, when using EfficientViT as the backbone and positioning the Tim CBAM attention network at position Figure 10d, the algorithm achieves the best object detection results in terms of mAP and FPS. Notably, compared to adding the CA attention network at the same site, adding the CBAM attention network in Figure 10d results in a 1.8-point gain in object detection accuracy and a 9.75 images per second increase in detection speed. Additionally, utilizing YOLOv5-EfficientViT without the attention mechanism results in a 0.1% improvement in detection accuracy.

In order to improve the YOLOv5-EfficientViT algorithm, this work introduces four loss functions, namely EIoU, SIoU, and WIoU. Table 5 makes it very evident that using the WIoU loss function increases the algorithm's detection accuracy in comparison to YOLOv5-EfficientViT by 0.2 percentage points. Additionally, the technique improves speed by 0.4 images per second. Incorporating the CBAM attention mechanism, the WIoU loss function, and the replacement of the YOLOv5 backbone with EfficientViT at position (d) in Figure 10 make up the entire algorithm structure of this study. The addition of the WIoU loss function improves the accuracy of traffic signage by 0.2 percentage points and improves the inference speed by 1 FPS. Table 5 displays the experimental findings. The algorithm used in this study improves the detection accuracy in terms of mAP by 4.76 percentage points in comparison to the YOLOv5s model and accelerates detection by 18.03 photos per second.

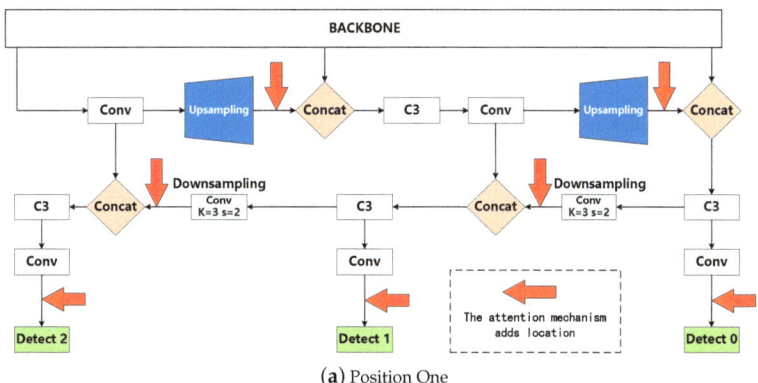

(**a**) Position One

Figure 10. *Cont.*

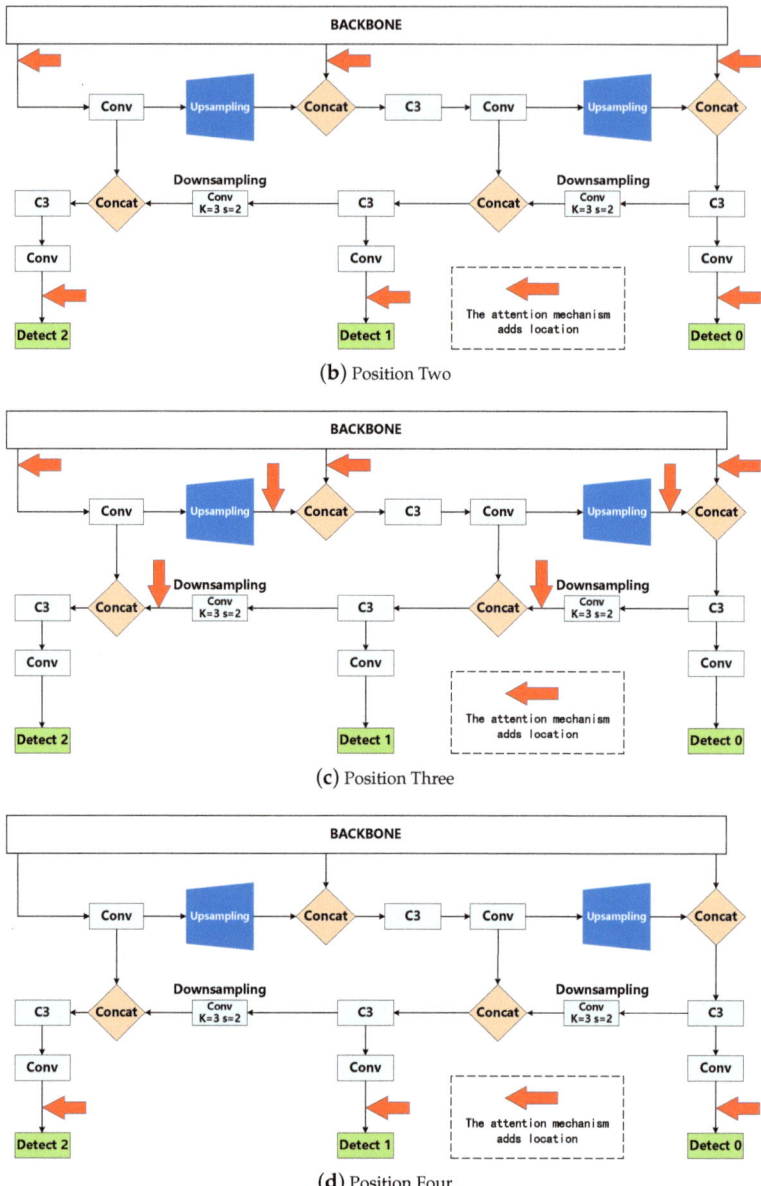

(b) Position Two

(c) Position Three

(d) Position Four

Figure 10. Comparison of total communication delay for different penetration rates of CAV.

Table 5. Comparison of ablation experiment results.

Number	Backbone	Attention Mechanisms	IoU Loss	mAP@0.5%	FPS (frame/s)
1	Mobilenetv3	-	-	83.2%	85.47
2	EfficientFormerv2(s1)	-	-	92.7%	32.26
3	EfficientFormerv2(l)	-	-	94.4%	29.59
4	EMO(1M)	-	-	93.5%	60.61
5	EMO(6M)	-	-	93.7%	54.05
6	EfficientViT(b1)	-	-	93.7%	62.89
7	EfficientViT(b2)	-	-	93.8%	53.19
8	EfficientViT(b1)	CA(a)	-	92.5%	56.50
9	EfficientViT(b1)	CA(b)	-	93.4%	56.50
10	EfficientViT(b1)	CA(c)	-	92.5%	55.56
11	EfficientViT(b1)	CA(d)	-	92%	52.36
12	EfficientViT(b1)	CBAM(a)	-	93.7%	54.64
13	EfficientViT(b1)	CBAM(b)	-	93%	57.14
14	EfficientViT(b1)	CBAM(c)	-	93.4%	53.48
15	EfficientViT(b1)	CBAM(d)	-	93.8%	62.11
16	EfficientViT(b1)	-	SIoU	90.8%	71.94
17	EfficientViT(b1)	-	EIOU	91.2%	67.57
18	EfficientViT(b1)	-	Wise IoU	93.9%	63.29
19	EfficientViT(Ours)	CBAM(d)	Wise IoU	94.1%	62.50

4.3.4. Comparative Analysis of Experimental Results of Algorithm Detection Accuracy

Using the 3L-TT100K dataset, the current algorithm is evaluated against the YOLOv5(s), YOLOv5(l), YOLOv4-tiny, YOLOv, and YOLOv8 algorithms. The mean average precision (mAP) for each algorithm is calculated after a thorough analysis of the average precision (AP) of each algorithm for several categories, as shown in Table 6 below. For all three types of tags in the 3L-TT100K dataset, the algorithm reported in this paper surpasses YOLOv5(s), YOLOv4-tiny, YOLOv7, and YOLOv8 algorithms in terms of detection accuracy. Compared with the method in this study, YOLOv5(l) has a higher detection accuracy, and according to the comprehensive analysis of Tables 4 and 6, the algorithm in this paper has the advantages of high detection accuracy and speed. In order to prove that the detection performance of this paper's algorithm is better than the existing state-of-the-art traffic sign detection algorithms, the algorithm in this paper is compared with ETSR-YOLO [30], TRD-YOLO [31], and CR-YOLOv8 [32], and the accuracy of traffic sign detection is better than the three traffic sign target detection algorithms mentioned above.

Table 6. Comparison of algorithm detection accuracy results.

Algorithm	Prohibitory AP	Mandatory AP	Warnin AP	mAP
YOLOv5(s)	89.37%	91.33%	87.32%	89.34%
YOLOv5(l)	93.11%	94.51%	94.69%	94.1%
YOLOv4-tiny	60.29%	60.01%	67.76%	62.69%
YOLOv7	78.8%	81.6%	72.2%	77.6%
YOLOv8	91.7%	92.6%	92.5%	92.3%
ETSR-YOLO	-	-	-	88.3%
TRD-YOLO	-	-	-	86.3%
CR-YOLOv8	-	-	-	86.9%
YOLOv5-EfficientViT(Ours)	93.7%	95.4%	93.2%	94.1%

4.4. Algorithm Detection Performance Comparison Analysis

This research assesses the algorithms by contrasting them with YOLOv5(s), YOLOv5(l), YOLOv4-tiny, YOLOv7, and YOLOv8 on the validation set of the 3L-TT100K dataset. This comparison helps to promote a more natural comparison of the detection performance among methods. Only the prediction frames with a confidence level higher than 0.5 are kept for the validation testing.

In the figures below, Figures 11–17, the validation findings are shown. The image under detection is shown in Figure 11, where Figure 11a shows how the backdrop and signage features are quite similar, interfering with the algorithm used to recognize the signs. The YOLOv7 algorithm's detection result, shown in Figure 15a, wrongly classifies background information as signage. On the other hand, Figure 17a shows the detection outcome produced by the algorithm suggested in this study. This approach improves the extraction of object information in the feature layer by including the CBAM attention mechanism, considerably lowering the incidence of false detections by the detection algorithm.

The YOLOv5l algorithm fails to identify mandatory-type signs in Figures 12b, 14b, and 15b when attempting to recognize the signage seen in Figure 11b. The detection results of the YOLOv5l method, which successfully detects the mandatory class flag, are shown in Figure 13b. However, compared to the 0.76 attained by the algorithm suggested in this research, the confidence level of the algorithm's detection is just 0.5. The algorithm presented in this research makes use of the self-attention mechanism in the EfficientViT backbone to extract information on the global feature layer order and content, enhancing detection precision and decreasing the number of missed detection cases. The detection effects of the YOLOv4-tiny algorithm and the YOLOv7 algorithm, respectively, are shown in Figures 14b and 15b. The findings show unequivocally that both methods provide prediction frames that considerably differ from the detection item, leading to subpar detection performance. The technique suggested in this paper proposes the WIoU loss function, which modifies the weights of superior and inferior prediction frames to minimize the deviation value between the prediction frame and the detection object, in order to address the problem of severe frame deviation.

(a) One (b) Two (c) Three

Figure 11. Original picture(Object detection model input image).

(a) One (b) Two (c) Three

Figure 12. YOLOv5(s) object detection model output results.

(**a**) One (**b**) Two (**c**) Three

Figure 13. YOLOv5(l) object detection model output results.

(**a**) One (**b**) Two (**c**) Three

Figure 14. YOLOv4-tiny object detection model output results.

(**a**) One (**b**) Two (**c**) Three

Figure 15. YOLOv7 object detection model output results.

(**a**) One (**b**) Two (**c**) Three

Figure 16. YOLOv8 object detection model output results.

(**a**) One (**b**) Two (**c**) Three

Figure 17. YOLOv5-EfficienntViT (Ours) object detection model output results.

Figure 16 shows the detection effect of the YOLOv8 algorithm. From Figure 16a,b, it can be seen that the overall detection accuracy is worse than the model in this paper. The methods suggested in this paper provide higher detection performance compared to existing mainstream detection algorithms for the warning class signage, especially taking into account the limited training samples available, as shown in Figures 12c–17c.

The YOLOv5-EfficientViT algorithm proposed in this paper, which effectively addresses the limitations of conventional networks, such as missed detections and errors, by leveraging its strong feature extraction capabilities and precise object frame positioning, has been verified through a comparative analysis of the aforementioned six groups of detection models. The experimental findings show that the algorithm performs quite well in terms of accuracy and real-time performance when it comes to detecting traffic signs. It excels in real-time traffic sign detection and outperforms currently used techniques.

5. Conclusions

The identification of traffic signs is crucial for study in the areas of traffic asset exclusion, aided driving, and autonomous driving. In this research, we offer an accurate and fast traffic sign identification system based on the single-stage YOLOv5 algorithm and using EfficientViT as the foundation. We overcome the problem of the CSPDarkNet network's failure to extract the global feature layer order and content information by relocating the self-attention mechanism from the transformer to object detection. The detection accuracy and real-time performance of traffic signage are both improved by this self-attention module. In order to improve the FPN stage's ability to extract features, we also incorporate the CBAM attention method. In addition, the model's convergence is sped up by using the WIoU loss function. Ablation experiments that contrast the impacts of the backbone network, attention mechanism, and loss function on the model serve to demonstrate the use of these modules.

On the 3L-TT100K dataset, our approach outperforms conventional mainstream techniques by achieving an mAP of 94.1% and a frame rate of 62.50 frames per second (FPS) for traffic sign detection. Our approach enhances the mAP by 4.76% when compared to the YOLOv5s algorithm on the same dataset. To balance the quantity of labels in the dataset and lessen the effect of label imbalances on accuracy, we plan to address the issue of label proportions during model training in future research.

Author Contributions: Conceptualization, G.Z.; methodology, G.Z.; software, G.Z.; validation, G.Z.; formal analysis, G.Z.; investigation, G.Z.; resources, G.Z.; data curation, G.Z.; writing—original draft preparation, G.Z.; writing—review and editing, G.Z.; visualization, G.Z.; supervision, Z.W.; project administration, L.X.; funding acquisition, Z.W. and Y.L. All authors have read and agreed to the published version of the manuscript.

Funding: This work is supported by the National Natural Science Foundation of China (Grant No. 52172330) and Hunan Provincial Natural Science Foundation of China (Grant No. 2023JJ40731).

Data Availability Statement: The data used to support the findings of this study are available from the corresponding author upon request.

Conflicts of Interest: The authors declare no conflicts of interest.

References

1. Wang, Z.; Wang, J.; Li, Y.; Wang, S. Traffic sign recognition with lightweight two-stage model in complex scenes. *IEEE Trans. Intell. Transp. Syst.* **2020**, *23*, 1121–1131. [CrossRef]
2. Kukkala, V.K.; Tunnell, J.; Pasricha, S.; Bradley, T. Advanced driver-assistance systems: A path toward autonomous vehicles. *IEEE Consum. Electron. Mag.* **2018**, *7*, 18–25. [CrossRef]
3. Nandi, D.; Saif, A.S.; Prottoy, P.; Zubair, K.M.; Shubho, S.A. Traffic sign detection based on color segmentation of obscure image candidates: A comprehensive study. *Int. J. Mod. Educ. Comput. Sci.* **2018**, *10*, 35. [CrossRef]
4. Zaklouta, F.; Stanciulescu, B. Real-time traffic sign recognition in three stages. *Robot. Auton. Syst.* **2014**, *62*, 16–24. [CrossRef]
5. Vitabile, S.; Pollaccia, G.; Pilato, G.; Sorbello, F. Road signs recognition using a dynamic pixel aggregation technique in the HSV color space. In Proceedings of the Proceedings 11th International Conference on Image Analysis and Processing, Palermo, Italy, 26–28 September 2001; pp. 572–577.

6. Yakimov, P.; Fursov, V. Traffic signs detection and tracking using modified hough transform. In Proceedings of the 2015 12th International Joint Conference on e-Business and Telecommunications (ICETE), Colmar, France, 20–22 July 2015; Volume 5, pp. 22–28.
7. Balali, V.; Jahangiri, A.; Machiani, S.G. Multi-class US traffic signs 3D recognition and localization via image-based point cloud model using color candidate extraction and texture-based recognition. *Adv. Eng. Inform.* **2017**, *32*, 263–274. [CrossRef]
8. Zhang, J.; Xie, Z.; Sun, J.; Zou, X.; Wang, J. A cascaded R-CNN with multiscale attention and imbalanced samples for traffic sign detection. *IEEE Access* **2020**, *8*, 29742–29754. [CrossRef]
9. Gao, B.; Jiang, Z.; zhang, J. Traffic Sign Detection based on SSD. In Proceedings of the 2019 4th International Conference on Automation, Control and Robotics Engineering, Shenzhen, China, 19–21 July 2019.
10. Ren, S.; He, K.; Girshick, R.; Sun, J. Faster r-cnn: Towards real-time object detection with region proposal networks. *Adv. Neural Inf. Process. Syst.* **2015**, *28*. [CrossRef] [PubMed]
11. Qian, R.; Liu, Q.; Yue, Y.; Coenen, F.; Zhang, B. Road surface traffic sign detection with hybrid region proposal and fast R-CNN. In Proceedings of the 2016 12th International Conference on Natural Computation, Fuzzy Systems and Knowledge Discovery (ICNC-FSKD), Changsha, China, 13–15 August 2016; pp. 555–559.
12. Zuo, Z.; Yu, K.; Zhou, Q.; Wang, X.; Li, T. Traffic signs detection based on faster r-cnn. In Proceedings of the 2017 IEEE 37th International Conference on Distributed Computing Systems Workshops (ICDCSW), Atlanta, GA, USA, 5–8 June 2017; pp. 286–288.
13. Liu, W.; Anguelov, D.; Erhan, D.; Szegedy, C.; Reed, S.; Fu, C.Y.; Berg, A.C. Ssd: Single shot multibox detector. In Proceedings of the Computer Vision–ECCV 2016: 14th European Conference, Amsterdam, The Netherlands, 11–14 October 2016; pp. 21–37.
14. Lin, T.Y.; Goyal, P.; Girshick, R.; He, K.; Dollár, P. Focal loss for dense object detection. In Proceedings of the IEEE International Conference on Computer Vision, Venice, Italy, 22–29 October 2017; pp. 2980–2988.
15. Redmon, J.; Farhadi, A. YOLO9000: Better, faster, stronger. In Proceedings of the IEEE Conference on Computer Vision and Pattern Recognition, Honolulu, HI, USA, 21–26 July 2017; pp. 7263–7271.
16. Redmon, J.; Farhadi, A. Yolov3: An incremental improvement. *arXiv* **2018**, arXiv:1804.02767.
17. Bochkovskiy, A.; Wang, C.Y.; Liao, H.Y.M. Yolov4: Optimal speed and accuracy of object detection. *arXiv* **2020**, arXiv:2004.10934.
18. Vaswani, A.; Shazeer, N.; Parmar, N.; Uszkoreit, J.; Jones, L.; Gomez, A.N.; Kaiser, Ł.; Polosukhin, I. Attention is all you need. *arXiv* **2017**, arXiv:1706.03762.
19. Dosovitskiy, A.; Beyer, L.; Kolesnikov, A.; Weissenborn, D.; Zhai, X.; Unterthiner, T.; Dehghani, M.; Minderer, M.; Heigold, G.; Gelly, S.; et al. An image is worth 16x16 words: Transformers for image recognition at scale. *arXiv* **2020**, arXiv:2010.11929.
20. Cai, H.; Gan, C.; Han, S. EfficientViT: Enhanced Linear Attention for High-Resolution Low-Computation Visual Recognition. *arXiv* **2022**, arXiv:2205.14756.
21. Woo, S.; Park, J.; Lee, J.Y.; Kweon, I.S. Cbam: Convolutional block attention module. In Proceedings of the European Conference on Computer Vision (ECCV), Munich, Germany, 8–14 September 2018; pp. 3–19.
22. Hou, Q.; Zhou, D.; Feng, J. Coordinate attention for efficient mobile network design. In Proceedings of the IEEE/CVF Conference on Computer Vision and Pattern Recognition, Nashville, TN, USA, 20–25 June 2021; pp. 13713–13722.
23. Yu, J.; Jiang, Y.; Wang, Z.; Cao, Z.; Huang, T. Unitbox: An advanced object detection network. In Proceedings of the 24th ACM International Conference on Multimedia, Amsterdam, The Netherlands, 15–19 October 2016; pp. 516–520.
24. Rezatofighi, H.; Tsoi, N.; Gwak, J.; Sadeghian, A.; Reid, I.; Savarese, S. Generalized intersection over union: A metric and a loss for bounding box regression. In Proceedings of the IEEE/CVF Conference on Computer Vision and Pattern Recognition, Long Beach, CA, USA, 15–20 June 2019; pp. 658–666.
25. Zheng, Z.; Wang, P.; Liu, W.; Li, J.; Ye, R.; Ren, D. Distance-IoU loss: Faster and better learning for bounding box regression. In Proceedings of the AAAI Conference on Artificial Intelligence, New York, NY, USA, 7–12 February 2020; Volume 34, pp. 12993–13000.
26. Zhang, Y.F.; Ren, W.; Zhang, Z.; Jia, Z.; Wang, L.; Tan, T. Focal and efficient IOU loss for accurate bounding box regression. *Neurocomputing* **2022**, *506*, 146–157. [CrossRef]
27. Gevorgyan, Z. SIoU loss: More powerful learning for bounding box regression. *arXiv* **2022**, arXiv:2205.12740.
28. Tong, Z.; Chen, Y.; Xu, Z.; Yu, R. Wise-IoU: Bounding Box Regression Loss with Dynamic Focusing Mechanism. *arXiv* **2023**, arXiv:2301.10051.
29. Zhu, Z.; Liang, D.; Zhang, S.; Huang, X.; Li, B.; Hu, S. Traffic-sign detection and classification in the wild. In Proceedings of the IEEE Conference on Computer Vision and Pattern Recognition, Las Vegas, NV, USA, 27–30 June 2016; pp. 2110–2118.
30. Liu, H.; Zhou, K.; Zhang, Y.; Zhang, Y. ETSR-YOLO: An improved multi-scale traffic sign detection algorithm based on YOLOv5. *PLoS ONE* **2023**, *18*, e0295807. [CrossRef] [PubMed]
31. Chu, J.; Zhang, C.; Yan, M.; Zhang, H.; Ge, T. TRD-YOLO: A real-time, high-performance small traffic sign detection algorithm. *Sensors* **2023**, *23*, 3871. [CrossRef] [PubMed]
32. Zhang, L.J.; Fang, J.J.; Liu, Y.X.; Feng Le, H.; Rao, Z.Q.; Zhao, J.X. CR-YOLOv8: Multiscale object detection in traffic sign images. *IEEE Access* **2023**, *12*, 219–228. [CrossRef]

Disclaimer/Publisher's Note: The statements, opinions and data contained in all publications are solely those of the individual author(s) and contributor(s) and not of MDPI and/or the editor(s). MDPI and/or the editor(s) disclaim responsibility for any injury to people or property resulting from any ideas, methods, instructions or products referred to in the content.

Article

Facial Beauty Prediction Combined with Multi-Task Learning of Adaptive Sharing Policy and Attentional Feature Fusion

Junying Gan *, Heng Luo, Junling Xiong, Xiaoshan Xie, Huicong Li and Jianqiang Liu

Faculty of Intelligent Manufacturing, Wuyi University, Jiangmen 529020, China; 2112104068@wyu.edu.cn (H.L.); 2112204092@wyu.edu.cn (J.X.); xiaoshanxie.xsx@gmail.com (X.X.); 2112204010@wyu.edu.cn (H.L.); liu.geigei0203@gmail.com (J.L.)
* Correspondence: junyinggan@163.com

Abstract: Facial beauty prediction (FBP) is a leading research subject in the field of artificial intelligence (AI), in which computers make facial beauty judgments and predictions similar to those of humans. At present, the methods are mainly based on deep neural networks. However, there still exist some problems such as insufficient label information and overfitting. Multi-task learning uses label information from multiple databases, which increases the utilization of label information and enhances the feature extraction ability of the network. Attentional feature fusion (AFF) combines semantic information and introduces an attention mechanism to reduce the risk of overfitting. In this study, the multi-task learning of an adaptive sharing policy combined with AFF is presented based on the adaptive sharing (AdaShare) network in FBP. First, an adaptive sharing policy is added to multi-task learning with ResNet18 as the backbone network. Second, the AFF is introduced at the short skip connections of the network. The proposed method improves the accuracy of FBP by solving the problems of insufficient label information and overfitting issues. The experimental results based on the large-scale Asia facial beauty database (LSAFBD) and SCUT-FBP5500 databases show that the proposed method outperforms the single-database single-task baseline and can be applied extensively in image classification and other fields.

Keywords: attentional feature fusion; facial beauty prediction; image classification; multi-task learning

Citation: Gan, J.; Luo, H.; Xiong, J.; Xie, X.; Li, H.; Liu, J. Facial Beauty Prediction Combined with Multi-Task Learning of Adaptive Sharing Policy and Attentional Feature Fusion. *Electronics* **2024**, *13*, 179. https://doi.org/10.3390/electronics13010179

Academic Editor: Eva Cernadas

Received: 21 November 2023
Revised: 23 December 2023
Accepted: 26 December 2023
Published: 30 December 2023

Copyright: © 2023 by the authors. Licensee MDPI, Basel, Switzerland. This article is an open access article distributed under the terms and conditions of the Creative Commons Attribution (CC BY) license (https://creativecommons.org/licenses/by/4.0/).

1. Introduction

Facial beauty prediction (FBP) is a leading research subject in the field of artificial intelligence (AI), in which computers make facial beauty judgments and predictions similar to those of humans. With the development of AI, the applications of FBP are constantly expanding, including virtual makeup, plastic surgery, portrait photography and other fields. Research on FBP not only helps people understand and interpret beauty more scientifically and objectively but also promotes the development of AI, which has important significance. Currently, deep learning methods are generally used in FBP, which requires large amounts of label information. Existing facial beauty databases have certain issues, such as insufficient label information. Solving the aforementioned issue has become a popular subject in the field of FBP research. At present, some progress has been made in FBP research [1–7]. In [1], a novel personalized FBP approach based on meta-learning was designed to apply in some small databases. In [2], a self-correcting noise labels method was proposed. It can automatically select clean samples for learning and can make full use of all data to reduce the negative impact of noise labels. In [3], a fusion model of pseudolabel and cross-network was applied to solve the problems of weak generalization ability and insufficient label information in FBP. In [4], an innovative method of broad learning fused with transfer learning was applied in FBP, which received better performance in prediction accuracy and training speed. In [5], an adaptive transformer with global and local multihead self-attention was proposed for FBP, which achieved better performance on several datasets of different scales. In [6], a dynamic convolution vision transformer named FBPFormer was proposed which aims to focus on both local and global facial beauty features. Furthermore, an instance-level dynamic exponential loss function was designed to adjust the optimization objectives of the model dynamically. In [7], a novel method was proposed to improve the facial beauty feature extraction ability of CNNs, in which generative adversarial networks (GAN) were used to generate facial data.

Although the research above improved the accuracy of FBP, it did not efficiently solve the problems of insufficient label information and overfitting. Multi-task learning improves the generalization ability of a network by training related tasks containing domain-specific information. In the era of deep learning, multi-task learning has been transformed into designing networks that can learn shared representations from the label information of multiple tasks. Compared with a single-task learning network, a multi-task learning network has greater advantages. For example, related tasks can share complementary information or act as regularizers, thereby improving the network performance. FBP based on multi-task learning has been extensively studied in recent years [8,9]. In [8], a neural architecture search (NAS) was applied to FBP to automatically determine the backbone network for multi-task learning. Moreover, a new preprocessing method was introduced to enhance the diversity of data and a nonlocal spatial attention module was proposed which further improved the performance of the network on the FBP task. By combining ResneXt-50 and Inception-v3, the dual-branch network can extract more facial beauty features and balance performance and parameter quantity [9]. Simultaneously, adaptive and dynamic loss functions are introduced.

At present, multi-task learning networks can be generally divided into hard parameter sharing and soft parameter sharing networks. In the hard parameter sharing network, the parameters are divided into a shared parameter and a task-specific parameter, and a hard parameter sharing network usually consists of several shared network layers and a task-specific network layer. In the soft parameter sharing network, each task has a separate feature extraction layer, with L_2-norm or trace norms to constrain the parameters of the shared feature extraction layer. However, these two kinds of multi-task learning mostly set up the network layer statically. The method for adaptively training the network has become one of the key issues of multi-task learning.

Adaptive training can be divided into three key methods. First, the optimal backbone network is adaptively obtained according to different tasks through the NAS. Auto-multi-task learning (AutoMTL) proposed an automatic and efficient multi-task learning network framework for vision tasks, which takes a backbone network and a set of tasks to be learned as input and automatically generates a high-precision multi-task learning model [10]. Although NAS can automatically generate a high-precision multi-task learning network, it requires high computing equipment and a long calculation time. Second, in the process of parameter backpropagation for network optimization, adaptive task weights are learned based on the importance of different tasks. A Bayesian task weight learner is used to adjust the task weights and back-propagate the joint loss of different tasks [11]. The adaptive weight learning method based on the verification loss trend can measure the importance of different tasks and adjust the weights of different tasks [12]. In [13], a new training algorithm was proposed to utilize the similarity between tasks to learn the task relationship coefficients and neural network parameters. Although the optimization algorithm consumed fewer resources, the improvement in the network performance was limited. Finally, the network layer parameters that can be shared across tasks are determined. In adaptive sharing (AdaShare) networks, researchers have investigated sharing policies between tasks to achieve the highest accuracy and improve resource efficiency [14]. However, in an AdaShare network, the atrous spatial pyramid pooling (ASPP) method loses local information when extracting multiscale information from images. Attentional feature fusion (AFF) combines local and global information with semantic information at different levels [15].

There were differences in the distributions of the means and variances in the different databases. Shared batch normalization (BN) layers tend to exhibit poor network performance. A dataset-aware block (DAB) was applied to capture the homogeneous convolutional representations and heterogeneous statistics across different datasets, where the dataset alternation training (DAT) mechanism was utilized to facilitate the optimization process [16]. Reference [17] proposed a different training mechanism. Each batch of training data consisted of data randomly selected from all the datasets for batch loss calculation.

The chief contributions of this study are summarized as follows:

- We extend the AdaShare network, introduce DAB to solve the issue of distribution differences between different databases in multi-task learning on FBP and apply the network in various databases.
- We propose multi-task learning of an adaptive sharing policy combined with AFF to solve the issue of insufficient label information and overfitting for FBP, in which the receptive field is expanded, and more semantic information is obtained from the images.
- The experimental results show that multi-task learning of the adaptive sharing policy combined with AFF outperforms the baseline model and the other method on FBP.

2. Methods

2.1. Network Model

A schematic diagram of the network model structure is shown in Figure 1, including the pre-trained network module, multi-task learning of the adaptive sharing policy combined with the AFF and classification module. The pre-training network module transfers the parameters to multi-task learning of the adaptive sharing policy combined with the AFF module through the ResNet18 [18] network trained by the ImageNet datasets. Multi-task learning of adaptive sharing policy combined with the AFF module contains multi-task learning of adaptive sharing policy with ResNet18 as the backbone network plus the AFF introduced at the short-skip connection. It primarily performs sharing policy learning, image feature extraction, and fusion. The classification module includes an average pooling layer, a fully connected layer, a Dropout [19] layer and a softmax classifier. Database1 and database2 are two different databases, task1 and task2 are two different tasks. First, the parameters of the pretrained network module are transferred to the multi-task learning of the adaptive sharing policy combined with the AFF module. Second, the images from database1 and database2 are simultaneously entered into the multi-task learning of the adaptive sharing policy combined with the AFF module. Meanwhile, the sharing policies and image features of task1 and task2 are learned from the module. Finally, the features are entered into the classification module, in which the categories of task1 and task2 are the outputs.

2.2. Multi-Task Learning of Adaptive Sharing Policy Combined with AFF Module

The multi-task learning of the adaptive sharing policy combined with the AFF module was extended with ResNet18 as the backbone network; its schematic is shown in Figure 2. Among them, the multi-task learning of the adaptive sharing policy combined with the AFF module contains four-layer blocks, and each layer block is composed of four BasicBlock structures. First, the images from database1 and database2 are entered into the network simultaneously. In the convolution, ReLU, and max-pooling layers, the network parameters of the two tasks are shared. Second, the image features must pass through four-layer blocks. The BasicBlock structure of each layer block includes an adaptive sharing policy and AFF. A schematic of the layered block structure is shown in Figure 3, and the BasicBlock structure is shown in Figure 4. Finally, the features produced by layer4 are entered into the classification module and the classification results of task1 and task2 are produced.

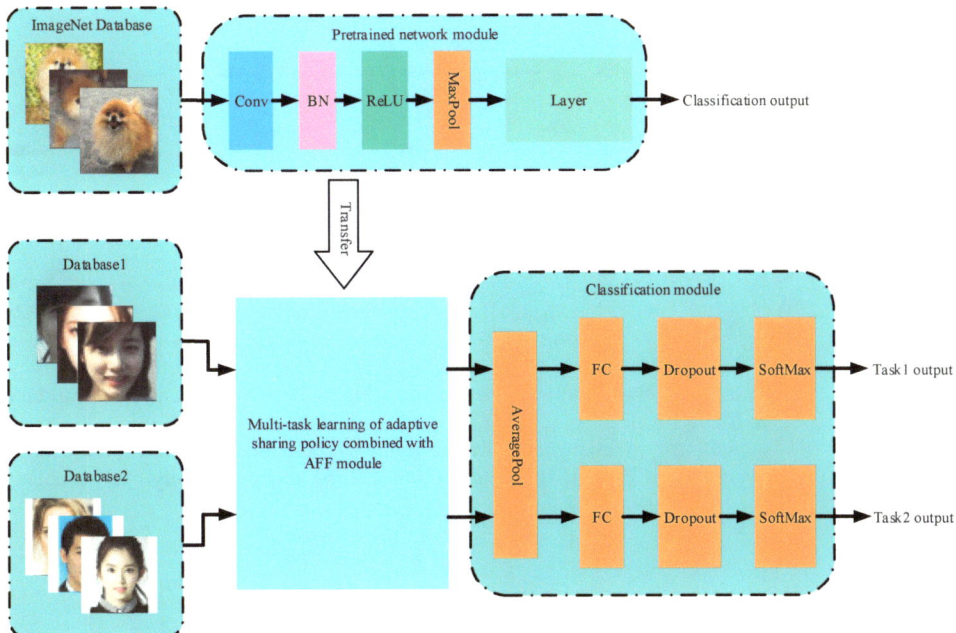

Figure 1. Schematic diagram of network model structure.

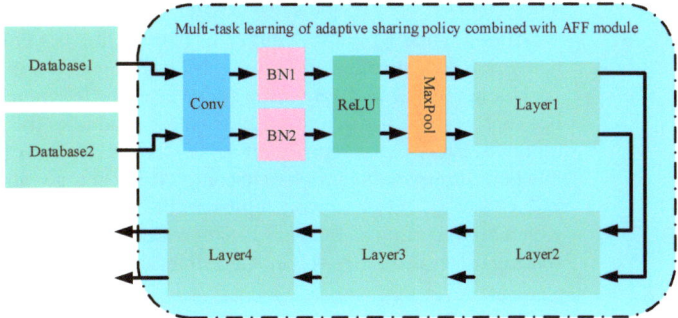

Figure 2. Schematic structure of multi-task learning of adaptive sharing policy combined with AFF module.

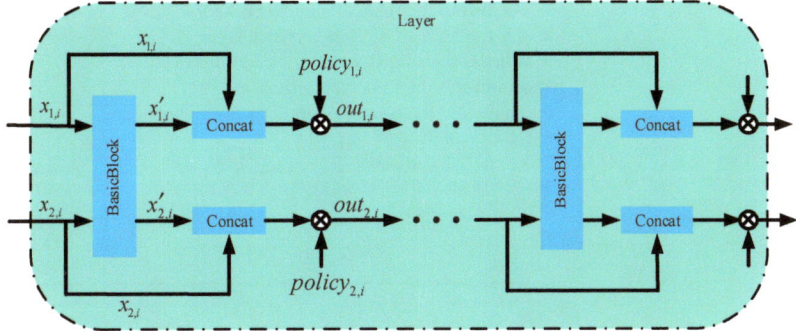

Figure 3. Schematic diagram of layer block structure.

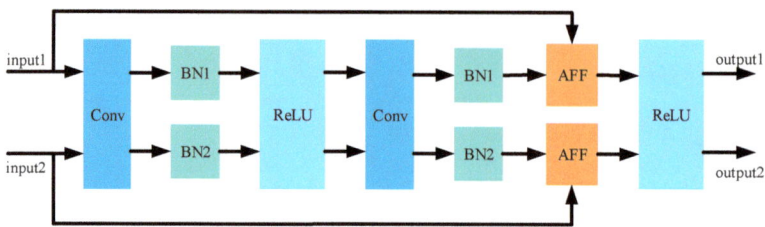

Figure 4. Schematic diagram of BasicBlock structure.

In Figure 3, $x_{1,i}, x'_{1,i}, out_{1,i}, policy_{1,i}$ are the variables of task1 in the $i-\text{th}(2 < i < 17)$ layer network. Among them, $x_{1,i}, x'_{1,i}$ are feature maps with a resolution of $m \times n$ and a channel number of l, that is $x_{1,i}, x'_{1,i} \in \mathbb{R}^{m \times n \times l}$. $policy_{1,i}$ represents the sharing policy of task1 on the $i-\text{th}$ layer network. In Figure 3, the specific process can be described as follows:

First, $x_{1,i}$ is changed into $x'_{1,i}$ through the BasicBlock structure. At the same time, $x_{1,i}$ concatenates $x'_{1,i}$ and its result is multiplied by $policy_{1,i}$. Finally, $out_{1,i}$ is obtained. $out_{1,i}$ can be expressed as follows:

$$out_{1,i} = [x'_{1,i}\ x_{1,i}] \cdot policy_{1,i} = \\ \begin{cases} x'_{1,i} \cdot 0 + x_{1,i} \cdot 1, \text{ when } policy_{1,i} = \begin{bmatrix} 0 \\ 1 \end{bmatrix} \\ x'_{1,i} \cdot 1 + x_{1,i} \cdot 0, \text{ when } policy_{1,i} = \begin{bmatrix} 1 \\ 0 \end{bmatrix} \end{cases} \quad (1)$$

where $policy_{1,i} = [0\ 1]^T$ indicates that the sharing policy of task1 in the $i-\text{th}$ layer network is skipped. $policy_{1,i} = [1\ 0]^T$ indicates that the sharing policy of task1 in the $i-\text{th}$ layer network is implemented. The multi-task learning of adaptive sharing policy aims to learn the sharing policy and network weights from the loss function through backpropagation. But each $policy_{1,i}$ is discrete and non-differentiable so the gradient of the entire network cannot be backpropagated. Therefore, the Gumbel Softmax [20] function is applied to solve this non-differentiable problem to complete backpropagation and update the parameters. $x_{2,i}, x'_{2,i}, x''_{2,i}, out_{2,i}, policy_{2,i}$ represent the variables of task2 in the i-th layer network, which are the same as the variables of task1 in the network. The details of the adaptive sharing policy are expressed in Algorithm 1.

Algorithm 1 Facial beauty prediction via adaptive sharing policy

---

Input: sample set x
Output: output set out
1: n is the number of layers in the backbone;
2: m is the number of blocks in each layer;
3: $policy$ is the adaptive policy of the current layer;
4: φ indicates the BasicBlock structure;
5: ϕ indicates the concatenation and multiplication;
6: for $i, i \leq n$ do
7:     for $j, j \leq m$ do
8:         Calculate $x' = \varphi(x)$
9:         Calculate $out = \phi(x, x', policy)$
10:     end
11: end

To improve the convergence speed of the network, a multi-stage training method is adopted during the training phase. Initially, the multi-task learning network shares all the parameters. As the number of training epochs increases, the deep network adopts a shared policy for training. In a deep convolutional network, the BN layer can be understood as a simplified whitening operation on the input value of each layer of the deep network. This whitening operation is significantly affected by the distribution of the databases. Therefore, to apply the label information of multiple databases and to solve the issue of distribution differences caused by different databases, DAB is introduced, which implies that different tasks will use different BN layers. Figure 4 shows a schematic of the improved BasicBlock structure proposed in this study, where input1 and input2 represent the Image features of database1 and database2 in Figure 2, and the tasks of each database use different BN layers. The AFF aims to extract features that are more relevant to the current task and fuse channel features at different scales.

2.3. Attentional Feature Fusion

The AFF module was introduced to fuse the semantic information of different network layers and generate the fusion weights for the mapping and residuals of the network [15]. Figure 5 shows a schematic of the AFF structure, where $b, r \in \mathbb{R}^{C \times H \times W}$ and C is the channels, H is the height, and W is the width. In ResNet [18], b is the mapping and r is the residual. Based on the multiscale channel attention module (MS-CAM), the AFF can be expressed as follows:

$$z = c' \otimes b \oplus (1 - c') \otimes r \tag{2}$$

where $z \in \mathbb{R}^{C \times H \times W}$ is the fusion feature of the $i-$th layer network, the $\otimes$ operation is the multiplication of each element, the $\oplus$ operation is the sum of each element, and $c' = \mathrm{MS}(c)$, $c = b \oplus r$, and $1 - c'$ is obtained from c' by passing it through the Diff operation. The output c' after the MS-CAM structure is a real number between 0 and 1, and $1 - c'$ is also a real number between 0 and 1. Therefore, the network can improve the feature extraction ability by learning the fusion weight of the mapping and residual, thereby improving the accuracy of the target task. Figure 6 shows a schematic of the MS-CAM structure.

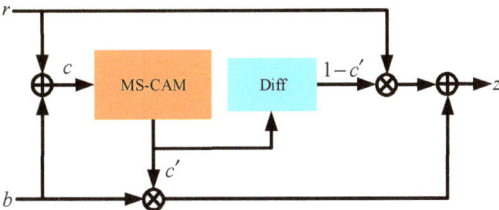

Figure 5. Schematic diagram of AFF structure.

In AFF, MS-CAM fuses local and global features in the attention mechanism, which not only assigns different weights to each channel but also gathers multi-scale feature context information. Thus, it improves the network's ability to extract the target task features. By aggregating multiscale contextual information along the channel dimension, MS-CAM can simultaneously emphasize global and local information [15]. Therefore, the MS-CAM was utilized as a multiscale feature extractor. The local information extractor can be computed as follows:

$$L(c) = B(\mathrm{PWConv}_2(\delta(B(\mathrm{PWConv}_1(c))))) \tag{3}$$

where PWConv_1 indicates that the channels of the input feature $c \in \mathbb{R}^{C \times H \times W}$ are reduced to the original $1/r$ by the point convolution of 1×1, B indicates the BN layer, δ indicates the ReLU activation layer, PWConv_2 indicates that the channels are restored to the original input channel by the point convolution of 1×1, and r is the channel-scaling ratio. The global information extractor can be represented as follows:

$$G(c) = B(\text{PWConv}_2(\delta(B(\text{PWConv}_1(A(c))))))\tag{4}$$

where $A(c)$ denotes the global average pooling layer. The final output c' can be calculated as follows:

$$c' = c \otimes \sigma(L(c) \oplus G(c))\tag{5}$$

where σ is the Sigmoid activation function. Therefore, a network with AFF not only fuses different semantic information but also introduces an attention mechanism that improves the feature extraction ability of the network, reduces the risk of overfitting, and improves the accuracy of the target task.

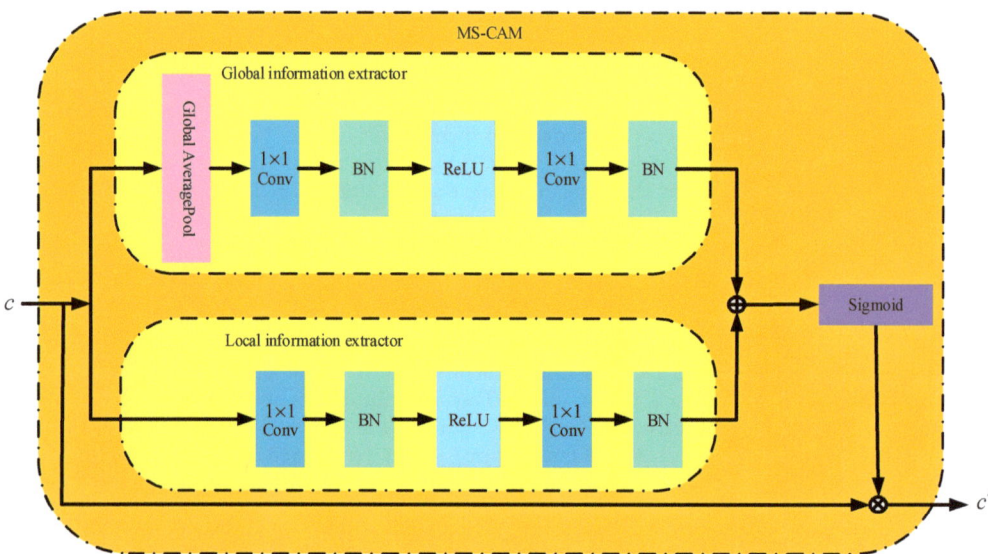

Figure 6. Schematic diagram of MS-CAM structure.

2.4. Loss Function

In this study, cross-entropy was adopted as the loss function for task1 and task2, which can be defined as follows:

$$L = \sum_{i=1}^{N} y_i * \log(p_i)\tag{6}$$

where N is the number of categories in task1 or task2, y_i is the label value of the $i-\text{th}$ category of the image, and p_i is the probability value of the image being predicted as the $i-\text{th}$ category. The total task loss function can be formalized as follows:

$$L_{\text{task}} = \lambda_1 L_1 + \lambda_2 L_2\tag{7}$$

where L_1 and L_2 represent the loss function value of task1 and task2, respectively; λ_1 and λ_2 represent the weight coefficient of task1 and task2, respectively. In multi-task learning, the weight ratio $\lambda_1 : \lambda_2$ of different tasks affects the accuracy of the target task.

3. Experiments and Analysis

3.1. Experimental Databases

3.1.1. LSAFBD Database

The authors established the LSAFBD database with 20,000 labeled facial images (including 10,000 male and 10,000 female facial images) and 80,000 unlabeled facial images, with a resolution of 144 × 144. It is divided into five categories, including "0", "1", "2", "3" and "4", which correspond to five attractiveness levels of facial beauty, with "0" being the lowest level and "4" being the highest level. This study primarily focused on experiments with 10,000 labeled female facial images from the LSAFBD database. The distribution of facial beauty labels in the LSAFBD database and some image samples in the LSAFBD database are shown in Figures 7 and 8, respectively.

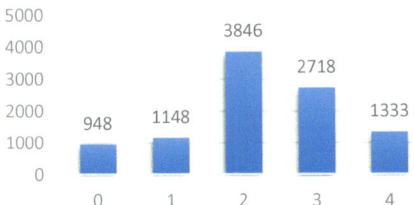

Figure 7. Distribution of facial beauty labels on LSAFBD.

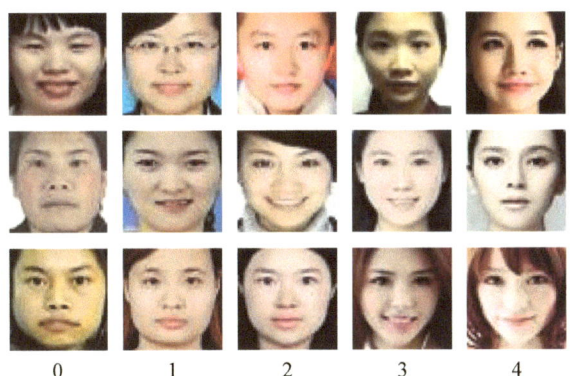

Figure 8. Facial images with different properties of LSAFBD.

3.1.2. SCUT-FBP5500 Database

The SCUT-FBP5500 database was established by the South China University of Technology and contains a total of 5,500 facial images with a resolution of 350 × 350. Each facial image contained various label information, including gender (male or female), race (Asian or White), and facial beauty. The facial beauty level of the SCUT-FBP5500 database is divided into five levels, namely "0", "1", "2", "3" and "4", which correspond to the five attractiveness levels of facial beauty, with "0" as the lowest grade, and "4" as the highest grade. The facial beauty grade of each image was given by 60 volunteers; therefore, this study takes the grade with the largest number of volunteers as the facial beauty grade of the image. The distribution of the facial beauty labels in the SCUT-FBP5500 database and some image samples of the SCUT-FBP5500 database are shown in Figures 9 and 10, respectively.

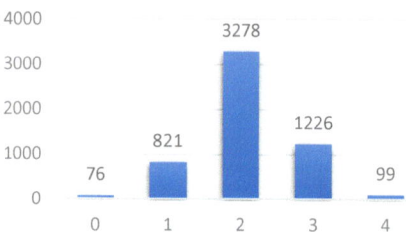

Figure 9. Distribution of facial beauty labels on SCUT-FBP5500.

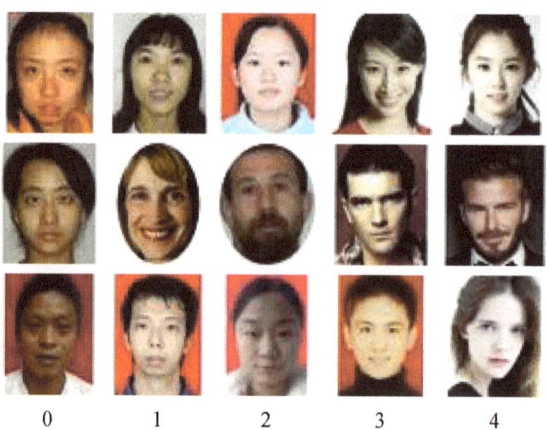

Figure 10. Facial images with different properties of SCUT-FBP5500.

3.2. Experimental Environment

Table 1 describes the experimental environment. In Figure 3, the variables $x_{1,i}$, $x'_{1,i}$, and $x''_{1,i}$ have a resolution of 56 × 56, the number of channels is 64, the task weight ratio $\lambda_1 : \lambda_2$ of the training phase is 1:0.6, the data batch size is 32, the initial learning rate is 0.001, and the optimizer is AdamW [21]. In this study, the accuracy (ACC) and F1 score were applied as the performance evaluation metric.

Table 1. Experimental environment configuration.

Environment	Parameters
Deep learning framework	Pytorch1.12.1
Operating system	Ubuntu20.04
Memory	64 G
Resolution $m \times n$	56 × 56
Channels l	64
Task weight ratio $\lambda_1 : \lambda_2$	1:0.6
Learning rate	0.001
Batch size	32
Optimizer	AdamW

The experimental setting in Figure 1, is shown in Table 2. Database1 and database2 represent the LSAFBD database and SCUT-FBP5500 database, respectively. Task1 and task2 represent the facial beauty prediction (FBP) and gender recognition (GR), respectively.

Table 2. Explanation of the experimental setting.

Experiment Settings	Explanation
Database1	LSAFBD
Database2	SCUT-FBP5500
Task1	FBP
Task2	GR

3.3. Comparison Experiment between the Proposed Method and the Baseline

3.3.1. Experiments Based on Different Databases

The experimental results of the proposed method and the baseline based on the LSAFBD database are shown in Tables 3–5. The ratio of the training, verification and testing set was 6:2:2, and the experiments included the training and testing phases. In the training phase, the facial beauty-labeled data from the LSAFBD database and gender-labeled data from the SCUT-FBP5500 database are used as an input of the network for the proposed method. In the testing phase, the proposed method was based on the testing set of the LSAFBD database for FBP. The baseline based on transfer learning was a single-database, single-task method with ResNet18 as the backbone network. In the training phase, the facial beauty-labeled data from the LSAFBD database are used as an input of the network of baseline. During the testing phase, the baseline was based on the testing set of the LSAFBD database for FBP.

Table 3. Experimental results based on LSAFBD (ACC(%), F1 score(%)).

Batch Size	Task	Method	Baseline without AFF ACC	Baseline without AFF F1 Score	Baseline with AFF ACC	Baseline with AFF F1 Score	Ours without AFF ACC	Ours without AFF F1 Score	Ours with AFF ACC	Ours with AFF F1 Score
32	FBP		58.01	56.51	59.52	57.70	59.12	57.72	**61.37**	**59.72**
16	FBP		58.02	56.53	59.77	57.76	59.02	57.62	**61.12**	**59.53**

Note: The bold is the optimal value.

Table 4. Experimental results of the proposed method based on LSAFBD (ACC(%), time (s), difference of ACC(%)).

Batch Size	Task	Method	Ours without AFF Training Time	Ours without AFF Training ACC	Ours without AFF Testing ACC	Ours without AFF Difference of ACC	Ours with AFF Training Time	Ours with AFF Training ACC	Ours with AFF Testing ACC	Ours with AFF Difference of ACC
32	FBP		2976.04	63.42	59.12	4.30%	3867.85	63.49	**61.37**	2.12%
16	FBP		3555.86	63.12	59.02	4.10%	4587.81	63.31	**61.12**	2.19%

Note: The bold is the optimal value.

Table 5. Experimental results of the baseline based on LSAFBD (ACC(%), time (s), difference of ACC(%)).

Batch Size	Task	Method	Baseline without AFF Training Time	Baseline without AFF Training ACC	Baseline without AFF Testing ACC	Baseline without AFF Difference of ACC	Baseline with AFF Training Time	Baseline with AFF Training ACC	Baseline with AFF Testing ACC	Baseline with AFF Difference of ACC
32	FBP		637.23	65.03	58.01	7.02%	853.19	61.61	59.52	2.09%
16	FBP		800.91	65.28	58.02	7.26%	1154.07	61.72	59.77	1.95%

It can be observed from Table 3 that with AFF, the accuracy of the FBP in the proposed method was 61.37%, which was 1.85% higher than the baseline accuracy of 59.52% and the F1 score of the FBP in the proposed method was 59.72%, which was 2.02% higher than the baseline F1 score of 57.70. Without AFF when the batch size was 32, the accuracy of the FBP in the proposed method was 59.12%, which was 1.11% higher than the baseline accuracy of 58.01% and the F1 score of the FBP in the proposed method was 57.72%, which was 1.21% higher than the baseline F1 score of 56.51%. The experimental results showed that the proposed multi-task learning of the adaptive sharing policy outperformed the baseline. In the current method, the accuracy of FBP with AFF was 61.37%, which was 2.25% higher than that without AFF (59.12%) and the F1 score of FBP with AFF was 59.72%, which was 2.00% higher than that without AFF (57.72%). At baseline, the accuracy of FBP with AFF was 59.52%, which was 1.51% higher than the accuracy of 58.01% and the F1 score of FBP with AFF was 57.70%, which was 1.19% higher than the F1 score of 56.51%. The experimental results showed that AFF can improve the network's ability to extract facial beauty features, thereby improving the accuracy of FBP. When the batch size was 16, the proposed method also achieved better performance than the baseline.

It can be observed from Table 4 to Table 5 that when the batch size was 32, the difference between the training accuracy and testing accuracy of the proposed method with AFF was 2.12%, which is 2.18% lower than that of the proposed method without AFF of 4.30%. The difference between the training accuracy and testing accuracy of the baseline with AFF was 2.09%, which was 4.93% lower than that of the baseline without AFF of 7.02%. The experimental results showed that the AFF truly reduces the risk of overfitting and improves the feature extraction capability of the network. The improvement also can be seen when the batch size was 16.

Table 6 shows the experimental results of the proposed method and the baseline method based on the SCUT-FBP5500 database, respectively. In the training phase, the facial beauty-labeled and gender-labeled data from the training set are used as an input of the network of the proposed method simultaneously. In the testing phase, the proposed method was based on a testing set for FBP and GR. In the training phase, the facial beauty-labeled data and gender-labeled data from the training set are used as an input of the network of baseline, respectively. In the testing phase, the baseline implemented FBP and GR, respectively, based on the testing set.

Table 6. Experimental results based on SCUT-FBP5500 (ACC(%), F1 score(%)).

Batch Size	Task	Method	Baseline without AFF		Baseline with AFF		Ours without AFF		Ours with AFF	
			ACC	F1 Score	ACC	F1 Score	ACC	F1 Score	ACC	F1 Score
32	FBP		73.41	70.64	74.50	71.72	74.23	72.02	75.41	73.82
	GR		98.27	98.26	98.55	98.55	96.52	96.52	97.09	97.09
16	FBP		73.67	70.13	74.61	71.91	73.95	71.91	75.13	73.27
	GR		98.45	98.45	98.73	98.73	96.43	96.40	96.89	96.88

It can be observed from Table 6 that with AFF, the FBP accuracy of the proposed method was 75.41%, which was 0.91% higher than the baseline accuracy of 74.50% and the F1 score was 73.82%, which was 1.1% higher than the baseline F1 score of 71.72%. Without AFF when the batch size was 32, the accuracy of the FBP in the proposed method was 74.23%, which was 0.82% higher than the baseline accuracy of 73.41% and the F1 score was 72.02%, which was 1.38% higher than the baseline F1 score of 70.64. The experimental results showed that the proposed multi-task learning of the adaptive sharing policy outperformed the baseline. In the current method, the accuracy of FBP with AFF was 75.41%, which was 1.18% higher than the accuracy of 74.23% without AFF and the F1 score of FBP with AFF was 73.82%, which was 1.8% higher than the F1 score of 72.02% without AFF. The accuracy of the GR with AFF was 97.09%, which was 0.57% higher than the accuracy of 96.52% and the F1 score of the GR with AFF was 97.09%, which was 0.57% higher than the F1 score of 96.52%. At baseline, the accuracy of FBP with AFF was 74.50%, which was 1.09% higher than the accuracy of 73.41% without AFF, and the F1 score of FBP with AFF was 71.72%, which was 1.08% higher than the F1 score of 70.64. The accuracy of GR with AFF was 98.55%, which was 0.28% higher than the accuracy of 98.27% without AFF and the F1 score of GR with AFF was 98.55%, which was 0.29% higher than the F1 score of 98.26%. The experimental results showed that AFF can improve the network's ability to extract facial beauty and gender features, thereby improving the accuracy of FBP in both the proposed method and the baseline. When the batch size was 16, the proposed method also achieved better performance than the baseline.

It can be observed from Table 7 to Table 8 that when the batch size was 32, the difference between FBP training accuracy and FBP testing accuracy of the proposed method with AFF was 1.43%, which was 2.02% lower than that of the proposed method without AFF of 3.45%. The difference between FBP training accuracy and FBP testing accuracy of the baseline with AFF was 0.61%, which was 6.45% lower than that of the baseline without AFF of 7.06%. The experimental results showed that the AFF truly reduces the risk of overfitting and improves the feature extraction capability of the network. The improvement also can be seen when the batch size was 16.

Table 7. Experimental results of the proposed method based on SCUT-FBP5500 (ACC(%), time (s), difference of ACC(%)).

Batch Size	Task	Method	Ours without AFF				Ours with AFF			
			Training Time	Training ACC	Testing ACC	Difference of ACC	Training Time	Training ACC	Testing ACC	Difference of ACC
32	FBP		1587.81	77.68	74.23	3.45	2073.85	76.84	75.41	1.43
	GR			97.36	96.52	0.84		97.63	97.09	0.54
16	FBP		1894.58	77.49	73.95	3.54	3076.09	76.44	75.13	1.31
	GR			97.13	96.43	0.70		97.50	96.89	0.61

Table 8. Experimental results of the baseline based on SCUT-FBP5500 (ACC(%), time (s), difference of ACC(%)).

Batch Size	Task	Method	Baseline without AFF				Baseline with AFF			
			Training Time	Training ACC	Testing ACC	Difference of ACC	Training Time	Training ACC	Testing ACC	Difference of ACC
32	FBP		372.69	80.47	73.41	7.06	482.48	75.11	74.50	0.61
	GR		362.23	98.49	98.27	0.22	484.57	98.64	98.55	0.09
16	FBP		442.85	79.49	73.67	5.82	653.17	75.24	74.61	0.63
	GR		443.31	98.61	98.45	0.16	619.89	98.86	98.73	0.13

From the experimental results, it is observed that in FBP multi-task learning of the adaptive sharing policy combined with AFF achieved the best results on the two different databases. The proposed method not only effectively utilizes GR to improve the network's ability to extract facial beauty features, but also reduces the risk of overfitting through attention feature fusion, thereby improving the accuracy of FBP. From the experimental results in Table 6, it can be observed that the accuracy of the proposed method is lower than that of the baseline method in terms of the GR. This is because the proposed method improves the accuracy of FBP through GR. Therefore, when the task weight ratio $\lambda_1 : \lambda_2$ was 1:0.6, the network learned more facial beauty features, resulting in a lower extraction ability for gender features than the baseline. From Tables 4, 5, 7 and 8, it can be observed that the proposed method requires more time for training. This is because the proposed method has a more complex network and more data to calculate.

3.3.2. Experiments with Different Weight Ratios Based on Different Databases

To study the effect of the weight ratio $\lambda_1 : \lambda_2$ on different tasks in FBP, the weight ratios of the three groups of FBP and GR were explored. The experimental results for different weight ratios based on the LSAFBD database are shown in Table 9. At a weight ratio of 1:0.6, FBP achieved an accuracy of 61.37%, surpassing the 58.91% by 2.46% at a weight ratio of 1:0.7, and exceeding the 58.62% by 2.75% at a weight ratio of 1:0.5. At a weight ratio of 1:0.6, FBP achieved an F1 score of 59.72%, surpassing the 56.94% by 2.78% at a weight ratio of 1:0.7, and exceeding the 56.70% by 3.02% at a weight ratio of 1:0.5. The experimental results showed that different weight ratios have a significant influence on the

FBP. When the weight ratio was 1:0.6, the proposed method achieved the best performance on the LSAFBD database.

Table 9. Different weight ratios of the experimental results based on LSAFBD (ACC(%), F1 score(%)).

Batch Size	Task	$\lambda_1:\lambda_2$ 1:0.7		1:0.6		1:0.5	
		ACC	F1 Score	ACC	F1 Score	ACC	F1 Score
32	FBP	58.91	56.94	**61.37**	**59.72**	58.62	56.70
16	FBP	58.88	56.86	**61.12**	**59.53**	58.53	56.37

Note: The bold is the optimal value.

The experimental results for different weight ratios based on the SCUT-FBP5500 database of the proposed method are shown in Table 10. When the weight ratio was 1:0.6, the accuracy of the FBP was 75.41%, which was 1.76% higher than 73.65% when the weight ratio was 1:0.7, and 1.83% higher than 73.58% when the weight ratio was 1:0.5. When the weight ratio was 1:0.7, the accuracy of the GR was 97.18%, which was 0.09% higher than 97.09% when the weight ratio was 1:0.6, and 0.73% higher than 96.45% when the weight ratio was 1:0.5. When the weight ratio was 1:0.6, the F1 score of the FBP was 73.82, which was 2.40% higher than 71.42 when the weight ratio was 1:0.7, and 2.42% higher than 71.40% when the weight ratio was 1:0.5. When the weight ratio was 1:0.7, the F1 score of the GR was 97.18%, which was 0.09% higher than 97.09% when the weight ratio was 1:0.6, and 0.77% higher than 96.41% when the weight ratio was 1:0.5. The experimental results showed that different weight ratios have a significant influence on the FBP. When the weight ratio was 1:0.6, the proposed method achieved the best performance on the SCUT-FBP5500 database.

Table 10. Different weight ratios of the experimental results based on SCUT-FBP5500 (ACC(%), F1 score(%)).

Batch Size	Task	$\lambda_1:\lambda_2$ 1:0.7		1:0.6		1:0.5	
		ACC	F1 Score	ACC	F1 Score	ACC	F1 Score
32	FBP	73.65	71.42	75.41	73.82	73.58	71.40
	GR	97.18	97.18	97.09	97.09	96.45	96.44
16	FBP	73.27	71.67	75.13	73.27	73.41	70.67
	GR	97.15	97.14	96.89	96.88	96.35	96.31

From the experimental results, it is observed that when the weight ratio is 1:0.6, the FBP accuracy of the proposed method based on two different databases reaches the highest value in the existing experiments. When the weight ratio was 1:0.7, the gender features learned by the network increased and the facial beauty features decreased, resulting in a slight improvement in the accuracy of the FBP compared with the single-task network. When the weight ratio was 1:0.5, the gender features learned by the network were insufficient, and compared with the single-task network, it could only slightly improve the accuracy of the FBP.

3.4. Comparison Experiments between the Proposed Method and Other Models

In this section, the proposed method is compared with other models based on the LSAFBD database and SCUT-FBP5500 databases. The experimental results for the proposed method and other models are shown in Table 11. Based on the LSAFBD database, during the training phase, the facial beauty-labeled data from the LSAFBD database and the gender-labeled data from the SCUT-FBP5500 database are used as an input of the network of the proposed method simultaneously. In the testing phase, the proposed method was based on the testing set of the LSAFBD database for FBP. In the training phase, the facial beauty-labeled data from the LSAFBD database are used as an input of the other models. In the testing phase, the other models were based on the testing set of the LSAFBD database for the FBP.

Table 11. Experimental results compared with other models (ACC(%)).

Method	Task	LSAFBD FBP	SCUT-FBP5500 FBP
GoogleNet [22]		56.06	72.77
MobileNetV2 [23]		50.70	72.13
MobileNetV3 [24]		52.35	72.31
ShuffleNetV2 [25]		59.97	75.14
DenseNet [26]		59.32	73.95
EfficientNet [27]		59.02	75.04
RegNet [28]		59.02	74.68
ConvNeXt [29]		60.67	75.32
Proposed method		**61.37**	**75.41**

Note: The bold is the optimal value.

Based on the SCUT-FBP5500 database, in the training phase, facial beauty labeled data and gender labeled data of the SCUT-FBP5500 database are used as an input of the network of the proposed method simultaneously. During the testing phase, the proposed method was based on the testing set of the SCUT-FBP5500 database for FBP. In the training phase, the facial beauty-labeled data from the SCUT-FBP5500 database are used as an input for the other models. During the testing phase, the other models were based on the testing set of the SCUT-FBP5500 database for FBP.

In Table 1, GoogleNet [22] improved the utilization of computing resources inside the network through the inception structure. MobileNetV2 [23] introduced a residual structure that ascended and descended the dimensions to enhance the propagation of gradients and significantly reduce the memory footprint required during inference. MobileNetV3 [24] added a lightweight attention model Squeeze Excitation (SE) structure based on MobileNetV2. ShuffleNetV2[25] proposed that the ratio of the input feature matrix channel to the output matrix channel should be equal to or close to one. The input to each network layer in DenseNet [26] is a concatenation of all previous network outputs. EfficientNet [27] was proposed to keep the channels of features, depth of the network model, and image resolution small, which can create a competitive and computationally efficient CNN model. RegNet [28] aims to determine the optimal search space. Using the search space, a series of design criteria for the model can be obtained and extended to other scenarios. In ConvNeXt [29], better CNN structures and parameter settings were determined through numerous experiments.

Based on the LSAFBD database, the FBP accuracy of the proposed method was 61.37%, which was 5.31% higher than 56.06% on GoogleNet, 11.3% higher than 50.70% on MobileNetV2, 9.02% higher than 52.35% on MobileNetV3, 1.4% higher than 59.97% on ShuffleNetV2, 2.05% higher than 59.32% on DenseNet, 2.35% higher than 59.02% on EfficientNet, 2.35% higher than 59.02% on RegNet, and 0.7% higher than 60.67% on ConvNeXt. The experimental results showed that the proposed method can effectively utilize GR to improve the accuracy of FBP, which is better than other single-task network models.

Based on the SCUT-FBP5500 database, the FBP accuracy of the proposed method was 75.41%, which was 2.64% higher than 72.77% on GoogleNet, 3.28% higher than 72.13% on MobileNetV2, 3.1% higher than 72.31% on MobileNetV3, 0.27% higher than 75.14% on ShuffleNetV2, 1.46% higher than 73.95% on DenseNet, 0.37% higher than 75.04% on EfficientNet, 0.73% higher than 74.68% on RegNet, and 0.09% higher than 75.32% on ConvNeXt. The experimental results showed that the proposed method can effectively apply GR to improve the accuracy of FBP, which is superior to other models.

3.5. Comparison Experiments between the Proposed Method and Other Methods

To further validate the effectiveness of the proposed method, we also compared the proposed method with other methods based on the LSAFBD and SCUT-FBP5500. The results are listed in Table 12. In [2], a self-correcting noise labels method was proposed, which can make full use of all data to reduce the negative impact of noise labels. In [3], a fusion model of pseudolabel and cross-stitch network was applied to solve the problems of weak generalization ability and insufficient label information in FBP. In [4], a network named E-BLS fusing EffeicientNet and a broad learning system was applied in FBP. In [5], a tiny network named TransBLS-T fusing transformer and broad learning system was proposed to improve FBP. The performance of the proposed method surpasses that of the other method. Based on the LSAFBD database, the method by way of self-correcting noise labels achieves poor results. This is because the method is based on single-task deep neural networks (DNNs) and does not utilize label information from multiple databases. The experimental results of the cross-network based on multi-task learning illustrate the superiority of multi-task learning. The methods by way of E-BLS and TransBLS-T are better than those of DNNs based on the LSAFBD database, which is attributed to the attention mechanism of the transformer. The proposed method in this paper combines the advantages of multi-task learning and attention feature fusion to achieve the best results.

Table 12. Experimental results compared with other methods (ACC(%)).

Method	Task	LSAFBD FBP	SCUT-FBP5500 FBP
Noise Labels [2]		60.80	75.30
Cross Network [3]		61.29	-
E-BLS [4]		60.82	73.13
TransBLS-T [5]		61.27	75.23
Proposed method		**61.37**	**75.41**

Note: The bold is the optimal value.

In summary, multi-task learning of the adaptive sharing policy combined with AFF utilizes the label information of two different databases, solves the problem of insufficient label information on the single-task network for FBP, and improves the network's ability to extract facial beauty features. Simultaneously, the network combines AFF to reduce the risk of overfitting, thereby improving the accuracy of the FBP.

4. Conclusions

To address the issue of insufficient label information and easy overfitting in FBP, multi-task learning of an adaptive sharing policy combined with AFF based on the AdaShare network is proposed. Among them, multi-task learning of the adaptive sharing policy utilizes the label information of two different databases to improve the accuracy of FBP by solving the insufficient label information issue. The AFF reduces the risk of overfitting and improves the feature extraction capability of the network by adding a feature fusion and attention mechanism at the short skip connections of ResNet. The experimental results based on the LSAFBD database and SCUT-FBP5500 databases showed that the multi-task learning of the adaptive sharing policy combined with AFF outperforms the single-task baseline method. Future studies will be focused on label information from multiple databases, how to set the weight ratio of different tasks adaptively, how to balance the category of databases, and on continuously optimizing the current method to obtain greater improvement.

Author Contributions: Conceptualization, J.G., H.L. (Heng Luo); methodology, H.L. (Heng Luo), J.X.; software, H.L. (Heng Luo), J.X., X.X.; validation, H.L. (Heng Luo), X.X., H.L. (Huicong Li); formal analysis, J.G., X.X.; investigation, J.G., X.X., H.L. (Huicong Li), J.L.; resources, J.G.; data curation, H.L. (Heng Luo), J.X., X.X.; writing—original draft preparation, J.G., H.L. (Heng Luo), J.X.; writing—review and editing, J.G., H.L. (Heng Luo), J.X., H.L. (Huicong Li), J.L.; supervision, J.G.; project administration, J.X., X.X., H.L. (Huicong Li), J.L.; funding acquisition, J.G. All authors have read and agreed to the published version of the manuscript.

Funding: This research was supported by the National Natural Science Foundation of China (Grant No. 61771347).

Data Availability Statement: SCUT-FBP5500: Dataset utilized in this research is publicly available: https://github.com/HCIILAB/SCUT-FBP5500-Database-Release (accessed on 20 November 2023). LSAFBD: The data presented in this study are available on request from the corresponding author. The data are not publicly available due to privacy.

Conflicts of Interest: The authors declare no conflict of interest.

References

1. Lebedeva, I.; Ying, F.; Guo, Y. Personalized facial beauty assessment: A meta-learning approach. *Vis. Comput.* **2023**, *39*, 1095–1107. [CrossRef]
2. Gan, J.; Wu, B.; Zhai, Y.; He, G.; Mai, C.; Bai, Z. Self-correcting noise labels for facial beauty prediction. *Chin. J. Image Graph.* **2022**, *27*, 2487–2495.
3. Gan, J.; Wu, B.; Zou, Q.; Zheng, Z.; Mai, C.; Zhai, Y.; He, G.; Bai, Z. Application Research for Fusion Model of Pseudolabel and Cross Network. *Comput. Intell. Neurosci.* **2022**, *2022*, 1–10. [CrossRef] [PubMed]
4. Gan, J.; Xie, X.; Zhai, Y.; He, G.; Mai, C.; Luo, H. Facial beauty prediction fusing transfer learning and broad learning system. *Soft Comput.* **2023**, *27*, 13391–13404. [CrossRef]
5. Gan, J.; Xie, X.; He, G.; Luo, H. TransBLS: Transformer combined with broad learning system for facial beauty prediction. *Appl. Intell.* **2023**, *53*, 26110–26125. [CrossRef]
6. Liu, Q.; Lin, L.; Shen, Z.; Yu, Y. FBPFormer: Dynamic Convolutional Transformer for Global-Local-Contexual Facial Beauty Prediction. In Proceedings of the Artificial Neural Networks and Machine Learning (ICANN), Heraklion, Greece, 26–29 September 2023; pp. 223–235. [CrossRef]
7. Laurinavičius, D.; Maskeliūnas, R.; Damaševičius, R. Improvement of Facial Beauty Prediction Using Artificial Human Faces Generated by Generative Adversarial Network. *Cogn. Comput.* **2023**, *15*, 998–1015. [CrossRef]
8. Zhang, P.; Liu, Y. NAS4FBP: Facial Beauty Prediction Based on Neural Architecture Search. In Proceedings of the Artificial Neural Networks and Machine Learning (ICANN), Bristol, UK, 6–9 September 2022; pp. 225–236.
9. Bougourzi, F.; Dornaika, F.; Taleb-Ahmed, A. Deep learning based face beauty prediction via dynamic robust losses and ensemble regression. *Knowl.-Based Syst.* **2022**, *242*, 108246–108251. [CrossRef]
10. Zhang, L.; Liu, X.; Guan, H. AutoMTL: A Programming Framework for Automating Efficient Multi-task Learning. In Proceedings of the Advances in Neural Information Processing Systems (NeuralPS), New Orleans, LA, USA, 28 November–9 December 2022; pp. 34216–34228.
11. Li, H.; Wang, Y.; Lyu, Z.; Shi, J. Multi-task learning for recommendation over heterogeneous information network. *IEEE Trans. Knowl. Data Eng.* **2020**, *34*, 789–802. [CrossRef]
12. Fan, X.; Wang, H.; Zhao, Y.; Li, Y.; Tsui, K.L. An adaptive weight learning-based multi-task deep network for continuous blood pressure estimation using electrocardiogram signals. *Sensors* **2021**, *21*, 1595. [CrossRef] [PubMed]
13. Zhou, F.; Shui, C.; Abbasi, M.; Robitaille, L.-E.; Wang, B.; Gagne, C. Task similarity estimation through adversarial multi-task neural network. *IEEE Trans. Neural Netw. Learn. Syst.* **2020**, *32*, 466–480. [CrossRef] [PubMed]
14. Sun, X.; Panda, R.; Feris, R.; Saenko, K. AdaShare: Learning What to Share for Efficient Deep Multi-task Learning. In Proceedings of the Advances in Neural Information Processing Systems (NeuralPS), Virtual, 6–12 December 2020; pp. 8728–8740.
15. Dai, Y.; Gieseke, F.; Oehmcke, S.; Wu, Y.; Barnard, K. Attentional Feature Fusion. In Proceedings of the 2021 IEEE Winter Conference on Applications of Computer Vision (WACV), Virtual, 5–9 January 2021; pp. 3559–3568.
16. Wang, L.; Li, D.; Liu, H.; Peng, J.; Tian, L.; Shan, Y. Cross-dataset collaborative learning for semantic segmentation in autonomous driving. In Proceedings of the AAAI Conference on Artificial Intelligence, Virtual, 22 February–1 March 2022; pp. 2487–2494.
17. Kapidis, G.; Poppe, R.; Veltkamp, R.C. Multi-Dataset, Multi-task Learning of Egocentric Vision Tasks. *IEEE Trans. Pattern Anal. Mach. Intell.* **2023**, *45*, 6618–6630. [CrossRef] [PubMed]
18. He, K.; Zhang, X.; Ren, S.; Sun, J. Deep Residual Learning for Image Recognition. In Proceedings of the 2016 IEEE Conference on Computer Vision and Pattern Recognition (CVPR), Las Vegas, NV, USA, 27–30 June 2016; pp. 770–778.
19. Srivastava, N.; Hinton, G.E.; Krizhevsky, A.; Sutskever, I.; Salakhutdinov, R. Dropout: A simple way to prevent neural networks from overfitting. *J. Mach. Learn. Res.* **2014**, *15*, 1929–1958.
20. Jang, E.; Gu, S.; Poole, B. Categorical Reparameterization with Gumbel-Softmax. In Proceedings of the 5th International Conference on Learning Representations (ICLR), Toulon, France, 24–26 April 2017.
21. Loshchilov, I.; Hutter, F. Decoupled Weight Decay Regularization. In Proceedings of the 7th International Conference on Learning Representations (ICLR), New Orleans, LA, USA, 6–9 May 2019.
22. Szegedy, C.; Liu, W.; Jia, Y.; Sermanet, P.; Reed, S.; Anguelov, D.; Erhan, D.; Vanhoucke, V.; Rabinovich, A. Going deeper with convolutions. In Proceedings of the IEEE Conference on Computer Vision and Pattern Recognition (CVPR), Boston, MA, USA, 7–12 June 2015; pp. 1–9.

23. Sandler, M.; Howard, A.G.; Zhu, M.; Zhmoginov, A.; Chen, L.C. MobileNetV2: Inverted Residuals and Linear Bottlenecks. In Proceedings of the 2018 IEEE Conference on Computer Vision and Pattern Recognition (CVPR), Salt Lake City, UT, USA, 18–23 June 2018; pp. 4510–4520.
24. Howard, A.; Sandler, M.; Chu, G.; Chen, L.-C.; Chen, B.; Tan, M.; Wang, W.; Zhu, Y.; Pang, R.; Vasudevan, V.; et al. Searching for MobileNetV3. In Proceedings of the IEEE/CVF International Conference on Computer Vision (ICCV), Seoul, Republic of Korea, 27 October–2 November 2019; pp. 1314–1324.
25. Ma, N.; Zhang, X.; Zheng, H.T.; Sun, J. ShuffleNet V2: Practical Guidelines for Efficient CNN Architecture Design. In Proceedings of the European Conference on Computer Vision (ECCV), Munich, Germany, 8–14 September 2018; pp. 116–131.
26. Huang, G.; Liu, Z.; van der Maaten, L.; Weinberger, K.Q. Densely Connected Convolutional Networks. In Proceedings of the IEEE Conference on Computer Vision and Pattern Recognition (CVPR), Honolulu, HI, USA, 21–26 July 2017; pp. 4700–4708.
27. Tan, M.; Le, Q. EfficientNet: Rethinking Model Scaling for Convolutional Neural Networks. In Proceedings of the 36th International Conference on Machine Learning (ICML), Long Beach, CA, USA, 9–15 June 2019; pp. 6105–6114.
28. Radosavovic, I.; Kosaraju, R.P.; Girshick, R.; He, K.; Dollár, P. Designing Network Design Spaces. In Proceedings of the IEEE/CVF Conference on Computer Vision and Pattern Recognition (CVPR), Seattle, WA, USA, 13–19 June 2020; pp. 10428–10436.
29. Liu, Z.; Mao, H.; Wu, C.Y.; Feichtenhofer, C.; Darrell, T.; Xie, S. A ConvNet for the 2020s. In Proceedings of the IEEE/CVF Conference on Computer Vision and Pattern Recognition (CVPR), New Orleans, LA, USA, 18–24 June 2022; pp. 11976–11986.

Disclaimer/Publisher's Note: The statements, opinions and data contained in all publications are solely those of the individual author(s) and contributor(s) and not of MDPI and/or the editor(s). MDPI and/or the editor(s) disclaim responsibility for any injury to people or property resulting from any ideas, methods, instructions or products referred to in the content.

Article

Two-Stage Progressive Learning for Vehicle Re-Identification in Variable Illumination Conditions

Zhihe Wu [1,2,3], Zhi Jin [1,2,4] and Xiying Li [1,2,3,*]

1. School of Intelligent Systems Engineering, Sun Yat-sen University, Shenzhen 518107, China; wuzhh8@mail2.sysu.edu.cn (Z.W.); jinzh26@mail.sysu.edu.cn (Z.J.)
2. Shenzhen Campus of Sun Yat-sen University, Shenzhen 518107, China
3. Guangdong Provincial Key Laboratory of Intelligent Transportation System, Shenzhen 518107, China
4. Guangdong Provincial Key Laboratory of Fire Science and Technology, Shenzhen 518107, China
* Correspondence: stslxy@mail.sysu.edu.cn

Abstract: Vehicle matching in variable illumination environments can be challenging due to the heavy dependence of vehicle appearance on lighting conditions. To address this issue, we propose a two-stage progressive learning (TSPL) framework. In the first stage, illumination-aware metric learning is enforced using a two-branch network via two illumination-specific feature spaces, used to explicitly model differences in lighting. In the second stage, discriminative feature learning is introduced to extract distinguishing features from a given vehicle. This process consists of a local feature extraction attention module, a local constraint, and a balanced sampling strategy. During the metric learning phase, the model expresses the union of local features, extracted from the attention module, with illumination-specific global features to form joint vehicle features. As part of the study, we construct a large-scale dataset, termed VERI-DAN (vehicle re-identification across day and night), to address the current lack of vehicle datasets exhibiting variable lighting conditions. This set is composed of 200,004 images from 16,654 vehicles, collected in various natural illumination environments. Validation experiments conducted with the VERI-DAN and Vehicle-1M datasets demonstrated that our proposed methodology effectively improved vehicle re-identification Rank-1 accuracy.

Keywords: vehicle re-identification; dataset; illumination aware; detail aware; discriminative feature learning

1. Introduction

Vehicle re-identification (re-ID) aims to match a target vehicle across multiple non-overlapping surveillance cameras with varying viewpoints, illumination, and resolution. The proliferation of surveillance cameras in urban areas has led to a significant increase in the demand for vision-based re-ID techniques, which could facilitate the management of smart cities [1–3]. While the development of deep learning and existing annotated datasets have greatly facilitated vehicle re-ID research, vision-based vehicle re-ID still suffers from low resolution, blurred motion, and extreme weather conditions, such as fog, rain, and snow. Meanwhile, variations in viewpoint, illumination, and background can pose significant challenges for vehicle re-ID. Specifically, illumination presents a major challenge, as vehicle appearance can depend heavily on subtle changes in light intensity. Existing models have been trained primarily using datasets that exhibit limited lighting variability, while also ignoring the obstruction of notable visual cues caused by dramatic fluctuations in illumination. Furthermore, the conventional approach of collecting images in a single-feature space also underestimates the challenges posed by inconsistent lighting. As shown in Figure 1, two vehicles of the same model in similar lighting conditions (Figure 1a) may appear to be more similar than the same vehicle observed under different lighting (Figure 1b). In addition, lower lighting levels may obstruct visual cues, such as logos, stickers, and body features, as seen in Figure 1c. One possible solution to this problem is to

enhance images featuring poor illumination. Although low-light enhancement techniques have been successful in improving visual quality for classification tasks [4–8], extreme variations in illumination still pose significant challenges. As part of this study, experiments were conducted using images enhanced by a state-of-the-art (SOTA) method [6]. The results are summarized in Table 1, which indicates that re-ID accuracy experience a significant drop-off when images undergo enhancement. We suggest that some distinguishing details, which are essential for differentiating similar vehicles, may have been lost during enhancement. In addition, images containing unnatural noise may have further reduced re-ID accuracy.

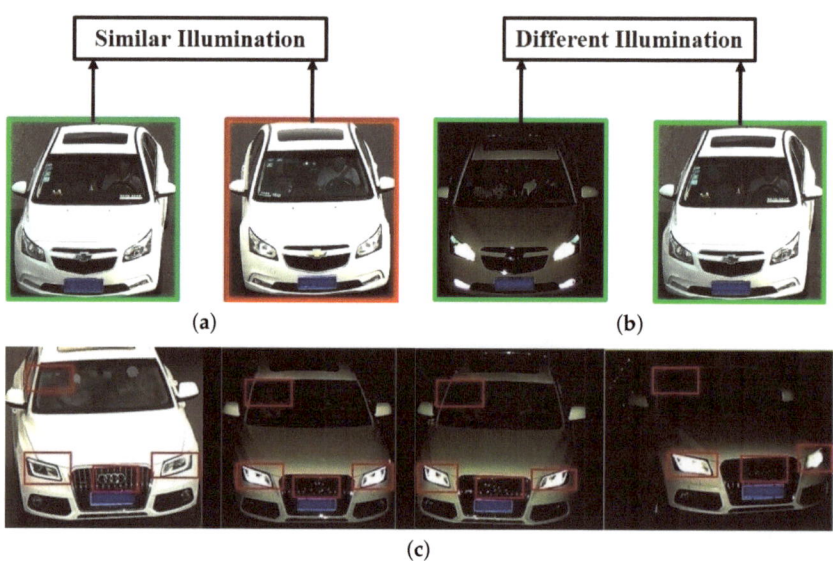

Figure 1. Challenges posed by variations in illumination. (**a**) Two different vehicles may appear to be similar under consistent lighting, especially when they are of the same model. (**b**) In contrast, images of the same vehicle may appear to be quite different if the illumination varies drastically. (**c**) Dramatic changes in lighting may also alter distinctive visual cues, such as inspection marks on windshields, headlights, and car logos.

Table 1. Re-ID performance with augmented images. Origin denotes the weight offered by the author. Retrain denotes a weight retrained on VERI-DAN. The best results are given in bold.

Setting	Augment		Origin			Retrain		
	Query	Gallery	Rank-1	Rank-5	mAP	Rank-1	Rank-5	mAP
Baseline	×	×	**88.9**	**94.4**	**56.5**	**88.9**	**94.4**	**56.5**
	✓	×	75.8	87.0	48.7	75.5	85.2	41.4
	×	✓	72.8	83.6	47.6	64.8	79.0	34.9
	✓	✓	84.0	91.0	52.1	81.1	90.2	47.2

Inspired by the manual process of recognizing vehicles, we propose to address this problem by using a two-stage progressive learning (TSPL) strategy, consisting of an illumination-aware metric-learning stage and a detail-aware discriminative feature-learning stage. In the first phase, we used coarse-grained labels to describe the illumination of each image (i.e., "daytime" and "nighttime"). Samples with the same illumination label were then assigned as S-IL image pairs, and samples with different illumination labels were assigned as D-IL image pairs, as illustrated in Figure 1. Two separate deep metrics were then learned for the S-IL and D-IL images in the two illumination-specific feature spaces. Specifically, we measured the similarity of images with the same illumination label in the S-IL feature space and images with different illumination labels in the D-IL feature space.

The within-space and cross-space constraints were then enforced to explicitly learn robust visual representations against variations in lighting. In the second stage, we designed a detail-aware discriminative feature learning process, which was learned with the guidance of a local constraint, to extract distinguishing features among similar types of vehicles (as shown in Figure 2). Specifically, a local feature extraction module was introduced to generate local features, and a triplet loss, optimized by triplets of the same model, was designed to enforce the local constraint. Experiments confirmed that both stages were critical for improving re-ID accuracy (see Section 5.4.1).

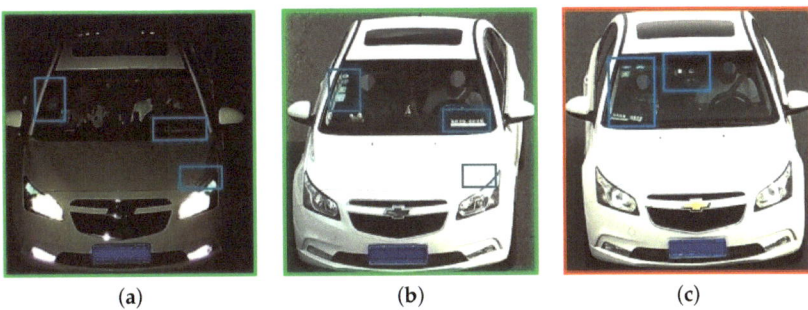

Figure 2. Visual markers that could be used to distinguish similar vehicles under varying illumination, especially when the negative sample includes the same model with a positive sample under similar illumination. Personalized decorations on the windshield were of particular importance, as shown in the blue boxes. (**a**) Anchor. (**b**) Positive. (**c**) Negative.

As part of the study, we constructed a comprehensive, large-scale dataset termed VERI-DAN (vehicle re-identification across day and night) to address the lack of re-ID datasets exhibiting significant changes in illumination across samples. VERI-DAN included 200,004 images from 16,654 vehicles, each of which was photographed at least 4 times in variable lighting conditions using real-world cameras. The primary contributions of this study can be summarized as follows:

- A large-scale dataset termed VERI-DAN is developed to facilitate vehicle re-ID in various illumination conditions. VERI-DAN is the first dataset of its type to represent changes in lighting on this scale. As such, it simulated a relatively challenging scenario (matching D-IL pairs), which is both common and useful in real-world scenes.
- A two-stage progressive learning strategy is proposed for vehicle re-ID with variable illumination. In Stage I, we introduced an illumination-aware network, which significantly improved the learning of robust visual representations in extreme lighting conditions. In Stage II, we developed a discriminative local feature learning process, which facilitated the ability to distinguish among vehicles with a similar appearance.
- We assessed the effectiveness of this approach using two datasets involving obvious lighting changes (VERI-DAN and Vehicle-1M). Despite only 12% of the training set being usable in Vehicle-1M (due to insufficient lighting variability), the proposed technique achieved SOTA performance for the original testing set.

2. Related Works

2.1. Vehicle Re-ID Methods

Vehicle re-ID, a variation of person re-ID [9], has received increasing attention in recent years, as its viability continues to improve. Zapletal and Herout [10] were the first to collect a large-scale dataset for this purpose, conducting a vision-based study by utilizing color and oriented gradient histograms. Liu et al. [11] combined traditional hand-crafted features with CNN-based deep features, thereby demonstrating that deep features were more discriminative. Liu et al. [12] proposed "PROVID" and made progress with the use of license plate information. Other studies [13,14] have shown that spatial and temporal information from vehicle images have contributed to improving vehicle re-ID performance. For example, PROVID [12] re-ranks vehicles using spatio-temporal properties based on a simple from-near-distant principle. Wang et al. [15] achieved spatio-temporal regularization for vehicle re-ID by considering the delay time between cameras. These techniques, however, are limited in their application because they require complex spatio-temporal labels.

Several studies have described vehicle re-ID as a metric learning problem and have introduced a series of metric losses to obtain better vehicle representations. Specifically, triplet loss has achieved great success in person re-ID0 [16–18] and has been adopted in vehicle re-ID. Zhang et al. [12] combined classification loss with triplet loss, providing further benefit. Yan et al. [19] proposed a multi-grain ranking loss to discriminate vehicles with a similar appearance. Studies have also shown that attributes, such as color, brand, and wheel pattern, can further improve re-ID efficacy [1,20–22]. Other strategies [20,21,23–27] have exploited the indirect attributes of a vehicle, such as camera perspective information and background information, making considerable improvements. These techniques, however, have overlooked valuable information present in the image beyond the vehicle itself, such as lighting conditions. In this study, we have suggested that the significance of an image extends beyond its perceptible features. By incorporating less apparent elements, such as illumination, the proposed deep learning model can produce more robust representations in a variety of lighting conditions. Table 2 summarizes related work on vehicle re-ID.

Table 2. Summary of related works on vehicle re-ID.

Classification Basis	Method Type	References	Advantage	Limitation
Feature representation approaches	Hand-crafted	Refs. [10,11]	Highly interpretable	High time complexity; low recognition accuracy
	Deep learning	Refs. [1,11–15,19–27]	High recognition accuracy	High cost; poor interpretability 2
Key aspects	Spatio-temporal information based	Refs. [12–14]	Works well for hard samples	Need extra complex spatio-temporal labels
	Metrics learning based	Refs. [12,19]	High recognition accuracy	High cost
	Multidimensional information based	Refs. [1,20–27]	Sensitivity to the special appearance of vehicles	Vulnerable to variations in viewpoints and illuminations

2.2. Vehicle Re-ID Datasets

Re-ID algorithms that have been applied to public datasets, such as VehicleID [28], VeRi-776 [12], VERI-Wild [29], and Vehicle-1M [30], have conventionally underestimated the importance of illumination. These conditions are limited in existing datasets, as the lighting in each image is typically consistent. For example, all of the samples in VeRi-776 were collected between 4:00 p.m. and 5:00 p.m. We inspected vehicle images in these public datasets and counted the number of samples collected during both the daytime and nighttime. This preliminary evaluation suggested that 90% of samples in VehicleID, 94% of samples in VERI-Wild, and 70% of samples in Vehicle-1M exhibited little variation in background luminance. In this paper, we propose a large-scale vehicle re-ID dataset termed VERI-DAN, which provides a more challenging classification task because each vehicle appears several times in different lighting conditions. The set contains 482 refined vehicle models (e.g., MG3-2016) with highly similar features. As such, this set was more suitable for evaluating the performance of vehicle re-ID methods in challenging scenarios.

3. Methodology

The network architecture for the proposed algorithm is illustrated in Figure 3. This framework constituted a two-stage progressive deep learning process involving illumination conditions and vehicle attributes. During the first stage (Section 3.2), we established an illumination-aware network (IANet) consisting of two branches with identical structures and applied it to both S-IL and D-IL image pairs. This two-branch network leveraged the coarse-grained illumination labels to supervise the learning of illumination-specific features. The Stage I model (IANet) then enabled the retrieval of samples under different lighting conditions. During the second stage (Section 3.3), we introduced a guided local feature extraction process to generate local features. This process included an illumination-aware local feature extraction module (IAM) and a detail-aware local feature extraction module (DAM). This attention mechanism facilitated the learning of distinguishing features among different vehicles with similar appearances, under the supervision of fine-grained model labels. The Stage II model was specifically designed to extract discriminative features from local areas to distinguish among similar types of vehicles. We adopted triplet loss as a learning baseline metric, as discussed in Section 3.1.

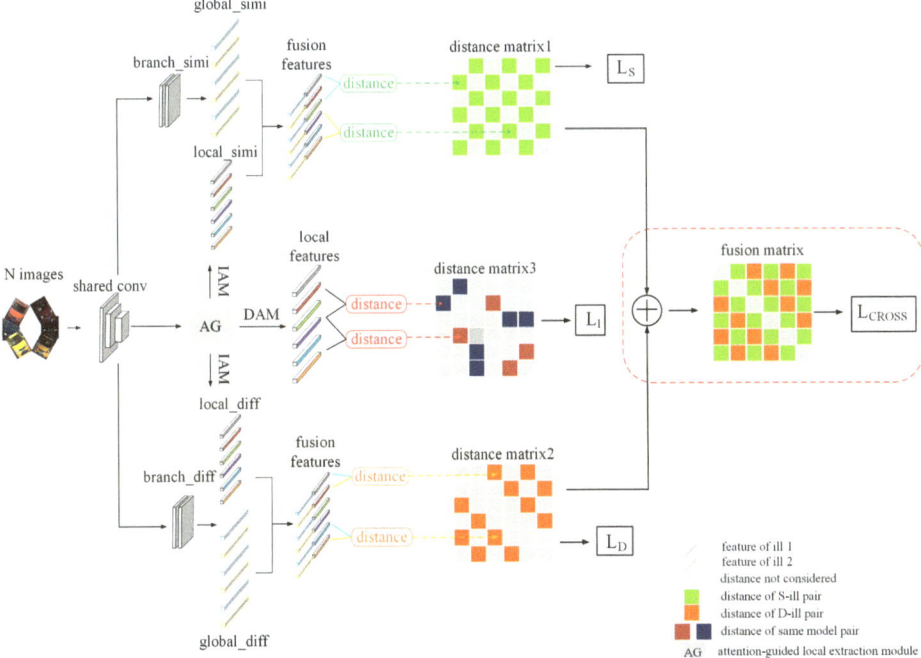

Figure 3. The TSPL architecture. The "branch_simi" and "branch_diff" modules accept the output of "shared conv" and transform N images into $2N$ features (i.e., $global\_simi$ and $global\_diff$). TSPL then appends an attention process to the "shared conv" to generate $3N$ local features (i.e., $local\_simi$, $local\_diff$, and $local\ features$). In the illumination-specific feature space, TSPL expresses the fusion of local features extracted from the IAM (with global features extracted from the $branch$) as joint vehicle features. TSPL also generates an $N \times N$ distance matrix using the local features and two $N \times N$ distance matrices from the fusion features (i.e., matrix3, matrix1, and matrix2). In matrix3, TSPL only uses distances from same-model pairs to calculate the loss function L_l. In matrix1 (matrix2), TSPL only uses the green cells (brown cells) to compute the loss function L_S (L_D). In addition, TSPL incorporates matrix1 and matrix2 into the fusion matrix to calculate L_{CROSS}.

3.1. Metric Learning Baseline

We adopted triplet loss to construct a metric learning baseline. Given an image pair $P = (x_i, x_j)$, distances were calculated using $D(P) = D(x_i, x_j) = \|f(x_i) - f(x_j)\|_2$, where x_i and x_j represent images from the dataset X and D denotes the Euclidean distance between features. The function f then mapped raw images to their respective features. An example is provided given three samples: x, x^+, and x^-, where x and x^+ belong to the same class (i.e., the same vehicle ID), while x and x^- belong to different classes. A positive pair $P^+ = (x, x^+)$ and a negative pair $P^- = (x, x^-)$ can then be formed, for which the triplet loss is defined as follows:

$$L_{Tri}(x, x^+, x^-) = \max\{D(P^+) - D(P^-) + \alpha, 0\}, \tag{1}$$

where α is a margin enforced between positive and negative pairs. Equation (1) aims to minimize the distance between samples with the same ID while maximizing the distance between samples with different IDs.

3.2. Illumination-Aware Metric Learning

Inspired by previous work [25], we propose an illumination-aware network that learns two separate deep metrics for S-IL and D-IL samples. A coarse-grained classification was included to divide the images into two distinct illumination types. We then employed IANet to learn illumination-specific metrics via the explicitly modeling of lighting conditions. Since it is difficult to manually annotate real-world environments with fine-grained labels, coarse-grained labels were assigned to the images (i.e., daytime and nighttime). Images including annotated timestamps ranging from 06:00 to 18:00 were labeled daytime, and those spanning from 18:00 to 06:00 were labeled nighttime. Datasets lacking a timestamp were categorized using an illumination predictor trained on VERI-DAN samples. Images with the same illumination label were denoted as S-IL pairs, and those with different labels were denoted as D-IL pairs. This convention produced four types of image pairs: P_s^+ (S-IL positive), P_d^+ (D-IL positive), P_s^- (S-IL negative), and P_d^- (D-IL negative).

Images were mapped into two distinct illumination-specific feature spaces using two convolutional branches with identical structures, which did not share any parameters. Each branch layer could be viewed as a function for illumination-specific feature extraction (i.e., f_s and f_d). For each image in a mini-batch, IANet generated two distinct features using $branch\_simi$ and $branch\_diff$, as illustrated in Figure 3. Pair-wise distances in the S-IL feature space were then calculated from $D_s(P) = \|f_s(x_i) - f_s(x_j)\|_2$, and distances in the D-IL feature space were determined by $D_d(P) = \|f_d(x_i) - f_d(x_j)\|_2$. Equation (1) was decomposed into two types of constraints: within-space and cross-space constraints. The within-space constraints expect $D_s(P_s^+)$ to be smaller than $D_s(P_s^-)$ in the S-IL feature space, and $D_d(P_d^+)$ to be smaller than $D_d(P_d^-)$ in the D-IL feature space. The cross-space constraints expect $D_d(P_d^+)$ to be smaller than $D_s(P_s^-)$, and $D_s(P_s^+)$ to be smaller than $D_d(P_d^-)$.

Within-space constraints: Two triplet loss terms were introduced, one in each of the S-IL and D-IL feature spaces, to ensure that positive samples were closer to each other than negative samples. Triplet loss in the S-IL feature space was defined as follows:

$$L_s = \max\{D_s(P_s^+) - D_s(P_s^-) + \alpha, 0\}, \tag{2}$$

and in the D-IL feature space as follows:

$$L_d = \max\{D_d(P_d^+) - D_d(P_d^-) + \alpha, 0\}. \tag{3}$$

Within-space constraints were then implemented through a summation of L_s and L_d as follows:

$$L_{within} = L_s + L_d. \tag{4}$$

Within each illumination-specific feature domain, the correlating loss function operated solely on illumination-specific samples. In other words, we used only S-IL pairs to calculate L_s, while L_d was optimized solely by D-IL pairs.

Cross-space constraints: Focusing solely on single-feature spaces runs the risk of underestimating the complex issue of illumination variability, which in turn could limit re-ID accuracy. As such, we further proposed cross-space constraints between (P_s^-, P_d^+) and (P_s^+, P_d^-), which were implemented using the following triplet loss function:

$$L_{cross} = \max\{D_d(P_d^+) - D_s(P_s^-) + \alpha, 0\} \\ + \max\{D_s(P_s^+) - D_d(P_d^-) + \alpha, 0\}. \quad (5)$$

Loss functions in the Stage I model: The total triplet loss enforced in the first stage can then be expressed as follows:

$$L = L_{within} + L_{cross}. \quad (6)$$

3.3. Detail-Aware Discriminative Feature Learning

We observed that vehicles with similar appearances often exhibited differences in localized regions, such as windshield decorations, as depicted in Figure 2. Thus, we suggested that re-ID accuracy could be improved by enhancing an algorithm's capacity to capture these distinctive local details in the second stage. The neural network encoded images in a progressive process [31,32], beginning with fine-grained details and gradually expanding to local and global information. Thus, mid-level features from the middle layers of the network facilitated the extraction of local area features for the vehicle. As such, based on this approach, we proposed a detail-aware discriminative feature learning process for vehicle re-ID. This process incorporated a local feature extraction module with attention mechanisms included to extract local features. Local constraints were then introduced to guide the generation of these features and devise an illumination-balanced sampling strategy to optimize local constraints.

Attention-guided local feature extraction module (AG): Different vehicle parts play varying roles in distinguishing among vehicles that are similar in appearance. Specifically, areas such as a car logo or windshield, for which marked dissimilarities exist between individual vehicles, are more important than common features, such as doors and hoods. To this end, we introduced an attention mechanism to learn from these distinctive areas. This attention-guided process consisted of a detail-aware local feature extraction module (DAM) and an illumination-aware local feature extraction module (IAM), as illustrated in Figure 4.

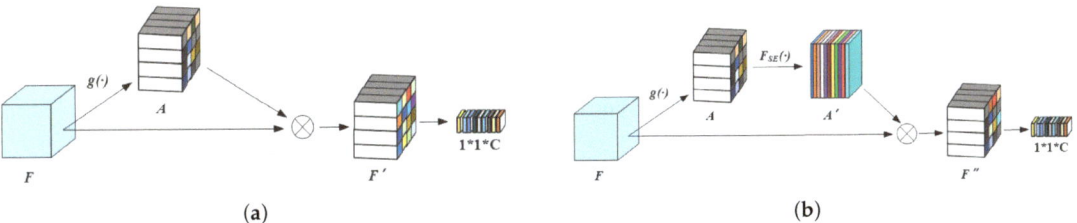

Figure 4. The attention-guided local feature extraction module (AG). (**a**) The detail-aware local feature extraction module (DAM). (**b**) The illumination-aware local feature extraction module (IAM).

The DAM generated detail-aware discriminative local features to enforce local constraints, as shown in Figure 4a. Mid-level features are denoted in the figure by F, with dimensions $H \times W \times C$, where H, W, and C represent the height, width, and number of channels in the feature layer, respectively. The attention local feature map F' was then generated with the following equation:

$$F' = A \otimes F = \sigma(g(F) \otimes F), \quad (7)$$

where $g(\cdot)$ is a convolution kernel, σ is the sigmoid function, and $\otimes$ denotes element-wise multiplication between two tensors. Global maximum pooling was then applied to F' to produce the final local feature vector (i.e., *local features* in Figure 3). Each channel in F' represents a specific vehicle region, and spatial points within the vector indicate the significance of each region. In this way, the incorporated attention map was able to guide the network's focus toward the significant areas of each vehicle.

As demonstrated in Figure 4b, IAM generated two different types of local features that were discriminative in S-IL and D-IL feature spaces, respectively. The appearance of certain distinguishing areas, such as headlights, differed significantly as the illumination changed. In other words, specific visual cues may become more or less significant in different feature spaces. To this end, we further introduced squeeze and excitation modules [33] to identify illumination-specific local features for the S-IL and D-IL space. The corresponding feature map F'' is obtained as follows:

$$F'' = A' \otimes F = F_{SE}(A) \otimes F = \sigma(F_{SE}(g(F)) \otimes F), \quad (8)$$

where F_{SE} denotes the squeeze-and-excitation block. Consequently, we obtained two different local features from IAM (i.e., *local_simi* and *local_diff*), as shown in Figure 3. We then employed the union of illumination-specific local features with global features (extracted from the branch network) to enforce within-space and cross-space constraints. This process was distinguished from the formulation defined in Section 3.2 by using L_S, L_D, and L_{CROSS} to denote corresponding loss terms calculated from the fusion features.

Detail-aware local constraints: In real-world scenarios, differences between vehicles of the same model were concentrated primarily in regions such as inspection marks and personalized decorations. As such, training a triplet loss function using hard negatives from the same vehicle model served as a guiding mechanism that directed network attention toward relevant discriminative local regions. In the following notation, x_m denotes a vehicle belonging to model m. A typical triplet in the local constraints is denoted by (x_m, x_m^+, x_m^-), where x_m and x_m^+ exhibit the same ID, while x_m^- has a different ID but shares a model type with x_m and x_m^+. Following these definitions, P_m^+ (same-model positive pair) and P_m^- (same-model negative pair) are denoted as (x_m, x_m^+) and (x_m, x_m^-), respectively. Formally, local constraints were enforced through triplet loss as follows:

$$L_l = L_l(x_m, x_m^+, x_m^-) = \max\{D(P_m^+) - D(P_m^-) + \beta, 0\}, \quad (9)$$

where β is a margin enforced between positive and negative pairs. All negative samples in the proposed local constraints shared a model type with the anchor, which was conducive to guiding the generation of discriminative local features. Note that L_l is an advanced version of L_cross, since different vehicles of the same model were prone to generate the hardest negatives in S-IL and D-IL feature spaces. Thus, we removed L_{CROSS} from the final model after introducing local constraints.

Loss functions in the Stage II model: The total triplet loss function in the Stage II model can be expressed as follows:

$$L = L_S + L_D + L_l. \quad (10)$$

Illumination-balanced sampling strategy: Maintaining a balance between S-IL and D-IL pairs is necessary in a mini-batch to train an illumination-aware network against variations in lighting. However, in most cases, the number of daytime images in each mini-batch is much larger than that of the nighttime images. As a result, the network may tend to learn from images captured in the daytime and may not be able to identify a robust correlation among samples with different illumination. To address this issue, we designed a function to ensure that each vehicle provided an equal number of images for both types of lighting. Specifically, the algorithm selected N daytime images and N nighttime images for each vehicle ID in a minibatch. If a vehicle ID exhibited fewer than N daytime images, the algorithm duplicated these samples to produce N images. The effectiveness of this balanced sampling strategy will be illustrated in Section 5.4.2.

3.4. Training and Inference

TSPL expressed the fusion of local features with global features extracted from "branch_conv" as joint vehicle features, as demonstrated in Figure 3. During training, "branch_conv" output dual global features for each image in different feature spaces (i.e., $global\_simi$ in S-IL and $global\_diff$ in D-IL). In contrast, IAM output dual illumination-specific local features to form joint representation with global features (i.e., $local\_simi$ and $local\_diff$). DAM then output detail-aware local features to optimize the local constraints. Given N input images, TSPL generated two illumination-specific distance matrices containing $N \times N$ distance value elements (i.e., matrix1 and matrix2). Only $D_s(P_s)$ and $D_d(P_d)$ (denoted by the green and brown cells in Figure 3) contributed to L_S and L_D loss, respectively. TSPL also generated a local distance matrix containing $N \times N$ distance value elements calculated from local features. Distances from the same model (denoted by the colored cells in matrix3) were then used to calculate the triplet loss L_l and to enforce detail-aware local constraints.

Note that L_{CROSS} was not incorporated into the final model but was a component of the ablation study. The generation of L_{CROSS} was illustrated by the red dashed line box shown in Figure 3. In the *fusion matrix*, the green cells were related to S-IL pair distance values in matrix1, while the brown cells were related to D-IL distance values in matrix2. During the testing phase, a specific procedure was followed based on the illumination conditions of query and gallery images. If these images were identified as a S-IL pair, their distance was calculated by $D_s(P_s)$ using a S-IL branch; otherwise, $D_d(P_d)$ was employed through a D-IL branch. Distances were also calculated from local features and the union of these results provided joint distances between the query and gallery images.

4. The VERI-DAN Dataset

Existing re-ID datasets either exhibit limited illumination variability or lack annotations to quantify luminance. Therefore, we carefully constructed the VERI-DAN dataset to provide a variety of lighting conditions for each vehicle. The set included 200,004 total images from 16,654 vehicles, collected by 120 cameras in a large urban district in natural environments. Statistics for this dataset are provided in Figure 5 and sample images are shown in Figure 6a. Table 3 presents a comparison of VehicleID [28], VeRI-776 [12], VERI-Wild [29], Vehicle-1M [30], and VERI-DAN. The distinctive properties of VERI-DAN can be summarized as follows:

Balanced illumination conditions: VERI-DAN was generated from $120 \times 24 \times 8 = 23,040$ h of video footage collected in various illumination conditions. Specifically, every vehicle appeared multiple times in both daytime and nighttime settings, as shown in Figure 6b.

Refined model information: We meticulously annotated each image with one of 482 refined vehicle classes, denoting the make, model, color, and year (e.g., "Audi-A6-2013"). VERI-DAN included many similar vehicles of the same model, which facilitated the training of a network to differentiate hard negative samples.

Spatio-temporal geographic coordinate information (S-T): Details such as camera ID, timestamp, and geodetic coordinates were provided to facilitate research based on camera networks [34–36].

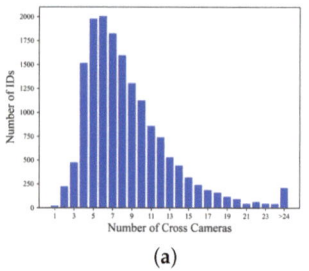 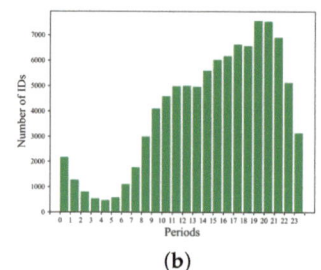 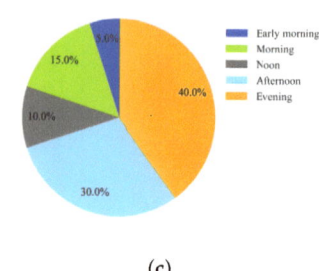

(a) (b) (c)

Figure 5. VERI-DAN dataset statistics. (**a**) The number of identities collected by camera (i.e., 1–120). (**b**) The number of IDs captured by hour. (**c**) The distribution of captured images by time of day.

(a) (b)

Figure 6. An overview of the VERI-DAN dataset, including (**a**) sample images and (**b**) examples of changes in illumination.

Table 3. A comparison of re-ID datasets. S-T, spatio-temporal geographic coordinate information; ID-DL, ID with diverse lighting.

Dataset	VehicleID	Vehicle-1M	VERI-Wild	VERI-DAN
Images	221,763	936,051	416,314	200,004
Identities	26,267	55,527	40,671	16,654
Models	250	400	153	482
S-T	×	×	✓	✓
ID-DL (%)	10.3%	29.9%	6.3%	100%

5. Experiments

5.1. Datasets

We evaluated the proposed method using the VERI-DAN and Vehicle-1M datasets, both of which included vehicles exhibiting significant illumination changes. Following a common practice [28], we divided VERI-DAN into a training set (141,470 images from 13,454 vehicles) and a test set, which contained the remaining 58,534 images from 4800 vehicles. We further divided the test set into three subsets, denoted Small, Medium, and Large, as shown in Table 4.

Table 4. Division of the training and testing sets (IDs/Images).

Dataset	Train	Test		
		Small	Medium	Large
Vehicle-1M	6448/525,808	1000/16,123	2000/32,539	3000/49,259
VERI-DAN	13,454/141,470	800/9723	1600/19,338	2400/29,473

5.2. Evaluation Protocols

During evaluation, we followed the protocol proposed by Liu et al. [12,28], in which mean average precision (mAP) and cumulative matching characteristics (CMC) were used as performance metrics. CMC estimates the probability of finding a correct match in the top K returned results, while MAP is a comprehensive index that considers both the precision and recall of the results. The final CMC and mAP values were averaged over 10 iterations.

5.3. Implementation Details

We adopted the InceptionV3 [37] network as the backbone model. All layers preceding the Inception (7a) module were implemented as "share conv", and layers ranging from Inception (7a) to the global average pooling layer were appended as "branch conv". Since mid-level features facilitated the extraction of discriminative local vehicle features, we added an attention module to the Inception (5d) layers to generate local feature maps of dimensions $35 \times 35 \times 288$. The input images were then resized to 299×299 without augmentation, using processes such as color jitter and horizontal flip. The model was trained for 120 epochs using the Adam optimizer with a momentum of 0.9 and a weight decay of 0.05. The learning rate was initialized to 0.001, and decreased by a factor of 0.1 every 20 epochs. The margins α and β were both set to 1.0. Each mini-batch contained 128 images (32 IDS, each with 4 images) on VERI-DAN as well as on Vehicle-1M. We adopted a batch hard-mining strategy to reduce the triplet loss.

The illumination predictor was trained using cross-entropy based on InceptionV3. We coarsely categorized all images into two illumination classes: daytime and nighttime. The daytime—daytime and nighttime—nighttime samples were then defined as the S-IL pairs, and the daytime—nighttime samples were defined as the D-IL pairs. In addition to triplet loss, we incorporated cross-entropy loss into the model to learn differences between the individual vehicle models, drawing inspiration from several existing re-ID methods [1,25,38]. Specifically, we appended the model classifier into the feature-embedding layer. The classifier was then implemented with a fully connected layer and a softmax layer. The output of the softmax was supervised by the model labels applied to the training images, and optimized by the cross-entropy loss step.

5.4. Ablation Study

We conducted ablation studies on the two large-scale datasets to validate the effectiveness of the proposed strategies both quantitatively and qualitatively. We provided a detailed analysis of the impacts arising from constraints in Section 5.4.1 and the sampling strategy in Section 5.4.2, respectively.

5.4.1. Constraint Influence

We conducted a series of comparison experiments to validate the effectiveness of the included illumination-aware metric learning and detail-aware discriminative feature learning. Specifically, we performed comprehensive ablation studies on combinations of L_l with L_{within} and L_{cross}. This was carried out to verify the benefits of fusing global and local features, as demonstrated in Table 5. Note that $TSPL_3^-$ and $TSPL_3$ used the same model to generate features, although $TSPL_3^-$ did not consider local features when calculating distances. It is evident from the table that our proposed strategy significantly improved vehicle re-ID performance over the baseline method.

Table 5. Evaluation results for the small VERI-DAN and Vehicle-1M test sets (%). The best results are shown in bold.

Method	L_{within}	L_{cross}	L_{local}	VERI-DAN		Vehicle-1M	
				Rank-1	Rank-5	Rank-1	Rank-5
(a) Baseline	-	-	-	96.26	99.23	85.86	96.67
(b) IANet	✓	✓		98.83	99.70	92.60	98.53
(c) $TSPL_1$	✓	✓	✓	**99.55**	99.93	96.29	99.13
(d) $TSPL_2$		✓	✓	99.40	99.94	95.51	98.65
(e) $TSPL_3^-$	✓		✓	99.52	99.95	96.59	99.18
(f) $TSPL_3$	✓		✓	99.54	**99.95**	**96.97**	**99.18**

IANet produced significant improvements despite relatively coarse-grained illumination classification. Comparing IANet with the single-branch baseline demonstrated Rank-1 accuracy improvements of +6.74% for Vehicle-1M and +2.57% for VERI-DAN. Consistent performance improvements across both datasets confirmed the effectiveness of a multi-branch network following the proposed progressive strategy.

Local constraints provide significant benefits for vehicle re-ID. Every variation of IANet, with the introduction of local constraints (i.e., TSPL1, TSPL2, and TSPL3) produced considerable improvements over IANet. Specifically, compared with IANet, local constraints yielded Rank-1 accuracy improvements of +3.69% for Vehicle-1M and +0.72% for VERI-DAN. In addition, combining either L_{within} or L_{cross} with L_{local} resulted in better performance than the combination of within-space and cross-space constraints. Combining cross-space constraints and local constraints resulted in Rank-1 accuracy increases of +2.91% for Vehicle-1M and +0.57% for VERI-DAN. The joint optimization of within-space and local constraints produced similar results, that is, +4.37% for Vehicle-1M and +0.71% for VERI-DAN. $TSPL_3$ achieved the best performance, while $TSPL_3^-$ outperformed IANet by ~1.8% (Rank-1 accuracy), even when local features were not involved in distance matrix calculations during testing. This result suggested that local constraints, which focus on extracting and leveraging local fine-grained visual cues, are also well suited for processing the variations and challenges introduced by illumination.

Within-space constraints are critical for re-ID. We observed a performance degradation when comparing $TSPL_2$ with $TSPL_1$ (−0.78% Rank-1 accuracy for Vehicle-1M and −0.15% Rank-1 accuracy for VERI-DAN.) In contrast, either $TSPL_3$ or $TSPL_3^-$ achieved better performance than $TSPL_2$ and $TSPL_1$. This was reasonable because without within-space constraints, TSPL was not able to learn from two relatively common scenarios: both the positive pairs and the negative pairs are observed under S-IL (or D-IL). We thus inferred that within-space constraints played a critical role in enhancing the retrieval capacity.

5.4.2. Sampling Strategy Influence

We developed a special test set to validate the importance of maintaining a balance between S-IL and D-IL pairs during training. All query and gallery samples were D-IL pairs, as summarized in Table 6. For each individual in a mini-batch, a ratio of 1:3 indicated that one image was captured during the daytime, while the other three images were taken during the nighttime. As demonstrated in Table 6, both the baseline and IANet achieved the best performance when this ratio was 2:2. This outcome suggested that maintaining an illumination-balanced sampling strategy was beneficial for query retrieval from the D-IL gallery.

Table 6. The effect of sampling strategy (%).

Method	Daytime: Nighttime	Test Size = 800		
		Rank-1	Rank-5	mAP
Baseline	Random	89.45	98.03	89.99
	1:3	88.8	97.83	88.54
	2:2	**92.05**	**98.03**	**91.27**
	3:1	89.60	97.58	89.93
IANet	Random	96.30	99.20	96.16
	1:3	96.37	99.35	95.41
	2:2	**96.82**	**99.40**	**95.82**
	3:1	96.15	99.23	95.02

5.5. Comparison with SOTA Methods

We compared the proposed method with a variety of SOTA vehicle re-ID methods on VERI-DAN and Vehicle-1M. We used InceptionV3 [37] as our baseline model, which was pretrained on ImageNet [39]. C2F-Rank [30] designed a multi-grain ranking loss to efficiently learn feature embedding with a coarse-to-fine structure. GSTN [40] automatically located vehicles and performed division for regional features to produce robust part-based features for re-ID. DFR-ST [13] involved appearance and spatio-temporal information to build robust features in the embedding space. DSN [41] utilized a cross-region attention to enhance spatial awareness of local features. The comparison results on the two datasets are detailed in Sections 5.5.1 and 5.5.2, respectively.

5.5.1. Evaluation with VERI-DAN

We verified the effectiveness of the proposed methodology in the presence of significant illumination changes by conducting comprehensive validation experiments using the VERI-DAN dataset, while also drawing comparisons among the InceptionV3 [37], IANet, and TSPL. As shown in Table 7, TSPL achieved significant improvements in Rank-1 accuracy and mAP over the baseline. The superiority of TSPL was evident through visual inspection as well, as illustrated in Figure 7. When compared with the baseline, we observed that TSPL could identify more correct matches among retrieved ranking lists in which the correct matches had lower rank values.

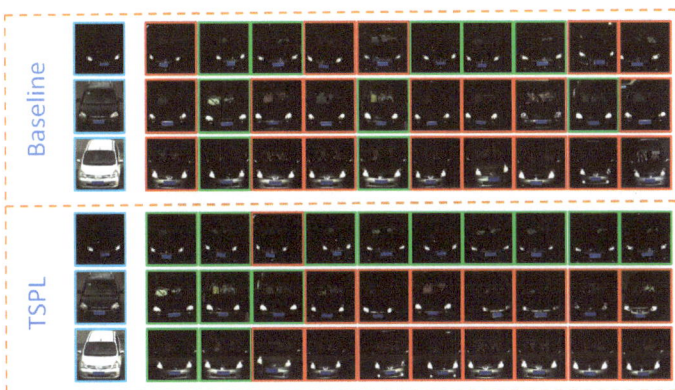

Figure 7. A visual comparison of baseline (**top**) and TSPL (**bottom**) performance. Images with blue contours show query vehicles, and images with green and red contours indicate correct and incorrect predictions, respectively.

Table 7. Performance with the VERI-DAN dataset (%). The best results are shown in bold.

Method	Small		Medium		Large	
	Rank-1	mAP	Rank-1	mAP	Rank-1	mAP
InceptionV3 [37]	96.26	93.59	93.27	89.25	91.10	85.36
IANet	98.83	97.65	98.42	96.31	98.03	95.35
TSPL	**99.54**	**98.91**	**99.51**	**98.41**	**99.33**	**97.80**

5.5.2. Evaluation with Vehicle-1M

We selected a group of 6448 (out of 50,000) vehicles in Vehicle-1M, whose images involved a variety of illumination conditions, as the training set. TSPL was compared with a variety of SOTA methods developed in recent years, including C2F-Rank [30], GSTN [40], DFR-ST [13], and DSN [41], as shown in Table 8. Despite the limited utilization of training samples, TSPL achieved remarkably competitive performance without any modified training strategies or additional detection modules. Specifically, compared with the second-place method, TSPL achieved +1.83%, +1.46%, and +1.66% Rank-1 improvements for the small, medium, and large test sets, respectively. This outcome demonstrated the superiority of the proposed two-stage progressive learning framework. Re-ranking and data augmentation may further improve performance.

Table 8. A comparison with SOTA algorithms applied to Vehicle-1M (%). The best results are shown in bold.

Method	Backbone	Training Set		Small		Medium		Large	
		IDS	Images	Rank-1	mAP	Rank-1	mAP	Rank-1	mAP
C2F-Rank (2018)	GoogLeNet	50,000	844,571	67.1	87.1	62.0	79.8	52.8	74.7
GSTN (2019)	ResNet18	50,000	844,571	95.14	96.29	92.79	**94.58**	90.75	**92.88**
DFR-ST (2022)	ResNet50	50,000	844,571	93.04	**96.70**	90.60	94.28	91.24	87.25
DSN (2023)	ResNet50	50,000	844,571	92.9	93.7	91.8	92.7	90.4	91.5
TSPL (Ours)	InceptionV3	6448	525,808	**96.97**	95.40	**94.25**	92.39	**92.90**	90.49

6. Conclusions

To address the challenging problem posed by dramatic changes in illumination, we proposed a novel two stage-progressive learning (TSPL) strategy for vehicle re-identification. This technique consisted of illumination-aware metric learning and detail-aware discriminative feature learning. Unlike existing methods that only learn a single metric for all types of lighting conditions, Stage I of TSPL aimed to learn proper vehicle representations under different illumination conditions using a two-branch network called IANet, which learned two separate metrics for images with similar and differing illumination conditions. By enforcing corresponding constraints (i.e., within-space constraints and cross-space constraints), IANet improved re-ID accuracy when retrieving D-IL images. Stage II in TSPL enabled the network to learn discriminative local features through an attention guided local feature extraction module (AG), which was optimized by local constraints. The proposed attention module not only facilitated the distinguishing of vehicles with similar appearances but also increased the associated robustness against variations in illumination. Additionally, the large-scale VERI-DAN was developed as part of the study, to provide images with significant changes in lighting. VERI-DAN is expected to facilitate the development of new re-ID methods by suppressing the distractions introduced by variable illumination. The implementation of each proposed metric learning strategy consistently improved re-ID performance with both VERI-DAN and Vehicle-1M, which further verified the effectiveness of TSPL. Despite the limited number of training samples in Vehicle-1M, TSPL achieved SOTA Rank-1 accuracy for the original test set, thereby demonstrating the superiority of this approach.

Author Contributions: Conceptualization, Z.W., Z.J. and X.L.; methodology, Z.W., Z.J. and X.L.; software, Z.W.; validation, Z.W., Z.J. and X.L.; formal analysis, Z.W.; investigation, Z.W.; resources, X.L.; data curation, Z.W.; writing—original draft preparation, Z.W.; writing—review and editing, Z.W., Z.J. and X.L.; visualization, Z.W.; supervision, Z.J. and X.L.; project administration, Z.J. and X.L.; funding acquisition, X.L. All authors have read and agreed to the published version of the manuscript.

Funding: This research was funded by the National Natural Science Foundation of China (grant No. U21B2090) and Natural Science Foundation of Guangdong Province, China (grant No. 2022A1515010361).

Data Availability Statement: The data presented in this study are available in the article. VERI-DAN is available at http://www.openits.cn/openData4/825.jhtml (accessed on 8 November 2023).

Conflicts of Interest: The authors declare no conflict of interest.

Abbreviations

The following abbreviations are used in this manuscript:

$P = (x_i, x_j)$	An image pair consists of image x_i and x_j
$D(x_i, x_j)$	Euclidean distance between x_i and x_j
x, x^+, and x^-	x and x^+ share the same vehicle ID, while x and x^- have different vehicle ID
S-IL	Similar-illumination
D-IL	Different-illumination
P_s^+	S-IL positive
P_d^+	D-IL positive
P_s^-	S-IL negative
P_d^-	D-IL negative
P_m^+	same-model positive pair
P_m^-	same-model negative pair
AG	Attention-guided local feature extraction module
CMC	Cumulative matching characteristics
DAM	Detail-aware local feature extraction module
IAM	Illumination-aware local feature extraction module
IANet	Illumination-aware network
mAP	Mean average precision
re-ID	Re-identification
SOTA	State-of-the-art
S-T	Spatio-temporal geographic coordinate information
TSPL	Two-stage progressive learning
VERI-DAN	Vehicle re-identification across day and night

References

1. Tang, Z.; Naphade, M.; Liu, M.-Y.; Yang, X.; Birchfield, S.; Wang, S.; Kumar, R.; Anastasiu, D.; Hwang, J.-N. CityFlow: A city-scale benchmark for multi-target multi-camera vehicle tracking and re-identification. In Proceedings of the 2019 IEEE/CVF Conference on Computer Vision and Pattern Recognition (CVPR), Long Beach, CA, USA, 15–20 June 2019; IEEE: New York, NY, USA, 2019; pp. 8789–8798.
2. Yang, H.; Cai, J.; Zhu, M.; Liu, C.; Wang, Y. Traffic-informed multi-camera sensing (TIMS) system based on vehicle re-identification. *IEEE Trans. Intell. Transp. Syst.* **2022**, *23*, 17189–17200. [CrossRef]
3. Chen, X.; Yu, H.; Zhao, F.; Hu, Y.; Li, Z. Global-local discriminative representation learning network for viewpoint-aware vehicle re-identification in intelligent transportation. *IEEE Trans. Instrum. Meas.* **2023**, *72*, 1–13. [CrossRef]
4. Lore, K.G.; Akintayo, A.; Sarkar, S. LLNet: A deep autoencoder approach to natural low-light image enhancement. *Pattern Recognit.* **2017**, *61*, 650–662. [CrossRef]
5. Jiang, Y.; Gong, X.; Liu, D.; Cheng, Y.; Fang, C.; Shen, X.; Yang, J.; Zhou, P.; Wang, Z. EnlightenGAN: Deep light enhancement without paired supervision. *IEEE Trans. Image Process.* **2021**, *30*, 2340–2349. [CrossRef]
6. Guo, C.; Li, C.; Guo, J.; Loy, C.C.; Hou, J.; Kwong, S.; Cong, R. Zero-reference deep curve estimation for low-light image enhancement. In Proceedings of the 2020 IEEE/CVF Conference on Computer Vision and Pattern Recognition (CVPR), Seattle, WA, USA, 13–19 June 2020; IEEE: New York, NY, USA, 2020; pp. 1777–1786.
7. Liu, Z.; Wang, K.; Wang, Z.; Lu, H.; Yuan, L. PatchNet: A tiny low-light image enhancement net. *J. Electron. Imaging* **2021**, *30*, 033023. [CrossRef]
8. Chen, Y.; Xia, R.; Zou, K.; Yang, K. FFTI: Image inpainting algorithm via features fusion and two-steps inpainting. *J. Vis. Commun. Image Represent.* **2023**, *91*, 103776. [CrossRef]

9. Watson, G.; Bhalerao, A. Person re-identification using deep foreground appearance modeling. *J. Electron. Imaging* **2018**, *27*, 1. [CrossRef]
10. Zapletal, D.; Herout, A. Vehicle re-identification for automatic video traffic surveillance. In Proceedings of the 2016 IEEE Conference on Computer Vision and Pattern Recognition Workshops (CVPRW), Las Vegas, NV, USA, 26 June–1 July 2016; IEEE: New York, NY, USA, 2016; pp. 1568–1574.
11. Liu, X.; Liu, W.; Ma, H.; Fu, H. Large-scale vehicle re-identification in urban surveillance videos. In Proceedings of the 2016 IEEE International Conference on Multimedia and Expo (ICME), Seattle, WA, USA, 11–15 July 2016; IEEE: New York, NY, USA, 2016; pp. 1–6.
12. Liu, X.; Liu, W.; Mei, T.; Ma, H. A deep learning-based approach to progressive vehicle re-identification for urban surveillance. In Proceedings of the Computer Vision—ECCV 2016, Amsterdam, The Netherlands, 11–14 October 2016; Leibe, B., Matas, J., Sebe, N., Welling, M., Eds.; Springer: Cham, Switzerland, 2016; Volume 9906, pp. 869–884.
13. Tu, J.; Chen, C.; Huang, X.; He, J.; Guan, X. DFR-ST: Discriminative feature representation with spatio-temporal cues for vehicle re-identification. *Pattern Recognit.* **2022**, *131*, 108887. [CrossRef]
14. Huang, W.; Zhong, X.; Jia, X.; Liu, W.; Feng, M.; Wang, Z.; Satoh, S. Vehicle re-identification with spatio-temporal model leveraging by pose view embedding. *Electronics* **2022**, *11*, 1354. [CrossRef]
15. Wang, Z.; Tang, L.; Liu, X.; Yao, Z.; Yi, S.; Shao, J.; Yan, J.; Wang, S.; Li, H.; Wang, X. Orientation invariant feature embedding and spatial temporal regularization for vehicle re-identification. In Proceedings of the 2017 IEEE International Conference on Computer Vision (ICCV), Venice, Italy, 22–29 October 2017; IEEE: New York, NY, USA, 2017; pp. 379–387.
16. Hermans, A.; Beyer, L.; Leibe, B. In defense of the triplet loss for person re-identification. *arXiv* **2017**, arXiv:1703.07737.
17. Zheng, Z.; Zheng, L.; Garrett, M.; Yang, Y.; Xu, M.; Shen, Y.-D. Dual-path convolutional image-text embeddings with instance loss. *ACM Trans. Multimed. Comput. Commun. Appl.* **2020**, *16*, 1–23. [CrossRef]
18. Ding, Y.; Fan, H.; Xu, M.; Yang, Y. Adaptive exploration for unsupervised person re-identification. *ACM Trans. Multimed. Comput. Commun. Appl.* **2020**, *16*, 1–19. [CrossRef]
19. Yan, K.; Tian, Y.; Wang, Y.; Zeng, W.; Huang, T. Exploiting multi-grain ranking constraints for precisely searching visually-similar vehicles. In Proceedings of the 2017 IEEE International Conference on Computer Vision (ICCV), Venice, Italy, 22–29 October 2017; pp. 562–570.
20. Lin, Y.; Zheng, L.; Zheng, Z.; Wu, Y.; Hu, Z.; Yan, C.; Yang, Y. Improving person re-identification by attribute and identity learning. *Pattern Recognit.* **2019**, *95*, 151–161. [CrossRef]
21. Wang, J.; Zhu, X.; Gong, S.; Li, W. Transferable joint attribute-identity deep learning for unsupervised person re-identification. In Proceedings of the 2018 IEEE/CVF Conference on Computer Vision and Pattern Recognition, Salt Lake City, UT, USA, 18–23 June 2018; IEEE: New York, NY, USA, 2018; pp. 2275–2284.
22. Li, H.; Li, C.; Zheng, A.; Tang, J.; Luo, B. Attribute and state guided structural embedding network for vehicle re-identification. *IEEE Trans. Image Process.* **2022**, *31*, 5949–5962. [CrossRef]
23. Zhou, Y.; Shao, L. Viewpoint-aware attentive multi-view inference for vehicle re-identification. In Proceedings of the 2018 IEEE/CVF Conference on Computer Vision and Pattern Recognition, Salt Lake City, UT, USA, 18–23 June 2018; IEEE: New York, NY, USA, 2018; pp. 6489–6498.
24. Zhou, Y.; Shao, L. Cross-view GAN based vehicle generation for re-identification. In Proceedings of the British Machine Vision Conference 2017, London, UK, 4–7 September 2017; British Machine Vision Association: London, UK, 2017; p. 186.
25. Chu, R.; Sun, Y.; Li, Y.; Liu, Z.; Zhang, C.; Wei, Y. Vehicle re-identification with viewpoint-aware metric learning. In Proceedings of the 2019 IEEE/CVF International Conference on Computer Vision (ICCV), Seoul, Republic of Korea, 27 October–2 November 2019; IEEE: New York, NY, USA, 2019; pp. 8281–8290.
26. Lu, Z.; Lin, R.; Lou, X.; Zheng, L.; Hu, H. Identity-unrelated information decoupling model for vehicle re-identification. *IEEE Trans. Intell. Transp. Syst.* **2022**, *23*, 19001–19015. [CrossRef]
27. Wang, S.; Wang, Q.; Min, W.; Han, Q.; Gai, D.; Luo, H. Trade-off background joint learning for unsupervised vehicle re-identification. *Vis. Comput.* **2023**, *39*, 3823–3835. [CrossRef]
28. Liu, H.; Tian, Y.; Wang, Y.; Pang, L.; Huang, T. Deep relative distance learning: Tell the difference between similar vehicles. In Proceedings of the 2016 IEEE Conference on Computer Vision and Pattern Recognition (CVPR), Las Vegas, NV, USA, 27–30 June 2016; IEEE: New York, NY, USA, 2016; pp. 2167–2175.
29. Lou, Y.; Bai, Y.; Liu, J.; Wang, S.; Duan, L. VERI-wild: A large dataset and a new method for vehicle re-identification in the wild. In Proceedings of the 2019 IEEE/CVF Conference on Computer Vision and Pattern Recognition (CVPR), Long Beach, CA, USA, 15–20 June 2019; IEEE: New York, NY, USA, 2019; pp. 3230–3238.
30. Guo, H.; Zhao, C.; Liu, Z.; Wang, J.; Lu, H. Learning coarse-to-fine structured feature embedding for vehicle re-identification. *Proc. AAAI Conf. Artif. Intell.* **2018**, *32*, 1. [CrossRef]
31. Lin, G.; Milan, A.; Shen, C.; Reid, I. RefineNet: Multi-path refinement networks for high-resolution semantic segmentation. In Proceedings of the 2017 IEEE Conference on Computer Vision and Pattern Recognition (CVPR), Honolulu, HI, USA, 21–26 July 2017; IEEE: New York, NY, USA, 2017; pp. 5168–5177.
32. Yosinski, J.; Clune, J.; Nguyen, A.; Fuchs, T.; Lipson, H. Understanding neural networks through deep visualization. *arXiv* **2015**, arXiv:1506.06579.

33. Hu, J.; Shen, L.; Sun, G. Squeeze-and-excitation networks. In Proceedings of the 2018 IEEE/CVF Conference on Computer Vision and Pattern Recognition, Salt Lake City, UT, USA, 18–23 June 2018; IEEE: New York, NY, USA, 2018; pp. 7132–7141.
34. Morris, B.T.; Trivedi, M.M. Learning, modeling, and classification of vehicle track patterns from live video. *IEEE Trans. Intell. Transp. Syst.* **2008**, *9*, 425–437. [CrossRef]
35. Javed, O.; Shafique, K.; Rasheed, Z.; Shah, M. Modeling inter-camera space–time and appearance relationships for tracking across non-overlapping views. *Comput. Vis. Image Underst.* **2008**, *109*, 146–162. [CrossRef]
36. Xu, J.; Jagadeesh, V.; Ni, Z.; Sunderrajan, S.; Manjunath, B.S. Graph-based topic-focused retrieval in distributed camera network. *IEEE Trans. Multimed.* **2013**, *15*, 2046–2057. [CrossRef]
37. Szegedy, C.; Vanhoucke, V.; Ioffe, S.; Shlens, J.; Wojna, Z. Rethinking the inception architecture for computer vision. In Proceedings of the 2016 IEEE Conference on Computer Vision and Pattern Recognition (CVPR), Las Vegas, NV, USA, 27–30 June 2016; IEEE: New York, NY, USA, 2016; pp. 2818–2826.
38. Redmon, J.; Farhadi, A. YOLOv3: An incremental improvement. *arXiv* **2018**, arXiv:1804.02767.
39. Krizhevsky, A.; Sutskever, I.; Hinton, G.E. ImageNet Classification with Deep Convolutional Neural Networks. In Proceedings of the Advances in Neural Information Processing Systems 25 (NIPS 2012), Lake Tahoe, NV, USA, 3–6 December 2012.
40. Ma, X.; Zhu, K.; Guo, H.; Wang, J.; Huang, M.; Miao, Q. Vehicle re-identification with refined part model. In Proceedings of the 2019 IEEE International Conference on Multimedia & Expo Workshops (ICMEW), Shanghai, China, 8–12 July 2019; IEEE: New York, NY, USA, 2019; pp. 603–606.
41. Zhu, W.; Wang, Z.; Wang, X.; Hu, R.; Liu, H.; Liu, C.; Wang, C.; Li, D. A dual self-attention mechanism for vehicle re-identification. *Pattern Recognit.* **2023**, *137*, 109258. [CrossRef]

Disclaimer/Publisher's Note: The statements, opinions and data contained in all publications are solely those of the individual author(s) and contributor(s) and not of MDPI and/or the editor(s). MDPI and/or the editor(s) disclaim responsibility for any injury to people or property resulting from any ideas, methods, instructions or products referred to in the content.

Article

DBENet: Dual-Branch Brightness Enhancement Fusion Network for Low-Light Image Enhancement

Yongqiang Chen [1], Chenglin Wen [2,*], Weifeng Liu [1] and Wei He [1]

[1] School of Electrical and Control Engineering, Shaanxi University of Science and Technology, Xi'an 710021, China; 210611029@sust.edu.cn (Y.C.); liuwf@sust.edu.cn (W.L.); 220612047@sust.edu.cn (W.H.)
[2] School of Automation, Guangdong University of Petrochemical Technology, Maoming 525000, China
* Correspondence: wencl@gdupt.edu.cn

Abstract: In this paper, we propose an end-to-end low-light image enhancement network based on the YCbCr color space to address the issues encountered by existing algorithms when dealing with brightness distortion and noise in the RGB color space. Traditional methods typically enhance the image first and then denoise, but this amplifies the noise hidden in the dark regions, leading to suboptimal enhancement results. To overcome these problems, we utilize the characteristics of the YCbCr color space to convert the low-light image from RGB to YCbCr and design a dual-branch enhancement network. The network consists of a CNN branch and a U-net branch, which are used to enhance the contrast of luminance and chrominance information, respectively. Additionally, a fusion module is introduced for feature extraction and information measurement. It automatically estimates the importance of corresponding feature maps and employs adaptive information preservation to enhance contrast and eliminate noise. Finally, through testing on multiple publicly available low-light image datasets and comparing with classical algorithms, the experimental results demonstrate that the proposed method generates enhanced images with richer details, more realistic colors, and less noise.

Keywords: low-light image enhancement; YCbCr space; dual-branch network; feature fusion

Citation: Chen, Y.; Wen, C.; Liu, W.; He, W. DBENet: Dual-Branch Brightness Enhancement Fusion Network for Low-Light Image Enhancement. *Electronics* **2023**, *12*, 3907. https://doi.org/10.3390/electronics12183907

Academic Editor: Eva Cernadas

Received: 17 August 2023
Revised: 11 September 2023
Accepted: 12 September 2023
Published: 16 September 2023

Copyright: © 2023 by the authors. Licensee MDPI, Basel, Switzerland. This article is an open access article distributed under the terms and conditions of the Creative Commons Attribution (CC BY) license (https://creativecommons.org/licenses/by/4.0/).

1. Introduction

In recent years, with the continuous improvement of computer hardware and algorithms, artificial intelligence has made remarkable progress in various fields, such as image recognition [1], object detection [2], semantic segmentation [3], and autonomous driving [4]. However, these technologies are mainly based on the assumption that images are captured under good lighting conditions, and there are few discussions on target recognition and detection technologies under weak illumination conditions such as insufficient exposure at night, unbalanced exposure, and insufficient illumination. Due to the low brightness, poor contrast, and color distortion of images and videos captured at night (example shown in Figure 1), the effectiveness of visual systems, such as object detection and recognition, is seriously weakened. Enhancing the quality of images captured under low-light conditions via low-light image enhancement (LLIE) can help improve the accuracy and effectiveness of many imaging-based systems. Therefore, LLIE is an essential technique in computer vision applications.

Currently, various methods have been proposed for LLIE, including histogram equalization (HE) [5,6], non-local means filtering [7], Retinex-based methods [8,9], multi-exposure fusion [10–12], and deep-learning-based methods [13–15], among others. While these approaches have achieved remarkable progress, two main challenges impede their practical deployment in real-world scenarios. First, it is difficult to handle extremely low illumination conditions. Deep-learning-based methods show satisfactory performance in slightly low-light images, but they perform poorly in extremely dark images. Additionally, due to the low signal-to-noise ratio, low-light images are usually affected by strong noise. Noise pollution and color distortion also bring difficulties to this task. Most of the previous studies on LLIE have focused on dealing with one of the above problems.

(a) LOL (b) VE-LOL (c) LIME (d) MEF

Figure 1. The comparison effect of various images taken in different scenes. From left to right, these images are derived from LOL, VE-LOL, LIME, and MEF datasets, respectively.

To explore the above problems, we counted the differences between 500 pairs of real low-/normal-light image pairs captured in the VE-LOL dataset in different color spaces and channels, as shown in Figure 2. In the RGB color space, all three channels exhibit significant degradation. However, in the YCbCr color space, the chrominance channels show higher PSNR and SSIM values compared to the luminance channel, indicating more severe image quality loss in the luminance channel. The inherent characteristics of the YCbCr color space indicate that the difference in luminance primarily resides in the Y channel, while the Cb and Cr channels are more susceptible to noise contamination. To achieve the goal of decoupling luminance distortion and noise interference, it is possible to employ channel-wise processing to handle different channels more appropriately. Therefore, in low-light image enhancement tasks, compared to the RGB color space, the YCbCr color space provides a favorable potential candidate space for separating luminance distortion and noise interference.

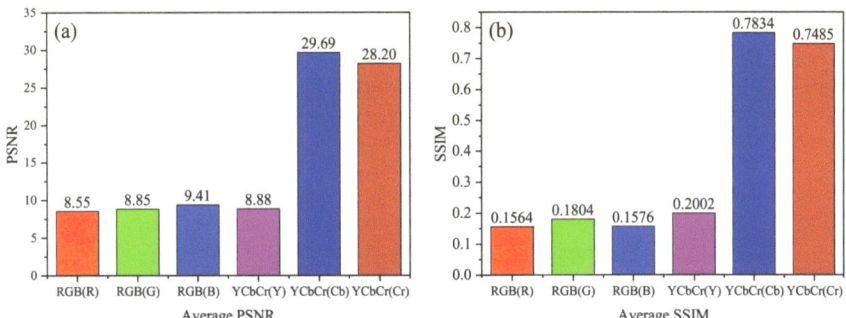

Figure 2. The difference between low-light images and normal images in RGB space and YCbCr space under the VE-LOL dataset. (**a**) The average PSNR values for each channel; (**b**) The average SSIM values for each channel.

In summary, the main contributions of this article are as follows:

- We propose a new hierarchical structure (DBENet) for enhancing low-light conditions in the real world. This framework includes networks for enhancing illumination maps, denoising chromatic information, and feature map fusion, respectively;
- We employed a CNN branch to predict the gamma matrix and utilized nonlinear mapping to regulate brightness variations, effectively suppressing overexposure during the enhancement process;

- Our method outperforms existing techniques on benchmark datasets, achieving significant improvements in evaluation metrics such as MAE, PSNR, SSIM, LPIPS (reference), and NIQE (no-reference), demonstrating its superior efficiency.

The rest of this paper is as follows: Section 2 introduces the proposed network framework. Section 3 explains the loss function used in each component. Section 4 presents the evaluation of our method via subjective and objective assessments of multiple datasets. Sections 5 and 6 are dedicated to the discussion and conclusion, respectively

2. Related Works

In general, image enhancement methods can be roughly divided into two categories: non-learning-based methods and learning-based methods.

2.1. Non-Learning-Based Methods

LLIE plays an irreplaceable role in recovering the intrinsic colors and details, as well as compressing noise in low-light images. In the following, we provide a comprehensive review of previous work on low-light image enhancement. Traditional LLIE methods encompass techniques such as tone mapping [16], gamma correction [17], histogram equalization [18], and those based on the Retinex theory [19–22]. Tone mapping is used to create more detailed, colorful, and high-contrast images while maintaining a natural appearance. However, linear mapping can lead to the loss of information in bright and dark areas. Gamma correction employs nonlinear tone mapping to handle the shadows and highlights in image signals, but selecting global parameters can be difficult and may result in overexposure or underexposure. Histogram equalization enhances image contrast by transforming the histogram, but it may yield unsatisfactory results in certain local regions. Adaptive histogram equalization [23] can map the histogram of local regions to a simpler distribution for improved effects. The Retinex theory [24] is a computational theory that simulates human visual perception and can achieve color constancy, color enhancement, and high dynamic range compression. However, there is still room for improvement in its processing mechanisms and universality, and its effectiveness may vary in different scenarios. In general, traditional model-based methods heavily rely on manually designed priors or statistical models, which may limit their applications.

2.2. Learning-Based Methods

In the field of LLIE, methods based on deep learning have currently become the mainstream research direction. LLNet [25] represents a seminal contribution from the LLIE group, which focuses on contrast enhancement and denoising via a depth autoencoder-based approach. However, it is worth noting that this work does not explore the intricate relationship between real-world illumination and noise, consequently leading to persistent issues such as residual noise and excessive smoothing. In contrast, Chen et al. [26] introduced Retinex-Net, a method that decomposes the input image into a reflectance map and an illumination map. It enhances the illumination map using a deep neural network for low-light conditions and then applies BM3D [27] for denoising, while Retinex-Net effectively enhances brightness and image details, it tends to suffer from inadequate image smoothing and severe color distortion. Lv et al. [28] proposed a comprehensive end-to-end multi-branch enhancement network (MBLLEN) encompassing feature extraction, enhancement, and fusion modules to boost the performance of LLIE. Drawing inspiration from super-resolution reconstruction techniques, UTVNet [29] and URetinex [30] introduced an adaptive unfolding network tailored for robustly denoising and enhancing low-light images. Another notable approach by Wang et al. [31] introduces a two-stage Fourier-based LLIE network, FourLLIE. This method enhances the brightness of low-light images by estimating amplitude transformation in the Fourier space. Furthermore, it leverages a signal-to-noise ratio (SNR) map to provide a priori information regarding global Fourier frequencies and local spatial details for image restoration. Notably, FourLLIE is both lightweight and highly effective in terms of enhancement.

Recently, zero-shot-learning-based methods has garnered substantial attention due to their efficiency, cost-effectiveness, and ability to leverage limited image data. For instance, Liu et al. [32] introduced Retinex-based Unrolling with Architecture Search (RUAS) and devised a collaborative reference-free learning strategy to discover low-light prior architectures from a compact search space. Guo et al. [33] presented Zero-DCE, a technique employing an intuitive nonlinear curve mapping. Subsequently, they improved upon this method with Zero-DCE++ [34], which is faster and lighter. However, it is important to note that Zero-DCE relies on multiple exposure training data and does not effectively address noise, especially in extreme enhancement scenarios. Zhu et al. [35] introduced RRDNet, a three-branch convolutional neural network designed for restoring underexposed images. RRDNet employs an iterative approach to decompose input images into their constituent parts: illumination, reflectance, and noise. This is achieved via the minimization of a customized loss function and the adjustment of the illumination map via gamma correction. The reconstructed reflectance and adjusted illumination map are then multiplied element-wise to generate the enhanced output. In another development, Ma et al. [36] proposed a learning framework called self-calibrating illumination (SCI) for rapid and adaptable enhancement in real-world low-illumination scene images. This method estimates a convergent illuminance map via a neural network and, following Retinex theory, divides the input low-illuminance image element-wise with the estimated illuminance map to derive an enhanced reflectance map. It is worth noting that while SCI achieves a convergence of the illuminance map through iterations, it does not explicitly address noise interference in the process. PSENet [37] offers an unsupervised approach for extreme-light image enhancement, effectively addressing image enhancement challenges in both overexposure and underexposure scenarios.

3. The Proposed Network

In the third section, we first introduced our proposed DBENet and provided a more detailed explanation of the components we proposed in the following subsections.

The architecture of the proposed dual-branch enhancement network (DBENet) is shown in Figure 3. DBENet consists of two branches (CNN branch and U-Net branch) and a fusion module. The network follows a divide-and-conquer strategy, where the input image is transformed from the original RGB color space to the YCbCr color space for separate processing. The CNN branch handles the luminance component (Y) based on the nonlinear function. The encoder–decoder branch network processes the chrominance component (CbCr) starting from global features. Finally, the cascaded fusion features (Y_{res} and W_{res}) from both branches are fed into the fusion module to aggregate the enhanced image.

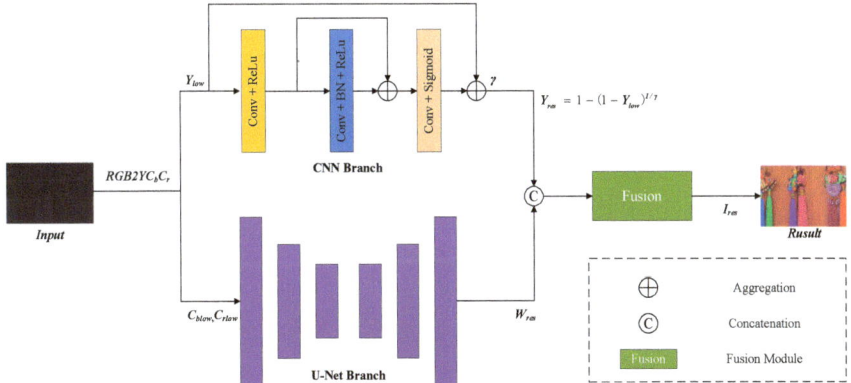

Figure 3. The proposed network structure framework diagram.

3.1. CNN Branch

The CNN branch based on the residual concept consists of three parts: the initial layer Conv + ReLU, the middle layer Conv + BatchNorm + ReLU, and the final layer Conv + Sigmoid. The convolutional kernel size is set uniformly to 3 × 3 with a dilation rate of 1, which enlarges the receptive field of the convolutional network and enhances the feature extraction ability without increasing the computational burden. The BatchNorm layer normalizes each channel to reduce inter-channel dependencies and accelerate network convergence. After obtaining the estimated gamma component γ through the network, we employ the gamma adjustment scheme [38] to enhance the visibility of details in both dark and bright regions. The nonlinear function is represented by the following equation:

$$Y_{res} = 1 - (1 - Y_{low})^{1/\gamma} \qquad (1)$$

In Equation (1), Y_{res} represents the enhanced result, and γ and Y_{low}, respectively, denote the predicted gamma map and the separated luminance component of the original image. This function is designed to address the issue of overexposure that often occurs when enhancing results in the presence of non-uniform lighting and complex light sources in the original image. Unlike directly applying the gamma function to the original image, we draw inspiration from dehazing techniques and apply it to the inverted image to obtain the enhanced output. This approach arises from the shared characteristics of blurred and low-light images, which often exhibit low dynamic range and high noise levels. Therefore, dehazing techniques, such as using inverted images, can be employed to enhance and alleviate this concern.

Within the CNN branch, the process begins by normalizing the image to a 0–1 range. Subsequently, the network learns the intermediate parameter gamma for predicting the mapping function and, finally, computes the predicted result. As illustrated in Figure 4's mapping curve, when the gamma value is less than 1, it brightens areas with underexposure, while gamma values greater than 1 darken areas with overexposure. The purpose of this function is to provide reasonable suppression, allowing the control and mitigation of the local intensity increase, while simultaneously enhancing the overall image quality.

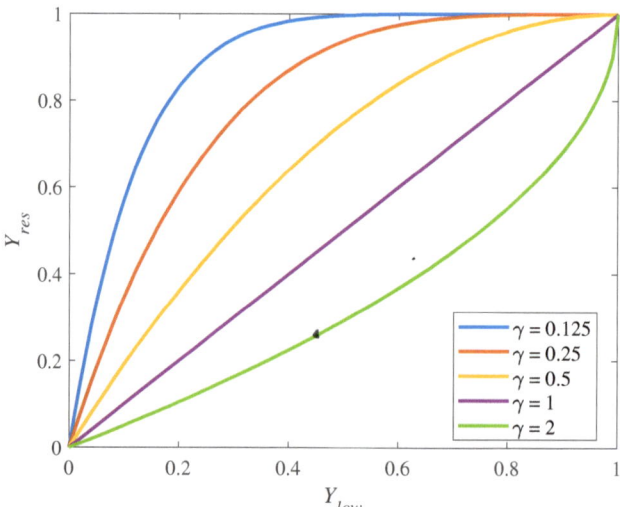

Figure 4. Function mapping curves corresponding to different γ values.

3.2. U-Net Branch

Due to the influence of the acquisition environment and equipment, low-illumination images often contain a lot of noise in dark areas. Noise will reduce image information and image quality. In order to better dealing with low-light images, it is necessary to achieve better denoising and detail preservation effects.

In an effort to reveal the details while avoiding the increase in distortion, we propose a chromaticity denoising module. The module uses the chrominance channel of the low-illumination image to mainly reflect the chrominance information of the image, which can be represented as W. Since the color information distortion is often non-local, in order to obtain the global color information of the image, the classical U-Net network structure is used to enrich the spatial information by extracting features of different sizes so that the semantic information is more diverse. Through the encoder–decoder structure, the U-Net branch can capture context information at different scales. In addition, the introduction of skip connections enables U-Net [39] to make full use of feature information and restore details and boundaries, as shown in Figure 5. In the U-Net branch, the encoder expands the receptive field of convolution via layer-by-layer pooling operation. In the bottleneck layer of the network, the larger receptive field can extract the non-local chrominance information for contrast recovery, and the decoder expands the non-local information to the global via layer-by-layer upsampling.

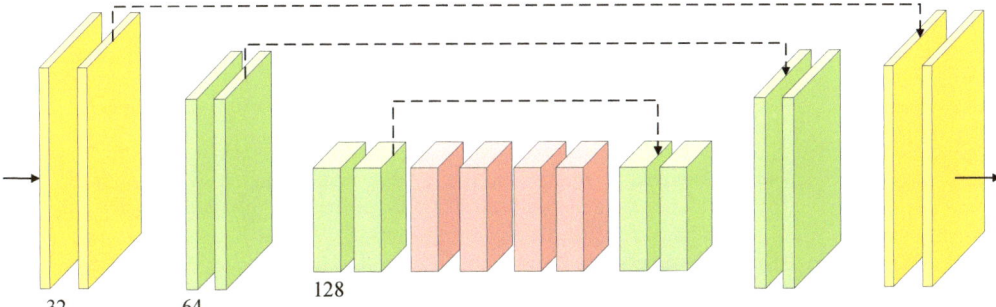

Figure 5. The structure of the U-Net Branch.

3.3. Fusion Module

In our method, we did not perform the corresponding transformation from YCbCr to RGB color space on the returned three components. Instead, we did not design a unique fusion rule but used a fusion module to generate the fused result I_{res}. As shown in Figure 6, the architecture of the fusion module consists of 10 layers, with Y_{res} and W_{res} concatenated as inputs. Each layer has a convolutional operation, followed by an activation function. The kernel size of all convolutional layers is set to 3×3, with a stride of 1. The padding mode is set to "reflect" to prevent edge artifacts. No pooling layers are used to avoid information loss. The activation function in the first nine layers is LeakyReLU with a slope of 0.2, while the activation function in the last layer is Sigmoid. Furthermore, studies [40] have shown that building short connections between layers close to the input and layers close to the output can significantly deepen and effectively train neural networks. Therefore, in the first seven layers, dense connection blocks are utilized to improve information flow and performance. In these layers, shortcut direct connections are established in a feed-forward manner between each layer and all preceding layers, reducing the problem of vanishing gradients.

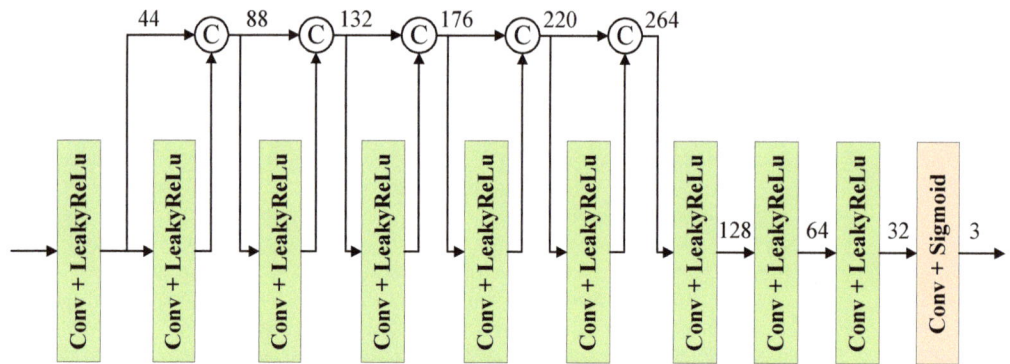

Figure 6. The structure of the fusion module. Numbers are the channels of corresponding feature maps.

3.4. Loss Function

During the training phase, due to the similar degradation patterns of the Cb and Cr chroma channels, for convenience, we use W to represent both the Cb and Cr channels simultaneously. The loss function of the entire network as follows:

$$\mathcal{L}_{Total} = \mathcal{L}_1(Y_{res}, Y_{high}) + \mathcal{L}_2(W_{res}, W_{high}) + \mathcal{L}_3(I_{res}, I_{high}) \tag{2}$$

Among these, I represents the output of the network, and Y and W represent the outputs of the CNN branch and the U-Net branch, respectively. The subscripts "res" and "high" indicate the enhanced result and the corresponding normal image.

In Equation (2), the three loss functions, $\mathcal{L}_1$, $\mathcal{L}_2$, and $\mathcal{L}_3$, share the same form. Taking $\mathcal{L}_1$ as an example, we have $\mathcal{L}_1 = L_2 + L_{ssim}$. The two components represent the mean square error loss and the structural similarity loss function, respectively. The first term of the loss function aims to measure the reconstruction error, while the second term measures the differences in brightness, contrast, and structural similarity between the two images. Similarly, taking $\mathcal{L}_1$ as an example, the L_2 loss is defined as shown in Equation (3), while the definition of the L_{ssim} is presented in Equation (4).

$$L_2 = \left\| Y_{res} - Y_{high} \right\|_2^2 \tag{3}$$

$$L_{ssim} = 1 - SSIM(Y_{res} - Y_{high}) \tag{4}$$

where SSIM [41] is the structural similarity, the function is defined as follows:

$$\text{SSIM}(x,y) = \frac{(2 \times u_x \times u_y + c_1)(2 \times \sigma_{xy} + c_2)}{\left(u_x^2 + u_y^2 + c_1\right)\left(\sigma_x^2 + \sigma_y^2 + c_2\right)} \tag{5}$$

4. Experimental Results and Analysis

In this part, we describe the experimental results and analysis in detail. First, we briefly introduce the experimental setting. Then, the qualitative and quantitative evaluation of paired and unpaired data sets is described. Finally, the experimental results are analyzed.

4.1. Experimental Settings

Parameter Settings: Parameter Settings: All experiments in this paper were conducted in the same configuration environment, i.e., training environment configuration: Ubuntu system, 32 GB RAM, and NVIDIA GeForce RTX3090 GPU. The network framework was constructed with the PyTorch framework and optimized using Admm [42] with parameters $\beta_1 = 0.9$, $\beta_2 = 0.99$, $\epsilon = 0.95$. In addition, the batch size was 16, the learning rate was 0.0002, and the training sample size was uniformly adjusted to 256 × 256. A total of 485 randomly selected paired images from the LOL dataset were used to train our model. The training epoch number was set to 3000.

Compared Methods: As for the low-light-level image intensifier, we conducted a visual evaluation of our proposed network on classic low-light image datasets (LOL and other datasets) and compared it with other state-of-the-art methods and available codes, including the traditional methods HE [5] and tone mapping [16], deep-learning-based methods Retinex-Net [26], RUAS [32], Zero-DCE [33], SCI [36], and RRDNet [35].

Evaluation Criteria: We employ quantitative image quality assessment metrics for comparative analysis to illustrate the effectiveness of the algorithms presented in this paper. To gauge the disparities in color, structural, and high-level feature similarity, we utilize MAE, PSNR, SSIM [41], LPIPS [43], and NIQE [44] as measurement indices. In addition, two paired data sets (LOL and VE-LOL) and two unpaired data sets (LIME and MEF) were selected for verification experiments to test their performance in image enhancement.

4.2. Subjective Visual Evaluation

Figures 7 and 8 show some representative results of the visual comparison of various algorithms. Figures 7 and 8 belong to the LOL and VE-LOL datasets, respectively. In Figure 7, it can be seen that HE has obvious image distortion and color distortion; Retinex-Net amplifies inherent noise, losing image details; SCI, Zero-DCE, and RRD-Net have weak brightness enhancement capabilities; tone mapping, RUAS, and our method perform extremely well in brightness and color aspects. From Figure 8, the enhanced results show that HE can significantly increase the brightness of low-light images. However, it applies contrast enhancement to each channel of RGB separately, causing color distortion. Retinex-Net significantly improves the visual quality of low-light images, but it overly smooths out details, enlarges noise, and even causes color deviation. Tone mapping can stretch the dynamic range of the image, but it still has insufficient enhancement for the grandstand seating section in the image. Although the image effect of RUAS is delicate and has no obvious noise interference, it does not successfully brighten the image in extremely dark areas (such as the central seat part). SCI and RRD-Net perform poorly in darker images and cannot effectively enhance low-light images. Zero-DCE can preserve the details of the image relatively completely, but the brightness enhancement is not obvious, and the color contrast of the image is significantly reduced. Compared with the ground truth, our method not only significantly improves brightness but also preserves colors and details to a large extent, thereby improving image quality.

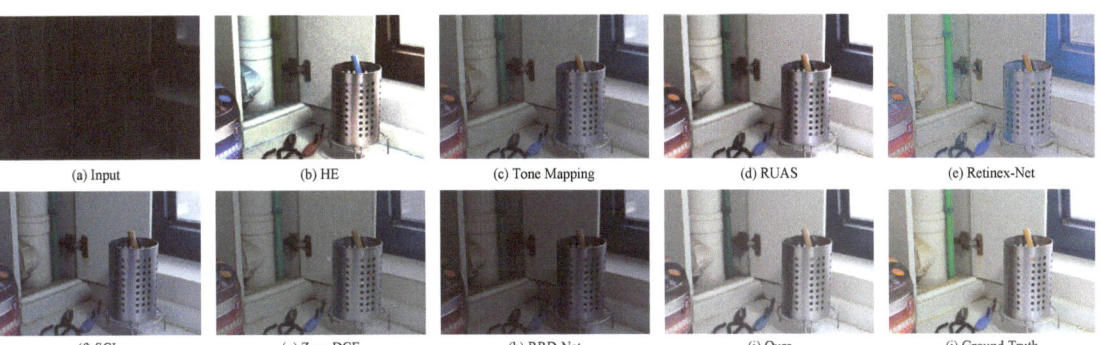

Figure 7. Visual comparisons of different approaches on the LOL benchmark.

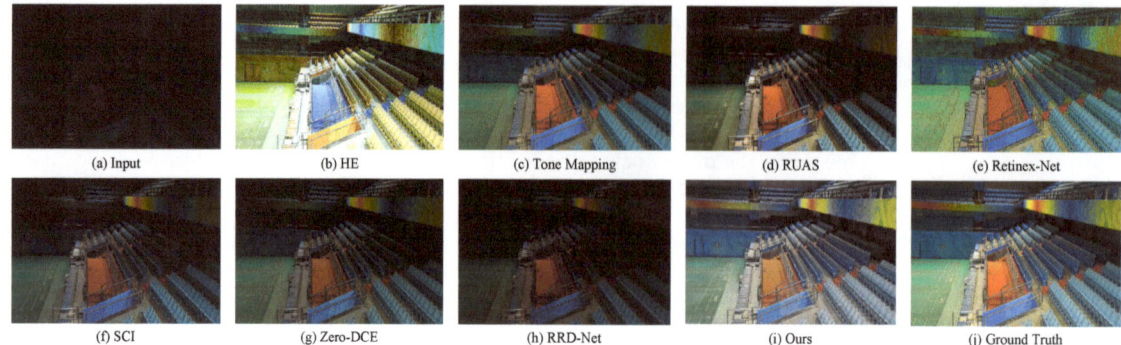

Figure 8. Visual comparisons of different approaches on the VE-LOL benchmark.

To comprehensively evaluate various algorithms, we also selected two unpaired benchmarks (LIME, MEF) for the verification experiments. As shown in Figures 9 and 10, we show the visual contrast effects produced via these cutting-edge methods under various benchmarks. From these enhancement results, it is evident that HE greatly improves the contrast of the image, but there is also a significant color shift phenomenon. Retinex-Net introduces visually unsatisfactory artifacts and noise. Tone mapping and RRD-Net can preserve image details, but the overall enhancement strength is not significant, and they fail to effectively enhance local dark areas. RUAS and SCI can effectively enhance low-contrast images, but during the enhancement process, they tend to excessively enhance originally bright areas, such as the sky and clouds in Figure 10, which are replaced by an overly enhanced white-ish tone. Among all the methods, Zero-DCE and our proposed method perform well on these two benchmarks, effectively enhancing image contrast while maintaining color balance and detail clarity.

Figure 9. Visual comparisons of different approaches on the LIME benchmark.

Figure 10. Visual comparisons of different approaches on the MEF benchmark.

4.3. Objective Evaluation

We evaluate the results of the proposed method and seven other representative methods on the LOL and VE-LOL paired datasets. Table 1 shows the average MAE, PSNR, SSIM, and LPIPS scores of these two public datasets. Among these evaluation indexes, the higher the PNSR and SSIM values, the better the image quality. On the contrary, the smaller the MAE and LPIPS, the better the image quality. From Table 1, it is evident that our method outperforms other approaches significantly on both test sets, demonstrating the effectiveness of the DBENet framework we proposed.

Table 1. Quantitative comparison on LOL and VE-LOL datasets. The best result is in bold, whereas the second best results are in underline, respectively.

Dataset	Method	MAE↓	PSNR↑	SSIM↑	LPIPS↓
LOL	Input	0.3914	7.7733	0.1952	0.4191
	HE	0.1879	12.918	0.3369	0.4376
	Tone Mapping	0.1517	16.5034	0.5092	0.2312
	RUAS	0.1534	16.4047	0.4997	<u>0.1937</u>
	Retinex-Net	<u>0.1255</u>	<u>16.7740</u>	0.4196	0.3758
	SCI	0.1912	14.784	0.5220	0.2385
	Zero-DCE	0.1860	14.7971	<u>0.5573</u>	0.2368
	RRDNet	0.2739	11.4037	0.4575	0.2480
	Ours	**0.1007**	**19.8625**	**0.8149**	**0.1152**
VE-LOL (real)	Input	0.3131	9.7168	0.1989	0.3472
	HE	0.4901	13.1314	0.3760	0.4140
	Tone Mapping	<u>0.1298</u>	<u>17.2469</u>	0.5262	0.2349
	RUAS	0.1621	15.3255	<u>0.4878</u>	0.2165
	Retinex-Net	0.1313	16.0971	0.4011	0.4368
	SCI	0.1470	17.3035	0.5336	0.2021
	Zero-DCE	0.1320	17.9992	0.5719	0.2154
	RRDNet	0.2089	13.9818	0.4832	<u>0.1896</u>
	Ours	**0.0099**	**19.8285**	**0.8437**	**0.1086**

In addition, we also evaluated these datasets using the non-reference image quality evaluator (NIQE), as shown in Table 2. With the exception of Zero-DCE, which had the best score on some datasets, our NIQE scores outperformed most of the other methods. Overall, Tables 1 and 2 provide stronger evidence for the effectiveness and applicability of our proposed method.

Table 2. NIQE scores on low-light image sets (LOL, VE-LOL, LIME, and MEF). The best result is in bold, whereas the second best results are in underline, respectively. Smaller NIQE scores indicate a better quality of perceptual tendency.

Method	LOL	VE-LOL (Real)	LIME	MEF
HE	8.1541	8.7654	6.8883	3.5638
Tone Mapping	7.8310	7.9683	**3.9201**	3.5254
RUAS	<u>6.3400</u>	<u>6.5330</u>	5.3642	5.4255
Retinex-Net	8.8781	9.4276	4.7669	4.4097
SCI	7.8766	8.0461	4.2064	3.6277
Zero-DCE	7.7925	8.0449	<u>3.9733</u>	**3.3023**
RRDNet	7.4777	7.7131	4.0689	<u>3.4796</u>
Ours	**5.2485**	**5.0481**	4.3475	4.2920

4.4. Ablation Study

We conducted ablation studies on the dual-branch network, and the data results are shown in Table 3. The CNN branch is based on spatially extracting local features from the image, which may overlook global contextual relationships that are crucial for understanding the overall representation. On the other hand, the encoder–decoder branch-based method captures global contextual relationships via skip connections but may overlook local features, which can affect the fusion outcome. We performed experiments on three different methods, including a single branch and a combination of both branches. The experimental results indicate that our proposed dual-branch fusion network outperforms the CNN branch or U-Net branch methods in all metrics. Therefore, combining the capture of global contextual relationships and local features can improve the fusion-enhancement effect for low-light images.

Table 3. Data of ablation experiment.

Methods	PSNR	SSIM
CNN branch	18.6481	0.7128
U-Net branch	17.5846	0.7813
DBENet	19.8625	0.8149

5. Discussion

To shed light on the core mechanisms underpinning our model's exceptional performance, we introduce DBENet, a deep-learning framework designed explicitly for enhancing and denoising low-light images. Our model adopts a divide-and-conquer strategy, breaking down the intricacies into manageable components for separate handling. Furthermore, we combine the improved gamma correction with deep learning, as illustrated in Figure 11. The regions highlighted within the red boxes demonstrate that our approach avoids excessive amplification of well-exposed parts of the input image. This approach enables us to carefully balance image fidelity while enhancing brightness.

Figure 11. Visual comparison examples of non-uniform illumination images. The top images represent the input, while the bottom images depict the model's output. In particular, within the red rectangles, the light sources are not excessively enhanced.

Moreover, this research opens opportunities for future investigations. These prospects include the reduction in model inference time, enabling the real-time processing of high-resolution visuals, and exploring applications in low-light video enhancement. These endeavors hold significant potential for advancing the frontiers of image and video enhancement across a diverse range of real-world scenarios.

6. Conclusions

We propose an end-to-end dual-branch low-light enhancement architecture network based on the YCbCr color space, inspired by the separation of luminance and chrominance information in YCbCr color space. This network aims to address the issues of brightness distortion, color distortion, and noise pollution in enhanced images caused by the high coupling between brightness and RGB channels in low-light images. The enhancement network adopts a dual-branch structure to enhance the contrast of the luminance channel and suppress the noise in the chrominance channel. The experimental results demonstrate that our proposed method effectively enhances brightness, restores image textures, and produces images with richer details, more realistic colors, and less noise. Compared to classical low-light enhancement algorithms, our approach achieves significant improvements in multiple metrics and multiple datasets, while being more lightweight and faster in processing speed.

Author Contributions: Conceptualization, Y.C., C.W. and W.L.; methodology, C.W.; software, Y.C.; validation, Y.C. and W.H.; formal analysis, Y.C.; investigation, Y.C.; resources, Y.C.; data curation, Y.C.; writing—original draft preparation, Y.C.; writing—review and editing, C.W. and W.L.; visualization, W.H.; supervision, C.W. and W.L.; project administration, C.W.; funding acquisition, C.W. and W.L. All authors have read and agreed to the published version of the manuscript.

Funding: This work was supported in part by the National Natural Science Foundation of China under Grant No. 62125307 and supported by the Opening Project of Guangdong Provincial Key Lab of Robotics and Intelligent System.

Institutional Review Board Statement: Not applicable.

Informed Consent Statement: Not applicable.

Data Availability Statement: These data can be found here: LOL https://daooshee.github.io/BMVC2018website/, VE-LOL https://flyywh.github.io/IJCV2021LowLight_VELOL/, and LIME and MEF https://drive.google.com/drive/folders/1lp6m5JE3kf3M66Dicbx5wSnvhxt90V4T, accessed on 10 August 2018, 11 January 2021, and 23 June 2019, respectively.

Conflicts of Interest: The authors declare no conflict of interest.

Nomenclatures

DBENet	Dual-Branch Brightness Enhancement Fusion Network
FM	Fusion Module
MAE	Mean Absolute Error
PSNR	Peak Signal-to-Noise Ratio
SSIM	Structural Similarity Index Measure
LPIPS	Learned Perceptual Image Patch Similarity
NIQE	Natural Image Quality Evaluator

References

1. Meng, L.; Li, H.; Chen, B.C.; Lan, S.; Wu, Z.; Jiang, Y.G.; Lim, S.N. Adavit: Adaptive vision transformers for efficient image recognition. In Proceedings of the IEEE/CVF Conference on Computer Vision and Pattern Recognition, New Orleans, LA, USA, 18–24 June 2022; pp. 12309–12318.
2. Fang, W.; Wang, L.; Ren, P. Tinier-YOLO: A real-time object detection method for constrained environments. *IEEE Access* **2019**, *8*, 1935–1944. [CrossRef]
3. Strudel, R.; Garcia, R.; Laptev, I.; Schmid, C. Segmenter: Transformer for semantic segmentation. In Proceedings of the IEEE/CVF International Conference on Computer Vision, Montreal, BC, Canada, 11–17 October 2021; pp. 7262–7272.
4. Fujiyoshi, H.; Hirakawa, T.; Yamashita, T. Deep learning-based image recognition for autonomous driving. *IATSS Res.* **2019**, *43*, 244–252. [CrossRef]
5. Stark, J.A. Adaptive image contrast enhancement using generalizations of histogram equalization. *IEEE Trans. Image Process.* **2000**, *9*, 889–896. [CrossRef]
6. Reza, A.M. Realization of the contrast limited adaptive histogram equalization (CLAHE) for real-time image enhancement. *J. Vlsi Signal Process. Syst. Signal, Image Video Technol.* **2004**, *38*, 35–44. [CrossRef]
7. Li, L.; Si, Y.; Jia, Z. Remote sensing image enhancement based on non-local means filter in NSCT domain. *Algorithms* **2017**, *10*, 116. [CrossRef]
8. Lam, E.Y. Combining gray world and retinex theory for automatic white balance in digital photography. In Proceedings of the Ninth International Symposium on Consumer Electronics, Macau SAR, China, 14–16 June 2005; pp. 134–139.
9. Xie, C.; Tang, H.; Fei, L.; Zhu, H.; Hu, Y. IRNet: An Improved Zero-Shot Retinex Network for Low-Light Image Enhancement. *Electronics* **2023**, *12*, 3162. [CrossRef]
10. Park, J.S.; Soh, J.W.; Cho, N.I. Generation of high dynamic range illumination from a single image for the enhancement of undesirably illuminated images. *Multimed. Tools Appl.* **2019**, *78*, 20263–20283. [CrossRef]
11. Xu, H.; Ma, J.; Jiang, J.; Guo, X.; Ling, H. U2Fusion: A unified unsupervised image fusion network. *IEEE Trans. Pattern Anal. Mach. Intell.* **2020**, *44*, 502–518. [CrossRef]
12. Deng, X.; Zhang, Y.; Xu, M.; Gu, S.; Duan, Y. Deep Coupled Feedback Network for Joint Exposure Fusion and Image Super-Resolution. *IEEE Trans. Image Process. Publ. IEEE Signal Process. Soc.* **2021**, *30*, 3098–3112. [CrossRef]
13. Lu, H.; Gong, J.; Liu, Z.; Lan, R.; Pan, X. FDMLNet: A Frequency-Division and Multiscale Learning Network for Enhancing Low-Light Image. *Sensors* **2022**, *22*, 8244. [CrossRef]
14. Guo, X.; Hu, Q. Low-light image enhancement via breaking down the darkness. *Int. J. Comput. Vis.* **2023**, *131*, 48–66. [CrossRef]
15. Zhang, J.; Ji, R.; Wang, J.; Sun, H.; Ju, M. DEGAN: Decompose-Enhance-GAN Network for Simultaneous Low-Light Image Lightening and Denoising. *Electronics* **2023**, *12*, 3038. [CrossRef]
16. Ahn, H.; Keum, B.; Kim, D.; Lee, H.S. Adaptive local tone mapping based on retinex for high dynamic range images. In Proceedings of the 2013 IEEE International Conference on Consumer Electronics (ICCE), Las Vegas, NV, USA, 11–14 January 2013; pp. 153–156.
17. Huang, S.C.; Cheng, F.C.; Chiu, Y.S. Efficient contrast enhancement using adaptive gamma correction with weighting distribution. *IEEE Trans. Image Process.* **2012**, *22*, 1032–1041. [CrossRef] [PubMed]
18. Ooi, C.H.; Isa, N.A.M. Quadrants dynamic histogram equalization for contrast enhancement. *IEEE Trans. Consum. Electron.* **2010**, *56*, 2552–2559. [CrossRef]
19. Guo, X.; Li, Y.; Ling, H. LIME: Low-light image enhancement via illumination map estimation. *IEEE Trans. Image Process.* **2016**, *26*, 982–993. [CrossRef]
20. Jobson, D.J.; Rahman, Z.u.; Woodell, G.A. Properties and performance of a center/surround retinex. *IEEE Trans. Image Process.* **1997**, *6*, 451–462. [CrossRef]
21. Rahman, Z.u.; Jobson, D.J.; Woodell, G.A. Multi-scale retinex for color image enhancement. In Proceedings of the 3rd IEEE International Conference on Image Processing, Austin, TX, USA, 19 September 1996; Volume 3, pp. 1003–1006.
22. Jobson, D.J.; Rahman, Z.u.; Woodell, G.A. A multiscale retinex for bridging the gap between color images and the human observation of scenes. *IEEE Trans. Image Process.* **1997**, *6*, 965–976. [CrossRef]

23. Pizer, S.M.; Amburn, E.P.; Austin, J.D.; Cromartie, R.; Geselowitz, A.; Greer, T.; ter Haar Romeny, B.; Zimmerman, J.B.; Zuiderveld, K. Adaptive histogram equalization and its variations. *Comput. Vision Graph. Image Process.* **1987**, *39*, 355–368. [CrossRef]
24. Land, E.H.; McCann, J.J. Lightness and retinex theory. *Josa* **1971**, *61*, 1–11. [CrossRef]
25. Lore, K.G.; Akintayo, A.; Sarkar, S. LLNet: A deep autoencoder approach to natural low-light image enhancement. *Pattern Recognit.* **2017**, *61*, 650–662. [CrossRef]
26. Wei, C.; Wang, W.; Yang, W.; Liu, J. Deep Retinex Decomposition for Low-Light Enhancement. In Proceedings of the British Machine Vision Conference, British Machine Vision Association, Newcastle, UK, 3–6 September 2018.
27. Dabov, K.; Foi, A.; Katkovnik, V.; Egiazarian, K. Image denoising by sparse 3-D transform-domain collaborative filtering. *IEEE Trans. Image Process.* **2007**, *16*, 2080–2095. [CrossRef] [PubMed]
28. Lv, F.; Lu, F.; Wu, J.; Lim, C. MBLLEN: Low-Light Image/Video Enhancement Using CNNs. In Proceedings of the BMVC, Newcastle, UK, 3–6 September 2018; Volume 220, p. 4.
29. Zheng, C.; Shi, D.; Shi, W. Adaptive Unfolding Total Variation Network for Low-Light Image Enhancement. In Proceedings of the IEEE/CVF International Conference on Computer Vision (ICCV), Montreal, BC, Canada, 11–17 October 2021; pp. 4439–4448.
30. Wu, W.; Weng, J.; Zhang, P.; Wang, X.; Yang, W.; Jiang, J. URetinex-Net: Retinex-Based Deep Unfolding Network for Low-Light Image Enhancement. In Proceedings of the IEEE/CVF Conference on Computer Vision and Pattern Recognition (CVPR), New Orleans, LA, USA, 18–24 June 2022; pp. 5901–5910.
31. Chenxi Wang Hongujun Wu and Zhi Jin. FourLLIE: Boosting Low-Light Image Enhancement by Fourier Frequency Information. In Proceedings of the ACM MM, Thessaloniki, Greece, 12–15 June 2023.
32. Liu, R.; Ma, L.; Zhang, J.; Fan, X.; Luo, Z. Retinex-inspired unrolling with cooperative prior architecture search for low-light image enhancement. In Proceedings of the IEEE/CVF Conference on Computer Vision and Pattern Recognition, Nashville, TN, USA, 20–25 June 2021; pp. 10561–10570.
33. Guo, C.; Li, C.; Guo, J.; Loy, C.C.; Hou, J.; Kwong, S.; Cong, R. Zero-reference deep curve estimation for low-light image enhancement. In Proceedings of the IEEE/CVF Conference on Computer Vision and Pattern Recognition, Seattle, WA, USA, 13–19 June 2020; pp. 1780–1789.
34. Li, C.; Guo, C.; Feng, R.; Zhou, S.; Loy, C.C. CuDi: Curve Distillation for Efficient and Controllable Exposure Adjustment. *arXiv* **2022**, arXiv:2207.14273.
35. Zhu, A.; Zhang, L.; Shen, Y.; Ma, Y.; Zhao, S.; Zhou, Y. Zero-shot restoration of underexposed images via robust retinex decomposition. In Proceedings of the 2020 IEEE International Conference on Multimedia and Expo (ICME), Virtual, 6–10 July 2020; pp. 1–6.
36. Ma, L.; Ma, T.; Liu, R.; Fan, X.; Luo, Z. Toward fast, flexible, and robust low-light image enhancement. In Proceedings of the IEEE/CVF Conference on Computer Vision and Pattern Recognition, New Orleans, LA, USA, 18–24 June 2022; pp. 5637–5646.
37. Hue Nguyen and Diep Tran and Khoi Nguyen and Rang Nguyen. PSENet: Progressive Self-Enhancement Network for Unsupervised Extreme-Light Image Enhancement. In Proceedings of the IEEE/CVF Winter Conference on Applications of Computer Vision (WACV), Waikoloa, HI, USA, 2–7 January 2023.
38. Ko, K.; Kim, C.-S. IceNet for interactive contrast enhancement. *IEEE Access* **2021**, *9*, 168342–168354. [CrossRef]
39. Ronneberger, O.; Fischer, P.; Brox, T. U-net: Convolutional networks for biomedical image segmentation. In *Medical Image Computing and Computer-Assisted Intervention–MICCAI 2015, Proceedings of the 18th International Conference, Munich, Germany, 5–9 October 2015*; Proceedings, Part III 18; Springer: Berlin/Heidelberg, Germany, 2015; pp. 234–241.
40. Huang, G.; Liu, Z.; Van Der Maaten, L.; Weinberger, K.Q. Densely connected convolutional networks. In Proceedings of the IEEE Conference on Computer Vision and Pattern Recognition, Honolulu, HI, USA, 21–26 July 2017; pp. 4700–4708.
41. Wang, Z.; Bovik, A.C.; Sheikh, H.R.; Simoncelli, E.P. Image quality assessment: From error visibility to structural similarity. *IEEE Trans. Image Process.* **2004**, *13*, 600–612. [CrossRef] [PubMed]
42. Kingma, D.P.; Ba, J. Adam: A method for stochastic optimization. *arXiv* **2014**, arXiv:1412.6980.
43. Zhang, R.; Isola, P.; Efros, A.A.; Shechtman, E.; Wang, O. The unreasonable effectiveness of deep features as a perceptual metric. In Proceedings of the IEEE Conference on Computer Vision and Pattern Recognition, Salt Lake City, UT, USA, 18–23 June 2018; pp. 586–595.
44. Mittal, A.; Moorthy, A.K.; Bovik, A.C. No-reference image quality assessment in the spatial domain. *IEEE Trans. Image Process.* **2012**, *21*, 4695–4708. [CrossRef]

Disclaimer/Publisher's Note: The statements, opinions and data contained in all publications are solely those of the individual author(s) and contributor(s) and not of MDPI and/or the editor(s). MDPI and/or the editor(s) disclaim responsibility for any injury to people or property resulting from any ideas, methods, instructions or products referred to in the content.

Article

RSLC-Deeplab: A Ground Object Classification Method for High-Resolution Remote Sensing Images

Zhimin Yu, Fang Wan, Guangbo Lei *, Ying Xiong, Li Xu, Zhiwei Ye, Wei Liu, Wen Zhou and Chengzhi Xu

School of Computer Science, Hubei University of Technology, Wuhan 430068, China; 102111135@hbut.edu.cn (Z.Y.)
* Correspondence: 20000012@hbut.edu.cn

Abstract: With the continuous advancement of remote sensing technology, the semantic segmentation of different ground objects in remote sensing images has become an active research topic. For complex and diverse remote sensing imagery, deep learning methods have the ability to automatically discern features from image data and capture intricate spatial dependencies, thus outperforming traditional image segmentation methods. To address the problems of low segmentation accuracy in remote sensing image semantic segmentation, this paper proposes a new remote sensing image semantic segmentation network, RSLC-Deeplab, based on DeeplabV3+. Firstly, ResNet-50 is used as the backbone feature extraction network, which can extract deep semantic information more effectively and improve the segmentation accuracy. Secondly, the coordinate attention (CA) mechanism is introduced into the model to improve the feature representation generated by the network by embedding position information into the channel attention mechanism, effectively capturing the relationship between position information and channels. Finally, a multi-level feature fusion (MFF) module based on asymmetric convolution is proposed, which captures and refines low-level spatial features using asymmetric convolution and then fuses them with high-level abstract features to mitigate the influence of background noise and restore the lost detailed information in deep features. The experimental results on the WHDLD dataset show that the mean intersection over union (mIoU) of RSLC-Deeplab reached 72.63%, the pixel accuracy (PA) reached 83.49%, and the mean pixel accuracy (mPA) reached 83.72%. Compared to the original DeeplabV3+, the proposed method achieved a 4.13% improvement in mIoU and outperformed the PSP-NET, U-NET, MACU-NET, and DeeplabV3+ networks.

Keywords: high-resolution remote sensing images; semantic segmentation; feature fusion; attention mechanism

Citation: Yu, Z.; Wan, F.; Lei, G.; Xiong, Y.; Xu, L.; Ye, Z.; Liu, W.; Zhou, W.; Xu, C. RSLC-Deeplab: A Ground Object Classification Method for High-Resolution Remote Sensing Images. *Electronics* **2023**, *12*, 3653. https://doi.org/10.3390/electronics12173653

Academic Editor: Byung Cheol Song

Received: 23 July 2023
Revised: 12 August 2023
Accepted: 28 August 2023
Published: 30 August 2023

Copyright: © 2023 by the authors. Licensee MDPI, Basel, Switzerland. This article is an open access article distributed under the terms and conditions of the Creative Commons Attribution (CC BY) license (https://creativecommons.org/licenses/by/4.0/).

1. Introduction

High-resolution remote sensing images contain rich geographic information and have many potential applications in areas including agricultural monitoring, land use, and urban planning [1,2], making the intelligent analysis of remote sensing images a topic of considerable interest. The semantic segmentation of remote sensing images is a significant image processing task [3,4], aiming to categorize each pixel and mark it as the corresponding category [5]. Remote sensing images are characterized by high quantities, complex backgrounds, and large scale changes. The process of manually annotating data is labor-intensive and prone to error. The rapid and accurate automatic extraction of object information from remote sensing images has become an urgent need.

There are three main semantic segmentation methods used for remote sensing images: traditional methods, machine learning, and deep learning. In the early days, traditional remote sensing image segmentation mostly relied on shallow features of the image, including the texture, edges, and geometric shapes of the target. Common segmentation methods based on image pixels include thresholding, edge detection, and region-based segmentation.

Cuevas et al. [6] presented an automatic image segmentation approach that implements multi-thresholding through differential evolution optimization. This method is capable of dynamically selecting optimal thresholds while maintaining the primary features of the original image. Chen et al. [7] employed the Canny edge detector for edge detection on multispectral images and performed multi-scale segmentation on the detected edge features. The integration of edge information and segmentation scale effectively controlled the merging procedure of neighboring image objects. Byun et al. [8] achieved initial segmentation through an improved seed region-growing program and obtained segmentation results using a region adjacency graph to merge regions. To cope with complex remote sensing image segmentation scenarios, the simple linear iterative clustering (SLIC) superpixel segmentation algorithm, which utilizes the K-means clustering algorithm, is widely utilized in the remote sensing field. Csillik et al. [9] used SLIC superpixels to quickly segment and classify remote sensing data. Model-based segmentation methods based on Markov random fields are also widely used, which improve segmentation accuracy by introducing contextual information. Sziranyi et al. [10] applied unsupervised clustering to fused image series using cross-layer similarity measures and then performed multi-layer Markov random field segmentation. To overcome the constraints of single shallow-feature-based segmentation approaches, hybrid feature combination segmentation methods have been proposed, such as combining edge detection with region-based segmentation to enhance the quality of the segmentation outcomes. Zhang et al. [11] introduced a hybrid approach to region merging. This method utilizes the globally most similar region to establish the initial point for region growing and enhances the optimization ability for local region merging. These traditional methods rely too heavily on shallow features of the image, and pixel features are easily affected by factors such as the lighting, the presence of clouds and fog, and the sensors, resulting in insufficient reliability. The ability of machine learning to learn features and geometric relationships between images has received attention. Mitra et al. [12] used the support vector machine (SVM) algorithm to solve the problem of insufficient labeled pixels required for supervised pixel classification in remote sensing images. Bruzzone et al. [13] introduced an enhanced support-vector-machine-based semi-supervised approach for remote sensing image classification. By leveraging both labeled and unlabeled samples, this method effectively tackles the ill-posed problem. Pal et al. [14] used a random forest classifier to select the best category. Mellor et al. [15] used a random forest classification model to classify forest cover areas on multispectral remote sensing images. These methods heavily rely on handcrafted features, which result in a poor generalization capability [16,17].

With a high-resolution background, due to the impact of the spatiotemporal environment, objects of the same type present different spectral features, and the utilization of shallow features is inadequate for capturing the complexity of remote sensing images, thereby leading to limited segmentation accuracy. Deep learning methods have begun to attract attention as computing power has improved rapidly, since deep neural networks can automatically learn features in large datasets and extract deep semantic features of images, showing excellent performance. Classic segmentation models have begun to emerge. Long et al. [18] pioneered the fully convolutional network (FCN) semantic segmentation model, enabling pixel-level image classification. In a FCN, the traditional fully connected layer in the final layer of the network is replaced by a convolutional layer, allowing the network to accept inputs of arbitrary sizes and produce feature maps of the same size as the input. Zhong et al. [19] used an FCN to extract buildings and roads, which could better capture ground target features compared to traditional neural networks, but the eight-fold upsampling method lost image detail information. A series of segmentation networks using an encoder–decoder structure have been proposed, such as SegNet [20] and U-Net [21]. Cao et al. [22] proposed the Res-UNet network, which addresses the problems of gradient vanishing and feature loss in deep neural networks by introducing residual connections. Although it has achieved high segmentation accuracy in high-resolution remote sensing forest images, its segmentation performance for small target tree species is poor. Based on U-Net, Li et al. proposed MACU-Net [23], which utilizes asymmetric convolutions to replace regular convolutions and enhance the feature extraction capability, thus improving the utilization rate of features, but the segmentation of ground object boundaries is still not clear enough. To avoid reducing the size of the receptive field when obtaining feature maps at various scales, the utilization of dilated convolution [24] to perform convolution operations on input images is widespread. PSPNet [25] is a model based on pyramid pooling that implements the pyramid pooling module at the last layer to extract contextual information at different scales. DeeplabV1 was proposed in [26], which utilizes dilated convolution to perform convolution operations on input images in VGG [27] and then adds a conditional random field (CRF) module at the output end for post-processing to obtain relatively accurate contours. In DeeplabV2 [28], dilated convolutions are extensively applied to feature maps at multiple scales to capture contextual information at different levels, thereby improving segmentation accuracy. DeeplabV3 [29] optimized the ASPP module by adding average pooling and batch normalization operations to improve the feature representation and model generalization capabilities. Removing the CRF as a post-processing module still achieved good segmentation results. DeeplabV3+ [30] included a decoder module to fuse shallow features in the encoder with deep features output by the encoder in order to further optimize the edges and details of the segmentation results. Compared with classical semantic segmentation methods, DeeplabV3+ can segment ground objects in complex remote sensing images, but it still faces challenges such as the inaccurate segmentation of small targets and blurred boundary information. Wang et al. [31] introduced a class feature attention mechanism into the DeeplabV3+ network to enhance the correlation between different categories and effectively extract and process semantic information of diverse categories.

The attention mechanism holds great importance in the field of deep learning. It can assist a model in identifying useful information within the input data, suppressing irrelevant information, and enhancing performance and efficiency. SENet [32] assigns different weights to each channel by learning the correlation between feature channels. The Efficient Channel Attention Network (ECA-Net) [33] models the interactions between convolutional feature channels and introduces an adaptive channel attention mechanism, optimizing the negative impact of dimensionality reduction in SENet. To account for information interaction in the spatial dimension, Woo et al. [34] introduced the Convolutional Block Attention Module (CBAM), which uses a channel attention module and a spatial attention module in series to perform adaptive feature refinement, in contrast to methods that employ costly and complex techniques such as non-local or self-attention blocks. The Coordinate Attention (CA) mechanism [35] encodes each spatial position, which aids in capturing global contextual information and long-range dependencies. It proves particularly effective for remote sensing images, where spatial relationships and geometric information play a crucial role, enabling neural networks to better comprehend input data and improve prediction accuracy.

To address the intricate scenarios encountered in object classification for remote sensing images, the proposed RSLC-Deeplab model was designed by combining attention mechanisms and feature fusion methods to automatically extract different ground objects from remote sensing images. To compare the segmentation performance, various segmentation networks including RSLC-Deeplab, DeeplabV3+, U-Net, PSP-NET, and MACU-Net were evaluated on the publicly available WHDLD dataset through experiments. The experimental results showed that RSLC-Deeplab outperformed other comparison networks, effectively enhancing the segmentation ability and reducing the training cost.

2. Methodology

The traditional DeeplabV3+ model was proposed by a team at Google. On the basis of DeeplabV3, DeeplabV3+ has undergone fundamental architectural changes. DeeplabV3+ uses Xception [36] as the backbone network, eliminates the use of fully connected Conditional Random Fields (CRF), and uses DeeplabV3 as the encoder to design a new encoder–decoder structure. In the encoder, a deep convolutional neural network is employed to extract features from the input image. Then, ASPP obtains rich contextual information by utilizing multi-scale atrous convolution and pyramid pooling from the output features of the backbone network. The semantic information features of various scales are integrated, and the fused high-level semantic features with multiple scales are adjusted in terms of channel number and upsampled using bilinear interpolation. In the decoder, the upsampled high-level semantic features are used to restore spatial resolution. During the process of feature map resolution recovery, the low-level features extracted from the backbone network are concatenated with the high-level features. The low-level features possess better perceptual abilities for capturing fine-grained details, such as small objects or edges, resulting in improved accuracy when localizing and segmenting small objects within the image. Finally, four-times bilinear interpolation upsampling is used to generate the final prediction image.

The feature extraction process in the DeeplabV3+ network utilizes the Xception backbone network. The Xception backbone network possesses a substantial amount of layers and parameters, resulting in high model complexity and a slow training speed. Based on improvements made to the original DeeplabV3+ model, RSLC-Deeplab is proposed to enhance the segmentation performance and training efficiency, as shown in Figure 1. The main contributions of the RSLC-Deeplab model proposed in this paper are as follows:

1. In the encoder, ResNet-50 is used instead of the original Xception as the feature extraction module, which can capture more refined features.
2. After the backbone network, the CA module is introduced to embed positional information into the channel attention mechanism, enabling neural networks to better comprehend input data and improve prediction accuracy.
3. In the decoder, we designed an MFF module, which captures and refines low-level spatial features using asymmetric convolution and then fuses them with high-level abstract features to mitigate the influence of background noise and restore the lost detailed information in deep features.

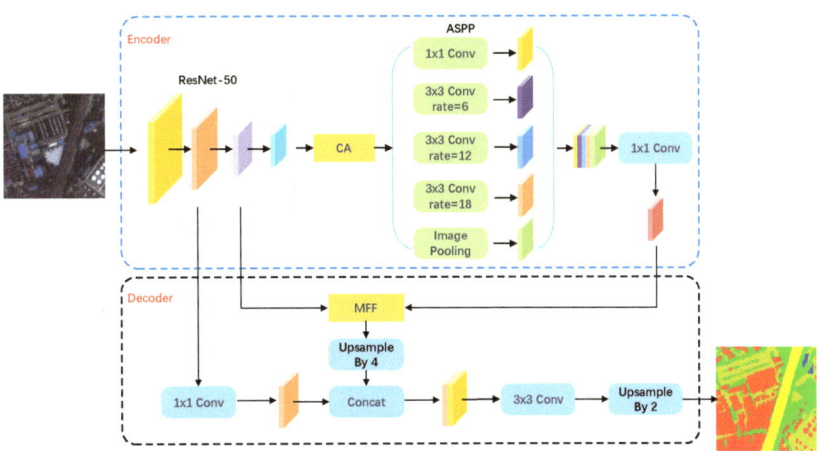

Figure 1. Structure diagram of RSLC-Deeplab.

2.1. Optimized Feature Extraction Module

In the encoder, the feature extraction network for RSLC-Deeplab is ResNet-50 [37], and Table 1 depicts its structure. We know that the depth of a network is crucial for effective feature extraction. Deep convolutional networks utilize an end-to-end multi-layer approach to integrate features at different levels, achieved through the stacking of convolutional layers and downsampling layers. When the network is stacked to a certain depth, gradient vanishing and gradient explosion problems will occur. Data preprocessing and the incorporation of batch normalization (BN) in the network are effective solutions to address these issues. However, as the network depth increases and convergence is achieved, another challenge emerges: the accuracy tends to reach a plateau and subsequently deteriorate rapidly. Therefore, ResNet introduces a residual structure to alleviate the degradation problem of network performance.

Table 1. ResNet-50 network structure.

Output Size	Network	Output Channel	Module Repetitions
128 × 128	7 × 7, 64	64	1
64 × 64	3 × 3, max pool	64	1
64 × 64	Bottleneck	256	3
32 × 32	Bottleneck	512	4
16 × 16	Bottleneck	1024	6
8 × 8	Bottleneck	2048	3

Compared to traditional convolutional neural networks, the residual structure can directly pass low-level features to high-level layers through shortcut connections, which enhances the smooth flow of information within the network. This helps the network to better capture details and local features and improves the reusability of features, thereby enhancing the network's performance. The shortcut connection skips the connection of one or more layers and directly combines its output with the output of the stacked layers. This approach not only avoids introducing additional parameters or computational complexity, but also facilitates gradient propagation and enables feature reuse. The formula is as follows:

$$y = F(x) + x \quad (1)$$

where x and y represent the input and output features, respectively, and the function $F(x)$ represents the residual mapping composed of stacked nonlinear layers. For residual networks with different network depths, there are two different residual structures. The residual structure on the left of Figure 2 is suitable for networks with fewer layers, while the residual structure on the right is more suitable for networks with more layers. In ResNet-50, the $F(x)$ function of the residual structure is composed of three stacked layers: 1×1, 3×3, and 1×1 convolution. The channel number is first reduced by 1×1 convolution, then 3×3 convolution is performed, and finally the channel number is restored by 1×1 convolution.

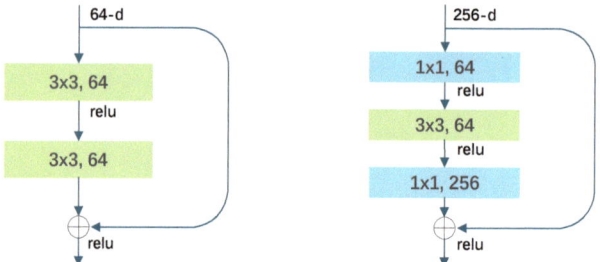

Figure 2. A deeper residual structure. Left: ResNet-34 building block. Right: "Bottleneck" building block for ResNet-50/101/152.

2.2. CA Module

The origin of attention mechanisms can be traced back to studies on human vision, where researchers aimed to develop models of visual selective attention that could simulate the intricate process of human visual perception. It has been empirically established that incorporating attention mechanisms into convolutional neural networks enhances the ability to capture crucial information. The core principle underlying attention mechanisms entails learning the regions of interest in each image via the process of forward propagation and negative feedback, followed by the assignment of appropriate attention weights. In order to effectively capture the relationships between channels, a Coordinate Attention (CA) module is introduced subsequent to the feature extraction network module. The CA module is mainly implemented through two steps: embedding coordinate information and generating coordinate attention. The CA module dynamically adjusts weights to model dependencies between different distances, enabling the model to better capture global information within images. The specific structure is depicted in Figure 3.

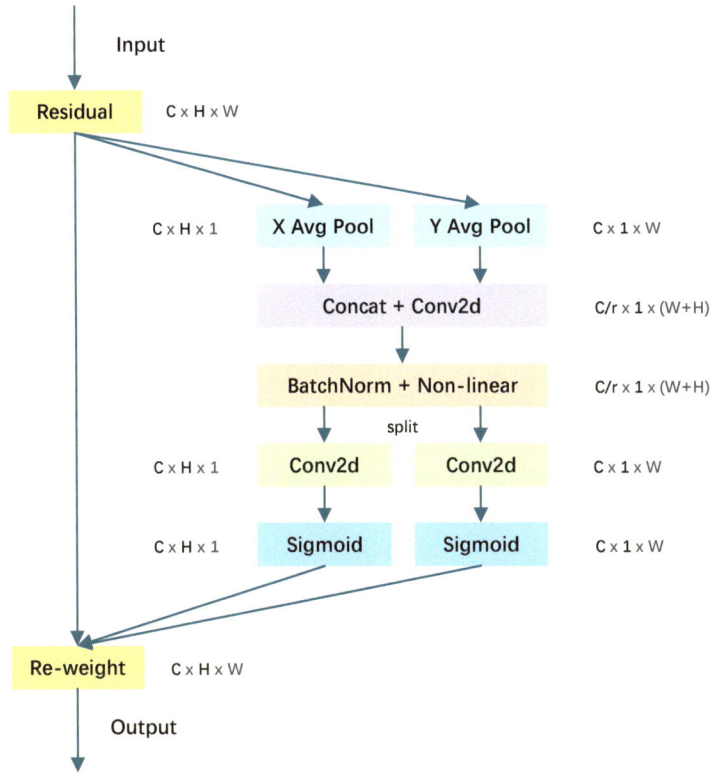

Figure 3. The CA module.

Due to the prevalent utilization of global pooling in channel attention mechanisms for the purpose of globally encoding spatial information, there exists a potential risk of losing positional information. In the coordinate information embedding module, for the input feature X, a pooling kernel of dimensions (H,1) and (1,W) is employed to encode each channel along the horizontal and vertical coordinate directions, respectively. By using a pair of one-dimensional features to encode the features of each location into a unique vector, the network can better understand and utilize location information. Consequently, the output of the c-th channel, characterized by a height (h) and width (w), can be expressed as follows:

$$z_c^h(h) = \frac{1}{W} \sum_{0 \leq i \leq W} x_c(h, i) \tag{2}$$

$$z_c^w(w) = \frac{1}{H} \sum_{0 \leq j \leq H} x_c(j, w) \tag{3}$$

By combining features along both the horizontal and vertical directions, a set of feature maps that are sensitive to directional information is generated. This pair of transformations helps the attention block gain the ability to apprehend distant correlations within a particular spatial orientation while upholding the integrity of precise positional data in the alternative spatial orientation. Consequently, such operations assist the network in effectively locating desired objects. After performing cascaded operations on the aggregated feature maps, they are further processed using a 1×1 convolutional transformation function, F_1, which is expressed as follows:

$$f = \delta\left(F_1\left[z^h, z^w\right]\right) \tag{4}$$

where $[\cdot, \cdot]$ denotes the concatenation operation along the horizontal and vertical coordinate directions, δ denotes the non-linear activation function, and f represents the intermediate feature map that encodes spatial information. Subsequently, f is partitioned into two separate tensors, namely $f^h \in R^{C/r \times H}$ and $f^w \in R^{C/r \times W}$, along the spatial dimension. Here, the variable r specifically denotes the reduction ratio employed to regulate the block size within the SE block. Subsequently, f^h and f^w undergo separate 1×1 convolutions, denoted as F_h and F_w, respectively, to match the channel dimensions of the input tensor X, as follows:

$$g^h = \sigma\left(F_h\left(f^h\right)\right) \tag{5}$$

$$g^w = \sigma(F_w(f^w)) \tag{6}$$

where σ represents the sigmoid activation function. Then, g^h and g^w are expanded as attention weights, and the final output Y of CA is as follows:

$$y_c(i,j) = x_c(i,j) \times g_c^h(i) \times g_c^w(j) \tag{7}$$

2.3. MFF Module

Due to the three downsampling operations in the feature extraction process of the backbone network, the decrease in resolution leads to the loss of spatial information for finer details. In the decoder part of the original DeeplabV3+ network model, the problem of lost segmentation object detail is improved to some extent by directly concatenating the deep features output by the encoder with the shallow features from the backbone network, but it is still not precise enough for segmenting complex objects such as object boundaries and small targets. To further improve segmentation accuracy, a multilevel feature fusion module (MFF) is introduced, as illustrated in Figure 4.

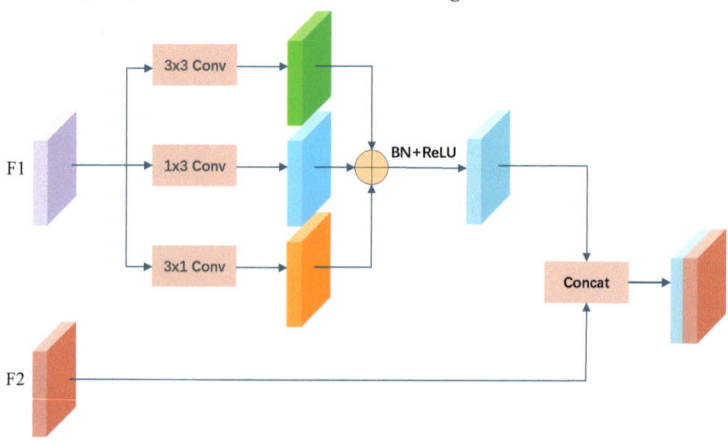

Figure 4. Structure of the MFF.

During the process of multilevel feature fusion, the shallow features. F_1, obtained from the third downsampling of the backbone network and the deep features, F_2, from the encoder output are used as inputs. To fuse the local spatial information in F_1 with the global semantic information in F_2, asymmetric convolution is utilized to extract features from the shallow features, F_1, which are then concatenated and fused with the deep features, F_2. By effectively combining shallow and deep features, this method enhances the overall accuracy of the segmentation model.

Compared to normal convolution, asymmetric convolution has a stronger feature representation ability. The weights of the square convolution kernel are typically larger than those of the corners, which can lead to uneven feature refinement. Asymmetric convolution uses three parallel convolutional layers: 3 × 3 convolution, 1 × 3 convolution, and 3 × 1 convolution. The 3 × 3 convolution obtains features from a larger receptive field, while the 1 × 3 and 3 × 1 convolutions can obtain receptive fields in the horizontal and vertical directions, respectively. This allows the network to effectively collect the correlation information of different spatial scales, which is particularly useful for tasks such as semantic segmentation, where capturing detailed spatial information is crucial. Finally, the outcomes of three convolution operations are added to further enrich the spatial features. The formula for asymmetric convolution is

$$x'_i = F_{3\times 3}(x_{i-1}) + F_{1\times 3}(x_{i-1}) + F_{3\times 1}(x_{i-1}) \tag{8}$$

$$x_i = \sigma\left(\gamma \frac{x'_i - \mu(x'_i)}{\sqrt{v(x'_i) + \varepsilon_i}} + \beta\right) \tag{9}$$

where x_{i-1} is the input feature, x_i is the output feature, v is the expected value of the input, ε_i is a small constant to ensure numerical stability, γ and β represent the two trainable parameters of the BN layer, and σ represents the ReLU activation function.

3. Experiment

3.1. Experimental Data

The dataset used in this study was the publicly available remote sensing image dataset WHDLD (https://sites.google.com/view/zhouwx/dataset#h.p_hQS2jYeaFpV0 (accessed on 27 August 2023)), which was released by Wuhan University. It consists of 4940 images captured by GF-1 and ZY-3, with each image being an RGB image and having a resolution of 256 × 256 pixels. The pixel-level annotations of the dataset include six classes: water, vegetation, building, road, bare soil, and pavement.

According to the statistics, the WHDLD dataset exhibits an issue of imbalanced pixel distribution among different classes. Therefore, we employed augmentation techniques, including horizontal flipping, vertical flipping, 90-degree rotation, 180-degree rotation, 270-degree rotation, and brightness adjustment, to enhance classes with a lower pixel count, such as road, bare soil, and building. The dataset was expanded to a total of 6700 images, and the augmented samples are illustrated in Figure 5. The dataset was divided into training, validation, and testing sets in an 8:1:1 ratio. The example images and labels of the WHDLD dataset are shown in Figure 6.

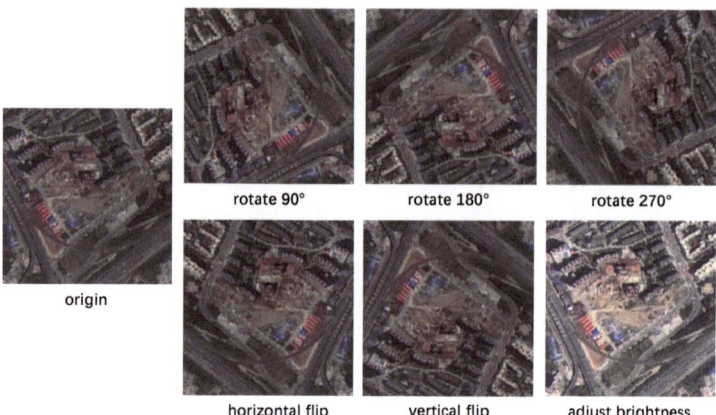

Figure 5. The augmented samples.

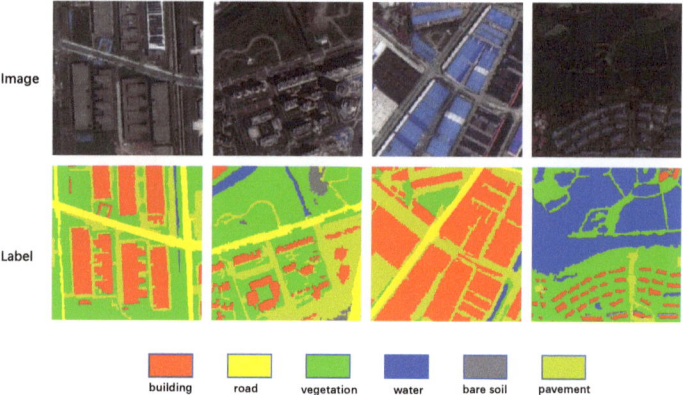

Figure 6. Dataset samples.

3.2. Implementation Details

Experimental verification was conducted on the proposed algorithm, and the configuration parameters of the experimental platform are shown in Table 2. The transfer learning approach was used in the experiment, where the pre-trained model weights of the backbone network were loaded before training to accelerate the model's convergence. The SGD optimizer was selected for network gradient updates. The initial learning rate of the experiment was 0.007, the momentum coefficient was 0.9, the batch size was 12, and the training epoch was 200.

The experiment utilized the cross-entropy loss function to quantify the disparity between the model's predictions and the actual results, a technique that is well-suited for classification tasks. It has the benefits of being easy to compute and optimize and usually produces good results in training neural networks, so it can effectively guide a model to learn the task objectives. Since the pixels in the input image of this experiment had six categories, the experiments used the following multi-category cross-entropy loss function:

$$Loss = -\frac{1}{N}\sum_{i=1}^{N}\sum_{k=1}^{K} y_{i,k} \log p_{i,k} \tag{10}$$

where $y_{i,k}$ is the true class of the i-th sample, taking a value of 1 if it belongs to the k-th class and 0 otherwise, with N samples and K classes in total. Meanwhile, $p_{i,k}$ is the probability of the i-th sample being predicted as the k-th class.

Table 2. Information about the experimental platform.

Experimental Environment	Configuration Information
Operating system	Windows 10
CPU	Intel(R) Core(TM) i7-11700F
GPU	NVIDIA GeForce RTX 3060
Cuda	Cuda 11.3
Framework	Pytorch 1.10.0

3.3. Evaluation Metrics

After the model was trained, the trained weights were used for testing with the test set. The accuracy of classification was analyzed using a confusion matrix, as shown in Table 3. TP (true positive) represents correctly classified positive samples, while FP (false positive) represents incorrectly classified negative samples. Conversely, FN (false negative) represents incorrectly classified positive samples, and TN (true negative) represents correctly classified negative samples.

Table 3. Confusion matrix.

		Predicted Label	
		True	False
GT data	True	TP (true positive)	FN (false negative)
	False	FP (false positive)	TN (true negative)

The experiment employed key metrics such as pixel accuracy (PA), mean pixel accuracy (mPA), and mean intersection over union (mIoU) were used in the experiment to measure the differences between the predicted and ground-truth images. The formulas are as follows:

$$PA = \frac{\sum_{i=0}^{n} p_{ii}}{\sum_{i=0}^{n} \sum_{j=0}^{n} p_{ij}} \quad (11)$$

$$mPA = \frac{1}{n} \sum_{i=0}^{n} \frac{p_{ii}}{\sum_{i=0}^{n} \sum_{j=0}^{n} p_{ij}} \quad (12)$$

$$mIoU = \frac{1}{n} \sum_{k=1}^{n} \frac{TP_k}{TP_k + FP_k + FN_k} \quad (13)$$

where n is the number of classes including the background class, p_{ii} is the count of pixels of class i predicted as class i, and p_{ij} is the count of pixels of class i predicted as class j.

3.4. Comparative Experiment of Different Backbone Networks

A backbone network is a pre-trained model utilized for extracting image features and providing enhanced feature representation for subsequent semantic segmentation tasks. To select an appropriate backbone network as the feature extraction network for the model, five comparative experiments were conducted using different backbone networks within the original DeeplabV3+ [30] network architecture. Table 4 presents the experimental data.

Table 4. Comparative experimental results of different backbone networks.

Method	Backbone	mIoU (%)	Parameters (M)	Flops (G)	Model Size (M)
Scheme 1	Xception	68.50	54.71	41.72	209.70
Scheme 2	MobileNetV2	67.44	5.81	13.23	22.44
Scheme 3	EfficientNetV2	69.68	31.25	100.10	120.12
Scheme 4	ResNet-101	70.81	59.33	76.29	226.98
Scheme 5	ResNet-50	70.48	40.34	66.54	154.23

In Table 4, Scheme 5 used ResNet-50 [37] as the backbone network, with an mIoU of 70.48%, a parameter count of 40.34 M, a computational cost of 66.54 G, and a model size of 154.23 M. Scheme 1 used Xception [36] as the backbone network, and Scheme 5 had an mIoU increase of 1.98% compared to Scheme 1, with a significantly smaller parameter count and model size. Scheme 2 used MobileNetv2 [38] as the backbone network, and although the parameter count and model size were greatly reduced, its mIoU was 3.04% lower than that of Scheme 5, indicating insufficient segmentation accuracy. Scheme 3 used EfficientNetV2 [39] as the backbone network, and its mIoU was 0.80% lower than that of Scheme 5, with a smaller parameter count but a much larger computational cost than Scheme 5. Scheme 4 used ResNet-101 as the backbone network, and although its mIoU was 0.33% higher than that of Scheme 5, its parameter count and model size were much larger than those of Scheme 5. After a comprehensive analysis, ResNet-50 was chosen as the feature extraction module of this task, not only improving the semantic segmentation accuracy, but also optimizing the model complexity.

3.5. Ablation Experiment

To validate the efficacy of the ResNet-50 network, the CA module, and the MFF module, a set of experiments were designed by gradually introducing the ResNet-50 backbone network, CA attention module, and MFF module. Table 5 presents the experimental data.

Scheme 1: The original Deeplabv3+ network, which employed Xception as the feature extraction network, was used as the baseline.

Scheme 2: ResNet-50 was used as the feature extraction network to replace Xception in Scheme 1.

Scheme 3: The CA module was introduced on the basis of Scheme 2, which enhanced the feature representation generated by the network, enabling neural networks to better comprehend input data and improve prediction accuracy.

Scheme 4: The MFF module was introduced on the basis of Scheme 2, which captured and refined low-level spatial features using asymmetric convolution and then fused them with high-level abstract features to improve segmentation accuracy.

Scheme 5: On the basis of Scheme 2, both the CA module and the MFF module were introduced simultaneously.

Table 5. Results of ablation experiments on different modules.

Method	Backbone	CA	MFF	PA (%)	mPA (%)	mIoU (%)
Scheme 1	Xception			80.38	80.47	68.50
Scheme 2	ResNet-50			81.92	81.89	70.48
Scheme 3	ResNet-50	✓		82.63	82.45	71.67
Scheme 4	ResNet-50		✓	82.78	82.86	71.73
Scheme 5	ResNet-50	✓	✓	83.49	83.72	72.63

As shown in Table 5, the PA, mPA, and mIoU values of Scheme 1 were 80.38%, 80.47%, and 68.50%, respectively. Scheme 2 utilized ResNet-50 as the feature extraction network, and its PA, mPA, and mIoU values were 81.92%, 81.89%, and 70.48%, respectively. Compared to Scheme 1, the PA, mPA, and mIoU values improved by 1.54%, 1.42%, and 1.98%, respectively. Based on Scheme 2, Scheme 3 introduced a CA module, yielding PA, mPA, and mIoU values of 82.63%, 82.45%, and 71.67%, respectively. Compared to Scheme 2, the PA, mPA, and mIoU values improved by 0.71%, 0.56%, and 1.19%, respectively. Scheme 4 introduced an MFF module to further restore the edge details of the segmentation image by fusing low-level and high-level features, with PA, mPA, and mIoU values of 82.78%, 82.86%, and 71.73%, respectively. Compared to Scheme 2, the PA, mPA, and mIoU values improved by 0.86%, 0.97%, and 1.25%, respectively. Scheme 5 simultaneously introduced both the CA and MFF modules, with PA, mPA, and mIoU values of 83.49%, 83.72%, and 72.63%, respectively. Compared to the original DeepLabV3+ model, the PA, mPA, and mIoU values improved by 3.11%, 3.25%, and 4.13%, respectively. The experimental results indicate that RSLC-Deeplab exhibited impressive segmentation performance.

The experiments used SGD as the optimizer, which updated the model parameters by computing the gradients of each training sample and gradually reducing the model's loss function. The performance variation of different approaches at different stages is depicted in Figure 7. Using ResNet-50 as the backbone network, the mIoU value increased rapidly at the beginning and then tended to converge, with a significant improvement in mIoU values. After gradually introducing the CA and MFF modules, the model had the ability to fit the training data faster and achieve better segmentation results, indicating that the design and training methods of the model were effective. The training and validation loss values of the RSLC-Deeplab algorithm on the WHDLD dataset are shown in Figure 8. During the initial stages of the experiment, both the training and validation losses decreased rapidly; then, the decreasing trend slowed down after a certain number of iterations, before finally tending to converge.

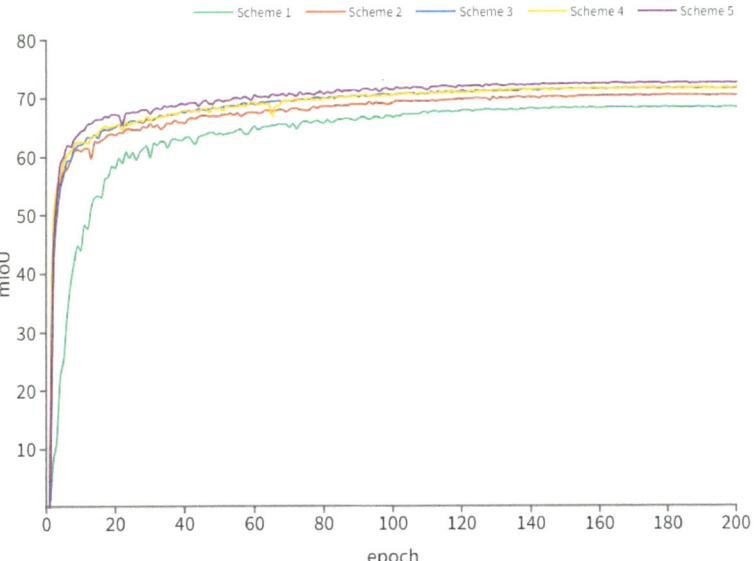

Figure 7. The mIoU values of different schemes in ablation experiments.

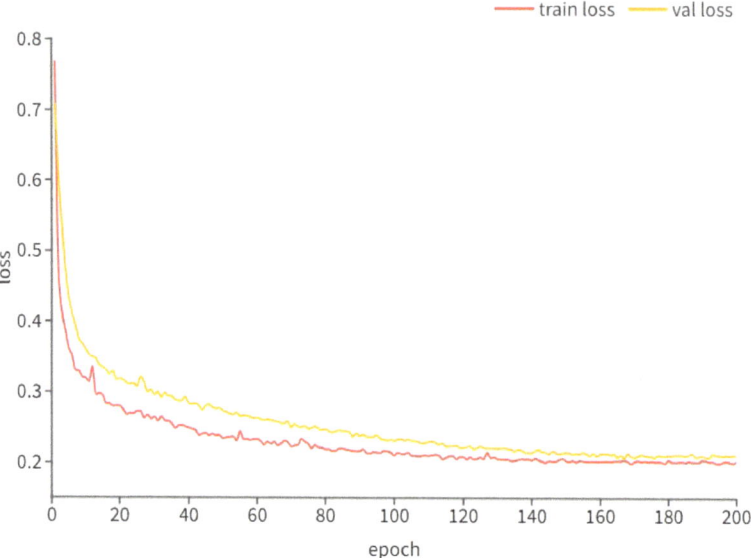

Figure 8. The loss values of RSLC-Deeplab on the training and validation sets.

3.6. Comparative Experiment of Different Methods

We conducted comparative experiments between RSLC-Deeplab and other models, including DeeplabV3+ [30], U-Net [21], PSP-Net [25], and MACU-Net [23], on the WHDLD dataset to verify the segmentation performance of RSLC-Deeplab. The experimental results of different network models are shown in Table 6. The results obtained in this study reveal that RSLC-Deeplab outperformed the other networks. The PA, mPA, and mIoU of the proposed method were 83.49%, 83.72%, and 72.63%, respectively, which were 3.11%, 3.25%, and 4.13% higher than those of DeeplabV3+ and 5.56%, 3.91%, and 4.99% higher than those of MACU-Net.

Table 6. Comparative experimental results of different segmentation methods.

Method	PA (%)	mPA (%)	mIoU (%)
DeeplabV3+	80.38	80.47	68.50
U-Net	72.73	75.35	63.31
PSPNet	69.54	72.32	60.36
MACU-Net	77.93	79.81	67.64
RSLC-Deeplab	83.49	83.72	72.63

At the same time, the remote sensing image segmentation results produced by RSLC-Deeplab and the comparative methods are presented in Figure 9. As illustrated in the diagram, PSPNet, and U-Net could roughly segment large-scale ground objects, but their segmentation ability for small-scale targets and object edges was poor, resulting in many misclassifications and omissions. MACU-Net demonstrated a certain improvement in segmentation ability compared to U-Net, but there were still problems of misclassification and omission in categories such as buildings, vegetation, and water bodies. DeeplabV3+ showed a greater improvement in segmentation ability than the classical semantic segmentation methods, but it still could not accurately segment the edge feature information of small-scale categories such as buildings, water bodies, and bare soil. The proposed RSLC-Deeplab improved the segmentation accuracy of small-scale landform targets, and the edge segmentation of categories such as buildings, roads, and vegetation was clearer, without many misclassifications and omissions. The experiment proved that RSLC-Deeplab captured more detailed features and improved the segmentation accuracy of small targets.

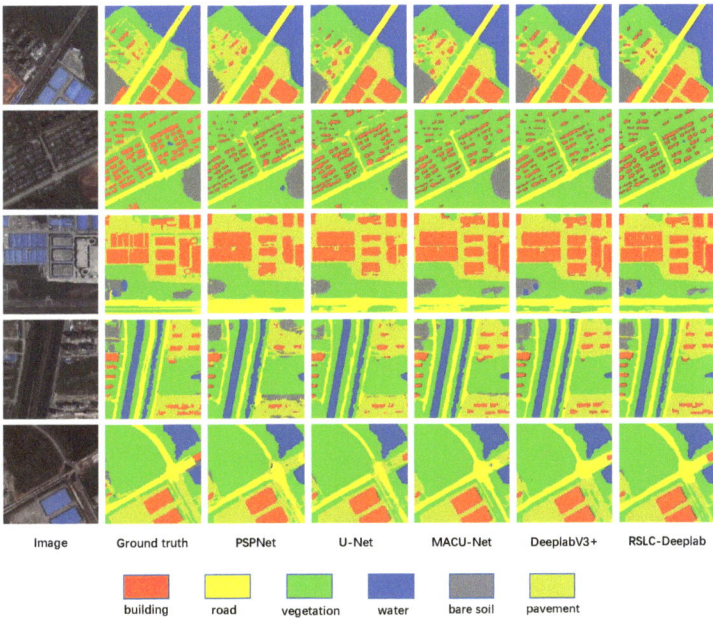

Figure 9. Diagram of the segmentation effect of different methods.

This study also took into account the metrics of parameter size and training time. The parameter size and training time per epoch of the compared methods are presented in Table 7. The parameter size of RSLC-Deeplab was 47.62M, and the training time was 239s. The experimental results demonstrated a significant reduction in both training time and parameter size for RSLC-Deeplab compared to the original DeeplabV3+ network. MACU-Net showed a smaller parameter size, but it had a more complex model structure, resulting in a longer training time. RSLC-Deeplab used ResNet-50 as the feature extraction network, which significantly reduced the model's parameter size and computation amount.

Table 7. Comparison of training time and parameter size of different methods.

Method	Training Time (s)/Epoch	Parameters (M)
PSPNet	181	48.97
U-Net	217	34.53
MACU-Net	266	5.17
DeeplabV3+	304	54.71
RSLC-Deeplab	239	47.62

4. Conclusions

This paper proposed RSLC-Deeplab for high-resolution remote sensing image semantic segmentation. Firstly, ResNet-50 was used as the backbone network, which had a stronger feature extraction ability while reducing the parameter size and computation amount, providing better feature representation for subsequent segmentation. Secondly, the CA mechanism was used after the feature extraction module to embed positional information into the channel attention mechanism, enabling neural networks to better comprehend input data and improve prediction accuracy. Finally, a multi-level feature fusion (MFF) module based on asymmetric convolution was proposed, which captured and refined low-level spatial features using asymmetric convolution and then fused them with high-level abstract features. The MFF module effectively eliminated background noise during feature extraction and improved the clarity of segmentation boundaries.

On the WHDLD remote sensing image dataset, our model achieved an mIoU of 72.63% and an mPA of 83.72%, which significantly improved issues such as mis-segmentation and edge detail blurring. Compared with other methods, our model obtained more accurate segmentation results. On this basis, we will further optimize the segmentation accuracy of the model for categories with a low segmentation accuracy and continue to study how to suppress the impact of interfering factors such as background noise and shadows in the image to enhance the model's overall segmentation capability.

Author Contributions: Conceptualization, Z.Y. (Zhimin Yu) and F.W.; methodology, Z.Y. (Zhimin Yu); software, Z.Y. (Zhimin Yu) and G.L.; validation, Z.Y. (Zhimin Yu); formal analysis, Y.X., L.X. and W.L.; investigation, F.W., G.L. and C.X.; resources, L.X. and W.Z.; data curation, Z.Y. (Zhimin Yu); writing—original draft preparation, Z.Y. (Zhimin Yu); writing—review and editing, F.W., G.L. and Z.Y. (Zhiwei Ye); visualization, Z.Y. (Zhimin Yu); supervision, Y.X., W.L. and C.X.; project administration, W.Z.; funding acquisition, L.X. and W.Z. All authors have read and agreed to the published version of the manuscript.

Funding: This research was funded by the National Natural Science Foundation of China (grant No. 62202147) and the Science and Technology Research Project of the Education Department of Hubei Province (grant No. B2021070).

Data Availability Statement: The WHDLD dataset can be found at: https://sites.google.com/view/zhouwx/dataset#h.p_hQS2jYeaFpV0 (accessed on 27 August 2023).

Conflicts of Interest: The authors declare no conflict of interest.

References

1. Kemker, R.; Salvaggio, C.; Kanan, C. Algorithms for semantic segmentation of multispectral remote sensing imagery using deep learning. *ISPRS J. Photogramm. Remote Sens.* **2018**, *145*, 60–77. [CrossRef]
2. Yao, H.; Qin, R.; Chen, X. Unmanned aerial vehicle for remote sensing applications—A review. *Remote Sens.* **2019**, *11*, 1443. [CrossRef]
3. Zhao, Q.; Liu, J.; Li, Y.; Zhang, H. Semantic segmentation with attention mechanism for remote sensing images. *IEEE Trans. Geosci. Remote Sens.* **2021**, *60*, 1–13. [CrossRef]
4. Zhang, Q.; Yang, G.; Zhang, G. Collaborative network for super-resolution and semantic segmentation of remote sensing images. *IEEE Trans. Geosci. Remote Sens.* **2021**, *60*, 1–12. [CrossRef]
5. Yuan, Y.; Chen, X.; Wang, J. Object-contextual representations for semantic segmentation. In Proceedings of the Computer Vision–ECCV 2020: 16th European Conference, Glasgow, UK, 23–28 August 2020; Proceedings, Part VI 16; Springer: Berlin/Heidelberg, Germany, 2020; pp. 173–190.
6. Cuevas, E.; Zaldivar, D.; Pérez-Cisneros, M. A novel multi-threshold segmentation approach based on differential evolution optimization. *Expert Syst. Appl.* **2010**, *37*, 5265–5271. [CrossRef]
7. Chen, J.; Li, J.; Pan, D.; Zhu, Q.; Mao, Z. Edge-guided multiscale segmentation of satellite multispectral imagery. *IEEE Trans. Geosci. Remote Sens.* **2012**, *50*, 4513–4520. [CrossRef]
8. Byun, Y.; Kim, D.; Lee, J.; Kim, Y. A framework for the segmentation of high-resolution satellite imagery using modified seeded-region growing and region merging. *Int. J. Remote Sens.* **2011**, *32*, 4589–4609. [CrossRef]
9. Csillik, O. Fast segmentation and classification of very high resolution remote sensing data using SLIC superpixels. *Remote Sens.* **2017**, *9*, 243. [CrossRef]
10. Sziranyi, T.; Shadaydeh, M. Segmentation of remote sensing images using similarity-measure-based fusion-MRF model. *IEEE Geosci. Remote Sens. Lett.* **2014**, *11*, 1544–1548. [CrossRef]
11. Zhang, X.; Xiao, P.; Feng, X.; Wang, J.; Wang, Z. Hybrid region merging method for segmentation of high-resolution remote sensing images. *ISPRS J. Photogramm. Remote Sens.* **2014**, *98*, 19–28. [CrossRef]
12. Mitra, P.; Shankar, B.U.; Pal, S.K. Segmentation of multispectral remote sensing images using active support vector machines. *Pattern Recognit. Lett.* **2004**, *25*, 1067–1074. [CrossRef]
13. Bruzzone, L.; Chi, M.; Marconcini, M. A novel transductive SVM for semisupervised classification of remote-sensing images. *IEEE Trans. Geosci. Remote. Sens.* **2006**, *44*, 3363–3373. [CrossRef]
14. Pal, M. Random forest classifier for remote sensing classification. *Int. J. Remote Sens.* **2005**, *26*, 217–222. [CrossRef]
15. Mellor, A.; Haywood, A.; Stone, C.; Jones, S. The performance of random forests in an operational setting for large area sclerophyll forest classification. *Remote Sens.* **2013**, *5*, 2838–2856. [CrossRef]
16. Li, R.; Zheng, S.; Zhang, C.; Duan, C.; Wang, L.; Atkinson, P.M. ABCNet: Attentive bilateral contextual network for efficient semantic segmentation of Fine-Resolution remotely sensed imagery. *ISPRS J. Photogramm. Remote Sens.* **2021**, *181*, 84–98. [CrossRef]

17. Yang, X.; Li, S.; Chen, Z.; Chanussot, J.; Jia, X.; Zhang, B.; Li, B.; Chen, P. An attention-fused network for semantic segmentation of very-high-resolution remote sensing imagery. *ISPRS J. Photogramm. Remote Sens.* **2021**, *177*, 238–262. [CrossRef]
18. Long, J.; Shelhamer, E.; Darrell, T. Fully convolutional networks for semantic segmentation. In Proceedings of the IEEE Conference on Computer Vision and Pattern Recognition, Boston, MA, USA, 7–15 June 2015; pp. 3431–3440.
19. Zhong, Z.; Li, J.; Cui, W.; Jiang, H. Fully convolutional networks for building and road extraction: Preliminary results. In Proceedings of the 2016 IEEE International Geoscience and Remote Sensing Symposium (IGARSS), Beijing, China, 10–15 July 2016; pp. 1591–1594.
20. Badrinarayanan, V.; Kendall, A.; Cipolla, R. Segnet: A deep convolutional encoder-decoder architecture for image segmentation. *IEEE Trans. Pattern Anal. Mach. Intell.* **2017**, *39*, 2481–2495. [CrossRef]
21. Ronneberger, O.; Fischer, P.; Brox, T. U-net: Convolutional networks for biomedical image segmentation. In Proceedings of the Medical Image Computing and Computer-Assisted Intervention–MICCAI 2015: 18th International Conference, Munich, Germany, 5–9 October 2015; Proceedings, Part III 18; Springer: Berlin/Heidelberg, Germany, 2015; pp. 234–241.
22. Cao, K.; Zhang, X. An improved res-unet model for tree species classification using airborne high-resolution images. *Remote Sens.* **2020**, *12*, 1128. [CrossRef]
23. Li, R.; Zheng, S.; Duan, C.; Su, J.; Zhang, C. Multistage attention ResU-Net for semantic segmentation of fine-resolution remote sensing images. *IEEE Geosci. Remote Sens. Lett.* **2021**, *19*, 1–5. [CrossRef]
24. Yu, F.; Koltun, V. Multi-scale context aggregation by dilated convolutions. *arXiv* **2015**, arXiv:1511.07122.
25. Zhao, H.; Shi, J.; Qi, X.; Wang, X.; Jia, J. Pyramid scene parsing network. In Proceedings of the IEEE Conference on Computer Vision and Pattern Recognition, Honolulu, HI, USA, 21–26 July 2017; pp. 2881–2890.
26. Chen, L.C.; Papandreou, G.; Kokkinos, I.; Murphy, K.; Yuille, A.L. Semantic image segmentation with deep convolutional nets and fully connected crfs. *arXiv* **2014**, arXiv:1412.7062.
27. Simonyan, K.; Zisserman, A. Very deep convolutional networks for large-scale image recognition. *arXiv* **2014**, arXiv:1409.1556.
28. Chen, L.C.; Papandreou, G.; Kokkinos, I.; Murphy, K.; Yuille, A.L. Deeplab: Semantic image segmentation with deep convolutional nets, atrous convolution, and fully connected crfs. *IEEE Trans. Pattern Anal. Mach. Intell.* **2017**, *40*, 834–848. [CrossRef]
29. Chen, L.C.; Papandreou, G.; Schroff, F.; Adam, H. Rethinking atrous convolution for semantic image segmentation. *arXiv* **2017**, arXiv:1706.05587.
30. Chen, L.C.; Zhu, Y.; Papandreou, G.; Schroff, F.; Adam, H. Encoder-decoder with atrous separable convolution for semantic image segmentation. In Proceedings of the European Conference on Computer Vision (ECCV), Munich, Germany, 8–14 September 2018; pp. 801–818.
31. Wang, Z.; Wang, J.; Yang, K.; Wang, L.; Su, F.; Chen, X. Semantic segmentation of high-resolution remote sensing images based on a class feature attention mechanism fused with Deeplabv3+. *Comput. Geosci.* **2022**, *158*, 104969. [CrossRef]
32. Hu, J.; Shen, L.; Sun, G. Squeeze-and-excitation networks. In Proceedings of the IEEE Conference on Computer Vision and Pattern Recognition, Salt Lake City, UT, USA, 18–23 June 2018; pp. 7132–7141.
33. Wang, Q.; Wu, B.; Zhu, P.; Li, P.; Zuo, W.; Hu, Q. ECA-Net: Efficient channel attention for deep convolutional neural networks. In Proceedings of the IEEE/CVF Conference on Computer Vision and Pattern Recognition, Seattle, WA, USA, 13–19 June 2020; pp. 11534–11542.
34. Woo, S.; Park, J.; Lee, J.Y.; Kweon, I.S. Cbam: Convolutional block attention module. In Proceedings of the European Conference on Computer Vision (ECCV), Munich, Germany, 8–14 September 2018; pp. 3–19.
35. Hou, Q.; Zhou, D.; Feng, J. Coordinate attention for efficient mobile network design. In Proceedings of the IEEE/CVF Conference on Computer Vision and Pattern Recognition, Nashville, TN, USA, 20–25 June 2021; pp. 13713–13722.
36. Chollet, F. Xception: Deep learning with depthwise separable convolutions. In Proceedings of the IEEE Conference on Computer Vision and Pattern Recognition, Honolulu, HI, USA, 21–26 July 2017; pp. 1251–1258.
37. He, K.; Zhang, X.; Ren, S.; Sun, J. Deep residual learning for image recognition. In Proceedings of the IEEE Conference on Computer Vision and Pattern Recognition, Las Vegas, NV, USA, 26–30 June 2015; pp. 770–778.
38. Sandler, M.; Howard, A.; Zhu, M.; Zhmoginov, A.; Chen, L.C. Mobilenetv2: Inverted residuals and linear bottlenecks. In Proceedings of the IEEE Conference on Computer Vision and Pattern Recognition, Salt Lake City, UT, USA, 18–23 June 2018; pp. 4510–4520.
39. Tan, M.; Le, Q. Efficientnetv2: Smaller models and faster training. In Proceedings of the International Conference on Machine Learning, Virtual Event, 18–24 July 2021; pp. 10096–10106.

Disclaimer/Publisher's Note: The statements, opinions and data contained in all publications are solely those of the individual author(s) and contributor(s) and not of MDPI and/or the editor(s). MDPI and/or the editor(s) disclaim responsibility for any injury to people or property resulting from any ideas, methods, instructions or products referred to in the content.

Article

YOLO-CID: Improved YOLOv7 for X-ray Contraband Image Detection

Ning Gan [†], Fang Wan [†], Guangbo Lei *, Li Xu, Chengzhi Xu, Ying Xiong and Wen Zhou

School of Computer Science, Hubei University of Technology, Wuhan 430068, China; 102101054@hbut.edu.cn (N.G.); 20021026@hbut.edu.cn (F.W.); 20040038@hbut.edu.cn (L.X.); xcz911@hbut.edu.cn (C.X.); 19980052@hbut.edu.cn (Y.X.); zw_mmwh@hbut.edu.cn (W.Z.)
* Correspondence: 20000012@hbut.edu.cn
[†] These authors contributed equally to this work.

Abstract: Currently, X-ray inspection systems may produce false detections due to factors such as the varying sizes of contraband images, complex backgrounds, and blurred edges. To address this issue, we propose the YOLO-CID method for contraband image detection. Firstly, we designed the MP-OD module in the backbone network to enhance the model's ability to extract key information from complex background images. Secondly, at the neck of the network, we designed a simplified version of BiFPN to add cross-scale connection lines in the feature fusion structure, to preserve deeper semantic information and enhance the network's ability to represent objects in low-contrast or occlusion situations. Finally, we added a new object detection layer to improve the model's accuracy in detecting small objects in dense environments. Experimental results on the PIDray public dataset show that the average accuracy rate of the YOLO-CID algorithm is 82.7% and the recall rate is 81.2%, which are 4.9% and 3.2% higher than the YOLOv7 algorithm, respectively. At the same time, the mAP on the CLCXray dataset reached 80.2%. Additionally, it can achieve a real-time detection speed of 40 frames per second and 43 frames per second in real scenes. These results demonstrate the effectiveness of the YOLO-CID algorithm in X-ray contraband detection.

Keywords: contraband detection; X-ray images; YOLOv7; BiFPN; object detection

Citation: Gan, N.; Wan, F.; Lei, G.; Xu, L.; Xu, C.; Xiong, Y.; Zhou, W. YOLO-CID: Improved YOLOv7 for X-ray Contraband Image Detection. *Electronics* **2023**, *12*, 3636. https://doi.org/10.3390/electronics12173636

Academic Editor: KC Santosh

Received: 14 July 2023
Revised: 25 August 2023
Accepted: 28 August 2023
Published: 28 August 2023

Copyright: © 2023 by the authors. Licensee MDPI, Basel, Switzerland. This article is an open access article distributed under the terms and conditions of the Creative Commons Attribution (CC BY) license (https:// creativecommons.org/licenses/by/ 4.0/).

1. Introduction

In contemporary society, with the diversification of transportation modes and the reduction of travel costs, the density of human traffic in public places is gradually increasing. Therefore, it becomes more and more important to protect people's personal safety and property security in public places. X-rays have the qualities of high energy, a short wavelength, and the ability to penetrate substances, which make them widely used in the fields of video surveillance [1], drone cruising [2], image security inspection [3], etc. At present, security work mainly relies on X-rays to identify contraband such as knives, firearms, and flammable goods, but this identification method mainly relies on the analysis and judgment of the security inspector, so there is greater subjectivity, even among experienced professionals, in the face of a constant stream of X-ray images. This will also produce visual fatigue and thus, in the processing of complex scenes, to the phenomenon of missed or mis-inspection. Therefore, in order to ensure the maximum possible safety of individuals and accelerate the detection efficiency, it is necessary to devise an intelligent detection algorithm with high accuracy and timeliness to identify contraband. However, the poor recognition of objects in the X-ray imaging process, susceptibility to the imaging environment, and high noise levels pose considerable challenges to the construction of X-ray detection models.

There are several traditional methods for the detection of targets in infrared images, including threshold detection [4], the Hough transform [5], and wavelet detection [6]. However, the sensitivity of these methods is influenced by thermal emissivity, making them vulnerable to interference from the specimen's surface and background radiation. Traditional X-ray detection methods also have two main drawbacks. Firstly, the resulting images have complex structures, poor resolutions, and weak anti-interference abilities and are easily damaged. This makes it difficult to determine the target's shape, size, and location using traditional methods, resulting in low detection accuracy. Secondly, the imaging speed is slow and cannot meet practical demands.

In recent years, object detection algorithms based on deep learning have been widely used in various industries. The YOLO family, a family of regression-based single-stage algorithms, has played an important role in X-ray object detection. [7] YOLO's regression method eliminates the need for complex frameworks, thus reducing the detection time. However, the YOLO algorithm struggles to perform optimally in complex backgrounds where objects overlap and occlude each other. In addition, the problem of multiple color overlaps caused by objects made of different materials when exposed to X-rays needs to be addressed.

YOLOv7 is the latest and most advanced object detection tool in the YOLO series. Its exceptional performance has made it one of the leading real-time object detection methods. Additionally, it has applications in fields such as healthcare, national defense, and security [8–10]. It uses the scalable and efficient layer aggregation network E-ELAN to accelerate model convergence. Rep [11] (RepVGG Block) reparameterization is used to achieve the best trade-off between speed and accuracy during training. Label assignment and auxiliary training heads improve the performance of object detectors in multi-task training. These advantages enable the model to ensure good accuracy and timeliness when detecting X-ray images. However, when directly applied to the X-ray suspected contraband detection field, the YOLO algorithm may encounter some problems:

1. Compared with common scenes, most targets in X-ray images are placed arbitrarily and have directional characteristics. However, the YOLOv7 network's positioning of key information is relatively vague, making it easy to lose key feature information about the directionality of the target. This further increases the difficulty of contraband detection.
2. The objects in X-ray images form a complex background due to overlapping and occlusion. However, there is no corresponding attention mechanism to deal with this complex background, resulting in the inaccurate detection of contraband under such conditions.
3. Although the PAFPN structure in the feature fusion module can enhance the network's representation ability, it does not make full use of the feature map output of each node and does not take into account the different fusion capabilities of each module for features. In response to these challenges, this article targets improvements on the basis of YOLOv7.

This paper proposes an X-ray contraband detection algorithm, YOLO-CID, based on an improved version of YOLOv7 for use in complex scenes. Experiments demonstrate that, in the challenging environment of contraband identification with complex backgrounds, the algorithm can achieve high levels of detection speed and accuracy.

The main contributions of this paper are as follows.

1. This paper proposes the YOLO-CID algorithm for X-ray contraband detection. We conducted ablation and comparative experiments of YOLO-CID on the PIDray [12] dataset and CLCXray [13] dataset. The experimental results show that, compared with current mainstream algorithms, our algorithm has significantly improved detection accuracy and speeds.
2. We implemented a robust new architecture and an enhanced MP-OD model, which builds upon and extends the original MPConv model. We added skip connections between the models and completed the second part (ODConv [14]). This results in a more accurate model with less redundant feature information, greater resilience against background X-ray images, and a faster feature localization speed.
3. We designed the P3-BiFPN module by replacing the original model's PAFPN [15] network with a BIFPN [16] network while retaining the P3 feature fusion layer to preserve shallow semantic information. This improves the network's reasonable application of path resources.

4. We introduced the shuffle attention mechanism [17], an efficient spatial channel dual attention mechanism, in the neck to improve the network's focus on tiny features.

2. Related Works

2.1. Traditional Machine Learning Methods for Contraband Detection in X-ray Images

In early machine learning studies of X-ray detection using single-view correlation detection, Turcsany et al. [18] proposed a visual bag-of-words model based on SVM and SURF features. They used starter visual words obtained from clustering to identify contraband in X-ray images, demonstrating the effectiveness of large and distinctly characterized datasets. Riffo et al. also achieved good results by designing an implicit shape model (ISM) for single-view contraband recognition [19]. Kundegorski et al. conducted extensive experiments on X-ray image classification and detection tasks using traditional manual features [20]. By combining multiple manual features, they demonstrated the effectiveness of traditional manual features in X-ray image detection tasks.

Later, multi-view detection techniques were developed to improve the object detection performance by compensating for the incomplete information of single-view imaging. Franzel et al. introduced multi-view imaging for rotating objects and combined SVM with gradient histograms in sliding window detection to improve detection [21]. Bastan et al.conducted a comprehensive evaluation of standard local features for image classification and target detection using the visual bag-of-words model [22]. They extended these features to obtain additional useful information from X-ray images, improving the detection performance.

2.2. Deep Learning for Contraband X-ray Image Detection

In recent years, deep-learning-based target detection algorithms have been rapidly developed and have played an important role in X-ray contraband detection, significantly improving the detection accuracy and efficiency compared to traditional algorithms. Mery et al. provided the GDXrays dataset, which contains 8150 X-ray luggage images with guns, hand swords, and blades. The images in the GDXray dataset are grayscale maps with clear target outlines, simple backgrounds, and low object overlap and occlusion [23]. Miao et al. (2019) introduced the larger SIXray dataset, with over 1 million X-ray images containing six types of targets: guns, knives, wrenches, pliers, scissors, and hammers. The SIXray dataset has 8929 labeled images containing targets and a high degree of randomness in target object stacking [24]. Zhao et al. (2022) published the CLCXray dataset to address the overlapping problem in X-ray security images [13]. This dataset has a large amount of data with overlapping phenomena and more accurate annotations compared to previous datasets. The paper also proposes a label-aware mechanism with an attention mechanism that adjusts the feature map according to label information to distinguish different objects in overlapping regions at the high-dimensional feature layer. These large, publicly available datasets provide stable data support for deep learning experiments in this domain and motivate continued development and progress.

In 2012, Krizhevsky et al. proposed the AlexNet network, which achieved excellent results in image classification and demonstrated the potential of deep learning in image processing [25]. Following the success of AlexNet, various classification networks, such as VGG [26], GoogleNet [27], and ResNet [28], YOLOX[29], YOLOv5 [30], and YOLOv, were developed, continuously improving deep learning's classification performance. Akcay [31] et al. applied the AlexNet network to X-ray luggage classification using transfer learning and achieved excellent detection performance compared to traditional machine learning methods. Mery et al. conducted experiments on the GDXray dataset, comparing X-ray luggage classification using bag-of-words models, sparse representation, deep learning, and classical pattern recognition schemes [32]. The results showed that both AlexNet and GoogleNet achieved high recognition rates, indicating the feasibility of using deep learning to design automatic contraband recognition devices. Xu et al. used an attention mechanism to quickly locate unlabeled information in weakly supervised environments where image information labels were missing [33]. Liu et al. proposed the Faster R-CNN object detection framework based on deep convolutional neural networks (DCNNs) to address detection failures caused by complex image backgrounds [34]. Li et al. improved the YOLOv5 model by compressing channels, optimizing parameters, and proposing a new YOLO-FIRI model for infrared target detection problems such as low recognition rates and high false alarm rates due to long distances, weak energy, and low resolutions [35]. Xiang et al. integrated both MCA and SCA modules into the YOLOx framework, enabling the acquisition of material information for contraband while expanding the model's receptive field, thereby enhancing the detection efficiency [36]. These improvements have significantly impacted the detection quality of contraband detection algorithms. However, real-world contraband detection still faces challenges such as varying item scales and complex backgrounds.

To address existing issues and leverage the unique characteristics of X-ray contraband images, this paper introduces improvements to the MPConv module and feature pyramid module of the YOLOv7 network. Additionally, we incorporate a shuffle attention mechanism and propose the YOLOv7-based YOLO-CID network model. Through ablation and comparative experiments, we demonstrate that the YOLO-CID model is more effective and practical than current mainstream methods and has significant value in the field of X-ray security.

3. YOLO-CID

3.1. Network Architecture

YOLOv7 is the most advanced object detector in the YOLO series. Its high accuracy and real-time performance have garnered widespread recognition in the field of object detection. In light of this, we propose the YOLO-CID algorithm for X-ray contraband detection, which is based on YOLOv7.

The structure of the YOLO-CID model is shown in the figure below. The model consists of three components: an efficient full-dimensional feature extraction network (MP-OD), an improved bidirectionally weighted feature pyramid network (P3-BiFPN) for feature fusion, and a neck component combined with a shuffle attention mechanism.

In Figure 1, the input image is resized to a uniform size of 640×640 pixels to meet the format requirements of the entire network. The resized images are then fed into the backbone network, where the BConv convolutional layer extracts image features at different scales. The MP-OD convolutional layer adopts a parallel strategy to learn the four-dimensional complementary attention of the input channel, output channel, kernel space, and number of kernels without disrupting the original gradient path. This process quickly locates effective features in the model feature map and improves its feature extraction ability. The neck part uses an improved weighted bidirectional feature pyramid, BiFPN-P3. The red line represents our improvement on the original PAFPN. We use the P3 layer, which is the top layer of the neck E-ELEAN module and the MPConv module. The node is deleted, and the root node and end node of the P3 and P4 layers are connected simultaneously. Through a top-down and bottom-up model structure, semantic information of different scales is transferred from shallow to deep layers, outputting three-layer fusion feature maps of different scales. The SA mechanism redistributes the weights in the fused feature map to suppress irrelevant features while enhancing contraband features for more robust representations. Finally, four detection layers at the prediction end predict the confidence, category, and anchor box of the result to obtain the final detection outcome.

Compared to the original YOLOv7 network, this network has shown significant improvements in detection accuracy, speed, and model parameters.

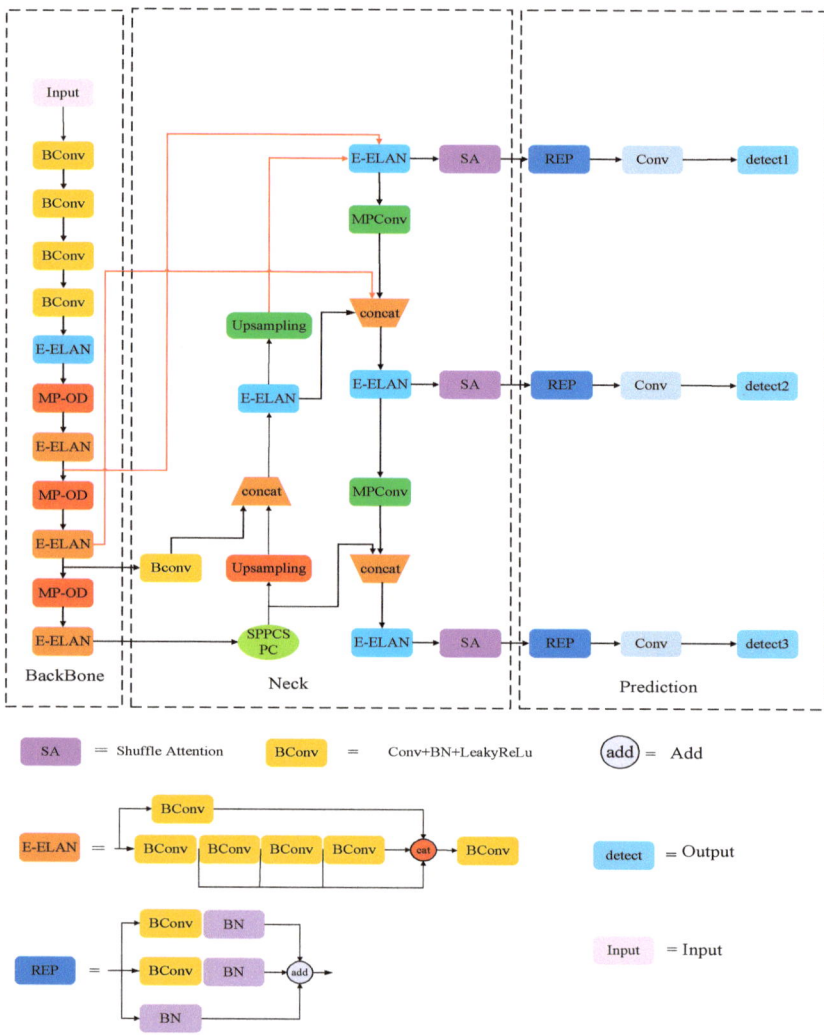

Figure 1. YOLO-CID network architecture.

3.2. MP-OD Module

The diversity of items in contraband recognition images and their random and variable stacking positions pose a major challenge for the network to effectively extract feature information. To maximize the extraction of key features for X-ray dangerous goods image detection, it is necessary to increase the parameters, depth, and number of channels of the network. However, this leads to increased computational complexity and a larger model size, making deployment more difficult. In the field of contraband identification, it is essential to control the number of model parameters and the amount of computation to ensure timely detection. To solve this problem, we improved the MPconv module of the backbone network and created the OD-MP module, enabling the YOLOv7 model to locate valid features in images more quickly. This improves the timeliness of feature extraction and enhances the object detection performance in complex situations.

In Figure 2, we replace the convolution (CBS) module of the lower branch of the central module with a full-dimensional dynamic convolution (ODConv) module. This allows the model to increase its complexity without increasing the network depth or width, reducing resource waste. We added a skip connection to the lower branch. When the network generates gradient dispersion due to the introduction of the ODConv module, it can independently select an appropriate path during the backpropagation of the gradient, avoiding branches that produce gradient dispersion. This makes the network fitting more stable and rapid. The specific ODConv structure diagram is shown in Figure 3.

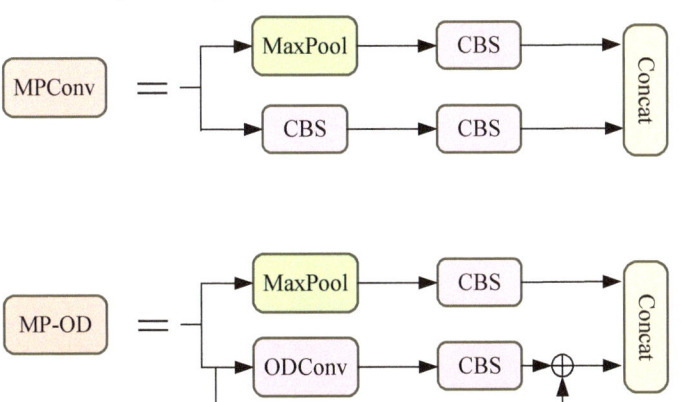

Figure 2. Structural comparison of MPConv and MP-OD modules.

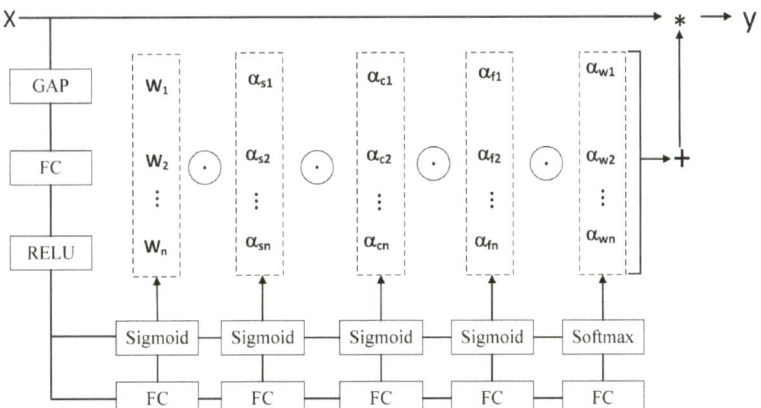

Figure 3. ODConv module.

In the convolution kernel W_i, α_{w_i} represents the attention scalar, while α_{s_i}, α_{c_i}, and α_{f_i} represent the attention weights along the spatial dimension, input channel dimension, and output channel dimension, respectively. The input feature vector X has a uniform length through GAP. As shown in the figure, ODConv compresses X into a feature vector of the input channel length through channel average pooling GAP. The feature vector is then mapped to a low-dimensional space through the fully connected layer (FC). After being activated by the ReLU function, it is divided into four head branches. The sigmoid or SoftMax function normalizes it to generate four different types of attention values: α_{w_i}, α_{s_i}, α_{c_i}, and α_{f_i}. Its working principle is shown in Formula (1).

$$Z_n = \alpha_{w_n} \odot \alpha_{f_n} \odot \alpha_{c_n} \odot \alpha_{s_n} \odot W_n \tag{1}$$

$$Z_n = \sum_{i=1}^{n} Z_t * X \tag{2}$$

In the equation, Z_n represents the final weight obtained by multiplication in each of the four dimensions of the dynamic convolution kernel. The input feature vector X is length-unified by GAP.

Unlike conditional parameter convolution (CondConv) [37] and dynamic filter convolution (DynamicConv) [38], which only focus on the weight ratio of a single dimension, ODConv uses SE's multi-head attention module to emphasize the importance of the spatial dimension, input channel dimension, and output channel dimension of the convolution kernel space for feature extraction. This module multiplies different attentions along the dimensions of the position, channel, filter, and kernel by progressively multiplying the convolution, providing better performance in capturing rich contextual information. As a result, ODConv greatly improves the feature extraction ability of convolution. More importantly, ODConv achieves better performance with fewer convolution kernels than CondConv and DyConv. Its high-efficiency and lightweight features enable the model to improve its perception of direction, position, and channel information without sacrificing accuracy or incurring a significant computational overhead.

3.3. BiFPN-P3 Module

Due to the varying scales of targets to be detected in images, a feature pyramid model (FPN) is commonly used in the feature fusion process of target detection to improve the situation wherein key information from small target objects is ignored during deep convolution. This approach utilizes hierarchical semantic information for feature fusion. The pixel aggregation network (PAFPN) used in the YOLOv7 model adds a low-dimensional to high-dimensional network layer on top of the FPN and transfers semantic information of different scales from shallow to deep. This enriches the semantic information transfer without affecting the location information of the fused feature map, enhancing the network integration effect. However, PAFPN does not fuse the original feature information, resulting in the partial loss of this information and affecting the model's detection accuracy. To address this issue, this paper introduces a bidirectional feature pyramid network (BiFPN) network based on the neck part of the original model. This is a weighted bidirectional (top-down and bottom-up) feature pyramid network, as shown in Figure 4b.

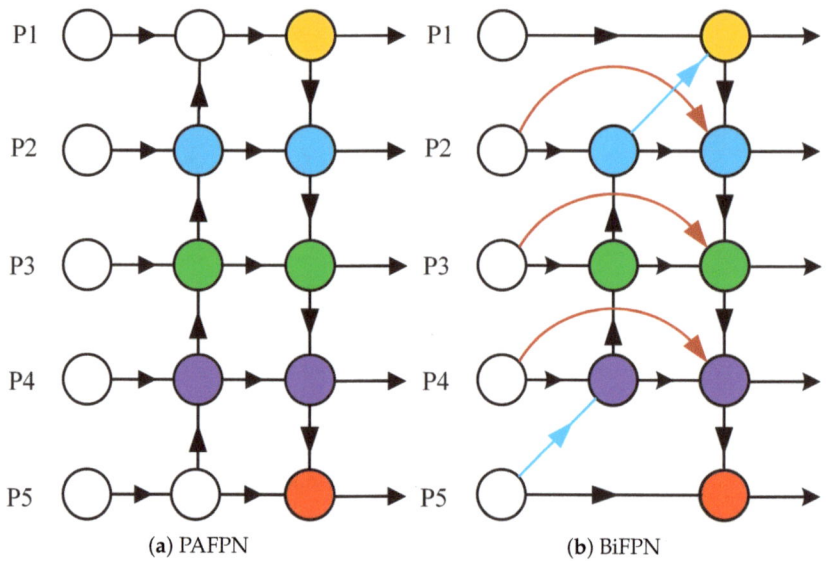

Figure 4. Structural comparison of PANFPN and BiFPN modules.

Compared to PAFPN, BiFPN can enhance network feature fusion through a simple residual operation by adding a residual link to the original feature. This strengthens the network's representation ability. At the same time, BiFPN recognizes that input feature maps of different scales have varying contributions to the network. Therefore, single-input edge nodes that contain less information and have lower contributions to feature fusion are removed from the PAFPN network. This reduces the computational overhead and allows for the better adjustment of each scale feature map's contribution by increasing the weight value after fusion, thereby improving the network's detection speed.

Similar to traditional target detection networks, the feature fusion layer of the YOLOv7 original network is its third layer. Although the BiFPN network adds a new fusion step to the original features and carefully optimizes the network structure to enhance its feature fusion and representation capabilities, the actual detection process of prohibited objects is affected by complex environments. The chaotic placement of contraband and small target objects that are easily obstructed by obstacles during the shooting process can result in the low efficiency of feature fusion and false or missed detections. This paper improves upon the BiFPN network and proposes the BiFPN-P3 model to enhance its ability to locate high-quality features, accelerate the flow of semantic information at different scales, and improve the detection accuracy.

In Figure 5, we retain the feature fusion layer of P3 in the original BiFPN network to preserve its shallow semantic information. Although this approach resulted in a slight increase in computational cost, the improved network architecture enhanced the attention to key information during feature fusion. This made the model more suitable for detecting contraband in complex scenarios.

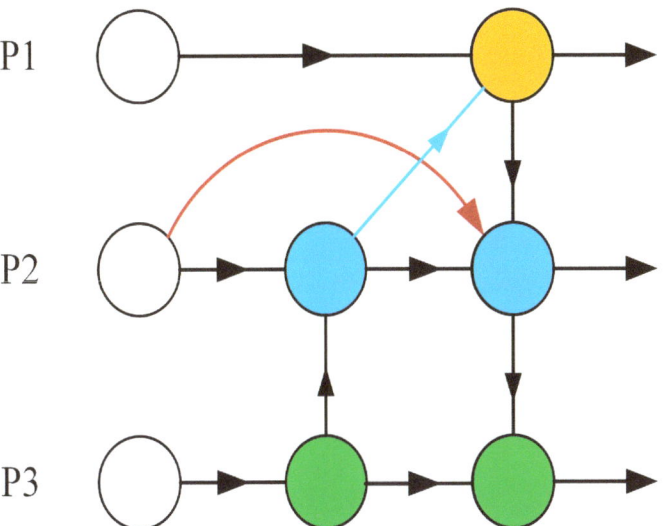

Figure 5. The BiFPN-P3 module.

3.4. SA Module

Channel attention and spatial attention are used to capture the dependency relationships between image channels and the pixel-level relationships in space, respectively. The SA module efficiently combines these two attention mechanisms without increasing the computational requirements. By adding the SA module to the neck module of YOLOv7, the efficient spatial channel dual attention mechanism (SA) can be fused simultaneously to effectively improve the model's detection performance. As shown in Figure 6, the SA module first groups image channel feature maps to obtain grouped sub-feature maps. The shuffle unit [39] is then used to apply the channel attention mechanism and spatial attention mechanism to each sub-feature map to extract features and capture feature map dependencies. Finally, the channel shuffle operation is used to fuse the summarized feature maps, establish information communication between sub-feature maps, and use the fused feature maps as the output of the SA module.

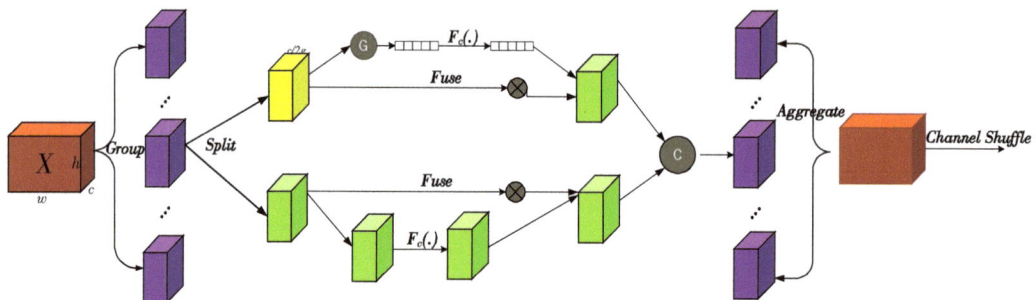

Figure 6. Shuffle attention mechanism structure.

The processing steps of the SA mechanism in the network are divided into the following three steps.

1. Feature grouping: The feature map $S \in R^{CHW}$ of a given length, width, and channel number W, H, and C is divided into G groups along the channel dimension, denoted as $X = [X_1, \ldots, X_G]$, $X_k \in R^{CHW}$. Each sub-feature X_k will gradually capture specific semantic information with training. This part corresponds to the section marked as Group on the leftmost side of the figure above.

2. Attention mixing: The generated feature X_k is divided into two branches along the channel dimension. The two sub-features are denoted as X_{k1}, $X_{k2} \in R^{CHW}$, as shown in the section marked as Split in the middle of the figure. During the processing of feature X_{k1}, a group normalization operation is used to accelerate convergence and avoid excessive differences in the values of different features, which can lead to confusion in the learning of lower layer networks. The representation of the enhanced input is then transformed through $F_{c(\cdot)}$. The specific formula is as follows:

$$X'_{k1} = \sigma(W_1 GN(X_{k1}) + b_1) X_{k1} \qquad (3)$$

In the equation, GN represents group normalization; W_1 and b_1 denote the scaling and shifting of the processed feature map. The enhanced feature representation is obtained through the sigmoid activation function.

For feature X_{k2}, the channel attention mechanism is employed. To reduce the complexity of the module and improve the processing efficiency, a fast and effective single-layer transformation mode consisting of global average pooling (GAP), scaling, and sigmoid activation is utilized for feature processing. First, channel statistics are generated through GAP to produce channel-level statistics. The specific formula is as follows:

$$s = F_{gp}(X_{k2}) = \frac{1}{H \times W} \sum_{i=1}^{H} \sum_{j=1}^{W} X_{k2}(i,j) \qquad (4)$$

In the equation, $\frac{1}{H \times W} \sum_{i=1}^{H} \sum_{j=1}^{W} X_{k2}(i,j)$ denotes the contraction calculation of X_{k2} along the spatial dimension HW. The generated S is then screened to obtain the final feature map X'_{k2}. The specific formula is as follows:

$$X'_{k2} = \sigma(W_2 \cdot (s) + b2) \cdot X_{k2} \qquad (5)$$

Finally, the results of the two types of attention are combined through a concatenation layer to obtain $X'_k = [X'_{k1}, X'_{k2}]$.

3. Feature aggregation: Similar to ShuffleNetv2, a channel shuffle operation is employed to aggregate all features and facilitate cross-group information exchange along the channel dimension, resulting in the final output feature map.

The aforementioned operations on the feature maps effectively integrate semantic and spatial information across different scales. The terminal attention mechanism improves the model's focus and enhances its detection efficiency in complex scenes.

4. Experimental Results and Analysis

4.1. Dataset

In order to verify the practicality and effectiveness of YOLO-CID in the field of X-ray contraband detection, we used two public datasets: PIDray and CLCXray. PIDray is a large-scale X-ray benchmark dataset for real-world contraband item detection, covering the detection of prohibited items in various situations, especially intentionally hidden items. The dataset contains more than 47,000 images of prohibited items in 12 categories with pixel-level annotations, including high-quality annotated segmentation masks and bounding boxes. It is currently the largest prohibited item detection dataset. The distribution of each class is shown in Figure 7. The test set is divided into three subsets, easy, hard, and hidden, with the hidden test set focusing on detecting contraband intentionally hidden in clutter. We used the hidden test set as our experiment's test set and divided the PIDray dataset into a training set and a test set at a ratio of 8:2.

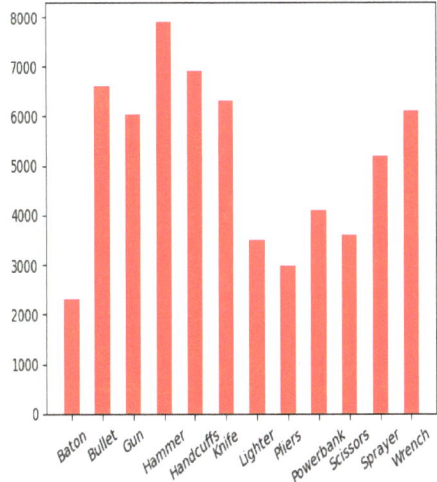

Figure 7. Class distribution of the PIDray dataset. The red bar represents the number of each class in the PIDray dataset.

CLCXray was jointly constructed by Tongji University, Beijing University of Posts and Telecommunications, and the University of the Chinese Academy of Sciences. It contains 9565 X-ray security images in 12 categories, including five types of knives (blades, daggers, knives, scissors, Swiss Army knives) and seven types of liquid containers (cans, beverage cartons, glass bottles, plastic bottles, vacuum cups, spray cans, tin cans). The distribution of each class is shown in Figure 8. In our experiment, we used 6696 images as the training set and 2869 images as the test set. Our partitioning of the modified dataset was consistent with that of PIDray.

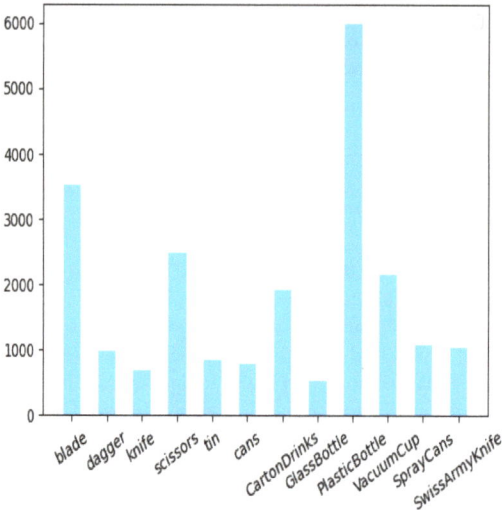

Figure 8. Class distribution of the CLCXray dataset. The blue bar represents the number of each class in the CLCXray dataset.

We demonstrated the superiority of the YOLO-CID algorithm through ablation and comparative experiments on the PIDray dataset and CLCXray dataset. The experiments were conducted on a Windows 10 64-bit operating system with an Intel i7-9700k processor and GeForce GTX3060 GPU. The acceleration environment was CUDA 11.6, the deep learning framework was Pytorch 1.12.1, and the programming language was Python 3.7.17. The experimental parameter settings are presented in Table 1.

Table 1. Configuration parameters of the experimental platform.

Parameters	Settings
Weights	Yolov7.pt
Epochs	300
Batch size	16
Hyperparameter file	hyp.scratch.p5.yaml

4.2. Analysis of Ablation Experiments

Three improvements were proposed for the original YOLOv7 algorithm. To verify the value of the proposed modules, ablation experiments were designed by gradually adding the improved modules. The model was trained and tested; '√' indicates the use of this modular approach. The results are shown in Table 2.

Table 2. Experimental results of MCS algorithm ablation on the test set of the PIDray dataset and CLCXray dataset.

Group	MP-OD	BiFPN-P3	SA	mAP (%)		F_1 Score (%)	
				PIDray	CLCXray	PIDray	CLCXray
G1				64.2	75.2	72.7	78.5
G2	√			66.1	77.8	73.4	80.4
G3	√	√		69.3	78.7	75.3	81.9
G4	√	√	√	70.3	80.2	77.4	82.5

The results show that all three improvement points of the YOLO-CID algorithm improved the model's detection performance. In scheme 1, the MP-OD module was used in the backbone network to improve the model's positioning rate. Compared with the original model, the mAP increased by 1.9% and 2.6%, and the F1 score increased by 0.6% and 1.9%. In scheme 2, the PAFPN network of the original model was modified. The results show that the mAP increased by 5.1% and 3.5%, and the F1 score increased by 2.6% and 3.4%. Finally, the shuffle attention mechanism was introduced to increase the detection accuracy by 6.1% and 5.0%, and the F1 score increased by 4.7% and 4.0%. These three changes effectively increased the network's accuracy in identifying contraband.

4.3. Algorithm Performance Analysis

According to the experimental results of scheme 1 and scheme 4, under the same conditions, the evaluation index of YOLO-CID exceeded that of the original YOLOv7 algorithm. The mAP50 values on the PIDray and CLCXray datasets reached 70.3% and 80.2%, respectively. The YOLO-CID algorithm significantly improves the detection ability of contraband in complex situations and effectively addresses the issues of missed and false detections in X-ray object detection.

Figure 9 compares the detection accuracy of each category between YOLO-CID and the original YOLOv7 algorithm on the PIDray dataset. As shown, the detection accuracy of our proposed algorithm is higher than that of the original YOLOv7 for all categories. In particular, the detection of lighters, sprayers, and knives has been significantly improved compared to the original model.

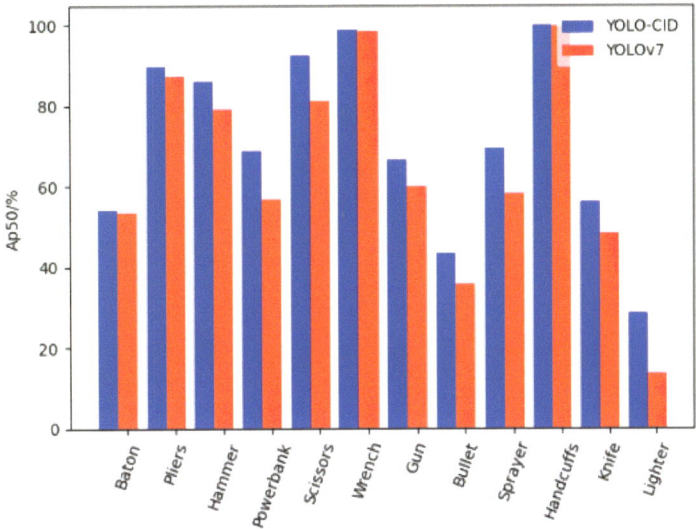

Figure 9. Single-class average precision comparison.

Figure 10 presents the confusion matrix for the PIDray dataset using the YOLOv7 model, while Figure 11 displays the confusion matrix for the same test set using the YOLO-CID model. A comparison of the two figures reveals that the detection accuracy for each class has been significantly improved with the YOLO-CID algorithm relative to the original algorithm. This suggests that the YOLO-CID model places greater emphasis on feature information and exhibits superior performance.

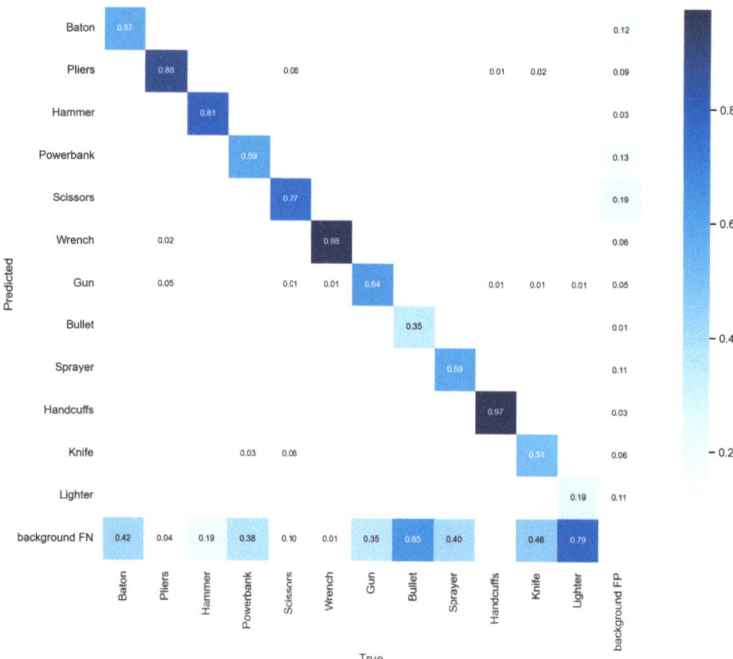

Figure 10. Confusion matrix for YOLOv7 network model.

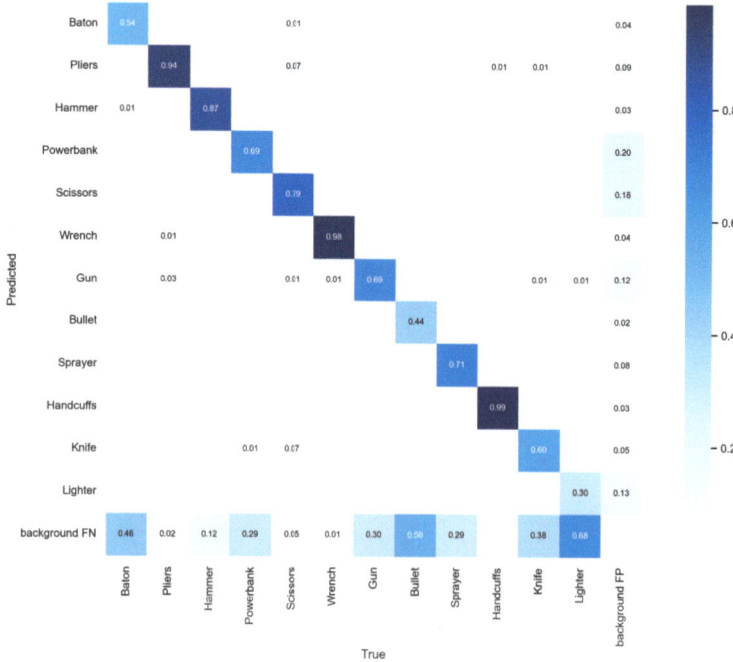

Figure 11. Confusion matrix for YOLO-CID network model.

Figure 12 presents the detection results for the YOLO-CID network model and the original YOLOv7 network model on the hidden test set, while Figure 13 presents the detection results for the YOLO-CID network model and the original YOLOv7 network model on the CLCXray test set. It can be seen that YOLO-CID exhibits stronger adaptability and generalization ability in detecting X-ray contraband under simulated real conditions. Compared to the YOLOv7 algorithm, YOLO-CID displays a higher level of confidence when detecting the same object. Additionally, the YOLO-CID algorithm has greatly improved the issues of missed and false detections in contraband detection, demonstrating its superiority and practicality.

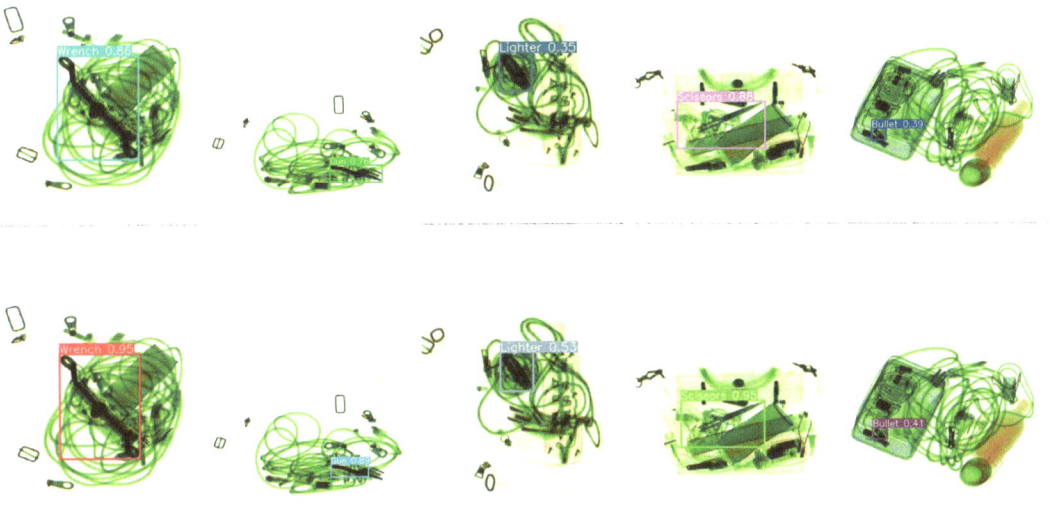

Figure 12. Some examples of the detection result on the test set of the PIDray dataset. The first row is the result of YOLOv7, and the second row is the result of YOLO-CID. We used the same four images to compare the performance of the detection models.

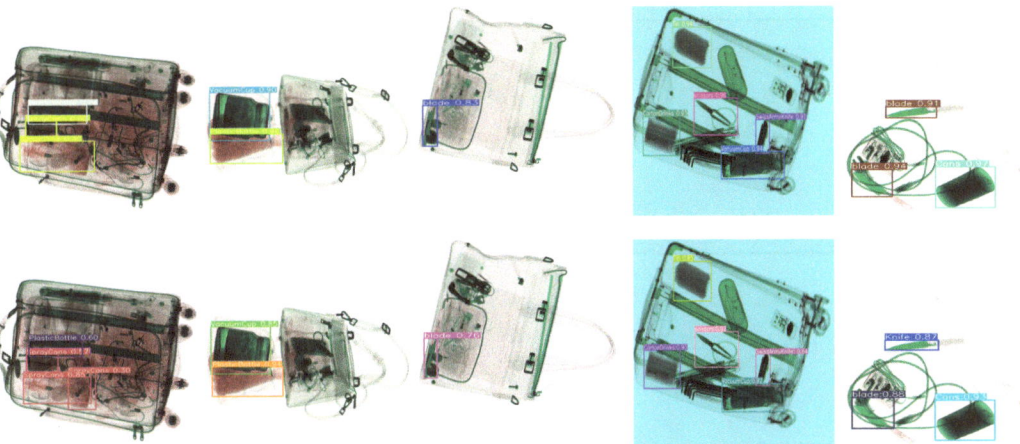

Figure 13. Some examples of the detection result on the test set of the CLCXray dataset. The first row is the result of YOLOv7, and the second row is the result of YOLO-CID. We used the same four images to compare the performance of the detection models.

4.4. Comparative Experimental Analysis

Table 3 shows the experimental results of different algorithm models on the test set of the PIDray dataset, while Table 4 presents the results on the test set of the CLCXray dataset. The average accuracy of the YOLO-CID algorithm is 70.3% and 80.2%, which are 6.1% and 5.0% higher than in the case of YOLOv7, respectively. The real-time detection speed is 40 frames per second and 43 frames per second, respectively. These results demonstrate that the YOLO-CID algorithm outperforms both single-stage and two-stage algorithms, exhibiting high detection accuracy while meeting the requirements of real-time detection.

Table 3. Experimental results comparing different algorithmic models on the PIDray dataset test set.

Model	AP50 (50%)	FPS
Faster R-CNN [40]	42.1	13.9
SSD512 [41]	43.8	16.1
YOLOv3 [42]	69.0	34.9
YOLOv5s [30]	65.5	39.2
YOLOv7	64.2	39.0
Ours	70.3	40.6

Table 4. Experimental results comparing different algorithmic models on the CLCXray dataset test set.

Model	AP50 (50%)	FPS
Cascade R-CNN [43]	71.4	18.0
SSD512 [41]	66.4	21.6
YOLOv3 [42]	67.2	36.7
YOLOv6s [44]	71.2	39.9
YOLOv7	75.2	41.2
Ours	80.2	43.3

Figure 14 illustrates the convergence of the loss functions for various models on the PIDray dataset. As depicted, the bounding box loss of the YOLO-CID algorithm decreased more rapidly during training and it exhibited lower loss values compared to other algorithms. Additionally, its mean average precision (mAP) value was higher. These results demonstrate that the improved algorithm converges more quickly and exhibits a higher degree of alignment between predicted and ground truth frames, thereby proving its effectiveness and superiority.

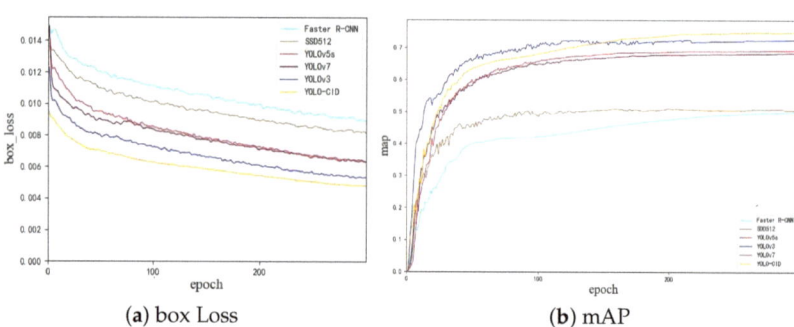

(a) box Loss   (b) mAP

Figure 14. Comparison of evaluation indexes under different models: (**a**) bounding box loss curve, (**b**) map curve.

5. Conclusions

To perform real-time X-ray contraband detection, we improved the original YOLOv7 network. We designed the MP-OD module in the backbone of YOLOv7 to enhance the timeliness of feature extraction, optimize the convolutional layer structure of the network, improve the model's ability to extract key information from complex background images, and reduce resource waste. In the neck component, we replaced the path aggregation network of the original model with a simplified version of BiFPN-P3, a bidirectional weighted feature pyramid network, and removed single-input edge nodes containing less PAN information to reduce the computational overhead. We also added an SA mechanism to enhance the model's attention to effective feature information without increasing the computational complexity. Ablation experiments on the extended PIDray and CLCXray datasets showed that these strategies effectively improved the timeliness and detection accuracy in complex background scenes. Comparative experiments with other classic object detection algorithms showed that under the same conditions, our improved YOLOv7 model achieved the highest F1 score and AP value and had a faster detection speed than the other five algorithms, demonstrating its effectiveness for real-time contraband detection.

Author Contributions: Conceptualization, N.G. and F.W.; methodology, N.G.; software, N.G. and G.L.; validation, N.G.; formal analysis, L.X. and C.X.; investigation, F.W. and Y.X.; resources, W.Z. and L.X.; data curation, N.G. and G.L.; writing—original draft preparation, N.G.; writing—review and editing, F.W. and G.L.; visualization, N.G.; supervision, C.X. and Y.X.; project administration, W.Z.; funding acquisition, W.Z. and L.X. All authors have read and agreed to the published version of the manuscript.

Funding: This research was funded by the National Natural Science Foundation of China (Grant No. 62202147) and the Science and Technology Research Project of the Education Department of Hubei Province (Grant No. B2021070).

Data Availability Statement: Not applicable.

Conflicts of Interest: The authors declare no conflict of interest.

References

1. Zhang, H.; Luo, C.; Wang, Q.; Kitchin, M.; Parmley, A.; Monge-Alvarez, J.; Casaseca-De-La-Higuera, P. A novel infrared video surveillance system using deep learning based techniques. *Multimed. Tools Appl.* **2018**, *77*, 26657–26676. [CrossRef]
2. Cazzato, D.; Cimarelli, C.; Sanchez-Lopez, J.L.; Voos, H.; Leo, M. A survey of computer vision methods for 2d object detection from unmanned aerial vehicles. *J. Imaging* **2020**, *6*, 78. [CrossRef] [PubMed]
3. Kim, H.Y.; Cho, S.J.; Baek, S.J.; Jung, S.W.; Ko, S.J. Learning-based image synthesis for hazardous object detection in X-ray security applications. *IEEE Access* **2021**, *9*, 135256–135265. [CrossRef]
4. Giełczyk, A.; Marciniak, A.; Tarczewska, M.; Lutowski, Z. Pre-processing methods in chest X-ray image classification. *PLoS ONE* **2022**, *17*, e0265949. [CrossRef]
5. Larhmam, M.A.; Mahmoudi, S.; Benjelloun, M. Semi-automatic detection of cervical vertebrae in X-ray images using generalized Hough transform. In Proceedings of the 2012 3rd International Conference on Image Processing Theory, Tools and Applications (IPTA), Istanbul, Turkey, 15–18 October 2012; pp. 396–401.
6. Dong, H.; Zhao, L.; Shu, Y.; Xiong, N.N. X-ray image denoising based on wavelet transform and median filter. *Appl. Math. Nonlinear Sci.* **2020**, *5*, 435–442. [CrossRef]
7. Wang, C.Y.; Bochkovskiy, A.; Liao, H.Y.M. YOLOv7: Trainable bag-of-freebies sets new state-of-the-art for real-time object detectors. *arXiv* **2022**, arXiv:2207.02696.
8. Santosh, K.; Dhar, M.K.; Rajbhandari, R.; Neupane, A. Deep neural network for foreign object detection in chest X-rays. In Proceedings of the 2020 IEEE 33rd International Symposium on Computer-Based Medical Systems (CBMS), Rochester, MN, USA, 28–30 July 2020; pp. 538–541.
9. Santosh, K.; Roy, S.; Allu, S. Generic Foreign Object Detection in Chest X-rays. In Proceedings of the International Conference on Recent Trends in Image Processing and Pattern Recognition, Kingsville, TX, USA, 1–2 December 2021; pp. 93–104.
10. Xue, Z.; Candemir, S.; Antani, S.; Long, L.R.; Jaeger, S.; Demner-Fushman, D.; Thoma, G.R. Foreign object detection in chest X-rays. In Proceedings of the 2015 IEEE International Conference on Bioinformatics and Biomedicine (BIBM), Washington, DC, USA, 9–12 November 2015; pp. 956–961.
11. Xie, J.; Miao, Q.; Liu, R.; Xin, W.; Tang, L.; Zhong, S.; Gao, X. Attention adjacency matrix based graph convolutional networks for skeleton-based action recognition. *Neurocomputing* **2021**, *440*, 230–239. [CrossRef]

12. Zhang, L.; Jiang, L.; Ji, R.; Fan, H. PIDray: A Large-scale X-ray Benchmark for Real-World Prohibited Item Detection. *arXiv* **2022**, arXiv:2211.10763.
13. Zhao, C.; Zhu, L.; Dou, S.; Deng, W.; Wang, L. Detecting overlapped objects in X-ray security imagery by a label-aware mechanism. *IEEE Trans. Inf. Forensics Secur.* **2022**, *17*, 998–1009. [CrossRef]
14. Li, C.; Zhou, A.; Yao, A. Omni-dimensional dynamic convolution. *arXiv* **2022**, arXiv:2209.07947.
15. Chen, C.P.; Li, H.; Wei, Y.; Xia, T.; Tang, Y.Y. A local contrast method for small infrared target detection. *IEEE Trans. Geosci. Remote Sens.* **2013**, *52*, 574–581. [CrossRef]
16. Tan, M.; Pang, R.; Le, Q.V. Efficientdet: Scalable and efficient object detection. In Proceedings of the IEEE/CVF Conference on Computer Vision and Pattern Recognition, Seattle, WA, USA, 13–19 June 2020; pp. 10781–10790.
17. Zhang, Q.L.; Yang, Y.B. Sa-net: Shuffle attention for deep convolutional neural networks. In Proceedings of the ICASSP 2021–2021 IEEE International Conference on Acoustics, Speech and Signal Processing (ICASSP), Toronto, ON, Canada, 6–11 June 2021; pp. 2235–2239.
18. Turcsany, D.; Mouton, A.; Breckon, T.P. Improving feature-based object recognition for X-ray baggage security screening using primed visualwords. In Proceedings of the 2013 IEEE International conference on industrial technology (ICIT), Cape Town, South Africa, 25–28 February 2013; pp. 1140–1145.
19. Riffo, V.; Mery, D. Automated detection of threat objects using adapted implicit shape model. *IEEE Trans. Syst. Man Cybern. Syst.* **2015**, *46*, 472–482. [CrossRef]
20. Kundegorski, M.E.; Akçay, S.; Devereux, M.; Mouton, A.; Breckon, T.P. On using feature descriptors as visual words for object detection within X-ray baggage security screening. In Proceedings of the 7th International Conference on Imaging for Crime Detection and Prevention (ICDP 2016), Madrid, Spain, 23–25 November 2016.
21. Franzel, T.; Schmidt, U.; Roth, S. Object detection in multi-view X-ray images. In Proceedings of the Pattern Recognition: Joint 34th DAGM and 36th OAGM Symposium, Graz, Austria, 28–31 August 2012; pp. 144–154.
22. Bastan, M.; Byeon, W.; Breuel, T.M. Object Recognition in Multi-View Dual Energy X-ray Images. In Proceedings of the BMVC, Bristol, UK, 9–13 September 2013; Volume 1, p. 11.
23. Mery, D.; Riffo, V.; Zscherpel, U.; Mondragón, G.; Lillo, I.; Zuccar, I.; Lobel, H.; Carrasco, M. GDXray: The database of X-ray images for nondestructive testing. *J. Nondestruct. Eval.* **2015**, *34*, 1–12. [CrossRef]
24. Miao, C.; Xie, L.; Wan, F.; Su, C.; Liu, H.; Jiao, J.; Ye, Q. Sixray: A large-scale security inspection x-ray benchmark for prohibited item discovery in overlapping images. In Proceedings of the IEEE/CVF Conference on Computer Vision and Pattern Recognition, Long Beach, CA, USA, 15–20 June 2019; pp. 2119–2128.
25. Krizhevsky, A.; Sutskever, I.; Hinton, G.E. Imagenet classification with deep convolutional neural networks. *Commun. ACM* **2017**, *60*, 84–90. [CrossRef]
26. Simonyan, K.; Zisserman, A. Very deep convolutional networks for large-scale image recognition. *arXiv* **2014**, arXiv:1409.1556.
27. Szegedy, C.; Liu, W.; Jia, Y.; Sermanet, P.; Reed, S.; Anguelov, D.; Erhan, D.; Vanhoucke, V.; Rabinovich, A. Going deeper with convolutions. In Proceedings of the IEEE Conference on Computer Vision and Pattern Recognition, Boston, MA, USA, 7–12 June 2015; pp. 1–9.
28. He, K.; Zhang, X.; Ren, S.; Sun, J. Deep residual learning for image recognition. In Proceedings of the IEEE Conference on Computer Vision and Pattern Recognition, Las Vegas, NV, USA, 27–30 June 2016; pp. 770–778.
29. Zhang, Y.; Xu, W.; Yang, S.; Xu, Y.; Yu, X. Improved YOLOX detection algorithm for contraband in X-ray images. *Appl. Opt.* **2022**, *61*, 6297–6310. [CrossRef] [PubMed]
30. Song, B.; Li, R.; Pan, X.; Liu, X.; Xu, Y. Improved YOLOv5 Detection Algorithm of Contraband in X-ray Security Inspection Image. In Proceedings of the 2022 5th International Conference on Pattern Recognition and Artificial Intelligence (PRAI), Xiamen, China, 23–25 September 2022; pp. 169–174.
31. Akçay, S.; Kundegorski, M.E.; Devereux, M.; Breckon, T.P. Transfer learning using convolutional neural networks for object classification within X-ray baggage security imagery. In Proceedings of the 2016 IEEE International Conference on Image Processing (ICIP), Phoenix, AZ, USA, 25–28 September 2016; pp. 1057–1061.
32. Mery, D.; Svec, E.; Arias, M.; Riffo, V.; Saavedra, J.M.; Banerjee, S. Modern computer vision techniques for x-ray testing in baggage inspection. *IEEE Trans. Syst. Man Cybern. Syst.* **2016**, *47*, 682–692. [CrossRef]
33. Xu, M.; Zhang, H.; Yang, J. Prohibited item detection in airport X-ray security images via attention mechanism based CNN. In Proceedings of the Pattern Recognition and Computer Vision: First Chinese Conference, PRCV 2018, Guangzhou, China, 23–26 November 2018; pp. 429–439.
34. Liu, J.; Leng, X.; Liu, Y. Deep convolutional neural network based object detector for X-ray baggage security imagery. In Proceedings of the 2019 IEEE 31st International Conference on Tools with Artificial Intelligence (ICTAI), Portland, OR, USA, 4–6 November 2019; pp. 1757–1761.
35. Li, S.; Li, Y.; Li, Y.; Li, M.; Xu, X. Yolo-firi: Improved yolov5 for infrared image object detection. *IEEE Access* **2021**, *9*, 141861–141875. [CrossRef]
36. Xiang, N.; Gong, Z.; Xu, Y.; Xiong, L. Material-Aware Path Aggregation Network and Shape Decoupled SIoU for X-ray Contraband Detection. *Electronics* **2023**, *12*, 1179. [CrossRef]

37. Yang, B.; Bender, G.; Le, Q.V.; Ngiam, J. Condconv: Conditionally parameterized convolutions for efficient inference. In Proceedings of the Advances in Neural Information Processing Systems 32: Annual Conference on Neural Information Processing Systems 2019, NeurIPS 2019, Vancouver, BC, Canada, 8–14 December 2019.
38. Chen, Y.; Dai, X.; Liu, M.; Chen, D.; Yuan, L.; Liu, Z. Dynamic convolution: Attention over convolution kernels. In Proceedings of the IEEE/CVF Conference on Computer Vision and Pattern Recognition, Seattle, WA, USA, 13–19 June 2020; pp. 11030–11039.
39. Ma, N.; Zhang, X.; Zheng, H.T.; Sun, J. Shufflenet v2: Practical guidelines for efficient cnn architecture design. In Proceedings of the European Conference on Computer Vision (ECCV), Munich, Germany, 8–14 September 2018; pp. 116–131.
40. Ren, S.; He, K.; Girshick, R.; Sun, J. Faster r-cnn: Towards real-time object detection with region proposal networks. In Proceedings of the Advances in Neural Information Processing Systems 28: Annual Conference on Neural Information Processing Systems 2015, Montreal, QC, Canada, 7–12 December 2015.
41. Liu, W.; Anguelov, D.; Erhan, D.; Szegedy, C.; Reed, S.; Fu, C.Y.; Berg, A.C. Ssd: Single shot multibox detector. In Proceedings of the Computer Vision–ECCV 2016: 14th European Conference, Amsterdam, The Netherlands, 11–14 October 2016; pp. 21–37.
42. Redmon, J.; Farhadi, A. Yolov3: An incremental improvement. *arXiv* **2018**, arXiv:1804.02767.
43. Cai, Z.; Vasconcelos, N. Cascade r-cnn: Delving into high quality object detection. In Proceedings of the IEEE Conference on Computer Vision and Pattern Recognition, Salt Lake City, UT, USA, 18–23 June 2018; pp. 6154–6162.
44. Li, C.; Li, L.; Jiang, H.; Weng, K.; Geng, Y.; Li, L.; Ke, Z.; Li, Q.; Cheng, M.; Nie, W.; et al. YOLOv6: A single-stage object detection framework for industrial applications. *arXiv* **2022**, arXiv:2209.02976.

Disclaimer/Publisher's Note: The statements, opinions and data contained in all publications are solely those of the individual author(s) and contributor(s) and not of MDPI and/or the editor(s). MDPI and/or the editor(s) disclaim responsibility for any injury to people or property resulting from any ideas, methods, instructions or products referred to in the content.

Article
Enhancing the Accuracy of an Image Classification Model Using Cross-Modality Transfer Learning

Jiaqi Liu, Kwok Tai Chui * and Lap-Kei Lee *

Department of Electronic Engineering and Computer Science, School of Science and Technology, Hong Kong Metropolitan University, Hong Kong, China; s1304012@live.hkmu.edu.hk
* Correspondence: jktchui@hkmu.edu.hk (K.T.C.); lklee@hkmu.edu.hk (L.-K.L.)

Abstract: Applying deep learning (DL) algorithms for image classification tasks becomes more challenging with insufficient training data. Transfer learning (TL) has been proposed to address these problems. In theory, TL requires only a small amount of knowledge to be transferred to the target task, but traditional transfer learning often requires the presence of the same or similar features in the source and target domains. Cross-modality transfer learning (CMTL) solves this problem by learning knowledge in a source domain completely different from the target domain, often using a source domain with a large amount of data, which helps the model learn more features. Most existing research on CMTL has focused on image-to-image transfer. In this paper, the CMTL problem is formulated from the text domain to the image domain. Our study started by training two separately pre-trained models in the text and image domains to obtain the network structure. The knowledge of the two pre-trained models was transferred via CMTL to obtain a new hybrid model (combining the BERT and BEiT models). Next, GridSearchCV and 5-fold cross-validation were used to identify the most suitable combination of hyperparameters (batch size and learning rate) and optimizers (SGDM and ADAM) for our model. To evaluate their impact, 48 two-tuple hyperparameters and two well-known optimizers were used. The performance evaluation metrics were validation accuracy, F1-score, precision, and recall. The ablation study confirms that the hybrid model enhanced accuracy by 12.8% compared with the original BEiT model. In addition, the results show that these two hyperparameters can significantly impact model performance.

Keywords: batch size; cross-modality; deep learning; image classification; learning rate; overfitting; text classification; transfer learning

1. Introduction

Image classification problems have been leading research in computer vision. With the continual development of the Internet in recent decades, people can easily create, access, and analyze all types of images, which has resulted in the rapid expansion of the number of images. Images are an important way of carrying information and are essential in all aspects of people's daily communication, life, and work. In this context, there has been an emphasis on finding accurate and valuable images in a short amount of time from many images. The potential of machine learning algorithms (particularly deep learning algorithms) is increasingly being explored as technology advances, and it has produced beneficial effects in various sectors, including, but not limited to, natural language processing (NLP), traffic prediction, medical diagnosis, and image classification [1]. Attention is drawn to image classification problems because of their state-of-the-art performance in the field. However, machine learning must improve with lengthy training times, the large sample sizes required, and limited computer ability [2].

With the advent of deep learning algorithms, automatic feature extraction from images can be achieved. Convolutional neural networks (CNNs) [3] are one of the most mainstream image analysis methods [4]. Regarding deep learning models, it is desirable to have sufficient labeled training data to achieve promising model performance (e.g., accurate and unbiased classification). However, some real-world problems are linked to small-scale labeled datasets, such as rare diseases [5], mental health [6], and legal areas [7]. Transfer learning has recently been suggested as a solution to this issue, which has several benefits for enhancing the performance of target models from single or multiple source models [8,9]. The general idea of transfer learning is to transfer knowledge learned from the source domain to the target domain, speeding up training and lowering the requirement for sample size in the target dataset. Some studies have demonstrated the improvement of transfer learning on image classification accuracy and the effect of transfer learning on CNN, which performs better in image classification after pre-training compared to traditional CNN [10,11]. In the methodologies of [12–14], including another domain as the source domain becomes redundant if the training samples are large enough and an impressive performance can be achieved while restricted in the target domain. There are various levels of disagreement between different source and target domain data pairs. Regardless of their disagreement, imposing knowledge from the source domain into the target domain can lead to some performance degradation or, in worse cases, disrupt data consistency in the target domain [15]. On the other hand, traditional transfer learning is only partially applicable to some tasks and requires a good degree of similarity or common information between the source and target domains. As mentioned above, the key part of the transfer learning algorithm is to discover the similarity between the source domain $P_S(X,Y)$ and the target domain $P_T(X,Y)$. When the labeled target data are not available ($n_l = 0$), one has to resort to the similarity between the marginal $P_S(X)$ and $P_T(X)$; although this does have a theoretical limitation [14]. In contrast, this problem can be solved if a significant number of samples $(x_l, y_l) \sim P_T(X,Y)$ and $(x_s, y_s) \sim P_s(X,Y)$ are available. Thus, a reasonable migration learning algorithm may be able to use datasets with labeled target domains to mitigate the negative impact of irrelevant source information [16]. In other words, transferring learning between domains with low similarity will be prone to negative transfer [16–18], i.e., resulting in degradation of the performance of the target model.

Such a problem of transfer learning between domains with low similarity is known as cross-modality transfer learning, which involves transfer learning between heterogeneous datasets [19]. In this paper, a breakthrough is desired to alleviate the limits of traditional transfer learning when the source and target domains differ. A cross-modality transfer approach from text to images is chosen. It is believed that the machine learning methods used for text classification could be used for image classification, known as cross-modality transfer.

1.1. Related Work on Cross-Modality Transfer Learning

The discussion of existing works includes only research studies using cross-modality transfer learning, i.e., existing works using traditional transfer learning with high similarity between the source and target domains are not considered. Therefore, cross-modality transfer learning was proposed to tackle the issue of negative transfer between heterogeneous source and target domains [20–25].

Image to Image. Lei et al. [20] performed cross-modality transfer learning using ResNet-50 with three convolutional layers from ImageNet (the source dataset) to the ICPR2012 dataset or the ICPR2016 dataset (the target datasets). The ratio between the training and testing datasets was 80:20. The model achieved an accuracy of 97.1% (an improvement of 6.12%) for the ICPR 2012 dataset and an accuracy of 98.4% (an improvement of 0.163%) for the ICPR 2016 dataset. In another work [21], knowledge was transferred from the NPHEp-2 dataset (source dataset) to the LSHEp-2 dataset (target dataset) using a parallel deep residual network with a two-dimensional discrete wavelet transform. The training-testing dataset was in an 80:20 ratio. The proposed method enhanced the accuracy by 0.417% (from 95.9% to 96.3%). Hadad et al. [22] proposed using cross-modality transfer learning to improve the recognition rate of masses in breast MRI images. They trained a network on X-ray images and then transferred the pre-trained network to the target domain (MRI images). Performance evaluation revealed that cross-modality transfer learning improved the classification performance from an overall accuracy of 90% to 93%. Their study's limitation is that it involves transferring between different types of images, specifically from X-ray images to MRI images. While X-ray images have a relatively small dataset compared to other domains (e.g., the text domain), the transfer process still fails to fully utilize the benefits of CMTL due to the relatively large amount of data in MRI images. Another work [23] proposed a cross-modality transfer learning approach from 2D to 3D sensors in which different modalities shared the same observation targets. They employed a pre-trained model network based on 2D images and then transferred the pre-trained model to the visual system of 3D sensors. The model achieved an average precision improvement of 13.2% and 16.1% compared to ConvNets and ViTs, respectively. A cross-modality transfer learning algorithm was proposed for transferring a network trained on a large dataset in the source domain (RGB) to the target domains (depth and infrared) [24], which was used for the task of transferring knowledge from one source modality to another target modality without accessing task-related source data. The model achieved an accuracy of 90.2% in the single-source cross-modality knowledge transfer task from RGB to NIR using the RGB-NIR dataset without task-related source data and 92.7% from NIR to RGB. However, their designed model has yet to be tested in tasks with larger modality gaps as it was only applied in cases with smaller modality differences.

Text to Image. Du et al. [25] described a chest X-Ray quality assessment method that combined image-text contrastive learning and medical domain knowledge fusion. The proposed method integrated large-scale real clinical chest X-rays and diagnostic report text information and fine-tuned the pretrained model based on contrastive text-image pairs. The model yielded an accuracy of 89.7–97.2% for 13 classes. Another work [26] proposed a zero-shot transfer learning model that can recognize objects in images without any training samples available. The model acquired knowledge by learning from an unsupervised, large-scale text corpus. In the performance evaluation, the images were split into visible and invisible categories. The model achieved about 80% accuracy in the training categories. The research study also suggested that if two zero-shots had no remote similarity with any visible class, the performance was relatively poor, resulting in suboptimal zero-shot classification. Chen et al. [27] presented a history-aware multimodal transformer (HAMT) approach for visual linguistic navigation (VLN). The HAMT encoded all past panoramic observations by a hierarchical visual transformer, which can effectively incorporate far-future history into multimodal decision-making. The model joins text, history, and current observations to predict the following actions. Another work [28] compared pre-trained and fine-tuned representations at the visual, verbal, and multimodal levels using a set of detection tasks and introduced a new dataset specifically for multimodal detection. While their visual-linguistic models could understand color at the multimodal level, they relied on biases in the textual data concerning object position and size. This suggests that fine-tuning the visual-linguistic model in a multimodal task does not necessarily improve its multimodal capabilities. In [29], a new efficient and flexible multimodal fusion method called prompt-based multimodal fusion (PMF) was proposed that utilized a unimodal pre-trained transformer. The authors presented a modular multimodal fusion framework that enabled bidirectional interactions between different modalities to dynamically learn different objectives of multimodal learning. The proposed method is memory-efficient, which can significantly reduce the use of training memory and achieve comparable performance to existing fine-tuning methods with fewer trainable parameters. However, the performance of PMF on all three datasets still lags behind the baseline tuning with the same pre-trained backbone and no tuning of hyperparameters. In addition, CLiMB consisted of several implementations of CL algorithms and an improved visual language translator (ViLT) model that could be deployed on both multimodal and unimodal tasks [30]. It was found that common language learning methods could help mitigate forgetting in multimodal task learning but did not enable cross-task knowledge transfer.

Other. Falco et al. [31] collected a visual dataset and a tactile dataset to form the nature of the distant source and target domains. Cross-modality transfer learning was supported by subspace alignment and transfer component analysis for dimensionality reduction and a geodesic flow kernel for characterizing geodesic flow. The model achieved an accuracy of 89.7%. A multimodal transformer framework with variable-length memory (MTVM) was proposed for VLN [32]. The framework also included an explicit memory bank for storing past activations. It enabled the agent to easily update the temporal context by adding the current output activation corresponding to the action at each step to learn a strong relationship between the instruction and the temporal context, thus further improving navigation performance.

1.2. Research Limitations of Existing Works

By analyzing existing research papers, we can identify their limitations. Most current research involves similar domains, such as cross-domain studies within the Image-to-Image field. In the Text-to-Image field, good performance can be achieved by making an ideal model if the data in the source and target domains are similar [25]. However, considering the zero-shot transfer learning problem [26], when the data in the source and target domains are dissimilar or have low similarity, the performance of the target model is poor, which illustrates that the current research in the Text-to-Image field is still limited by the similarity between the source and target domains. In other fields, such as the previously mentioned research from the visual to the tactile domain, the performance is good, with high accuracy. However, the applicability is limited, making it suitable for niche areas but not widely applicable.

1.3. Our Research Contributions

Cross-modality transfer learning is considered for text-to-image classification problems. First, we adopt bidirectional encoder representations from the transformer (BERT) model, typically trained in two stages [33]. The first stage uses MaskLM to train the language model, mask a random portion of words in a sentence, and predict the masked words by understanding the context. In the second stage, the BERT model predicts the following sentence, which helps it better understand the relationship between individual sentences. We used BERT to train text sentiment classification on the IMDb reviews dataset, which contains 25,000 movie reviews for training and 25,000 movie reviews for testing, explicitly used for sentiment classification. In addition, we employ a bidirectional encoder representation from the image transformer (BEiT) model [34]. This self-supervised learning model applies a similar idea to the BERT model to the image classification task. The idea is to obtain image features by masking the image modeling pre-training task, achieving an accuracy of 83.2 in the ImageNet-1K classification task, which we used to train on the ImageNet-1K dataset for image classification. Finally, a novel hybrid model is designed by joining the first ten layers of the pre-trained BERT model and the last two layers of the pre-trained BEiT model. An ablation study showed that the contribution of the BEiT model enhanced accuracy by 12.8%.

Regarding the performance evaluation of the hybrid model, we have conducted an in-depth analysis of the model's performance with the batch size, learning rate, and types of optimizers.

1.4. Organization of the Paper

The rest of the paper is organized as follows: Section 2 introduces the datasets and illustrates the methodology of the novel hybrid model. Then, a performance evaluation of the proposed model is conducted, comparing the proposed work with existing work. To study the contributions of the standalone BERT model and the standalone BEiT model, an ablation study is carried out in Section 4. Finally, a conclusion is drawn, and research implications and future research directions are discussed.

2. Materials and Methods

In this section, all stages of cross-modality transfer learning are illustrated. First, two datasets are used to train the models in two different domains, i.e., the image and text domains, and save the training results as the pre-trained models for the next stage. In the second stage, we combined the two pre-trained models and selected CIFAR-10 as the dataset for the next stage of training. In the third stage, to obtain the most suitable optimizer, batch size, and learning rate for the model, we used both GridSearchCV and K-Fold cross-validation methods. The performance is evaluated using different hyperparameters and optimizers by calculating the F1-score, precision, and recall. The whole process of cross-modal transfer learning will be summarized. Following the workflow, the BERT and BEiT models are first pretrained using the IMDb reviews and ImageNet-1K datasets, respectively. Then, the knowledge is transferred to the novel hybrid model. Afterward, the CIFAR-10 dataset is pre-processed to determine whether the 5-fold cross-validation has been completed. If it is not yet complete, the combination of optimizers and hyperparameters is fed into the unique hybrid model, and if it is, training and testing are finished using the best optimizer and hyperparameters. In the 5-fold cross-validation process, the dataset is first divided into five parts, with one part selected as the testing data and four parts as the training data for each training session. Each set of hyperparameters is cross-validated five times, and the mean result is calculated. The results were then compared to select the best combination of hyperparameters. In normal model training, we calculated the results without averaging them.

2.1. Pre-Training Models

The main objective of this section is to use the pre-trained model as a feature extractor by pre-training the model on a large dataset. We first trained the model on a large underlying dataset; in the text domain, we chose to use the BERT model on the IMDb review dataset, a widely used sentiment binary classification dataset, as a benchmark for sentiment classification, which consists of 100,000 text reviews of films. Half (50,000) of the reviews contained no labels, and these were used for testing, with the other 50,000 reviews paired with labels of 0 or 1, representing negative and positive sentiment, respectively. These reviews with tags were split into two groups, with each group having 12,500 positive and 12,500 negative reviews to keep the data balanced. These labels are linearly mapped from IMDb's star rating system, in which critics can rate a film with a certain number of stars from 1 to 10 [35]. Figure 1 shows the split of the IMDb review dataset and two examples of reviews. The BERT model is a pre-trained model proposed by the Google AI Institute that has demonstrated impressive performance in all aspects, using a network architecture with a multi-layer transformer structure, which is most distinctive in that it does not use traditional recurrent neural networks (RNNs) and CNNs; instead, it uses an attention mechanism to convert the distance between two arbitrarily placed positions. This solves the problem of long-term dependency in NLP. It has already achieved wide application in the field of NLP.

	Positive	Negative
Training	12,500	12,500
Validation	12,500	12,500

Positive Example:
Someone release this movie on DVD so it can take its hallowed place as on of the greatest films of all time in ten to twenty years when critics and film historians look back on the so-called films of the 1990's and see how vapid they were for the most part, and how Lars Von Trier tried to revolutionize and revitalize the international film world with this masterpiece.

Negative Example:
I have this film out of the library right now and I haven't finished watching it. It is so bad I am in disbelief. Audrey Hepburn had totally lost her talent by then, although she'd pretty much finished with it in 'Robin and Marian.' This is the worst thing about this appallingly stupid film. It's really only of interest because it was her last feature film and because of the Dorothy Stratten appearance just prior to her homicide.

Figure 1. The split of the IMDb review dataset and two examples of reviews.

In the image domain, we chose to use the BEiT model for training on the ImageNet-1K dataset, which is currently the largest image recognition dataset in the world and is mainly used in machine vision, target detection, and image classification. The ImageNet-1K dataset introduced for the ILSVRC 2012 visual recognition challenge has been at the center of modern advances in deep learning. ImageNet-1K is the primary dataset for pre-training computer vision migration learning models, and improving the performance of ImageNet-1K is often seen as a litmus test for general applicability to downstream tasks. ImageNet-1K is a subset of the full ImageNet dataset, which consists of 14197122 images divided into 21841 classes. We will refer to the full dataset as ImageNet-21K, and ImageNet-1K was created by selecting a subset of 1.2 million images belonging to 1000 mutually exclusive classes from ImageNet-21K [36]. In contrast, the BEiT model is a self-supervised visual representation model proposed by Microsoft, which is similar to BERT in that it uses the transformer's masked image modeling task. Specifically, in pre-training, each image has two views. The developer converts the original image into a tokenizer, then randomly masks some patches and feeds them into the transformer. Experimental results in image classification and semantic segmentation show that the BEiT model achieves better results. Figure 2 shows the whole process of pre-training the BERT and BEiT models. The BERT model was trained using the IMDb Reviews dataset as an input, whereas the BEiT model was trained using the ImageNet-1K dataset. Their weights and network structures after pre-training are saved, and some of them (knowledge) will be transferred to a novel hybrid model in a later step, which is known as knowledge transfer. The selection of the number of layers from the pre-trained BERT and BEiT models will be elaborated in Section 2.2. The left half of Figure 3 illustrates the pre-training process for BERT and BEiT, with BERT being pre-trained in the IMDb reviews dataset and BEiT being pre-trained in ImageNet-1K.

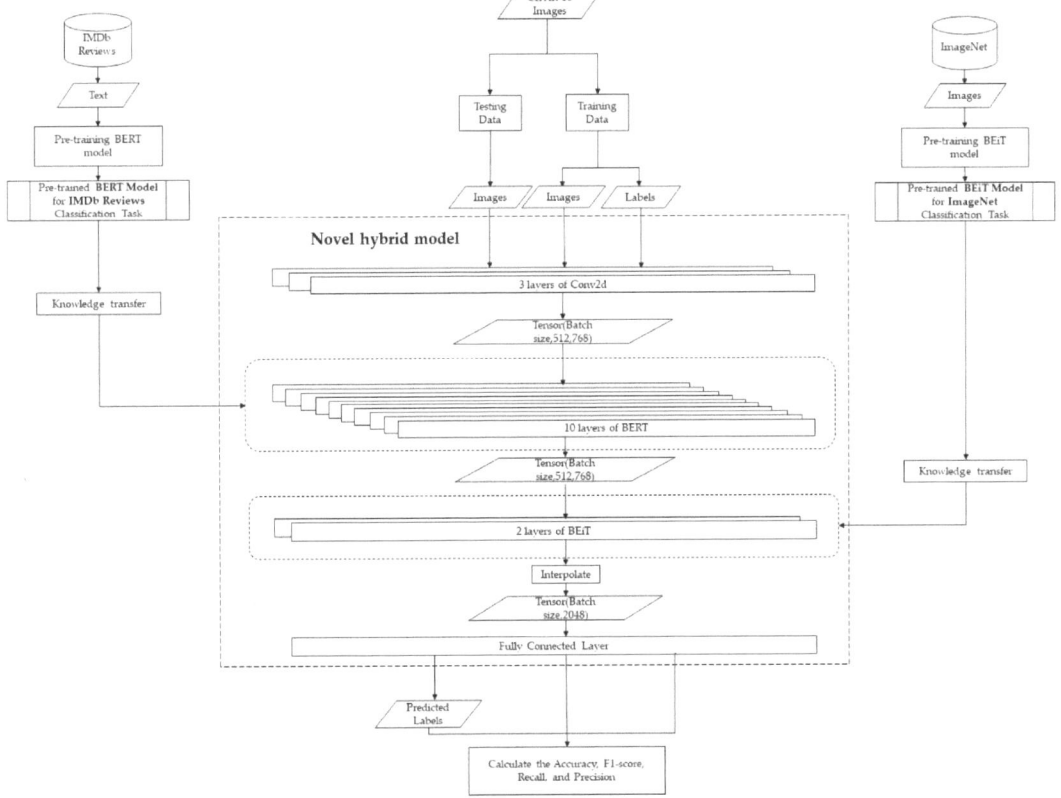

Figure 2. The process of pre-training the BERT and BEiT models.

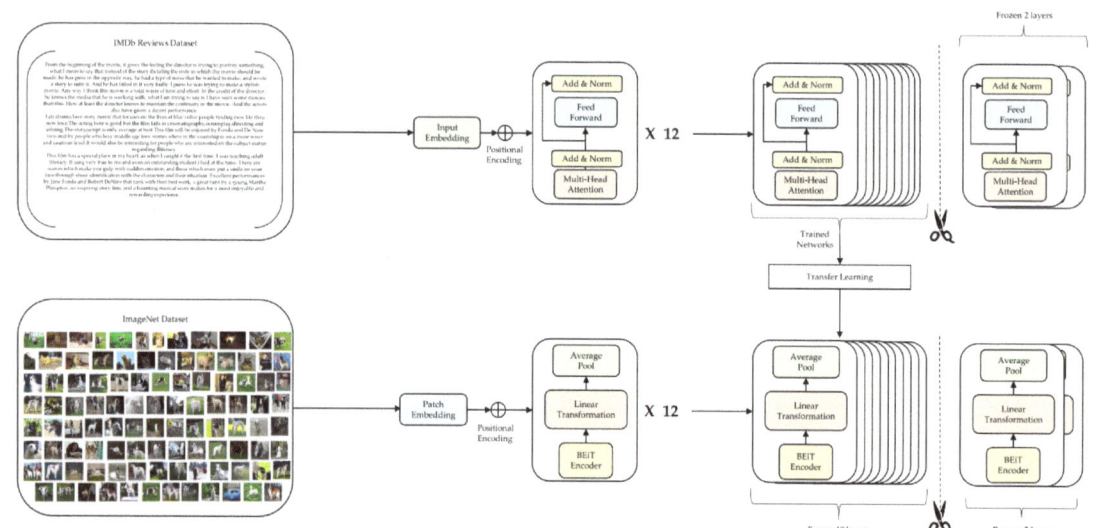

Figure 3. The process of pre-training and transfer learning for BERT and BEiT and the structure of the new hybrid model.

2.2. Design of a Novel Hybrid Model

To achieve cross-modal transfer learning, we combined the BERT and BEiT models. By merging the two models, we can transfer a large amount of knowledge learned by the BERT model in the source domain to the task in the target domain to compensate for the lack of data in the target domain. The first ten layers of the BERT model and the last two layers of the BEiT model are retained. The last few layers of a neural network are usually specialized; Yosinski et al.'s study [37] claims that the last layer allows features to transition from general to specific with some specificity. In contrast, the first few layers are usually not specific to a particular dataset or task but generic as they apply to many datasets and tasks; therefore, we chose to retain the last two layers of BEiT, which would make the novel hybrid model better suited to image classification tasks. The other layers are frozen and are not used for training. Liu et al. [38] showed that the transformer-based structure is more transferable to other tasks in the middle layer, while the higher layers are more task-specific. Kirichenko et al. [39] demonstrated that the retraining of the last layer improves the performance of the model and improves its robustness. This suggests that the results are heavily influenced by the last linear layer of the model and that even though the model has acquired the features of the data in the previous layers, the last layer can still assign higher weights to the data. Kovaleva et al.'s study [40] calculated the similarity between pre-trained and fine-tuned BERT weights by finding that the weights of the last two layers changed the most after fine-tuning. This suggests that the last two layers of the BERT model learn the most information in a given task and that the previous layers mainly capture more underlying base information. Based on these studies, we believe that removing the last two layers of BERT can help the new hybrid model better learn the basics of BERT while retaining the specificity of the BEiT model for better classification tasks. Then, we add the corresponding network structures and weights of the pre-trained BERT and BEiT models to a new hybrid model for the next stage of training. Cross-modality transfer learning is used to extract information features from the pre-trained datasets, which could be used to extract deep features from new images. Therefore, these models may help accomplish image classification tasks. Our novel hybrid model processes the input image through 3 convolutional layers and the ReLU activation function; then, the processed image is considered a tensor with shape (batch size, 512, 768); next, this tensor is passed into the first ten layers of the BERT encoder, and the output tensor is passed as an input to the

BEiT model; then, using the interpolation method, the output tensor is resized to (batch size, 2048) using interpolation; the elements of the first dimension are extracted; finally, these elements are passed to the fully connected layers; the final output with shape (batch size, 10) is obtained through the fully connected layers. The right half of Figure 3 shows the transfer learning process of the two pre-trained models and the structure of the new hybrid model, where the knowledge of the first ten layers of BERT is transferred to the new model. In contrast, the first ten layers of BEiT are frozen, keeping the last two layers for the image classification task. Table A1 (Appendix A) explains the detailed structure of our new hybrid model, including the layer's type, output shape, and parameters, and concludes with a summary of the model's parameters and sizes.

2.3. GridSearchCV and K-Fold Cross-Validation

To find the best combination of batch size and learning rate for the new hybrid model, the traditional GridSearchCV method is used to find the best hyperparameters. In this process, the CIFAR-10 dataset is trained using 48 combinations of BS (4, 8, 12, 16, 20, 24, 28, and 32), LR (0.005, 0.001, 0.0005, 0.0001, 0.00005, and 0.00001), optimizers (stochastic gradient descent with momentum (SGDM), and adaptive moment estimation (ADAM)). Because of the momentum involved, SGDM is faster than SGD, training will be faster than SGD, and local minima can be an escape to achieve global minima. Simply put, momentum enables SGD to locate the global minima more quickly and precisely. Both SGDM and ADAM are two of the most popular optimizers. In typical applications, the ADAM optimizer takes advantage of faster initial learning, whereas the SGDM optimizer yields a more accurate model in the later stage. It can be explained by the fact that the ADAM optimizer has added the adaptive learning rate mechanism on top of the SGDM optimizer, which enables the ADAM optimizer to increase the optimization speed by assigning different learning rates for different parameters. Being an adaptive learning rate algorithm, ADAM determines unique learning rates for various parameters. RMSprop and stochastic gradient descent with momentum can be combined to form ADAM. Similar to RMSprop, it scales the learning rate using gradient squaring, and like SGDM, it leverages momentum by utilizing a moving average of the gradient rather than the gradient itself. Figure 4 illustrates this process and all combinations of the hyperparameters used in the 5-fold cross-validation. Figure 5 illustrates the CIFAR-10 dataset with 5-fold cross-validation and training in our novel hybrid model.

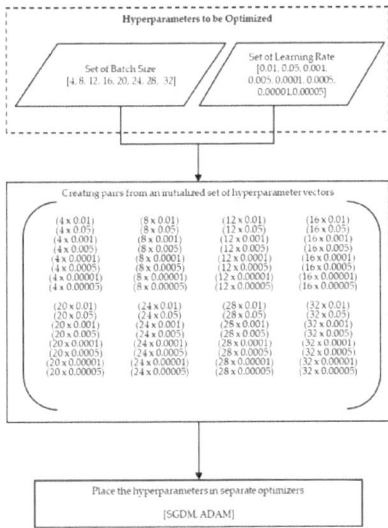

Figure 4. All combinations of hyperparameters were used in the 5-fold cross-validation.

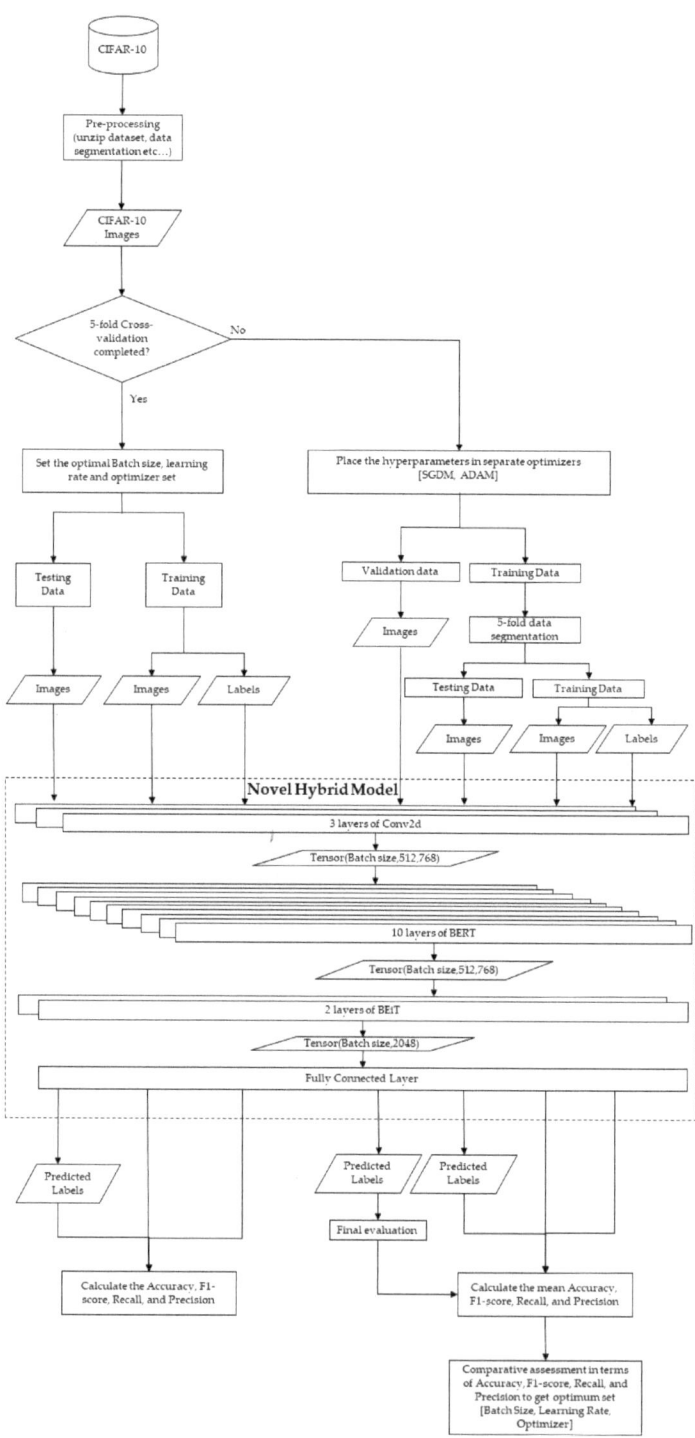

Figure 5. CIFAR-10 dataset with 5-fold cross-validation and training in novel hybrid model.

The performance of this hybrid model is then evaluated using K-fold cross-validation with K = 5 [41], which divides the dataset into K groups, with each subset of data serving as a separate validation set and the remaining K-1 subset of data serving as the training set. Each fold takes 10 epochs to complete. The reason for this design is that we found in the training of our previous hybrid model that the model was usually overfitted at around 10 calendar hours. The validation set results are evaluated separately, and the final mean squared error (MSE) is summed and averaged to obtain the cross-validation error. Figure 6 shows the process of 5-fold cross-validation. Cross-validation efficiently uses the limited data available, and the evaluation results are as close to the model's performance on the test set as possible. Unique values for the optimal hyperparameters batch size and learning rate were determined by comparing the F1-score (Equation (1)), precision (Equation (2)), and recall (Equation (3)) of each set of hyperparameters after K-fold cross-validation [42]. When the hybrid model is used to classify the CIFAR-10 dataset, we obtain the optimal hyperparameter values (BS = 24 and LR = 0.0005) for the SGDM optimizer, which results in an F1-score of 57.79%, a precision of 59.6481%, and a recall of 61.6944%.

$$F1 - score = 2 \times \frac{Recall \times Precision}{Recall + Precision} \tag{1}$$

$$Precision = \frac{TP}{TP + FP} \tag{2}$$

$$Recall = \frac{TP}{TP + FN} \tag{3}$$

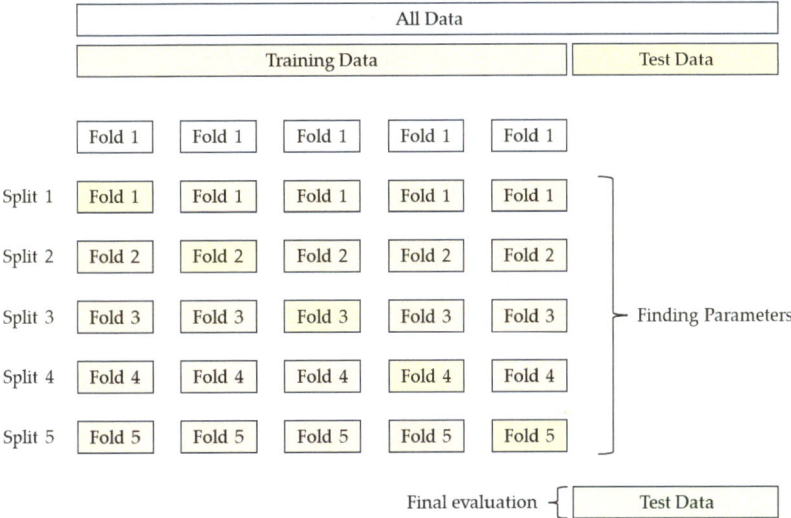

Figure 6. Process of 5-fold cross-validation.

3. Experimental Setup and Results Analysis

The experimental setup is based on the methodology described in Section 2. All simulations are conducted using a PC with NVIDIA GEFORCE GTX 3090—24 GB Graphics, a 15 vCPU AMD EPYC 7543 32-Core Processor, and Python 3.8.

3.1. 5-Fold Cross-Validation

Regarding 5-fold cross-validation, the dataset was divided into 80% and 20% for training and testing of the model, respectively. To evaluate and validate the impact of both hyperparameters, we increased the number of samples in the specified ranges of the LR (Equation (4)) and BS (Equation (5)) to obtain a detailed output distribution for better interpretation. In determining the range of LR, we found that both optimizers were prone to non-convergence when they used LRs greater than 0.005, so the maximum LR is set at 0.005. For other specific values of LR, they refer to Usmani et al.'s research [43] to finalize the range of LR. For the range of BS, we chose the most common from 4 to 32, with BS increasing by eight at a time. This study used an extended Cartesian product matrix consisting of 48 two-tuple hyperparameters generated from the following two vectors:

$$LR\epsilon[0.005, 0.001, 0.0005, 0.0001, 0.00005, 0.0001] \quad (4)$$

$$BS\epsilon[4, 8, 12, 16, 20, 24, 28, 32] \quad (5)$$

In addition, the model is evaluated using SGDM and ADAM. Table 1 summarizes the performance of each set of hyperparameters, including the average of all parameters and standard deviation of validation accuracy for 5-fold at each cross-validation. The summarized parameters are used in addition to the validation accuracy, and we use three measures: F1-score, recall, and precision.

Table 1. The performance of each set of hyperparameters.

BS	LR	Optimizer	Standard Deviations (%)	Validation Accuracy (%)	F1-Score (%)	Recall (%)	Precision (%)
4	0.00001	SGDM	1.5727	56.32	32.889	34.667	33.833
		ADAM	3.0496	59.18	32.333	33.999	31.500
	0.00005	SGDM	0.9613	61.31	41.667	43.333	40.833
		ADAM	0.2296	9.97	4.666	11.666	2.916
	0.0001	SGDM	1.9611	59.15	36.333	37.333	36.833
		ADAM	0.2872	9.91	3.775	14.167	2.239
	0.0005	SGDM	24.8728	40.49	34.444	38.333	32.500
		ADAM	0.3000	9.95	4.000	10.000	2.500
	0.001	SGDM	0.1523	9.95	6.444	11.667	4.583
		ADAM	0.3968	9.95	6.444	11.667	4.583
	0.005	SGDM	0.2340	10.00	4.444	6.667	3.333
		ADAM	0.2028	10.12	2.000	5.000	1.250
8	0.00001	SGDM	1.0712	51.43	40.444	41.845	43.155
		ADAM	0.3269	57.49	47.500	50.575	50.238
	0.00005	SGDM	0.5180	44.00	43.996	46.607	47.698
		ADAM	0.3088	9.96	2.222	10.000	1.250
	0.0001	SGDM	3.5695	60.03	44.978	48.714	47.000
		ADAM	0.3309	10.05	2.222	10.000	1.250
	0.0005	SGDM	18.3248	45.78	42.306	45.250	44.806
		ADAM	0.2555	10.15	3.704	14.000	2.167
	0.001	SGDM	21.3882	26.95	13.534	23.048	11.869
		ADAM	0.2740	9.96	3.111	14.000	1.750
	0.005	SGDM	0.2279	10.04	2.182	4.000	1.500
		ADAM	0.2098	10.03	3.111	14.000	1.750
12	0.00001	SGDM	0.8184	48.61	35.667	36.167	36.667
		ADAM	0.9671	57.77	53.299	55.867	53.001
	0.00005	SGDM	1.3184	59.23	42.667	42.000	44.000
		ADAM	24.6269	29.94	12.667	12.000	14.000
	0.0001	SGDM	1.5544	60.93	40.899	42.107	42.024
		ADAM	0.2972	9.99	4.444	6.667	3.333

Table 1. *Cont.*

BS	LR	Optimizer	Standard Deviations (%)	Validation Accuracy (%)	F1-Score (%)	Recall (%)	Precision (%)
12	0.0005	SGDM	0.7146	59.27	37.133	35.833	40.333
		ADAM	0.1212	9.93	10.444	21.667	7.083
	0.001	SGDM	0.1469	10.01	4.667	11.667	2.917
		ADAM	0.1937	10.09	4.667	11.667	2.917
	0.005	SGDM	0.1754	10.06	6.444	11.667	4.583
		ADAM	0.2196	10.02	2.000	5.000	1.250
16	0.00001	SGDM	1.3853	44.46	28.779	32.283	29.200
		ADAM	0.5009	56.74	52.315	56.839	53.749
	0.00005	SGDM	1.5716	58.73	42.184	47.870	43.685
		ADAM	24.3304	39.23	36.593	42.256	37.370
	0.0001	SGDM	1.9416	58.47	51.295	54.241	55.635
		ADAM	0.2595	9.87	3.257	11.944	1.910
	0.0005	SGDM	2.1745	60.06	50.436	53.204	53.153
		ADAM	0.0963	9.88	2.795	11.944	1.667
	0.001	SGDM	24.2741	39.84	31.150	35.167	32.365
		ADAM	0.2001	10.11	1.373	9.444	0.747
	0.005	SGDM	0.1659	9.92	1.373	7.222	0.764
		ADAM	0.0508	9.87	1.987	9.413	0.908
20	0.00001	SGDM	0.9337	41.47	32.568	36.577	34.750
		ADAM	1.1632	57.38	47.456	50.374	50.921
	0.00005	SGDM	1.2411	58.17	49.420	52.798	55.075
		ADAM	20.2989	50.38	43.375	48.237	44.785
	0.0001	SGDM	1.2448	57.15	49.800	55.042	50.093
		ADAM	0.2402	10.08	1.070	6.944	0.583
	0.0005	SGDM	1.9982	59.45	47.849	49.890	51.778
		ADAM	0.0837	9.76	1.575	9.722	0.861
	0.001	SGDM	19.3078	48.44	38.313	40.950	41.583
		ADAM	0.0989	10.11	2.334	11.944	1.319
	0.005	SGDM	0.3008	10.00	0.666	4.722	0.361
		ADAM	0.2338	10.17	1.530	9.444	0.847
24	0.00001	SGDM	1.3658	38.26	30.969	36.472	32.122
		ADAM	0.4772	57.42	45.392	49.330	47.431
	0.00005	SGDM	1.1611	54.64	51.796	57.306	55.889
		ADAM	0.7211	59.47	52.799	59.652	56.463
	0.0001	SGDM	1.3350	58.77	52.867	56.043	54.927
		ADAM	0.1209	9.68	1.638	1.638	0.903
	0.0005	SGDM	2.2888	60.47	57.789	61.694	59.648
		ADAM	0.2597	10.01	2.160	11.944	1.198
	0.001	SGDM	19.1042	46.75	39.269	43.170	41.476
		ADAM	0.1559	10.01	1.634	9.444	0.903
	0.005	SGDM	0.1629	10.09	1.078	6.944	0.590
		ADAM	0.3708	10.24	1.837	8.615	1.031
28	0.00001	SGDM	2.8993	36.81	14.667	14.000	16.000
		ADAM	0.4116	57.33	32.667	32.000	34.000
	0.00005	SGDM	0.9147	54.74	34.667	33.167	37.667
		ADAM	20.0329	50.07	36.667	39.000	37.250

Table 1. *Cont.*

BS	LR	Optimizer	Standard Deviations (%)	Validation Accuracy (%)	F1-Score (%)	Recall (%)	Precision (%)
28	0.0001	SGDM	1.3348	56.45	38.167	39.167	40.333
		ADAM	0.1785	10.02	2.000	5.000	1.250
	0.0005	SGDM	2.1328	58.73	30.556	33.000	30.167
		ADAM	0.1679	9.96	0.000	0.000	0.000
	0.001	SGDM	19.4801	49.05	26.190	27.524	25.524
		ADAM	0.2318	9.80	0.000	0.000	0.000
	0.005	SGDM	0.1875	10.02	2.667	6.667	1.667
		ADAM	0.2691	9.94	0.000	0.000	0.000
32	0.00001	SGDM	1.8973	35.88	22.401	26.796	23.499
		ADAM	0.9375	56.38	42.033	46.230	42.611
	0.00005	SGDM	0.9352	52.98	48.248	51.367	55.033
		ADAM	2.5092	59.13	46.719	51.293	48.148
	0.0001	SGDM	1.2391	57.47	47.486	50.344	50.344
		ADAM	0.1832	10.00	1.868	9.444	1.059
	0.0005	SGDM	0.2294	59.84	49.280	53.456	51.630
		ADAM	0.1931	10.14	1.866	9.444	1.042
	0.001	SGDM	1.7214	58.68	43.959	49.241	44.963
		ADAM	0.2317	9.88	3.444	11.944	2.049
	0.005	SGDM	0.1667	9.98	1.634	9.444	0.903
		ADAM	0.1481	9.76	1.863	10.743	1.125

Table A2 in Appendix B details all the results of GridSearchCV and 5-fold cross-validation for various combinations of optimizers and hyperparameters, including mean validation accuracy, F1-score, precision, and recall.

In addition, the distribution of the results collected by the optimizer SGDM and ADAM is shown on the new hybrid model retrained on the CIFAR-10 dataset. On the left side of the table, the distribution of the measurement accuracy for a given BS ranges from 0.00001 to 0.005 for each specific LR. On the right side of the table, the distribution of the validation accuracy, F1-score, precision, and recall for a given LR range starting from 4 to 32 for each specific BS is shown.

When using SGDM with BS = 24 and LR = 0.0005, a maximum accuracy of 60.474%, an F1-score of 57.79%, a recall of 61.6944%, and a precision of 59.6481% were observed. In ADAM, the maximum accuracy = 59.47% was observed for BS = 24 and LR = 0.0005, while the maximum F1-score was 52.8%, recall was 59.6519%, and precision was 56.463%. Thus, using our new hybrid model on CIFAR-10, SGDM has better performance compared to ADAM as it achieves the maximum accuracy and F1-score, while also performing better in terms of recall and precision.

Figure 7a,b, Figure 8a,b, Figure 9a,b and Figure 10a,b depict the resulting curves of the validating accuracy, F1-score, recall, and precision for all parameters of SGDM and ADAM, respectively. The numerical labels of the best-performing dataset will be labeled with the specific values of BS = 24 and LR = 0.0005 in the SGDM optimizer and BS = 24 and LR = 0.00005 in the ADAM optimizer.

When using the SGDM optimizer, we observed that the difference in validation accuracy between different batch sizes was not significant when the learning rate was less than or equal to 0.005. However, when the learning rate was greater than or equal to 0.005, the difference in validation accuracy was more sensitive to changes in the learning rate. The F1-score, recall, and precision remained regular and stable across different batch size combinations.

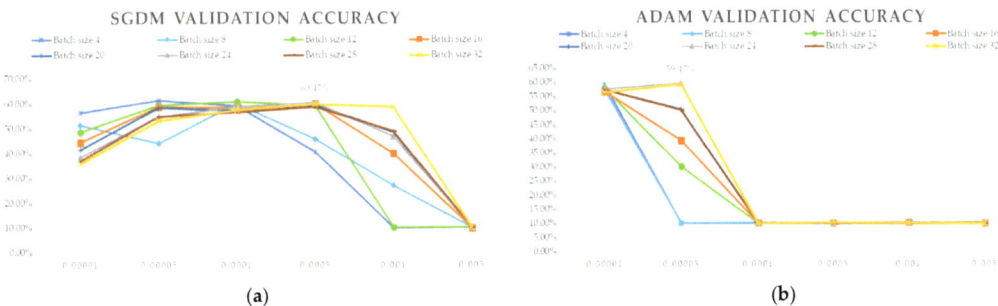

Figure 7. Validation accuracy. (**a**) SGDM optimizer. (**b**) ADAM optimizer.

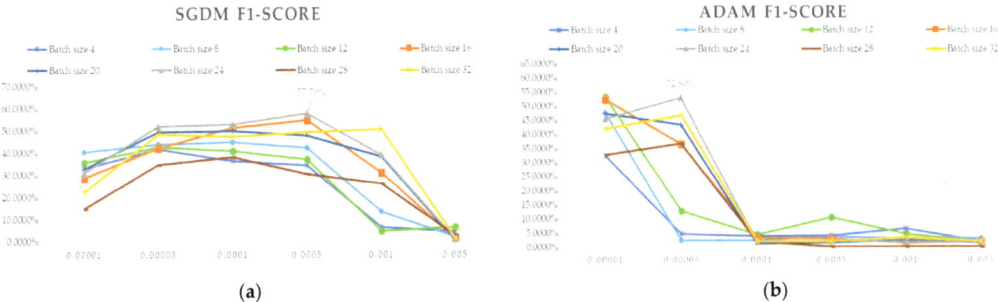

Figure 8. F1-score. (**a**) SGDM optimizer. (**b**) ADAM optimizer.

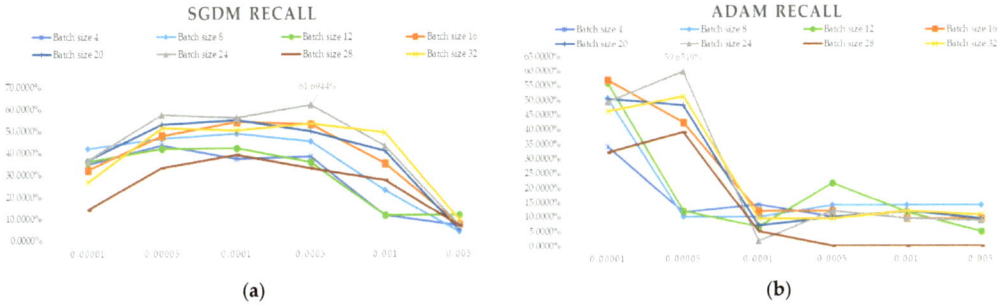

Figure 9. Recall. (**a**) SGDM optimizer. (**b**) ADAM optimizer.

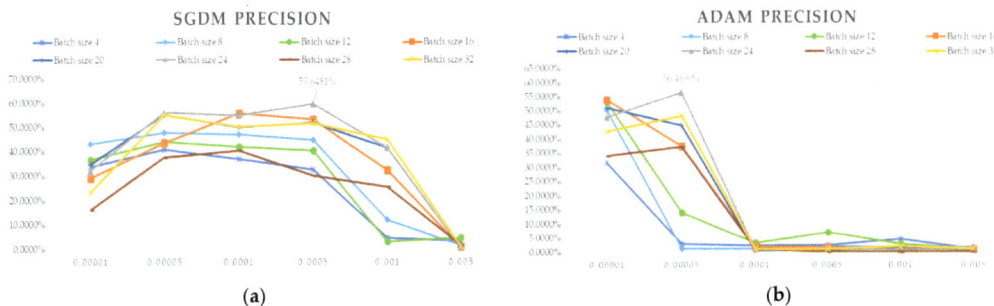

Figure 10. Precision. (**a**) SGDM optimizer. (**b**) ADAM optimizer.

When using the ADAM optimizer, we found that the difference in validation accuracy between different batch sizes was most significant when the learning rate was set to 0.0005. However, when the learning rate was greater than 0.001, the change in validation accuracy was negligible. The F1-score, recall, and precision showed some changes but not significant ones. Previous research has shown the use of an exponential moving average of the squares of the gradients generated by previous iterations [44]. This moving average is used to scale the current gradient after taking the square root of the average to update the weights. The contribution of the exponential mean is positive, and this approach should prevent the learning rate from becoming nearly infinitesimal during the learning process, which is a key drawback of the ADAM optimizer. However, the short-term memory capacity of this gradient becomes an obstacle in other cases. During the convergence of the ADAM optimizer to a suboptimal solution, it has been observed that some small batches of data provide large and informative gradients. Since these small batches occur very rarely, exponential averaging will reduce their impact. As a result, the ADAM optimizer corrects the gradient only when the learning rate is high, which can cause the algorithm to converge to suboptimal minima or even fail to converge, resulting in skipping local minima. The derivative can become too large, resulting in an infinite loss. This shows that ADAM does not generalize as well as SGDM.

3.2. Ablation Study between the Novel Hybrid Model and Original BEiT Model

We trained and tested the original BEiT model for 50 epochs on the CIFAR-10 dataset using the official default hyperparameters and optimizer configuration (batch size = 64, optimizer = ADAM, optimizer Epsilon = 1×10^{-8}, and learning rate = 5×10^{-4}). We then trained and tested our hybrid model for 50 epochs on the same dataset using the optimal configuration (batch size = 24, optimizer = SGDM, and learning rate = 5×10^{-4}). Table 2 shows the loss and test accuracy for each epoch and the test accuracy for both models. Figure 11 illustrates the process of training CIFAR-10 in the original BEiT model.

Table 2. The loss, testing accuracy for each epoch, and test accuracy for the original BEiT model and novel hybrid model.

Epoch	Original BEiT Model			Novel Hybrid Model			Epoch	Original BEiT Model			Novel Hybrid Model		
	Loss	Training Accuracy	Testing Accuracy	Loss	Training Accuracy	Testing Accuracy		Loss	Training Accuracy	Testing Accuracy	Loss	Training Accuracy	Testing Accuracy
0	4.457	4.00%	4.27%	1.987	24.23%	37.80%	25	3.078	32.80%	44.57%	0.000	100.00%	64.70%
1	4.224	7.47%	8.93%	1.547	43.26%	47.09%	26	3.059	33.41%	44.72%	0.000	100.00%	64.72%
2	4.121	9.49%	11.64%	1.353	51.38%	54.00%	27	3.041	34.02%	45.54%	0.000	100.00%	64.70%
3	4.066	10.49%	15.29%	1.211	56.45%	56.46%	28	3.045	34.07%	45.94%	0.000	100.00%	64.70%
4	4.026	11.27%	18.78%	1.085	61.25%	59.58%	29	3.034	34.12%	47.23%	0.000	100.00%	64.66%
5	3.973	12.52%	20.79%	0.956	66.00%	61.15%	30	2.826	34.67%	47.23%	0.000	100.00%	64.63%
6	3.913	13.60%	24.13%	0.837	70.27%	62.09%	31	2.780	35.00%	48.02%	0.000	100.00%	64.60%
7	3.856	14.74%	25.46%	0.715	74.53%	63.20%	32	2.735	35.33%	48.64%	0.000	100.00%	64.57%
8	3.803	15.94%	27.54%	0.588	79.06%	63.51%	33	2.689	35.66%	48.89%	0.000	100.00%	64.54%
9	3.747	17.04%	29.12%	0.468	83.28%	61.87%	34	2.643	35.99%	48.89%	0.000	100.00%	64.51%
10	3.710	17.90%	30.36%	0.355	87.26%	61.76%	35	2.597	36.32%	49.18%	0.000	100.00%	64.48%
11	3.651	18.94%	32.30%	0.258	90.74%	61.89%	36	2.551	36.65%	50.02%	0.000	100.00%	64.45%
12	3.608	20.04%	33.48%	0.191	93.38%	61.89%	37	2.505	36.98%	50.02%	0.000	100.00%	64.42%
13	3.561	21.15%	34.45%	0.150	94.72%	62.38%	38	2.459	37.31%	50.02%	0.000	100.00%	64.39%
14	3.517	22.23%	35.51%	0.105	62.38%	62.92%	39	2.413	37.64%	50.39%	0.000	100.00%	64.36%
15	3.476	23.36%	36.29%	0.084	97.10%	62.20%	40	2.368	37.97%	50.63%	0.000	100.00%	64.37%
16	3.423	24.35%	37.22%	0.072	97.48%	61.98%	41	2.322	38.30%	50.98%	0.000	100.00%	64.40%
17	3.379	25.34%	38.95%	0.055	98.17%	62.96%	42	2.276	38.63%	50.98%	0.000	100.00%	64.41%
18	3.332	26.46%	39.29%	0.045	98.53%	62.57%	43	2.230	38.96%	51.41%	0.000	100.00%	64.38%
19	3.286	27.87%	40.51%	0.041	98.67%	62.69%	44	2.184	39.29%	51.41%	0.000	100.00%	64.38%
20	3.243	28.71%	41.20%	0.019	99.41%	63.57%	45	2.138	39.62%	51.63%	0.000	100.00%	64.39%
21	3.193	29.72%	41.71%	0.011	99.68%	63.47%	46	2.092	39.95%	51.63%	0.000	100.00%	64.42%
22	3.147	30.53%	42.28%	0.005	99.86%	64.37%	47	2.046	40.28%	51.65%	0.000	100.00%	64.43%
23	3.100	31.30%	43.16%	0.001	100.00%	64.78%	48	1.977	40.61%	51.65%	0.000	100.00%	64.42%
24	3.054	32.42%	43.91%	0.000	100.00%	64.67%	49	1.928	40.94%	51.65%	0.000	100.00%	64.42%

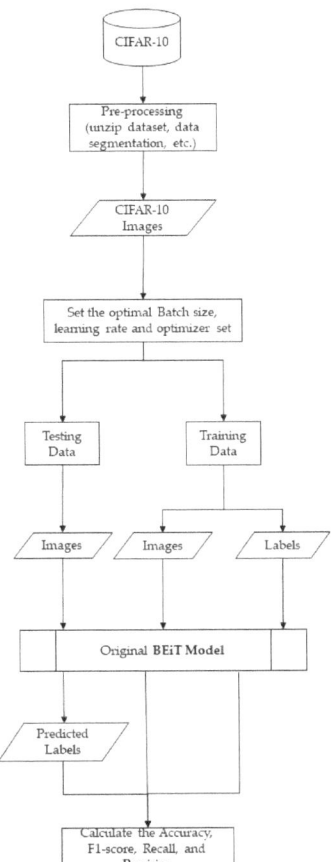

Figure 11. Process of training CIFAR-10 in the original BEiT model.

During training, the new hybrid model achieved 100% accuracy in 23 calendar hours, with loss dropping to 0. During validation, overfitting occurred in 10 epochs, with little improvement in accuracy during the subsequent validation process. On the other hand, the original BEiT model consistently improved in accuracy and decreased in loss during the training period. During validation, the original model never overfitted, but the performance improvement became smaller and smaller as the epochs increased. Due to the nature of cross-modality transfer learning, our model is pre-trained in the source domain using a completely different dataset from the target domain, which is a necessary condition for cross-modality transfer learning. In the comparison session, we do not compare the training accuracy of the two models but rather the testing accuracy. From the training results, the accuracy of our new hybrid model at the beginning of training was 12.77% higher compared to the original BEiT model. This is mainly due to pre-training; as the number of training sessions increased, both the original BEiT model and our hybrid model showed overfitting, but our hybrid model showed overfitting earlier, which made the difference between the accuracy of the original BEiT model and our model smaller. We performed Wilcoxon rank-sum tests between the novel hybrid model and the original BEiT model using training accuracy and testing accuracy. The null hypothesis H_0: accuracy of the novel hybrid model < accuracy of the original BEiT model is being rejected for all experimental settings (Table 2). Therefore, it is concluded that the novel hybrid model is statistically outperforming the original BEiT model. Figure 12 compares the accuracy of the two models tested over 50 epochs. The graph clearly shows that our model appears to overfit earlier and that the difference between the accuracy of the two models becomes smaller and smaller until they both seem to overfit.

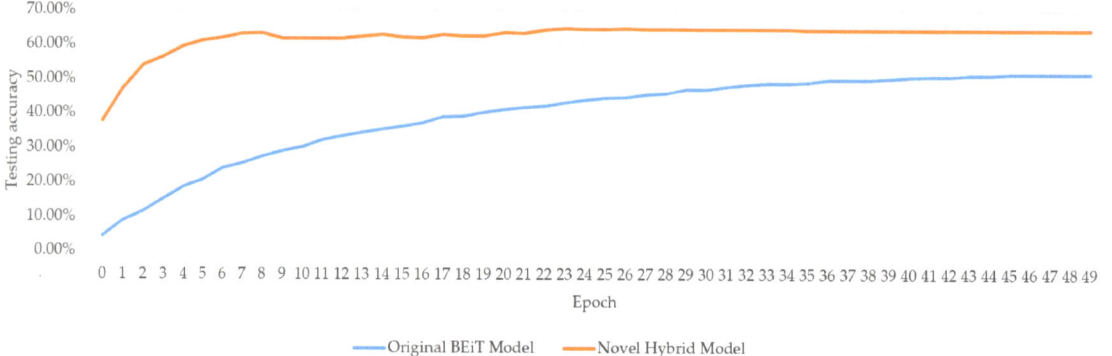

Figure 12. Comparison between the original BEiT model and the novel hybrid model.

4. Conclusions and Future Works

In this work, we propose a cross-modal transfer learning algorithm from the text domain to the image domain for image classification problems to solve tasks in the image classification domain. In the first phase of our work, two pre-trained models from different domains are trained on different source domains, and a new hybrid model is designed based on them. In the second phase of the work, we used GridSearchCV and 5-fold cross-validation to determine the best combination of hyperparameters by evaluating the validation accuracy, F1-score, precision, and recall of the model for different combinations. The results of the experiments not only allowed us to select the most efficient hyperparameters from various combinations of optimizers (SGDM, ADAM) and hyperparameters but also showed us that the optimizers and the two hyperparameters (BS and LR) had a significant impact on our model. In addition to these results, after several comparisons of BS and LR, we found that each hyperparameter affected our model's performance independently, suggesting that trade-offs should be made in the selection of BS and LR to obtain the highest F1-score. In the third stage, after our tests, we showed that, compared to the traditional BEiT model, the new hybrid model we designed had a higher accuracy.

It is worth noting that CMTL can facilitate knowledge transfer between the source and target domains of different modalities (low similarity between domains), where some knowledge cannot be learned from traditional transfer learning (domains with high similarity) [16,45,46]. Therefore, a comparison with non-CMTL approaches is not included in Section 3. Intuitively, combining traditional transfer learning with CMTL will further enhance the performance of the target model because more knowledge (from similar and dissimilar source domains) can be transferred, given that the issue of negative transfer is suppressed. We have thus suggested future work in this area. In future work, we would like to consider the application of migration learning to more different pre-trained models of text domains for image classification tasks, allowing a broader range of application scenarios for migration learning to occur. We believe that it is possible to study the effect of different layers on the results by adjusting the number of layers of the retained or frozen pre-trained model to study the importance of the last few layers in the overall model as well as the performance of the model on new datasets by reducing or increasing the number of layers in which the original model is retained, an approach that is considered an interesting direction for improving the effectiveness of migration learning in the future. Indeed, in addition to the text domain, many different source domains can be migrated to the image domain. In the future, higher accuracy can be achieved in the image classification domain by migrating to other domains. Furthermore, in our work, the evaluation of batch sizes larger than 32 is a current limitation due to GPU performance limitations. More analysis can be conducted to evaluate the performance of the novel hybrid model using other datasets, such as the Visual Question Answering (VQA) 2.0 dataset [47].

Author Contributions: Formal analysis, J.L., K.T.C. and L.-K.L.; investigation, J.L., K.T.C. and L.-K.L.; methodology, J.L.; validation, J.L., K.T.C. and L.-K.L.; visualization, J.L.; writing—original draft, J.L., K.T.C. and L.-K.L.; writing—review and editing, J.L., K.T.C. and L.-K.L. All authors have read and agreed to the published version of the manuscript.

Funding: The work described in this paper was supported by the Katie Shu Sui Pui Charitable Trust—Research Training Fellowship (KSRTF/2022/07).

Data Availability Statement: Not applicable.

Conflicts of Interest: The authors declare no conflict of interest.

Appendix A

Table A1. The table explains the detailed structure of our new hybrid model, including the types of layers, output shapes, and parameters, in order from left column to right column, and concludes with a summary of the model's parameters and sizes.

Layer (Type)	Output Shape	No. of Params	Layer (Type)	Output Shape	No. of Params
Conv2d-1	[−1, 64, 32, 32]	1792	Linear-127	[−1, 512, 768]	590,592
Conv2d-3	[−1, 128, 32, 32]	73,856	Linear-128	[−1, 512, 768]	590,592
Conv2d-5	[−1, 384, 32, 32]	442,752	Linear-129	[−1, 512, 768]	590,592
Linear-7	[−1, 512, 768]	590,592	Linear-130	[−1, 512, 768]	590,592
Linear-8	[−1, 512, 768]	590,592	Linear-131	[−1, 512, 768]	590,592
Linear-9	[−1, 512, 768]	590,592	Linear-132	[−1, 512, 768]	590,592
Linear-10	[−1, 512, 768]	590,592	Linear-135	[−1, 512, 768]	590,592
Linear-11	[−1, 512, 768]	590,592	Linear-136	[−1, 512, 768]	590,592
Linear-12	[−1, 512, 768]	590,592	LayerNorm-139	[−1, 512, 768]	1536
Linear-15	[−1, 512, 768]	590,592	LayerNorm-140	[−1, 512, 768]	1536
Linear-16	[−1, 512, 768]	590,592	Linear-141	[−1, 512, 3072]	2,362,368
LayerNorm-19	[−1, 512, 768]	1536	Linear-142	[−1, 512, 3072]	2,362,368
LayerNorm-20	[−1, 512, 768]	1536	Linear-145	[−1, 512, 768]	2,360,064
Linear-21	[−1, 512, 3072]	2,362,368	Linear-146	[−1, 512, 768]	2,360,064
Linear-22	[−1, 512, 3072]	2,362,368	LayerNorm-149	[−1, 512, 768]	1536
Linear-25	[−1, 512, 768]	2,360,064	LayerNorm-150	[−1, 512, 768]	1536
Linear-26	[−1, 512, 768]	2,360,064	Linear-151	[−1, 512, 768]	590,592
LayerNorm-29	[−1, 512, 768]	1536	Linear-152	[−1, 512, 768]	590,592
LayerNorm-30	[−1, 512, 768]	1536	Linear-153	[−1, 512, 768]	590,592
Linear-31	[−1, 512, 768]	590,592	Linear-154	[−1, 512, 768]	590,592
Linear-32	[−1, 512, 768]	590,592	Linear-155	[−1, 512, 768]	590,592
Linear-33	[−1, 512, 768]	590,592	Linear-156	[−1, 512, 768]	590,592
Linear-34	[−1, 512, 768]	590,592	Linear-159	[−1, 512, 768]	590,592
Linear-35	[−1, 512, 768]	590,592	Linear-160	[−1, 512, 768]	590,592
Linear-36	[−1, 512, 768]	590,592	LayerNorm-163	[−1, 512, 768]	1536
Linear-39	[−1, 512, 768]	590,592	LayerNorm-164	[−1, 512, 768]	1536
Linear-40	[−1, 512, 768]	590,592	Linear-165	[−1, 512, 3072]	2,362,368
LayerNorm-43	[−1, 512, 768]	1536	Linear-166	[−1, 512, 3072]	2,362,368
LayerNorm-44	[−1, 512, 768]	1536	Linear-169	[−1, 512, 768]	2,360,064
Linear-45	[−1, 512, 3072]	2,362,368	Linear-170	[−1, 512, 768]	2,360,064
Linear-46	[−1, 512, 3072]	2,362,368	LayerNorm-173	[−1, 512, 768]	1536
Linear-49	[−1, 512, 768]	2,360,064	LayerNorm-174	[−1, 512, 768]	1536
Linear-50	[−1, 512, 768]	2,360,064	Linear-175	[−1, 512, 768]	590,592
LayerNorm-53	[−1, 512, 768]	1536	Linear-176	[−1, 512, 768]	590,592
LayerNorm-54	[−1, 512, 768]	1536	Linear-177	[−1, 512, 768]	590,592
Linear-55	[−1, 512, 768]	590,592	Linear-178	[−1, 512, 768]	590,592
Linear-56	[−1, 512, 768]	590,592	Linear-179	[−1, 512, 768]	590,592

Table A1. *Cont.*

Layer (Type)	Output Shape	No. of Params	Layer (Type)	Output Shape	No. of Params
Linear-57	[−1, 512, 768]	590,592	Linear-180	[−1, 512, 768]	590,592
Linear-58	[−1, 512, 768]	590,592	Linear-183	[−1, 512, 768]	590,592
Linear-59	[−1, 512, 768]	590,592	Linear-184	[−1, 512, 768]	590,592
Linear-60	[−1, 512, 768]	590,592	LayerNorm-187	[−1, 512, 768]	1536
Linear-63	[−1, 512, 768]	590,592	LayerNorm-188	[−1, 512, 768]	1536
Linear-64	[−1, 512, 768]	590,592	Linear-189	[−1, 512, 3072]	2,362,368
LayerNorm-67	[−1, 512, 768]	1536	Linear-190	[−1, 512, 3072]	2,362,368
LayerNorm-68	[−1, 512, 768]	1536	Linear-193	[−1, 512, 768]	2,360,064
Linear-69	[−1, 512, 3072]	2,362,368	Linear-194	[−1, 512, 768]	2,360,064
Linear-70	[−1, 512, 3072]	2,362,368	LayerNorm-197	[−1, 512, 768]	1536
Linear-73	[−1, 512, 768]	2,360,064	LayerNorm-198	[−1, 512, 768]	1536
Linear-74	[−1, 512, 768]	2,360,064	Linear-199	[−1, 512, 768]	590,592
LayerNorm-77	[−1, 512, 768]	1536	Linear-200	[−1, 512, 768]	590,592
LayerNorm-78	[−1, 512, 768]	1536	Linear-201	[−1, 512, 768]	590,592
Linear-79	[−1, 512, 768]	590,592	Linear-202	[−1, 512, 768]	590,592
Linear-80	[−1, 512, 768]	590,592	Linear-203	[−1, 512, 768]	590,592
Linear-81	[−1, 512, 768]	590,592	Linear-204	[−1, 512, 768]	590,592
Linear-82	[−1, 512, 768]	590,592	Linear-207	[−1, 512, 768]	590,592
Linear-83	[−1, 512, 768]	590,592	Linear-208	[−1, 512, 768]	590,592
Linear-84	[−1, 512, 768]	590,592	LayerNorm-211	[−1, 512, 768]	1536
Linear-87	[−1, 512, 768]	590,592	LayerNorm-212	[−1, 512, 768]	1536
Linear-88	[−1, 512, 768]	590,592	Linear-213	[−1, 512, 3072]	2,362,368
LayerNorm-91	[−1, 512, 768]	1536	Linear-214	[−1, 512, 3072]	2,362,368
LayerNorm-92	[−1, 512, 768]	1536	Linear-217	[−1, 512, 768]	2,360,064
Linear-93	[−1, 512, 3072]	2,362,368	Linear-218	[−1, 512, 768]	2,360,064
Linear-94	[−1, 512, 3072]	2,362,368	LayerNorm-221	[−1, 512, 768]	1536
Linear-97	[−1, 512, 768]	2,360,064	LayerNorm-222	[−1, 512, 768]	1536
Linear-98	[−1, 512, 768]	2,360,064	Linear-223	[−1, 512, 768]	590,592
LayerNorm-101	[−1, 512, 768]	1536	Linear-224	[−1, 512, 768]	590,592
LayerNorm-102	[−1, 512, 768]	1536	Linear-225	[−1, 512, 768]	590,592
Linear-103	[−1, 512, 768]	590,592	Linear-226	[−1, 512, 768]	590,592
Linear-104	[−1, 512, 768]	590,592	Linear-227	[−1, 512, 768]	590,592
Linear-105	[−1, 512, 768]	590,592	Linear-228	[−1, 512, 768]	590,592
Linear-106	[−1, 512, 768]	590,592	Linear-231	[−1, 512, 768]	590,592
Linear-107	[−1, 512, 768]	590,592	Linear-232	[−1, 512, 768]	590,592
Linear-108	[−1, 512, 768]	590,592	LayerNorm-235	[−1, 512, 768]	1536
Linear-111	[−1, 512, 768]	590,592	LayerNorm-236	[−1, 512, 768]	1536
Linear-112	[−1, 512, 768]	590,592	Linear-237	[−1, 512, 3072]	2,362,368
LayerNorm-115	[−1, 512, 768]	1536	Linear-238	[−1, 512, 3072]	2,362,368
LayerNorm-116	[−1, 512, 768]	1536	Linear-241	[−1, 512, 768]	2,360,064
Linear-117	[−1, 512, 3072]	2,362,368	Linear-242	[−1, 512, 768]	2,360,064
Linear-118	[−1, 512, 3072]	2,362,368	LayerNorm-245	[−1, 512, 768]	1536
Linear-121	[−1, 512, 768]	2,360,064	LayerNorm-246	[−1, 512, 768]	1536
Linear-122	[−1, 512, 768]	2,360,064	LayerNorm-247	[−1, 197, 768]	1536
LayerNorm-125	[−1, 512, 768]	1536	Linear-249	[−1, 197, 768]	590,592
LayerNorm-126	[−1, 512, 768]	1536	LayerNorm-252	[−1, 197, 768]	1536
Total params: 152,928,522			Linear−253	[−1, 197, 3072]	2,362,368
Trainable params: 152,928,522			Linear−256	[−1, 197, 3072]	2,360,064
Non-trainable params: 0			LayerNorm−259	[−1, 197, 768]	1536
Input size (MB): 0.011719			Linear−261	[−1, 197, 768]	590,592
Forward/backward pass size (MB): 1562.278091			LayerNorm−264	[−1, 197, 768]	1536
Params size (MB): 583.376015			Linear−265	[−1, 197, 3072]	2,362,368
Estimated Total Size (MB): 2145.665825			Linear−268	[−1, 197, 768]	2,360,064
			Linear−271	[−1, 10]	20,490

Appendix B

Table A2. This table shows all results for GridSearchCV and 5-fold cross-validation for various combinations of optimizers and hyperparameters, including mean validation accuracy, F1-score, precision, and recall.

				SGDM									
Batch Size	LR	Fold	Val Accuracy	F1-Score	Recall	Precision	Batch Size	LR	Fold	Val Accuracy	F1-Score	Recall	Precision
4	0.00001	1	53.52%	33.33%	40.00%	30.00%	8	0.00001	1	49.53%	43.33%	45.83%	43.75%
		2	57.86%	33.33%	30.00%	40.00%			2	51.91%	61.90%	64.29%	64.29%
		3	57.3%	66.67%	75.00%	62.50%			3	52.70%	63.89%	66.67%	66.67%
		4	55.7%	20.00%	20.00%	20.00%			4	51.87%	8.33%	6.25%	12.50%
		5	57.22%	11.11%	8.33%	16.67%			5	51.13%	24.76%	26.19%	28.46%
		Mean	56.32%	32.89%	34.67%	33.83%			Mean	51.43%	40.44%	41.85%	43.15%
	0.00005	1	62.00%	33.33%	33.33%	33.33%		0.00005	1	61.63%	54.76%	61.90%	57.14%
		2	60.55%	50.00%	50.00%	50.00%			2	61.62%	52.38%	57.14%	57.14%
		3	61.33%	66.67%	75.00%	62.50%			3	60.74%	74.44%	75.00%	77.78%
		4	60.01%	33.33%	33.33%	33.33%			4	60.70%	23.81%	28.57%	21.43%
		5	62.68%	25.00%	25.00%	25.00%			5	61.98%	14.58%	10.42%	25.00%
		Mean	61.31%	41.67%	43.33%	40.83%			Mean	44.00%	44.00%	46.61%	47.70%
	0.0001	1	56.5%	16.67%	16.67%	16.67%		0.0001	1	61.92%	34.26%	33.33%	35.71%
		2	59.8%	50.00%	50.00%	50.00%			2	61.26%	40.48%	42.86%	42.86%
		3	62.45%	41.67%	50.00%	37.50%			3	60.67%	55.56%	58.33%	58.33%
		4	58.63%	60.00%	60.00%	60.00%			4	53.09%	28.57%	35.71%	31.43%
		5	58.36%	13.33%	10.00%	20.00%			5	63.20%	66.00%	73.33%	66.67%
		Mean	59.15%	36.33%	37.33%	36.83%			Mean	60.03%	44.98%	48.71%	47.00%
	0.0005	1	61.17%	33.33%	33.33%	33.33%		0.0005	1	55.87%	39.58%	41.67%	43.75%
		2	62.00%	50.00%	50.00%	50.00%			2	56.74%	58.33%	56.25%	62.50%
		3	10.22%	0.00%	0.00%	0.00%			3	47.04%	80.00%	83.33%	77.78%
		4	59.19%	66.67%	75.00%	62.50%			4	59.18%	29.17%	25.00%	37.50%
		5	9.88%	22.22%	33.33%	16.67%			5	10.06%	4.44%	2.00%	2.50%
		Mean	40.49%	34.44%	38.33%	32.50%			Mean	45.78%	42.31%	45.25%	44.81%
	0.001	1	10.2%	0.00%	0.00%	0.00%		0.001	1	9.69%	0.00%	0.00%	0.00%
		2	9.92%	0.00%	0.00%	0.00%			2	45.19%	40.48%	50.00%	40.48%
		3	9.74%	10.00%	25.00%	6.25%			3	59.85%	19.05%	28.57%	14.29%
		4	10.01%	0.00%	0.00%	0.00%			4	9.98%	3.70%	16.67%	2.08%
		5	9.88%	22.22%	33.33%	16.67%			5	10.03%	4.44%	20.00%	2.50%
		Mean	9.95%	6.44%	11.67%	4.58%			Mean	26.95%	13.53%	23.05%	11.87%
	0.005	1	10.20%	0.00%	0.00%	0.00%		0.005	1	10.20%	0.00%	0.00%	0.00%
		2	10.33%	0.00%	0.00%	0.00%			2	10.33%	0.00%	0.00%	0.00%
		3	9.91%	0.00%	0.00%	0.00%			3	9.91%	0.00%	0.00%	0.00%
		4	9.68%	0.00%	0.00%	0.00%			4	9.68%	0.00%	0.00%	0.00%
		5	9.88%	22.22%	33.33%	16.67%			5	10.10%	10.91%	20.00%	7.50%
		Mean	10.00%	4.44%	6.67%	3.33%			Mean	10.04%	2.18%	4.00%	1.50%
12	0.00001	1	48.55%	33.33%	33.33%	33.33%	16	0.00001	1	44.38%	38.52%	43.33%	41.67%
		2	48.11%	66.67%	62.50%	75.00%			2	46.77%	46.87%	56.25%	45.00%
		3	47.46%	33.33%	40.00%	30.00%			3	44.78%	30.50%	32.50%	29.17%
		4	49.04%	20.00%	20.00%	20.00%			4	43.87%	14.00%	15.00%	15.83%
		5	49.87%	25.00%	25.00%	25.00%			5	42.51%	14.00%	14.33%	14.33%
		Mean	48.60%	35.67%	36.17%	36.67%			Mean	44.46%	28.78%	32.28%	29.20%
	0.00005	1	57.77%	60.00%	60.00%	60.00%		0.00005	1	58.00%	41.48%	48.89%	43.52%
		2	61.49%	100.00%	100.00%	100.00%			2	61.71%	66.93%	66.67%	69.44%
		3	59.22%	20.00%	20.00%	20.00%			3	58.89%	31.69%	44.44%	26.30%
		4	59.59%	20.00%	20.00%	20.00%			4	57.47%	27.67%	37.50%	29.17%
		5	58.08%	13.33%	10.00%	20.00%			5	57.58%	43.15%	41.85%	50.00%
		Mean	59.23%	42.67%	42.00%	44.00%			Mean	58.73%	42.18%	47.87%	43.69%
	0.0001	1	61.68%	14.29%	14.29%	14.29%		0.0001	1	57.37%	55.37%	62.22%	53.70%
		2	62.67%	66.67%	62.50%	75.00%			2	63.05%	59.26%	57.41%	62.96%
		3	58.44%	33.33%	40.00%	30.00%			3	61.01%	49.01%	56.48%	53.17%
		4	62.01%	65.21%	68.75%	65.83%			4	61.52%	45.00%	42.50%	50.00%
		5	59.87%	25.00%	25.00%	25.00%			5	59.38%	47.83%	52.59%	58.33%
		Mean	60.93%	40.90%	42.11%	42.02%			Mean	60.47%	51.29%	54.24%	55.63%
	0.0005	1	59.34%	33.33%	33.33%	33.33%		0.0005	1	63.73%	61.46%	70.00%	63.54%
		2	58.71%	33.33%	33.33%	33.33%			2	60.60%	41.67%	50.00%	37.50%
		3	59.36%	45.67%	42.50%	55.00%			3	57.44%	48.89%	52.78%	46.76%
		4	60.51%	40.00%	40.00%	40.00%			4	58.33%	45.67%	42.50%	55.00%
		5	58.44%	33.33%	30.00%	40.00%			5	60.22%	54.50%	50.74%	62.96%
		Mean	59.27%	37.13%	35.83%	40.33%			Mean	60.06%	50.44%	53.20%	53.15%

Table A2. *Cont.*

						SGDM						
Batch Size	LR	Fold	Val Accuracy	F1-Score	Recall	Precision	Batch Size	LR	Fold	Val Accuracy	F1-Score	Recall	Precision
12	0.001	1	10.11%	10.00%	25.00%	6.25%	16	0.001	1	10.01%	5.95%	12.50%	3.91%
		2	10.14%	0.00%	0.00%	0.00%			2	58.75%	70.42%	70.83%	72.92%
		3	10.00%	0.00%	0.00%	0.00%			3	59.32%	34.05%	45.00%	30.00%
		4	9.73%	0.00%	0.00%	0.00%			4	60.89%	45.33%	47.50%	55.00%
		5	10.06%	13.33%	33.33%	8.33%			5	10.24%	0.00%	0.00%	0.00%
		Mean	10.01%	4.67%	11.67%	2.92%			Mean	39.84%	31.15%	35.17%	32.36%
	0.005	1	10.20%	0.00%	0.00%	0.00%		0.005	1	10.20%	0.00%	0.00%	0.00%
		2	10.33%	0.00%	0.00%	0.00%			2	9.92%	2.78%	12.50%	1.56%
		3	9.91%	0.00%	0.00%	0.00%			3	9.91%	1.31%	11.11%	0.69%
		4	9.98%	10.00%	25.00%	6.25%			4	9.68%	0.00%	0.00%	0.00%
		5	9.88%	22.22%	33.33%	16.67%			5	9.88%	2.78%	12.50%	1.56%
		Mean	10.06%	6.44%	11.67%	4.58%			Mean	9.92%	1.37%	7.22%	0.76%
20	0.00001	1	42.66%	35.19%	41.85%	33.33%	24	0.00001	1	40.49%	32.08%	43.75%	31.67%
		2	42.15%	59.26%	65.63%	62.50%			2	38.41%	52.28%	51.85%	60.00%
		3	40.08%	31.33%	37.50%	29.17%			3	38.54%	22.52%	32.50%	18.33%
		4	41.68%	19.60%	19.76%	29.00%			4	37.56%	18.33%	25.00%	18.33%
		5	40.76%	17.46%	18.15%	19.75%			5	36.32%	29.63%	29.26%	32.28%
		Mean	41.47%	32.57%	36.58%	34.75%			Mean	38.26%	30.97%	36.47%	32.12%
	0.00005	1	56.44%	58.81%	65.83%	58.33%		0.00005	1	55.67%	44.81%	57.78%	49.07%
		2	59.93%	67.10%	71.88%	76.88%			2	52.94%	63.81%	64.58%	71.67%
		3	58.99%	44.36%	47.50%	44.33%			3	54.86%	52.65%	58.33%	50.37%
		4	57.21%	31.67%	32.62%	38.33%			4	56.01%	28.00%	32.50%	33.33%
		5	58.30%	45.17%	46.17%	57.50%			5	53.71%	69.71%	73.33%	75.00%
		Mean	58.17%	49.42%	52.80%	55.08%			Mean	54.64%	51.80%	57.31%	55.89%
	0.0001	1	60.15%	56.16%	60.00%	60.37%		0.0001	1	59.66%	45.33%	51.00%	42.50%
		2	62.88%	63.65%	66.67%	62.04%			2	58.20%	67.56%	68.75%	73.75%
		3	59.50%	47.35%	51.85%	44.44%			3	60.64%	38.70%	47.22%	34.26%
		4	61.04%	37.12%	40.95%	39.17%			4	58.66%	52.00%	52.50%	56.67%
		5	62.16%	44.71%	55.74%	44.44%			5	56.70%	60.74%	60.74%	67.46%
		Mean	61.15%	49.80%	55.04%	50.09%			Mean	58.77%	52.87%	56.04%	54.93%
	0.0005	1	57.81%	53.41%	56.67%	55.56%		0.0005	1	59.01%	53.39%	60.00%	53.70%
		2	58.31%	54.29%	55.00%	59.17%			2	62.81%	65.21%	68.75%	65.83%
		3	63.36%	57.17%	60.00%	61.00%			3	62.92%	67.65%	72.22%	64.44%
		4	59.04%	37.00%	35.95%	41.67%			4	56.93%	37.00%	37.50%	46.67%
		5	58.73%	37.38%	41.83%	41.50%			5	60.70%	65.70%	70.00%	67.59%
		Mean	59.45%	47.85%	49.89%	51.78%			Mean	60.47%	57.79%	61.69%	59.65%
	0.001	1	57.07%	37.08%	42.50%	35.42%		0.001	1	59.05%	53.70%	56.67%	58.33%
		2	58.38%	61.57%	60.00%	69.17%			2	61.08%	57.78%	57.41%	62.96%
		3	9.86%	2.02%	11.11%	1.11%			3	9.86%	1.31%	11.11%	0.69%
		4	59.46%	40.33%	40.95%	46.67%			4	46.66%	38.89%	41.67%	38.89%
		5	57.43%	50.56%	50.19%	55.56%			5	57.11%	44.67%	49.00%	46.50%
		Mean	48.44%	38.31%	40.95%	41.58%			Mean	46.75%	39.27%	43.17%	41.48%
	0.005	1	9.73%	2.27%	12.50%	1.25%		0.005	1	10.20%	0.00%	0.00%	0.00%
		2	10.46%	0.00%	0.00%	0.00%			2	9.93%	2.78%	12.50%	1.56%
		3	9.91%	1.06%	11.11%	0.56%			3	9.86%	1.31%	11.11%	0.69%
		4	9.68%	0.00%	0.00%	0.00%			4	10.23%	1.31%	11.11%	0.69%
		5	10.24%	0.00%	0.00%	0.00%			5	10.24%	0.00%	0.00%	0.00%
		Mean	10.00%	0.67%	4.72%	0.36%			Mean	10.09%	1.08%	6.94%	0.59%
28	0.00001	1	31.34%	0.00%	0.00%	0.00%	32	0.00001	1	36.77%	21.11%	32.22%	23.52%
		2	37.39%	0.00%	0.00%	0.00%			2	39.12%	31.10%	37.50%	31.25%
		3	38.16%	40.00%	40.00%	40.00%			3	34.83%	27.46%	33.33%	24.81%
		4	39.94%	20.00%	20.00%	20.00%			4	34.98%	15.67%	15.00%	18.33%
		5	37.20%	13.33%	10.00%	20.00%			5	33.69%	16.67%	15.93%	19.58%
		Mean	36.81%	14.67%	14.00%	16.00%			Mean	35.88%	22.40%	26.80%	23.50%
	0.00005	1	56.21%	33.33%	33.33%	33.33%		0.00005	1	52.80%	55.24%	60.00%	66.67%
		2	53.35%	66.67%	62.50%	75.00%			2	52.40%	62.14%	62.50%	71.67%
		3	54.51%	20.00%	20.00%	20.00%			3	53.83%	39.52%	47.50%	35.83%
		4	54.93%	40.00%	40.00%	40.00%			4	51.65%	43.33%	42.50%	55.00%
		5	54.70%	13.33%	10.00%	20.00%			5	54.21%	41.00%	44.33%	46.00%
		Mean	54.74%	34.67%	33.17%	37.67%			Mean	52.98%	48.25%	51.37%	55.03%
	0.0001	1	61.51%	33.33%	33.33%	33.33%		0.0001	1	56.69%	57.22%	62.22%	59.26%
		2	59.69%	66.67%	62.50%	75.00%			2	58.72%	72.92%	75.00%	75.00%
		3	60.92%	40.00%	40.00%	40.00%			3	57.91%	29.10%	41.67%	23.15%
		4	58.24%	37.50%	50.00%	33.33%			4	55.45%	52.00%	47.50%	66.67%
		5	61.90%	13.33%	10.00%	20.00%			5	58.58%	26.19%	25.33%	35.00%
		Mean	60.45%	38.17%	39.17%	40.33%			Mean	57.47%	47.49%	50.34%	50.34%

Table A2. Cont.

			SGDM									
Batch Size	LR	Fold	Val Accuracy	F1-Score	Recall	Precision	Batch Size	LR	Fold	Val Accuracy	F1-Score	Recall	Precision
28	0.0005	1	56.86%	16.67%	16.67%	16.67%	32	0.0005	1	59.85%	58.20%	60.00%	63.89%
		2	61.44%	50.00%	50.00%	50.00%			2	60.23%	57.30%	61.11%	54.63%
		3	63.29%	41.67%	50.00%	37.50%			3	59.80%	44.71%	50.00%	42.96%
		4	61.54%	33.33%	40.00%	30.00%			4	59.51%	46.67%	52.50%	48.33%
		5	60.50%	11.11%	8.33%	16.67%			5	59.82%	39.52%	43.67%	48.33%
		Mean	60.73%	30.56%	33.00%	30.17%			Mean	59.84%	49.28%	53.46%	51.63%
	0.001	1	58.72%	14.29%	14.29%	14.29%		0.001	1	60.31%	36.67%	42.22%	34.81%
		2	59.69%	50.00%	50.00%	50.00%			2	60.94%	37.50%	50.00%	33.33%
		3	58.04%	33.33%	40.00%	30.00%			3	58.44%	39.00%	43.33%	40.00%
		4	58.68%	33.33%	33.33%	33.33%			4	56.43%	40.33%	42.50%	46.67%
		5	10.10%	0.00%	0.00%	0.00%			5	57.29%	66.30%	68.15%	70.00%
		Mean	49.05%	26.19%	27.52%	25.52%			Mean	58.68%	43.96%	49.24%	44.96%
	0.005	1	10.20%	0.00%	0.00%	0.00%		0.005	1	10.20%	0.00%	0.00%	0.00%
		2	9.70%	13.33%	33.33%	8.33%			2	9.70%	2.78%	12.50%	1.56%
		3	9.91%	0.00%	0.00%	0.00%			3	9.91%	1.31%	11.11%	0.69%
		4	10.17%	0.00%	0.00%	0.00%			4	10.01%	1.31%	11.11%	0.69%
		5	10.10%	0.00%	0.00%	0.00%			5	10.06%	2.78%	12.50%	1.56%
		Mean	10.02%	2.67%	6.67%	1.67%			Mean	9.98%	1.63%	9.44%	0.90%

			ADAM									
Batch size	LR	Fold	Val Accuracy	F1-score	Recall	Precision	Batch size	LR	Fold	Val Accuracy	F1-score	Recall	Precision
4	0.00001	1	58.63%	40.00%	40.00%	40.00%	8	0.00001	1	56.96%	63.81%	66.67%	64.29%
		2	65.19%	20.00%	20.00%	20.00%			2	57.84%	45.83%	43.75%	50.00%
		3	57.11%	41.67%	50.00%	37.50%			3	57.31%	40.00%	42.86%	38.10%
		4	57.33%	40.00%	40.00%	40.00%			4	57.54%	29.52%	35.71%	32.14%
		5	57.64%	20.00%	20.00%	20.00%			5	57.80%	58.33%	63.89%	66.67%
		Mean	59.18%	32.33%	34.00%	31.50%			Mean	57.49%	47.50%	50.58%	50.24%
	0.00005	1	9.73%	0.00%	0.00%	0.00%		0.00005	1	10.20%	0.00%	0.00%	0.00%
		2	10.17%	13.33%	33.33%	8.33%			2	10.14%	3.70%	16.67%	2.08%
		3	10.25%	10.00%	25.00%	6.25%			3	10.25%	3.70%	16.67%	2.08%
		4	9.68%	0.00%	0.00%	0.00%			4	9.73%	3.70%	16.67%	2.08%
		5	10.03%	0.00%	0.00%	0.00%			5	9.46%	0.00%	0.00%	0.00%
		Mean	9.97%	4.67%	11.67%	2.92%			Mean	9.96%	2.22%	10.00%	1.25%
	0.0001	1	9.94%	10.00%	25.00%	6.25%		0.0001	1	10.20%	0.00%	0.00%	0.00%
		2	10.17%	3.70%	16.67%	2.08%			2	9.93%	3.70%	16.67%	2.08%
		3	9.73%	3.70%	16.67%	2.08%			3	10.25%	3.70%	16.67%	2.08%
		4	9.46%	1.47%	12.50%	0.78%			4	10.40%	3.70%	16.67%	2.08%
		5	10.24%	0.00%	0.00%	0.00%			5	9.46%	0.00%	0.00%	0.00%
		Mean	9.91%	3.77%	14.17%	2.24%			Mean	10.05%	2.22%	10.00%	1.25%
	0.0005	1	9.94%	10.00%	25.00%	6.25%		0.0005	1	10.37%	3.70%	16.67%	2.08%
		2	9.92%	0.00%	0.00%	0.00%			2	9.70%	6.67%	16.67%	4.17%
		3	10.03%	0.00%	0.00%	0.00%			3	10.22%	0.00%	0.00%	0.00%
		4	10.40%	10.00%	25.00%	6.25%			4	10.40%	3.70%	16.67%	2.08%
		5	9.46%	0.00%	0.00%	0.00%			5	10.06%	4.44%	20.00%	2.50%
		Mean	9.95%	4.00%	10.00%	2.50%			Mean	10.15%	3.70%	14.00%	2.17%
	0.001	1	10.37%	10.00%	25.00%	6.25%		0.001	1	9.72%	3.70%	16.67%	2.08%
		2	9.60%	22.22%	33.33%	16.67%			2	10.46%	0.00%	0.00%	0.00%
		3	9.86%	0.00%	0.00%	0.00%			3	9.86%	3.70%	16.67%	2.08%
		4	10.44%	0.00%	0.00%	0.00%			4	9.73%	3.70%	16.67%	2.08%
		5	9.46%	0.00%	0.00%	0.00%			5	10.03%	4.44%	20.00%	2.50%
		Mean	9.95%	6.44%	11.67%	4.58%			Mean	9.96%	3.11%	14.00%	1.75%
	0.005	1	10.03%	0.00%	0.00%	0.00%		0.005	1	10.11%	3.70%	16.67%	2.08%
		2	10.14%	0.00%	0.00%	0.00%			2	10.33%	0.00%	0.00%	0.00%
		3	10.22%	0.00%	0.00%	0.00%			3	9.86%	3.70%	16.67%	2.08%
		4	10.40%	10.00%	25.00%	6.25%			4	9.73%	3.70%	16.67%	2.08%
		5	9.79%	0.00%	0.00%	0.00%			5	10.10%	4.44%	20.00%	2.50%
		Mean	10.12%	2.00%	5.00%	1.25%			Mean	10.03%	3.11%	14.00%	1.75%
12	0.00001	1	57.81%	33.33%	33.33%	33.33%	16	0.00001	1	56.61%	58.33%	62.22%	64.81%
		2	57.96%	100.00%	100.00%	100.00%			2	56.60%	66.55%	68.75%	67.71%
		3	59.22%	33.33%	40.00%	30.00%			3	56.23%	50.51%	50.44%	50.67%
		4	56.18%	60.00%	60.00%	60.00%			4	57.70%	41.00%	45.00%	38.33%
		5	57.68%	39.83%	46.00%	41.67%			5	56.55%	45.19%	57.78%	47.22%
		Mean	57.77%	53.30%	55.87%	53.00%			Mean	56.74%	52.31%	56.84%	53.75%
	0.00005	1	9.73%	0.00%	0.00%	0.00%		0.00005	1	60.28%	41.00%	46.00%	41.00%
		2	9.82%	0.00%	0.00%	0.00%			2	59.55%	70.71%	75.00%	73.96%
		3	10.00%	0.00%	0.00%	0.00%			3	57.40%	65.33%	66.67%	68.33%
		4	58.26%	50.00%	50.00%	50.00%			4	9.44%	4.44%	11.11%	2.78%
		5	61.87%	13.33%	10.00%	20.00%			5	9.46%	1.47%	12.50%	0.78%
		Mean	29.94%	12.67%	12.00%	14.00%			Mean	39.23%	36.59%	42.26%	37.37%

Table A2. Cont.

						SGDM						
Batch Size	LR	Fold	Val Accuracy	F1-Score	Recall	Precision	Batch Size	LR	Fold	Val Accuracy	F1-Score	Recall	Precision
12	0.0001	1	10.20%	0.00%	0.00%	0.00%	16	0.0001	1	9.94%	2.78%	12.50%	1.56%
		2	9.60%	22.22%	33.33%	16.67%			2	9.82%	2.78%	12.50%	1.56%
		3	10.03%	0.00%	0.00%	0.00%			3	10.25%	3.51%	11.11%	2.08%
		4	9.73%	0.00%	0.00%	0.00%			4	9.44%	4.44%	11.11%	2.78%
		5	10.41%	0.00%	0.00%	0.00%			5	9.88%	2.78%	12.50%	1.56%
		Mean	9.99%	4.44%	6.67%	3.33%			Mean	9.87%	3.26%	11.94%	1.91%
	0.0005	1	10.11%	10.00%	25.00%	6.25%		0.0005	1	10.01%	5.95%	12.50%	3.91%
		2	9.93%	0.00%	0.00%	0.00%			2	9.82%	2.78%	12.50%	1.56%
		3	9.74%	10.00%	25.00%	6.25%			3	9.91%	1.31%	11.11%	0.69%
		4	9.98%	10.00%	25.00%	6.25%			4	9.73%	2.47%	11.11%	1.39%
		5	9.88%	22.22%	33.33%	16.67%			5	9.93%	1.47%	12.50%	0.78%
		Mean	9.93%	10.44%	21.67%	7.08%			Mean	9.88%	2.80%	11.94%	1.67%
	0.001	1	10.20%	0.00%	0.00%	0.00%		0.001	1	10.20%	1.47%	12.50%	0.78%
		2	9.93%	0.00%	0.00%	0.00%			2	9.92%	2.78%	12.50%	1.56%
		3	9.86%	0.00%	0.00%	0.00%			3	9.86%	1.31%	11.11%	0.69%
		4	10.40%	10.00%	25.00%	6.25%			4	10.17%	1.31%	11.11%	0.69%
		5	10.06%	13.33%	33.33%	8.33%			5	10.41%	0.00%	0.00%	0.00%
		Mean	10.09%	4.67%	11.67%	2.92%			Mean	10.11%	1.37%	9.44%	0.75%
	0.005	1	10.37%	10.00%	25.00%	6.25%		0.005	1	9.94%	2.78%	12.50%	1.56%
		2	10.14%	0.00%	0.00%	0.00%			2	9.92%	2.78%	12.50%	1.56%
		3	9.91%	0.00%	0.00%	0.00%			3	9.96%	1.31%	11.11%	0.69%
		4	9.73%	0.00%	0.00%	0.00%			4	9.82%	0.00%	0.00%	0.00%
		5	9.93%	0.00%	0.00%	0.00%			5	9.95%	1.47%	12.50%	0.78%
		Mean	10.02%	2.00%	5.00%	1.25%			Mean	9.87%	1.99%	9.41%	0.91%
20	0.00001	1	57.32%	68.81%	69.58%	80.21%	24	0.00001	1	57.68%	39.83%	46.00%	41.67%
		2	59.61%	62.78%	62.96%	63.89%			2	57.35%	45.93%	50.00%	46.30%
		3	56.62%	61.48%	69.44%	59.26%			3	57.34%	43.46%	48.15%	41.48%
		4	56.34%	41.94%	37.38%	50.00%			4	56.63%	28.00%	30.00%	31.67%
		5	57.02%	2.27%	12.50%	1.25%			5	58.08%	69.74%	72.50%	76.04%
		Mean	57.38%	47.46%	50.37%	50.92%			Mean	57.42%	45.39%	49.33%	47.43%
	0.00005	1	60.15%	48.24%	49.00%	60.33%		0.00005	1	60.55%	63.54%	70.00%	66.67%
		2	61.36%	70.63%	71.13%	70.33%			2	60.09%	49.63%	51.85%	48.15%
		3	59.93%	42.95%	53.33%	38.17%			3	59.16%	68.52%	76.85%	72.22%
		4	60.65%	52.59%	56.61%	53.70%			4	58.80%	39.26%	47.22%	44.44%
		5	9.79%	2.47%	11.11%	1.39%			5	58.76%	43.05%	52.33%	50.83%
		Mean	50.38%	43.38%	48.24%	44.79%			Mean	59.47%	52.80%	59.65%	56.46%
	0.0001	1	9.72%	2.27%	12.50%	1.25%		0.0001	1	9.72%	1.47%	12.50%	0.78%
		2	10.33%	0.00%	0.00%	0.00%			2	9.82%	2.78%	12.50%	1.56%
		3	9.86%	2.02%	11.11%	1.11%			3	9.74%	2.47%	11.11%	1.39%
		4	10.23%	1.06%	11.11%	0.56%			4	9.68%	0.00%	0.00%	0.00%
		5	10.24%	0.00%	0.00%	0.00%			5	9.46%	1.47%	12.50%	0.78%
		Mean	10.08%	1.07%	6.94%	0.58%			Mean	9.68%	1.64%	1.64%	0.90%
	0.0005	1	9.72%	2.27%	12.50%	1.25%		0.0005	1	10.37%	2.78%	12.50%	1.56%
		2	9.70%	2.27%	12.50%	1.25%			2	9.92%	2.78%	12.50%	1.56%
		3	9.91%	1.06%	11.11%	0.56%			3	10.22%	1.31%	11.11%	0.69%
		4	9.68%	0.00%	0.00%	0.00%			4	9.73%	2.47%	11.11%	1.39%
		5	9.79%	2.27%	12.50%	1.25%			5	9.73%	1.47%	12.50%	0.78%
		Mean	9.76%	1.58%	9.72%	0.86%			Mean	10.01%	2.16%	11.94%	1.20%
	0.001	1	10.11%	3.26%	12.50%	1.88%		0.001	1	10.11%	2.78%	12.50%	1.56%
		2	10.14%	3.26%	12.50%	1.88%			2	9.82%	2.78%	12.50%	1.56%
		3	10.22%	2.90%	11.11%	1.67%			3	9.86%	1.31%	11.11%	0.69%
		4	10.17%	1.06%	11.11%	0.56%			4	10.01%	1.31%	11.11%	0.69%
		5	9.93%	1.19%	12.50%	0.63%			5	10.24%	0.00%	0.00%	0.00%
		Mean	10.11%	2.33%	11.94%	1.32%			Mean	10.01%	1.63%	9.44%	0.90%
	0.005	1	10.37%	2.27%	12.50%	1.25%		0.005	1	9.73%	2.78%	12.50%	1.56%
		2	10.46%	0.00%	0.00%	0.00%			2	10.17%	1.47%	12.50%	0.78%
		3	9.81%	1.06%	11.11%	0.56%			3	10.78%	4.44%	11.11%	2.78%
		4	10.17%	1.06%	11.11%	0.56%			4	9.94%	2.78%	12.50%	1.56%
		5	10.03%	3.26%	12.50%	1.88%			5	9.86%	1.31%	11.11%	0.69%
		Mean	10.17%	1.53%	9.44%	0.85%			Mean	10.24%	1.84%	8.61%	1.03%
28	0.00001	1	57.46%	40.00%	40.00%	40.00%	32	0.00001	1	54.92%	43.17%	46.00%	43.33%
		2	57.47%	50.00%	50.00%	50.00%			2	57.72%	39.31%	42.59%	45.19%
		3	56.73%	40.00%	40.00%	40.00%			3	56.87%	42.59%	55.56%	37.04%
		4	57.94%	20.00%	20.00%	20.00%			4	55.91%	42.00%	45.00%	40.00%
		5	57.05%	13.33%	10.00%	20.00%			5	56.46%	43.10%	42.00%	47.50%
		Mean	57.33%	32.67%	32.00%	34.00%			Mean	56.38%	42.03%	46.23%	42.61%
	0.00005	1	10.01%	10.00%	25.00%	6.25%		0.00005	1	60.60%	41.67%	51.11%	41.67%
		2	60.19%	50.00%	50.00%	50.00%			2	60.71%	42.67%	48.33%	44.17%
		3	60.61%	50.00%	50.00%	50.00%			3	65.97%	59.26%	68.52%	57.41%
		4	59.38%	40.00%	40.00%	40.00%			4	59.06%	30.00%	27.50%	35.00%
		5	60.15%	33.33%	30.00%	40.00%			5	59.31%	60.00%	61.00%	62.50%
		Mean	50.07%	36.67%	39.00%	37.25%			Mean	59.13%	46.72%	51.29%	48.15%

Table A2. Cont.

Batch Size	LR	Fold	SGDM Val Accuracy	F1-Score	Recall	Precision	Batch Size	LR	Fold	Val Accuracy	F1-Score	Recall	Precision
28	0.0001	1	10.03%	0.00%	0.00%	0.00%	32	0.0001	1	10.20%	0.00%	0.00%	0.00%
		2	9.92%	0.00%	0.00%	0.00%			2	9.70%	2.78%	12.50%	1.56%
		3	9.74%	10.00%	25.00%	6.25%			3	9.91%	1.31%	11.11%	0.69%
		4	10.17%	0.00%	0.00%	0.00%			4	10.17%	1.31%	11.11%	0.69%
		5	10.24%	0.00%	0.00%	0.00%			5	10.03%	3.95%	12.50%	2.34%
		Mean	10.02%	2.00%	5.00%	1.25%			Mean	10.00%	1.87%	9.44%	1.06%
	0.0005	1	10.20%	0.00%	0.00%	0.00%		0.0005	1	10.20%	0.00%	0.00%	0.00%
		2	9.93%	0.00%	0.00%	0.00%			2	9.82%	2.78%	12.50%	1.56%
		3	9.86%	0.00%	0.00%	0.00%			3	10.22%	1.31%	11.11%	0.69%
		4	9.73%	0.00%	0.00%	0.00%			4	10.40%	2.47%	11.11%	1.39%
		5	10.10%	0.00%	0.00%	0.00%			5	10.06%	2.78%	12.50%	1.56%
		Mean	9.96%	0.00%	0.00%	0.00%			Mean	10.14%	1.87%	9.44%	1.04%
	0.001	1	9.69%	0.00%	0.00%	0.00%		0.001	1	10.11%	2.78%	12.50%	1.56%
		2	9.82%	0.00%	0.00%	0.00%			2	9.93%	2.78%	12.50%	1.56%
		3	9.86%	0.00%	0.00%	0.00%			3	10.02%	4.44%	11.11%	2.78%
		4	10.17%	0.00%	0.00%	0.00%			4	9.44%	4.44%	11.11%	2.78%
		5	9.46%	0.00%	0.00%	0.00%			5	9.88%	2.78%	12.50%	1.56%
		Mean	9.80%	0.00%	0.00%	0.00%			Mean	9.88%	3.44%	11.94%	2.05%
	0.005	1	9.94%	0.00%	0.00%	0.00%		0.005	1	9.72%	1.47%	12.50%	0.78%
		2	10.17%	0.00%	0.00%	0.00%			2	10.17%	1.47%	12.50%	0.78%
		3	10.22%	0.00%	0.00%	0.00%			3	9.86%	1.31%	11.11%	0.69%
		4	9.92%	0.00%	0.00%	0.00%			4	9.94%	2.68%	12.42%	1.57%
		5	9.46%	0.00%	0.00%	0.00%			5	9.86%	2.14%	10.21%	1.38%
		Mean	9.94%	0.00%	0.00%	0.00%			Mean	9.76%	1.86%	10.74%	1.12%

References

1. Pouyanfar, S.; Sadiq, S.; Yan, Y.; Tian, H.; Tao, Y.; Reyes, M.P.; Shyu, M.-L.; Chen, S.-C.; Iyengar, S.S. A Survey on Deep Learning: Algorithms, Techniques, and Applications. *ACM Comput. Surv.* **2018**, *51*, 1–36. [CrossRef]
2. Zhu, W.; Braun, B.; Chiang, L.H.; Romagnoli, J.A. Investigation of Transfer Learning for Image Classification and Impact on Training Sample Size. *Chemom. Intell. Lab. Syst.* **2021**, *211*, 104269. [CrossRef]
3. Alzubaidi, L.; Zhang, J.; Humaidi, A.J.; Al-Dujaili, A.; Duan, Y.; Al-Shamma, O.; Santamaría, J.; Fadhel, M.A.; Al-Amidie, M.; Farhan, L. Review of Deep Learning: Concepts, CNN Architectures, Challenges, Applications, Future Directions. *J. Big Data* **2021**, *8*, 53. [PubMed]
4. Li, Q.; Cai, W.; Wang, X.; Zhou, Y.; Feng, D.D.; Chen, M. Medical Image Classification with Convolutional Neural Network. In Proceedings of the 2014 13th International Conference on Control Automation Robotics & Vision (ICARCV), Singapore, 10–12 December 2014; pp. 844–848.
5. Decherchi, S.; Pedrini, E.; Mordenti, M.; Cavalli, A.; Sangiorgi, L. Opportunities and Challenges for Machine Learning in Rare Diseases. *Front. Med.* **2021**, *8*, 1696. [CrossRef]
6. Han, J.; Zhang, Z.; Mascolo, C.; André, E.; Tao, J.; Zhao, Z.; Schuller, B.W. Deep Learning for Mobile Mental Health: Challenges and Recent Advances. *IEEE Signal Process. Mag.* **2021**, *38*, 96–105. [CrossRef]
7. Sovrano, F.; Palmirani, M.; Vitali, F. Combining Shallow and Deep Learning Approaches against Data Scarcity in Legal Domains. *Gov. Inf. Q.* **2022**, *39*, 101715. [CrossRef]
8. Morid, M.A.; Borjali, A.; Del Fiol, G. A Scoping Review of Transfer Learning Research on Medical Image Analysis Using ImageNet. *Comput. Biol. Med.* **2021**, *128*, 104115. [CrossRef]
9. Chui, K.T.; Gupta, B.B.; Jhaveri, R.H.; Chi, H.R.; Arya, V.; Almomani, A.; Nauman, A. Multiround transfer learning and modified generative adversarial network for lung cancer detection. *Int. J. Intell. Syst.* **2023**, *2023*, 6376275. [CrossRef]
10. Hussain, M.; Bird, J.J.; Faria, D.R. A Study on Cnn Transfer Learning for Image Classification. In *Advances in Computational Intelligence Systems: Contributions Presented at the 18th UK Workshop on Computational Intelligence, Nottingham, UK, 5–7 September 2018*; Springer: Berlin/Heidelberg, Germany, 2019; pp. 191–202.
11. Salehi, A.W.; Khan, S.; Gupta, G.; Alabduallah, B.I.; Almjally, A.; Alsolai, H.; Siddiqui, T.; Mellit, A. A Study of CNN and Transfer Learning in Medical Imaging: Advantages, Challenges, Future Scope. *Sustainability* **2023**, *15*, 5930. [CrossRef]
12. Wang, Y.; Mori, G. Max-Margin Hidden Conditional Random Fields for Human Action Recognition. In Proceedings of the 2009 IEEE Conference on Computer Vision and Pattern Recognition, Miami, FL, USA, 20–25 June 2009; pp. 872–879.
13. Yao, A.; Gall, J.; Van Gool, L. A Hough Transform-Based Voting Framework for Action Recognition. In Proceedings of the 2010 IEEE Computer Society Conference on Computer Vision and Pattern Recognition, San Francisco, CA, USA, 13–18 June 2010; pp. 2061–2068.
14. Xia, T.; Tao, D.; Mei, T.; Zhang, Y. Multiview Spectral Embedding. *IEEE Trans. Syst. Man Cybern. B* **2010**, *40*, 1438–1446.
15. Shao, L.; Zhu, F.; Li, X. Transfer Learning for Visual Categorization: A Survey. *IEEE Trans. Neural Netw. Learn. Syst.* **2014**, *26*, 1019–1034. [CrossRef] [PubMed]

16. Zhuang, F.; Qi, Z.; Duan, K.; Xi, D.; Zhu, Y.; Zhu, H.; Xiong, H.; He, Q. A Comprehensive Survey on Transfer Learning. *Proc. IEEE* **2020**, *109*, 43–76.
17. Wang, Z.; Dai, Z.; Póczos, B.; Carbonell, J. Characterizing and Avoiding Negative Transfer. In Proceedings of the IEEE/CVF Conference on Computer Vision and Pattern Recognition, Long Beach, CA, USA, 15–20 June 2019; pp. 11293–11302.
18. Chui, K.T.; Arya, V.; Band, S.S.; Alhalabi, M.; Liu, R.W.; Chi, H.R. Facilitating Innovation and Knowledge Transfer between Homogeneous and Heterogeneous Datasets: Generic Incremental Transfer Learning Approach and Multidisciplinary Studies. *J. Innov. Knowl.* **2023**, *8*, 100313. [CrossRef]
19. Niu, S.; Jiang, Y.; Chen, B.; Wang, J.; Liu, Y.; Song, H. Cross-Modality Transfer Learning for Image-Text Information Management. *ACM Trans. Manag. Inf. Syst.* **2021**, *13*, 1–14. [CrossRef]
20. Lei, H.; Han, T.; Zhou, F.; Yu, Z.; Qin, J.; Elazab, A.; Lei, B. A Deeply Supervised Residual Network for HEp-2 Cell Classification via Cross-Modal Transfer Learning. *Pattern Recognit.* **2018**, *79*, 290–302. [CrossRef]
21. Vununu, C.; Lee, S.-H.; Kwon, K.-R. A Classification Method for the Cellular Images Based on Active Learning and Cross-Modal Transfer Learning. *Sensors* **2021**, *21*, 1469. [CrossRef]
22. Hadad, O.; Bakalo, R.; Ben-Ari, R.; Hashoul, S.; Amit, G. Classification of Breast Lesions Using Cross-Modal Deep Learning. In Proceedings of the 2017 IEEE 14th International Symposium on Biomedical Imaging (ISBI 2017), Melbourne, VIC, Australia, 18–21 April 2017; IEEE: Piscataway, NJ, USA; pp. 109–112.
23. Shen, Y.; Stamos, I. SimCrossTrans: A Simple Cross-Modality Transfer Learning for Object Detection with ConvNets or Vision Transformers. *arXiv* **2022**, arXiv:2203.10456.
24. Ahmed, S.M.; Lohit, S.; Peng, K.-C.; Jones, M.J.; Roy-Chowdhury, A.K. Cross-Modal Knowledge Transfer Without Task-Relevant Source Data. In *Computer Vision–ECCV 2022: Proceedings of the 17th European Conference, Tel Aviv, Israel, 23–27 October 2022, Proceedings, Part XXXIV*; Springer: Berlin/Heidelberg, Germany, 2022; pp. 111–127.
25. Du, S.; Wang, Y.; Huang, X.; Zhao, R.-W.; Zhang, X.; Feng, R.; Shen, Q.; Zhang, J.Q. Chest X-ray Quality Assessment Method with Medical Domain Knowledge Fusion. *IEEE Access* **2023**, *11*, 22904–22916. [CrossRef]
26. Socher, R.; Ganjoo, M.; Manning, C.D.; Ng, A. Zero-Shot Learning through Cross-Modal Transfer. *Adv. Neural Inf. Process. Syst.* **2013**, *26*.
27. Chen, S.; Guhur, P.-L.; Schmid, C.; Laptev, I. History Aware Multimodal Transformer for Vision-and-Language Navigation. *Adv. Neural Inf. Process. Syst.* **2021**, *34*, 5834–5847.
28. Salin, E.; Farah, B.; Ayache, S.; Favre, B. Are Vision-Language Transformers Learning Multimodal Representations? A Probing Perspective. In Proceedings of the AAAI Conference on Artificial Intelligence, Online, 22 February–1 March 2022; Volume 36, pp. 11248–11257.
29. Li, Y.; Quan, R.; Zhu, L.; Yang, Y. Efficient Multimodal Fusion via Interactive Prompting. In Proceedings of the IEEE/CVF Conference on Computer Vision and Pattern Recognition, Seattle, WA, USA, 17–21 June 2023; pp. 2604–2613.
30. Srinivasan, T.; Chang, T.-Y.; Pinto Alva, L.; Chochlakis, G.; Rostami, M.; Thomason, J. Climb: A Continual Learning Benchmark for Vision-and-Language Tasks. *Adv. Neural Inf. Process. Syst.* **2022**, *35*, 29440–29453.
31. Falco, P.; Lu, S.; Natale, C.; Pirozzi, S.; Lee, D. A Transfer Learning Approach to Cross-Modal Object Recognition: From Visual Observation to Robotic Haptic Exploration. *IEEE Trans. Robot.* **2019**, *35*, 987–998. [CrossRef]
32. Lin, C.; Jiang, Y.; Cai, J.; Qu, L.; Haffari, G.; Yuan, Z. Multimodal Transformer with Variable-Length Memory for Vision-and-Language Navigation. In *European Conference on Computer Vision*; Springer: Cham, Switzerland, 2022; pp. 380–397.
33. Koroteev, M. BERT: A Review of Applications in Natural Language Processing and Understanding. *arXiv* **2021**, arXiv:2103.11943.
34. Bao, H.; Dong, L.; Piao, S.; Wei, F. Beit: Bert Pre-Training of Image Transformers. *arXiv* **2021**, arXiv:2106.08254.
35. Yenter, A.; Verma, A. Deep CNN-LSTM with Combined Kernels from Multiple Branches for IMDb Review Sentiment Analysis. In Proceedings of the 2017 IEEE 8th Annual Ubiquitous Computing, Electronics and Mobile Communication Conference (UEMCON), New York, NY, USA, 19–21 October 2017; pp. 540–546.
36. Ridnik, T.; Ben-Baruch, E.; Noy, A.; Zelnik-Manor, L. Imagenet-21k Pretraining for the Masses. *arXiv* **2021**, arXiv:2104.10972.
37. Yosinski, J.; Clune, J.; Bengio, Y.; Lipson, H. How Transferable Are Features in Deep Neural Networks? *Adv. Neural Inf. Process. Syst.* **2014**, *27*.
38. Liu, N.F.; Gardner, M.; Belinkov, Y.; Peters, M.E.; Smith, N.A. Linguistic Knowledge and Transferability of Contextual Representations. *arXiv* **2019**, arXiv:1903.08855.
39. Kirichenko, P.; Izmailov, P.; Wilson, A.G. Last Layer Re-Training Is Sufficient for Robustness to Spurious Correlations. *arXiv* **2022**, arXiv:2204.02937.
40. Kovaleva, O.; Romanov, A.; Rogers, A.; Rumshisky, A. Revealing the Dark Secrets of BERT. *arXiv* **2019**, arXiv:1908.08593.
41. Fushiki, T. Estimation of Prediction Error by Using K-Fold Cross-Validation. *Stat. Comput.* **2011**, *21*, 137–146. [CrossRef]
42. Goutte, C.; Gaussier, E. A Probabilistic Interpretation of Precision, Recall and F-Score, with Implication for Evaluation. In *Advances in Information Retrieval: Proceedings of the 27th European Conference on IR Research, ECIR 2005, Santiago de Compostela, Spain, 21–23 March 2005, Proceedings 27*; Springer: Berlin/Heidelberg, Germany, 2005; pp. 345–359.
43. Usmani, I.A.; Qadri, M.T.; Zia, R.; Alrayes, F.S.; Saidani, O.; Dashtipour, K. Interactive Effect of Learning Rate and Batch Size to Implement Transfer Learning for Brain Tumor Classification. *Electronics* **2023**, *12*, 964. [CrossRef]
44. Reddi, S.J.; Kale, S.; Kumar, S. On the Convergence of Adam and Beyond. *arXiv* **2019**, arXiv:1904.09237.

45. Niu, S.; Liu, Y.; Wang, J.; Song, H. A decade survey of transfer learning (2010–2020). *IEEE Trans. Artif. Intell.* **2020**, *1*, 151–166. [CrossRef]
46. Chui, K.T.; Gupta, B.B.; Chi, H.R.; Arya, V.; Alhalabi, W.; Ruiz, M.T.; Shen, C.W. Transfer learning-based multi-scale denoising convolutional neural network for prostate cancer detection. *Cancers* **2022**, *14*, 3687. [CrossRef] [PubMed]
47. Antol, S.; Agrawal, A.; Lu, J.; Mitchell, M.; Batra, D.; Zitnick, C.L.; Parikh, D. Vqa: Visual question answering. In Proceedings of the IEEE International Conference on Computer Vision, Santiago, Chile, 7–13 December 2015.

Disclaimer/Publisher's Note: The statements, opinions and data contained in all publications are solely those of the individual author(s) and contributor(s) and not of MDPI and/or the editor(s). MDPI and/or the editor(s) disclaim responsibility for any injury to people or property resulting from any ideas, methods, instructions or products referred to in the content.

Article

Three-Dimensional Measurement of Full Profile of Steel Rail Cross-Section Based on Line-Structured Light

Jiajia Liu, Jiapeng Zhang, Zhongli Ma *, Hangtian Zhang and Shun Zhang

College of Automation, Chengdu University of Information Technology, Chengdu 610103, China; liujj@cuit.edu.cn (J.L.); zhangjp11@126.com (J.Z.); 18339523310@163.com (H.Z.); zchuangye.zs@gmail.com (S.Z.)
* Correspondence: mazl@cuit.edu.cn

Abstract: The wear condition of steel rails directly affects the safety of railway operations. Line-structured-light visual measurement technology is used for online measurement of rail wear due to its ability to achieve high-precision dynamic measurements. However, in dynamic measurements, the random deviation of the measurement plane caused by the vibration of the railcar results in changes in the actual measured rail profile relative to its cross-sectional profile, ultimately leading to measurement deviations. To address these issues, this paper proposes a method for three-dimensional measurement of steel rail cross-sectional profiles based on binocular line-structured light. Firstly, calibrated dual cameras are used to simultaneously capture the profiles of both sides of the steel rail in the same world coordinate system, forming the complete rail profile. Then, considering that the wear at the rail waist is zero in actual operation, the coordinate of the circle center on both sides of the rail waist are connected to form feature vectors. The measured steel rail profile is aligned with the corresponding feature vectors of the standard steel rail model to achieve initial registration; next, the rail profile that has completed the preliminary matching is accurately matched with the target model based on the iterative closest point (ICP) algorithm. Finally, by comparing the projected complete rail profile onto the rail cross-sectional plane with the standard 3D rail model, the amount of wear on the railhead can be obtained. The experimental results indicate that the proposed line-structured-light measurement method for the complete rail profile, when compared to the measurements obtained from the rail wear gauge, exhibits smaller mean absolute deviation (MAD) and root mean square error (RMSE) for both the vertical and lateral dimensions. The MAD values for the vertical and lateral measurements are 0.009 mm and 0.039 mm, respectively, while the RMSE values are 0.011 mm and 0.048 mm. The MAD and RMSE values for the vertical and lateral wear measurements are lower than those obtained using the standard two-dimensional rail profile measurement method. Furthermore, it effectively eliminates the impact of vibrations during the dynamic measurement process, showcasing its practical engineering application value.

Keywords: steel rail wear; dynamic measurement; line-structured light; binocular vision; ICP algorithm

Citation: Liu, J.; Zhang, J.; Ma, Z.; Zhang, H.; Zhang, S. Three-Dimensional Measurement of Full Profile of Steel Rail Cross-Section Based on Line-Structured Light. *Electronics* **2023**, *12*, 3194. https://doi.org/10.3390/electronics12143194

Academic Editor: Eva Cernadas

Received: 27 June 2023
Revised: 20 July 2023
Accepted: 20 July 2023
Published: 24 July 2023

Copyright: © 2023 by the authors. Licensee MDPI, Basel, Switzerland. This article is an open access article distributed under the terms and conditions of the Creative Commons Attribution (CC BY) license (https://creativecommons.org/licenses/by/4.0/).

1. Introduction

The surface wear condition of a rail directly affects the stability and safety of train operation. With the continuous development of railway transportation towards heavier loads and higher speeds, the surface wear of rails exhibits characteristics of shorter cycles and more severe wear. Therefore, higher requirements are placed on the accuracy and efficiency of online rail profile measurement. Currently, railway maintenance departments primarily rely on measuring the cross-sectional profile of rails to assess their wear condition. Rail wear measurement methods are mainly divided into two categories: contact-based and non-contact-based methods [1]. Contact-based measurement methods include mechanical gauges such as the P110B and SKM by Vogel and Plötscher from Germany, as well as the Miniprof profilometer by Greenwood Engineering from Denmark [2]. This type of equipment has mature technology but has the disadvantages of low measurement efficiency and difficulties in equipment maintenance. Compared to contact-based measurement methods, non-contact measurement methods have the advantages of fast measurement and high accuracy [3,4]. They mainly utilize laser displacement sensor and structured-light vision measurement. The laser displacement sensor is based on the principle of triangular ranging. The position of the rail profile can be determined according to the geometric relationship between the laser and the camera and the imaging position on the laser line array CCD, for example, the laser displacement sensors developed by Optimess in Switzerland and the laser portable track inspection instrument. This type of equipment offers simple operation and rapid measurement. However, the obtained rail cross-sectional profiles may have sparse sampling points, and the measurement data can be affected by ambient light interference. Additionally, these devices can be expensive [5]. Structure light photogrammetry technology is used to extract rail cross-sectional profiles from captured images of line-structured light on the rail surface. This method involves system calibration, image extraction, and coordinate transformation [6,7]. Examples of such measurement systems include KLD Labs' ORIAN™ (optical rail inspection and analysis) optical inspection and analysis system for rails, and the rail full-profile onboard measurement system by MERMEC. These measurement methods provide more detailed rail cross-sectional profile data, higher system flexibility in setup, and are relatively cost-effective [8].

To achieve dynamic measurement of the full cross-sectional profile of a rail using line-structured light, the use of binocular line-structured-light technology is a prevalent approach. In order to dynamically obtain rail cross-sectional profile data, the line-structured-light measurement system is typically installed on the underside of a rail inspection vehicle or grinding vehicle positioned close to the inner side of the rail. This allows for continuous acquisition of the cross-sectional profile of one side of the rail [9,10]. The railhead of the track undergoes deformation due to long-term train pressure, and the detection of one side profile cannot accurately assess the condition of rail usage. Moreover, the vibrations during the vehicle's motion cause the plane of the line-structured-light measurement to deviate from the vertical cross-section of the rail. To address the vibration issue, researchers have proposed various methods, including dynamic vibration correction based on multiple line-structured lights [11–13], estimation of vibration deviation by measuring the variation in the rail profile features compared to the standard rail profile [14–16], and combining multiple rail cross-sections for three-dimensional global registration to measure wear [17]. The multi-line-structured-light measurement method proposed by Wang Chao and Sun Junhua [12,13] involves extracting feature points from the measured cross-section to calculate an auxiliary projection plane. The distorted rail section is then projected onto the auxiliary plane to correct the deviation; however, inaccurate feature point extraction may occur due to the presence of outliers in the measured cross-section and inherent geometric distortions in the rail profile. Zhan dong [16] proposed a vehicle multiple degrees-of-freedom vibration decoupling and compensation method based on orthogonal decomposition. It corrects the deviations caused by vehicle vibrations by considering the changes in the rail waist profile; however, the rail profile after the deviation correction is not the cross-sectional profile that is perpendicular to the radial direction of the rail, which can still lead to measurement errors. Yang Yue [17] proposed merging multiple rail sections into a three-dimensional surface of the rail and aligning the measured three-dimensional profile with a standard rail model using global registration methods to calculate rail wear; however, merging the sections into a three-dimensional profile can introduce deviations in the radial direction of the rail.

To address the issue of low measurement accuracy in rail section profiles caused by the deviation of the line-structured-light measurement plane due to vehicle vibrations, this paper proposes a three-dimensional measurement of the full profile of the rail cross-section based on line-structured light. The proposed method begins by establishing a measurement model based on dual-camera vision with line-structured light and calibrating the line-structured-light measurement plane. Next, a two-step railhead profile measurement method is introduced, which starts with a coarse measurement and gradually refines the measurement to obtain the complete rail profile. The measured rail profile is then compared with a standard rail 3D point cloud model in three-dimensional space to quantify the rail wear. Finally, the line-structured-light dual-camera rail full-profile vision measurement system is tested and validated at a railway infrastructure maintenance base to assess the measurement accuracy of the proposed method.

2. Rail Cross-Section Full-Profile Measurement System Based on Binocular Line-Structured Light

2.1. Binocular Measurement System and Model

The structure of the binocular-structured light-based steel rail cross-section full-profile measurement system is shown in Figure 1. The system consists of a measurement unit comprising two sets of line lasers and CCD cameras, a data switch, an odometer, and a data processing computer. The structured light vision acquisition front-end uses a Basler acA1600-120uc CCD camera with an image resolution of 1600 × 1200. The lens used has a target size of 1/1.8″ and a resolution of 5 million, and the accuracy of the image can be guaranteed. During the inspection, the line lasers are projected vertically onto the surface of the steel rail, forming a curve of full-profile light stripes on the rail section. The odometer triggers the cameras at a fixed frequency to capture the images of the rail profile light stripes. The computer, using an established binocular vision imaging model based on structured light, reconstructs the full profile of the rail section from the captured light stripe images.

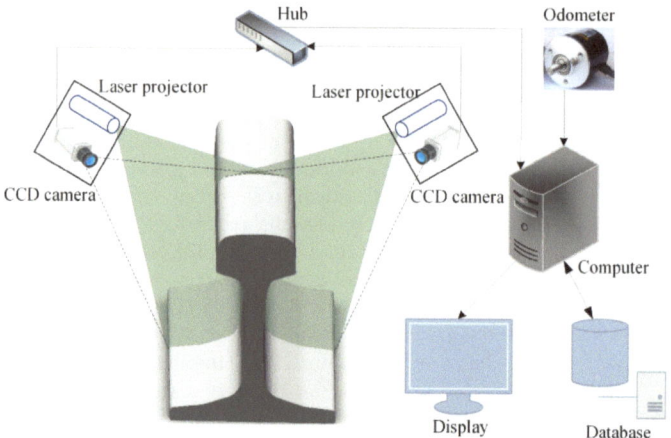

Figure 1. Steel rail full-profile measuring system based on binocular-structured light.

The binocular-structured-light vision system model is shown in Figure 2. $O_w X_w Y_w Z_w$ is the world coordinate system, $O_c X_c Y_c Z_c$ and $O_c' X_c' Y_c' Z_c'$ are the camera coordinate system, $o_c xy$ and $o_c' x' y'$ are the camera imaging plane coordinate system, $o_1 uv$ and $o_1' u' v'$ are the camera imaging plane pixel coordinate system, $[R\ t]$ and $[R'\ t']$ are the transformation matrix between the camera coordinate system and the world coordinate system. Suppose point $P_M = (x_w, y_w, z_w)^T$ is an intersection point M between the light plane and the surface of the steel rail in the world coordinate system, then $P_c = (x_c, y_c, z_c)^T$ and $p_c' = (x_c', y_c', z_c')^T$ are the coordinates of point M in the camera coordinate system, $p_m = (u_m, v_m)^T$ and $p_m' = (u_m', v_m')^T$ are the pixel coordinates of the point imaged by the camera. Taking the $O_c X_c Y_c Z_c$ camera as an example, a camera is modeled by the usual pinhole: the relationship between a 3D point M and its image projection m is given by

$$s\tilde{p}_m = A p_c = A[R\ t]\tilde{P}_M \tag{1}$$

where s is the scale factor, A is the matrix of the camera's intrinsic parameters, R and t are the rotation matrix and translation vector from the world coordinate system to the camera coordinate system, and $\tilde{p}_m$ and $\tilde{P}_M$ are the homogeneous coordinates of p_m and P_M. In addition, P_M satisfies

$$ax_c + bx_c + cz_c + d = 0 \tag{2}$$

where $(a, b, c,$ and $d)$ are the parameters of the light plane in the camera coordinate system. The light plane in the world coordinate system satisfies

$$Z_W = 0 \tag{3}$$

Referring to (1) to (3), the binocular-structured-light vision model can be represented as

$$\begin{cases} s\tilde{p}_m = AP_c = A[R\ t]\tilde{P}_M \\ ax_c + bx_c + cz_c + d = 0 \\ s'\tilde{p}'_m = A'p'_c = A'[R'\ t']\tilde{P}_M \\ a'x'_c + b'x'_c + c'z'_c + d' = 0 \\ Z_W = 0 \end{cases} \tag{4}$$

where the camera's intrinsic parameters A and A' can be obtained using the chessboard calibration method [18]. If the external parameters $[R\ t]$ and $[R'\ t']$ of the transformation from the line-structured-light plane $Z_W = 0$ in the world coordinate system to the $O_c X_c Y_c Z_c$ and $O'_c X'_c Y'_c Z'_c$ camera coordinate systems can be obtained, the unique coordinates of the complete rail profile on the line-structured-light plane P_M in the world coordinate system can be determined.

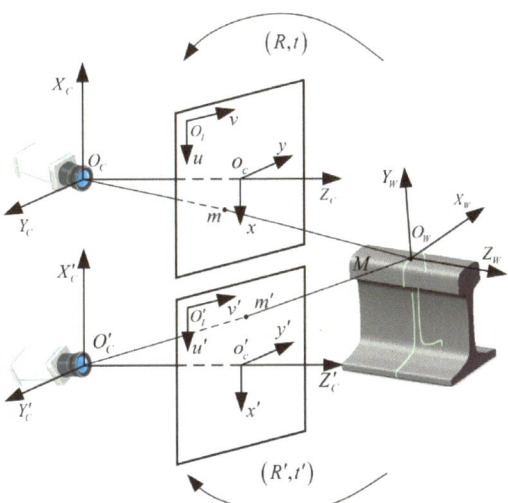

Figure 2. Binocular-structured-light vision model.

2.2. Determination of the Measurement Plane for Line-Structured Light

To achieve simultaneous calibration of the cameras on both sides of the rail, the checkerboard calibration board is adjusted so that it is within the common field of view of the two cameras. Then, the line projectors on both sides are adjusted to align the light planes, as shown in Figure 3. The cameras and projectors are symmetrically distributed on both sides, and the angle between the camera optical axis and the light plane is approximately $\beta = 60°$. The vertical distance d between the projectors and the cameras is

$$d = fH/h \times sin\beta \tag{5}$$

where f is the focal length of the camera, H is the height of target, and h is the optical size of camera.

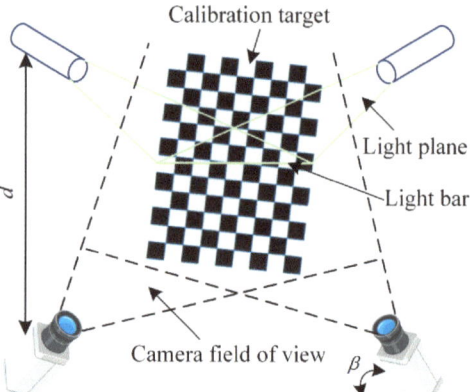

Figure 3. Line-structured-light plane calibration model.

The target plane is fixed in the common viewing area of the cameras on both sides. An image of the target plane is captured, denoted as image F_i, and an image of the intersection between the target plane and the line-structured-light plane is captured, denoted as image F'_i. Image F_i is used to extract corner points, while image F'_i is used to extract feature points formed by the intersection between the line-structured-light plane and the calibration board, the images captured by the cameras on both sides are shown in Figure 4. Then, the target plane is moved i (≥ 3) times, and the above steps are repeated to obtain i pairs of images.

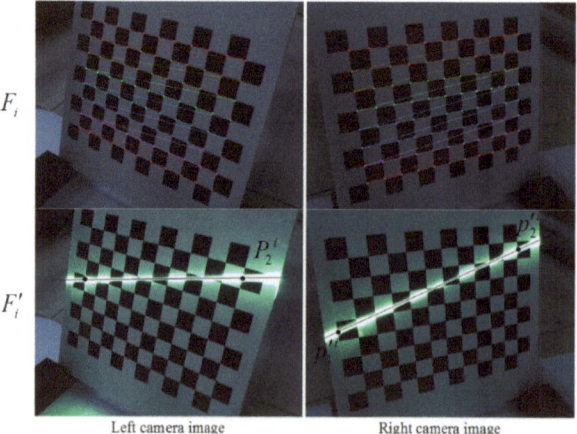

Figure 4. Calibration images.

The chessboard calibration method [18] is used to solve the external parameters $[R_i, t_i]$ and $[R'_i, t'_i]$ that transform each set of captured target planes from the world coordinate system $Z_W = 0$ to the coordinate systems of the cameras on both sides; the origin of the world coordinate system is set to the top-left corner point of the target plane. The feature points formed by the intersection of the light stripes and the chessboard target plane are shown in Figure 5 as points P_1^i and P_2^i.

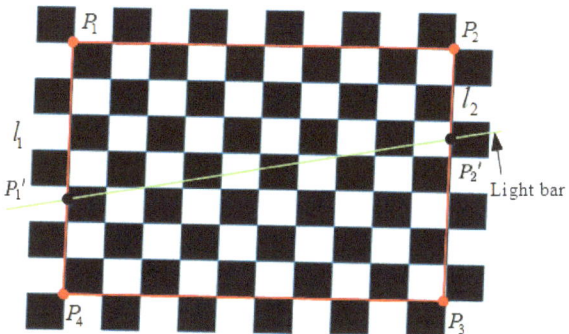

Figure 5. Feature points extraction on the light plane.

In the figure, points P_1, P_2, P_3, and P_4 represent the four corner points of the target plane, in the image, the corresponding corner points are denoted as P_{m1}, P_{m2}, P_{m3}, and P_{m4}. By moving the target plane times, the line-structured-light plane will generate a total of $2m$ feature points in the coordinate systems of the cameras on both sides. The coordinates of feature points p_1^i, p_2^i in the camera coordinate system are as follows:

$$\begin{cases} P_{c1}^i = [R_i \, t_i] P_1^i \\ P_{c2}^i = [R_i \, t_i] P_2^i \\ P_{c1}^{'i} = [R_i' \, t_i'] P_1^i \\ P_{c2}^{'i} = [R_i' \, t_i'] P_2^i \end{cases}, i = 1, 2 \ldots m \tag{6}$$

In the equation, points P_1^i and P_2^i are unknown and can be obtained through the processing of images F_i and F_i'. In image F_i', the pixel coordinates $(u_j, v_j), j = 1, 2 \ldots, n$ that correspond to the light stripe satisfy the following condition:

$$v = mu + c \tag{7}$$

The pixel points $(u_j, v_j), j = 1, 2 \ldots, n$ occupied by the light stripe can be extracted from images F_i and F_i' using the differential method. Then, the line parameters of the light stripe in the images can be solved using the least squares method:

$$\begin{cases} m = \dfrac{n(\sum u_j v_j) - (\sum u_j)(\sum v_j)}{n(\sum u_j^2) - (\sum u_j)^2} \\ c = \dfrac{(\sum u_j^2)(\sum v_j) - (\sum u_j)(\sum u_j v_j)}{n(\sum u_j^2) - (\sum u_j)^2} \end{cases} \tag{8}$$

The subpixel coordinates of the $P_{m1} P_{m2} P_{m3} P_{m4}$ corner point can be obtained from the F_i' image [19]. Using line intersection calculations, the intersection points P_{m1}^i and P_{m2}^i can be determined for the lines formed by the corner points $P_{m1} P_{m4}$ and $P_{m2} P_{m3}$ in the image, and the lines representing the structure of the light stripe. The chessboard target plane has a square size of 15 mm, according to the projective transformation and the principle of invariant ratios [20], the points P_{m1}^j and P_{m2}^j in the image and their corresponding feature points P_1^i and P_2^i in the world coordinate system satisfy the following relationship:

$$\frac{P_1^i - P_1}{P_1^i - P_4} = \frac{P_{m1}^i - P_{m1}}{P_{m1}^i - P_{m4}}, \frac{P_2^i - P_2}{P_2^i - P_3} = \frac{P_{m2}^i - P_{m2}}{P_{m2}^i - P_{m3}} \tag{9}$$

From (6) to (9), by applying the singular value decomposition (SVD) method to the feature points P_{c1}^i, P_{c2}^i and $P_{c1}^{'i}, P_{c2}^{'i}, i = 1, 2 \ldots m$, we can individually fit the equations of the line-structured-light plane in the coordinate systems of the two cameras:

$$\begin{cases} ax_c + bx_c + cz_c + d = 0 \\ a'x_c' + b'x_c' + c'z_c' + d' = 0 \end{cases} \quad (10)$$

Based on Equations (3) and (10), and using the Rodrigues transformation [21], we can calculate the external parameter matrices $[R\ t]$ and $[R'\ t']$, which represent the transformation from the line-structured-light plane to the coordinate systems of the two cameras.

3. Full-Profile Wear Measurement of Rail Section Based on Binocular Line-Structured Light

3.1. Extraction of Full Profile of Steel Rail Section

The rail geometry information can be obtained by means of distance measuring equipment such as rail height, rail waist height, rail waist width, and rail waist inclination, and the curve shape information can be obtained using a laser scanner. First, the contour images of the inner and outer sides of the steel rail are captured. Then, the subpixel coordinates of the center points of the steel rail contour light stripes are extracted [22,23]. Based on the established dual-camera vision model and the calibration of the line-structured-light plane's external parameters, the steel rail contour points on the line-structured-light plane are calculated using Equation (11):

$$\begin{cases} \tilde{P}_M = s[R\ t]^{-1} A^{-1} \tilde{P}_m \\ \tilde{P}_M' = s[R'\ t']^{-1} A^{-1} \tilde{P}_m' \end{cases} \quad (11)$$

To convert the subpixel coordinates of the center points of the rail profile light stripes in the image to the coordinates of the actual rail profile points on the measured light plane in the world coordinate system, the curved shape information of the rail is obtained using a laser scanner. The two locations on the top and bottom of the rail can be marked as "right" and "left", respectively. Then, the image undergoes median filtering and subpixel processing to obtain the contours of one side of the rail. Based on this, the complete contour of the rail on both sides is merged, as shown in Figure 6.

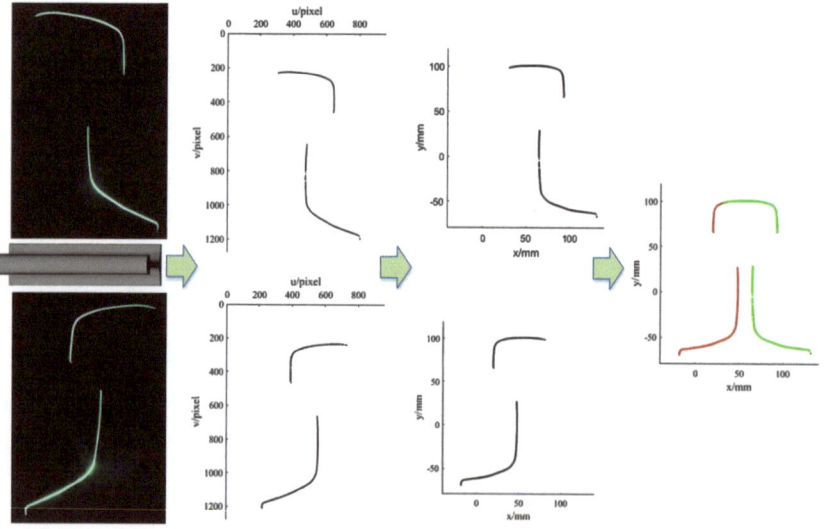

Figure 6. Full-profile collection of railway tracks.

3.2. Measurement of Railhead Contour Based on Two-Step Method

According to the "Maintenance Rules for Ballastless Track of High-speed Railway" [24], the measurement of vertical wear on the rail is taken at a width of one-third of the rail's top surface, and the measurement of side wear on the rail is taken 16 mm below the rail's running surface. As shown in Figure 7, W_V represents the vertical wear of the rail, and W_H represents the side wear of the rail. In general, by comparing the measured rail profile with the standard 2D profile, we can obtain W_V and W_H. However, the visual measurement system is installed on a moving train, and the vibrations of the train body can cause the random deflection of the line-structured-light measurement plane.

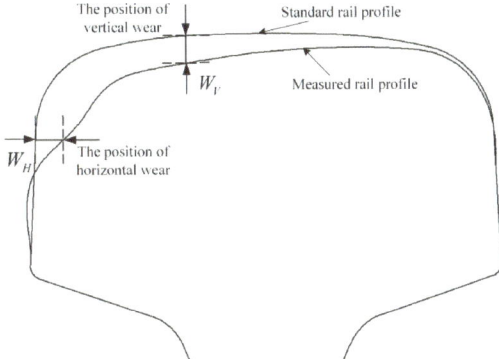

Figure 7. Rail vertical wear and horizontal wear.

As shown in Figure 8, a yaw angle deviation around the Y-axis, denoted as α, results in the measured rail profile being horizontally stretched compared to the standard rail profile. Similarly, a pitch angle deviation around the X-axis, denoted as β, leads to the measured rail profile being vertically stretched compared to the standard profile. Directly comparing the measured rail profile obtained under the train's vibration with the standard 2D rail profile will introduce measurement deviation. Therefore, the two-step method for measuring the railhead profile is adopted, which involves comparing the measured full rail profile with a standard 3D steel rail point cloud model in three-dimensional space. This approach helps to eliminate the influence of vibrations during the measurement process. Please refer to Sections 3.2.1 and 3.2.2 for detailed procedures.

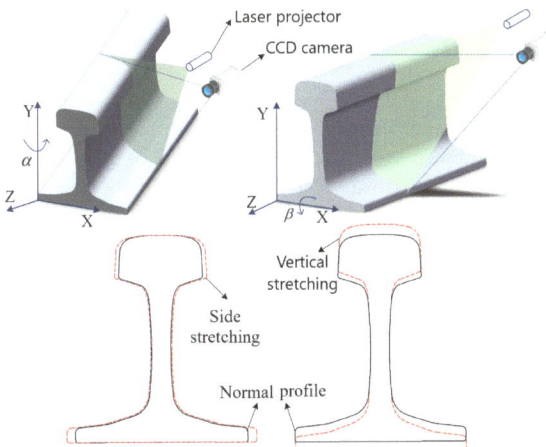

Figure 8. Measuring the plane pitch and heading offset.

3.2.1. Step 1: Initial Alignment of Rail Waist Contour Based on Rail Waist Feature Vectors

Due to the random deviation of the line-structured-light plane, the initial position of the measured steel rail profile in three-dimensional space differs significantly from the standard rail model. This misalignment prevents accurate alignment, requiring adjustment of the initial position of the measured rail profile to achieve initial registration with the standard rail model. By analysis, the complete rail profile can be divided into the railhead and rail waist sections, with the rail waist section experiencing no wear during actual operation. Therefore, the rail waist profile can be used as the reference. Two different feature vectors are formed by connecting the centers of the small circular arcs on both sides of the rail waist profile of the measured rail profile and the standard rail model, respectively, and the initial registration of the measured rail profile and the standard rail model is realized by aligning the two feature vectors. The specific process is as follows:

First, to minimize interference during the alignment between the measured rail profile and the standard rail model, the railhead bottom surface and rail bottom surface data of the standard steel rail model are removed before matching with the measured rail profile. Then, the standard rail model is transformed into a point cloud model. Specifically, for each triangle in the standard steel rail model with three vertices A, B, and C, a random uniformly distributed point cloud $Q_k, k = 1, 2 \ldots$ is generated on the surface of the triangle.

$$Q_k = A + s\overrightarrow{AB} + t\overrightarrow{AC} \tag{12}$$

where s and t are random numbers in [0, 1], if $s + t > 1$, then $s = 1 - s$ and $t = 1 - t$ [25]. Establish a Kd-tree index for the measured rail profile points to enable fast searching based on neighborhood relationships. Specifically, the measured rail profile points are denoted as Q, with the railhead contour points represented by Q_H, and the rail waist contour points represented by Q_W. Due to the significant distance between Q_H and Q_W, we can use Euclidean clustering to segment and extract them.

Then, as shown in Figure 9, the approximate centroid coordinates of the small arc contours on both sides of the steel rail waist can be extracted using techniques such as Hough circle detection. The radius of the small arc contour is $r = 20$ mm. The centroid coordinates o_r and o_l can be obtained, and the position of the centroid can be determined based on the grayscale values in the image. Specifically, in the steel rail waist curve, where each pixel point represents 1 mm, we can draw a circle with radius $r = 20\pi$ centered at the steel rail waist contour point, and the value of the corresponding pixel point increases by 1 when the arc passes through the pixel point. The approximate coordinates of the maximum pixel value point correspond to the centroid coordinates o_r and o_l of the small arc contour; the resulting steel rail waist feature point vector is denoted as $\overrightarrow{o_l o_r}$. Furthermore, for the standard rail model, the corresponding approximate coordinates on both sides of the rail waist contour are denoted as O_R and O_L, and the corresponding rail waist feature point vector is $\overrightarrow{O_R O_L}$. The corresponding points of the measured steel rail contour after initial registration are denoted as Q', the rail waist contour points become Q'_W, the rotation matrix and translation vector for the initial registration are represented as R_1 and t_1, the detailed solution process can be found in Equations (13)–(15).

$$\begin{cases} Q' = R_1 Q + t_1 \\ Q_W' = R_1 Q_W + t_1 \end{cases} \tag{13}$$

$$\begin{cases} R_1 = I + sin(\theta)K + (1 - cos(\theta))K^2 \\ t_1 = O_L - o_l \end{cases} \tag{14}$$

$$\begin{cases} k = \overrightarrow{o_l o_r} \times \overrightarrow{O_R O_L} \\ \theta = acos \dfrac{\overrightarrow{o_l o_r} \cdot \overrightarrow{O_R O_L}}{\|\overrightarrow{o_l o_r}\| * \|\overrightarrow{O_R O_L}\|} \end{cases} \tag{15}$$

In this formula, k represents the rotation axis vector for the rotation transformation, θ represents the rotation angle, K represents the cross-product matrix of k, and I represents the identity matrix.

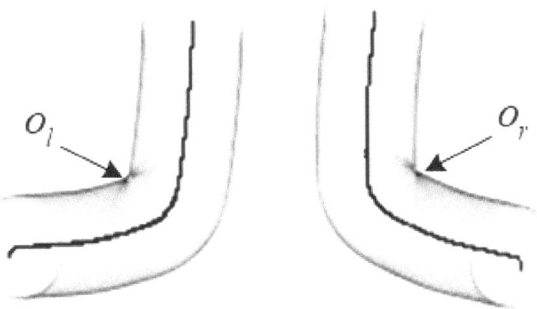

Figure 9. Rail waist feature point extraction.

3.2.2. Step 2: Accurate Measurement of Railhead Profile Based on ICP Algorithm and Model Registration

Using the initially aligned measured contour as a reference, and using the the ICP (iterative closest point) algorithm to achieve precise registration of the measured contour and the standard rail model, this ultimately enables the measurement of the railhead profile. In the ICP algorithm for precise registration, the total number of iterations [26], total deviation, and threshold for the difference between consecutive deviations are set to limit the number of iterations. The algorithm utilizes singular value decomposition (SVD) to estimate the rigid transformation. The rotation matrix and translation vector for precise registration are denoted as R_2 and t_2, respectively, to achieve the following transformation:

$$f(R_2, t_2) = \sum \|Q_k - (R_2 Q' + t_2)\|^2 = min \quad (16)$$

Finally, the transformation of the measured full rail contour points Q is given by:

$$Q'' = R_2(R_1 Q + t_1) + t_2 \quad (17)$$

Projecting the full rail contour points Q'' onto a plane perpendicular to the longitudinal direction of the rail and establishing a Kd-tree index, we can use the nearest neighbor point search to find the distances between the measured rail contour and the standard rail contour. This allows us to calculate the rail's overall wear condition based on the contour.

In summary, the alignment and comparison process between the measured rail contour points and the standard rail point cloud is shown in Figure 10. The process involves two steps: initial alignment and precise alignment. (a) The measured steel rail's full contour points are imported into the initial state of the standard steel rail point cloud in 3D space; (b) based on the feature vector formed by connecting the centers of the small circular arcs on both sides of the steel rail contour, the initial alignment between the measured steel rail contour and the standard steel rail model is performed; (c) the precise alignment is achieved by aligning the measured steel rail's full contour points with the standard steel rail point cloud model. The measured steel rail's waist section fits perfectly with the standard steel rail point cloud model, enabling accurate measurement and detection of railhead contour wear.

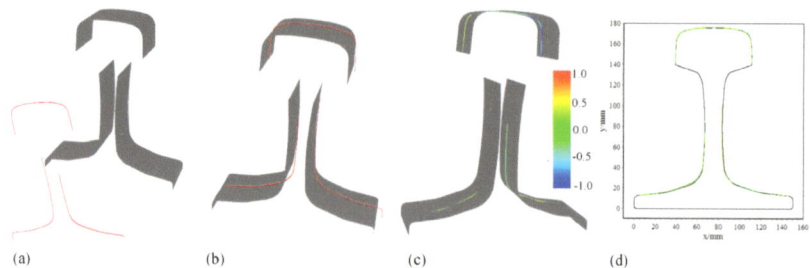

(a) (b) (c) (d)

Figure 10. The process of steel rail full−profile measuremen (**a**–**d**).

4. Experiment and Analysis

4.1. Test Experiment Platform

The measurement system was tested at the railway maintenance base of the railway bureau, as shown in Figure 11. The vision sensor was installed on the upper side of the railhead, about 70 mm above, and the vision sensor and line laser were fixed at a certain relative angle. The resolution of the vision sensor was 1600×1200, and the system was capable of capturing and processing rail contour images, system calibration, and measuring rail wear on the entire contour. The experimental process included the following steps: first, verifying the accuracy of the system's stereo calibration method [27]; then, using the proposed binocular vision measurement system and wear gauge measurement, comparing the vertical and side wear of the same rail to validate the measurement accuracy.

Figure 11. The experimental platform built on the rail inspection vehicle.

4.2. Calibration of Measurement System and Accuracy Analysis

The line-structured-light binocular camera system employs a 9×12 chessboard calibration board with square size of 15×15 mm. Thirteen sets of images of light stripe targets are captured using the two cameras. The method described in Section 2.2 is used to extract feature points at the intersections of the light stripes and the chessboard grid. The fitted equations of the light planes in the coordinate systems of the left and right cameras are as follows:

$$\begin{cases} -0.476x_c - 0.543x_c + 0.692z_c - 196.001 = 0 \\ 0.391x_c' - 0.528x_c' + 0.754z_c' - 202.922 = 0 \end{cases} \quad (18)$$

The calculated internal parameters A and A' of the two cameras, as well as the external parameters $[R, t]$ and $[R', t']$ of the line-structured-light plane, are shown in Table 1.

Table 1. Results of camera calibration parameters of left and right cameras.

Name	Solution Results
Internal External	$A = \begin{bmatrix} 1899.792 & 0 & 785.809 \\ 0 & 1898.065 & 621.232 \\ 0 & 0 & 1 \end{bmatrix}$
	$A' = \begin{bmatrix} 1904.880 & 0 & 804.499 \\ 0 & 1904.684 & 613.186 \\ 0 & 0 & 1 \end{bmatrix}$
External Parameters	$[R, t] = \begin{bmatrix} 0.877 & -0.236 & 0.418 & -52.677 \\ -0.064 & 0.806 & 0.588 & 8.064 \\ -0.476 & -0.543 & 0.692 & 253.306 \end{bmatrix}$
	$[R', t'] = \begin{bmatrix} 0.920 & 0.240 & -0.309 & -95.225 \\ -0.018 & 0.815 & 0.579 & -24.717 \\ 0.391 & -0.528 & 0.754 & 301.256 \end{bmatrix}$

In order to evaluate the calibration accuracy of the line-structured-light stereo camera system, and to verify the feasibility of the system, this paper proposes an analysis of the calibration errors of the cameras' internal parameters and the fitting degree of the line-structured-light plane. By using the calibration of the planar target, the cameras' internal and external parameters are obtained. The corner coordinates of the planar target in the world coordinate system are projected onto the images and compared with the corresponding corner coordinates in the images. The deviations of each image captured by the left and right cameras are shown in Figure 12. The overall average deviations are 0.0149 px and 0.0118 px, respectively.

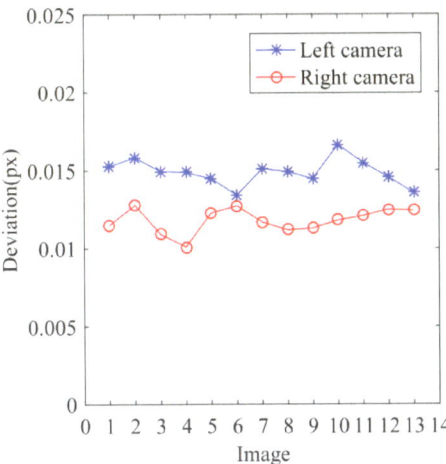

Figure 12. Camera calibration deviation.

In the coordinate systems of the left and right cameras, the distance deviations between the line-structured-light plane fitted using SVD decomposition and the feature points are shown in Figure 13, and only the edge points within the plane have relatively larger errors due to the quality of the projected line-structured light. The evaluation parameters for the fitting of the line-structured-light plane are shown in Table 2, where a determination coefficient close to 1 indicates a good fitting degree of the line-structured-light plane.

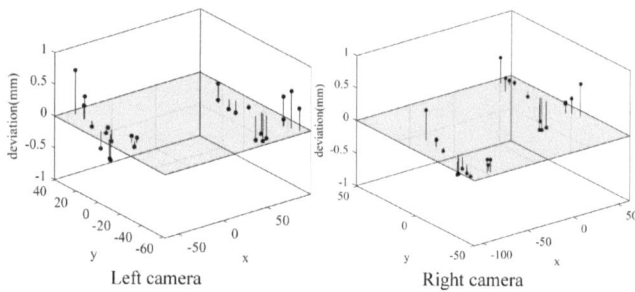

Figure 13. Analysis of fitting plane error.

Table 2. Fitting plane evaluation parameters.

	Coordinate System of the Left Camera	Coordinate System of the Right Camera
Sum of squared errors (SSE)	2.358	1.761
Coefficient of determination (R-square)	0.9999	0.9999
Standard deviation (RMSE)	0.3202	0.2767

4.3. Analysis of Rail Wear Measurement Accuracy

For the measurement of one section of the 60# steel rail at 20 different positions, the rail wear gauge, the standard rail-based 2D contour measurement and the proposed method in this paper were used. Among them, the cameras used in this experiment have a resolution of 1600 × 1200. The field of view of each camera is approximately 167 × 122 units, and the pixel accuracy is 0.1 mm/pixel. The measurement accuracy for rail wear using the gauge is 0.01 mm, which is one order of magnitude higher than the image accuracy. The vertical wear and side wear obtained based on the rail wear gauge measurement are shown in Table 3.

There was no obvious data fluctuation in the two groups of data. Therefore, the rail wear gauge measurement data are taken as the reference standard, and the measurement results obtained from the standard rail-based 2D contour measurement and the proposed method in this paper are compared with it. The measurement results are shown in Table 3.

Table 3 shows that compared to the measurement results of the rail wear gauge, the average absolute errors of vertical wear for the two methods are 0.038 mm and 0.009 mm, and the average absolute errors of the side wear measurements are 0.086 mm and 0.039 mm, respectively. The root mean square errors of the vertical wear measurements are 0.046 mm and 0.011 mm, and the root mean square errors of the side wear measurements are 0.097 mm and 0.048 mm, respectively. The proposed method in this paper exhibits smaller average absolute deviations and root mean square errors for both vertical and side wear measurements compared to the results obtained from the standard rail-based 2D contour measurement.

Furthermore, the measurements using the proposed method are closer to the standard measurements obtained from the rail wear gauge, as shown in Figures 14 and 15.

The method proposed in this paper for measuring the railhead contour, has the ability to correct measurement errors caused by random deviations in the measurement plane of the line-structured light. By bringing the measured steel rail's complete contour into a 3D space and comparing it with the standard 3D point cloud model of the steel rail, the wear can be accurately measured. This approach eliminates the influence of vibrations during the measurement process, and obtains more precise wear measurements.

Table 3. Results of wear measurement for 60 kg/m rail.

No	Results by Standard Rail Wear Gauge		Results by Standard 2D Profile				Results by the Proposed Method			
	Vertical Wear	Side Wear	Vertical Wear	Deviation	Side Wear	Deviation	Vertical Wear	Deviation	Side Wear	Deviation
1	0.020	−0.390	0.011	−0.009	−0.601	−0.211	0.021	0.001	−0.455	−0.065
2	0.020	−0.410	0.013	−0.007	−0.511	−0.101	0.017	−0.003	−0.402	0.008
3	0.060	−0.350	0.024	−0.036	−0.461	−0.111	0.065	0.005	−0.353	−0.003
4	0.070	−0.320	0.044	−0.026	−0.428	−0.108	0.062	−0.008	−0.305	0.015
5	0.110	−0.340	0.037	−0.073	−0.408	−0.068	0.090	−0.020	−0.350	−0.010
6	0.070	−0.300	0.033	−0.037	−0.428	−0.128	0.065	−0.005	−0.301	−0.001
7	0.060	−0.310	0.028	−0.032	−0.399	−0.089	0.045	−0.015	−0.286	0.024
8	0.080	−0.230	0.004	−0.076	−0.261	−0.031	0.076	−0.004	−0.173	0.057
9	0.110	−0.350	0.035	−0.075	−0.441	−0.091	0.104	−0.006	−0.340	0.010
10	0.060	−0.390	0.004	−0.056	−0.490	−0.100	0.048	−0.012	−0.305	0.085
11	0.140	−0.220	0.074	−0.066	−0.292	−0.072	0.108	−0.032	−0.244	−0.024
12	0.030	−0.260	0.004	−0.026	−0.365	−0.105	0.036	0.006	−0.264	−0.004
13	0.080	−0.240	0.039	−0.041	−0.296	−0.056	0.070	−0.010	−0.190	0.050
14	0.010	−0.430	0.001	−0.009	−0.474	−0.044	0.006	−0.004	−0.383	0.047
15	0.020	−0.440	0.001	−0.019	−0.469	−0.029	0.028	0.008	−0.374	0.066
16	0.050	−0.380	0.001	−0.049	−0.375	0.005	0.037	−0.013	−0.292	0.088
17	0.040	−0.210	0.004	−0.036	−0.248	−0.038	0.050	0.010	−0.177	0.033
18	0.030	−0.050	0.012	−0.018	−0.128	−0.078	0.020	−0.010	−0.002	0.048
19	0.050	−0.180	0.002	−0.048	−0.316	−0.136	0.055	0.005	−0.267	−0.087
20	0.060	−0.310	0.033	−0.027	−0.428	−0.118	0.056	−0.004	−0.361	−0.051
MAD (mm)				0.038		0.086		0.009		0.039
RMSE (mm)				0.046		0.097		0.011		0.048

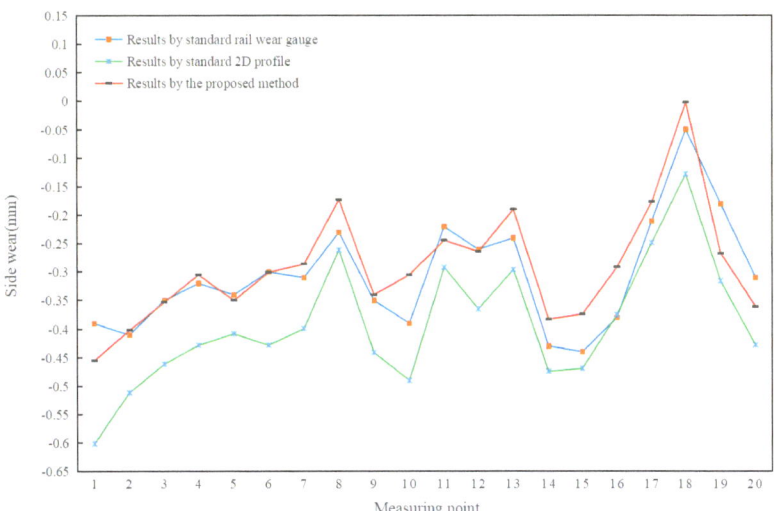

Figure 14. The measured values of side wear obtained from different methods.

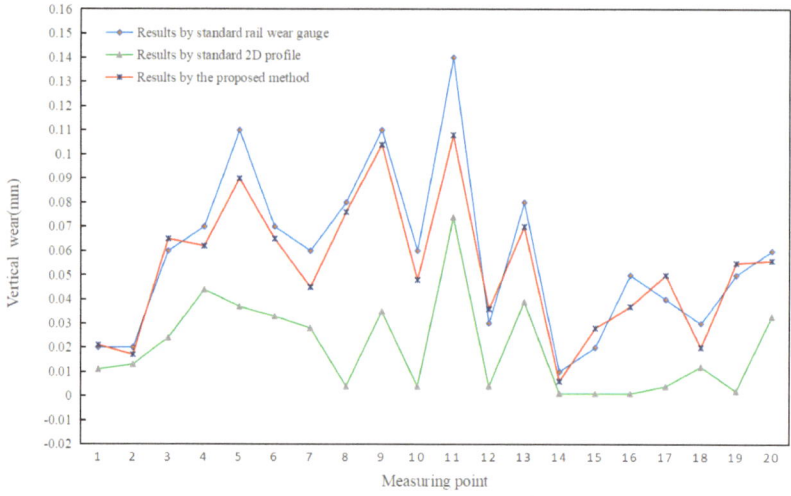

Figure 15. The measured values of vertical wear obtained from different methods.

5. Conclusions

In this paper, a full profile of rail cross-section measurement method based on line-structured light was established, and further, a coarse alignment and precise registration approach was proposed for measuring the railhead contour. The method involved comparing the measured rail contour with a three-dimensional point cloud model of a standard steel rail to obtain rail wear measurements and mitigate the influence of light plane deviations caused by vibrations during the measurement process. The experiments demonstrated the following conclusions: (1) The establishment of the binocular line-structured-light vision system model, with a camera's internal parameter calibration deviation of approximately 0.01px and a fitting degree of the line-structured-light plane reaching 0.9999, validated the feasibility of the binocular calibration method. (2) The proposed full profile of rail cross-section measurement method based on line-structured light and stereo vision achieved accurate measurement of the railhead contour in a two-step process. The on-site comparative measurement tests showed that the average absolute error in the vertical wear measurement obtained through this method was 0.009 mm, and the average absolute error in the side wear measurement was 0.039 mm. This measurement method effectively corrected measurement plane deviations and met the accuracy requirements for rail wear measurement.

Author Contributions: Writing—original draft preparation, J.L.; writing—review and editing, J.Z.; methodology and formal analysis, Z.M.; resources and data curation, H.Z.; data curation, S.Z. All authors have read and agreed to the published version of the manuscript.

Funding: This paper is supported by International Cooperation Project of Science and Technology Bureau of Chengdu (No. 2019-GH02-00051-HZ), Sichuan unmanned system and intelligent perception Engineering Laboratory Open Fund, and Research Fund of Chengdu University of information engineering, under Grant (No. WRXT2020-001, No. WRXT2020-002, No. WRXT2021-002 and No. KYTZ202142), and the Sichuan Science and Technology Program China, under Grant (No. 2022YFS0565); This paper is also supported by the Key R&D project of Science and Technology Department of Sichuan Province, under Grant (2023YFG0196 and 2023YFN0077), Science and Technology achievements transformation Project of Science and Technology Department of Sichuan Province, under Grant (2023JDZH0023), Sichuan Provincial Science and Technology Department, Youth Fund project, under Grant (2023NSFSC1429).

Data Availability Statement: Data is not available due to privacy or ethical restrictions.

Conflicts of Interest: The authors declare no conflict of interest.

References

1. Wang, C.; Zeng, J. Combination-Chord Measurement of Rail Corrugation Using Triple-Line Structured-Light Vision: Rectification and Optimization. *IEEE Trans. Intell. Transp. Syst.* **2021**, *22*, 7256–7265. [CrossRef]
2. Minbashi, N.; Bagheri, M.; Golroo, A.; Arasteh Khouy, I.; Ahmadi, A. Turnout degradation modelling using new inspection technologies: A literature review. In *Current Trends in Reliability, Availability, Maintainability and Safety: An Industry Perspective*; Springer: Cham, Switzerland, 2016; pp. 49–63.
3. Steinbuch, M.; Henselmans, R. Non-contact Measurement Machine for Freeform Optics. *Macromolecules* **2009**, *35*, 607–624.
4. Modjarrad A. Non-contact measurement using a laser scanning probe. In-Process Optical Measurements. *SPIE* **1989**, *1012*, 229–239.
5. Giri, P.; Kharkovsky, S. Detection of Surface Crack in Concrete Using Measurement Technique with Laser Displacement Sensor. *IEEE Trans. Instrum. Meas.* **2016**, *65*, 1951–1953. [CrossRef]
6. Alippi, C.; Casagrande, E.; Scotti, F.; Piuri, V. Composite real-time image processing for railways track profile measurement. *IEEE Trans. Instrum. Meas.* **2000**, *49*, 559–564. [CrossRef]
7. Ran, Y.; He, Q.; Feng, Q.; Cui, J. High-Accuracy On-Site Measurement of Wheel Tread Geometric Parameters by Line-Structured Light Vision Sensor. *IEEE Access* **2021**, *9*, 52590–52600. [CrossRef]
8. Chugui, Y.; Verkhoglyad, A.; Poleshchuk, A.; Korolkov, V.; Sysoev, E.; Zavyalov, P. 3D Optical Measuring Systems and Laser Technologies for Scientific and Industrial Applications. *Meas. Sci. Rev.* **2013**, *13*, 322–328. [CrossRef]
9. Guerrieri, M.; Parla, G.; Celauro, C. Digital image analysis technique for measuring steel rail defects and ballast gradation. *Meas. J. Int. Meas. Confed.* **2018**, *113*, 137–147. [CrossRef]
10. Liu, Z.; Sun, J.; Wang, H.; Zhang, G. Simple and fast rail wear measurement method based on structured light. *Opt. Lasers Eng.* **2011**, *49*, 1343–1351. [CrossRef]
11. Wang, C.; Liu, H.; Ma, Z.; Zeng, J. Dynamic inspection of rail wear via a three-step method: Auxiliary plane establishment, self-calibration, and projecting. *IEEE Access* **2018**, *6*, 36143–36154. [CrossRef]
12. Wang, C.; Li, Y.; Ma, Z.; Zeng, J.; Jin, T.; Liu, H. Distortion Rectifying for Dynamically Measuring Rail Profile Based on Self-Calibration of Multiline Structured Light. *IEEE Trans. Instrum. Meas.* **2018**, *67*, 678–689. [CrossRef]
13. Sun, J.; Liu, Z.; Zhao, Y.; Liu, Q.; Zhang, G. Motion deviation rectifying method of dynamically measuring rail wear based on multi-line structured-light vision. *Opt. Laser Technol.* **2013**, *50*, 25–32. [CrossRef]
14. Wang, C.; Ma, Z.; Li, Y.; Zeng, J.; Jin, T.; Liu, H. Deviation rectification for dynamic measurement of rail wear based on coordinate sets projection. *Meas. Sci. Technol.* **2017**, *28*, 105203. [CrossRef]
15. Zhan, D.; Yu, L.; Xiao, J.; Lu, M. Study on dynamic matching algorithm in inspection of full cross-section of rail profile. *Tiedao Xuebao J. China Railw. Soc.* **2015**, *37*, 71–77.
16. Zhan, D.; Yu, L.; Xiao, J.; Chen, T. Study on High-accuracy Vision Measurement Approach for Dynamic Inspection of Full Cross-sectional Rail Profile. *J. China Railw. Soc.* **2015**, *37*, 96–106.
17. Yang, Y.; Liu, L.; Yi, B.; Chen, F. An accurate and fast method to inspect rail wear based on revised global registration. *IEEE Access* **2018**, *6*, 57267–57278. [CrossRef]
18. Zhang, Z.Y. A flexible new technique for camera calibration. *IEEE Trans. Pattern Anal. Mach. Intell.* **2000**, *22*, 1330–1334. [CrossRef]
19. Lucchese, L.; Mitra, S.K. Using saddle points for subpixel feature detection in camera calibration targets. In Proceedings of the Asia-Pacific Conference on Circuits and Systems, Denpasar, Indonesia, 28–31 October 2002; pp. 191–195.
20. Zhang, G.J.; He, J.J.; Yang, X.M. Calibrating camera radial distortion with cross-ratio invariability. *Opt. Laser Technol.* **2003**, *35*, 457–461. [CrossRef]
21. Xu, G. *Image Based Modelling and Rendering*, 1st ed.; Wuhan University Press: Wuhan, China, 2006.
22. Steger, C. An unbiased detector of curvilinear structures. *IEEE Trans. Pattern Anal. Mach. Intell.* **1998**, *20*, 113–125. [CrossRef]
23. Zhai, H.; Ma, Z. Detection algorithm of rail surface defects based on multifeature saliency fusion method. *Sens. Rev.* **2022**, *42*, 402–411. [CrossRef]
24. Yang, S.; Liu, C. Discrete modeling and calculation of traction return-current network for 400 km/h high-speed railway. *Proc. Inst. Mech. Eng. Part F J. Rail Rapid Transit* **2023**, *237*, 445–457. [CrossRef]
25. Turk, G. *Generating Random Points in Triangles*; Elsevier Inc.: Amsterdam, The Netherlands, 1990; pp. 24–28.
26. Jiang, Y.; Niu, G. Rail Local Damage Detection based on Recursive Frequency-domain Envelope Tracking Filter and Rail Impact Index. In Proceedings of the 2022 Global Reliability and Prognostics and Health Management (PHM-Yantai), Yantai, China, 13–16 October 2022; pp. 1–7.
27. Zang, L.; Wang, H.; Han, Q.; Fang, Y.; Wang, S.; Wang, N.; Li, G.; Ren, S. A Laser Plane Attitude Evaluation Method for Rail Profile Measurement Sensors. *Sensors* **2023**, *23*, 4586.

Disclaimer/Publisher's Note: The statements, opinions and data contained in all publications are solely those of the individual author(s) and contributor(s) and not of MDPI and/or the editor(s). MDPI and/or the editor(s) disclaim responsibility for any injury to people or property resulting from any ideas, methods, instructions or products referred to in the content.

Article

A Workpiece-Dense Scene Object Detection Method Based on Improved YOLOv5

Jiajia Liu [1], Shun Zhang [1], Zhongli Ma [1,*], Yuehan Zeng [1] and Xueyin Liu [2]

[1] College of Automation, Chengdu University of Information Technology, Chengdu 610255, China; liujj@cuit.edu.cn (J.L.); zchuangye.zs@gmail.com (S.Z.); cuitno3@gmail.com (Y.Z.)
[2] Sichuan Machinery Research and Design Institute, Chengdu 610063, China; liuxueyin@ccjys.com
* Correspondence: mazl@cuit.edu.cn

Abstract: Aiming at the problem of detection difficulties caused by the characteristics of high similarity and disorderly arrangement of workpieces in dense scenes of industrial production lines, this paper proposes a workpiece detection method based on improved YOLOv5, which embeds a coordinate attention mechanism in the feature extraction network to enhance the network's focus on important features and enhance the model's ability to pinpoint targets. The pooling structure of the space pyramid has been replaced, which reduces the amount of calculation and further improves the running speed. A weighted bidirectional feature pyramid is introduced in the feature fusion network to realize efficient bidirectional cross-scale connection and weighted feature fusion, and improve the detection ability of small targets and dense targets. The SIoU loss function is used to improve the training speed and further improve the detection performance of the model. The average accuracy of the improved model on the self-built artifact dataset is improved by 5% compared with the original model and the number of model parameters is 14.6MB, which is only 0.5MB higher than the original model. It is proved that the improved model has the characteristics of high detection accuracy, strong robustness and light weight.

Keywords: workpiece detection; YOLOv5s; attention mechanism feature fusion; loss function

Citation: Liu, J.; Zhang, S.; Ma, Z.; Zeng, Y.; Liu, X. A Workpiece-Dense Scene Object Detection Method Based on Improved YOLOv5. *Electronics* 2023, *12*, 2966. https://doi.org/10.3390/electronics12132966

Academic Editor: Eva Cernadas

Received: 28 May 2023
Revised: 28 June 2023
Accepted: 4 July 2023
Published: 5 July 2023

Copyright: © 2023 by the authors. Licensee MDPI, Basel, Switzerland. This article is an open access article distributed under the terms and conditions of the Creative Commons Attribution (CC BY) license (https://creativecommons.org/licenses/by/4.0/).

1. Introduction

Workpiece sorting is a common task in manufacturing and industrial production. Due to its high repeatability, workpiece sorting has become one of the important application scenarios of industrial robots [1]. Traditional sorting robots are pre-programmed. Although they can carry out repetitive actions, such robots cannot be adjusted according to the actual situation and must strictly set the location of the sorting workpiece. Therefore, the robots lack the ability of independent identification and have low requirements for object detection technology, leading to an increase in the error rate and lower production efficiency [2]. Hence, in the automatic production line, improving the speed and accuracy of workpiece positioning and identification has important research significance for sorting robots. However, the problem of small and dense workpieces and workpieces blocking each other in industrial automation scenarios poses a greater challenge for workpiece inspection.

The disadvantages of the traditional object detection method are that it requires a large amount of manpower to extract effective features, the model lacks generalization ability when the target features change, and the detection algorithm of single feature or multiple features loses most of the feature information of the object, which cannot be applied to the actual industrial detection scene. Liu et al. [3] used the improved SURF-FREAK algorithm to recognize and grasp the workpiece. The algorithm adopted the improved SIFT for feature extraction but the experimental results of the algorithm were poor under complex illumination conditions. Jiang et al. [4] used the contour Hu moment invariant characteristic to match and recognize the workpiece image but this algorithm needs to manually design the feature extraction algorithm, which has some shortcomings in universality. In recent years, deep learning has been widely applied in object detection. Luigi Bibbo et al. [5] have developed a facial expression recognition system based on the Ensemble AI model that could help improve healthcare. Wang et al. [6] proposed the Faster R-CNN algorithm for identification and classification of small automotive parts under complex working conditions, which can accurately detect scattered parts, but there is a problem of missed detection for mutually occluded parts. Gong et al. [7] applied the YOLOv3 algorithm to the part recognition model, which solved the problem that it was difficult for stacked board parts to identify the blocked parts and improved the detection accuracy. However, when the workpiece was densely stacked, false detection and missed detection would also be caused. In most production lines, there are many kinds and irregular quantities of workpieces and they are placed randomly, which requires that the designed object detection algorithm and network not only have good robustness for workpiece detection in complex situations, but also have strong detection ability for dense small targets, so as to reduce the rate of missed detection.

In this paper, aiming at the problem that it is difficult to identify a large number of small targets in the industrial production line due to the dense workpieces, we compare the widely used object detection algorithms at present, and choose to improve the YOLOv5 algorithm with both speed and precision. The detection effect of the original YOLOv5 model is slightly insufficient in the detection of small targets, which are easy to miss, and false detection. Moreover, it has a large positioning error when there are many targets and dense distribution. To solve the above problems, a workpiece detection method based on improved YOLOv5 is proposed in this paper. Firstly, the coordinate attention mechanism is embedded in the backbone feature extraction network to make the network pay more attention to the region of interest and increase the feature extraction capability of the network. Secondly, the space pyramid pool structure is replaced to reduce the computation and improve the running speed. Secondly, BiFPN is used as the feature fusion network to enhance the feature fusion capability of the network, so that the location information and semantic information are fully integrated. Finally, the SIoU loss function is used to replace the CIoU loss function in the original model to accelerate the training speed and increase the convergence of the network. The comparison of multiple existing object detection algorithms shows that the improved algorithm in this paper has a higher detection accuracy for dense workpieces and can achieve accurate detection effects.

2. Workpiece Detection Algorithm Based on the Improved YOLOv5

2.1. YOLOv5 Object Detection Algorithm

YOLOv5 has high detection accuracy and speed, more flexible network deployment, and is widely used in real-time object detection research [8].

The network structure of YOLOv5 is shown in Figure 1, which is composed of the backbone, neck and head. The backbone mainly performs feature extraction and is composed of structures such as the Focus layer, CBS layer, C3 layer, SPP layer [9] and Bottleneck layer. The neck network adopts the structure of FPN (Feature Pyramid Network) [10] + PAN (Path Aggregation Network) [11], which can fuse shallow position features and deep semantic features of images, and enhance the feature fusion capability of the network, and generate feature maps of different sizes. The head part obtains the feature maps extracted from the backbone or fused from the neck to obtain the location and class of the detected targets.

As shown in Figure 2, the recovery and reuse of workpieces has become increasingly important in industry [12], for example, automobile workpiece recycling, including screws, bearings, bolts, etc. These parts come from a variety of different automobile brands and models, and are in large and disorganized quantities, making the identification and classification of the parts in recycling extremely time-consuming and labor-intensive.

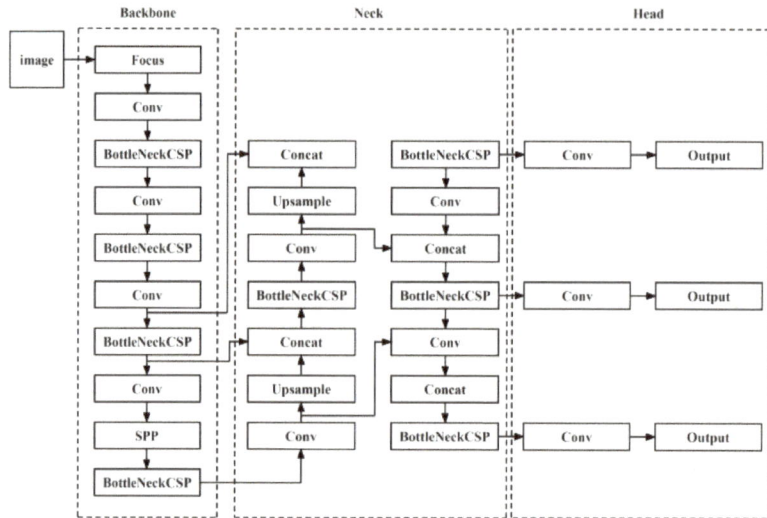

Figure 1. YOLOv5 network structure.

Figure 2. Workpiece sorting robot operation diagram.

In order to improve efficiency and accuracy, an efficient object detection algorithm is needed to identify and classify workpieces. However, the YOLOv5 model used has poor generalization for dense and small volume workpieces under different illumination; it is not suitable for practical application, so it has to be improved.

2.2. Improvements to the YOLOv5 Model

In order to solve the problem that it is difficult to accurately identify a large number of small targets formed by dense workpieces, the following improvements are made to the YOLOv5 model in this paper.

1. The coordinate attention mechanism is integrated into the backbone feature extraction network to increase the network's interest in important features and improve the feature extraction capability of the network.
2. The SPP in the original model is improved to SimSPPF, which reduces the computation and increases the running speed.
3. BiFPN structure is used for cross-layer feature fusion, which fully combines semantic information and location information to enhance the feature fusion capability of the network.

4. The CIoU loss function in the original model is improved to the SIoU loss function, and the direction matching between the real box and the predicted box is fully considered to improve the convergence performance of the model.

2.2.1. Coordinate Attention Mechanism

In view of the density and small size of some parts in industrial sorting, coordinate attention (CA) was introduced into the feature extraction network of YOLOv5 [13], which could effectively extract the feature information of small and dense targets of the workpiece and further improve the accuracy of detection.

Different from most attention mechanisms [14,15], which use maximum pooling or average pooling to process channels, the coordinate attention mechanism introduced in this paper adds location information to channel attention; the mobile network can participate in a larger area under the premise of avoiding a large number of calculations, so as to avoid the loss of location information. The introduced attention mechanism decomposes channel attention into two parallel one-dimensional feature coding processes, which aggregate features in two directions: one direction to obtain remote dependence, the other direction to retain accurate location information, and then encode the generated feature maps to form a pair of direction-aware and position-sensitive feature maps. The structure of the introduced CA module is shown in Figure 3, which uses coordinate information embedding and coordinate attention to generate the relationship between the channel and the position of the captured features.

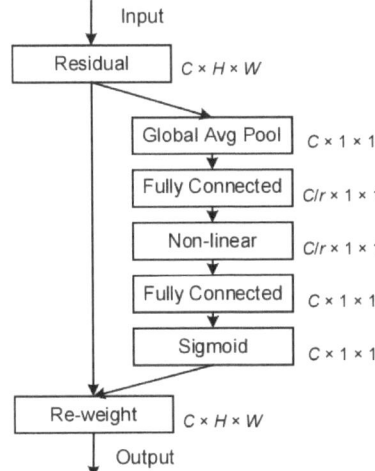

Figure 3. CA module structure.

In order to obtain the attention in the horizontal and vertical directions of the image and encode the exact position information, CA first divides the input feature graph x into horizontal $x_c(h,i)$ and vertical $x_c(i,w)$ directions for global averaging pooling. The two directions of the output $z_c^h(h)$ at the height h of channel c and the output $z_c^w(w)$ at the width w of channel are obtained.

$$z_c^h(h) = \frac{1}{W} \sum_{i=0}^{W} | x_c(h,i) \tag{1}$$

$$z_c^w(w) = \frac{1}{H} \sum_{j=0}^{H} | x_c(j,w) \tag{2}$$

Next, the horizontal feature graph z^h and vertical feature graph z^w obtained from the global receptive field are stitched together, and then they are sent into the shared 1×1 convolution transform F_1 to reduce their dimensions to the original c/r, and then the batch normalized feature graphs are sent into the nonlinear activation function δ to get the shaped $1 \times (W + H) \times c/r$ feature graph f.

$$f = \delta(F_1(|z^h, z^w|)) \quad (3)$$

Then, the feature graph f is divided into two feature vectors f^h and f^w according to the original horizontal and vertical directions, and two 1×1 convolution transform F_h and F_w, respectively, to get the feature graph with the same number of channels. After sigmoid activation function, the attention weight g^h of the feature graph in the horizontal direction and the attention weight g^w in the vertical direction are obtained.

$$g^h = \sigma(F_h()f^h) \quad (4)$$
$$g^w = \sigma(F_w()f^w) \quad (5)$$

Finally, the feature graph with attention weights in both horizontal and vertical directions will be obtained through multiplication weighting on the original feature graph.

$$y_c(i,j) = x_c(i,j) \times g_h^c \times g_c^w(j) \quad (6)$$

The CA module is a novel attention mechanism for mobile networks. It has the characteristics of being simple, flexible, and plug and play, which can improve the accuracy of the network without any extra computing overhead.

2.2.2. Simple and Fast Space Pyramid Pool

In traditional convolutional neural networks, the size of the input image must be fixed. However, in practical applications, the size of the input image is often uncertain, while the spatial pyramid pooling (SPP) [16] can flexibly obtain the output of any available dimension by increasing the number of layers of the feature pyramid or changing the size of the window. Its structure is shown in Figure 4. If the convolutional feature map of size (w, h) is input, the spatial pyramid of the first layer uses a 4×4 scale to divide the feature map into 16 pieces and the size of each piece is $(w/4, h/4)$. The second layer uses a 2×2 scale to divide the feature map into four blocks; the size of each is $(w/2, h/2)$. The third layer directly takes the whole feature map as a block, carries on the feature extraction operation and finally gets the feature vector of $21 = 16 + 4 + 1$ dimensions. SPP can not only solve the problem of inconsistent input image size, but also carry out multi-angle feature extraction and reaggregation of the feature map after convolution and pooling. SPP can significantly improve model performance and detection accuracy when used for target detection, while reducing the risk of over-fitting.

SimSPPF uses a cascade of multiple small-sized pooling kernels instead of a single large-sized pooling kernel in the SPP module while increasing the perceptual field of view. Specifically, it serial processing inputs through multiple maximum pooling layers of 5×5 size, replacing a 9×9 convolution operation with two 5×5 convolution operations and a 13×13 convolution operation with three 5×5 convolution operations. This design can not only retain the original function, but also reduce the amount of computation, improve the running speed and make the SimSPPF structure more efficient. The specific structure of SimSPPF is shown in Figure 5.

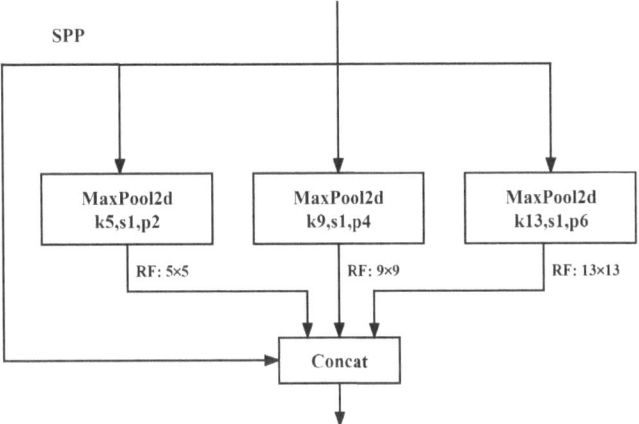

Figure 4. SPP structure diagram.

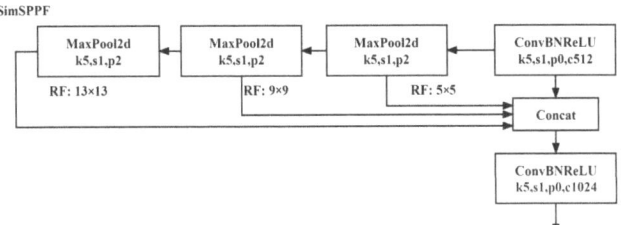

Figure 5. Structure diagram of SimSPPF.

2.2.3. Bidirectional Feature Pyramid

The purpose of the feature pyramid structure FPN is to fuse shallow position information and deep semantic information, as shown in Figure 6a. The original pyramid structure adopts the information fusion from top to bottom, which improves the information extraction ability of the network, but the fusion process will also lead to the loss of information. YOLOv5 adopts PANet structure, as shown in Figure 6b. Based on the idea of an FPN image feature pyramid, PANet not only carries out feature fusion from top to bottom but also adds feature fusion from bottom to top, so as to reduce information loss and achieve good detection results. However, the number of parameters in network training is increased. For workpiece detection, the original model has the problem of low detection accuracy due to the presence of more small target objects. Bidirectional Feature Pyramid Network (BiFPN) [17], as shown in Figure 6c, enhances the information extraction capability of the network, so that low-level position information can better combine with high-level semantic information, thus further improving the detection performance of the network for targets. The PANet structure of the original network is only stacked on the channel, while the BiFPN takes the weight information into account and implements bidirectional cross-scale feature fusion.

In this paper, BiFPN is integrated into the YOLOv5 structure to reduce the loss of feature information, improve the extraction efficiency of position information and enhance the detection ability of the network for small targets. Meanwhile, this improvement hardly increases the cost and has little impact on the size of model parameters.

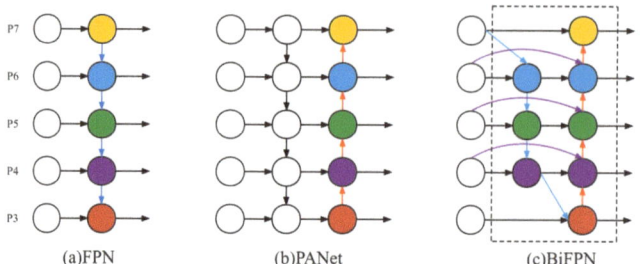

Figure 6. Schematic diagram of FPN, PANet and BiFPN structures.

2.2.4. SIoU Loss Function

The traditional object detection loss function relies on the aggregation of boundary box regression indicators [18], such as the distance between the predicted box and the real box, and the overlap area and the aspect ratio, but it ignores the direction of the mismatch between the desired real box and the predicted box. This deficiency leads to a slow convergence rate and correspondingly low efficiency of the model. For this SIoU loss function [19], the vector angle between the real box and the predicted box is introduced, and the angle, distance, shape and intersection ratio losses are redefined.

1. Angle cost

   The model first makes predictions on either the X or Y axes, and then approximates along the correlation axis. To achieve this, the convergence process will first attempt to minimize the angle, so the angle costing formula is introduced and defined.

$$\Lambda = 1 - 2 * \sin^2\left(\arcsin(x) - \frac{\Pi}{4}\right) \tag{7}$$

2. Distance cost

   Angle cost is introduced into distance cost and distance cost is redefined.

$$\Delta = \sum_{t=x}^{y}(1 - e^{-\gamma \rho t}) \tag{8}$$

3. Shape cost

   Shape cost is defined.

$$\Omega = \sum_{t=w}^{h}(1 - e^{-w_t})^\theta \tag{9}$$

4. Cross and compare costs

   The crossover cost is defined.

$$L_{IoUCost} = 1 - IoU \tag{10}$$

Finally, the SIoU loss function is defined.

$$L_{box} = 1 - IoU + \frac{\Delta + \Omega}{2} \tag{11}$$

3. Experimental Research and Result Analysis

3.1. Workpiece Dataset Establishment

3.1.1. Workpiece Data Acquisition

The sample types are common parts (screws, nuts, washers and wire screw sleeves) in industrial sorting. Taking into full account the interference brought by the external environment, different numbers and types of workpieces are randomly placed for collection in the actual environment, so as to improve the robustness of the model. The size of the image is uniformly processed into 640 × 480; part of the image dataset is shown in Figure 7.

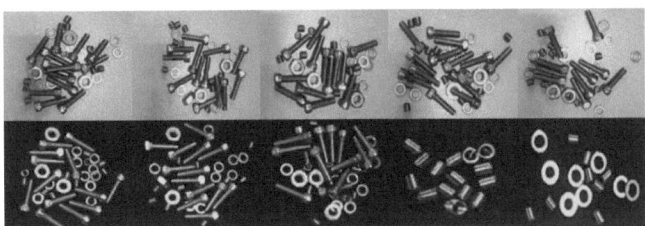

Figure 7. Part of image dataset sample.

In the training process of the deep learning network model, it is necessary to obtain the information of the target in the image accurately. In this paper, LabelImg is used to mark the image. After marking, the number, type and four vertex positions of the target can be obtained, and the corresponding .xml format tag file can be generated. The file contains the category, length, width and height information of the marked target, which is convenient for decoding and parsing.

3.1.2. Data Enhancement

A total of 1000 pictures were collected in this paper. In order to enrich the dataset, data enhancement strategies such as horizontal flip, vertical flip, cropping, affine transform, Gaussian blur, translation, adaptive Gaussian noise and brightness change were randomly introduced for the scenes of workpiece contamination, motion blur and brightness transformation in industrial sorting. And the above data enhancement strategies are randomly combined to process the training samples. After processing, the number of datasets increased to 18,000. Some random data enhancement samples are shown in Figure 8. The training set, test set and verification set were divided in a ratio of 8:1:1.

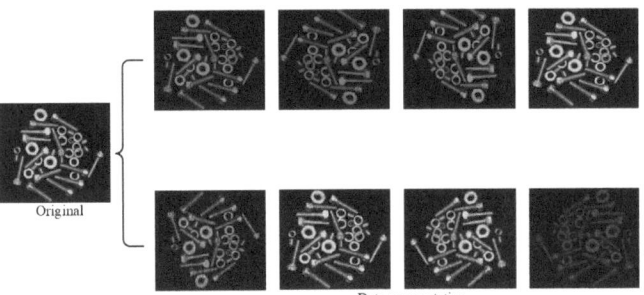

Figure 8. A sample of partial random data enhancement.

Figure 9 shows the visualization analysis results after dataset enhancement, where Figure 9a represents the distribution of object classes in the dataset, Figure 9b represents the distribution of object sizes, and horizontal and vertical represent the width and height of objects. It can be seen that the size distribution of small targets in the dataset is concentrated and occupies a large proportion.

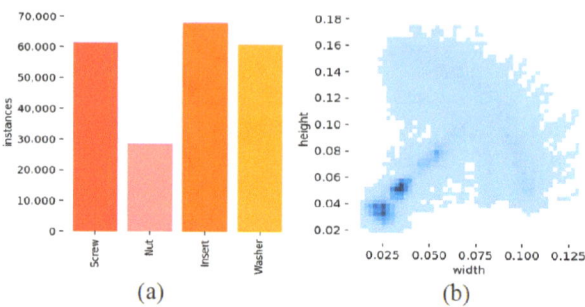

Figure 9. Data and analysis. (**a**) category distribution of objects in the data set; (**b**) size distribution of objects.

3.2. Experimental Environment and Evaluation Indicators

3.2.1. Setting the Experimental Environment and Parameters

The CPU model of the computer used in the experiment is i9-10900k, the GPU model is NVIDI A RTX3080 and the video memory size is 10 GB. The operating system is windows11 and the deep learning frame is Pytorch. In the comparison experiment of object detection algorithms, all algorithms are trained with the same dataset and the same parameter. Settings are at the same stage to ensure the comparability of experimental results. In the training process, the learning rate was set as 0.01, the momentum gradient descent algorithm was adopted for optimization, the momentum parameter was 0.937, the batch of each iteration was 16, the weight attenuation coefficient was 0.0005 and the number of iterations was uniformly set to 300.

3.2.2. Evaluation Index

In this paper, evaluation indexes such as recall, precision, AP (average precision) and mAP (mean average precision) were used to verify the accuracy of the model.

The precision rate refers to the probability that all predicted positive samples are actually positive samples, which can be calculated by

$$Precision = \frac{TP}{TP+FP} \tag{12}$$

The recall rate represents the probability of being predicted as a positive sample in the actual positive sample, calculated by

$$Recall = \frac{TP}{TP+FN} \tag{13}$$

The average accuracy refers to the area under a curve drawn with the recall rate as the axis and the accuracy rate as the axis, given by

$$AP = \int_0^1 p(r)dr \tag{14}$$

where p represents the accuracy rate, r represents the recall rate and the larger the area surrounded by the PR curve the higher the average accuracy.

The mean average precision represents the average precision of all categories in the dataset, which can reflect the accuracy and robustness of the model in target detection of different categories.

$$mAP = \frac{1}{m}\sum_{i=1}^{m} AP_i \tag{15}$$

3.3. Experimental Research

3.3.1. Contrast Experiment

Comparison experiments are conducted to better demonstrate the advantages of the improved model. In this experiment, the performance of Ours-YOLOv5 model, Faster-RCNN [20], SSD [21] and YOLOv5s model was compared on the self-built workpiece dataset. Table 1 shows the comparison results of each model in mAP@0.5, weight size, parameter number and reasoning time. In addition, Figure 10 shows the curve comparison of mAP@0.5.

Table 1. Comparison of experimental results.

Model	Weight/MB	mAP@0.5/%	Params/10^6	Inference/ms
SSD	100.3	77.8	23.7	123
Faster-RCNN	159	84.6	136.0	207
YOLOv5s	14.1	89.3	7.0	12
Ours-YOLOv5	14.6	94.3 (↑ 5.0)	7.1	13

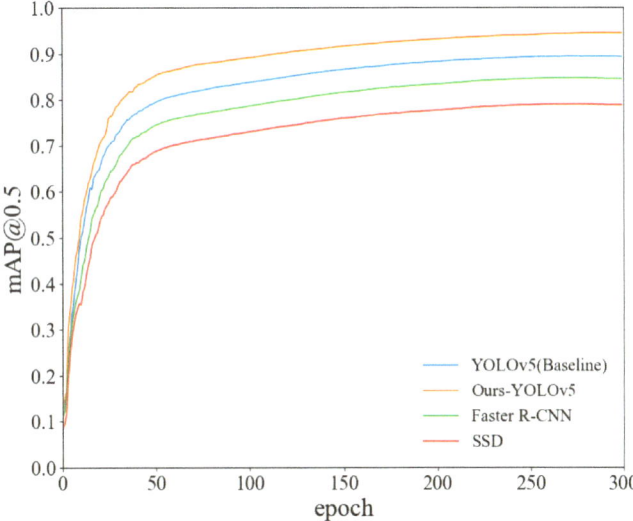

Figure 10. mAP@0.5 curve comparison.

By comparing the experimental results of different algorithm models in Table 1 and Figure 10, it can be seen that the model proposed in this paper has the highest detection accuracy compared with other mainstream models in the self-built dataset. Compared with the two-stage Faster-RCNN and first-stage SSD, the YOLOv5s model is a lightweight network model, while the improved model Ours-YOLOv5 proposed in this paper has a weight only 0.5 MB higher than that of YOLOv5s and 5.0% higher than that of YOLOv5s in mAP@0.5. Moreover, the reasoning speed is similar. The improved model in this paper has the highest detection accuracy while maintaining light weight and the original detection speed at the same time. Compared with Faster-RCNN, the average duration of reasoning video per frame is 194 ms faster and the overall performance is relatively outstanding, thus proving the superiority of the performance of Ours-YOLOv5 proposed in this paper.

In order to more intuitively evaluate the performance of the improved model proposed in this paper, Figure 11 shows the comparison of the detection effect of the model of Faster-RCNN, SSD and Ours-YOLOv5 in the actual scene. As can be seen from the figure, the Ours-YOLOv5 model has the best detection effect without missing or false detection, while the Faster-RCNN and SSD models have multiple missing and false detections.

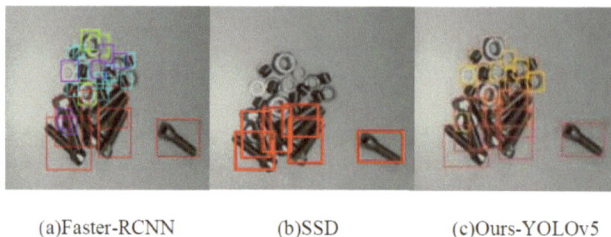

(a)Faster-RCNN (b)SSD (c)Ours-YOLOv5

Figure 11. Comparison of different model detection results.

Next, the detection effects of the YOLOv5s model and Ours-YOLOv5 model in different scenarios are compared, as shown in Figure 12a; the figure represents the detection of occluded targets; the left figure is the detection result of the YOLOv5s model; the white circle is the false detection target in the left figure; the right figure is the detection result of the Ours-YOLOv5 model. It can be seen that, in the white circle, parts of nuts were mistakenly detected in the left figure, while in the right figure they were successfully detected. Figure 12b shows the detection of cross-dense targets. In the left picture, when screws and nuts overlap, the original YOLOv5s model produces false detection, while, in the right picture, the improved model detects normally. Figure 12c shows the detection of small targets in a scene of strong illumination. The gasket was not identified in the left image due to the influence of illumination, while in the right image it was accurately identified successfully. To sum up, compared with the original YOLOv5s model, the improved Ours-YOLOv5 shows advantages in terms of performance, but the YOLOv5s model has poor performance in complex and diverse detection scenes, and there are cases of missing and false detection in the detection of small targets and dense targets. The Ours-YOLOv5 model has a better detection effect on small targets and dense targets, and has better robustness to different scenes, thus showing superior performance and more accurate positioning accuracy.

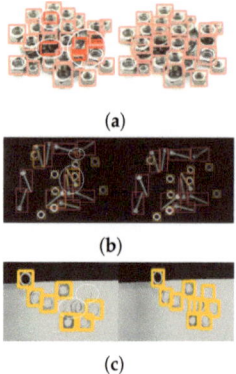

(a)

(b)

(c)

Figure 12. Comparison of test results before and after improvement. (**a**) Detection of occluded targets. (**b**) Detection of intersecting dense targets. (**c**) Detection of strong light scenes.

3.3.2. Ablation Experiment

The ablation experiment was conducted to verify the optimization effects of each improved module. The experimental results are shown in Table 2, where AAM represents adding an attention mechanism to the backbone network, RSP represents replacing the spatial pyramid pool structure, MFP represents modifying the feature pyramid structure and MTF represents modifying the loss function. Models 1 to 4 correspond to the addition of the AAM, RSP, MFP and MTF modules. Figure 13 shows the comparison of mAP@0.5 curves of the ablation experiment. All the improvements are combined into the model. The improved model is 5% higher than the original model mAP@0.5, and the detection of small targets and dense targets is greatly improved.

Table 2. Ablation experiment comparison results.

Model	AAM	RSP	MFP	MTF	mAP@0.5/%
YOLOv5s	×	×	×	×	89.3
Model 1	√	×	×	×	91.2 (↑1.9)
Model 2	×	√	×	×	90.1 (↑0.8)
Model 3	×	×	√	×	91.5 (↑2.2)
Model 4	×	×	×	√	91.0 (↑1.7)
Ours-YOLOv5	√	√	√	√	94.3 (↑5.0)

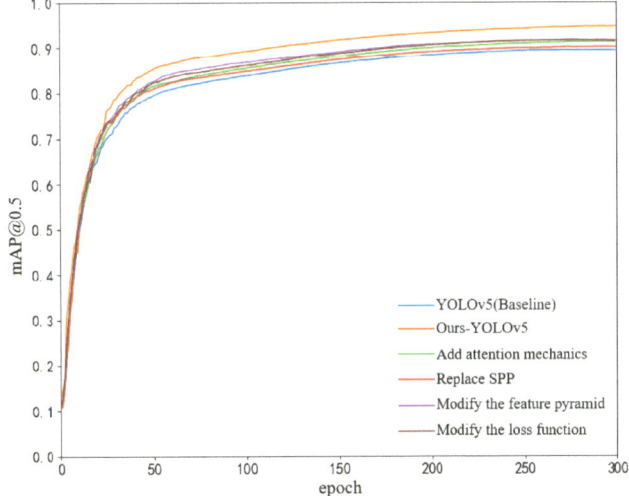

Figure 13. Ablation experiment mAP@0.5 curve comparison.

1. Analysis of the model test of increased attention mechanism

   In this paper, the CA module is added to the backbone network after feature extraction, so that it has clearer low-level contour information and coordinate information but also contains rich high-level semantic information. It can not only ensure the integrity of the feature information, but also improve the information expression ability of the feature map. According to the data in Table 2, it can be found that the index of mAP@0.5 of the model with the introduction of the attention mechanism is 1.9% higher than that of the original model, which indicates that adding the attention mechanism after the backbone network can effectively enhance the feature information.

   The accuracy rate–recall curve of the model introduced with the attention mechanism and the original YOLOv5s model on the self-built dataset is shown in Figure 14. In Figure 14a on the left, the area surrounded by the YOLOv5s blue curve is smaller than that surrounded by the axes, while in Figure 14b on the right, the area surrounded by the YOLOv5s-CA blue curve is larger than that surrounded by the axes, indicating that the classification performance of the model with the attention mechanism on the self-built dataset is improved compared with that of the YOLOv5s model.

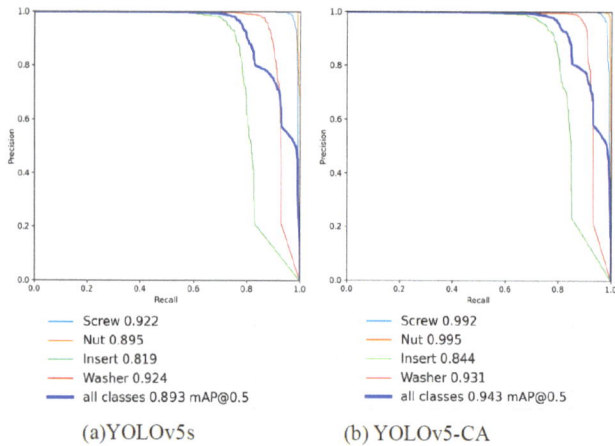

Figure 14. PR curve comparison.

Figure 15 shows the comparison of detection effects between the model with attention mechanism proposed in this paper and the YOLOv5s model. It can be seen that some wire sleeves are very small and dense, and the YOLOv5s model fails to correctly detect the targets and produces some false detections, while the YOLOv5-CA model can successfully detect these targets, indicating that it has become more accurate in the detection of small targets and dense targets after the introduction of the attention mechanism.

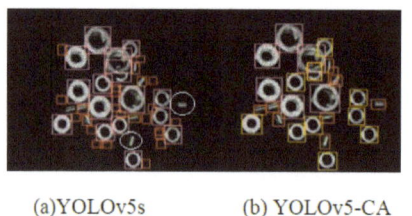

(a)YOLOv5s   (b) YOLOv5-CA

Figure 15. Test performance comparison.

2. Improved spatial pyramid pool model test analysis

In this paper, SPP in YOLOv5 was replaced by SimSPPF to increase the receptive field and uses multiple small-size pooling kernel cascades instead of a single large-size pooling kernel. Table 3 shows the comparison of the parameters of SPP and SimSPPF. Compared with SPP, the number of parameters and the amount of computation for SimSPPF decreased.

Table 3. Parameter comparison 1.

Model	Params/10^6	GFLOPs
SPP	7,225,885	16.5
SimSPPF	7,030,417	16.0

According to Table 2, the improved spatial pyramid pool model mAP@0.5 has an improvement of 0.8% over the original. The models configured with YOLOv5 and YOLOv5+simSPPF were, respectively, subjected to 50 times of reasoning and a comparison test of 100 images. The experimental comparison index was reasoning time, which could reflect the speed of image reasoning by the image processing module.

Figure 16 shows the curve comparison of reasoning time. It can be seen that the improved spatial pyramid pool model reasoning was faster than the original model. This proves that, while retaining the original function, SimSPPF reduces the amount of computation, further improving the speed and efficiency of operation.

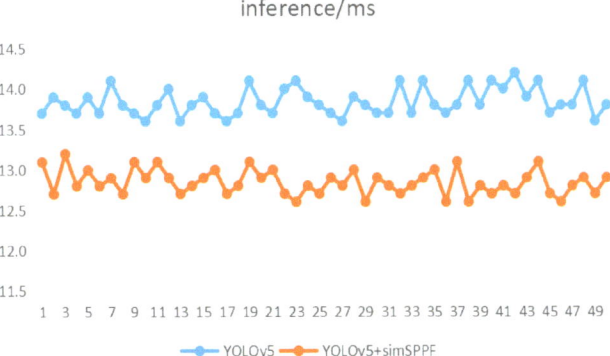

Figure 16. Inference time curve comparison plot.

3. Improved feature pyramid model test analysis

In order to verify the performance of BiFPN added in this paper, the number of model parameters, model weight, and mAP@0.5 of FPN, PANet and BiFPN in the mainstream feature pyramid network are compared. The results are shown in Table 4. It can be seen that the detection accuracy of the FPN network in the top-down single-order direction is not high. Adding the bottom-up path on the basis of FPN improves the detection performance of the PANet network; adding the cross-layer BiFPN network on the basis of PANet has the best detection performance; mAP@0.5 increased by 2.2% compared with PANet. At the same time, the number of parameters and the weight of the BiFPN network do not increase greatly, which proves that it enhances the information extraction ability of the network, so that the low level of location information can better combine with the high level of semantic information.

Table 4. Parameter comparison 2.

Model	Params/10^6	Weight/MB	mAP@0.5/%
FPN	6.2	13.2	87.4
PANet	7.0	14.0	89.3
BiFPN	7.1	14.6	94.3

Figure 17 shows the comparison between the test effect of the improved feature pyramid model and the original model. It can be seen that the improved feature pyramid model has a better detection effect on small targets and less false detection. Therefore, it is proved that the BiFPN can extract position information more fully, reduce the loss of feature information and increase the ability of the network to detect small targets.

(a)Yolov5s   (b)YOLOv5-Bi FPN

Figure 17. Comparison of test effects.

4. Improved loss function model test analysis

In this paper, the SIoU loss function is used to replace the CIoU loss function in the original model. According to Table 2, after using the SIoU loss function, mAP@0.5 improves by 1.7% compared with using CIoU. Meanwhile, Figure 18 shows the comparison of loss curves before and after the improvement of the loss function. After the improvement, the convergence speed of the model is faster, the loss value is gradually reduced and the convergence ability is enhanced. This indicates that SIoU is used instead of CIoU in this paper to solve the problem of direction matching between the real box and the predicted box, and the convergence performance of the model is improved.

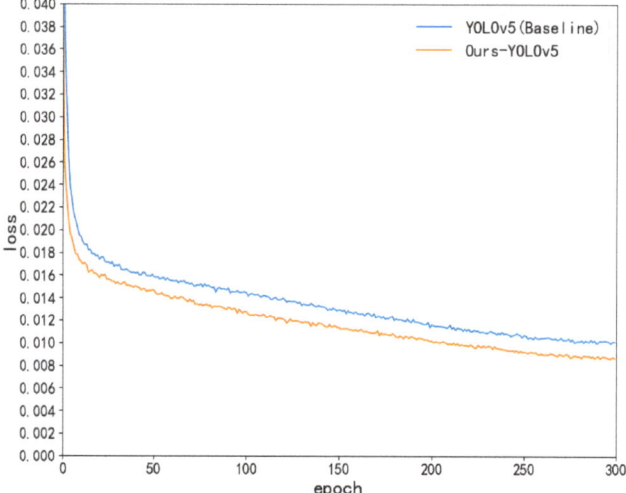

Figure 18. Improved before and after loss curve comparison.

4. Conclusions

In order to solve the problem of difficult identification caused by small and dense workpieces in industrial production lines, a workpiece detection method based on an improved YOLOv5 is proposed in this paper. Corresponding improvements are made in the backbone network, spatial pyramid pool structure, feature fusion network and loss function. The experimental results show that, compared with the current mainstream object detection algorithms, the improved model has the characteristics of small volume, high detection accuracy and fast reasoning speed, and can accurately detect the target and meet the real-time detection. Compared with the original YOLOv5s, the average accuracy of dense workpiece detection by the improved model is increased by 5% in the case of a small volume increase. In the industrial production line, sorting errors, missed inspection and other problems can cause great losses to the assets of the factory; increasing the accuracy by 5% can improve the assets of the factory, by providing a feasible method for actual workpiece detection.

Author Contributions: Methodology, Z.M.; Formal analysis, Z.M.; Resources, Y.Z.; Data curation, Y.Z. and X.L.; Writing—original draft, J.L.; Writing—review & editing, S.Z. All authors have read and agreed to the published version of the manuscript.

Funding: This research was funded by the International Cooperation Project of Science and Technology Bureau of Chengdu OF FUNDER grant number No.2019-GH02-00051-HZ. Sichuan unmanned system and intelligent perception Engineering Laboratory Open Fund and Research Fund of Chengdu University of information engineering, under Grants (No.WRXT2020-001, No.WRXT2020-002, No.WRXT2021-002 and No.KYTZ202142) and the Sichuan Science and Technology Program China, under Grant (No.2022YFS0565). This paper is also supported by the Key R&D project of the Science and Technology Department of Sichuan Province, under Grants (2023YFG0196 and 2023YFN0077), the Science and Technology achievements transformation Project of Science and Technology Department of Sichuan Province, under Grant (2023JDZH0023) and the Sichuan Provincial Science and Technology Department, Youth Fund project, under Grant (2023NSFSC1429).

Data Availability Statement: Due to privacy or ethical restrictions, we are unable to disclose self-built datasets. We suggest that other datasets related to small target detection can be used.

Acknowledgments: The authors are grateful to the College of Automation, Chengdu University of Information Technology. This paper is supported by the International Cooperation Project of Science and Technology Bureau of Chengdu (No.2019-GH02-00051-HZ), Sichuan unmanned system and intelligent perception Engineering Laboratory Open Fund and Research Fund of Chengdu University of information engineering, under Grants (No.WRXT2020-001, No.WRXT2020-002, No.WRXT2021-002 and No.KYTZ202142), and the Sichuan Science and Technology Program China, under Grant (No.2022YFS0565). This paper is also supported by the Key R&D project of the Science and Technology Department of Sichuan Province, under Grants (2023YFG0196 and 2023YFN0077), the Science and Technology achievements transformation Project of Science and Technology Department of Sichuan Province, under Grant (2023JDZH0023) and the Sichuan Provincial Science and Technology Department, Youth Fund project, under Grant (2023NSFSC1429).

Conflicts of Interest: The authors declare no conflict of interest. The funders had no role in the design of the study; in the collection, analyses, or interpretation of data; in the writing of the manuscript; or in the decision to publish the results.

References

1. Zhu, Y. Development of Robotic Arm Sorting System Based on Deep Learning Object Detection. Master's Thesis, Zhejiang University, Hangzhou, China, 2019.
2. Dang, H.; Hou, J.; Qiang, H.; Zhang, C. SCARA robot based on visual guiding automatic assembly system. *J. Electron. Technol. Appl.* **2017**, *43*, 21–24. [CrossRef]
3. Liu, J.; Zhong, P.; Liu, M. Research on Workpiece Recognition and Grasping Method Based on Improved SURF_FREAK Algorithm. *Mach. Tool Hydraul.* **2019**, *47*, 52–55+82.
4. Jiang, B.; Xu, X.; Wu, G.; Zuo, Y. Contour Hu invariant moments of workpiece, image matching and recognition. *J. Comb. Mach. Tools Autom. Process. Technol.* **2020**, 104–107+111. [CrossRef]
5. Bibbo', L.; Cotroneo, F.; Vellasco, M. Emotional Health Detection in HAR: New Approach Using Ensemble SNN. *Appl. Sci.* **2023**, *13*, 3259. [CrossRef]
6. Wang, B. Positioning and Grasping Technology of Small Parts of Automobile Based on Visual Guidance. Master's Thesis, Yanshan University, Qinghuangdao, China, 2019. [CrossRef]
7. Gong, W.; Zhang, K.; Yang, C.; Yi, M.; Wu, J. Adaptive visual inspection method for transparent label defect detection of curved glass bottle. In Proceedings of the 2020 International Conference on Computer Vision, Image and Deep Learning (CVIDL), Chongqing, China, 10–12 July 2020; pp. 90–95.
8. Chen, Y.; Alifu, K.; Lin, W. CA-YOLOv5 for crowded pedestrian detection. *Comput. Eng. Appl.* **2022**, *1*, 1–10.
9. Tan, M.; Le, Q. Efficientnet: Rethinking model scaling for convolutional neural networks. In Proceedings of the International Conference on Machine Learning, Long Beach, CA, USA, 9–15 June 2019; pp. 6105–6114.
10. Lin, T.Y.; Dollár, P.; Girshick, R.; He, K.; Hariharan, B.; Belongie, S. Feature pyramid networks for object detection. In Proceedings of the IEEE Conference on Computer Vision and Pattern Recognition, Honolulu, HI, USA, 21–26 July 2017; pp. 2117–2125.
11. Liu, S.; Qi, L.; Qin, H.; Shi, J.; Jia, J. Path aggregation network for instance segmentation. In Proceedings of the IEEE Conference on Computer Vision and Pattern Recognition, Salt Lake City, UT, USA, 18–22 June 2018; pp. 8759–8768.
12. Shen, X. *Analysis of Automobile Recyclability*; Heilongjiang Science and Technology Information: Harbin, China, 2012; Volume 90.
13. Hou, Q.; Zhou, D.; Feng, J. Coordinate attention for efficient mobile network design. In Proceedings of the IEEE Conference on Computer Vision and Pattern Recognition, Virtual, 19–25 June 2021; pp. 13713–13722.

14. Hu, J.; Shen, L.; Sun, G. Squeeze-and-excitation networks. In Proceedings of the IEEE Conference on Computer Vision and Pattern Recognition, Salt Lake City, UT, USA, 18–22 June 2018; pp. 7132–7141.
15. Woo, S.; Park, J.; Lee, J.Y.; Kweon, I.S. Cbam: Convolutional block attention module. In Proceedings of the European Conference on Computer Vision (ECCV), Munich, Germany, 8–14 September 2018; pp. 3–19.
16. He, K.; Zhang, X.; Ren, S.; Sun, J. Spatial pyramid pooling in deep convolutional networks for visual recognition. *IEEE Trans. Pattern Anal. Mach. Intell.* **2015**, *37*, 1904–1916. [CrossRef] [PubMed]
17. Tan, M.; Pang, R.; Le, Q.V. Efficientdet: Scalable and efficient object detection. In Proceedings of the IEEE Conference on Computer Vision and Pattern Recognition, hlSeattle, WA, USA, 13–19 June 2020; pp. 10781–10790.
18. Zheng, Z.; Wang, P.; Liu, W.; Li, J.; Ye, R.; Ren, D. Distance-IoU loss: Faster and better learning for bounding box regression. *Proc. AAAI Conf. Artif. Intell.* **2020**, *34*, 12993–13000. [CrossRef]
19. Gevorgyan, Z. SIoU loss: More powerful learning for bounding box regression. *arXiv* **2022**, arXiv:2205.12740.
20. Ren, S.; He, K.; Girshick, R.; Sun, J. Faster r-cnn: Towards real-time object detection with region proposal networks. *IEEE Trans. Pattern. Anal. Mach. Intell.* **2017**, *39*, 1137–1149. [CrossRef] [PubMed]
21. Liu, W.; Anguelov, D.; Erhan, D.; Szegedy, C.; Reed, S.; Fu, C.Y.; Berg, A.C. Ssd: Single shot multibox detector. In *Computer Vision–ECCV 2016, Proceedings of the 14th European Conference, Amsterdam, The Netherlands, 11–14 October 2016*; Springer International Publishing: Berlin/Heidelberg, Germany, 2016; pp. 21–37.

Disclaimer/Publisher's Note: The statements, opinions and data contained in all publications are solely those of the individual author(s) and contributor(s) and not of MDPI and/or the editor(s). MDPI and/or the editor(s) disclaim responsibility for any injury to people or property resulting from any ideas, methods, instructions or products referred to in the content.

Article

Improving the Performance of the Single Shot Multibox Detector for Steel Surface Defects with Context Fusion and Feature Refinement

Yiming Li, Lixin He *, Min Zhang *, Zhi Cheng, Wangwei Liu and Zijun Wu

School of Artificial Intelligence and Big Data, Hefei University, Hefei 230601, China; liyiming@stu.hfuu.edu.cn (Y.L.); cz_ganen108@126.com (Z.C.); liuwangwei@stu.hfuu.edu.cn (W.L.); wuzj@hfuu.edu.cn (Z.W.)
* Correspondence: hlxiniim@mail.ustc.edu.cn (L.H.); hfuuzhangmin@hfuu.edu.cn (M.Z.)

Abstract: Strip surface defects have large intraclass and small interclass differences, resulting in the available detection techniques having either a low accuracy or very poor real-time performance. In order to improve the ability for capturing steel surface defects, the context fusion structure introduces the local information of the shallow layer and the semantic information of the deep layer into multiscale feature maps. In addition, for filtering the semantic conflicts and redundancies arising from context fusion, a feature refinement module is introduced in our method, which further improves the detection accuracy. Our experimental results show that this significantly improved the performance. In particular, our method achieved 79.5% mAP and 71 FPS on the public NEU-DET dataset. This means that our method had a higher detection accuracy compared to other techniques.

Keywords: context fusion; feature refinement; steel defect detection; SSD

1. Introduction

For various reasons, including continuous casting billets and the production equipment and process, strip steel surfaces may have defects, such as surface pitting, rolled scale, scratches, and so on. These defects seriously affect the strip steel quality and may even destroy the subsequent production object. Therefore, the efficient detection of surface defects is pivotal for strip steel production.

Surface defect detection is essentially a kind of target detection, to which various convolutional neural network methods have been applied. Nonetheless, the surface defects of a strip steel differ significantly from other types of target. They are usually characterized by large intraclass and small interclass differences, resulting in the existing convolutional neural network methods failing to achieve a good balance between detection accuracy and efficiency.

To solve this problem, we propose a single-stage target detection method based on the single-shot multibox detector (SSD) [1]. The method consists of three stages, as follows: The first is the feature extraction stage. As the residual structure helps to build a deep network that can extract high-dimensional semantic features, ResNet50 [2] is used as the feature extraction network, and the feature maps extracted from its fourth residual block are sequentially downsampled by five additional layers, to construct five feature maps of different scales to detect defective targets of different sizes.

The second is the encoding stage. A context fusion structure was designed to introduce more contextual information for the multiscale feature maps, which increases the inference speed, while improving the ability of the model to capture defects.

The third is a decoding stage. A feature refinement module is added to the predicted feature map. Via the channel and spatial attention mechanisms, the model is guided to better integrate the context information, which solves the semantic conflict and redundancy

caused by the context fusion, and the detection accuracy of the model is thus further improved. Finally, six simple predictors are used to predict the six predicted feature maps, respectively. We evaluated our method with the NEU-DET [3] dataset. The results showed that our method significantly outperformed the other methods. Moreover, our method achieved a better balance between accuracy and efficiency.

We summarize our contributions below:

1. We propose a novel method based on the framework of the SSD, which achieves a better balance between detection accuracy and efficiency. For instance, on the NEU-DET dataset, our method achieved an accuracy of 79.5% mAP at a speed of 71 FPS, thereby outperforming other methods.
2. We designed a context fusion structure for the framework, which is able to more closely capture the surface defects, while maintaining the inference speed. Our structure is simpler than that in [4,5], as we only use a dilated convolution to transfer location information from the bottom to the top and a deconvolution to transfer semantic information from the top to the bottom.
3. We introduced a feature refinement module into the framework, which efficiently rules out the semantic conflicts and redundancies that result from context fusion. This improved the resulting detection accuracy. This idea stemmed from [6,7], where we combine the channel and spatial attention mechanisms for adaptive feature refinement and replace the fully connected layer in channel attention with 1×1 convolution.

2. Related Works

Early rolling steel enterprises generally used manual methods to detect defects. These methods obviously had a poor efficiency [8–10] and could suffer from poor performance caused by fatigue. However, nondestructive testing technologies have been used to detect surface defects (e.g., ultrasonic flaw detection), these methods present shortcomings, such as a high equipment installation cost and energy consumption and slow detection speed. With the combination of computer technology and vision, detection methods based on machine vision have been proposed [11–15]. However, their defect features need to be manually extracted and the resulting low-dimensional artificial features are difficult to generalize to complex strip surface defects. Therefore, the application of these methods needs to be combined with specific scenarios [15,16].

With the increase of computing power, detection methods based on convolutional neural networks have gradually become mainstream and can mainly be divided into two categories: The first is a two-stage target detection method, and the second is a single-stage target detection method. The two-stage target detection method includes a region proposal stage and a target bounding box regression and classification stage. While this has high accuracy, it generally has slow inference, because of its complex structure. Typical examples include the RCNN [17], Fast R-CNN [18], and Faster R-CNN [19]. The single-stage target detection method has a higher inference speed and integrates these two stages into an end-to-end network. Thus, its accuracy is slightly lower than that of a two-stage target detection method. Typical examples of single-stage target detection methods include the SSD [1], RetinaNet [20], YOLOv3 [21], YOLOv4 [22], YOLOv5 [23], YOLOX [24] and so on.

Since surface defects are characterized by large intraclass and small interclass differences, these classic target detection methods cannot usually be applied directly, as the targets in applications differ significantly from the surface defects in this study, as shown in Figure 1.

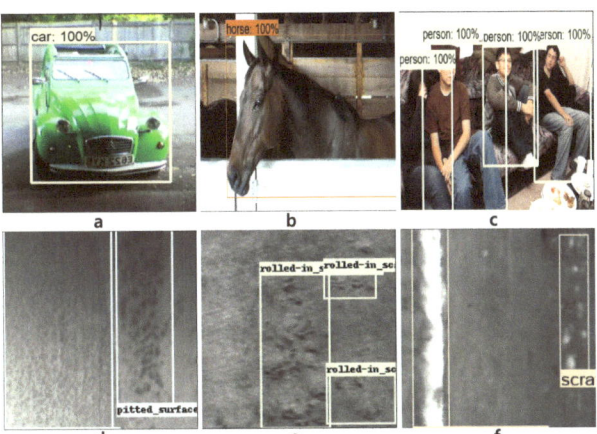

Figure 1. Samples of targets: (**a**–**c**) are sample Classic dataset. (**d**–**f**) are sample steel surface defects.

While these classic methods cannot be applied directly, they provide deep insights for detecting the surface defects of strip steel. We direct the readers to references [25–29] for detailed introductions to these methods.

To improve the performance of the Faster-RCNN in surface defect detection, Zhao et al. [25] proposed a refined Faster-RCNN method, which is a two-stage target detection model that first extracts the target region with a RPN network and achieved 75% mAP on the NEU-DET dataset. While this performance is excellent, the detection speed is still slow and insufficient to cope with practical demands. Moreover, Hatab et al. [26] designed a defect detection method based on the YOLO network and obtained 70.66% mAP on the NEU-DET dataset. Thereafter, Kou et al. [27] proposed a defect detection model based on anchor-free YOLO-v3 and achieved 72.2% mAP. He et al. [28] then proposed a two-stage defect detection model based on multifeature map fusion and achieved 82.3% mAP. However, when the model increased the detection speed to 20 FPS, the mAP dropped to 70%. In addition, Cheng et al. [29] recently proposed a single-stage defect detection method based on RetinaNet, which exhibited 78.25% mAP. Although the accuracy has been improved with these models, their detection speed cannot meet the requirements of an actual production line.

While there are various methods for strip surface defect detection, they are still unable to achieve a good balance between detection accuracy and efficiency. Thus, this remains an open technical problem. The method proposed in this study provides insights into this challenge, by achieving a good balance when using the NEU-DET dataset.

3. Model

We use the SSD as the overall framework. Compared to the Faster R-CNN, RetinaNet, YOLOv3, YOLOv4, YOLOv5, YOLOX, and so on, the SSD has a simple structure and fast detection speed. In particular, it is easy to deploy and integrate with industrial equipment.

Our model consists of three stages. The first stage is a feature extraction stage, which includes a feature extraction network with additional layers, as shown in Figure 2. From this network, six feature maps of different scales can be obtained ($L_0 \sim L_5$ layer feature maps in Figure 2). The second stage is a coding stage, which builds a context fusion structure (CFS) based on six feature maps and introduces more contextual information into the model through a location augmentation module (LAM) and semantic augmentation module (SAM), to obtain the final predicted feature maps ($P_0 \sim P_5$ layer feature maps in Figure 2). The third stage is a decoding stage, which adds a feature refinement module (FRM) after the first four predicted feature maps ($P_0 \sim P_3$ layer feature maps in Figure 2), to filter out the semantic conflicts and redundancy caused by contextual feature fusion.

Finally, we use six predictors to regress the offset of the defect target location and classify the defect targets.

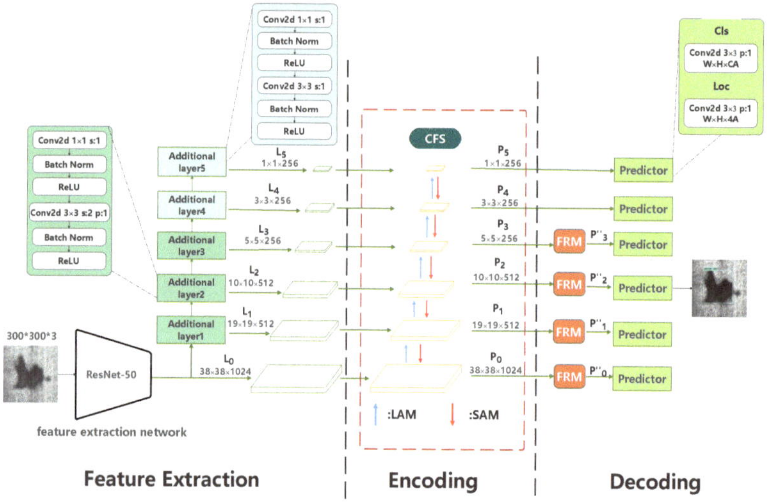

Figure 2. Model structure.

3.1. Feature Extraction Stage

The feature extraction stage first extracts a high-dimensional feature map from a 300 × 300 image using a feature extraction network and then obtains five different scales of feature maps ($L_1 \sim L_5$ layer feature maps in Figure 2) using five additional layers on this high-dimensional feature map, before finally sending this to the encoding stage. It should be noted that we use ResNet50 [2] instead of VGG16 [30] in the feature extraction network. ResNet50 is better than VGG16 in terms of its computational power and characterization ability. We only use the first seven layers of ResNet50 as the feature extraction network. Moreover, we refer readers to NVIDIA's code (available online at https://github.com/NVIDIA/DeepLearningExamples/tree/master/PyTorch/Detection/SSD (accessed on 8 December 2021)), where the stride of the first residual block of the Conv-4x layer is modified to 1 to improve the resolution.

Although multiscale feature maps can improve the performance for detecting targets of different sizes, these predictive feature maps ($L_0 \sim L_5$ layer feature maps in Figure 2) can only be obtained with a series of additional layers of recursive relationships on top of the feature extraction network. Therefore, they differ only in the size of the receptive fields and cannot make good use of the multiscale features, whose receptive field sizes are defined as:

$$R_L = R_{L-1} + \left[F_{L-1} \times \prod_{i=1}^{L-1} S_i \right] \quad (1)$$

where L represents the number of layers ($0 <= L <= 5$); R_L denotes the receptive field size of the L_{th} layer, which is related to the receptive field size of the preceding layer; F_L denotes the size of the pooling or convolution kernel of the L-th layer; and S_i denotes the stride of the i_{th} layer.

According to the definition of the receptive field size, we assume that the receptive field size of the L_0 layer is 1. We can then derive the receptive field expansion multipliers of the feature maps extracted from the additional layers ($L_1 \sim L_5$ layer feature maps in Figure 2), as shown in Table 1. It can be seen that the receptive field size of the last layer is 58-times larger than that of the first layer and it can therefore extract richer and more concise semantic features compared to the L_0 layer and detect large targets better. However, it also weakens the ability to perceive more local information compared to the L_0 layer, thus influencing the detection of small targets.

Table 1. Expansion of receptive field relative to the L_0 layer.

Feature Map	L_1	L_2	L_3	L_4	L_5
Multiplier	4	10	22	40	58

3.2. Encoding Stage

As shown in Section 3.1, the L_0~L_5 layer feature maps do not make good use of the contextual information. For this, Fu et al. [4] used deconvolution and skip connections on the basis of SSD to transfer the semantic information of deep layers to shallow layers using element-wise multiplication. Meanwhile, Jeong et al. [5] not only used deconvolution to directly connect the semantic information of deep layers with the shallow feature map in a stacked manner in the channel dimension, but also used the pooling layers to stack the local information of shallow layers to the deep feature map in the same way.

To introduce context information, our method not only transfers the semantic information of deep layers to shallow layers, but also transfers the local information of shallow layers to deep layers. At the same time, in the process of transmitting local information, we do not use pooling layers, as in [5], but replace them with dilated convolution.

We therefore designed a CFS that contains a LAM and a SAM, as shown in Figure 3. The CFS fuses the rich and concise semantic information in the deep layer together with the relatively accurate local position details in the shallow layer into the predicted feature map. This improves the ability to capture the surface defects, while maintaining the inference speed.

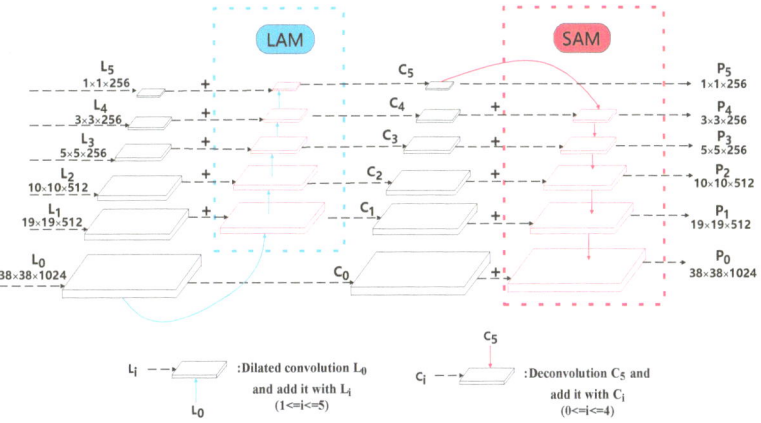

Figure 3. Context fusion structure.

As shown in Figure 3, the LAM transfers the relatively accurate local position information in the L_0 layer to the deep layer. This makes the feature map size of the L_0 layer consistent with the L_1 layer through a downsampling operation. The L_1 layer then joins to obtain the C_1 layer. After that, the L_0 layer continues to downsample and the L_2 layer joins to obtain C_2. By repeating this, we eventually obtain $\{C_3 \sim C_5\}$. Note that the C_0 layer is obtained by the L_0 layer without any other operations. Although traditional downsampling (pooling or convolution) can increase the receptive field, it might raise the problem of spatial resolution degradation, which does not transfer the rich position information of the L_0 layer to subsequent layers well. Therefore, we use dilated convolution with kernels of size 3×3, a stride size of 2, and a dilation rate of 2 for downsampling. For the last two downsampling operations, the stride size is adjusted to 1, since the feature map is small and a larger stride size may lead to information loss.

The SAM transfers the rich and concise semantic information from the C_5 layer to the shallow layer, which makes the feature map size of the C_5 layer consistent with the C_4 layer through a upsampling operation. The C_4 layer is then summed, to obtain the P_4 layer, after which the C_5 layer continues to be upsampled and summed with the C_3 layer to obtain the P_3 layer. By repetition, we eventually obtain $\{P_0 \sim P_2\}$. Note that the P_5 layer is obtained from the C_5 layer without any operations. Here, we do not use the same nearest-neighbor upsampling as the feature pyramid network [31]. In its place, a deconvolution operation with learning capability is applied, which has a stronger ability to reduce the resolution than nearest-neighbor upsampling and has shown effectiveness in detection and segmentation [4,32–34]. All deconvolution kernels have a size of 3×3 and a stride size of 2. For the first two upsampling operations, we use a stride size of 1.

3.3. Decoding Stage

The decoding stage contains a FRM and a predictor. After passing through the FRM, the predicted feature maps are fed into six predictors that do not share parameters and are independent. Here, each predictor contains two branches. One is for regressing the offset of the defect target location and the other classifies the defect target.

In context fusion, although the CFS introduces more contextual information for predicting feature maps, directly fusing feature information of different scales will result in semantic conflicts. This reduces the characterization ability of multiscale feature maps and influences the resulting defect detection.

For this, Woo et al. [6] used an spatial attention mechanism and a channel attention mechanism for adaptive feature refinement. However, in the channel attention mechanism, two of these fully connected layers were used as features after average pooling and maximum pooling, to learn a set of mappings. At the same time, in order to reduce the parameters of the fully connected layers, the dimensions of these two fully connected layers were reduced. In [7], it was found that the dimensionality reduction of these fully connected layers had a negative impact on the channel attention mechanism, and 1×1 convolution was used to solve this problem.

Inspired by CBAM [6] and ECANet [7], we add a FRM after $\{P_0 \sim P_3\}$ to refine the channel and spatial information of the predicted feature maps fused with the contextual information, and use 1×1 convolution to replace the fully connected layers in the channel attention mechanism, so as to guide the contextual fusion and filter out the semantic conflicts and redundancies brought by direct information fusion of different scales.

As shown in Figure 4, given the prediction feature map $P_i \in R^{H \times W \times C}, (0 \leq i \leq 3)$ as input, the channel and spatial refinements $F_c \in R^{1 \times 1 \times C}$ and $F_s \in R^{H \times W \times 1}$ are obtained in turn and then the final prediction feature map $P_i'' \in R^{H \times W \times C}$ using the following steps:

$$P_i' = F_c \times P_i \qquad (2)$$

$$P_i'' = F_s \times P_i' \qquad (3)$$

where $\times$ is the element-wise multiplication, and F_c and F_s can be regarded as weights in the channel and space dimensions, respectively.

As shown in Figure 5, channel feature refinement uses the channel attention mechanism to obtain the weights of the feature maps, so that the model gives more attention to the information that should be learned and filters out the semantic conflicts and redundancies. Given a prediction feature map $P_i \in R^{H \times W \times C}, (0 \leq i \leq 3)$ as input, the feature map is squeezed into two feature longs with dimensions $1 \times 1 \times C$ by global average and global maximum pooling operations, respectively. These two feature longs are then fed into $Conv_1$ with a convolution kernel size of 1×1, compressing its channel number to $C \times \frac{1}{ratio}$, and activated by the activation function $\phi : ReLU()$ to obtain $F_c' \in R^{1 \times 1 \times C \times \frac{1}{ratio}}$ and $F_c'' \in R^{1 \times 1 \times C \times \frac{1}{ratio}}$:

$$F_c' = \phi(Conv_1(AvgPooling(P_i))) \qquad (4)$$

$$F_c^{''} = \phi(Conv_1(MaxPooling(P_i))) \quad (5)$$

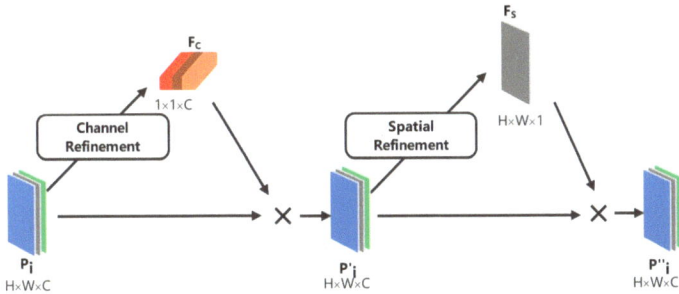

Figure 4. Feature refinement module.

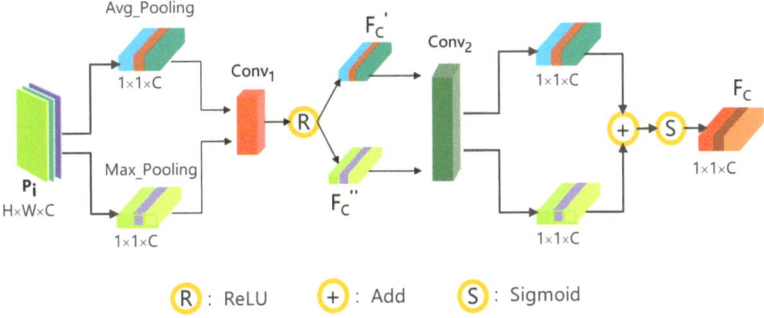

Figure 5. Channel refinement.

Finally, $F_c^{'}$ and $F_c^{''}$ are fed into $Conv_2$ with a convolution kernel of size 1×1 and their channel numbers are reduced back to $1 \times 1 \times C$. These two are then summed to obtain $F_c \in R^{1 \times 1 \times C}$ using the activation function $\theta : Sigmoid()$:

$$F_c = \theta(Conv_2(F_c^{'}) + Conv_2(F_c^{''})) \quad (6)$$

As shown in Figure 6, the spatial feature refinement uses a spatial attention mechanism to obtain the weights of the feature maps in the spatial dimension, so that the model gives more attention to the information learned in the spatial dimension and filters out the semantic conflicts and redundancies brought by the direct fusion of the feature maps in the spatial dimension. Given a prediction feature map $P_i^{'} \in R^{H \times W \times C}$, $(0 \leq i \leq 3)$ as input, this is squeezed into two eigenfaces of dimensions $H \times W \times 1$ using an averaging operation and a maximizing operation in the channel dimension, respectively. Moreover, the process stacks them together in the channel dimension, restores the number of channels using a convolution kernel of size 3×3, and then activates them again using $\theta : Sigmoid()$ to obtain $F_s \in R^{H \times W \times 1}$:

$$F_s = \theta(Conv(Concat(Avg(P_i^{'}), Max(P_i^{'})))) \quad (7)$$

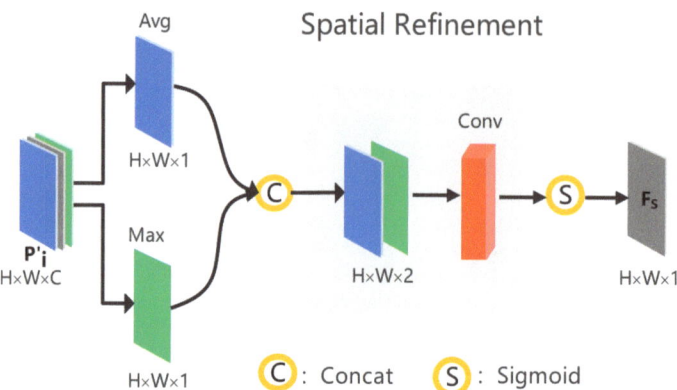

Figure 6. Spatial refinement.

4. Experiments

4.1. Experimental Settings and Dataset

4.1.1. Experimental Platform

Pytorch v1.7, 4-core CPU and 2 NVIDIA RTX 3090 GPUs.

4.1.2. Training Parameter Setting

The input image size was 300 × 300 and the total iteration number was set at 1500. The first 500 iterations were trained by freezing the feature extraction layer and the additional layer, with a batch setting of 8 and a learning rate of 0.01. We then thawed the additional layer for another 500 training sessions, with a batch setting of 16 and a learning rate of 0.001. Finally, we thawed the feature extraction layer for global fine-tuning training, with a batch setting of 32 and a learning rate 0.0001. To optimize the training process, the momentum method was used, with a momentum parameter of 0.9 and a weight decay parameter of 0.3. The decay frequency was once per 30 iterations. To prevent overfitting, image augmentation methods, such as random cropping and flipping, were also used.

4.1.3. Evaluation Metrics

In classification tasks, Params is the total number of parameters that need to be trained during model training, and floating point operations (FLOPs) were used to measure the computational performance of the model, with the smaller the better. Accuracy was used to measure the prediction accuracy of the model, as shown in Table 2. Taking the classification result of the binary classification model as an example, the calculation formula of accuracy was as follows:

$$Accuracy = \frac{TP + TN}{TP + TN + FP + FN} \tag{8}$$

For the target detection task, not only the classification accuracy, but also the accuracy of the target frame positioning must be considered. This study considered the IoU coincidence degree between the target frame predicted by the model and the real frame as a measure. When the IoU threshold between the target frame and the real frame was greater than 0.5, the model prediction was positive (*TP*); otherwise, it was negative (*TP*). The precision and recall were then calculated as follows:

$$Precision = \frac{TP}{TP + FP} \tag{9}$$

$$Recall = \frac{TP}{TP + FN} \tag{10}$$

Precision and recall were then calculated according to different classification probabilities, by taking recall as the abscissa and precision as the ordinate and plotting the obtained values to obtain the P-R curve. The area under this curve is the average precision (AP). Finally, the mAP was obtained by averaging the AP of each class.

Table 2. Model prediction results.

		True Value	
		Positive	Negative
Predicted value	Positive	TP	FP
	Negative	FN	TN

4.1.4. Dataset

We used the NEU-DET [3] steel surface defect detection dataset created by Northeastern University, China. As shown in Figure 7, this dataset contains six types of hot-rolled strip steel surface defects; namely, crazing (Cr), inclusion (In), patches (Pa), pitted surface (Ps), rolled-in scale (Rs), and scratches (Sc). Each of these classes has 300 images. The dataset thus has 1800 images in total. For each target detection task in this study, we randomly chose 80% of the images as the training set (i.e., 1440 images) and 20% of the images as the test set (i.e., 360 images).

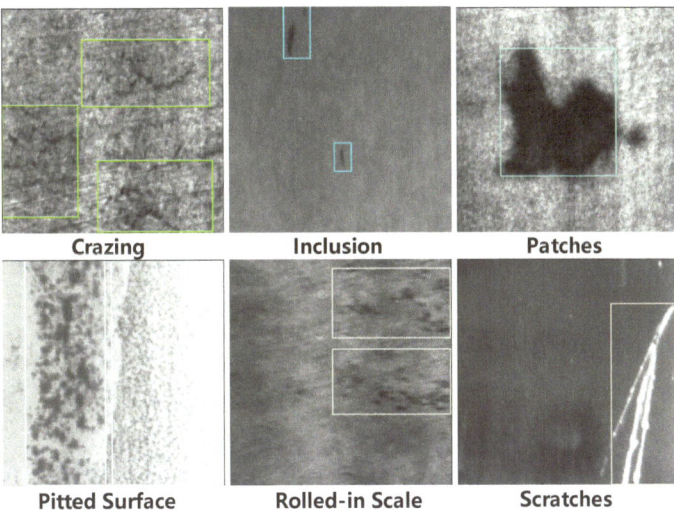

Figure 7. NEU-DET dataset.

4.1.5. Experiment Design

Our experiment consisted of three steps. In first step, we used an extensive experimental study to show why we used ResNet50 as our feature extraction network. The corresponding experiment results are reported in Section 4.2.

We then report the experimental performance of our framework in Section 4.3. The results showed that our framework outperformed the other methods in detection accuracy and efficiency.

In the third step, we reported a more detailed comparison with other methods. The corresponding experiment showed that our method achieved a much better average performance (Section 4.4).

Finally, we performed an ablation experiment. In our ablation analysis, we showed the impacts of distinct components of the CFS and FRM on the performance of our framework. With this experiment, we eventually chose dilated convolution and deconvolution as the respective downsampling and upsampling methods, and used element-by-element addition to fuse the two feature maps, which, together with FRM and a compression ratio of 32 in layers $P_0 \sim P_3$, achieved an optimal balance between the detection accuracy and efficiency. The details regarding the ablation experiment are presented in Section 4.5.

4.2. Selection of Feature Extraction Network

A good feature extraction network is very important for the performance of a defect detection model. We divided the NEU-DET dataset, according to the defect categories, into six classes, with 10% of the images in each class selected for the test set. This resulted in a steel defect classification dataset with 1620 images in the training set and 180 images in the test set. Different classification models were then applied to classify this steel defect classification dataset, and all models were trained using weights loaded with pretrained weights on the ImageNet [35] dataset. The results are shown in Table 3. Only Resnet50 [2] achieved 100% accuracy. Although Params was 0.53M larger than Resnetxt50 [36], it had the smallest computational effort (FLOPs).

Table 3. Performance of the different classification models.

Models	VGG16 [30]	Resnet50 [2]	Resnet101 [2]	Resnetxt50 [36]
Accuracy(%)	97.2	**100**	99.4	98.9
Params(M)	138.36	25.56	44.5	**25.03**
FLOPs(G)	15.61	**4.14**	7.87	4.29

We used Resnet50 and VGG16 for the feature extraction network, where the details are described in Section 3.1 for Resnet50 and in the original study of the SSD [1] for VGG16. Table 4 shows the depths of the feature maps (i.e., the $L_0 \sim L_5$ layer feature maps in Figure 2) in the network derived from the feature extraction stage. Here, only the convolutional and pooling layers were considered when we calculated the depths. The results show that the feature map had the deepest network depth at the same resolution while using Resnet50. This means that the semantic information characterized by Resnet50 was stronger than VGG16, while the improvement in the prediction performance was greater.

Table 4. Depth of feature maps composed of VGG and Resnet.

	L_0	L_1	L_2	L_3	L_4	L_5
Resolution	38×38	19×19	10×10	5×5	3×3	1×1
VGG	13	20	22	24	26	27
Resnet50	41	43	45	47	49	51

In summary, both the Params and FLOPs of Resnet50 were smaller, and the resulting semantic information at the same resolution was stronger. Thus, we used Resnet50 in this study as the feature extraction network.

4.3. Detection Performance of the Model

4.3.1. Detection Accuracy of Model

As mentioned above, we used the SSD as the overall framework and Resnet50 as the feature extraction network. In addition, a CFS was used in the encoding stage to introduce more contextual information into the multiscale feature map. This ensured a higher inference speed and improved the characterization ability of the multiscale feature map. Furthermore, in the decoding stage, in order to filter out the semantic conflicts and redundancies brought by feature fusion, a FRM was added after the first four layers of predicted feature maps, to further improve the detection accuracy. The results are shown in Figure 8.

Our model achieved 79.5% mAP and 71 FPS on the NEU-DET dataset. Our accuracy outperformed those of SSD-resnet50 and SSD-vgg16 at rates of 7.4/72.1 and 7.5/72.0, respectively. Compared to the other methods, our model achieved the best accuracy (mAP) and had a sufficient detection speed (FPS).

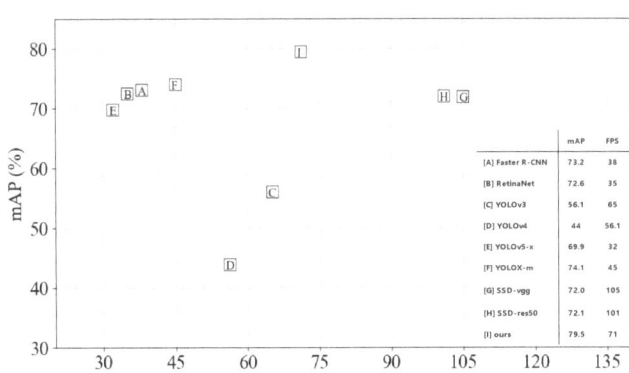

Figure 8. Model detection performance.

4.3.2. Efficiency

The inference of the image, including the execution of non-maximum suppression, took only 0.014 s and the detection speed reached 71 FPS. In a real production line, a single camera has a range of 50–100 cm and the maximum production speed is usually 30 m/s, which requires a detector speed of at least 30~60 FPS [37]. Therefore, the detection speed of our model meets such requirements of practical applications.

4.4. Detailed Comparison with Other Models

To further evaluate its effectiveness, we compared our model with several existing methods using the NEU-DET dataset. For a comprehensive comparison, we considered both two- and single-stage target detection methods. We used Faster R-CNN [19] as an example two-stage target detection method, which uses a region proposal network to generate candidate target frames. For the single-stage target detection method, we chose RetinaNet [20] configured with the feature pyramid network and different YOLO methods, namely YOLOv3 [21], YOLOv4 [22], YOLOv5 [23], YOLOX [24], YOLOv8 [38], and SSD [1]. The comparison results are shown in Table 5. Compared to these existing methods, our model again achieved the best accuracy. Moreover, the detection speed was only poorer than the SSD and YOLOv8.

Table 5. Comparison results with other models.

Methods	Backbone	mAP(%)	FPS	Cr(%)	In(%)	Pa (%)	Ps(%)	Rs(%)	Sc(%)
Faster R-CNN [19]	Resnet50+FPN	73.2	38	33	79	92	84	54	95
RetinaNet [20]	Resnet50+FPN	72.6	35	38	78	94	85	54	84
YOLOv3 [21]	Darknet53	67.4	65	29	73	89	79	50	85
YOLOv4 [22]	CSPDarknet53	23.9	44	5	24	43	46	5	20
YOLOv5-s [23]	CSPDarknet	59.6	68	17	72	86	68	37	77
YOLOv5-m [23]	CSPDarknet	63.8	50	19	73	89	75	46	81
YOLOv5-l [23]	CSPDarknet	69.6	44	32	75	91	75	58	88
YOLOv5-x [23]	CSPDarknet	69.9	32	28	76	92	76	57	90
YOLOX-s [24]	CSPDarknet	71.2	60	35	73	92	82	56	90
YOLOX-m [24]	CSPDarknet	74.1	45	38	80	91	84	57	96
YOLOX-l [24]	CSPDarknet	73.8	41	39	76	92	**86**	57	93
YOLOX-x [24]	CSPDarknet	73.5	30	37	78	93	84	58	93
YOLOv8-n [38]	CSPDarknet	72.0	**144**	33.7	78.1	89.9	79.7	56.7	93.6
YOLOv8-s [38]	CSPDarknet	69.8	116	28.0	74.8	89.9	80.6	54.5	91.0
YOLOv8-m [38]	CSPDarknet	71.8	103	35.6	78.1	91.2	77.6	57.3	91.1
YOLOv8-x [38]	CSPDarknet	72.3	56	35.9	77.8	90.8	79.3	59.5	90.2
SSD [1]	VGG16	72.0	105	37	76	91	**86**	61	77
SSD	Resnet50	72.1	101	37	76	91	81	60	86
Ours	Resnet50	**79.5**	71	**48**	**82**	**94**	**86**	**73**	92

4.5. Ablation Experiments

Finally, we conducted ablation experiments for further evaluation of the CFS and FRM.

4.5.1. CFS

The CFS involves information fusion of two feature maps of different sizes and needs to use upsampling and downsampling to adjust the sizes of the feature maps. We designed two different strategies for upsampling and downsampling. One was dilated convolution and deconvolution with a LAM and a SAM, as discussed in Section 3.2. These are self-adaptive and so can optionally fuse two feature maps during training. The other was a combination of a LAM-S and a SAM-S. As in the method in [5], the LAM-S uses a maximum pooling as downsampling, so as to pass the local position detail information to the rest of the layers. The SAM-S uses a nearest neighbor interpolation as upsampling, to pass the semantic information to the rest of the layers. In addition, we needed a suitable fusion approach to fuse feature maps after their sizes become identical. Figure 9 shows the performance of three fusion methods in the CFS. The first was element-by-element addition (Add) fusion. The second was element-by-element multiplication (Multiply) fusion. The third stacks two feature maps in the channel dimension and then downscales them to the original channel number using 1×1 convolution and is usually shorted as Concat.

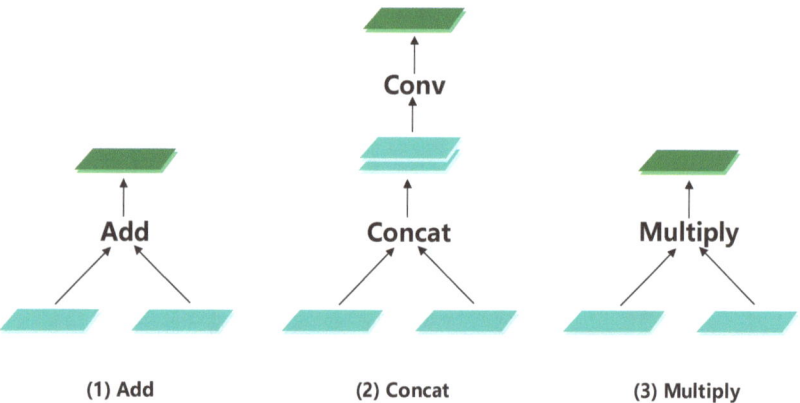

Figure 9. Three types of feature map fusion in CFS.

Table 6 shows the experimental results. Add achieved the best performance for both upsampling and downsampling. Furthermore, the performance of LAM and SAM was better than the LAM-S and SAM-S. Hence, the combination of Add with upsampling and downsampling with a learning capability was a good choice.

We eventually choose the combination of Add with LAM and SAM as the two optional components of the CFS. Table 7 shows the resulting effectiveness of the four possible combinations of these two components in terms of mAP and FPS.

Table 6. Three types of feature map fusion and two strategies of downsampling and upsampling. ✓ represents the use of this module.

Module	Add	Concat	Multiply	mAP
LAM	✓			**76.8**
LAM		✓		55.0
LAM			✓	76.5
LAM-S	✓			75.7
LAM-S		✓		71.6
LAM-S			✓	39.3
SAM	✓			**76.2**
SAM		✓		47.5
SAM			✓	73.9
SAM-S	✓			55.7
SAM-S		✓		46.2
SAM-S			✓	53.4

Table 7. Components of the CFS module. ✓ represents the use of this module.

LAM	SAM	mAP	FPS
		72.1	101
✓		76.4	90
	✓	76.2	91
✓	✓	78.5	89

Without the LAM and SAM, our method degenerated to the baseline model SSD-resnet50, which had a detection accuracy of 72.1 mAP on the NEU-DET dataset. With only the LAM or the SAM, the detection accuracy was improved by 4.3 and 4.1 percentage points, respectively. Moreover, the LAM improved the performance more significantly, especially for small instances, see, for example, Figure 10.

When the LAM and SAM were used together, the mAP was improved by 6.4 percentage points compared to the baseline model and the detection accuracy of small targets was improved by 7 percentage points. This means that introducing contextual information into the prediction feature maps indeed improved the detection accuracy, especially for small targets. In particular, the inference speed reached 89 FPS and was still comparable with that of the baseline model.

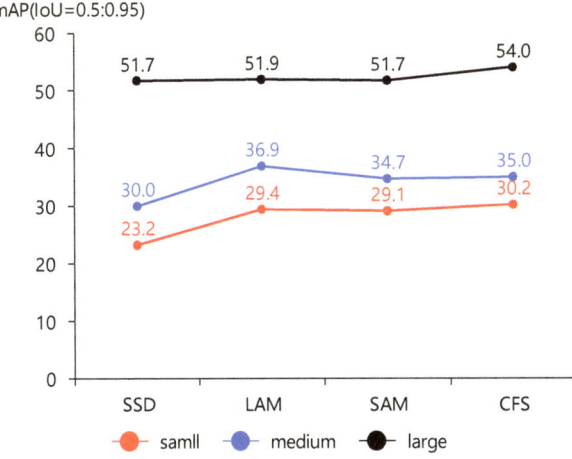

Figure 10. Detection accuracy of multiscale targets.

4.5.2. FRM

Our model used the CFS to introduce more contextual information to the multiscale feature map, to improve its detection capability. Then, we validated the effectiveness of the FRM in filtering out semantic conflicts and redundancies.

Table 8 shows that we obtained a 1 percentage point improvement when we combined the CFS with the FRM. This achieved a 7.4 percentage point improvement compared to the baseline model (without the CFS and FRM).

Table 8. CFS and FRM modules. ✓ represents the use of this module.

CFS	FRM	CBAM	mAP	FPS
			72.1	101
✓			78.5	89
✓		✓	75.6	71
✓	✓		79.5	71

We also implemented a comparative experimental study to show the effectiveness of using 1×1 convolutional layers to replace the fully connected layers in CBAM, see the results in Table 8. With 1×1 convolution, the detection accuracy of our model was considerably improved.

In the channel refinement part of the FRM, we had to feed the channel weights obtained from pooling into $Conv_1$ to compress the number of channels and then reduced them in $Conv_2$. The choice of compression ratio thus affected the detection performance. Figure 11 shows a plot of accuracy over compression ratio. The detection accuracy gradually increased but the detection speed decreased. Therefore, a different ratio can be chosen according to the actual production needs. To balance accuracy and speed, a final ratio of 32 was chosen here, which was compressed to 1/32 of the original.

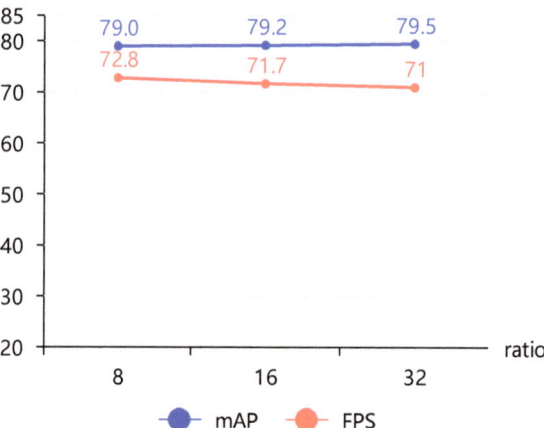

Figure 11. Different compression ratios.

As shown in Figure 12, we extracted the same layers in the CFS and FRM to generate the feature class activation map Eigen-CAM [39] and visualize the features learned by both. We can see that the features learned by CFS were more scattered, due to the semantic conflict and redundancy brought by the fusion of different scale feature maps and the features learned by the FRM being more focused after filtering and guiding, which also proved the effectiveness of our FRM.

Our model only adds the FRM in layers $P_0 \sim P_3$ (as shown in Figure 2), while the FRM is not applied in layers P_4 and P_5, since the feature maps of these two layers are small (3×3 and 1×1, respectively) and they do not have much conflict and redundant information by themselves. If the FRM was added in this case, then it would reduce the detection performance. As shown in Table 9, we added the FRM to P_4 and P_5 layers after adding the FRM to $P_0 \sim P_3$ but the results became worse.

Table 9. Results of adding FRM in order from P_0 to P_5 layers.

Layer	Ratio	mAP	FPS
$P_0 \sim P_3$	8	**79.0**	72.8
$P_0 \sim P_4$	8	78.7	70
$P_0 \sim P_5$	8	78.8	67
$P_0 \sim P_3$	16	**79.2**	71.7
$P_0 \sim P_4$	16	78.7	69
$P_0 \sim P_5$	16	78.9	67
$P_0 \sim P_3$	32	**79.5**	71.3
$P_0 \sim P_4$	32	78.8	68
$P_0 \sim P_5$	32	78.3	65

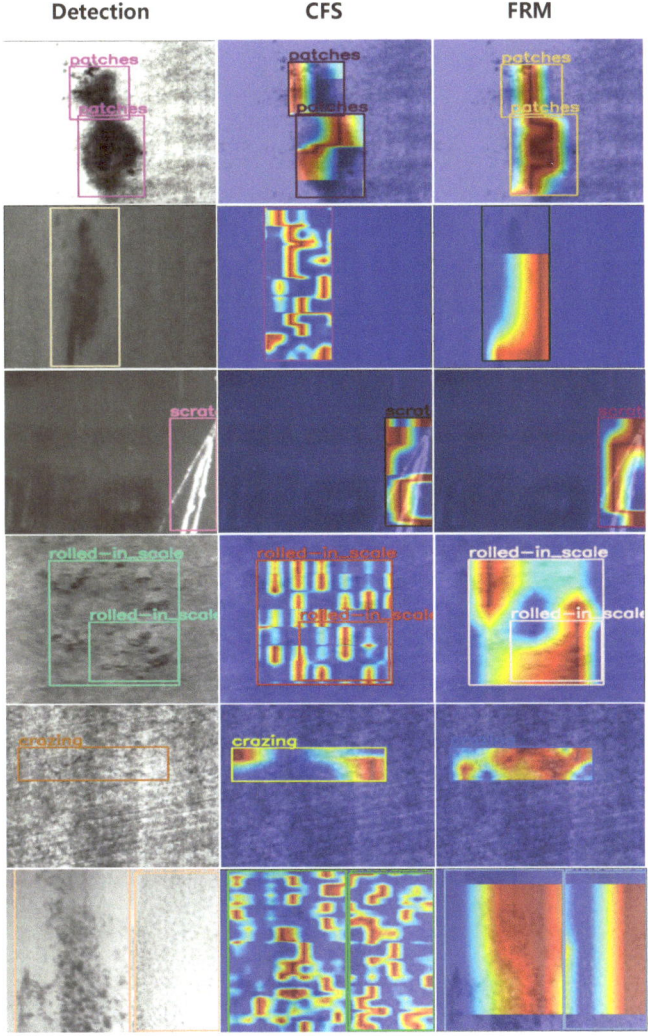

Figure 12. Comparison of the effects of the class activation map of FRM and CFS.

5. Discussion

While our model achieved a very good average performance on NEU-DET, there were still a few cases of detection failure. In Table 5, the accuracy of Cr and Rs was the lowest, followed by In. In particular, the accuracy of Cr was only 47%. Therefore, the model had different degrees of detection errors in these categories, as shown in Figure 13. The main reason for this was that with a low resolution and low contrast, the objects are smaller and widely scattered, which is difficult for anchor-based models to detect. In particular, the shape of crazing is very thin and widely distributed, which caused great difficulties for the target positioning of the model.

Some possible methods we can develop to improve the performance include the following: First, expand the data set, to enable the model to learn more information. Second, use anchor-free techniques for detection. Third, combine a transformer model to extract global features, which would help the model to better locate target defects.

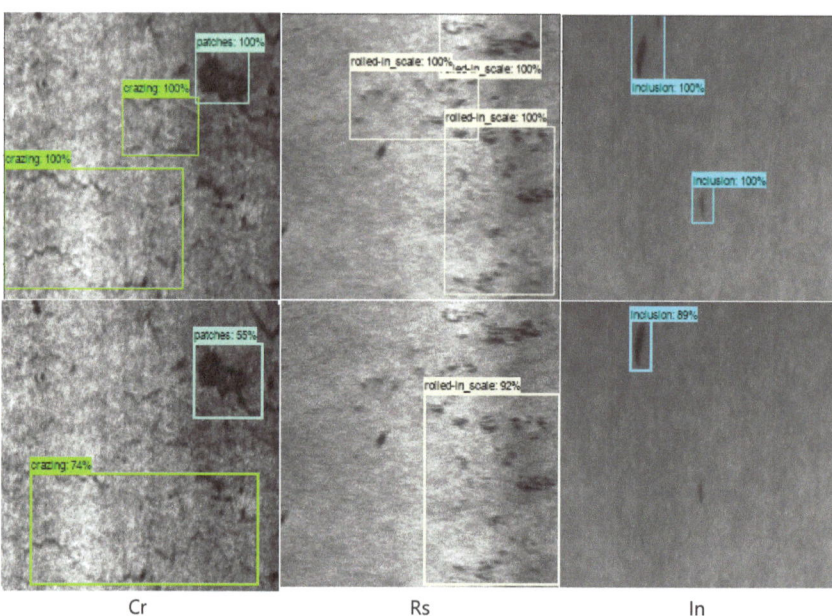

Figure 13. Examples of failed detection with our model on NEU-DET, where the first line is the ground truth. Cr: crazing, Rs: rolled-in scale, In: inclusion.

6. Conclusions

Steel defects with small interclass and large intraclass differences and the high requirement for detection speed in industrial production raise significant challenges regarding their detection. These are the two main problems that hinder the development of strip steel surface defect detection. In order to solve these issues, this study proposed a new detection method, which is a lightweight model with high detection accuracy and speed. We followed the classic frame of the SSD. We design a CFS in the encoding stage, which introduced more contextual information for the multiscale feature map and improved the detection accuracy, while maintaining the speed. In the decoding stage, a FRM was used after the predicted feature map, in order to filter out the semantic conflicts and redundancies brought by the feature map fusion of different scales. This further improved the detection accuracy. Our experiments validated our method. In particular, our experiments showed that our method achieved a comparatively better performance than the other methods, in terms of both accuracy and efficiency.

Author Contributions: Data curation, Y.L., L.H., M.Z., Z.C., W.L. and Z.W.; methodology, Y.L. and L.H.; writing—original draft preparation, Y.L. and L.H.; writing—review and editing, Y.L., L.H., M.Z. and Z.W. All authors have read and agreed to the published version of the manuscript.

Funding: The authors would like to acknowledge the support of the Hefei University graduate innovation and entrepreneurship program (Grant 21YCXL23), the support of Natural Science Foundation of China (Grants 61906062 and 72271085), the support of the Talent Foundation of Hefei University (Grants 18-29RC28 and 18-19RC29), the support of the Distinguished Young Scientist Foundation of Anhui Education Department (Grant 2022AH020095), and the support of the Visiting and Research Foundation for Outstanding Young Talents of Anhui Province (Grant gxgnfx2019060).

Institutional Review Board Statement: Not applicable.

Informed Consent Statement: Not applicable.

Data Availability Statement: The datasets generated during and/or analyzed during the current study are available from the corresponding author on reasonable request.

Conflicts of Interest: The authors declare no conflict of interest.

References

1. Liu, W.; Anguelov, D.; Erhan, D.; Szegedy, C.; Reed, S.; Fu, C.Y.; Berg, A.C. SSD: Single Shot MultiBox Detector. In Proceedings of the Computer Visio (ECCV 2016), Amsterdam, The Netherlands, 11–14 October 2016; Leibe, B., Matas, J., Sebe, N., Welling, M., Eds.; Springer International Publishing: Cham, Switzerland, 2016; pp. 21–37. [CrossRef]
2. He, K.; Zhang, X.; Ren, S.; Sun, J. Deep Residual Learning for Image Recognition. In Proceedings of the IEEE Conference on Computer Vision and Pattern Recognition (CVPR), Las Vegas, NV, USA, 27–30 June 2016. [CrossRef]
3. Song, K.; Yan, Y. A noise robust method based on completed local binary patterns for hot-rolled steel strip surface defects. *Appl. Surf. Sci.* **2013**, *285*, 858–864. [CrossRef]
4. Fu, C.Y.; Liu, W.; Ranga, A.; Tyagi, A.; Berg, A.C. Dssd: Deconvolutional single shot detector. *arXiv* **2017**, arXiv:1701.06659. https://doi.org/10.48550/arXiv.1701.06659.
5. Jeong, J.; Park, H.; Kwak, N. Enhancement of SSD by concatenating feature maps for object detection. *arXiv* **2017**, arXiv:1705.09587. https://doi.org/10.48550/arXiv.1705.09587.
6. Woo, S.; Park, J.; Lee, J.Y.; Kweon, I.S. CBAM: Convolutional Block Attention Module. In Proceedings of the European Conference on Computer Vision (ECCV), Munich, Germany, 8–14 September 2018. [CrossRef]
7. Wang, Q.; Wu, B.; Zhu, P.; Li, P.; Zuo, W.; Hu, Q. Supplementary material for 'ECA-Net': Efficient channel attention for deep convolutional neural networks. In Proceedings of the 2020 IEEE/CVF Conference on Computer Vision and Pattern Recognition, Seattle, WA, USA, 14–19 June 2020; IEEE: Seattle, WA, USA, 2020; pp. 13–19. [CrossRef]
8. Di, H.; Ke, X.; Peng, Z.; Dongdong, Z. Surface defect classification of steels with a new semi-supervised learning method. *Opt. Lasers Eng.* **2019**, *117*, 40–48. [CrossRef]
9. Li, Z.; Wu, C.; Han, Q.; Hou, M.; Chen, G.; Weng, T. CASI-Net: A Novel and Effect Steel Surface Defect Classification Method Based on Coordinate Attention and Self-Interaction Mechanism. *Mathematics* **2022**, *10*, 963. [CrossRef]
10. Fu, G.; Sun, P.; Zhu, W.; Yang, J.; Cao, Y.; Yang, M.Y.; Cao, Y. A deep-learning-based approach for fast and robust steel surface defects classification. *Opt. Lasers Eng.* **2019**, *121*, 397–405. [CrossRef]
11. Tang, l.B.; Kong, J.; Wu, S. Review of surface defect detection based on machine vision. *J. Image Graph.* **2017**, *22*, 1640–1663.
12. Luo, Q.; Sun, Y.; Li, P.; Simpson, O.; Tian, L.; He, Y. Generalized completed local binary patterns for time-efficient steel surface defect classification. *IEEE Trans. Instrum. Meas.* **2018**, *68*, 667–679. [CrossRef]
13. Liu, K.; Wang, H.; Chen, H.; Qu, E.; Tian, Y.; Sun, H. Steel surface defect detection using a new Haar–Weibull-variance model in unsupervised manner. *IEEE Trans. Instrum. Meas.* **2017**, *66*, 2585–2596. [CrossRef]
14. Mei, S.; Yang, H.; Yin, Z. An unsupervised-learning-based approach for automated defect inspection on textured surfaces. *IEEE Trans. Instrum. Meas.* **2018**, *67*, 1266–1277. [CrossRef]
15. Luo, Q.; Fang, X.; Sun, Y.; Liu, L.; Ai, J.; Yang, C.; Simpson, O. Surface defect classification for hot-rolled steel strips by selectively dominant local binary patterns. *IEEE Access* **2019**, *7*, 23488–23499. [CrossRef]
16. Li, H.; Fu, X.; Huang, T. Research on surface defect detection of solar pv panels based on pre-training network and feature fusion. In *Proceedings of the IOP Conference Series: Earth and Environmental Science*; IOP Publishing: Bristol, UK, 2021; Volume 651, p. 022071. [CrossRef]
17. Girshick, R.; Donahue, J.; Darrell, T.; Malik, J. Rich feature hierarchies for accurate object detection and semantic segmentation. In Proceedings of the IEEE Conference on Computer Vision and Pattern Recognition, Columbus, OH, USA, 23–28 June 2014; pp. 580–587. [CrossRef]
18. Girshick, R. Fast r-cnn. In Proceedings of the IEEE International Conference on Computer Vision, Santiago, Chile, 7–13 December 2015; pp. 1440–1448. [CrossRef]

19. Ren, S.; He, K.; Girshick, R.; Sun, J. Faster r-cnn: Towards real-time object detection with region proposal networks. *IEEE Trans. Pattern Anal. Mach. Intell.* **2017**, *39*, 1137–1149. [CrossRef] [PubMed]
20. Lin, T.Y.; Goyal, P.; Girshick, R.; He, K.; Dollár, P. Focal loss for dense object detection. In Proceedings of the IEEE International Conference on Computer Vision, Venice, Italy, 22–29 October 2017; pp. 2980–2988. [CrossRef]
21. Redmon, J.; Farhadi, A. Yolov3: An incremental improvement. *arXiv* **2018**, arXiv:1804.02767. https://doi.org/10.48550/arXiv.1804.02767.
22. Bochkovskiy, A.; Wang, C.Y.; Liao, H.Y.M. Yolov4: Optimal speed and accuracy of object detection. *arXiv* **2020**, arXiv:2004.10934. https://doi.org/10.48550/arXiv.2004.10934.
23. Jocher, G.; Stoken, A.; Borovec, J.; Chaurasia, A.; Changyu, L.; Laughing, A.; Hogan, A.; Hajek, J.; Diaconu, L.; Marc, Y.; et al. ultralytics/yolov5: v5. 0-YOLOv5-P6 1280 models AWS Supervise. ly and YouTube integrations. *Zenodo* **2021**, *11*, 4679653.
24. Ge, Z.; Liu, S.; Wang, F.; Li, Z.; Sun, J. Yolox: Exceeding yolo series in 2021. *arXiv* **2021**, arXiv:2107.08430. https://doi.org/10.48550/arXiv.2107.08430.
25. Zhao, W.; Chen, F.; Huang, H.; Li, D.; Cheng, W. A new steel defect detection algorithm based on deep learning. *Comput. Intell. Neurosci.* **2021**, *2021*, 5592878. [CrossRef] [PubMed]
26. Hatab, M.; Malekmohamadi, H.; Amira, A. Surface defect detection using YOLO network. In Proceedings of the SAI Intelligent Systems Conference, London, UK, 3–4 September 2020; pp. 505–515. [CrossRef]
27. Kou, X.; Liu, S.; Cheng, K.; Qian, Y. Development of a YOLO-V3-based model for detecting defects on steel strip surface. *Measurement* **2021**, *182*, 109454. [CrossRef]
28. He, Y.; Song, K.; Meng, Q.; Yan, Y. An end-to-end steel surface defect detection approach via fusing multiple hierarchical features. *IEEE Trans. Instrum. Meas.* **2019**, *69*, 1493–1504. [CrossRef]
29. Cheng, X.; Yu, J. RetinaNet with difference channel attention and adaptively spatial feature fusion for steel surface defect detection. *IEEE Trans. Instrum. Meas.* **2020**, *70*, 1–11. [CrossRef]
30. Simonyan, K.; Zisserman, A. Very deep convolutional networks for large-scale image recognition. *arXiv* **2014**, arXiv:1409.1556. https://doi.org/10.48550/arXiv.1409.1556.
31. Lin, T.Y.; Dollár, P.; Girshick, R.; He, K.; Hariharan, B.; Belongie, S. Feature pyramid networks for object detection. In Proceedings of the IEEE Conference on Computer Vision and Pattern Recognition, Honolulu, HI, USA, 21–26 July 2017; pp. 2117–2125. [CrossRef]
32. Long, J.; Shelhamer, E.; Darrell, T. Fully convolutional networks for semantic segmentation. In Proceedings of the IEEE Conference on Computer Vision and Pattern Recognition, Boston, MA, USA, 7–12 June 2015; pp. 3431–3440. [CrossRef]
33. Noh, H.; Hong, S.; Han, B. Learning deconvolution network for semantic segmentation. In Proceedings of the IEEE International Conference on Computer Vision, Santiago, Chile, 11–18 December 2015; pp. 1520–1528. [CrossRef]
34. Zeiler, M.D.; Fergus, R. Visualizing and understanding convolutional networks. In Proceedings of the European Conference on Computer Vision, Zurich, Switzerland, 6–12 September 2014; pp. 818–833. [CrossRef]
35. Russakovsky, O.; Deng, J.; Su, H.; Krause, J.; Satheesh, S.; Ma, S.; Huang, Z.; Karpathy, A.; Khosla, A.; Bernstein, M.; et al. Imagenet large scale visual recognition challenge. *Int. J. Comput. Vis.* **2015**, *115*, 211–252. [CrossRef]
36. Xie, S.; Girshick, R.; Dollár, P.; Tu, Z.; He, K. Aggregated residual transformations for deep neural networks. In Proceedings of the IEEE Conference on Computer Vision and Pattern Recognition, Honolulu, HI, USA, 21–26 July 2017; pp. 1492–1500. [CrossRef]
37. Li, J.; Su, Z.; Geng, J.; Yin, Y. Real-time detection of steel strip surface defects based on improved yolo detection network. *IFAC-PapersOnLine* **2018**, *51*, 76–81. [CrossRef]
38. Jocher, G.; Chaurasia, A.; Qiu, J. YOLO by Ultralytics, 2023. Available online: https://doi.org/10.5281/zenodo.7347926 (accessed on 17 May 2023).
39. Muhammad, M.B.; Yeasin, M. Eigen-cam: Class activation map using principal components. In Proceedings of the 2020 International Joint Conference on Neural Networks (IJCNN), Glasgow, UK, 19–24 July 2020; pp. 1–7. [CrossRef]

Disclaimer/Publisher's Note: The statements, opinions and data contained in all publications are solely those of the individual author(s) and contributor(s) and not of MDPI and/or the editor(s). MDPI and/or the editor(s) disclaim responsibility for any injury to people or property resulting from any ideas, methods, instructions or products referred to in the content.

Article

Object Detection Algorithm of UAV Aerial Photography Image Based on Anchor-Free Algorithms

Qi Hu [1], Lin Li [2], Jin Duan [2,*], Meiling Gao [2], Gaotian Liu [2], Zhiyuan Wang [2] and Dandan Huang [2]

[1] College of Artificial Intelligence, Chang Chun University of Science and Technology, Changchun 130022, China
[2] College of Electronic Information Engineering, Chang Chun University of Science and Technology, Changchun 130022, China
* Correspondence: duanjin@vip.sina.com

Abstract: Aiming at the problems of the difficult extraction of small target feature information, complex background, and variable target scale in unmanned aerial vehicle (UAV) aerial photography images. In this paper, an anchor-free target detection algorithm based on fully convolutional one-stage object detection (FCOS) for UAV aerial photography images is proposed. For the problem of complex backgrounds, the global context module is introduced in the ResNet50 network, which is combined with feature pyramid networks (FPN) as the backbone feature extraction network to enhance the feature representation of targets in complex backgrounds. To address the problem of the difficult detection of small targets, an adaptive feature balancing sub-network is designed to filter the invalid information generated at all levels of feature fusion, strengthen multi-layer features, and improve the recognition capability of the model for small targets. To address the problem of variable target scales, complete intersection over union (CIOU) Loss is used to optimize the regression loss and strengthen the model's ability to locate multi-scale targets. The algorithm of this paper is compared quantitatively and qualitatively on the VisDrone dataset. The experiments show that the proposed algorithm improves 4.96% on average precision (AP) compared with the baseline algorithm FCOS, and the detection speed is 35 frames per second (FPS), confirming that the algorithm has satisfactory detection performance, real-time inference speed, and has effectively improved the problem of missed detection and false detection of targets in UAV aerial images.

Keywords: object detection; drone aerial photography; global context block; multi-scale feature fusion; adaptive equalization network

Citation: Hu, Q.; Li, L.; Duan, J.; Gao, M.; Liu, G.; Wang, Z.; Huang, D. Object Detection Algorithm of UAV Aerial Photography Image Based on Anchor-Free Algorithms. *Electronics* **2023**, *12*, 1339. https://doi.org/10.3390/electronics12061339

Academic Editor: Donghyeon Cho

Received: 18 January 2023
Revised: 14 February 2023
Accepted: 26 February 2023
Published: 11 March 2023

Copyright: © 2023 by the authors. Licensee MDPI, Basel, Switzerland. This article is an open access article distributed under the terms and conditions of the Creative Commons Attribution (CC BY) license (https://creativecommons.org/licenses/by/4.0/).

1. Introduction

In recent years, Unmanned aerial vehicles (UAVs) have been widely used in traffic monitoring, sea area search and rescue, aerial photography, and other fields due to their small size, convenient operation, and high imaging resolution. UAV object detection is one of the important branches of computer vision tasks, and the target instances in the images can be captured efficiently by processing the images captured by UAVs.

The design of traditional object detection algorithms is mainly based on artificially constructed features, such as scale invariant feature transform (SIFT) [1], Haar-like (Haar) [2], Deformable Part Model (DPM) [3], etc.

However, its limitations are that the manually designed features require a large amount of prior knowledge, fail to make full use of deep semantic information, and have weak generalization ability. In recent years, with the rise and development of deep learning technology, the use of Convolutional Neural Networks (CNNs) has been applied to object detection tasks.

CNN-based object detection algorithms are generally divided into two categories, namely, two-stage algorithms and single-stage algorithms. The two-stage algorithm is to first generate a series of candidate frames as samples by the algorithm, and then classify the samples through CNNs. The single-stage object detection algorithm does not need to generate a candidate frame, but directly predicts the bounding box and target type of the object. Typical representatives of two-stage algorithms include region-CNN (R-CNN) [4], Faster R-CNN [5], Mask R-CNN [6], etc. Typical representatives of single-stage algorithms include You Only Look Once (YOLO) [7], single shot multi-box detector (SSD) [8], RetinaNet [9], etc. Aiming at the problems of object detection in UAV aerial images, many scholars have carried out a series of studies. Liu et al. [10] designed and added a multi-branch parallel feature pyramid network (MPFPN) on the Faster R-CNN and introduced a supervised spatial attention module (SSAM) to effectively improve the detection performance of UAV image targets in complex backgrounds, but the detection of small targets still needs to be improved. Liang et al. [11] proposed a spatial context analysis method for object re-inference based on the SSD algorithm, which greatly improves the detection accuracy of small targets, but there are false detection cases for targets in complex contexts. Zhou et al. [12] designed a metric-based object classification method to solve the classification problem of untrained subclass objects and modified the localization loss function to improve the localization performance of small objects.

As for the object detection algorithm, it can be divided into anchor-based algorithm and anchor-free algorithm according to the setting of anchor frame or not. The anchor-based method needs to pre-set a certain number of anchors at each position in the feature map of the image, and then classify and regress each anchor. The anchor-free method does not need to pre-set the anchor and directly detects the object on the image. The main difference between the two methods is whether to use anchor to generate proposal. Compared with the anchor-based algorithm, the anchor-free algorithm can greatly reduce the amount of additional parameters and reduce the memory occupied by the calculation. Many anchor-free networks that have emerged in recent years are also suitable for object detection of UAV aerial images. For example, CornerNet [13] proposed for the first time to predict the target as a pair of key points through a single neural network, using box-to-corner prediction instead of anchor for localization and target detection. CenterNet [14] models the detection object as a single center point of the bounding box and uses the heat map generated by the convolutional network to predict and classify the single centroid. Zhang et al. [15] improved on the basis of YOLOX network and proposed the skip scale feature enhancement module BiNet, which effectively improved the detection accuracy of small targets. Inspired by FoveaBox, Liu et al. [16] reset the target detection layer and proposed a HollowBox algorithm for multi-size features, which effectively reduces the false detection probability of drone detection. Hou et al. [17] applied the fully convolutional one-stage object detection (FCOS) algorithm to ship detection to further improve the detection performance of ship targets. Mao et al. [18] proposed ResSARNet based on the improvement of FCOS to obtain powerful detection performance by compressing the model parameters. The above anchor-free frame algorithm, in which FCOS performs detection by pixel-by-pixel point-wise regression, not only gets rid of the anchor frame but also outperforms most target detection algorithms in terms of performance. However, it still has limitations. Although the algorithm uses feature pyramid network (FPN) for multi-level prediction, the detection effect is still unsatisfactory for targets with large scale changes and cases where different targets overlap each other.

Therefore, this paper uses the single-stage target detection algorithm FCOS without anchor frames as the benchmark algorithm to improve it. The main contributions of the article are as follows: (1) To improve the backbone network, introduce the Global Context Block (GC-Block) into the residual block of the ResNet50 network, and improve the network's capture of UAV targets in complex backgrounds ability. (2) Propose the Adaptive Feature Balancing Subnet (AFBS) structure, which can effectively balance the low-level and high-level features from the multi-level feature map, avoiding the dilution of its information flow when passing across layers, thus effectively improving the detection accuracy of small targets. (3) Use complete intersection over union (CIOU) Loss to optimize the regression loss, thus giving the model regression process scale sensitivity and strengthening the algorithm's ability to detect multi-scale targets.

2. Materials and Methods

2.1. Baseline

FCOS is a single-stage anchor-free object detection algorithm based on FCN proposed by Tian Z et al. [19], which detects by means of pixel-by-pixel regression. The specific method is that FCOS performs a regression operation on each feature point on the feature map to predict four values (l,r,t,d), which, respectively, represent the distance from the feature point to the upper, lower, left, and right sides of the target boundary frame. As shown in Figure 1, the network consists of three parts: the backbone network (Backbone), the feature pyramid (Feature Pyramid Network, FPN) [20], and the output section Detection head, which includes Classification, Regression, and Center-ness branches.

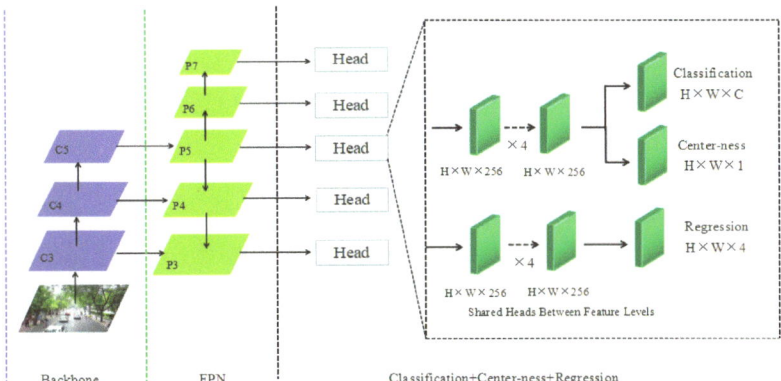

Figure 1. FCOS network architecture.

FCOS mainly has the following advantages: (1) By getting rid of the anchor box, it avoids the complex intersection over union (IOU) calculation and reduces the training memory footprint. (2) It can be used as a Region Proposal Network (RPN) for two-stage detectors, and its performance is significantly better than anchor-based RPN. (3) Strong universality, the improved model can be applied to other visual tasks. In summary, this paper chooses the FCOS algorithm as the benchmark algorithm.

2.2. Algorithm of This Paper

The algorithmic network architecture of this paper is shown in Figure 2.

The model uses the ResNet50 network for feature extraction of the input image to obtain the initial features, selects the obtained C3, C4, and C5 features to send to FPN for feature fusion, and then uses the outputs P3, P4, and P5 as the input feature map of adaptively spatial feature fusion (ASFF) [21]. Firstly, ASFF adjusts and integrates the features of other levels to the same resolution and then multiplies and, finally, sums the fusion with the corresponding weights of the feature maps at each level, and the features of different levels are adaptively fused to achieve the purpose of filtering conflicting information. The output feature maps from this network are M3, M4, M5, and M5 are down-sampled twice to obtain M6 and M7, respectively. The five-level features of M3, M4, M5, M6, and M7 are used as the input of balanced feature pyramid (BFP) [22], which first integrates the five-level features to generate more balanced semantic features and then refines to obtain the more differentiated feature maps N3, N4, N5, N6, and N7. Finally, the identity (layer-by-layer addition) operation is executed to add M3~M7 to N3~N7, correspondingly, to enhance the original features. The detection head located at the end of the network detects the enhanced 5-layer features, which enter the detection head first through 4 H×W×256 convolutional layers for feature enhancement and then upstream in parallel through H×W×C and H×W×1 convolution to obtain two branches of classification and center-ness. The center-ness reflects the distance of a point on the feature map from the target center. By multiplying the predicted category probability with the corresponding center-ness, the bounding boxes with high scores are kept in order according to their scores, so that low-quality bounding boxes are filtered out in the non-maximum suppression (NMS) process, and the regression detection results are obtained by H×W×4 convolution in the downstream.

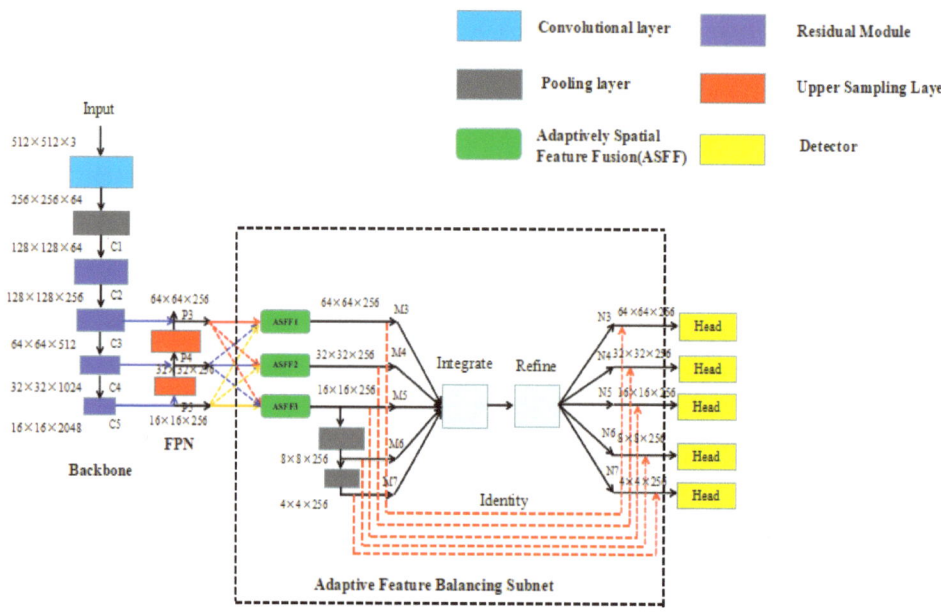

Figure 2. The algorithm network architecture of this paper.

2.2.1. Improved Backbone Network

The general target detection model uses convolution operation to extract image features, but, since the convolution kernel only acts on the local receptive field, only the depth stacking of the convolution layer can associate all the regional information of the image. Multiple convolution stacking will increase the difficulty of training, and the network learning efficiency will be low, which will greatly reduce the positioning accuracy of the model for UAV image targets. In order to solve the above problems, this paper introduces the global context block (GC-Block) [23] to improve the residual block of ResNet50, strengthens the ability of ResNet50 to capture long-distance dependencies, and uses the self-attention mechanism in the module to model the dependencies between long-distance pixels on the image. The improved backbone network is shown in Figure 3.

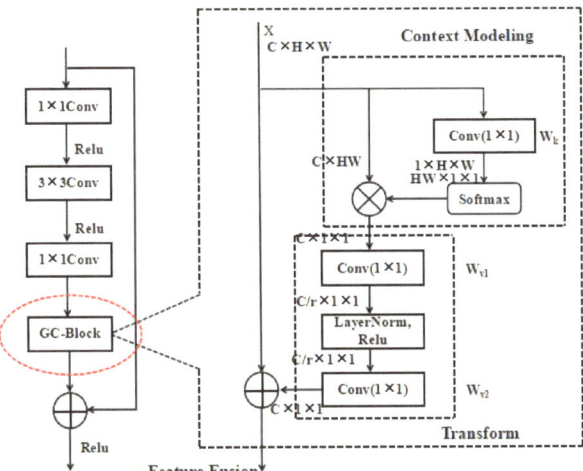

Figure 3. Improved backbone network structure.

2.2.2. Adaptive Feature Equalization Subnetwork

Adaptive Feature Balancing Subnet (AFBS) consists of two parts: ASFF and BFP. The sub-network can not only adaptively learn the spatial weight of the multi-scale feature map, but also use the deeply integrated balanced semantic features to balance and strengthen the multi-level feature information, thus the information of small objects can be completely displayed. The network structure is shown in Figure 4.

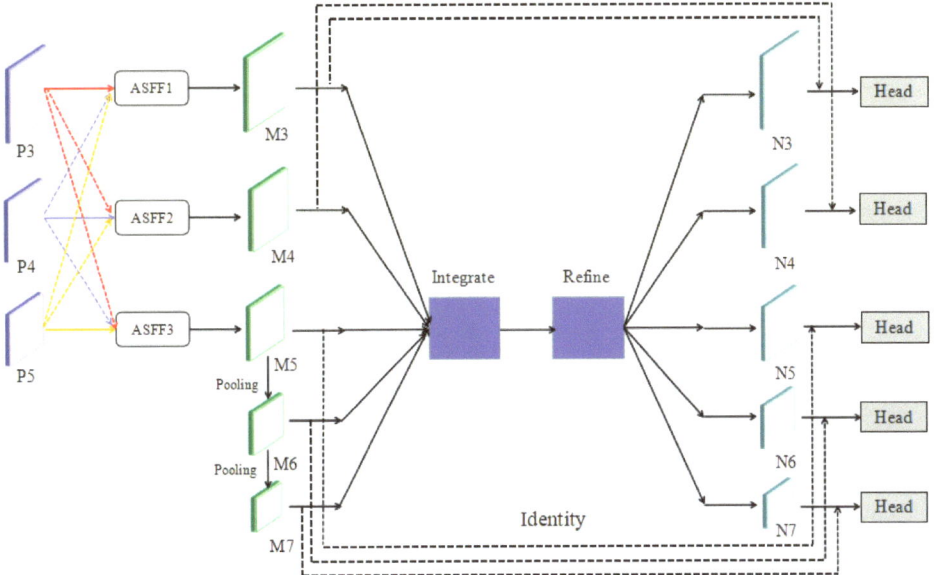

Figure 4. Architecture diagram of Adaptive Feature Equalization Subnetwork.

Adaptive Spatial Feature Fusion Module

The key idea of adaptive spatial feature fusion is to learn the fused spatial weights of features at different scales. multiply the learned parameters of each weight with the input to filter conflicting information and retain useful information to solve the problem of conflicting information when multi-layer features are fused. The specific implementation steps of this method are as follows:

(1) Feature input. Input the feature maps of different scales in the backbone network.
(2) Feature scaling. Scaling is to keep the channel of feature fusion the same. For the feature layer that needs to be upsampled, first use 1×1 convolution to adjust the number of channels to be consistent with the target layer, and then use interpolation to increase the resolution and adjust the size. For the 1/2 scale downsampling layer, a convolution of size 3×3 with stride 2 is used. For the 1/4 scale downsampling layer, it is necessary to add a maximum pooling layer with a stride of 2 to the convolution with a size of 3×3 and a stride of 2.
(3) Feature Fusion. Assuming that the target layer is l, $x_{i,j}^{n \to l}$ represents the feature vector adjusted from layer n to layer l at feature map (i, j), and α_{ij}^l, β_{ij}^l, and γ_{ij}^l are the spatial weight parameters of features $x^{1 \to l}$, $x^{2 \to l}$, and $x^{3 \to l}$ fused to layer (i, j) at l, respectively. The feature vectors of different feature maps at (i, j) are multiplied with their respective weights and then summed. l layer fusion outputs the following equation:

$$F_{ij}^l = \alpha_{ij}^l \cdot x_{ij}^{1 \to l} + \beta_{ij}^l \cdot x_{ij}^{2 \to l} + \gamma_{ij}^l \cdot x_{ij}^{3 \to l} \tag{1}$$

where the weights α, β, γ represent the spatial importance of the features at different levels, ranging from [0, 1] and summing to 1, generated using the Softmax function and with $\lambda_{\alpha_{ij}}^l, \lambda_{\beta_{ij}}^l, \lambda_{\gamma_{ij}}^l$ as control parameters, calculated as follows:

$$\alpha_{ij}^l = \frac{e^{\lambda_{\alpha ij}^l}}{e^{\lambda_{\alpha ij}^l} + e^{\lambda_{\beta ij}^l} + e^{\lambda_{\gamma ij}^l}} \tag{2}$$

Balanced Feature Pyramid

The balanced feature pyramid fully fuses the multi-dimensional features of different depth feature maps; thus, the fused features take into account both powerful semantic information and rich geometric information. The work process is divided into four steps:

(1) Feature size adjustment

The five features M3, M4, M5, M6, and M7 participating in feature fusion are adjusted to the same resolution through interpolation and maximum pooling operations. Because choosing a larger resolution will increase the network computing burden, a smaller resolution will be detrimental to small target detection. Therefore, this paper uniformly adjusts the same size as M5, and this process can avoid the input of additional parameters.

(2) Feature fusion

Feature fusion is to integrate features of different sizes and resolutions to remove redundant information, as to obtain better feature expression. The fusion is performed as follows to obtain balanced semantic features:

$$C = \frac{1}{L} \sum_{min}^{max} C_l \tag{3}$$

Among them, C_l represent the l layer feature, l_{min} and l_{max} denote the highest and lowest layer features, respectively.

(3) Feature refinement

The Gaussian non-local module [24] is used to refine the fused features. This module can refine the fused semantic features to make them more distinguishable, thereby further improving the performance of object detection in the UAV scene.

(4) Feature enhancement

The idea of strengthening comes from the design concept of the residual structure. M3~M7 are added correspondingly to the optimized features through cross-connection and finally output N3~N7.

2.2.3. Loss Function

The loss function, as the basis for the deep neural network to judge the false detection samples, largely influences the model's convergence effect, while providing optimization direction for the training of object detection network. The loss function of the algorithm in this paper contains three main components: Focal Loss is used as the classification loss function, Binary Cross Entropy (BCE) is used as the loss function of center-ness branch, and CIOU [25] is used as the regression loss function. The total loss L is defined as follows:

$$L = L_{cls} + L_{center} + L_{reg} \tag{4}$$

L_{cls} is the classification loss, L_{center} is the loss of center-ness branch, and L_{reg} is the regression loss.

(1) Classification loss function

Focal Loss is a loss function used to deal with unbalanced sample classification. When there are too many negative samples, the classification accuracy will be reduced. By reducing the weight of easily classified samples, Focal loss enables the model to learn difficult classified samples in a centralized manner, as to prevent a large number of easily classified negative samples from dominating model training in the training process. The formula is as follows:

$$L_{Focal} = \begin{cases} -(1-\alpha)y*^\gamma \log(1-y*), y = 0 \\ -\alpha(1-y*)^\gamma \log y*, y = 1 \end{cases} \tag{5}$$

Among them, y is the real value, $y*$ is the predicted value, which α is a balance factor to balance the importance of positive and negative samples, and the value range is [0, 1], which γ is an adjustable focal length parameter.

(2) Binary Cross Entropy loss function.

FCOS uses the center-ness branch to suppress low-quality detection frames in UAV image samples. The regression object's center-ness of a certain position in the sample is defined as follows:

$$Centerness* = \sqrt{\frac{\min(l*, r*)}{\max(l*, r*)} \times \frac{\min(t*, b*)}{\max(t*, b*)}} \tag{6}$$

Among them, the $l*, r*, t*, b*$ represent vertical distances from the point to the upper, lower, left, and right boundaries of the ground truth box, respectively.

(3) Improved regression loss function

The regression loss is mainly used to train the ability of the model to accurately locate the small target of the UAV. The benchmark algorithm uses IOU Loss as the regression loss. The value of IOU is 0 when the two boundary frames do not overlap. It is effective only when the two boundary frames overlap, the actual distance between the predicted frame and the real frame cannot be judged.

Therefore, this paper adopts CIOU Loss instead of IOU Loss. CIOU not only considers the overlap area and center point distance but also the aspect ratio in the process of bounding box regression, CIOU Loss can overcome its own defects while making full use of the advantages of IOU Loss and is sensitive to the transformation of the target's bounding box shape, which is more conducive to the detection of UAV multi-scale targets. The expressions of IOU and CIOU are as follows:

$$IOU = \frac{B \cap B^{gt}}{B \cup B^{gt}} \tag{7}$$

$$L_{CIOU} = 1 - IOU + \frac{\rho^2(B, B^{gt})}{C^2} + \beta v \tag{8}$$

Among them:

$$\beta = \frac{v}{(1 - IOU) + v} \tag{9}$$

$$v = \frac{4}{\pi^2}(\arctan\frac{w^{gt}}{h^{gt}} - \arctan\frac{w}{h})^2 \tag{10}$$

β is a positive trade-off parameter, and v is used to measure the consistency of the aspect ratio. B is the predicted frame, B_{gt} is the ground truth, and C is the minimum frame diagonal length containing two frames.

2.3. Experimental Conditions

2.3.1. Dataset

The data used in this paper comes from the VisDrone [26] image target detection public dataset. The dataset includes 10 categories: pedestrians (people with walking or standing posture), people (people with other posture), cars, vans, buses, trucks, motorcycles, bicycles, awning tricycles, and tricycles. The VisDrone dataset is composed of 288 video clips, providing a total of 10,209 static images captured by drones of different heights, including 6471 images for training, 548 images for validation, and 3190 images for testing, totaling 2.6 million target instance samples.

2.3.2. Experiment Settings

The experimental platform in this paper used the Ubuntu 18.04 operating system. The GPU was an RTX A4000 16 G, and the CPU was an Intel(R) Xeon(R) Gold 5320 CPU @ 2.20 GHz. The deep learning framework chosen was PyTorch, and the input image size was 512 × 512. When building the network, the batch size was 8, the training was 100 epochs, the initial learning rate was set to 0.001, and the Adam optimizer was used.

2.4. Evaluation Metrics

In order to verify the effectiveness of the algorithm in this paper, evaluation was performed from both qualitative and quantitative aspects. Qualitative analysis was mainly evaluated from a subjective perspective, and quantitative analysis was mainly evaluated from objective evaluation indexes as a reference.

In this paper, comprehensive average precision AP (Average Precision), AP_S, AP_M, AP_L, FPS (Frame Per Second), Params (Parameters), and FLOPs (Floating Point Operations) indicators are used to evaluate the performance of the model. AP means that the IOU is within the range of [0.50, 0.95], with a step of 0.05. A total of 10 thresholds are used to change the comprehensive average precision. The higher the AP value, the better the detection effect of the algorithm. The formula is shown in (11).

$$AP = \frac{1}{classses}\sum_c(\frac{1}{|thresholds|}\sum_t \frac{TP(t)}{TP(t) + FP(t)}) \tag{11}$$

In the formula, classes and thresholds represent the number of target categories and the IOU threshold, respectively. c is the element in classes, and t represents the value in the threshold interval. TP is True Positives, representing positive samples that are correctly classified. FP stands for False Positives, which represent positive samples that have been misclassified. FPS is used to evaluate the real-time performance of the model, and the higher the value the better the real-time performance of the algorithm. According to the COCO evaluation system, AP_S, AP_M, and AP_L, respectively, represent the absolute pixel area of the object under small (area less than 32^2), medium (area greater than 32^2, less than 96^2), and large (area greater than 96^2) average precision.

Params is the total number of parameters in the network layer including parameters, which measures the space resource occupation of the model, the formula is shown in (12).

$$Params = \sum_{l=1}^{D} K_l^2 \times N_{l-1} \times N_l \quad (12)$$

Among them, D represents the total number of layers of the network, K_l, N_{l-1}, and N_l are the convolution kernel size, the number of input and output channels, respectively.

FLOPs measure the number of floating-point operations of the model, reflecting the computational complexity of the model. The formula is shown in (13).

$$FLOPs = \sum_{l=1}^{D} H_l \times W_l \times K_l^2 \times N_{l-1} \times N_l \quad (13)$$

In the formula, D represents the total number of layers of the network, H_l, W_l represent the height and width of the output feature map of the layer, and K_l, N_{l-1}, and N_l are the convolution kernel size and the number of input and output channels, respectively.

3. Results

3.1. Module Ablation Experiment

Baseline is FCOS algorithm, M1 is FCOS + GC-Block, M2 is FCOS + GC-Block + AFBS, M3 is FCOS + GC-Block + AFBS + CIOU, which is the algorithm in this paper. All experiments are tested on the VisDrone dataset, using AP, FLOPs, Params as metrics. The final performance comparison results are shown in Table 1.

Table 1. Comparison of ablation experiments.

Model	Baseline	GC-Block	AFBS	CIOU	AP (%)	FLOPs (G)	Params (M)
FCOS	√				18.86	77.79	32.02
M1	√	√			19.95	77.83	34.12
M2	√	√	√		23.43	82.73	39.32
M3	√	√	√	√	23.82	82.73	39.32

According to the experimental results in Table 1, compared with the baseline algorithm, it can be seen that, the AP of M1 has increased by 1.09%, and the Params increased by 2.1 M, the FOLPs have only increased by 0.04 G, which shows that the introduction of GC-Block increased the detection accuracy while generating negligible computational overhead. Compared with the baseline algorithm, M2 has increased AP by 4.57%, FLOPs increased by 4.94 G, and Params increased by 7.3 M, which shows that although AFBS improves the detection accuracy of the model through a stronger ability to adaptively fuse different feature information, the complex network structure increases the computational complexity of the model. M3 is the algorithm proposed in this paper, and the overall performance of the network reached the highest gain. Compared with the baseline algorithm, it increased AP by 4.96%. The values of the two evaluation indicators PLOPs and Params are basically the same as those in M2, which also shows that changing the loss function does not affect the calculation amount of the model.

In order to further evaluate the detection effect of the improved algorithm proposed in this paper in real special scenes, UAV aerial images with dense distribution of small targets, multi-scale targets and complex backgrounds are selected in the VisDrone dataset, and the FCOS algorithm and the algorithm in this paper are tested. The effect comparison is shown in Figure 5.

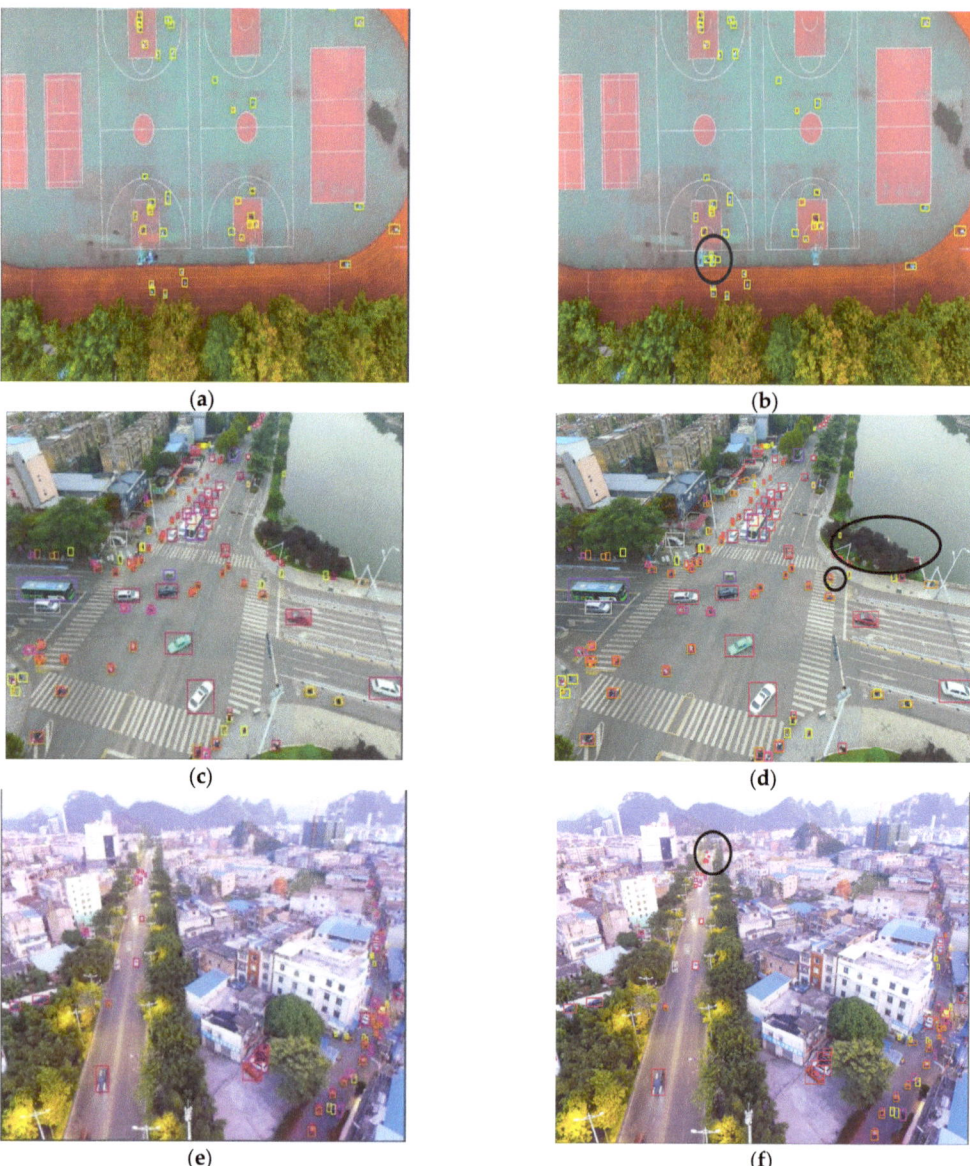

Figure 5. Visual comparison of detection effect between the FCOS algorithm and the improved algorithm in this paper. (**a**,**c**,**e**) are the detection results of FCOS ; (**b**,**d**,**f**) are the detection results of the algorithm in this paper.

Comparing Figure 5a,b, in the case of dense distribution of small targets, the FCOS algorithm mistakenly recognizes the school uniforms stacked next to the basketball poles as people, while the algorithm in this paper does not have this error. Comparing Figure 5c,d, there are a large number of targets of different scales in the figure. The FCOS algorithm did not recognize the cars on the river bank, the people in the grass, and the tricycle driving on the sidewalk on the right, and missed detection. The algorithm in this paper can better adapt to the change in the target size and thus accurately identify it. Comparing Figure 5e,f, in the case of complex background environments, the algorithm in this paper can still identify vehicles farther away on the road, and it can also detect overlapping targets normally, while FCOS misses detection. According to the comparison, it can be seen that the algorithm in this paper can better combine the superior information in high-level features and low-level features by adaptively fusing multi-layer features and has stronger identification and positioning capabilities for small targets and multi-scale targets.

3.2. Comparative Experiment

In order to verify the effectiveness of the algorithm in this paper, the model in this paper is compared with the current classic model. All experiments are trained on the VisDrone dataset and tested under the same hardware conditions. The experimental results are shown in Table 2.

Table 2. Performance comparison of each algorithm.

Method	Backbone	AP (%)	AP_S (%)	AP_M (%)	AP_L (%)	FPS	FLOPs (G)	Params (M)
Faster R-CNN	ResNet50	16.49	7.25	25.32	37.73	16	79.21	41.18
SSD	VGG-16	12.03	5.75	20.12	35.04	40	37.60	26.47
RetinaNet	ResNet50	16.85	7.91	23.97	36.82	23	84.35	37.03
R-FCN	ResNet101	19.65	9.89	26.35	41.28	19	132.38	78.16
YOLOV3	CSPDarkNet	15.05	6.28	21.45	36.18	38	75.14	61.50
FCOS	ResNet50	18.86	8.65	25.01	36.32	25	77.79	32.02
Proposal	ResNet50	**23.82**	**14.11**	**27.25**	**41.85**	35	82.73	39.32

As can be seen from Table 2, the Params of the single-stage target detection algorithm SSD is 26.47 M, the FLOPs are 37.60 G, and the AP value is 12.03% lower than other algorithms, but this algorithm has a greater advantage in Params. It can also be seen that although the R-FCN algorithm has relatively high detection accuracy, its computational complexity is also the highest. Compared with several other classical algorithms, the proposed algorithm has achieved the best detection effect. Among them, the improvement of small target detection accuracy is the most evident. Compared with the suboptimal R-FCN algorithm, the AP has increased by 4.22%, and the inference speed is relatively high. The FPS value is 35, and the FLOPs and Params are 82.73 G and 39.32 M, respectively. To sum up, the proposed algorithm achieves better detection performance on the premise of maintaining a small computational overhead, and it has great advantages compared with other algorithms in processing UAV aerial photography image target detection tasks.

Figure 6 is a visual comparison between the algorithm in this paper and other mainstream algorithms, which more intuitively reflects the detection accuracy and speed of each algorithm.

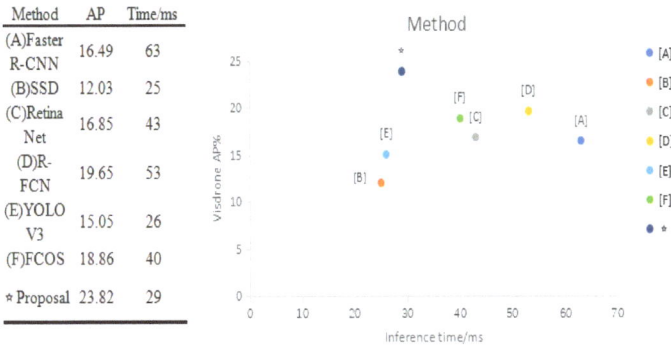

Figure 6. VisDrone test comparison visualization.

It can be seen from Figure 6 that the SSD algorithm has the highest inference speed, and the detection time of a single picture is only 50 ms. Faster R-CNN has the lowest detection efficiency, and the reasoning time for a single image takes 63 ms. Compared with several other algorithms, the reasoning efficiency of the algorithm in this paper is relatively high, and it has good real-time performance.

This paper also compares the three classic target detection algorithms selected on the VisDrone dataset, and the detection effect is shown in Figure 7:

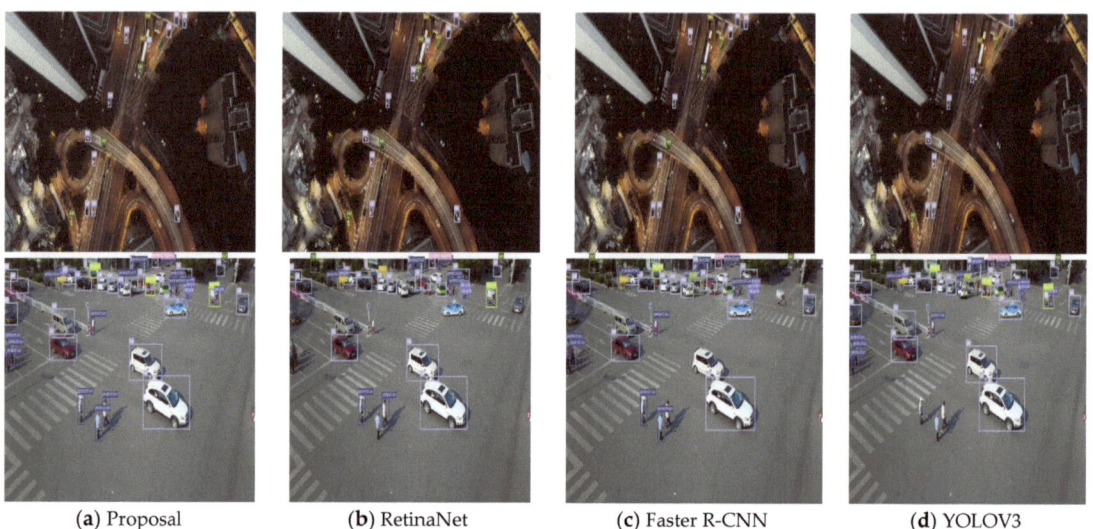

Figure 7. Comparison chart of the detection effect between the algorithm in this paper and some classic algorithms. (**a**) Proposal; (**b**) RetinaNet; (**c**) Faster R-CNN; (**d**) YOLOV3.

This paper extracts target sample instances during the day and night, respectively, and compares the detection results of the four algorithms. It can be seen that RetinaNet, Faster R-CNN, and YOLOV3 have different degrees of missing detection for small targets and targets with similar distances, while the algorithm feature learning in this paper is relatively sufficient. Compared with the other three algorithms, there were no missed or false detections. In summary, the detection accuracy of the proposed algorithm for all kinds of targets is higher than the other three, especially for small targets. This is because AFBS can better combine the superior information of high-level features and low-level features in the feature map through the adaptive fusion of multi-layer features and has stronger identification and localization ability for small targets and multi-scale targets. In the case of low illumination at night, the other three algorithms also have some missing detections. The algorithm in this paper weakens the background noise interference and strengthens the multi-scale features of interest in the network, showing strong anti-interference ability in the face of complex background information and effectively improves the missed alarm situation. In general, it has stronger recognition ability for small-scale, complex backgrounds and large scale transformation UAV image targets when processing UAV image target detection tasks, and it effectively avoids false alarms and missed alarms.

4. Conclusions

In this paper, we made improvements based on the FCOS algorithm to improve the effect of target detection for UAV aerial images. (1) Improvements were made to the backbone network by embedding the global context module in the backbone network and combining it with the FPN to enhance the algorithm's perception and understanding of the relevance of the environment in which the target is located and to improve the detection accuracy of small UAV targets in complex backgrounds. (2) An adaptive feature balancing sub-network was designed to effectively balance the dominant information in multi-layer features and reduce the false detection probability of the algorithm for small targets. (3) Finally, CIOU Loss was used to improve the regression loss function to enhance the detection capability of the algorithm for targets with larger scale transformations. The results show that the algorithm in this paper has a better detection effect on different scale targets in different aerial photography scenes. Compared with the baseline algorithm, the algorithm in this paper improves the AP by 4.96%. Compared with other mainstream algorithms, the algorithm in this paper has strong competitiveness and reduces the cases of missing detection and false positives. It is an effective aerial image target detection algorithm. In addition, the proposed algorithm has good real-time performance, which is far better than Faster R-CNN, and the detection speed is comparable to that of YOLOV3.

Author Contributions: L.L. and M.G. conducted the algorithm design; G.L. and Z.W. made a Python implementation of the proposed algorithm and formulated the proposed algorithm. J.D., Q.H. and D.H. contributed to prepare and analyze the experimental data and the results. All authors were involved in modifying the article, the literature review, and the discussion of the results. All authors have read and agreed to the published version of the manuscript.

Funding: This research was Supported by the Jilin Provincial Science and Technology Department Development Project (20210203181SF).

Institutional Review Board Statement: Not applicable.

Informed Consent Statement: Not applicable.

Data Availability Statement: Not applicable.

Acknowledgments: The authors are grateful to the reviewers for enhancing the clarity and completeness of this article.

Conflicts of Interest: The authors have no conflicts of interest to declare that are relevant to the content of this article.

References

1. Lowe, D.G. Distinctive image features from scale invariant keypoint. *Int. J. Comput. Vis.* **2004**, *60*, 91–110. [CrossRef]
2. Viola, P.; Jones, M.J. Robust real-time face detection. *Int. J. Comput. Vis.* **2004**, *57*, 137–154. [CrossRef]
3. Felzenszwalb, P.; McAllester, D.; Ramanan, D. A discriminatively trained, multiscale, deformable part mode. In Proceedings of the 2008 IEEE Conference on Computer Vision and Pattern Recognition, Anchorage, AK, USA, 23–28 June 2008; IEEE: Anchorage, AK, USA, 2008; pp. 1–8.
4. Girshick, R.; Donahue, J.; Darrell, T.; Malik, J. Rich Feature Hierarchies for Accurate Object Detection and Semantic Segmentation. In Proceedings of the IEEE Conference on Computer Vision and Pattern Recognition, Columbus, OH, USA, 23–28 June 2014.
5. Ren, S.; He, K.; Girshick, R.; Sun, J. Faster R-CNN: Towards Real-Time Object Detection with Region Proposal Networks. *IEEE Transcations Pattern Anal. Mach. Intell.* **2017**, *39*, 1137–1149. [CrossRef] [PubMed]
6. He, K.; Gkioxari, G.; Dollár, P.; Girshick, R. Mask R-CNN. In Proceedings of the 2017 IEEE International Conference on Computer Vision (ICCV), Venice, Italy, 22–29 October 2017; IEEE Press: Venice, Italy, 2017; pp. 2980–2988.
7. Redmon, J.; Divvala, S.; Girshick, R.; Farhadi, A. You only look once: Unified, real-time object detection. In Proceedings of the IEEE International Conference on Computer Vision and Pattern Recognition, Las Vegas, NV, USA, 27–30 June 2016; pp. 779–788.
8. Liu, W.; Anguelov, D.; Erhan, D.; Szegedy, C.; Reed, S.; Fu, C.Y.; Berg, A.C. SSD: Single Shot MultiBox Detector. In Proceedings of the Computer Vision–ECCV 2016: 14th European Conference, Amsterdam, The Netherlands, 11–14 October 2016.
9. Lin, T.Y.; Goyal, P.; Girshick, R.; He, K.; Dollár, P. Focal loss for dense object detection. In Proceedings of the IEEE International Conference on Computer Vision, Venice, Italy, 22–29 October 2017; pp. 2980–2988.
10. Liu, Y.; Yang, F.; Hu, P. Small-Object Detection in UAV-Captured Images Multi-Branch Parallel Feature Pyramid Networks. *IEEE Access* **2020**, *8*, 145710–145750. [CrossRef]
11. Liang, X.; Zhang, J.; Zhuo, L.; Li, Y.; Tian, Q. Small object detection in unmanned aerial vehicle images using feature fusion and scaling-based single shot detector with spatial context analysis. *IEEE Trans. Circuits Syst. Video Technol.* **2019**, *30*, 1758–1770. [CrossRef]
12. Zhou, H.; Ma, A.; Niu, Y.; Ma, Z. Small-Object Detection for UAV-Based Images Using a Distance Metric Method. *Drones* **2022**, *6*, 308. [CrossRef]
13. Law, H.; Deng, J. Cornernet: Detecting objects as paired keypoints. In Proceedings of the European Conference on Computer Vision (ECCV), Munich, Germany, 8–14 September 2018; pp. 734–750.

14. Zhou, X.; Koltun, V.; Krähenbühl, P. Objects as points. *arXiv* **2019**, arXiv:1904.07850.
15. Zhang, Q.; Zhang, H.; Lu, X.; Han, X. Anchor-Free Small Object Detection Algorithm Based on Multi-scale Feature Fusion. In Proceedings of the 2022 5th International Conference on Pattern Recognition and Artificial Intelligence (PRAI), Chengdu, China, 30 June 2022; pp. 370–374. [CrossRef]
16. Liu, S.; Qu, J.; Wu, R. HollowBox: An anchor-free UAV detection method. *LET Image Process* **2022**, *16*, 2922–2936. [CrossRef]
17. Hou, X.; Jin, G.; Tan, L. SAR Ship Target Detection Algorithm Based on Anchor—Free Frame Detection Network FCOS. In *National Security Geophysics Series (16) Big Data and Geophysics*; Xi'an Map Press: Xi'an, China, 2020; pp. 162–166.
18. Mao, Y.; Li, X.; Li, Z.; Li, M.; Chen, S. An Anchor-free SAR ship detector with only 1.17 M parameters. In Proceedings of the 2020 International Conference on Aviation Safety and Information Technology, Weihai, China, 14–16 October 2020; pp. 182–186.
19. Tian, Z.; Shen, C.; Chen, H.; He, T. FCOS: Fully convolutional one-stage object detection. In Proceedings of the IEEE International Conference on Computer Vision, Seoul, Republic of Korea, 27 October–2 November 2019; pp. 9627–9636.
20. Lin, T.Y.; Dollár, P.; Girshick, R.; He, K.; Hariharan, B.; Belongie, S. Feature pyramid networks for object detection. In Proceedings of the IEEE Conference on Computer Vision and Pattern Recognition, Honolulu, HI, USA, 21–26 July 2017; pp. 2117–2125.
21. Liu, S.; Huang, D.; Wang, Y. Learning spatial fusion for single-shot object detection. *arXiv* **2019**, arXiv:1911.09516.
22. Pang, J.; Chen, K.; Shi, J.; Feng, H.; Ouyang, W.; Lin, D. Libra R-CNN: Towards balanced learning for object detection. In Proceedings of the IEEE/CVF Conference on Computer Vision and Pattern Recognition, Long Beach, CA, USA, 15–20 June 2019; pp. 821–830.
23. Cao, Y.; Xu, J.; Lin, S.; Wei, F.; Hu, H. GCNet: Non-local networks meet squeeze-excitation networks and beyond. In Proceedings of the 2019 IEEE/CVF International Conference on Computer Vision Workshop, Seoul, Republic of Korea, 27–28 October 2019; pp. 1971–1980.
24. Wang, X.; Girshick, R.; Gupta, A.; He, K. Non-local neural networks. In Proceedings of the IEEE Conference on Computer Vision and Pattern Recognition, Salt Lake City, UT, USA, 18–23 June 2018; pp. 7794–7803.
25. Zheng, Z.; Wang, P.; Liu, W.; Li, J.; Ye, R.; Ren, D. Distance-IoU Loss: Faster and better learning for bounding box regression. In Proceedings of the AAAI Conference on Artificial Intelligence, Hilton, NY, USA, 7–12 February 2020; Volume 34, pp. 12993–13000.
26. Zhu, P.; Wen, L.; Du, D.; Bian, X.; Hu, Q.; Ling, H. Vision meets drones: Past, present and future. *arXiv* **2020**, arXiv:2001.06303.

Disclaimer/Publisher's Note: The statements, opinions and data contained in all publications are solely those of the individual author(s) and contributor(s) and not of MDPI and/or the editor(s). MDPI and/or the editor(s) disclaim responsibility for any injury to people or property resulting from any ideas, methods, instructions or products referred to in the content.

Article

A Vehicle Recognition Model Based on Improved YOLOv5

Lei Shao, Han Wu, Chao Li * and Ji Li

School of Electrical Engineering and Automation, Tianjin University of Technology, Tianjin 300384, China
* Correspondence: liton@email.tjut.edu.cn

Abstract: The rapid development of the automobile industry has made life easier for people, but traffic accidents have increased in frequency in recent years, making vehicle safety particularly important. This paper proposes an improved YOLOv5s algorithm for vehicle identification and detection to reduce vehicle driving safety issues based on this problem. In order to solve the problems of a disappearing model training gradient in the YOLOv5s algorithm, difficulty in recognizing small objects and poor recognition accuracy caused by the boundary frame regression function, it is necessary to implement a new function. These aspects have been enhanced in this article. On the basis of the traditional YOLOv5s algorithm, the ELU activation function is used to replace the original activation function. The attention mechanism module is then added to the YOLOv5s algorithm's backbone network to improve the feature extraction of small and medium-sized objects. The CIoU Loss function replaces the original regression function of YOLOv5s, thereby enhancing the convergence rate and measurement precision of the loss function. In this paper, the constructed dataset is utilized to conduct pertinent experiments. The experimental results demonstrate that, compared to the previous algorithm, the mAP of the enhanced YOLOv5s is 3.1% higher, the convergence rate is 0.8% higher, and the loss is 2.5% lower.

Keywords: deep learning; vehicle detection; YOLOv5; attention mechanism; artificial intelligence

Citation: Shao, L.; Wu, H.; Li, C.; Li, J. A Vehicle Recognition Model Based on Improved YOLOv5. *Electronics* **2023**, *12*, 1323. https://doi.org/10.3390/electronics12061323

Academic Editor: Eva Cernadas

Received: 8 February 2023
Revised: 6 March 2023
Accepted: 8 March 2023
Published: 10 March 2023

Copyright: © 2023 by the authors. Licensee MDPI, Basel, Switzerland. This article is an open access article distributed under the terms and conditions of the Creative Commons Attribution (CC BY) license (https://creativecommons.org/licenses/by/4.0/).

1. Introduction

In recent years, with the rapid development of China's industrial modernization, the number of Chinese automobiles has far surpassed the initial development of the industry. However, the frequency of traffic accidents has made the issue of safe driving one of the major research foci. Increasing attention has been paid to the development of Advanced Driver Assistance Systems (ADAS) [1] in an effort to reduce the number of accidents. ADAS systems primarily evaluate and predict the driving environment of vehicles by combining a number of sensors; in the event of a hazardous situation, the signal can be transmitted to the driver in a timely manner to ensure safe driving. Increasing numbers of people are becoming devoted to the research and development of ADAS systems as society evolves. Current ADAS systems include numerous subsystems, including Forward Collision Warning (FCW) [2]. The FCW system is an important functional component of the ADAS system, providing warning messages when a potential collision hazard is imminent, thereby preventing or reducing the severity of accident-related damage. Computer vision technology can now use advanced algorithms to detect, identify, and track objects in video [3–7] as a result of the ongoing research into computer vision by domestic and international researchers in recent years. Vehicle detection technology is a vital component of the system, and at present computer vision is primarily used to detect domestic and international targets. Using various advanced algorithms, computer vision identifies and detects objects in video [8–10].

In 2012, the proposal of the AlexNet [11,12] network sparked a new wave of deep learning algorithms, which became the predominant object detection algorithms at that time. Since then, improved object detection algorithms such as Fast RCNN [13,14], Faster RCNN [15], and R-FCN [16] have emerged. The accuracy of these proposed algorithms has reached the optimal level, but in some instances the recognition speed falls short of the requirements. In 2016, Redmon J. proposed the YOLO [5] algorithm to improve calculation speed and ensure calculation accuracy. In the same year, the SSD [17] (Single Shot Multibox Detector) algorithm based on VGG16 (Visual Geometry Group Network) was proposed to achieve multi-scale Feature Map prediction. The algorithm employs the feature layer to detect and enhance YOLO's inadequate detection of small targets. In 2018, the Redmon J. team improved YOLOv2 [18] and obtained YOLOv3 [19] algorithm, enhanced YOLO's inadequate detection of small targets.

Zhang Fukai et al. [20] enhanced the YOLOv3 algorithm to detect vehicles. Wang Fujian et al. [21] accomplished the enhancement of the YOLO algorithm dataset's target detection. By screening VOC datasets, Ding Bing et al. [22] improved the YOLOv3 algorithm and implemented the detection of parking in highway tunnels. On the basis of the concept of transfer learning, Fu Jingchao et al. [23] enhanced the adjustment learning strategy of YOLO to improve its target detection capability. YOLOv4 [24] and YOLOv5 [25] were born in 2020. The speed and accuracy of image recognition have been significantly enhanced, and the size of the YOLOv5 model has been reduced, allowing for improved detection results in the current environment. This paper employs the YOLOv5 algorithm as its starting point for vehicle target detection.

YOLOv5's engineering practicability has improved with each iteration of the YOLO series, making it the most widely used target detection algorithm at present. According to model size, YOLOv5 is available in four variants: YOLOv5s, YOLOv5m, YOLOv5l and YOLOV5x. The only difference between the Backbone and the Neck and Prediction settings is the model's depth and width settings. More feature maps are available the deeper the backbone network, and a deeper network is more complex. In addition, the YOLOV5s network has the narrowest depth feature map width and the fastest processing speed. This paper proposes an enhanced vehicle detection algorithm based on YOLOV5s, which improves the detection accuracy of small targets and accelerates the convergence rate in response to the issues of low detection accuracy and the gradient disappearance of small targets.

2. Materials and Methods

2.1. Development of Experimental Datasets

Currently, the most popular databases for vehicle detection are the KITTI database, the general dataset VOC and COCO dataset, and the general dataset VOC. In order to improve the applicability of the model, this paper combines the KITTI open-source dataset and Internet-collected road images to create a traffic target dataset. The dataset's format is VOC, and it contains images captured from various viewing angles and orientations. Figure 1 is a schematic representation of a portion of the dataset. This article selects the three dataset categories of Car, Van, and Trunk.

Python and Qt are used to develop labeling tools. When labeling datasets, rectangular boxes are used to frame vehicles and vehicle information is noted. The precise labeling procedure is depicted in Figure 2.

Once the annotation is complete, you must use the split.py file for classification, followed by the txt2yolo_label.py file to finish the conversion from .xml to .txt. You need to use the split.py file for classification, and then use the txt2yolo_label.py file to complete the conversion from .xml to .txt. The five values represent object-class, x_center, y_center, width and height attributes. In the end, 5000 images were used for training. The experiment has a training set of 4500 and a test set of 500. The ratio of the two sets was 9:1, with approximately 12,000 vehicle targets.

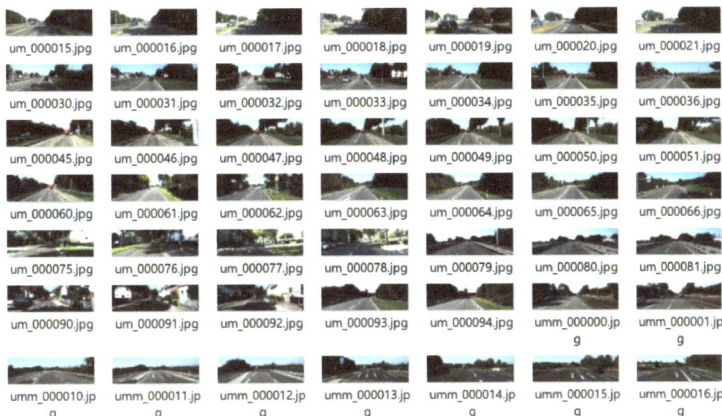

Figure 1. Portioned images extracted from the dataset.

Figure 2. Vehicle identification interface.

2.2. YOLOv5s Network Design

The YOLOV5s model is an improvement over its predecessor. The adaptive anchor frame is utilized, initially. In the training process, an expected frame is created to roughly estimate the target's position, which is then compared to the actual frame. The coordinate algorithm is used to iteratively calculate their difference. Based on this calculation, reverse update is conducted. As depicted in Figure 3, the initial predicted anchor coordinates of YOLOv5 can be obtained after multiple iterations.

```
anchors:
  - [10,13, 16,30, 33,23]      # P3/8
  - [30,61, 62,45, 59,119]     # P4/16
  - [116,90, 156,198, 373,326] # P5/32
```

Figure 3. Initial predicted coordinates for the anchor box.

YOLOv5s will optimize the algorithm so that the network's backbone can adapt to various image inputs. Before training, the majority of algorithms will, thus, unify and standardize the input images. For instance, the image size can be scaled or expanded to the sizes that YOLO uses most frequently, which significantly reduces the interference caused by the picture's unnecessary information to the running speed.

Additionally, YOLOv5s includes the CBL module, the Focus module, the SPP module, and the CSP module. It firstly performs convolution, batch standardization, and activation functions, which are then transferred to the Focus module for slicing processing, thereby minimizing the loss of image data. Then, it performs downsampling and the SPP module combines all parts, integrates the extracted features, and sends them to the CSP module for integration processing. The YOLOv5 network model is depicted in Figure 4.

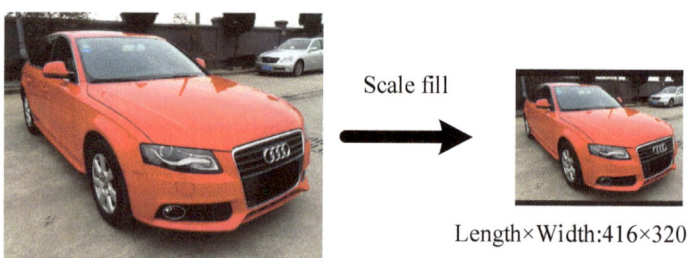

Figure 4. Size drawing after scaling.

YOLOv5s also adds CBL, Focus, SPP and CSP modules to the previous version. The CBL module mainly carries out convolution, batch standardization and function activation, and then gives it to the Focus module for slicing processing, which will greatly reduce the loss of picture information. Next, it carries out down sampling. SPP module pools all parts, fuses the extracted features, and finally sends it to CSP module for integration processing. The network model of YOLOv5 is shown in Figure 5.

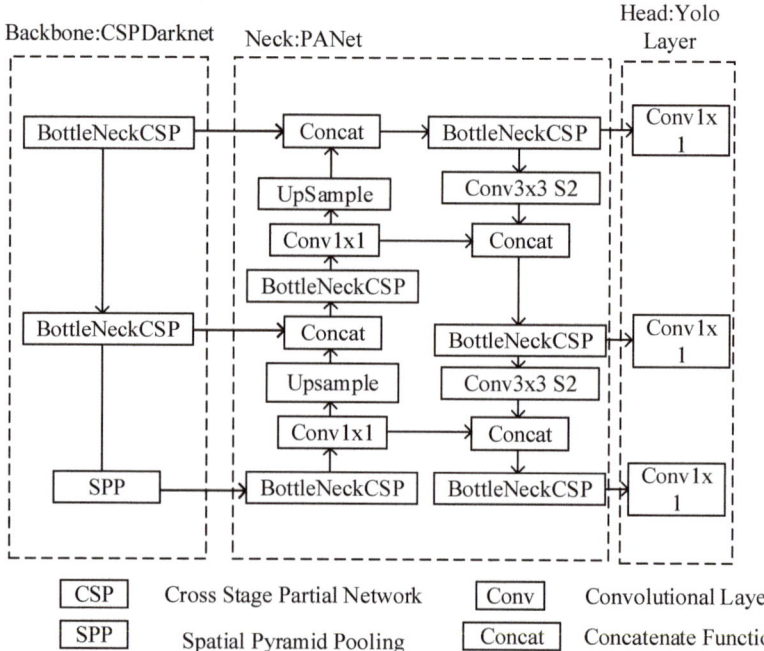

Figure 5. YOLOv5 network model diagram.

3. Methods

Due to the fact that the YOLOv5s algorithm is suitable for deployment on embedded devices with limited memory, while also meeting the accuracy requirements of the algorithm during driving and the algorithm's response speed, the YOLOv5s algorithm is currently a popular object detection algorithm. However, the YOLOv5s algorithm has numerous drawbacks: (1) YOLOv5s combines multiple activation functions in the activation function section. When multi-activation functions are combined, the training model will exhibit gradient disappearance and other issues that will further reduce its accuracy. (2) YOLOv5s has trouble identifying small objects that require identification; therefore, the algorithm's precision must be improved. (3) When a particular case exists between the detection box and the prediction box, the convergence speed of the loss function is slowed. Based on the aforementioned issues with the YOLOv5s algorithm, this chapter is based on the YOLOv5s method for vehicle detection. The activation function of YOLOv5s is first replaced. The attention mechanism module is then introduced to the backbone network in order to improve the extraction of features by YOLOv5s. The algorithm's loss function is optimized, utilizing complete intersection ratio function. Experiments were carried out to examine the algorithm's performance before and after its enhancement.

3.1. Activation Function Improvements

The CSP module of the original YOLOv5s used the Leaky ReLU function [26] and the Mish function as activation functions. When these two activation functions are utilized concurrently, the gradient will gradually diminish during back propagation and may eventually disappear. The Exponential Linear Units (ELU) activation function replaces the Leaky ReLU function and Mish function to tackle this issue. The formula for calculating the ELU activation function is depicted in the figure:

$$ELU(s) = \begin{cases} x & x > 0 \\ \alpha(e^x - 1)x \leq 0 \end{cases} \quad (1)$$

The ELU function curve is depicted in Figure 6.

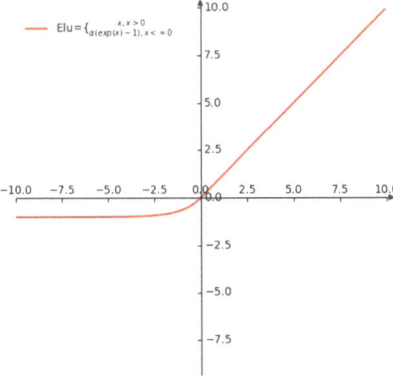

Figure 6. ELU function diagram.

The ELU function has a better linear distribution on the right side of the coordinate axis than the Leaky ReLU function, which effectively mitigates the disadvantage of gradient descent of the Leaky ReLU function. The left side of the coordinate axis is nonlinear, which may improve noise input robustness. In order to demonstrate the benefits of ELU function in a more intuitive manner, this activation function is compared to other activation functions in the COCO dataset and the results are presented in Table 1.

Table 1. Comparison table of activation functions under the COCO dataset.

Mosaic	Label Smoothing	Leaky ReLU	Mish	ELU	Top-1 Err (%)	Top-5 Err (%)
√	√	√			22.4	5.8
√	√	√	√		21.5	5.4
√	√			√	21.0	5.1

Table 1 demonstrates that the first and fifth error rates decreased by 0.9% and 0.4% when the Leaky ReLU function and Mish function were combined as compared to the Leaky ReLU function alone, and that the first and fifth error rates decreased by 0.5% and 0.3% when the ELU function was utilized alone. According to the experimental findings, it is possible to achieve the gradient descent caused by the combination of the two activation functions. The enhanced activation function can decrease the error rate and increase the calculation's precision.

3.2. Enhanced Attention Mechanism Module

The attention process resembles the attention mechanism used by humans for object recognition. The primary information is gained by allocating sufficient resources. Important data are collected and retrieved using a convolutional neural network, which significantly enhances the precision of data collecting. The attention mechanism module may typically be added to the backbone network, and the module's parameters are simple to alter, which significantly improves the model's performance. Currently, the attention mechanism is primarily separated into two types: a channel attention mechanism represented by SE [27] (Squeeze and Excitation) and a spatial attention mechanism represented by the Convolutional Block Attention Module (CBAM [28]).

In this paper, CBAM modules were added to three main parts of YOLOv5, as shown in Figure 7. In Figure 7a, the module is added to CSP1_3(feature fusion); in Figure 7b, the CBA module is added to the Neck part of YOLOv5s after the Concat layer; in Figure 7c, the CBMA module is added before the convolution of YOLOv5's prediction module.

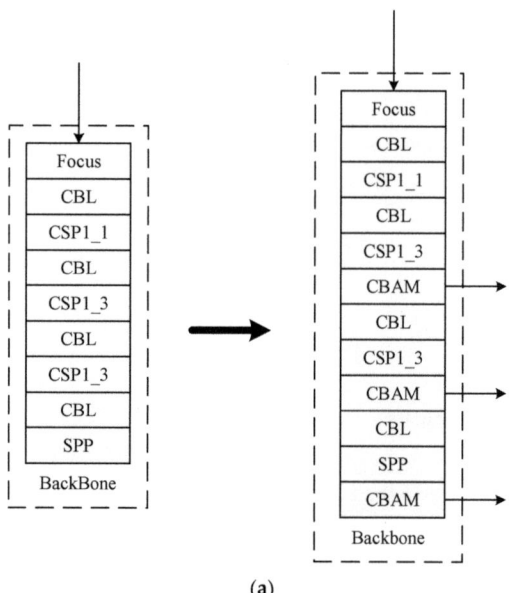

(a)

Figure 7. *Cont.*

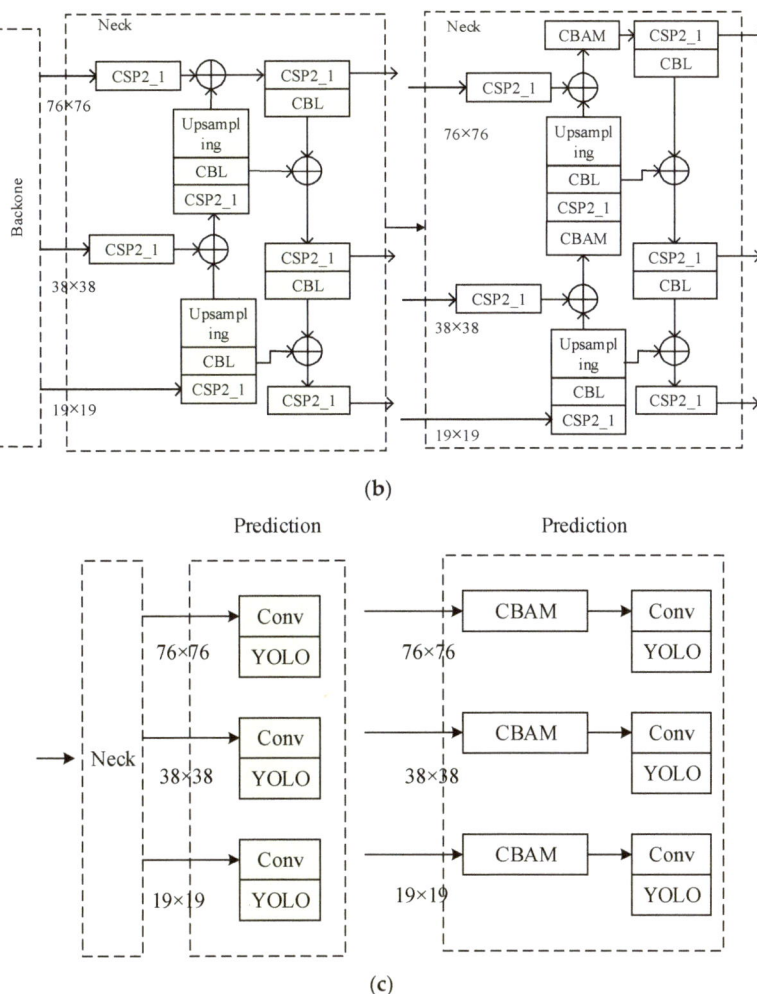

Figure 7. Network comparison before and after introducing CBMA attention mechanism. (**a**) CBAM YOLOv5s-Backbone, (**b**) CBAM YOLOv5s-Neck, (**c**) CBAM YOLOv5s-Prediction.

The comparison results of three CBAM modules in different positions and unfused YOLOv5s are shown in Table 2.

Table 2. Comparison of CBAM modules after fusion.

Network Model	AP 50%			P (%)	R (%)	mAP (%)
	Small Goal	Medium Goal	Big Goal			
YOLOv5s	83.0	97.9	99.3	76.4	92.5	92.7
CBAM_YOLOv5s-Backbone	90.4	98.2	99.4	81.2	93.8	94.1
CBAM_YOLOv5s-Neck	80.3	96.4	99.0	71.7	93.7	91.6
CBAM_YOLOv5s-Prediction	82.7	97.1	99.1	75.9	92.8	92.4

As can be seen from the table, not every fusion mode's accuracy is improved after CBAM module fusion is performed on different components of YOLOv5s. When CBAM modules are integrated into Backbone, the detection capability of small targets is greatly improved and mAP is increased by 1.4%. Since the semantic information in Backbone networks is not rich, CBAM is added to these modules to improve the accuracy. However, for Neck and Prediction, there is no improvement in accuracy. Therefore, this document adds the CBAM module to Backbone.

3.3. Improvement of CIoU Loss Function

An Intersection over Union (IoU) [29] is typically utilized to calculate the location relationship between the predicted and actual boxes in target detection using the following formula:

$$IoU = \frac{A \cap B}{A \cup B} \tag{2}$$

As depicted in Figure 8, the original IoU formula includes several weaknesses that have been rectified. In Figure 8a, when there is no intersection between the prediction box and the real box, the result of IoU computation is 0, impeding further training and algorithm execution. In Figure 8b,c, when the prediction box is the same size as the actual box, the IoU calculation yields the same result; therefore, no judgment can be formed.

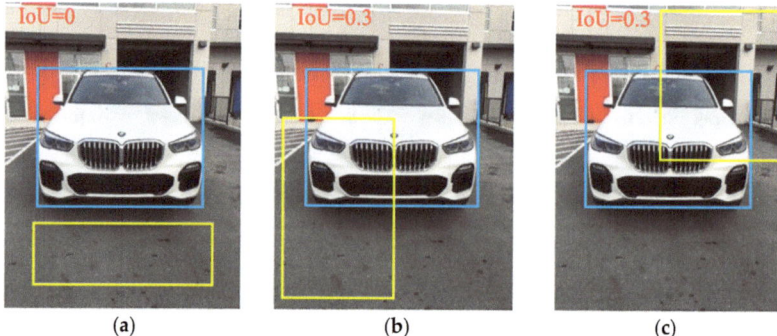

Figure 8. Network comparison before and after introducing the CBMA attention mechanism.

Therefore, in this paper, GIoU [30] (Generalized Intersection over Union) is used instead of IoU, In Figure 8, B is the yellow box, A is the blue box, and C is the red box (Figure 9). And the formulas for GIoU are shown in Equations (3) and (4):

$$GIoU = IoU - \frac{|C - (A \cup B)|}{|C|} \tag{3}$$

$$GIoU\_loss = 1 - GIoU = 1 - (IoU - \frac{|C - (A \cup B)|}{|C|}) \tag{4}$$

 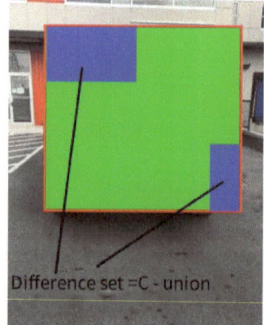

Figure 9. Schematic diagram of GIoU calculation.

GIoU introduced the test box C, which consisted of the combination of the yellow prediction box B and the blue actual box A. The GIoU calculation diagram is shown in Figure 9. In addition to considering the relationship between the prediction box and the actual box, GIoU also introduces the test box. Nevertheless, GIoU cannot play the actual effect while the two boxes are in the horizontal state. Here, the CIoU [31] function is substituted by the GIoU function, and the loss function equation for DIoU [32] is given in Equation (5):

$$DIoU\_Loss = 1 - IoU + \frac{\rho^2(b, b^{gt})}{c^2} \qquad (5)$$

here, b, b^{gt} denotes the center points of the prediction box and the real box, respectively, ρ represents the distance between the two center points, and c represents the diagonal distance of the minimal closure region that can encompass both the prediction box and the real box. In addition, the impact factor av is introduced, along with the horizontal to vertical ratio.

The improved formulas of GIoU and CIoU_Loss are shown in Equations (6) and (7).

$$CIoU = IoU - \frac{\rho^2(b, b^{gt})}{c^2} + \alpha v z_t = \sigma(W_z \cdot [h_{t-1}, x_t]) \qquad (6)$$

$$CIoU\_Loss = 1 - IoU + \frac{\rho^2(b, b^{gt})}{c^2} + \alpha v \qquad (7)$$

The parameter expression representing the penalty in the formula α is shown in Equation (8), and v represents the standard that can measure whether the aspect ratio is consistent, and the expression is shown in Equation (9):

$$\alpha = \frac{v}{(1 - IoU) + v} \qquad (8)$$

$$v = \frac{4}{\pi^2}(\arctan\frac{w^{gt}}{h^{gt}} - \arctan\frac{w}{h})^2 \qquad (9)$$

The modified formula demonstrates that the convergence rate of CIoU is substantially faster than that of IoU.

4. Test and Result Analysis

4.1. The Experiment Platform

Ubuntu18.06 is the operating system version of the training experiment machine for the model presented in this paper. Tables 3 and 4 detail the experimental setting and hardware and software configurations.

Table 3. The development environment.

Hardware Name	Version Number
Processor	AMD Ryzen 5 5600X 6-Core Processor (3701 MHz)
Graphics card	NVIDIA GeForce RTX 3060 12G
Memory	16 GB

Table 4. Software environment.

The Specific Environment	Version Number
Python	Python3.8
CUDA	11.1
CUDNN	11.3

4.2. Comparison of Training Results

Beginning with an initial learning rate of 0.01, SDG was used to optimize algorithm parameters and the cosine annealing approach was employed to dynamically modify the learning rate. The weight attenuation coefficient was set to 0.0005, the learning momentum was set to 0.937, and the Batch-Size to 8. In this experiment, 300 epochs were trained to examine the overfitting issue in the training process. Model A is denoted by the black curve, while model B is defined by the red curve. Models A and B are trained together, and the training outcomes are depicted in Figure 10.

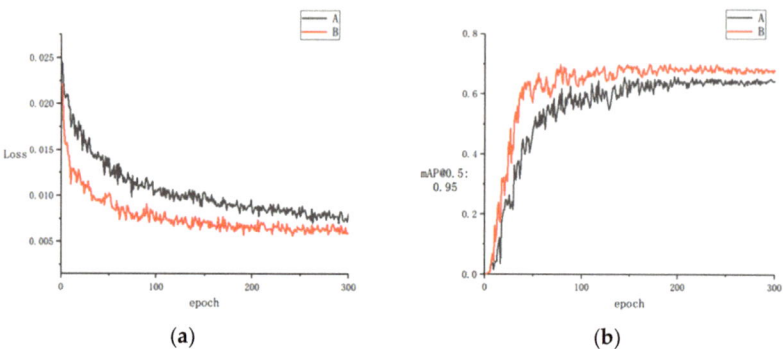

Figure 10. Comparison of AB model training parameters before and after improvement.

Figure 10a demonstrates that, compared to the loss value before improvement, the improved model exhibits a more pronounced drop and a faster convergence speed. Figure 10b demonstrates that the mAP value of the enhanced model is 3.1% greater than that of the previous model. Overall, the new model is more precise and has a faster convergence rate. The comparison of model performance before and after loss function enhancement is shown in Table 4. As shown in the Table 5, the loss value of model B's parameter was lowered by 2.8% compared to the model before improvement, showing that the convergence speed of the revised model was greatly increased. The mAP% value of the new model was 2.1% greater than previously, and its accuracy was enhanced. Furthermore, both Recall and Precision are greatly enhanced following enhancement. In conclusion, the enhancements to the YOLOv5 model presented in this research greatly increase the performance and convergence speed and precision.

Table 5. Performance comparison between model A and model B.

Model	Loss	mAP@0.5:0.95	Precision (%)	Recall (%)
Model A	0.0068	0.651	91.9	92.5
Model B	0.0070	0.672	93.9	94.5

4.3. Algorithm Improves Visual Contrast

The same image is used to examine the effect difference of the activation function of YOLOv5's algorithm improvement before and after, in order to more intuitively illustrate the improvement of the algorithm's accuracy and speed in image recognition. As shown in Figure 11a depicts the original input image, Figure 11b depicts the accuracy of vehicle recognition before the activation function is enhanced, and Figure 11c depicts the vehicle recognition after the activation function has been enhanced. After an object is discovered, there will be text indicating the sort of object detected, along with a recognition accuracy indicator.

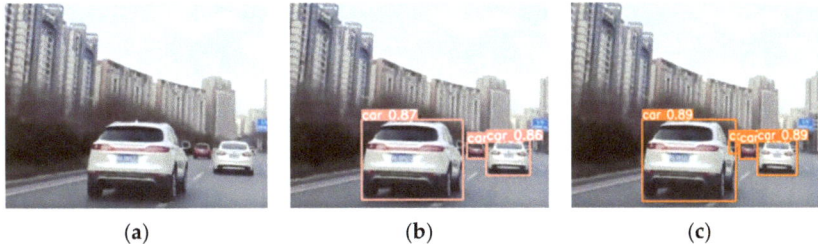

Figure 11. Visualization comparison before and after activation function improvement.

As shown in the picture above, the confidence level increases when the activation function in YOLOv5's algorithm is enhanced, the accuracy of target recognition is enhanced, and the model's performance is further enhanced.

The diagram depicts the experimental outcomes of adding the CBAM module to the YOLOV5s network architecture. As shown in Figure 12, Figure 12a is the original image, Figure 12b is the detection image before CBAM improvement, and Figure 12c is the detection image after CBAM improvement. The results indicate that the modified CBAM algorithm has significantly enhanced the detection of small objects. Tiny items that were previously undetectable can now be detected, and the confidence level has been increased; nevertheless, the improvement effect on the identification of large objects is not readily apparent. Hence, the algorithm's performance is further enhanced with the addition of the CBAM module.

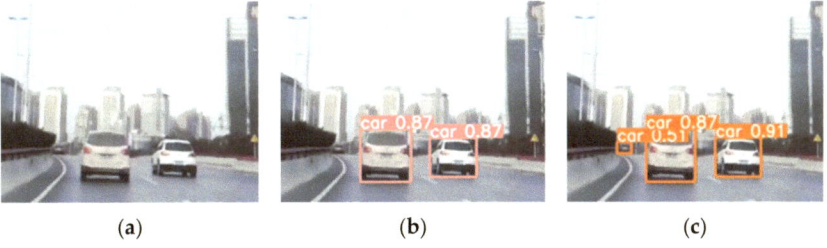

Figure 12. Visualization comparison before and after CBAM function improvement.

Figure 13 is a comparison of the experimental outcomes before and after the improvement of the loss function. Figure 13a is the original picture, Figure 13b is the detection graph before the improvement of the loss function, and Figure 13c is the detection graph after the improvement of the loss function. The preceding graph demonstrates that the modified algorithm increases the accuracy of vehicle detection, as well as the convergence speed of the loss function and the recognition speed.

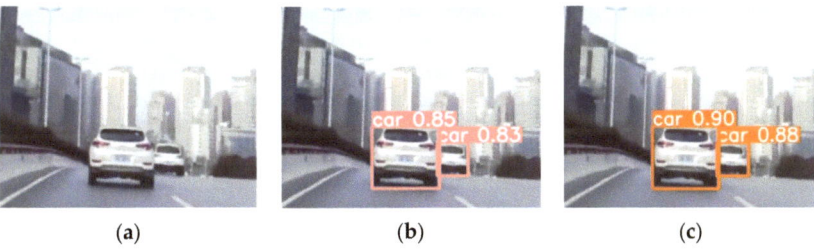

Figure 13. Visual comparison of loss function before and after improvement.

4.4. Experimental Verification of the Improved Algorithm

To further demonstrate the superiority of the enhanced algorithm, an ablation experiment was undertaken to evaluate the model's performance. The enhanced activation function, attention mechanism and loss function were utilized to validate the model's performance.

Table 6 demonstrates that after the activation function was enhanced the mAP value grew by 2.1%, while Precision and Recall also increased slightly. Adding the attention mechanism to the Backbone network increased the mAP value by 2.9%. mAP value increased by 1.5%, Precision increased by 0.9%, and Recall increased by 1.1% after the loss function was adjusted. After enhancing the three algorithmic components, the algorithm's Precision and Recall are enhanced by 2% and 2%, respectively. In conclusion, based on the ablation experiment conducted after the algorithm improvement, it can be concluded that the improved model performance was significantly enhanced in terms of confidence, precision, and recall compared to that of the previous model, thereby effectively improving the model performance.

Table 6. Comparison table of ablation experiments.

YOLOv5s	Activation Function	Mechanism of Attention	Loss Function	mAP@ 0.5:0.95(%)	P (%)	R (%)
√				65.1	91.9	92.5
√	√			66.5	92.2	92.8
√		√		67.0	93.1	94.1
√			√	66.1	92.8	93.6
√	√	√	√	67.2	93.9	94.5

In addition, YOLOv5s is compared to YOLOv4, YOLOV4-Tiny, and Faster-RCNN, which are typically used to evaluate the performance of each algorithm. Table 7 compares the performance of several algorithms.

Table 7. Performance comparison of different detection methods.

Method	Model Storage Size (MB)	mAP@0.5 (%)	P (%)
Faster-RCNN	186	83.7	83.8
YOLOv4	113.9	93.1	93.3
YOLOv4-tiny	30	83.4	87.3
YOLOv5s	24.5	87.4	91.9
Our approach	24.7	91.5	94.5

As seen in the table above, the YOLOv5s algorithm requires the minimum amount of memory to operate and performs well in terms of confidence level and precision. Following the enhancement of the experimental algorithm, the mAP@0.5 value and accuracy have been further enhanced and the method's overall performance has been enhanced.

In conclusion, the improved algorithm is superior to the previous algorithm in terms of object recognition speed and accuracy, effectively addresses the disadvantage of low accuracy in the recognition of small objects, and improves the shortcomings of the previous algorithm, such as vanishing gradient and low confidence, making the algorithm more practical and efficient.

5. Conclusions

In this paper, the original YOLOv5s algorithm was enhanced in order to address the issues present in the basic YOLOv5s algorithm, including the disappearing model training gradient, tiny target object recognition accuracy and poor convergence speed of loss function. First, the new activation function is substituted for the old model's activation function, which successfully mitigates the gradient descent of the Leaky ReLU function. Then, to address the issue that the YOLOv5s algorithm has a low recognition rate for small objects, the CBAM module is included to improve the algorithm's feature extraction for small and medium-sized objects. Lastly, the CIoU loss function replaces the original YOLOv5s loss function. The improved detection algorithm proposed in this paper is superior to the YOLOv5s algorithm prior to the improvement in terms of accuracy, mAP, Recall, etc., so the improvement of the algorithm can effectively solve the problems of gradient loss, low accuracy of small object recognition, and slow reasoning speed in the original algorithm, and the improved method has clear benefits.

Author Contributions: Conceptualization, L.S.; Data curation, C.L.; Formal analysis, J.L.; Investigation, H.W.; Methodology, L.S.; Supervision, C.L.; Validation, H.W.; Writing—original draft, H.W.; Writing—review & editing, H.W. and J.L. All authors have read and agreed to the published version of the manuscript.

Funding: This research received no external funding.

Data Availability Statement: The load forecasting data used to support the results of this study has not been provided because it is private data of enterprises.

Conflicts of Interest: The authors declare that there is no conflict of interest regarding the publication of this paper.

References

1. Divakarla, K.P.; Emadi, A.; Razavi, S.A. Cognitive advanced driver assistance systems architecture for autonomous-capable electrified vehicles. *IEEE Trans. Transp. Electrif.* **2019**, *5*, 48–58. [CrossRef]
2. Koustanaï, A.; Cavallo, V.; Delhomme, P.; Mas, A. Simulator training with a forward collision warning system: Effects on driver-system interactions and driver trust. *Hum. Factors* **2012**, *54*, 709–721. [CrossRef] [PubMed]
3. Vapnik, V.; Levin, E.; Cun, Y. Measuring the VC-Dimension of a Learning Machine. *Neural Comput.* **1994**, *6*, 851–876. [CrossRef]
4. Sri, M.S. Object detection and tracking using KLT algorithm. *Int. J. Eng. Dev. Res.* **2019**, *7*, 542–545.
5. Joseph, R.; Santosh, D.; Ross, G.; Ali, F. You Only Look Once: Unified, Real-Time Object Detection. In Proceedings of the IEEE Conference on Computer Vision and Pattern Recognition (CVPR), Las Vegas, NV, USA, 27–30 June 2016.
6. Lin, T.Y.; Maire, M.; Belongie, S.; Hays, J.; Perona, P.; Ramanan, D.; Dollár, P.; Zitnick, C.L. Microsoft COCO: Common Objects in Context. In Proceedings of the Computer Vision—ECCV 2014: 13th European Conference, Zurich, Switzerland, 6–12 September 2014.
7. Everingham, M.; Gool, L.V.; Williams, C.; Winn, J.; Zisserman, A. The Pascal Visual Object Classes (VOC) Challenge. *Int. J. Comput. Vis.* **2010**, *88*, 303–308. [CrossRef]
8. Hamsa, S.; Panthakkan, A.; Al Mansoori, S.; Alahamed, H. Automatic Vehicle Detection from Aerial Images using Cascaded Support Vector Machine and Gaussian Mixture Model. In Proceedings of the 2018 International Conference on Signal Processing and Information Security (ICSPIS), Dubai, United Arab Emirates, 7–8 November 2018; pp. 1–4.
9. Zhang, H.; Wang, Y.; Dayoub, F.; Sünderhauf, N. VarifocalNet: An IoU-aware Dense Object Detector. In Proceedings of the IEEE/CVF Conference on Computer Vision and Pattern Recognition, Seattle, WA, USA, 14–19 June 2020.
10. Wang, Z.; Jun, L. A review of object detection based on convolutional neural network. In Proceedings of the 2017 36th Chinese Control Conference (CCC), Dalian, China, 26–28 July 2017; pp. 11104–11109.
11. Krizhevsky, A.; Sutskever, I.; Hinton, G.E. ImageNet classification with deep convolutional neural networks. *Adv. Neural Inf. Process. Syst.* **2012**, *25*, 1097–1105. [CrossRef]
12. Han, X.; Zhong, Y.; Cao, L.; Zhang, L. Pre-Trained AlexNet Architecture with Pyramid Pooling and Supervision for High Spatial Resolution Remote Sensing Image Scene Classification. *Remote Sens.* **2017**, *9*, 848. [CrossRef]
13. Girshick, R. Fast R-CNN. In Proceedings of the 2015 IEEE International Conference on Computer Vision (ICCV), Santiago, Chile, 7–13 December 2015.
14. Cai, Z.; Vasconcelos, N. Cascade R-CNN: High Quality Object Detection and Instance Segmentation. *IEEE Trans. Pattern Anal. Mach. Intell.* **2021**, *43*, 1483–1498. [CrossRef] [PubMed]
15. Ren, S.; He, K.; Girshick, R.; Sun, J. Faster R-CNN: Towards Real-Time Object Detection with Region Proposal Networks. *IEEE Trans. Pattern Anal. Mach. Intell.* **2017**, *39*, 1137–1149. [CrossRef] [PubMed]
16. Girshick, R.; Donahue, J.; Darrell, T.; Malik, J. R-FCN: Object detection via region-based fully convolutional networks. In Proceedings of the 30th International Conference on Neural Information Processing Systems, Barcelona, Spain, 5–10 December 2016; pp. 379–387.
17. Liu, W.; Anguelov, D.; Erhan, D.; Szegedy, C.; Reed, S.; Fu, C.-Y.; Berg, A.C. SSD: Single shot multi-box detector. In *European Conference on Computer Vision*; Springer: Cham, Switzerland, 2016; pp. 21–37.

18. Redmon, J.; Farhadi, A. YOLO9000: Better, faster, stronger. In Proceedings of the IEEE Conference on Computer Vision and Pattern Recognition, Honolulu, HI, USA, 21–26 July 2017; pp. 7263–7271.
19. Redmon, J.; Farhadi, A. Yolov3: An incremental improvement. *arXiv* **2018**, arXiv:1804.02767.
20. Zhang, F.; Yang, F.; Li, C. Rapid Vehicle Detection Method Based on Improved YOLOv3. *Comput. Eng. Appl.* **2019**, *2*, 3–8.
21. Wang, F.; Zhang, J.; Lu, G. Vehic YOLOv4: Optimal Speed and Accle Information Detection and Tracking System Based on YOLO. *Ind. Control. Comput.* **2018**, *7*, 89–91.
22. Ding, B.; Yang, Z.; Ding, J.; Liu, J. Highway tunnel stop detection method based on improved YOLOv3. *Comput. Eng. Appl.* **2021**, *23*, 234–239.
23. Fu, J.; Su, Q.; Zhang, D.; Li, J. A Road Multi-Object Detection Method Based on YOLOv3. *Comput. Sci. Appl.* **2021**, *11*, 207–216. [CrossRef]
24. Bochkovskiy, A.; Wang, C.Y.; Liao, H.Y.M. YOLOv4: Optimal Speed and Accuracy of Object Detection. *arXiv* **2020**, arXiv:2004.10934.
25. Jocher, G. Yolov5[EB/OL]. Code Repository. 2020. Available online: https://github.com/ultralytics/yolov5 (accessed on 10 January 2022).
26. Jiang, T.; Cheng, J. Target recognition based on CNN with LeakyReLU and PReLU activation functions. In Proceedings of the 2019 International Conference on Sensing, Diagnostics, Prognostics, and Control (SDPC), Beijing, China, 15–17 August 2019; pp. 718–722.
27. Hu, J.; Shen, L.; Sun, G. Squeeze-and-excitation networks. In Proceedings of the IEEE Conference on Computer Vision and Pattern Recognition, Salt Lake City, UT, USA, 18–22 June 2018; pp. 7132–7141.
28. Liu, Y.; Shao, Z.; Hoffmann, N. Global Attention Mechanism: Retain Information to Enhance Channel-Spatial Interactions. *arXiv* **2021**, arXiv:2112.05561.
29. Jiang, B.; Luo, R.; Mao, J.; Xiao, T.; Jiang, Y. Acquisition of localization confidence for accurate object detection. In Proceedings of the European Conference on Computer Vision (ECCV), Munich, Germany, 8–14 September 2018; pp. 816–832.
30. He, J.; Erfani, S.; Ma, X.; Bailey, J.; Chi, Y.; Hua, X.S. α-IoU: A Family of Power Intersection over Union Losses for Bounding Box Regression. *Adv. Neural Inf. Process. Syst.* **2021**, *34*, 20230–20242.
31. Zheng, Z.; Wang, P.; Ren, D.; Liu, W.; Ye, R.; Hu, Q.; Zuo, W. Enhancing geometric factors in model learning and inference for object detection and instance segmentation. *IEEE Trans. Cybern.* **2021**, *52*, 8574–8586. [CrossRef] [PubMed]
32. Zheng, Z.; Wang, P.; Liu, W.; Li, J.; Ye, R.; Ren, D. Distance IoU Loss: Faster and Better Learning for Bounding Box Regression. In Proceedings of the 2020 Proceedings of the AAAI Conference on Artificial Intelligence (AAAI), New York, NY, USA, 7–12 February 2020; pp. 1–8.

Disclaimer/Publisher's Note: The statements, opinions and data contained in all publications are solely those of the individual author(s) and contributor(s) and not of MDPI and/or the editor(s). MDPI and/or the editor(s) disclaim responsibility for any injury to people or property resulting from any ideas, methods, instructions or products referred to in the content.

Article

Material-Aware Path Aggregation Network and Shape Decoupled SIoU for X-ray Contraband Detection

Nan Xiang [1], Zehao Gong [1], Yi Xu [1] and Lili Xiong [2],*

[1] Liangjiang International College, Chongqing University of Technology, Chongqing 400054, China
[2] Chongqing Academy of Science and Technology, Chongqing 401331, China
* Correspondence: sealilyxiong@163.com

Abstract: X-ray contraband detection plays an important role in the field of public safety. To solve the multi-scale and obscuration problem in X-ray contraband detection, we propose a material-aware path aggregation network to detect and classify contraband in X-ray baggage images. Based on YoloX, our network integrates two new modules: multi-scale smoothed atrous convolution (SCA) and material-aware coordinate attention modules (MCA). In SAC, an improved receptive field-enhanced network structure is proposed by combining smoothed atrous convolution, using separate shared convolution, with a parallel branching structure, which allows for the acquisition of multi-scale receptive fields while reducing grid effects. In the MCA, we incorporate a spatial coordinate separation material perception module with a coordinated attention mechanism. A material perception module can extract the material information features in X and Y dimensions, respectively, which alleviates the obscuring problem by focusing on the distinctive material characteristics. Finally, we design the shape-decoupled SIoU loss function (SD-SIoU) for the shape characteristics of the X-ray contraband. The category decoupling module and the long–short side decoupling module are integrated to the shape loss. It can effectively balance the effect of the long–short side. We evaluate our approach on the public X-ray contraband SIXray and OPIXray datasets, and the results show that our approach is competitive with other X-ray baggage inspection approaches.

Keywords: X-ray images; contraband detection; atrous convolution; attention mechanism; regression loss function

1. Introduction

With the development of the transportation industry, transportation security has become a key area of concern, where contraband detection is an important measure to maintain public safety and transportation security. However, the current excessive reliance on the experience and energy of security personnel has decreased the accuracy of manual reviews, and the accuracy rate of contraband detection by security personnel is generally between 80% and 90% [1]. Therefore, automatically searching for prohibited items in passenger packages from X-ray images is essential for reducing labor costs and improving efficiency and reliability.

Through the analysis of the dual-energy X-ray scanning contraband dataset and operation of related experiments, it is found that they compared with the photographic (optical) object detection dataset, MS-COCO [2] (Microsoft Common Object in Context), and the dataset PASCAL VOC [3]. In the past few years, artificial intelligence technology based on the neural network has been applied to X-ray contraband detection [4–6]. However, these algorithms have not yielded satisfactory achievements in contraband detection. Contraband security screening remains an open challenge for several key reasons [7]:

1. Multi-scale detection in X-ray datasets: Due to the scanning angle of the dual-energy X-ray scanner and the physical characteristics of the contraband, there is a seriously uneven scale, which includes an uneven scale between the different categories, an

Citation: Xiang, N.; Gong, Z.; Xu, Y.; Xiong, L. Material-Aware Path Aggregation Network and Shape Decoupled SIoU for X-ray Contraband Detection. *Electronics* **2023**, *12*, 1179. https://doi.org/10.3390/electronics12051179

Academic Editor: Eva Cernadas

Received: 21 January 2023
Revised: 17 February 2023
Accepted: 24 February 2023
Published: 28 February 2023

Copyright: © 2023 by the authors. Licensee MDPI, Basel, Switzerland. This article is an open access article distributed under the terms and conditions of the Creative Commons Attribution (CC BY) license (https://creativecommons.org/licenses/by/4.0/).

uneven scale between the same categories, and an uneven scale between the long–short sides, rendering it difficult to detect the contraband.
2. Extreme clutter and occlusion: Pieces of information obscure each other because of the penetrating nature of the X-ray scanning equipment and the resulting overlap between the deep and shallow high-density image. This has a negative impact on the accuracy of X-ray contraband detection.

To solve the above problems, this paper proposes a material-aware path aggregation network for X-ray object detection and shape-decoupled SIoU (SD-SIoU), which can not only detect items of contraband in common but also detect difficult samples in extreme cases, such as small objects and obscured items. Our model takes the YoloX [8] object detection network as the baseline and modifies its neck part for the differences between the X-ray images and the natural images in the OPIXray [9] dataset. Figure 1 shows the images of the dataset with the above problem.

Figure 1. Problem description in X-ray contraband dataset. The first three images show the scale difference problem caused by different views of the same type of contraband and its uneven aspect ratio, and the last image shows the complex occlusion and clutter problem.

Our main contributions are listed below:
1. Constructing a novel material-aware path aggregation network, which includes a smoothed atrous convolution module (SAC) and material-aware coordinate attention mechanism (MCA). The SAC is to handle the multi-scale problem by combining smoothed atrous convolution using separate shared convolutions with a parallel branching structure. The SAC effectively mitigates the grid effect caused by the atrous convolution, while improving the model's multi-scale detection capability. The MCA is designed to address the clutter and occlusion problem by incorporating a spatial coordinate separation material perception module with a coordinate attention mechanism. The MCA mitigates contraband obstruction by focusing deeply on the contraband material information.
2. A new shape-decoupled SIoU (SD-SIoU), based on the SIoU, is constructed for the uneven aspect ratio problem. First, we optimize the normalized penalty factor; a cen-

trosymmetric normalization function is constructed. Then, we decouple the predicted bounding box long–short side length information to construct a long–short-shape loss branch. Finally, we introduce the category long–short side coefficient, which is determined by category prior knowledge of the contraband datasets. The category long–short coefficient is embedded in the long–short-shape loss branch to handle the uneven aspect ratio by utilizing the category prior knowledge.

3. We evaluate our module on the OPIXray [9] and SIXray [10] datasets, then compare it to recent high-performing object detection networks and contraband detection networks. The experimental results confirm the superiority of our model over other contraband detection models.

2. Relate Work

X-ray security inspection task. Compared to the traditional photographic imagery generated by light reflection, an X-ray image is based on X-ray properties (penetrating, fluorescent and photographic effects). In X-ray images, the brightness and color of the pictures represent the density and material of the detected items, respectively. Therefore, objects scanned by X-ray lose their texture and original color information.

Traditional feature detection methods. X-ray contraband detection belongs to the category of object detection, and the early object detection feature extractors were mostly designed manually and purposefully. Turcsany et al. [11] used a Support Vector Machine (SVM) and SURF features (Speeded-UP Robust Features) to build a visual bag-of-words; Zhang et al. [12] extracted potential features of the image, such as the edges and color, by traditional image processing methods, and obtained a good detection performance improvement.

Deep learning detection methods. Deep learning comprises multiple layers of neural networks that outperform traditional machine learning algorithms. Akcay [13] et al. first introduced deep learning to luggage classification detection of X-ray images using transfer learning. Li et al. [14] combined a semantic segmentation network with Mask R-CNN [15] into a two-stage CNN model, using the semantic segmentation network as Mask R-CNN soft-attention coding to improve the performance degradation caused by overlapping objects in X-ray images. Zhang et al. [16] used an XMC R-CNN model, consisting of a material classification algorithm and an organic-inorganic separation algorithm, for object detection to mitigate the accuracy degradation caused by the occlusion problem effectively.

Multi-scale problem in contrabands detection. Few research studies focus on X-ray baggage threat detection in complex scenarios, including multi-scale detection. Wang et al. [17] utilized a dense attention module to contribute to SDANet, and Cascade Mask RCNN is used as the baseline for the extracted multi-scale features. Tao et al. [18] utilized bidirectional propagation to filter out the impact of the noisy region in the key part by constructing multi-scale features links. Chunjie et al. [19] proposed EAOD-Net, utilizing the learnable Gabor convolution and deformable convolution. ResNeXt is also used to improve the representative ability of multi-scale features. Nguyen et al. [20] used a task-specific deep feature extractor to reduce the multi-scale X-ray images to the same aspect ratio in the same size. This can enable a more efficient deep-detection pipeline. Chunjie et al. [21] constructed a global context feature extraction (GCFE) module and learnable Gabor convolution layer for the high-level and low-level features, which facilitates the detection of bands of different sizes while suppressing background noise.

Obscuration problem in contrabands detection. The obscuration problem has also been widely studied by many scholars. Gas et al. [22] explored the ability of the traditional CNN model to adapt different properties of the scanner and evaluated the prohibited items predicted result on the Dbf3 and SIXray datasets. Hassan et al. [23] obtained dual tensors with improved contour information in X-ray baggage images by levering the intensity transit transitions in low- and high-energy scans. Those contour features were then put into an edge suppression model to filter the noise information to a normal level. Li et al. [24] proposed a method based on GANs with a generator architecture with Res2Net for the natural occurrence problem. Hassan et al. [25] proposed a tensor pooling strategy to decompose the scans across various scales and then fuse them via a single multi-scale tensor to obtain more salient contour maps for boosting a framework's capacity for handling the overlap problem. Wei et al. [9]. proposed the de-occlusion module (DOAM), which combines the edge and material information of the contraband to refine the feature map, which enhances the detection performance.

However, edge information contains too many irrelevant gradients [26]. Therefore, it has a limited improvement in the model localization and classification; this leads to poor discrimination by the detection model in the case of occlusion and a multi-scale task. In addition, the above model does not take into account the effect of a severely unbalanced aspect ratio on the model predictions, which prevents the model from using the contraband shape information distribution to improve the model's prediction performance.

3. Method

The anchor-free detection method is able to learn multi-scale features better than the anchor-based method [27]. Therefore, the YoloX model using the anchor free detection method is chosen as the baseline model in this paper. A new shape-decoupled SIoU loss is also designed for YoloX's unique decoupling.

The block diagram of the proposed framework is depicted in Figure 2. The input origin image is fed into the CSP-DarkNet53 [28] backbone for multi-scale feature extraction. The extracted multi-scale features are separately fed into the material-aware coordinate attention mechanism (MCA) for recalibration. In the MCA, the material information related to the contraband can be extracted and integrated more accurately by utilizing a spatial coordinate separation material perception module. Afterward, these features containing the aggregated material information are then fed into an improved path aggregation network (PAN) [29], which is embedded in the multi-scale smoothed atrous convolution module (SAC), with the SAC levering the ability of the smoothed atrous convolution to increase the field of perception for further extraction and fusion of multi-scale object information. Finally, in the training stage, the contraband prediction results are output by the decoupling head. SD-SIoU is used in the bounding box loss calculation, which decouples the shape loss of the prediction box into the long-side and short-side shape loss. The specific details will be described in the following sections.

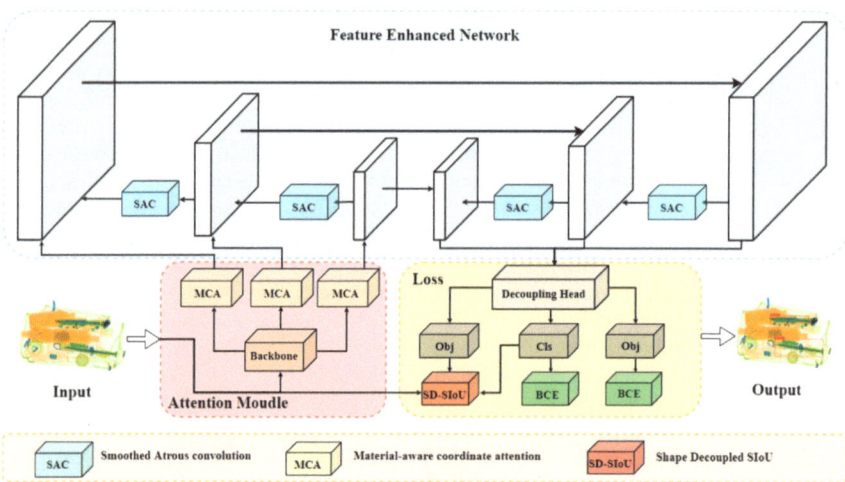

Figure 2. Overall architecture diagram. The network backbone for the feature extraction is CSP-Darknet53, which is the same in the detection network. The feature-enhanced network is a path aggregation network with a SAC module.

3.1. Material-Aware Path Aggregation Network

To further address the problem of multi-scale detection and occlusion in contraband images, a Material-aware Path Aggregation network is proposed, which consists of multi-scale smoothing atrous convolution (SAC) and a material-aware coordinate attention mechanism module (MCA).

3.1.1. Multi-Scale Smoothing Atrous Convolution (SAC)

Compared to the traditional convolutional method, atrous convolution increases the receptive field of the convolution kernel while keeping the number of parameters unchanged [30]. However, atrous convolution faces a serious grid effect, weakening the proximate connections while gaining long-distance dependence. To address this problem, inspired by the smoothed atrous convolution [31], a multi-scale parallel smoothed atrous convolution structure is designed, which is shown in Figure 3.

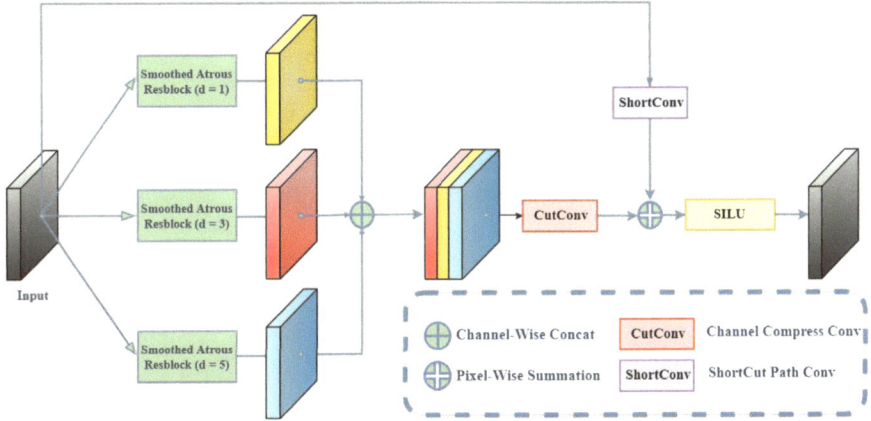

Figure 3. Smoothed atrous convolution (SAC) structure diagram.

As shown above, to limit the impact of the grid effect, this paper constructs parallel atrous convolution branches; each branch uses a different expansion rate to minimize the grid effect. Figure 4 shows the visualization of the atrous convolution grid effect rendering.

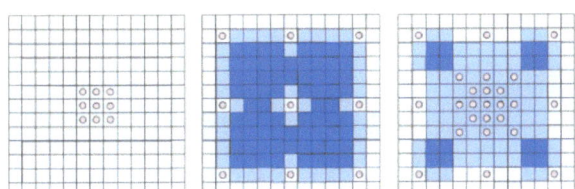

Figure 4. Visualization of receptive fields and grid effects.

A smoothed dilated residual block can effectively prevent the grid effect [31]; it addresses the gridding effect by levering separable and shared convolutions (SS), based on the idea of separable convolutions [32]. In SS convolutions, sharing means that the filters are the same and shared by all the input and output channel pairs. For both the input and output channels, the SS convolution uses only one filter to obtain all the spatial information and shares that filter over all the channels. Therefore, smoothed dilated convolutions can effectively amplify the receptive field to make this branch pay more attention to style features(e.g. edges and global colors) [33]. We therefore apply this module to our parallel multi-scale architecture. Finally, inspired by ResNet [34], the residual information is summed with the fused information in Pixel-Wise and activated by the SiLU activation function.

Although the use of null convolution is effective in reducing the computational effort, the model itself increases some of the parameters and computational effort because of the addition of extra convolution

By using the SAC in the path aggregation network, the weight of the contraband material information can be augmented, which significantly increases the capability of the features to describe the important objects.

3.1.2. Material-Aware Coordinate Attention Mechanism (MCA)

Due to the unique physical characteristics of the X-ray scanner, the material information of the contraband is greatly diminished and is ultimately represented as color information. This means that channel information has a greater contribution to the detection of contraband in X-ray scanned images. The channel attention mechanism can learn different weights of channel dimensions, so that the information from the key channels can be utilized to a greater extent. The coordinate attention (CA) mechanism [35], as a kind of channel attention module, embeds the spatial location information into the channel attention, which means adding extra information into the channels.

However, due to the weakness of spatial information in X-ray images, the original CA attention mechanism cannot fully extract the comprehensive spatial information of images. For this problem, inspired by SRM [36], a material-aware coordinate attention mechanism is designed, and the specific structure is shown in Figure 5.

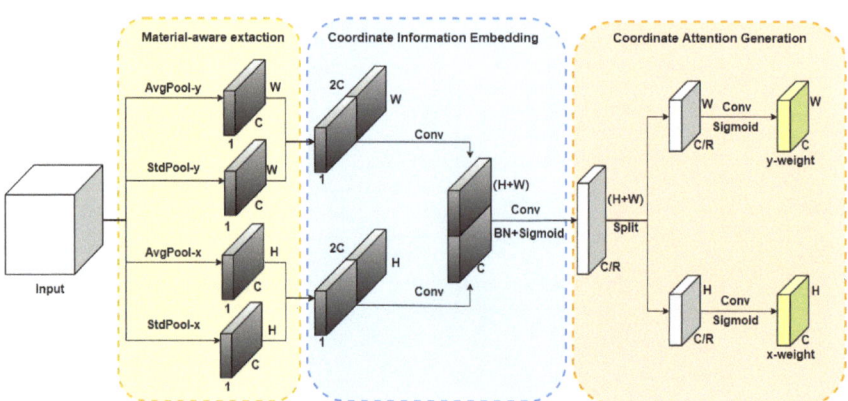

Figure 5. Material-aware coordinate attention (MCA) structure diagram.

First, the input feature maps are put into the material-aware extraction module, which is constructed by average pooling and standard pooling in the width and height directions, to obtain four feature maps, respectively. Specifically, given the input X, two special two-dimensional convolution kernels, (H,1) and (1, W), are used to encode the input data, and four different pooling methods are used to obtain the horizontal and vertical coordinate encoding information. The output of the height, h, at the c-th channel can be presented as

$$Avg_c^h(h) = \frac{1}{W} \sum_{0 \leq i < W} x_c(h, i) \qquad (1)$$

$$Std_c^h(h) = \sqrt{\frac{1}{W} \sum_{0 \leq i < W} (x_c(h, i) - Avg_c^h(h))^2} \qquad (2)$$

Similarly, the output of width, w, at the c-th channel can be formulated as

$$Avg_c^w(w) = \frac{1}{H} \sum_{0 \leq j < H} x_c(j, w) \tag{3}$$

$$Std_c^w(w) = \sqrt{\frac{1}{H} \sum_{0 \leq j < H} (x_c(j, w) - Avg_c^w(w))^2} \tag{4}$$

The above four branches integrate the information of two spatial dimensions, encoding the spatial information and channel information together. This serves as a summary description of the material information for each example, n, and channel, c.

After that, we enter the coordinate information embedding layer to splice and convolve the channel dimensions of the width and height feature information, which embeds the width and height information with the channel information into one feature map. Two feature maps with scales of H × 1 × C and 1 × W × C are obtained. These two directional feature maps of the width and height of the obtained global receptive field are put together according to the spatial dimension. Then, in the coordinate attention generation part, the two feature maps are fed into a convolution module with a shared convolution kernel of 1 × 1 to scale the dimension to C/r and, finally, to the sigmoid activation function and the BatchNorm operation.

3.2. Shape Decoupling SIoU (SD-SIoU)

In addition to the anchor-free detector, YoloX also introduces a decoupled head. The decoupled head decouples the classification task and the regression localization task into two separate branches for separate outputs. This enables the model to focus on the classification and localization tasks separately and improve the model performance. We further improve the decoupled localization task by introducing the SioU [37] loss function and improving it for the physical properties of the X-ray scanning object, which include the shape-decoupling module and normalized optimization algorithm

3.2.1. Revisit SIoU Loss Function

Traditional IoU losses, such as DIoU, CioU [38] and GioU [39], only consider the distance, overlap area and aspect ratio information, and do not consider the angle and ratio between the shape and the predicted bounding box and the target bounding box, resulting in a slight overlap. However, SIoU redefines the penalty matrix by considering the angle and shape. SIOU regression loss consists of four components: distance loss, IOU loss, angle loss and shape loss. The total loss is defined as:

$$L_{box} = 1 - IoU + \frac{\Delta + \Omega}{2} \tag{5}$$

The angle loss is defined as:

$$\Lambda = 1 - 2 * \sin^2(\arcsin(x) - \frac{\pi}{4}) \tag{6}$$

$$x = \frac{\max(b_{cy}^{gt}, b_{cy}) - \min(b_{cy}^{gt}, b_{cy})}{\sqrt{(b_{cx}^{gt} - b_{cx})^2 + (b_{cy}^{gt} - b_{cy})^2}} \tag{7}$$

The distance loss is defined as:

$$\Delta = \sum_{t=x,y} (1 - e^{(\Lambda-2)\rho_t}) \tag{8}$$

where

$$\rho_x = \left(\frac{b_{c_x}^{gt} - b_{c_x}}{\max(w, w^{gt})}\right)^2, \rho_y = \left(\frac{b_{c_y}^{gt} - b_{c_y}}{\max(h, h^{gt})}\right)^2 \tag{9}$$

The shape loss is defined as:

$$\Omega = \sum_{t=w,h} (1 - e^{-\omega_t})^\theta \tag{10}$$

where

$$\omega_w = \frac{|w - w^{gt}|}{\max(w, w_{gt})}, \omega_h = \frac{|h - h^{gt}|}{\max(h, h_{gt})} \tag{11}$$

b_{cy}^{gt} and b_{cy} represent the y coordinates of the center point for ground truth and prediction. w and h represent the width and height of the bounding box.

SIoU has been widely used in recent networks and has proven to be a key component in the implementation of advanced detectors [40–43]. However, although SIoU takes shape loss into account, it couples the long- and short-side information of the prediction bounding box together and assigns the same computational weight to them, which ignores the proportional relationship between the long and short sides. In addition, SIoU limits the shape loss to [0, 1] by dividing by the maximum of the predicted and true values, which causes asymmetry in the parameter convergence curve and convergence difficulties due to low proximity gradients.

In the following, we will reconsider the shape loss part for the above problem.

3.2.2. Shape Decoupling Module

In the X-ray contraband images, the distribution of the long side and short side is always not equal, and the aspect weight of contraband varies greatly among different categories. Giving the same weight to the long side and short side will affect the optimization of the model for the contraband shape information. Figure 6 shows the scatter plot of the OPIXray dataset consisting of information on the long side and short side of different types of contraband.

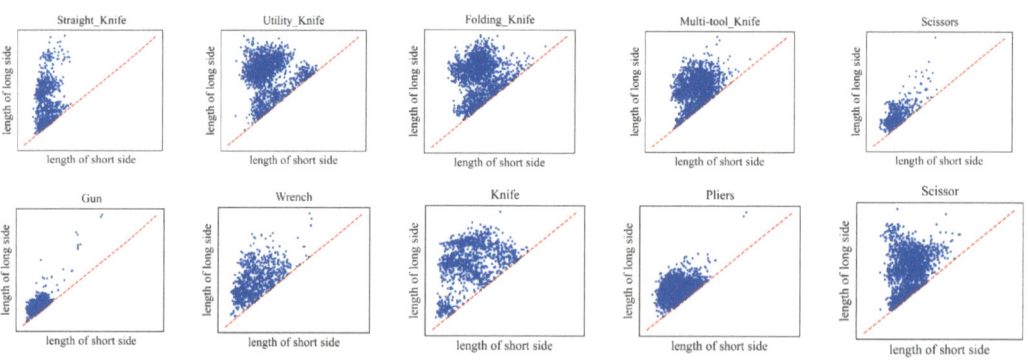

Figure 6. Comparison of length ratio of different categories under SIXray and OPIXray datasets.

As shown in Figure 6, there is a significant difference between the long–short sides of the target box. To address this problem, we designed the long–short side decoupling module and the category information embedding module, based on the special structure of the YoloX decoupling head. The detailed structure is shown in Figure 7.

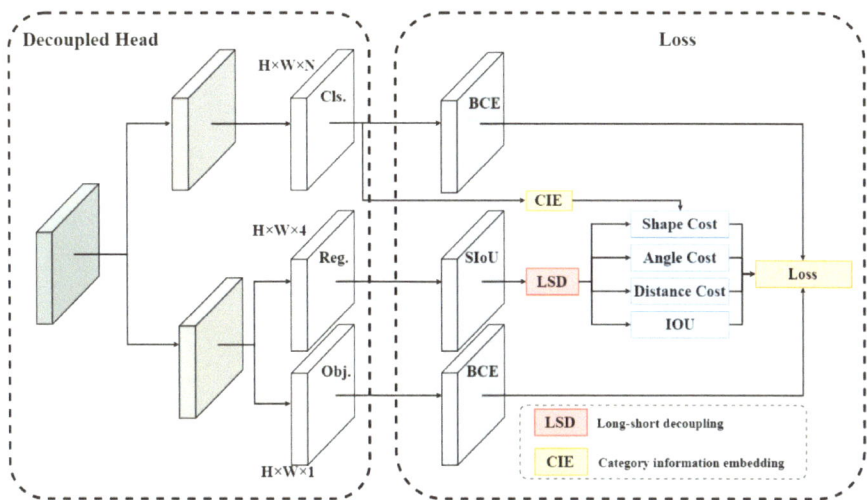

Figure 7. SD-SIoU structure diagram.

In the long–short side decoupling module, the length and width information of the input prediction bounding box is separated, and the lengths of the long side and the short side are extracted, respectively. Therefore, a new shape loss penalty factor is decoupled for the long length, l, and short length, s, as follows.

$$\omega_l = \frac{|l - l^{gt}|}{\max(l, l_{gt})}, \omega_s = \frac{|s - s^{gt}|}{\max(s, s_{gt})} \quad (12)$$

In the category information embedding module, we collect the long and short side information of the dataset by category and perform a cluster analysis to obtain the gathering point information. Finally, we construct the long–short scale matrix, $M_{n \times 1}$, which can be represented as follows.

$$M = [\alpha_1, \alpha_2, \alpha_3, \cdots, \alpha_n]_{n \times 1} \quad (13)$$

where n is the number of categories, and α_i is the aspect ratio of i-th category clustered. Then, multiplying the category prediction matrix, $C_{m \times n}$, with the long–short scale matrix, $M_{n \times 1}$, yields the category long–short side coefficient matrix, $A_{m \times 1}$.

Then, we embed the category information into the shape loss by dividing the long-side penalty factor by the category long–short side coefficient matrix, $A_{m \times 1}$. The equation is shown below.

$$\omega_{l+} = \omega_l / A_{m \times 1} \quad (14)$$

The above formula realizes the decoupling of the shape information and the embedding of the category information, effectively alleviating the impact of the long–short sides on detection accuracy.

3.2.3. Normalized Optimization Module

As we continue our research, we find that, in shape loss, the range of values is restricted to $\mathbb{R} \in (0, 1)$ by dividing by the maximum value of the ground truth box width and height and the predicted box width and height in Equation (7). However, this method leads to a symmetry problem. It can be seen, in Figure 8, the maximum normalization does not work consistently for the same distance gap between the target and predicted bounding box sizes in the positive and negative directions, and the optimized gradient is worse as distance between the target and prediction gets closer. Although the function has a very fast convergence speed in the early stage of training, the convergence ability of the model decreases as the prediction results approach.

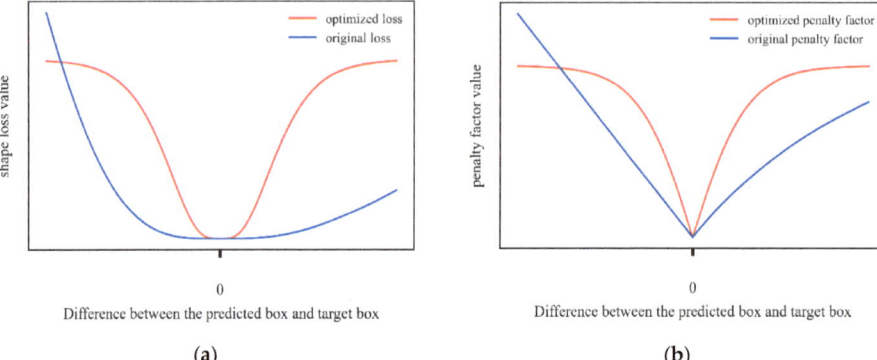

Figure 8. Comparison of shape loss and normalized penalty factor before and after improvement. (**a**) Shape loss; (**b**) normalized penalty factor.

To address this problem, we designed a symmetric normalization method for the shape loss part of the SIoU. The new shape loss composition is shown below.

$$\Omega = \sum_{t=w,h} \left(1 - e^{-\varphi_t}\right)^\theta \quad (15)$$

where the novel penalty factor is:

$$\omega_t^+ = b \times \frac{e^{k \times |w - w^{gt}|} - e^{-k \times |w - w^{gt}|}}{e^{k \times |w - w^{gt}|} + e^{-k \times |w - w^{gt}|}} \quad (16)$$

As shown above, the improved normalization function solves the left–right asymmetry problem caused by the max function and optimizes the penalty factor regularization algorithm, so that the loss decreases more smoothly during the training process and still has a certain descent gradient in the late training period.

4. Experiment

In this section, we conduct comprehensive experiments on OPIXray and SIXray datasets to evaluate the effectiveness of our method. OPIXray and SIXray are the common datasets for X-ray contraband images.

4.1. Experiment Setting Details

This paper is implemented by a Windows 10 64-bit operating system, 12th Gen Intel Core i9-12900K@3.2 GHz CPU, 32 GB RAM, NVIDIA 3080ti GPU with CUDA Toolkit 11.4 and Torch 1.11 in Python 3.8. As the benchmark of our model, YoloX uses the most primitive parameter settings. The backbone of YoloX uses CSP-Darknet53.

All the experiments of our model and baselines are optimized by an Adam optimizer. The initial learning rate is set to 0.001, and the Cosine Annealing learning rate reduction strategy is used. The momentum and weight decay are set to 0.93 and 0, respectively. The batch size is set to 16. We evaluate the mean Average Precision (mAP) to measure the performance of all the methods. In addition, the IoU threshold measuring the accuracy of the predicted bounding box is set to 0.5.

4.2. Comparing with SOTA Detection Methods

To verify the effectiveness of the proposed methods in this paper, as shown in Tables 1 and 2, we compared the mainstream contraband detection models and object detection models in the last two years on the OPIXray and SIXray datasets, respectively. The method involved included object detection models such as Swin Transformer [44], RetinaNet [45], DetectoRS [46], Yolov5 and baseline YoloX. It also includes the most advanced contraband detection models in the last two years such as CHR [10], FBS [47], CFPA-Net [48], MCIA-FPN [49] and POD-Y [21].

Table 1. Performance comparison results using different object detection methods on the OPIXray dataset.

Model	Year	Backbone	Category					mAP
			FO	ST	SC	UT	MU	
Swin Trans [44]	2021	Swin Trans	82.14	42.77	95.75	69.60	84.84	75.04
CHR [10]	2019	Resnet-50	87.94	84.53	95.23	50.99	74.47	78.63
RetinaNet [45]	2017	Resnet-50	89.27	55.66	98.15	79.79	85.27	81.63
FBS [47]	2022	CSPDarknet53	86.38	88.29	95.45	57.99	80.62	81.75
CFPA-Net [48]	2021	Resnet-50	87.72	76.10	90.52	85.94	84.87	81.84
DetectoRS [46]	2021	Resnet-50	88.51	64.01	89.86	81.02	86.59	82.00
DOAM [9]	2020	Resnet-50	86.71	68.58	90.23	78.84	87.67	82.41
Yolov5	2021	CSPDarknet53	90.36	64.85	97.69	80.93	94.44	85.65
MCIA-FPN [49]	2022	ResNet-101	89.08	74.48	89.99	86.13	89.75	85.89
ATSS-Lacls [50]	2022	ResNet-50	92.31	72.04	96.58	80.23	91.67	86.59
Chang et al. [5]	2022	Resnet-50	90.42	75.95	91.46	84.31	91.29	86.69
YoloX [8]	2021	CSPDarknet53	91.84	77.53	97.89	89.22	92.79	89.85
LIM [18]	2021	Resnet-50-FPN	94.79	77.66	98.20	88.92	93.75	90.43
POD-Y [21]	2022	CSP-Darknet53	94.5	77.8	98.2	89.5	94.5	90.9
Ours	N/A	CSPDarkNet53	94.53	86.68	98.88	89.56	94.96	92.92

Table 2. Performance comparison results using different object detection methods on the SIXray dataset.

Model	Year	Backbone	Category					mAP
			Gun	Knife	Wrench	Pliers	Scissors	
CHR [10]	2019	Resnet50	79.22	63.77	73.77	71.55	65.55	70.77
RetinaNet [45]	2017	Resnet-50	81.16	77.27	33.24	66.87	22.61	81.50
FBS [47]	2022	CSP-DarkNet53	79.72	64.14	74.96	71.19	66.17	71.24
DetectoRS [46]	2021	Resnet-50	81.61	80.52	84.48	87.40	81.4	83.10
CFPA-Net [48]	2021	Resnet-50	86.07	86.33	72.44	87.28	75.95	81.61
DOAM [9]	2020	CSP-Darknet53	81.37	64.25	73.26	70.17	61.98	70.21
MCIA-FPN [49]	2022	Resnet101	85.75	83.75	81.50	86.79	88.34	85.23
Yolo v5	2021	CSP-Darknet53	97.36	84.60	90.00	85.56	85.20	88.55
YoloX [8]	2021	CSP-Darknet53	96.74	85.94	91.48	86.94	87.89	89.80
POD-Y [21]	2022	CSP-Darknet53	92.6	87.9	87.6	92.1	91.8	90.4
Ours	N/A	CSP-Darknet53	97.01	87.63	88.66	92.48	89.70	91.10

As Tables 1 and 2 show, the proposed model can achieve the optimal detection performance on the OPIXray and SIXray datasets; the mAP values are 2.02% and 0.71% higher than those of the state-of-the-art model on the OPIXray and SIXray datasets. Compared with the existing one-stage prohibited items detection network, our model can achieve an optimal detection performance. Especially for the small target category "Straight Knife" in OPIXray, which faces the problem of obscuration and small scale, and its aspect ratio is extremely uneven, our model achieves an 8.88% improvement compared with POD-y. The above experimental results fully demonstrate that our proposed method is effective and efficient.

4.3. Comparing with Different Attention

To verify the effectiveness of the improved attention mechanisms in this paper, we compare the mainstream attention mechanisms, including the SE [51], GAM [52], CA [35] and PSA [53] attention mechanisms. The specific results are shown in Table 3, below.

Table 3. Comparison of different attention mechanism modules.

Model	MAP	GFLOPs	Parameters (M)
YoloX	90.45	155.331	54.152
YoloX + SE	90.75	156.017	54.383
YoloX + GAM	89.87	218.954	88.624
YoloX + CBAM	91.18	156.013	54.383
YoloX + CA	91.49	156.032	54.342
YoloX + DOAM	92.24	175.362	54.290
YoloX + MCA (ours)	92.36	156.037	54.382

It is obvious that our method performs better on the OPIXray dataset compared to the other methods, with results 2.11%, 1.81%, 2.69%, 1.38%, 1.17% and 0.21% higher than the other attention mechanisms, respectively. We also compare DOAM, an attention mechanism for contraband detection, and see that our model is 0.12% more accurate than DOAM, with a smaller number of computations and parameters than DOAM. It can be seen that our model maintains a high level of detection accuracy and speed without a significant increase in the number of computations and parameters.

4.4. Comparing with Different Receptive Field Enhancement Module

We further verify the effect of our multi-scale smoothed atrous convolution (SAC). As we can see in Table 4, we compare different receptive field enhancement modules include ASPP [54] and RFB [55]. Our method shows an improvement of 1.80% and 0.34% over the ASPP and RFB modules.

Table 4. Comparing with different receptive field modules.

Method	Category					mAP	FLOPs	Paras (m)	FPS
	FO	ST	SC	UT	MU				
Baseline	91.84	77.53	97.89	89.22	92.79	89.85	155.331	54.152	89.834
Baseline + ASPP	91.74	78.42	97.87	91.36	92.09	90.03	238.416	100.955	74.567
Baseline + RFB	89.83	86.04	99.3	87.4	94.91	91.49	209.604	83.812	79.058
Baseline + SAC (our)	89.71	88.68	99.32	86.67	94.29	91.83	233.403	96.834	74.350

To better show the superiority of our proposed model, we plot the P-R curves for different receptive field modules, as shown in Figure 9. The P-R curve of our module is closer to the upper right position compared to the other models, which means that our SAC has a better performance.

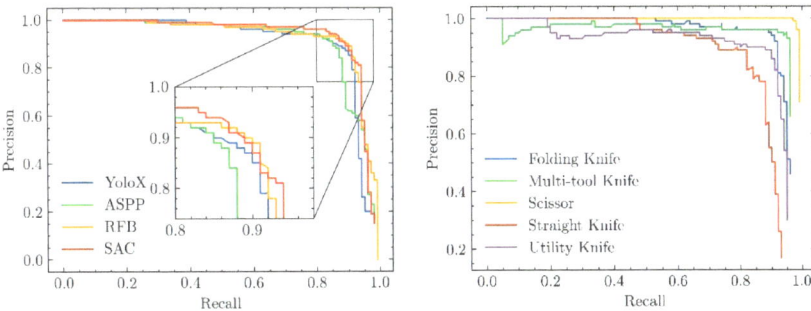

Figure 9. Comparison of P-R curves of different receptive field enhancement modules.

4.5. Ablation Study

To verify the effect of each module on the model performance, we perform ablation experiments on the OPIXray and SIXray datasets. The results are shown in Table 5. We compare the mAP of the model with different combinations of components. The same parameters were used for all the experiments performed in the ablation study to ensure the validity of the comparison. The SD-SIoU increases the mAP of the baseline from 89.85% to 91.76% and 89.80% to 90.94% on OPIXray and SIXray, respectively. This result shows that the SD-SIoU has considerably improved the detecting performance. Then, we split the material-aware path aggregation network into SAC and MCA, which represent the Smoothed Atrous Convolution and Material-aware Coordinate Attention. The MCA increases the mAP of the baseline with SD-SIoU by 0.29% on OPIXray and 0.18% on SIXray. SAC increases the mAP of the baseline with SD-SIoU by 0.60% on the OPIXray and 0.33% on the SIXray. The experiments shows that the SAC and MCA modules are helpful for the model to detect contraband accurately. Finally, when all the methods are used together, our model mAP achieves 92.65% and 91.31%. These are 2.80% and 1.51% higher than the YoloX baseline on OPIXray and SIXray, respectively. Each method can improve performance individually, and combining these methods results in the optimal performance. It is worth mentioning that the improvement on the OPIXray dataset is greater than on the SIXray dataset. The main gap is in the SD-SIoU section. It will be further investigated in the following.

Table 5. Ablation study on OPIXray and SIXray.

SD-SIoU	MCA	SAC	mAP (%) OPIXray	mAP (%) SIXray	GFLOPs	Parameters
			89.85	89.80	156.011	54.209
✓			91.76	90.94	156.011	54.209
✓	✓		92.05	91.12	156.037	54.385
✓		✓	92.36	91.27	256.835	109.284
✓	✓	✓	92.65	91.31	256.860	109.460

To further visualize the effectiveness of our SD-SIoU, we perform detailed ablation experiments on the SD-SIoU part, which we illustrate by two parts of the mAP and loss function curves.

As can be seen in Table 6, we compared the mAP of the SIoU loss function under different conditions. ON denotes the optimized normalized curve; LSside denotes the long–short side decoupling module. "Decoupling" means the category information embedding module. The optimized normalized curve improves the mAP of the model by 1.38% and 0.95%, which means this normalized method can improve the convergence results of the model. It is worth noting that, when introducing the long–short side decoupling module without the category information embedding module, the accuracy of the model decreases by 0.16% and 0.21%. The reason for this phenomenon is that there is a serious maldistribution after the construction of the long–short side shape loss. The weight of the long-side loss is not balanced with the weight of the short-side loss. Therefore, we continue to add the category length ratio decoupling module. It increases the mAP by 0.69% and 0.50% and achieves higher AP detection performance.

Table 6. Ablation study for OD-SIoU.

Method	mAP (%)	
	OPIXray	SIXray
SIoU	89.85	89.70
SIoU-ON	91.23	90.65
SIoU-ON-LSside	91.07	90.44
SIoU-NO-LSside-Decoupled	91.76	90.94

We recorded the shape loss curves and long–short loss curves of the SD-SIoU under different conditions. Since the loss data under different conditions varied widely and had small fluctuations, we normalized and denoised all the curves and indicated their validity by observing the decreasing trend of loss. The specific images are shown in the Figure 10.

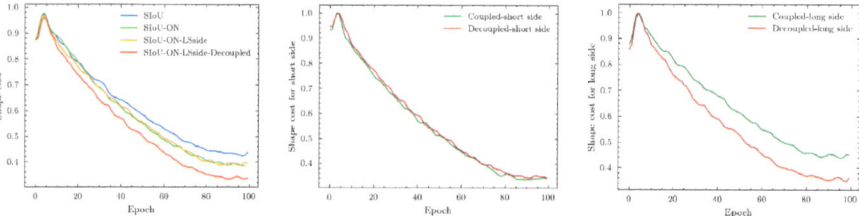

Figure 10. Ablation experiments on loss reduction curves for SD-SIoU.

The first figure shows the SD-SIoU loss curves under the ablation experiment. The loss value drops lower after improving the normalization function of the shape loss factor, but the trend is almost the same at the beginning of the training. This is because our new normalization method still has a good gradient in the late training period, while the gradient of the traditional normalization method is not significant in that period. We also find that the downward trend does not change significantly after adding the long–short side decoupling module, but there is a significant improvement after adding the category information embedding module. To address this issue, we conduct more detailed experiments.

Figure 10 splits the long side and short side from the shape loss. This represents the long-side loss and short-side loss before and after adding the category information embedding module. We can see that the addition of this module directly affects the decreasing trend of the long-side loss, while the decreasing trend of the short edge does not change significantly. This means that adding the classification module can effectively improve the convergence of the long side without affecting the short-side loss. In other words, this module alleviates the problem of uneven weights between the long–short sides.

Finally, we use the model proposed in this paper for visual inspection of the OPIXray and SIXray datasets, as shown in Figure 11 below.

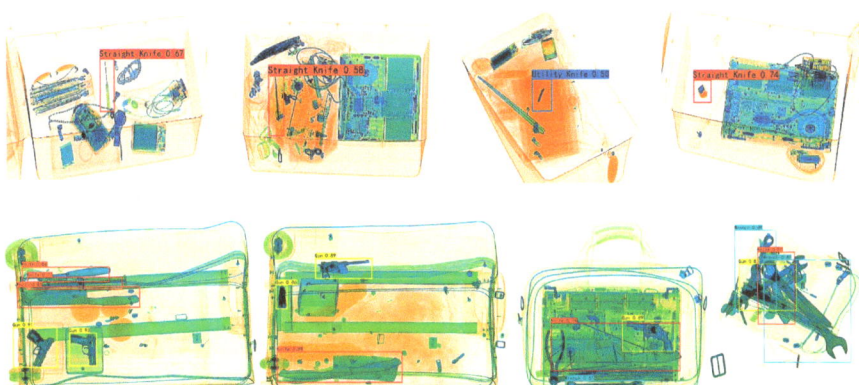

Figure 11. Detection performance in OPIXray and SIXray. The first line is the detection performance of OPIXray and the second line is that of the SIXray.

5. Conclusions

In this paper, a new feature extraction network is designed considering the specific physical characteristics of X-ray images. For the X-ray contraband multi-scale problem, a multi-scale smoothing atrous convolution module is designed to capture multi-scale contraband features by acquiring different sizes of the receptive field. For the occlusion and weak textural information in X-ray contraband images, we design a material-aware coordinate attention mechanism to enhance the material features' extraction ability in obscured X-ray images. In addition, an improved SIoU was designed, named SD-SIoU, which addresses the problem of inconsistent aspect ratios in contraband images. Through a large number of experiments and visualization results, we determine that the feature extraction and enhancement strategies proposed in this paper can effectively strengthen the ability of the model to detect contraband. Its validity is reflected in the evaluation index mAP. Our experimental results, based on the OPIXray and SIXray datasets, show that our method achieves an average accuracy of 92.65% and 91.31%, with a computational volume of 256.86G for 109.46M parameters, respectively. From the quantitative point of view, the proposed method has excellent performance in the field of contraband detection. The comparison results show that the method outperforms other contraband detection methods.

Author Contributions: Methodology, N.X.; software, Z.G.; validation, N.X. and Z.G.; writing—original draft preparation, Z.G.; writing—review and editing, Z.G. and Y.X.; visualization, Y.X.; supervision, N.X. and L.X.; funding acquisition, L.X. All authors have read and agreed to the published version of the manuscript.

Funding: This research was funded by the Natural Science Foundation of Chongqing Province of China, grant number CSTB2022NSCQ-MSX0786 and the Natural Science Foundation of Chongqing Province of China, grant number CSTB2022NSCQ-MSX1477.

Data Availability Statement: Not applicable.

Conflicts of Interest: The authors declare no conflict of interest.

References

1. Michel, S.; Koller, S.M. Computer-based training increases efficiency in X-ray image interpretation by aviation security screeners. In Proceedings of the 2007 41st Annual IEEE International Carnahan Conference on Security Technology, Ottawa, ON, Canada, 8–11 October 2007.
2. Lin, T.-Y.; Maire, M. Microsoft coco: Common objects in context. In Proceedings of the European Conference on Computer Vision, Zurich, Switzerland, 6–12 September 2014.
3. Everingham, M.; Van Gool, L. The pascal visual object classes (voc) challenge. *Int. J. Comput. Vis.* **2010**, *88*, 303–338. [CrossRef]
4. Thammasorn, P.; Oztan, B. Augmenting data with GANs for firearms detection in cargo X-ray images. In Proceedings of the Anomaly Detection and Imaging with X-rays (ADIX) VII, Orlando, FL, USA, 3 April–13 June 2022.

5. Chang, A.; Zhang, Y. Detecting prohibited objects with physical size constraint from cluttered X-ray baggage images. *Knowl. Based Syst.* **2022**, *237*, 107916. [CrossRef]
6. Velayudhan, D.; Hassan, T. Baggage threat recognition using deep low-rank broad learning detector. In Proceedings of the 2022 IEEE 21st Mediterranean Electrotechnical Conference (MELECON), Palermo, Italy, 14–16 June 2022.
7. Velayudhan, D.; Hassan, T. Recent advances in baggage threat detection: A comprehensive and systematic survey. *ACM Comput. Surv.* **2022**, *55*, 1–38. [CrossRef]
8. Ge, Z.; Liu, S. Yolox: Exceeding yolo series in 2021. *arXiv* **2021**, arXiv:2107.08430.
9. Wei, Y.; Tao, R. Occluded prohibited items detection: An X-ray security inspection benchmark and de-occlusion attention module. In Proceedings of the Proceedings of the 28th ACM International Conference on Multimedia, Seattle, WA, USA, 12–16 October 2020.
10. Miao, C.; Xie, L. Sixray: A large-scale security inspection X-ray benchmark for prohibited item discovery in overlapping images. In Proceedings of the IEEE/CVF Conference on Computer Vision and Pattern Recognition, Long Beach, CA, USA, 15–20 June 2019.
11. Turcsany, D.; Mouton, A. Improving feature-based object recognition for X-ray baggage security screening using primed visualwords. In Proceedings of the 2013 IEEE International conference on industrial technology (ICIT), Cape Town, South Africa, 25–28 February 2013.
12. Zhang, N.; Zhu, J. A study of X-ray machine image local semantic features extraction model based on bag-of-words for airport security. *Int. J. Smart Sens. Intell. Syst.* **2015**, *8*, 45–64. [CrossRef]
13. Akçay, S.; Kundegorski, M.E. Transfer learning using convolutional neural networks for object classification within X-ray baggage security imagery. In Proceedings of the 2016 IEEE International Conference on Image Processing (ICIP), Phoenix, AZ, USA, 25–28 September 2016.
14. Li, J.; Liu, Y. Segmentation and Attention Network for Complicated X-Ray Images. In Proceedings of the 2020 35th Youth Academic Annual Conference of Chinese Association of Automation (YAC), Zhanjiang, China, 16–18 October 2020.
15. He, K.; Gkioxari, G. Mask r-cnn. In Proceedings of the IEEE International Conference on Computer Vision, Venice, Italy, 22–29 October 2017.
16. Zhang, Y.; Kong, W. On using XMC R-CNN model for contraband detection within X-ray baggage security images. *Math. Probl. Eng.* **2020**, *2020*, 1823034. [CrossRef]
17. Wang, B.; Zhang, L. Towards real-world prohibited item detection: A large-scale X-ray benchmark. In Proceedings of the IEEE/CVF International Conference on Computer Vision, Montreal, QC, Canada, 10–17 October 2021.
18. Tao, R.; Wei, Y. Towards real-world X-ray security inspection: A high-quality benchmark and lateral inhibition module for prohibited items detection. In Proceedings of the IEEE/CVF International Conference on Computer Vision, Montreal, QC, Canada, 10–17 October 2021.
19. Ma, C.; Zhuo, L. EAOD-Net: Effective anomaly object detection networks for X-ray images. *IET Image Process.* **2022**, *16*, 2638–2651. [CrossRef]
20. Nguyen, H.D.; Cai, R. Towards More Efficient Security Inspection via Deep Learning: A Task-Driven X-ray Image Cropping Scheme. *Micromachines* **2022**, *13*, 565. [CrossRef]
21. Ma, C.; Zhuo, L. Occluded prohibited object detection in X-ray images with global Context-aware Multi-Scale feature Aggregation. *Neurocomputing* **2023**, *519*, 1–16. [CrossRef]
22. Gaus, Y.F.A.; Bhowmik, N. Evaluating the transferability and adversarial discrimination of convolutional neural networks for threat object detection and classification within X-ray security imagery. In Proceedings of the 2019 18th IEEE International Conference On Machine Learning And Applications (ICMLA), Boca Raton, FL, USA, 16–19 December 2019.
23. Hassan, T.; Shafay, M. Meta-transfer learning driven tensor-shot detector for the autonomous localization and recognition of concealed baggage threats. *Sensors* **2020**, *20*, 6450. [CrossRef]
24. Li, D.; Hu, X. A GAN based method for multiple prohibited items synthesis of X-ray security image. *Optoelectron. Lett.* **2021**, *17*, 112–117. [CrossRef]
25. Hassan, T.; Akcay, S. Tensor pooling-driven instance segmentation framework for baggage threat recognition. *Neural Comput. Appl.* **2022**, *34*, 1239–1250. [CrossRef]
26. Liu, D.; Tian, Y. Handling occlusion in prohibited item detection from X-ray images. *Neural Comput. Appl.* **2022**, *34*, 20285–20298. [CrossRef]
27. Yan, Y.; Li, J. Anchor-free person search. In Proceedings of the IEEE/CVF Conference on Computer Vision and Pattern Recognition, Nashville, TN, USA, 20–25 June 2021.
28. Bochkovskiy, A.; Wang, C.-Y. Yolov4: Optimal speed and accuracy of object detection. *arXiv* **2020**, arXiv:2004.10934.
29. Liu, S.; Qi, L. Path aggregation network for instance segmentation. In Proceedings of the IEEE Conference on Computer Vision and Pattern Recognition, Salt Lake City, UT, USA, 18–23 June 2018.
30. Cao, F.; Bao, Q. A survey on image semantic segmentation methods with convolutional neural network. In Proceedings of the 2020 International Conference on Communications, Information System and Computer Engineering (CISCE), Kuala Lumpur, Malaysia, 3–5 July 2020.
31. Wang, Z.; Ji, S. Smoothed dilated convolutions for improved dense prediction. In Proceedings of the 24th ACM SIGKDD International Conference on Knowledge Discovery & Data Mining, London, UK, 19–23 August 2018.

32. Chollet, F. Xception: Deep learning with depthwise separable convolutions. In Proceedings of the IEEE Conference on Computer Vision and Pattern Recognition, Honolulu, HI, USA, 21–26 July 2017.
33. Su, C.; Wu, X. Restoration of turbulence-degraded images using the modified convolutional neural network. *Appl. Intell.* **2022**, *53*, 5834–5844. [CrossRef]
34. He, K.; Zhang, X. Deep residual learning for image recognition. In Proceedings of the IEEE Conference on Computer Vision and Pattern Recognition, Las Vegas, NV, USA, 27–30 June 2016.
35. Hou, Q.; Zhou, D. Coordinate attention for efficient mobile network design. In Proceedings of the IEEE/CVF Conference on Computer Vision and Pattern Recognition, Nashville, TN, USA, 20–25 June 2021.
36. Lee, H.; Kim, H.-E. Srm: A style-based recalibration module for convolutional neural networks. In Proceedings of the IEEE/CVF International Conference on Computer Vision, Seoul, Republic of Korea, 27 October–2 November 2019.
37. Gevorgyan, Z. SIoU Loss: More Powerful Learning for Bounding Box Regression. *arXiv* **2022**, arXiv:2205.12740.
38. Zheng, Z.; Wang, P. Distance-IoU loss: Faster and better learning for bounding box regression. In Proceedings of the AAAI Conference on Artificial Intelligence, New York, NY, USA, 7–12 February 2020.
39. Rezatofighi, H.; Tsoi, N. Generalized intersection over union: A metric and a loss for bounding box regression. In Proceedings of the IEEE/CVF Conference on Computer Vision and Pattern Recognition, Long Beach, CA, USA, 15–20 June 2019.
40. Xue, Q.; Lin, H. FCDM: An Improved Forest Fire Classification and Detection Model Based on YOLOv5. *Forests* **2022**, *13*, 2129. [CrossRef]
41. Liu, B.; Luo, H. An Improved Yolov5 for Multi-Rotor UAV Detection. *Electronics* **2022**, *11*, 2330. [CrossRef]
42. Guo, Y.; Chen, S. LMSD-YOLO: A Lightweight YOLO Algorithm for Multi-Scale SAR Ship Detection. *Remote Sens.* **2022**, *14*, 4801. [CrossRef]
43. Yang, X.; Zhao, J. Detection of River Floating Garbage Based on Improved YOLOv5. *Mathematics* **2022**, *10*, 4366. [CrossRef]
44. Liu, Z.; Lin, Y. Swin transformer: Hierarchical vision transformer using shifted windows. In Proceedings of the IEEE/CVF International Conference on Computer Vision, Montreal, QC, Canada, 10–17 October 2021.
45. Lin, T.-Y.; Goyal, P. Focal loss for dense object detection. *IEEE Trans. Pattern Anal. Mach. Intell.* **2020**, *42*, 318–327. [CrossRef] [PubMed]
46. Qiao, S.; Chen, L.-C. Detectors: Detecting objects with recursive feature pyramid and switchable atrous convolution. In Proceedings of the IEEE/CVF Conference on Computer Vision and Pattern Recognition, Nashville, TN, USA, 20–25 June 2021.
47. Shao, F.; Liu, J. Exploiting foreground and background separation for prohibited item detection in overlapping X-ray images. *Pattern Recognit.* **2022**, *122*, 108261. [CrossRef]
48. Wei, Y.; Wang, Y. CFPA-Net: Cross-layer Feature Fusion And Parallel Attention Network For Detection And Classification of Prohibited Items in X-ray Baggage Images. In Proceedings of the 2021 IEEE 7th International Conference on Cloud Computing and Intelligent Systems (CCIS), Xi'an, China, 7–8 November 2021.
49. Wang, M.; Du, H. Material-aware Cross-channel Interaction Attention (MCIA) for occluded prohibited item detection. *Vis. Comput.* **2022**. [CrossRef]
50. Zhao, C.; Zhu, L. Detecting Overlapped Objects in X-ray Security Imagery by a Label-Aware Mechanism. *IEEE Trans. Inf. Forensics Secur.* **2022**, *17*, 998–1009. [CrossRef]
51. Hu, J.; Shen, L. Squeeze-and-excitation networks. In Proceedings of the IEEE Conference on Computer Vision and Pattern Recognition, Salt Lake City, UT, USA, 18–23 June 2018.
52. Liu, Y.; Shao, Z. Global Attention Mechanism: Retain Information to Enhance Channel-Spatial Interactions. *arXiv* **2021**, arXiv:2112.05561.
53. Zhang, H.; Zu, K. EPSANet: An efficient pyramid squeeze attention block on convolutional neural network. In Proceedings of the Asian Conference on Computer Vision, Macau, China, 4–8 December 2022.
54. Pu, R.; Ren, G. Autonomous Concrete Crack Semantic Segmentation Using Deep Fully Convolutional Encoder–Decoder Network in Concrete Structures Inspection. *Buildings* **2022**, *12*, 2019. [CrossRef]
55. Liu, S.; Huang, D. Receptive field block net for accurate and fast object detection. In Proceedings of the European Conference on Computer Vision (ECCV), Munich, Germany, 8–14 September 2018.

Disclaimer/Publisher's Note: The statements, opinions and data contained in all publications are solely those of the individual author(s) and contributor(s) and not of MDPI and/or the editor(s). MDPI and/or the editor(s) disclaim responsibility for any injury to people or property resulting from any ideas, methods, instructions or products referred to in the content.

Article

Fast Adaptive Binarization of QR Code Images for Automatic Sorting in Logistics Systems

Rongjun Chen [1], Weijie Li [1], Kailin Lan [1], Jinghui Xiao [2,*], Leijun Wang [1] and Xu Lu [1,*]

[1] School of Computer Science, Guangdong Polytechnic Normal University, Guangzhou 510665, China
[2] Guangdong Telecommunication Plan & Design Institute Co., Ltd., Guangzhou 510665, China
* Correspondence: 13312880077@189.cn (J.X.); bruda@126.com (X.L.)

Abstract: With the development of technology, QR codes play an important role in information exchange. In order to work out the problem of uneven illumination in automatic sorting in logistics systems, an adaptive method in binarization is presented. The proposed method defines the block windows' size adaptively for local binarization based on the traits of the QR code. It takes advantage of integral images to calculate the sum of gray values in a block. The method can binarize the QR code with high quality and speed under uneven illumination. Compared with several existing algorithms, it is shown that the proposed method is more effective. The experimental results validate that the proposed method has a higher recognition accuracy and is more efficient in binarization.

Keywords: binarization; QR code; integral image; logistics

Citation: Chen, R.; Li, W.; Lan, K.; Xiao, J.; Wang, L.; Lu, X. Fast Adaptive Binarization of QR Code Images for Automatic Sorting in Logistics Systems. *Electronics* 2023, 12, 286. https://doi.org/10.3390/electronics12020286

Academic Editor: Chiman Kwan

Received: 29 November 2022
Revised: 19 December 2022
Accepted: 27 December 2022
Published: 5 January 2023

Copyright: © 2023 by the authors. Licensee MDPI, Basel, Switzerland. This article is an open access article distributed under the terms and conditions of the Creative Commons Attribution (CC BY) license (https://creativecommons.org/licenses/by/4.0/).

1. Introduction

Shortly, the IoT will affect many fields, such as retail, agriculture, and transportation [1]. To be more specific, people may control the heating, lighting, and other home equipment by constructing intelligent home systems using IoT technologies [2]. Moreover, the IoT may boost logistics systems' flexibility, robustness, and productivity [3,4]. While building the IoT ecosystem, the QR code, the entrance to the Internet of Things, plays a significant role. QR codes can not only store a large amount of information but also have vital error correction functions and low production costs, which makes them very valuable. In logistics systems, the packages are transmitted onto the conveyor belt. When the scanner near the conveyer belt recognizes the QR code on the packages, the local computer will upload information to the cloud and obtain a response to change the moving direction of parts of the belt to sort the packages. Then, the packages with the same destination will be put together and delivered.

It can be seen from Figure 1 that the sorting operation depends on the QR code. Combined with QR code technology, it is possible that logistics companies then implement the unmanned management of sorting and package tracking. The accuracy and speed of QR code recognition will directly affect sorting efficiency. However, in complex environments, QR code recognition is often affected by other factors, such as uneven lighting. There are several ways to deal with this factor. Wellner [5] proposed a method that used an average of surrounding pixels as a threshold to segment the image. Sauvola [6] devised a way of utilizing the average and deviation of gray values in an area to set the threshold. Zhang and Yang [7] proposed an improved algorithm based on that of Sauvola to speed up the calculation process, but the size of the processing window limited the algorithm. Di et al. [8] proposed an improved method based on Wellner's, and the results can be obtained through simple calculations. However, the algorithm is not effective in the case of severe unevenness of light. Yang and Feng [9] came up with an algorithm combining the methods of Bersen [10] and Otsu [11]. The algorithm will modify the threshold to prevent misclassification. However, several parameters in the algorithm need to be set manually, lacking some adaptive ability. Wu et al. [12] found a method of using BTC to segment an image into multiple blocks for binarization. This method is computationally intensive, and its effect depends on the number of segmented blocks. Chen et al. [13] proposed a window-adaptive binarization algorithm before; the proposed method has a favorable adaptive ability. The algorithm meets the requirements of the warehouse sorting systems, but it cannot meet the needs of the logistics sorting system because the automatic scoring in the logistics system has a higher requirement for efficiency.

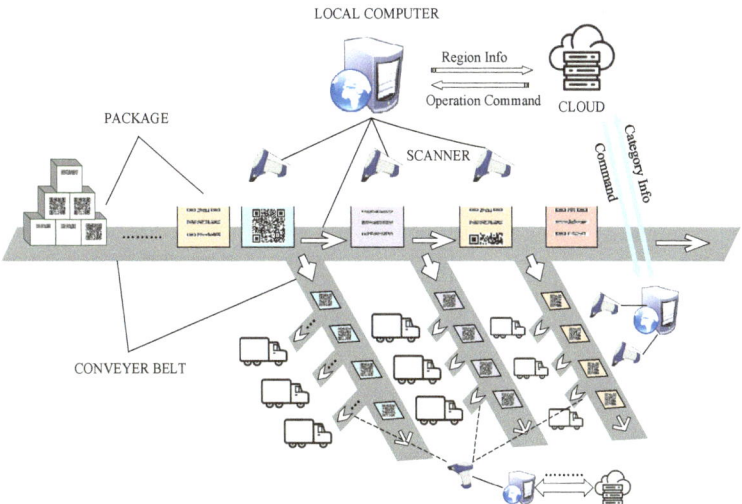

Figure 1. Workflow of automatic sorting in Logistics Systems.

In addition, feature extraction is a standard method in image processing. Ren et al. [14] presented an automatic end-to-end supervised deep learning framework to improve the accuracy of object segmentation and extraction. Sun et al. [15] proposed a novel SpaSSA approach for effective extraction and classification accuracy. Although there are substantial binarization methods in the QR code image, few feature extraction methods are utilized in QR code image processing.

Considering the needs of the logistics sorting system while extracting the features of the QR code, we propose a fast adaptive binarization algorithm, which solves the problem of difficult window definition and achieves a high recognition rating. The algorithm first determines the window size by searching for the position detection patterns and then combines the improved local binarization algorithm for processing. The experimental results show that the algorithm can not only process QR codes with different degrees of uneven illumination but also improve the quality of the fast-processed images.

2. Related Work
2.1. Features of QR Code

In the QR code, the information is encoded in a binary representation. As shown in Figure 2, the dark modules, or black modules, usually represent "1", while the light modules, or white modules, often represent "0". In the upper left, lower left, and upper right corners of the QR code are the position detection patterns. When the mobile device detects the three modules, it can determine the position and direction of the QR code and prepare for decoding. The three position-detection patterns in the QR code have the same size and are composed of three concentric squares. The width ratio of the dark module to the light module of the position detection pattern is 1:1:3:1:1.

Figure 2. Position detection patterns in QR code.

2.2. Some Binarization Algorithm

At present, traditional binarization algorithms can be divided into two categories. One is the global threshold algorithm, which divides the image according to a specific gray value. The most commonly used global threshold algorithm, the Otsu algorithm, determines the threshold T by calculating the maximum between-class variance and then calculates the gray value $f(x, y)$ of each pixel on the image according to Equation (1) to obtain the final value $g(x, y)$ of the pixel. The calculation process of this kind of algorithm is relatively simple, and the calculation speed is fast. However, because the algorithm uses a uniform threshold, image details and information are seriously lost in more complex environments, and the processing effect is poor.

$$g(x,y) = \begin{cases} 255, & f(x,y) > T \\ 0, & f(x,y) \leq T \end{cases} \quad (1)$$

The other is a local threshold algorithm. The core of this algorithm is to use different thresholds to binarize the pixels in the image. The processed image can well restore the details of the image. Similar to the idea of Sauvola's algorithm, first take one pixel as the center and create a local window of w × w size; second, calculate the average gray value $m(x, y)$ in the window, and then calculate the gray value standard deviation $\sigma(x, y)$ of the pixel in the window according to Equation (2); then calculate the threshold value $T(x, y)$ of the pixel according to Equation (3); afterward perform the same operation on each pixel to obtain the respective threshold value; finally, segment each pixel.

$$\sigma(x,y) = \sqrt{\frac{1}{w^2} \sum_{i=x-\frac{w}{2}}^{x+\frac{w}{2}} \sum_{j=y-\frac{w}{2}}^{y+\frac{w}{2}} (f(i,j) - m(x,y))^2} \quad (2)$$

$$T(x,y) = m(x,y)\left[1 + k\left(\frac{\sigma(x,y)}{R} - 1\right)\right] \quad (3)$$

Although the processing effect of such algorithms is relatively sound, the amount of calculation is often too large, resulting in slow operation speed. More importantly, the algorithm is often affected by the size of the processing window. If the window definition is too small, a block phenomenon will occur. On the other hand, if the size is too large, the algorithm's effectiveness will be reduced, and the amount of calculation will be further increased to reduce the processing speed.

Under complex lighting conditions, the traditional global binarization algorithm lacks advantages in recognition rate. At the same time, the traditional local binarization algorithm is also not ideal for processing speed and image segmentation effect. In order to accurately binarize QR codes under complex illumination, many researchers have proposed their methods. Zhou et al. [16] made improvements based on Sauvola's method, combined with the QR code feature definition parameter R in Equation (3). However, the problem of defining the window size was not resolved. Zhang's team [17] proposed an improved binarization method based on background grayscale. This method combines the joint interpolation algorithm and uses the Otsu method to segment the image. Nevertheless, the effect is general in the case of multiple light sources. Yao's team [18] proposed an algorithm that fuses the improved Niblack algorithm with Otsu's algorithm. The algorithm is faster than traditional local binarization methods but is not able to binarize QR code images under different degrees of uneven illumination.

Based on the analysis of the above methods, there is still a lack of an efficient and high-quality binarization algorithm, even under complex lighting conditions. Therefore, in this paper, we bring forward an adaptive fast binarization method combined with QR code features and an integral image method.

3. Method

Most local threshold binarization algorithms have the problems of slow operation speed and obstacles in window definition. In order to solve the problems above, we conducted research based on Sauvola's algorithm. In this paper, the problem of window selection of the local threshold algorithm is solved by combining the features of the QR code image. The method in this paper first finds the position detection pattern through preliminary binarization, then obtains the window size of the local threshold algorithm. Then, it uses Sauvola's and the integral image algorithm to accelerate the threshold calculation of the QR code image and finally reconstructs the image based on the threshold to obtain the binarized image.

3.1. Preprocessing

In daily life, the quality of the unprocessed QR code image is affected by the camera quality of the mobile device, the algorithm processed after shooting, and the environment. Due to these various factors, the image will be disturbed by noise, and the image will likely add noise, so we need to perform median filtering on the QR code image to eliminate the influence of noise.

Because the window size of the algorithm in this paper depends on the central black module of the position detection pattern, we need to pre-process the QR code image to enhance the contrast to ensure the integrity of the position detection pattern after the initial binarization. Top-hat transform and histogram equalization are commonly used methods to enhance contrast.

The top-hat transform can extract the image's dark features or bright regions [19]. So using top-hat transform, the dark module in the position detection pattern can be extracted from the QR code with uneven lighting. The top-hat transformation of the grayscale image I is performed according to

$$T_{hat} = I - (I \diamond b) \qquad (4)$$

where $I \diamond b$ represents the open operation and b is a structural element.

Because there is a width ratio of 1:1:3:1:1 between the modules in the position detection pattern, the size of the structure element is defined as follows:

$$b = \frac{\max(h, w)}{7} \qquad (5)$$

where h is the height of image I and w is the width. After obtaining the top-hat transformed image T_{hat}, we use Otsu algorithm to perform preliminary binarization processing on the image T_{hat}. The pre-processing flowchart is shown in Figure 3.

3.2. Define Window Size Adaptively

In order to solve the problem of window size selection, we performed a series of studies. Initially, we processed the QR code image P1 (Figure 4) with a size of 300 × 300 and iterated from a window size of 1 pixel until the window size was 1/4 of the image width. When the window size exceeds 1/4 of the image width, this will be too time-consuming to use in reality. Sauvola's algorithm was used for binarizing the QR code image. After obtaining several binarized QR code images after processing, we used two objective quality evaluation standards, peak signal-to-noise ratio (PSNR), to judge the results. The larger the calculated value of the evaluation standard, the higher the image quality after binarization. Based on the evaluation of the processed pictures, we have drawn Figure 5.

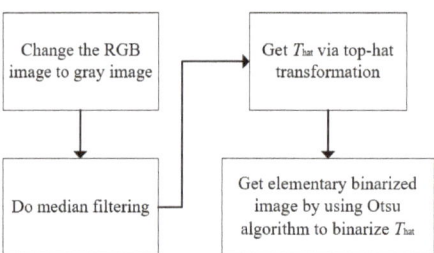

Figure 3. Flowchart of pre-processing.

Figure 4. Image P1.

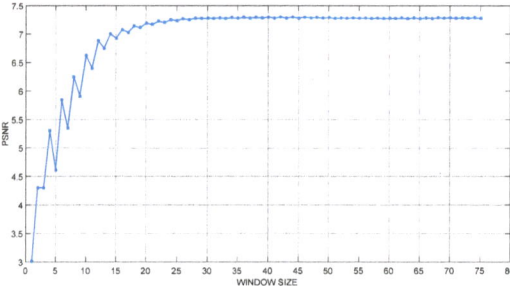

Figure 5. PSNR values after P1 processing.

From the figure, we found that when the window size is set to about 30, the values of PSNR reach the highest, after which the PSNR values remain stable. At the same time, by analyzing the QR code image in Figure 4, we found that the size of the middle black module in the position detection pattern of P1 is 30 × 30, as shown in Figure 6. When the size of the window is the same as the size of the middle black block of the position detection pattern, the PSNR values reach the highest after the QR code is binarized. Finally, in order to further verify the relationship between the window size and the position detection pattern, we performed the same experiment on five 300 × 300 size samples (as shown in Figure 7) and obtained the results shown in Figure 8.

Figure 6. The size of middle module.

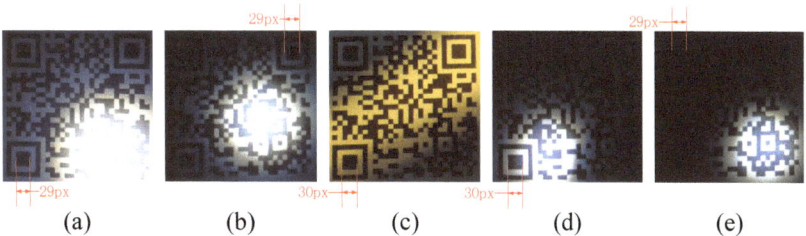

Figure 7. Experimental samples: (**a**) P2; (**b**) P3; (**c**) P4; (**d**) P5; (**e**) P6.

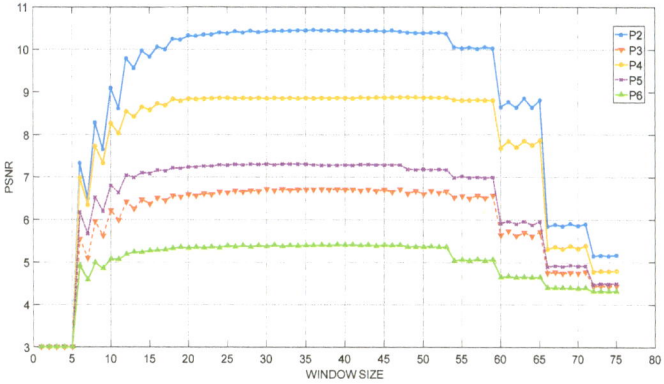

Figure 8. PSNR value curves of five 300 × 300 samples after processing.

As Figure 8 shows, when the window size increases, the image quality after binarization also increases. When the window size is close to the middle black module size of the position detection graphic, the binarized image quality effect reaches the best. As mentioned earlier, most local threshold algorithms currently have the problem of complicated window definitions. Therefore, the size of the black module in the center of the position detection pattern is used as the window size of the local threshold algorithm, which can effectively implement the adaptive selection of the processing window.

Subsequently, we used Adobe Photoshop to enlarge the proofs in Figure 7 to 450 × 450 and 900 × 900, two sets of samples, and gradually increased from a window size of 1, and then binarized the samples to obtain Figure 9.

When the size of the sample is 450 × 450, the middle dark module is close to 45 × 45. While the dark modules are near 90 × 90 in the 900 × 900 samples. From the processing results of the two sets of samples, it can be seen that when the window is close to the dark module in the middle of the position detection pattern, the PSNR values of the image tend to be stable. However, the PSNR values tend to decline as the window size becomes extensive. For each pixel, there is a local threshold algorithm with different thresholds. When traversing each pixel to calculate the threshold, the window size will affect the calculation speed. The larger the window, the slower the calculation speed.

Therefore, the size of the dark module can be defined as the window size of the local binarization algorithm.

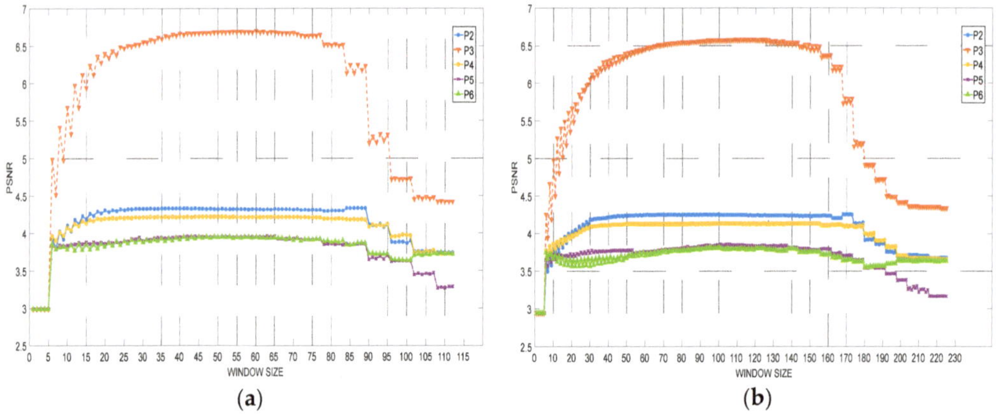

Figure 9. PSNR value curves of five samples in the same size: (**a**) 300 × 300; (**b**) 450 × 450.

As we know, an image can be viewed as a two-dimensional array. Therefore, in order to find the position detection pattern according to the characteristics of the module width ratio 1:1:3:1:1, after obtaining the preliminary binarized image, we transform the image into a one-dimensional array to obtain the array S. We can obtain the gray difference of the adjacent pixels according to

$$Gray_{diff} = S(i+1) - S(i) \qquad (6)$$

where $i \geq 1$. When $Gray_{diff} \neq 0$, we record the current value of i to obtain the index array Index_Array. Then, traverse Index_Array and find the 1:1:3:1:1 relationship. If the above proportional relationship is found, the window size can be determined according to the value of Index_Array.

3.3. Window Size Correction

It is found through experiments that in the case of slightly uneven illumination, the initial binarized image after the top-hat transformation sometimes has the situation that the position detection pattern cannot be determined. In order to improve the success rate of finding the position detection pattern, when the above method fails to obtain the window size, we try another method to obtain the window size again. Histogram equalization is an adaptive contrast enhancement tool [20]. We can use it on the grayscale image I to enhance its contrast and then perform preliminary binarization processing. Next, use the method of Section 3.2 to obtain the window size value again. If there is still no way to obtain the window size value for the histogram-equalized image, set the window size according to

$$window\ size = \frac{\min(h, w)}{10} \qquad (7)$$

Finally, the method flowchart for obtaining the window size is shown in Figure 10.

We used the window size definition method just mentioned in combination with Sauvola's algorithm to select several samples of different sizes for the binarization experiments. The original image and processing results are shown as follows.

It can be seen from Figure 11 that no matter what size the QR code image is, this window definition method is effective and can accurately segment the image.

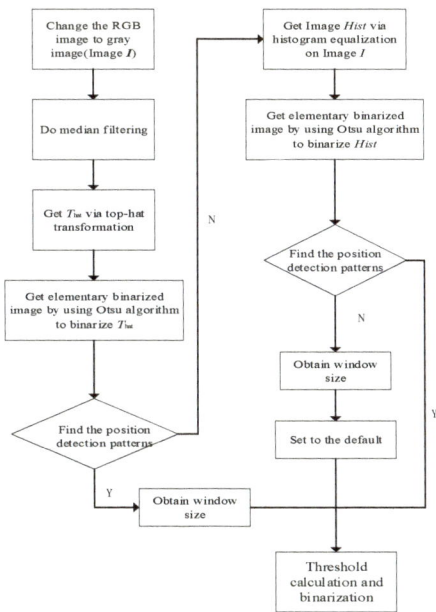

Figure 10. Flowchart of obtaining the window size.

Figure 11. The original image and processing result: (**a**) 300 × 300; (**b**) 50 × 450; (**c**) 600 × 600; (**d**) 900 × 900.

3.4. Threshold Calculation and Binarization

As we all know, the operation speed of the local binarization algorithm is relatively slow. Therefore, we use the integral image algorithm to speed up the operation speed of the algorithm. The integral image is mainly used to calculate the sum of gray values in a rectangular area [21]. Therefore, during the integral image algorithm of the QR code, an integral image needs to be created—the pixels on the integral image store the corresponding total gray values in the QR code. The values on the integral image are obtained by the formula

$$Inte(x,y) = \sum_{i=1}^{x} \sum_{j=1}^{y} G(i,j) \qquad (8)$$

where $G(i, j)$ represents the image T_{hat} obtained by the top-hat transformation or the image $Hist$ obtained by the histogram equalization.

Suppose there is an image A, the gray values of its image pixels are shown in Figure 12a, and the corresponding integral image is shown in Figure 12b.

1	2	3	4
1	2	3	4
1	2	3	4
1	2	3	4

(a)

1	3	6	10
2	6	12	20
3	9	18	30
4	12	24	40

(b)

Figure 12. The gray values of image A and its integral image: (**a**) image A; (**b**) integral image.

Generally, if you want to calculate the sum of gray values in the circled window in Figure 13a, you need to use

$$S(x,y) = \sum_{i=x-\frac{w}{2}}^{x+\frac{w}{2}} \sum_{j=y-\frac{w}{2}}^{y+\frac{w}{2}} I(x,y) \tag{9}$$

for calculation.

1	2	3	4
1	2	3	4
1	2	3	4
1	2	3	4

(a)

1	3	6	10
2	6	12	20
3	9	18	30
4	12	24	40

(b)

Figure 13. Pixel used to calculate the total gray value: (**a**) 9 pixels; (**b**) 4 pixels.

When using the local threshold algorithm, each time the threshold is calculated, the pixel values in the accumulation window need to be traversed, which is a time-consuming operation. In the case of using the integral image, the workload of the calculation is greatly reduced. We can just process by the formula as follows:

$$S(x,y) = Inte(x+d-1, y+d-1) + Inte(x-d, y-d) - Inte(x-d, y+d-1) - Inte(x+d-1, y-d), \tag{10}$$

where and $d = w/2$. Therefore, the calculation of the sum of gray values in the window in Figure 13a only needs to be calculated as follows:

$$S(3,3) = Inte(4,4) + Inte(1,1) - Inte(1,4) - Inte(4,1) = 40 + 1 - 10 - 4 = 27, \tag{11}$$

According to Equation (11), only four calculations are needed to obtain the result, while Equation (10) requires nine calculations. Therefore, calculating the sum of the gray values using the integral image algorithm is more straightforward and faster than the original Equation (10).

Because the method in this paper uses Sauvola's method to binarize the QR code image, when calculating the sum of the gray values in the window, combined with the integral image, the calculation amount can be effectively reduced and increase the calculation speed. Furthermore, the image can be binarized after the thresholds of all pixels are calculated using the improved Sauvola's algorithm.

We selected 30 proofs and used two methods for experiments. One is to use Sauvola's algorithm, and the other is to use Sauvola's algorithm combined with the integral image algorithm. Table 1 shows the result of the experiments.

Table 1. Average consume time of the two algorithms.

Algorithm	Average Time Consuming/s
Sauvola's	4.2544
Savuola's combined with integral image	0.0157

What can be learned from Table 1 is that the time consumption of Savuola's algorithm is far greater than that of another method. It proves that using the integral image algorithm can improve binarization efficiency.

3.5. Morphological Processing

Using the localized binarized image will inevitably lead to some loss of image detail and information, sometimes causing a pseudo-boundary. We can perform an opening operation on the image to reduce the impact. The opening operation smooths the outline of the image, breaking the narrow necks and eliminating fine protrusions. According to

$$A \circ B = (A \ominus B) \oplus B \qquad (12)$$

The opening operation can be understood as the structure element B is first used to corrode the image A, and then the structure element B is used to expand the result.

4. Experiments

In order to verify the effectiveness of the proposed method, we tested it in relation to image quality, recognition rate, and computation speed and used the methods in [6,8,13,18], for comparison. The parameters of the test environment are shown in Tables 2 and 3. The software used in the experiments was ZXing and WeChat. ZXing is an open-source project by Google. Most of the QR code identification software is improved based on this project. Moreover, WeChat is the most widely used QR identification software in China.

Table 2. Hardware parameters.

Hardware	Parameters
Processor	Intel(R) Core(TM) i7-6700HQ CPU @ 2.60 GHz (8 CPUs)
Memory	16 GB SAMSUNG DDR4 2133 MHz
Smart Phone	OnePlus 3 64 GB

Table 3. Software parameters.

Software	Versions
Operating System	Windows 10 Pro 64-bit (10.0, Build 18362)
MATLAB	R2016a 64-bit
ZXing AndroidSDK	3.4.0
WeChat	7.0.10

4.1. Image Quality

The experiments used two standards, PSNR and the measure of structural similarity (SSIM), to objectively evaluate the quality of the processed image. SSIM is the same as PSNR, the more significant the value, the better the image quality. Moreover, SSIM is well-matched to perceived visual quality [22]. We conducted the experiments with several types of uneven illumination QR code images.

(1) Figure 14 shows the effect of different algorithms in processing the QR code, which had a soft light in the lower right corner. We can still see the most details through our eyes.

(2) Figure 15 shows the effect of different algorithms in processing the QR code. Due to a beam of light passing through in a diagonal direction, the QR code had an increased uneven illumination phenomenon.
(3) Figure 16 shows the effect of different algorithms in processing the QR code. Two strong lights focused on the QR code made it have different illumination acquisition in different areas.
(4) Figure 17 shows the effect of different algorithms in processing the QR code. What caused the uneven illumination phenomenon was that a local highlight stayed in the middle part of the QR code. In this case, we can hardly see the modules in the image.
(5) Figure 18 shows the effect of different algorithms in processing the QR code. The original image was shot under the environment where a glare gathered in the lower right corner of the image. As a result, it is hard to recognize the position detection patterns with our eyes.

(a) (b) (c) (d) (e) (f)

Figure 14. The original image and experimental results of different algorithms: (**a**) Original image; (**b**) Sauvola's algorithm [6]; (**c**) Yao's algorithm [18]; (**d**) Di's algorithm [8]; (**e**) Chen's algorithm [13]; (**f**) Proposed method.

(a) (b) (c) (d) (e) (f)

Figure 15. The original image and experimental results of different algorithms: (**a**) Original image; (**b**) Sauvola's algorithm [6]; (**c**) Yao's algorithm [18]; (**d**) Di's algorithm [8]; (**e**) Chen's algorithm [13]; (**f**) Proposed method.

(a) (b) (c) (d) (e) (f)

Figure 16. The original image and experimental results of different algorithms: (**a**) Original image; (**b**) Sauvola's algorithm [6]; (**c**) Yao's algorithm [18]; (**d**) Di's algorithm [8]; (**e**) Chen's algorithm [13]; (**f**) Proposed method.

(a) (b) (c) (d) (e) (f)

Figure 17. The original image and experimental results of different algorithms: (**a**) Original image; (**b**) Sauvola's algorithm; (**c**) Yao's algorithm; (**d**) Di's algorithm; (**e**) Chen's algorithm; (**f**) Proposed method.

Figure 18. The original image and experimental results of different algorithms: (**a**) Original image; (**b**) Sauvola's algorithm [6]; (**c**) Yao's algorithm [18]; (**d**) Di's algorithm [8]; (**e**) Chen's algorithm [13]; (**f**) Proposed method.

According to the groups of experiments above, we obtained the values of PSNR and SSIM of different QR codes after using different algorithms. The exact data values are shown in Table 4. In order to compare the values more intuitively, we drew Figure 19 based on the data in Table 4.

Table 4. The values of PSNR and SSIM of different QR codes after using different algorithms.

Sample	Standard	Sauvola	Yao	Di	Chen	Proposed Method
(1)	PSNR	6.4850	6.3371	6.3560	6.5013	6.6319
	SSIM	0.1583	0.1611	0.1505	0.1540	0.1619
(2)	PSNR	7.4802	8.5616	8.0232	8.8290	8.8727
	SSIM	0.3377	0.3590	0.3415	0.3625	0.3649
(3)	PSNR	6.7898	6.4156	7.1323	7.2810	7.4410
	SSIM	0.2698	0.2650	0.2941	0.2999	0.3042
(4)	PSNR	4.0721	4.2207	4.6880	5.5986	5.6867
	SSIM	0.1101	0.1167	0.1072	0.1368	0.1371
(5)	PSNR	4.0956	4.2298	5.0369	4.5181	5.3828
	SSIM	0.1061	0.1058	0.1245	0.1028	0.1404

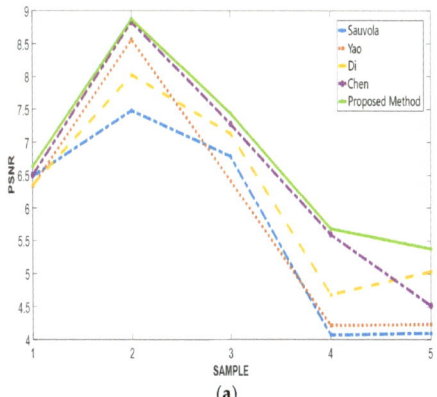
(**a**)

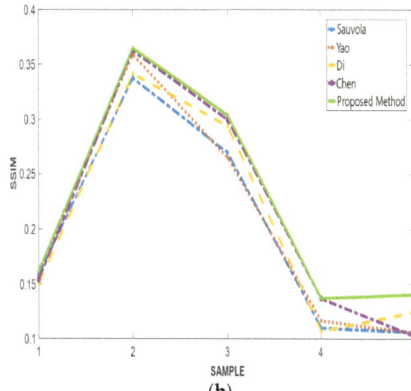
(**b**)

Figure 19. Curves of PSNR and SSIM values of different QR codes after using different algorithms: (**a**) PSNR; (**b**) SSIM.

From Figure 14 to Figure 18 above, we can see that the algorithm in this paper is significantly better than several other comparison algorithms. The algorithms of Sauvola and Yao can restore most of the image details in scenes with uneven lighting caused by dim light. However, unrelated dark modules are often introduced in more complex lighting scenes. Furthermore, the QR code processed by the algorithms of Sauvola and Yao has lower image quality. Di's algorithm has a better processing effect on the types mentioned above of QR codes, but occasionally details will be lost at the part that the light focuses on. The algorithm that we proposed previously can effectively deal with various types of QR codes, but in the case of identifying position detection patterns difficultly in the image, there will be a small number of details lost. It is worth noting that the PSNR and SSIM values of sample QR codes after using the proposed method in this paper are the largest, according to Table 4 and Figure 17. This proposed method gains an advantage over other comparison algorithms in the image quality of the QR code after binarization. Moreover, the proposed method hardly caused black blocks or information missing, even in the complex lighting environment.

4.2. Recognition Rate and Processing Speed

In order to test the recognition rate and processing speed of various algorithms, the experiment used 30 samples with slightly uneven illumination and 50 samples with strong uneven illumination. The size of the samples is 300×300. The results of the five algorithms are shown in Table 5.

Table 5. Recognition rates after processed by different algorithms.

Algorithm	Average Time Consume/s	Recognition Rate	
		ZXing	WeChat
None	——	35%	48.75%
Sauvola [6]	4.3871	37.5%	37.5%
Yao [18]	0.0113	37.5%	42.5%
Di [8]	1.5310	53.75%	71.25%
Chen [13]	0.1715	88.75%	92.5%
Proposed Method	0.0611	92.5%	97.5%

It is shown in Table 5 that the recognition rate of Sauvola's algorithms and Yao's are shallow, and the recognition rate of Sauvola's is even less ideal than when no algorithm is applied. The algorithm in this paper uses the integral image algorithm to speed up the threshold value calculation, and the processing speed has been greatly improved, making the processing efficiency much better than Sauvola's. Surprisingly, it is faster than the algorithm we proposed before. Compared with other methods, the algorithm proposed in this paper has the highest recognition rate on ZXing V3.4.0 and WeChat Version 7.0.10.

In a word, the algorithm proposed in this paper has advantages in terms of processing quality, speed, and recognition rate.

5. Conclusions

A new adaptive binarization method was put forward in this paper. This method, combined with the features of the QR code, looked for the position detection patterns to solve the problem of window size definition and dynamically define the size. In addition, using an integral image algorithm in the method significantly improved the speed of threshold calculation. After a lot of experiments and comparison with some excellent current algorithms, the algorithm in this paper has advantages in processing speed and quality of QR codes with uneven illumination. It meets the need for automatic sorting in logistics systems and can also be applied there.

Author Contributions: Conceptualization, R.C., J.X. and X.L.; Funding acquisition, R.C., W.L. and X.L.; Methodology, R.C. and W.L.; Project administration, J.X.; Resources, X.L.; Software, R.C. and W.L.; Validation, W.L. and K.L.; Writing—original draft, W.L. and R.C.; Writing—review and editing, R.C., K.L., J.X., L.W. and X.L. All authors have read and agreed to the published version of the manuscript.

Funding: This work was supported in part by the National Natural Science Foundation of China under Grant 62072122, in part by the Special Projects in Key Fields of Ordinary Universities of Guangdong Province under Grant 2021ZDZX1087, in part by the Special Project Enterprise Scitech Commissioner of Guangdong Province under Grant GDKTP2021033100, and the Undergraduate Universities Teaching Quality and Teaching Reform Project Construction Project of Guangdong Province (Yuejiao Gaohan [2021] No. 29)—Science, Industry and Education Integration Practice Teaching Base Construction Project (No. 31).

Institutional Review Board Statement: Not applicable.

Informed Consent Statement: Not applicable.

Data Availability Statement: Not applicable.

Acknowledgments: The authors would like to appreciate the contributions from Digital Content Processing and Security Technology of Guangzhou Key Laboratory of School of Computer Science, Guangdong Polytechnic Normal University.

Conflicts of Interest: The authors declare no conflict of interest.

References

1. Centenaro, M.; Costa, C.E.; Granelli, F.; Sacchi, C.; Vangelista, L. A Survey on Technologies, Standards and Open Challenges in Satellite Iot. *IEEE Commun. Surv. Tutor.* **2021**, *23*, 1693–1720. [CrossRef]
2. Laghari, A.A.; Wu, K.; Laghari, R.A.; Ali, M.; Khan, A.A. A Review and State of Art of Internet of Things (IoT). *Arch. Comput. Methods Eng.* **2022**, *29*, 1395–1413. [CrossRef]
3. Kumar, D.; Singh, R.K.; Mishra, R.; Wamba, S.F. Applications of the Internet of Things for Optimizing Warehousing and Logistics Operations: A Systematic Literature Review and Future Research Directions. *Comput. Ind. Eng.* **2022**, *171*, 108455. [CrossRef]
4. Su, J.-P.; Wang, C.-A.; Mo, Y.-C.; Zeng, Y.-X.; Chang, W.-J.; Chen, L.-B.; Lee, D.-H.; Chuang, C.-H. I-Logistics: An Intelligent Logistics System Based on Internet of Things. In Proceedings of the 2017 International Conference on Applied System Innovation (ICASI), Sapporo, Japan, 13–17 May 2017; IEEE: Piscataway, NJ, USA, 2017; pp. 331–334.
5. Wellner, P.D. Adaptive Thresholding for the DigitalDesk. *Xerox* **2021**, *EPC-1993-110*, 1–19.
6. Sauvola, J.; Pietikainen, M. Adaptive Document Image Binarization. *Pattern Recognit.* **2000**, *33*, 225–236. [CrossRef]
7. Zhang, W.; Yang, T. An Improved Algorithm for QR Code Image Binarization. In Proceedings of the 2014 International Conference on Virtual Reality and Visualization, Shenyang, China, 30–31 August 2014; IEEE: Piscataway, NJ, USA, 2014; pp. 154–159.
8. Di, Y.-J.; Shi, J.-P.; Mao, G.-Y. A QR Code Identification Technology in Package Auto-Sorting System. *Mod. Phys. Lett. B* **2017**, *31*, 1740035. [CrossRef]
9. Yang, L.; Feng, Q. The Improvement of Bernsen Binarization Algorithm for QR Code Image. In Proceedings of the 2018 5th IEEE International Conference on Cloud Computing and Intelligence Systems (CCIS), Nanjing, China, 23–25 November 2018; IEEE: Piscataway, NJ, USA, 2018; pp. 931–934.
10. Bernsen, J. Dynamic thresholding of gray-level images. In Proceedings of the Eighth International Conference on Pattern Recognition, Paris, France, 28-31 October 1986.
11. Otsu, N. A Threshold Selection Method from Gray-Level Histograms. *IEEE Trans. Syst. Man Cybern.* **1979**, *9*, 62–66. [CrossRef]
12. Wu, Y.; Yu, S.; Yang, M. Quick Response Code Binary Research Based on Basic Image Processing. *Sens. Mater.* **2019**, *31*, 859–871. [CrossRef]
13. Chen, R.; Yu, Y.; Xu, X.; Wang, L.; Zhao, H.; Tan, H.-Z. Adaptive Binarization of QR Code Images for Fast Automatic Sorting in Warehouse Systems. *Sensors* **2019**, *19*, 5466. [CrossRef] [PubMed]
14. Ren, J.; Sun, H.; Zhao, H.; Gao, H.; Maclellan, C.; Zhao, S.; Luo, X. Effective Extraction of Ventricles and Myocardium Objects from Cardiac Magnetic Resonance Images with a Multi-Task Learning U-Net. *Pattern Recognit. Lett.* **2022**, *155*, 165–170. [CrossRef]
15. Sun, G.; Fu, H.; Ren, J.; Zhang, A.; Zabalza, J.; Jia, X.; Zhao, H. SpaSSA: Superpixelwise Adaptive SSA for Unsupervised Spatial-Spectral Feature Extraction in Hyperspectral Image. *IEEE Trans. Cybern.* **2021**, *7*, 6158–6169. [CrossRef] [PubMed]
16. Zhou, J.; Liu, Y.; Li, P. Research on Binarization of QR Code Image. In Proceedings of the 2010 International Conference on Multimedia Technology, Ningbo, China, 29–31 October 2010; IEEE: Piscataway, NJ, USA, 2010; pp. 1–4.
17. Zhang, Y.; Gao, T.; Li, D.; Lin, H. An Improved Binarization Algorithm of QR Code Image. In Proceedings of the 2012 2nd International Conference on Consumer Electronics, Communications and Networks (CECNet), Yichang, China, 21–23 April 2012; IEEE: Piscataway, NJ, USA, 2012; pp. 2376–2379.
18. Yao, S.; Li, P.; He, L.; Li, Y. Uneven Illumination Two-Dimensional Code Image Recognition Algorithm Research. In Proceedings of the 2018 2nd IEEE Advanced Information Management, Communicates, Electronic and Automation Control Conference (IMCEC), Xi'an, China, 25–27 May 2018; IEEE: Piscataway, NJ, USA, 2018; pp. 2043–2046.
19. Mukhopadhyay, S.; Chanda, B. A Multiscale Morphological Approach to Local Contrast Enhancement. *Signal Process.* **2000**, *80*, 685–696. [CrossRef]
20. Gonzalez, R.C.; Woods, R.E. *Digital Image Processing*; Pearson Education India: Delhi, India, 2009; ISBN 81-317-2695-9.

21. Bradley, D.; Roth, G. Adaptive Thresholding Using the Integral Image. *J. Graph. Tools* **2007**, *12*, 13–21. [CrossRef]
22. Wang, Z.; Bovik, A.C.; Sheikh, H.R.; Simoncelli, E.P. Image Quality Assessment: From Error Visibility to Structural Similarity. *IEEE Trans. Image Process.* **2004**, *13*, 600–612. [CrossRef] [PubMed]

Disclaimer/Publisher's Note: The statements, opinions and data contained in all publications are solely those of the individual author(s) and contributor(s) and not of MDPI and/or the editor(s). MDPI and/or the editor(s) disclaim responsibility for any injury to people or property resulting from any ideas, methods, instructions or products referred to in the content.

Review

Surveying Racial Bias in Facial Recognition: Balancing Datasets and Algorithmic Enhancements

Andrew Sumsion *, Shad Torrie, Dah-Jye Lee and Zheng Sun

Electrical and Computer Engineering Department, Brigham Young University, Provo, UT 84602, USA; shad.torrie@byu.edu (S.T.); djlee@byu.edu (D.-J.L.); zsun2@student.byu.edu (Z.S.)
* Correspondence: andreww9@byu.edu

Abstract: Facial recognition systems frequently exhibit high accuracies when evaluated on standard test datasets. However, their performance tends to degrade significantly when confronted with more challenging tests, particularly involving specific racial categories. To measure this inconsistency, many have created racially aware datasets to evaluate facial recognition algorithms. This paper analyzes facial recognition datasets, categorizing them as racially balanced or unbalanced while limiting racially balanced datasets to have each race be represented within five percentage points of all other represented races. We investigate methods to address concerns about racial bias due to uneven datasets by using generative adversarial networks and latent diffusion models to balance the data, and we also assess the impact of these techniques. In an effort to mitigate accuracy discrepancies across different racial groups, we investigate a range of network enhancements in facial recognition performance across human races. These improvements encompass architectural improvements, loss functions, training methods, data modifications, and incorporating additional data. Additionally, we discuss the interrelation of racial and gender bias. Lastly, we outline avenues for future research in this domain.

Keywords: biometrics; deep learning; deep learning bias; facial recognition; race bias

1. Introduction

Although current facial recognition systems achieve high average accuracy, numerous current improvements are directed towards addressing the disproportionate accuracies across different categories, including race [1–4]. Many attribute the majority of these issues to unbalanced datasets [5–8]. Suresh and Guttag [9] from MIT explore the factors contributing to data bias. They categorize biases into five subcategories: historical, representational, measurement, evaluation, and aggregation. These biases frequently arise unintentionally, often remaining unnoticed by researchers and consequently impact results [9].

In an attempt to quantify and mitigate varying accuracy across race in facial recognition systems, many researchers have encouraged the use of racially balanced datasets over the use of those that are racially unbalanced [10–13]. When a racially balanced dataset is not available for training, a racially balanced evaluation is encouraged [14–17]. The use of racially balanced facial recognition systems is critical to applications that require high security, regardless of race. As such, we examine publicly available datasets and provide information on whether they are racially balanced or unbalanced.

Recently, large improvements have been made in the field of image generation [18]. The effects of these generated images on facial recognition tasks are now emerging. We provide a discussion on how image generation has impacted deep learning systems corresponding to the face in cross-race transformation. Many use this cross-race transformation to generate or balance through augmentation datasets that were originally racially unbalanced to be racially balanced. This is accomplished by transforming the race of individuals in the images through the use of generative adversarial networks (GANs) or latent diffusion models.

Various tradeoffs come from balancing datasets and point to the need for other improvements besides only balancing the dataset. In response to this need, various network improvements were developed that reduce variability in performance across different races. These improvements vary from loss functions and architectural changes to data modification and the use of additional data. We compile and analyze these contributions to demonstrate the field's current state of overcoming racial bias in facial recognition.

In summary, our contributions are as follows:

1. An analysis of both racially balanced and unbalanced datasets reveals significant imbalance across race in numerous widely used facial recognition datasets. Additionally, a list of the datasets that are racially balanced is included.

2. An examination of dataset balancing techniques through data generation, accompanied by an exploration of the implications of these methods.

3. Discussion on various network enhancements that effectively narrow the error gaps between different racial groups in facial recognition tasks.

Additionally, as gender bias is greatly interrelated with racial bias, we discuss gender bias in the context of these three contributions.

The rest of this paper is structured as follows: In Section 2, we present our methods. In Section 3, we discuss the differences between various facial recognition datasets comparing those that are racially unbalanced with those that are racially balanced. In Section 4, we discuss balancing datasets through image generation and the impact of data generation. In Section 5, we discuss various network improvements to decrease the skew of accuracies of facial recognition across race. We recommend future research directions in Section 6 and conclude in Section 7.

2. Methods

This section describes the approach for our survey paper for the dataset comparison in Section 2.1, balancing datasets through data generation in Section 2.2, the network improvements across the human race in Section 2.3, and our decision on terminology in Section 2.4. We consulted the PRISMA review methodology [19] and incorporated the majority of its checklist items to enhance the organization and clearly demonstrate the contributions of this work.

2.1. Datasets Methods

In this work, we selected 22 datasets for comparison in Section 3 based on Google Scholar searches for facial recognition datasets and selected the most popular datasets as defined by Serna et al. [20]. We analyzed the 22 datasets by reviewing the title, the abstract, and the dataset collection description. Each paper was initially reviewed by a single researcher. If inconsistencies or questions arose, a second researcher conducted an additional review. To maintain consistency and minimize bias, the primary researcher performed all initial reviews. Although this does not eliminate all potential biases, it ensures consistent biases throughout the analysis. Any papers that contained grayscale image datasets, such as that from the work of Samaria and Harter [21], were removed from the analysis.

After the datasets were selected, we compiled the racial and gender distributions for each dataset using the original publication of the dataset. When these distributions were not provided by the original publication, we referenced Serna et al. [20] to report the available distributions. When neither source provided the required data, we extracted the racial and gender labels directly from the dataset to obtain the distributions. These three methods allowed us to identify each dataset's racial and gender distributions without the need for hand labeling. We acknowledge that the varying methods may result in inconsistencies in race classification.

We then determined which racially balanced datasets contained overlap with racially unbalanced datasets, as discussed in Section 3.3. Our definition of a racially balanced dataset is when the proportionate difference between the most and least represented races in the dataset does not exceed 5 percentage points. As described by the following equation:

$$\left|\frac{n_{\max} - n_{\min}}{N}\right| \leq 0.05 \quad (1)$$

where $n_{\max}$ is the number of samples of the most represented race, $n_{\min}$ is the number of samples of the least represented race, and N is the total number of samples in the dataset. This definition is based on the principle of an alpha value of 0.05 in statistics. Our decision on the 0.05 alpha value is discussed more in depth in Section 3. The papers for the racially balanced datasets were further analyzed to determine the details of creation, benefits, tradeoffs, and what overlap exists with other popular datasets.

2.2. Dataset Balancing through Generation Methods

One of the first papers to propose generating a balanced dataset through generation was the work by Yucer et al. [22] as discussed more fully in Section 4.2. For this work, we examined all papers on Google Scholar that cited the work of Yucer et al. [22] and additionally searched for works that balance datasets through generation for facial recognition. The titles and abstracts were used to identify papers of interest. Papers were removed that did not focus on generating faces for creating a racially balanced dataset for facial recognition. Each paper's contributions were retrieved and reported in this work.

As the impact of generating images is a growing research field with the growth of additional image generation platforms and networks, we chose to include a discussion on the impacts of data generation. We acknowledge that entire survey papers are made to discuss the impact of data generation. This paper provides a small sample from the literature to highlight the use and benefits of data generation to reduce racial bias. Not including this small sample of data generation impacts would do the reader a disservice by not demonstrating the tradeoffs of the given approach.

2.3. Network Improvements across Human Race Methods

Upon reviewing various network improvements using Google Scholar we chose to focus our review of network improvements across the human race on loss/training, architecture, dataset modification, and the use of additional data. To compare works that made network improvements, we focus on works that were trained on the BUPT-Balancedface dataset while using the ArcFace loss and evaluated on the RFW dataset. The only exceptions are when the improvement is an adjustment to the loss function. This limitation allows for accurate comparison on the RFW dataset.

As we reviewed the articles surveyed in this paper, we discovered many approaches benefit from race classification. As such, we discuss the field of racial classification with articles found through Google Scholar. These articles were analyzed and the split between the two-class and multiple-class race classification categories.

2.4. Terminology

Across the facial recognition literature, the terms "race" and "ethnicity" are used interchangeably. For example, the work by Wang et al. [15] uses the term "race" while the work by Li et al. [16] uses the term "ethnicity" to define the same concept—varying physical appearance that comes from ancestral heritage. In our work, we use the similar, but distinct definitions of race and ethnicity provided by the Merriam-Webster Dictionary. Race is defined as "any one of the groups that humans are often divided into based on physical traits regarded as common among people of shared ancestry" [23], and ethnicity is defined as "ethnic quality or affiliation" [24] with ethnic being defined as "of or relating to large groups of people classed according to common racial, national, tribal, religious, linguistic, or cultural origin or background" [25]. Thus, we refer to "race" as the physical characteristics of the face and "ethnicity" as the cultural aspects of the individual. This clarification is provided to shed light on the use of these terms throughout the paper, acknowledging that others may use different definitions for these terms.

Notably, this survey paper's referenced works refer to 2–7 racial classifications. We acknowledge that there are many more racial classifications than these 2–7 categories and that many individuals identify as multicultural. As evident by the publication of a statistical policy directive defining what classifications and definitions of race ought to be used throughout the United States by the Office of Information and Regulatory Affairs and the Office of Management and Budget, racial classification best practices are still evolving [26]. This lengthy report discusses the various intricacies of racial identification, and includes multiple recent changes that demonstrate the complexity of classifying racial groups.

While we acknowledge the complexities of racial classification, in this work, we maintain the 2–7 categories used in previous racial facial recognition scholarships for consistency's sake. In line with one of the first racially balanced datasets, RFW, which created the standard across the field of racially aware facial recognition tasks [15], we primarily use the following ordering and groupings for racial classification: Caucasian, African, Indian, and Asian. In addition, throughout this paper, various approaches refer to "White" and "Non-White" classifications. We acknowledge that this definition may vary depending on where the authors of the various approaches reside. However, the use in this paper is primarily to emphasize the differing accuracies between different races.

Overall, our method is centered around using Google Scholar's search to find relevant papers. Titles and abstracts were manually checked to identify articles of interest. Further analysis of the articles was then performed to remove any articles that did not meet the focus of this work. Finally, for a paper to be included, a complete analysis of the paper was performed to identify contributions, results, and any pertinent background information. We used the PRISMA checklist [19] as a guide in the process of the creation of this paper with many of the checklist items included throughout the content of this paper.

3. Facial Recognition Dataset Comparison

Early facial recognition datasets often implemented constraints for what variation was acceptable in lighting, head pose, background, and facial expression. One early dataset, the AT&T Database of Faces (originally known as the ORL Database of Faces), incorporated several of these constraints [21]. Although this was a novel task in 1994, after only two years researchers shifted towards performing facial recognition in an unconstrained fashion seeking a model to increase generalization beyond the specified constraints [27]. In 2007, the Labeled Faces in the Wild (LFW) dataset was released with images containing a variety of head poses, lightings, camera parameters, and resolutions moving toward generalization across more scenarios [28]. However, in the last 5 years, the racial imbalance of these web-scraped datasets and the overfitting to the distribution of these datasets were demonstrated [15]. To overcome these datasets' inaccurate distributions, recent datasets synthetically generate images to enforce the prior of proper data distributions [29].

A recent dataset, Digi-Face 1M, released in 2023, is generated with synthetic images with a focus placed on previously overlooked biases such as race, lighting, and even make-up [29]. Although synthetic image generation has advanced significantly, authentic images remain essential in certain aspects of deep learning training pipelines [30]. Although approaches have identified the need for proper racial distributions across training datasets [15,29], there is no standard criteria to measure racial equality in deep learning systems [31].

To address the absence of criteria for measuring racially balanced datasets, we define a racially balanced dataset as a dataset with a 5 (or less) percentage point difference in the proportion of images from the highest to the lowest represented racial categories. This 5 percentage point difference is chosen based on statistics containing a p-value of less than 0.05 considered statistically significant for an alpha of 0.05. The 0.05 alpha value was originally proposed by Fisher [32] and was adopted as the default alpha value across many statistical approaches [33]. Following this trend, we set our alpha value to 0.05 resulting in the 5 percentage point maximum difference between race distributions to be considered a racially balanced dataset. A graph demonstrating the racial distribution across prevalent datasets is given in Figure 1.

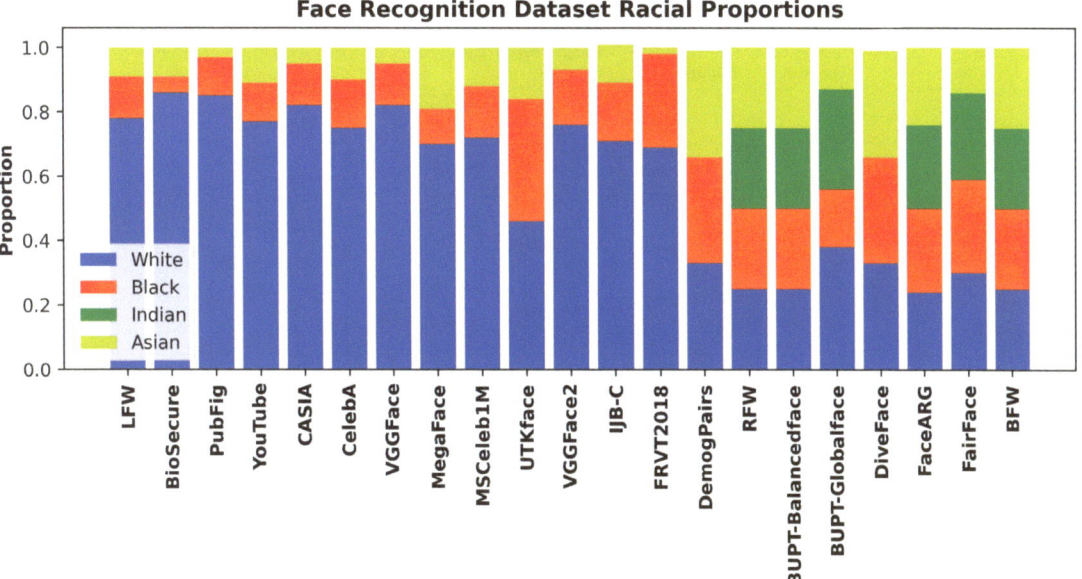

Figure 1. Dataset Racial Distributions: Visualization of racial distributions across prevalent facial recognition datasets. Consistent with the literature, we report only the races included in the RFW dataset [15].

3.1. Unbalanced Datasets

The pursuit to improve facial recognition led to the creation of many datasets. To create the largest datasets possible, web scraping Yahoo, Flickr, and other internet platforms are popular methods for compiling datasets. Some of the prevalent datasets include LFW [28], BioSecure [34], PubFig [35], YouTube Faces [36], CASIA [37], CelebA [38], VGGFace [39], MegaFace [40], MSCeleb1M [41], UTKFace [42], VGGFace2 [43], IJB-C [44], and FRVT2018 [45]. Each of these datasets was collected using different methods. However, each of these datasets was collected with a focus on obtaining the most images in the most cost-effective and efficient method available. Convenience sampling is defined as a method of focusing on ease of access when selecting participants from a target population [46]. When the population of interest is the entire human race, these datasets can be considered a convenience sample. The racial distribution of each of these datasets is provided in Table 1. We define a racially unbalanced dataset as a dataset that contains larger than a five percentage point difference from the most represented race to the least represented. As such, we define each of these datasets as racially unbalanced.

Despite being unbalanced, some racially unbalanced datasets remain valuable for racially focused facial recognition systems. These racially aware datasets employ targeted data collection methodologies. One of these datasets is the BUPT-Globalface dataset. Rather than basing the racial distribution on maintaining equal proportions across the dataset, they base their distribution on the worldwide distribution of race [10].

Table 1. Dataset Distribution Information: Descriptions of various racially balanced and unbalanced datasets. The datasets are sorted chronologically by release year, then alphabetically by dataset name. For those papers that did not originally report the race distribution, the distribution was taken from the work of Serna et al. [20].

Dataset	Year	Number of Images (In Thousands)	Number of Identities (In Thousands)	Average Images Per Identity	Caucasian	African	Indian	Asian	Racially Balanced/ Unbalanced
LFW [28]	2008	13	5.7	2	77.6%	12.9%	** Combined In African	9.4%	Unbalanced
BioSecure [34]	2009	2.7	0.667	4	86.1%	5.2%	** Combined In African	8.8%	Unbalanced
PubFig [35]	2011	58	0.2	294	85.0%	12.0%	** Combined In African	3.0%	Unbalanced
YouTube Faces [36]	2011	621	1.6	390	77.2%	11.7%	** Combined In African	10.9%	Unbalanced
CASIA [37]	2014	500	10.5	48	82.0%	12.9%	** Combined In African	5.2%	Unbalanced
CelebA [38]	2015	203	10.2	20	75.4%	14.6%	** Combined In African	9.9%	Unbalanced
VGGFace [39]	2015	2600	2.6	1000	82.3%	12.7%	** Combined In African	5.0%	Unbalanced
MegaFace [40]	2016	4700	660	7	70.3%	10.9%	** Combined In African	18.7%	Unbalanced
MSCeleb1M [41]	2016	10,000	100	100	71.6%	16%	** Combined In African	12.2%	Unbalanced
UTKFace [42]	2017	24	-	-	46.2%	37.8%	** Combined In African	16.0%	Unbalanced
IJB-C [44]	2018	21	3.5	6	70.5%	17.8%	** Combined In African	11.6%	Unbalanced
VGGFace2 [43]	2018	3300	9	370	76.1%	16.8%	** Combined In African	7%	Unbalanced
DemogPairs [14]	2019	10.8	0.6	18	33.3%	33.3%	** Combined In African	33.3%	Balanced
FRVT2018 [45]	2019	2700	1200	2	64.9%	27.3%	** Combined In African	1.6%	Unbalanced
RFW [15]	2019	40	12	3.3	25%	25%	25%	25%	Balanced
BUPT-Balancedface [10]	2020	1300	28	46.4	25%	25%	25%	25%	Balanced
BUPT-Globalface [10]	2020	2000	38	52.6	38%	13%	18%	31%	Unbalanced
CeFA [16]	2020	23.5	1.6	14.7	N/A	33.3%	33.3%	33.3%	Balanced
DiveFace [11]	2020	125	24	5.2	33.3%	33.3%	** Combined In African	33.3%	Balanced
FaceARG [12]	2021	175	-	-	24.42%	24.02%	25.94%	25.60%	Balanced
FairFace [13]	2021	108	-	-	* 29.7%	* 29.5%	* 26.6%	* 14.2%	* Unbalanced
BFW [17]	2023	20	0.8	25	25%	25%	25%	25%	Balanced

* The FairFace dataset [13] distributions are 14.1% Black 19.0% Caucasian, 14.1% East Asian, 14.2% Indian, 15.3% Latino, 10.7% Middle Eastern, and 12.5% Southeast Asian. Despite its emphasis on capturing diverse racial distributions, we classify this dataset as unbalanced due to the maximum difference of 8.3 percentage points.
** The Indian column is classified along with the African column.

In contrast to the majority of racially aware datasets that collected their images by subsampling existing facial recognition datasets, the FairFace dataset [13] collected new images for facial recognition. FairFace used a large public dataset not originally designed for facial recognition purposes, Yahoo YFCC100M [47], and detected faces in the images. They note that another dataset, Diversity in Faces (DIF) [48], also created a dataset in this manner. However, DIF does not focus on racial distribution. Additionally, FairFace varies from other racially aware datasets as they used seven race classifications based on the accepted race classification from the U.S. Census Bureau: Black, East Asian, Indian, Latino, Middle-East, South East Asian, and White. While we acknowledge that the U.S. Census Bureau's definition of race is not based on entirely visual aspects, the FairFace dataset is based on visual aspects as the race, gender, and age groups were manually labeled using images that were labeled on Amazon's Mechanical Turk. The racial distribution proportions for the FairFace dataset found in Table 1 were derived from the dataset labels as they were not specified in the original work. Despite the FairFace dataset's clear emphasis on racial equality, it is classified as unbalanced according to our criteria due to a maximum racial disparity of 8.3 percentage points, which exceeds the limit of 5 percentage points.

3.2. Balanced Datasets

While there are many scenarios in which convenience sampling is sufficient to represent a population of interest, strata sampling is a more structured approach to ensure proportionate representation. Strata sampling is defined as taking proportionately equal samples from each category or stratum from the population of interest [49]. Many assert that strata sampling is optimal for facial recognition datasets, as it employs proportional sampling from each race [10–15,48].

One of the first datasets presented with relatively proportionally equal distributions across race was the Racial Faces in the Wild (RFW) dataset. The RFW dataset was created by subsampling the MS-Celeb-1M dataset [50] with an equal proportion of images across the Caucasian, African, Indian, and Asian races. To identify the race, the researchers used the nationality attribute in FreeBase celebrities [51] to select individuals of Asian or Indian race. Then, they used the Face++ API [52] to estimate race for Caucasians and Africans. Afterward, the dataset was manually and thoroughly cleaned. This resulted in a dataset of four racial subsets (African, Asian, Caucasian, and Indian), each with 10K images of 3K individuals [15]. We acknowledge that their race labels came from the "nationality" label, and nationality is defined as "a people having a common origin, tradition, and language and capable of forming or actually constituting a nation-state" [53]. The nationality label is not equivalent to a race label but is more in line with the ethnicity of an individual. While the nationality label is not directly correlated to race, we acknowledge their manual cleaning to ensure the racial labels' accuracy. The racial distribution of the RFW dataset is compared with other unbalanced and balanced datasets in Table 1.

Released in the same year as the RFW dataset, the DemogPairs dataset followed a similar pattern of taking a subsample of unbalanced datasets [14]. However, instead of taking the samples all from one dataset, samples were taken from the CWF, VGGFace, and VGGFace2 datasets. The DemogPairs dataset is designed to be a validation dataset that can be used to evaluate model performance across the full spectrum of human racial diversity. If a model is trained on CWF, VGGFace, or VGGFace2, and validated on DemogPairs, the overlapping images must be removed from the training dataset to prevent polluting the test set. The DemogPairs dataset contains 0.13% of VGGFace2, 0.02% of VGGFace, and 1.27% of CWF [14].

In a trend to increase the size of racially balanced datasets, DiveFace [11] was assembled as a subset of the Megaface datasets MF2 [11]. This sampling brought variation in head pose, lighting, age, facial expression, and quality from the Flickr scraped images. However, they limit their racial categories to three races: combining the Indian and African categories. In Table 1, we have placed the African and Indian categories into the African category as African falls before Indian in alphabetical order.

Among the largest racially balanced datasets to date are the BUPT-Globalface and BUPT-Balancedface datasets. BUPT-Balancedface follows our racially balanced definition while the BUPT-Globalface represents each race according to the global proportions of that race and is racially unbalanced by our definition [10]. Both are subsets of the MS-Celeb-1M dataset and are extended using the one-million FreeBase celebrity list [50] and used the nationality labels in the FreeBase celebrities [51] along with the Face++ API [52], similar to RFW [15]. In addition, they removed any overlapping images with RFW, allowing for models that are trained on BUPT-Balancedface and BUPT-Globalface to be evaluated on the RFW dataset.

Another racially balanced dataset is the CASIA-SURF Cross-ethnicity Face Antispoofing (CeFA) dataset. The CeFA dataset was designed as an anti-spoofing dataset with 3 races, 1607 subjects, 3 modalities, and 2D plus 3D spoofing attack types [16]. This dataset was designed to counteract spoofing attacks by providing balanced races and depth information collected by infrared sensors.

The FaceARG dataset was collected by scraping the web for pictures of celebrities and resulted in over 175,000 facial images. The individuals' race was assigned labels corresponding to four main races, following the RFW split [12]. This dataset is referred to as an "in the wild" dataset due to the variety of head poses and orientations of the individuals' faces. More information about the racial distribution of the FaceARG dataset is given in Table 1.

The Balanced Faces in the Wild (BFW) dataset [17] was released recently in 2023 as a subset of the VGG2 dataset [43]. The BFW dataset was balanced across identity, gender, and race. The BFW dataset demonstrates the ongoing research on racially aware facial recognition systems along with the need to balance across multiple attributes in addition to balancing across race. However, to achieve the desired balance, the BFW dataset is less than 1% the size of the VGGFace2 dataset. Balancing datasets across race often requires significantly reducing the size of large datasets, resulting in a severe tradeoff.

In this work, we focus on datasets with images of individuals taken from monocular and stationary cameras. It is important to acknowledge other datasets exist with different emphases, such as those stated in past review articles [54]. Since the introduction of the RFW and DemogPairs datasets in 2019, there has been an ongoing effort to create racially balanced datasets. We emphasize that although using an authentic racially balanced dataset for training is ideal, the tradeoff tends to decrease the overall size of the dataset. To overcome this tradeoff, dataset balancing through data generation and various network improvements have been developed; these are discussed in Sections 4 and 5.

3.3. Evaluating Networks Trained on Unbalanced Datasets

The impact of training on a racially unbalanced dataset is best seen when evaluated on a racially balanced dataset. To properly evaluate network performance on facial recognition across race, it is crucial to have no overlap between the training and testing datasets. As many of the racially balanced datasets contain overlap with frequently used training datasets, we analyze which data should be partially excluded to ensure valid evaluation, as detailed for each of the racially conscious datasets in Table 2.

Table 2. Dataset Overlap: To properly use the racially conscious datasets as a test dataset, there needs to be no overlap between the training dataset and the test dataset. This table lists what racially balanced datasets contain overlap with popular racially unbalanced facial recognition datasets. We note that BUPT-Balancedface and BUPT-Globalface do not supply what percentage came from MS-Celeb-1M.

Dataset	Overlaps with Other Datasets	Percentage Overlap
DemogPairs [14]	VGGFace2, VGGFace, and CWF	0.13%, 0.02% and 1.27%
RFW [15]	MS-Celeb-1M	0.4%
BUPT-Balancedface [10]	MS-Celeb-1M	Not Available
BUPT-Globalface [10]	MS-Celeb-1M	Not Available
DiveFace [11]	Megaface dataset MF2	2.7%

In addition to publishing the RFW dataset, Wang et al. [15] also evaluated many state-of-the-art facial recognition methods on the RFW dataset. They demonstrated that certain races had lower individual accuracies, as seen in Table 3. For example, African individuals had nearly twice the average error rate than their Caucasian counterparts. To simplify comparison, we also report the skewed error ratio (SER) as defined by $SER = \frac{MaxError_r}{MinError_r}$ with r being the races: Caucasian, Indian, Asian, and African.

Table 3. Commercial API comparison: This table compares commercial APIs and popular algorithms trained on racially unbalanced datasets and evaluated on racially unbalanced (Labeled Faces in the Wild (LFW)) and racially balanced (Racial Faces in the Wild (RFW)) datasets as reported by Wang et al. [15]. The algorithms that are trained on racially unbalanced datasets have high accuracies on unbalanced datasets. Their generalization to balanced datasets such as RFW is limited. These accuracies and skewed error ratio (SER) values can be compared to the results of networks trained on racially balanced approaches discussed in Section 5. Reprinted/adapted with permission from Ref. Wang et al. [15]. 2019, IEEE.

	Model	LFW Verification Accuracy	RFW Caucasian	Indian	Asian	African	SER (↓)
Commercial API	Microsoft [55]	-	87.60%	82.83%	79.67%	75.83%	1.95
	Face++ [52,56]	99.5%	93.90%	88.55%	92.47%	87.50%	2.05
	Baidu [57]	-	89.13%	86.53%	90.27%	77.97%	2.26
	Amazon [58]	-	90.45%	87.20%	84.87%	86.27%	1.58
	mean	-	90.27%	86.28%	86.82%	81.89%	1.96
Algorithms trained on racially unbalanced datasets	Center-loss [59]	99.0%	87.18%	81.92%	79.32%	78.00%	1.72
	Sphereface [60]	99.42%	90.80	87.02	82.95	82.28	1.93
	Arcface [61]	99.40%	92.15%	88.00%	83.98%	84.93	2.04
	VGGface2 [43]	99.0%	89.90%	86.13%	84.93%	83.38	1.64
	mean	99.21%	90.01%	85.77%	82.80%	82.15%	1.83

3.4. Intersection of Racially Balanced Datasets and Gender Bias

As our survey focuses primarily on racial bias, we do not conduct an in depth analysis of gender bias across the datasets. However, as gender and race bias intersection is well known [62], we provide an analysis of the gender bias that remains in multiple racially balanced and racially unbalanced datasets.

In Table 4, we provide the distribution across race of both racially balanced and racially unbalanced datasets. We note that the BUPT-Balancedface and BUPT-Globalface datasets are not presented in the table as the initial work, nor subsequent works, have published labels for gender across these two datasets. In addition, the CeFA dataset only provides the distribution across gender and not the gender across the different races. We obtained the gender distributions for the FaceARG, DiveFace, and FairFace datasets by manually analyzing the datasets' provided gender labels. The RFW dataset distribution was obtained from Sarridis et al. [63]. We note that the BFW dataset is the most gender-balanced network that is also racially balanced. In contrast, the RFW dataset's gender distribution contains the greatest unbalance across gender for racially balanced datasets. In the discussion of racially balanced datasets, it is critical to understand which datasets are also balanced across gender.

Table 4. Dataset Gender Distributions: In the discussion of racial bias, gender bias is closely related. The gender distribution across multiple datasets is presented in this table. The table is sorted initially by the difference in percentage points between the overall Male and Female distributions (labeled in the table as Δ) and then by publication year. Although certain datasets are racially balanced, many remain unbalanced across gender.

Dataset	Racially Balanced	Caucasian Female	Male	African Female	Male	Indian Female	Male	Asian Female	Male	Overall Female	Male	Δ $|F-M|$
LFW [28]	✗	18.7%	58.9%	3.3%	9.6%	–	–	2.2%	7.2%	24.2%	75.7%	51.5%
RFW [15]	✓	7.9%	17.2%	1.3%	24.4%	9.1%	14.7%	7.7%	17.6%	26.1%	73.9%	47.8%
YouTube Faces [36]	✗	20.3%	56.9%	4.0%	7.7%	–	–	3.0%	7.9%	27.3%	72.5%	45.2%
FRVT2018 [45]	✗	16.5%	48.4%	7.4%	19.9%	–	–	0.4%	1.2%	24.3%	69.5%	45.2%
MSCeleb1M [41]	✗	19.2%	52.4%	3.9%	12.1%	–	–	4.5%	7.7%	27.6%	72.2%	44.6%
VGGFace2 [43]	✗	30.2%	45.9%	6.3%	10.5%	–	–	3.6%	3.4%	40.1%	59.8%	19.7%
CASIA [37]	✗	33.2%	48.8%	5.7%	7.2%	–	–	2.6%	2.6%	41.5%	58.6%	17.1%

Table 4. *Cont.*

Dataset	Racially Balanced	Caucasian Female	Caucasian Male	African Female	African Male	Indian Female	Indian Male	Asian Female	Asian Male	Overall Female	Overall Male	Δ $|F-M|$
PubFig [35]	✗	35.5%	49.5%	5.5%	6.5%	–	–	1.0%	2.0%	42.0%	58.0%	16.0%
IJB-C [44]	✗	30.2%	40.3%	6.0%	11.8%	–	–	6.2%	5.4%	42.4%	57.5%	15.1%
BioSecure [34]	✗	36.0%	50.1%	2.1%	3.1%	–	–	4.5%	4.3%	42.6%	57.5%	14.9%
MegaFace [40]	✗	30.3%	40.0%	4.7%	6.2%	–	–	8.1%	10.6%	43.1%	56.8%	13.7%
FaceARG [12]	✓	14.5%	9.8%	10.3%	13.8%	15.7%	10.3%	16.2%	9.5%	56.7%	43.3%	13.4%
CeFA [16]	✓	–	–	–	–	–	–	–	–	43.9%	56.1%	12.2%
CelebA [38]	✗	41.5%	33.9%	8.2%	6.4%	–	–	5.5%	4.4%	55.2%	44.7%	10.5%
UTKFace [42]	✗	20.0%	26.2%	16.3%	21.5%	–	–	8.9%	7.1%	45.2%	54.8%	9.6%
FairFace [13]	✗	12.3%	17.4%	14.8%	14.7%	6.8%	7.3%	13.1%	13.6%	47.0%	53.0%	6%
VGGFace [39]	✗	38.6%	43.7%	6.9%	5.8%	–	–	2.9%	2.1%	48.4%	51.6%	3.2%
DiveFace [11]	✓	19.7%	20.2%	14.0%	15.0%	–	–	16.3%	14.8%	50.5%	49.5%	1.0%
DemogPairs [14]	✓	16.7%	16.7%	16.7%	16.7%%	–	–	16.7%	16.7%	50%	50%	0%
BFW [17]	✓	12.5%	12.5%	12.5%	12.5%	12.5%	12.5%	12.5%	12.5%	50.0%	50.0%	0%

3.5. Discussion on Racially Balanced Datasets

As the field of facial recognition continues to grow, certain biases, such as bias across race begin to be more understood. Many point to the unbalance of training and validation datasets as the cause for this bias. We provide a definition for racially balanced and racially unbalanced datasets based on statistical principles. We define racially balanced datasets as those datasets that contain less than a 5 percentage point difference between the least represented race and the most represented race. In contrast, a racially unbalanced dataset contains a greater than five percentage point difference.

The first racially balanced dataset was released in 2019, with continual releases of additional racially balanced datasets. We provide a list of racially balanced datasets in Table 1 and describe the overlap between racially balanced and racially unbalanced datasets in Table 3.

As racially balanced datasets are becoming more available, the intersection of race and gender is highlighted. We identify that although many racially balanced datasets are created to decrease the racial bias, the gender bias often remains. The most recently released racially balanced dataset, BFW, is not only balanced across race but also gender.

4. Balancing Datasets through Data Generation

While there are various datasets that are balanced [10–12,14–17], many of the largest datasets remain unbalanced [39–41,43,45]. One method for obtaining racially balanced datasets from a racially unbalanced dataset is to augment the dataset through race transformations. The concept is centered around taking all images of people in one race and transferring the images to also be in all other races, creating an equally balanced dataset. Facial recognition focused on racially balancing datasets through race transformation frequently uses generative adversarial networks (GANs) [64] and diffusion models [65,66] to perform this augmentation.

Since the original publication of the GAN by Goodfellow et al. [64] in 2014, GANs have continued to increase in complexity and ability. Some of the top research papers on GANs are written on topics including adding details to segmentations or outlines of items such as handbags or cars [67], style-based networks that generate human faces [68] and even creating anime characters simply off of a list of attributes given in text [69]. In this paper, we focus on the effect that GANs have on increasing and decreasing racial equality as well as cross-race transformation.

Although stable diffusion was created in 2015 [65], it significantly grew in popularity and performance in 2022 with the release of stable diffusion in the latent space [66]. Latent stable diffusion is currently the leading method for image generation in various applications [70]. A recent variant, the diffusion transformer [71], has shown promising results in further enhancing this technology's capabilities.

4.1. Understanding the Impact of Data Generation

As GANs and latent stable diffusion continuously improve, many users remain unaware of the unintended consequences of data generation. One team of researchers demonstrated unintended consequences by using headshots of engineers to train a deep donvolutional GAN [72], resulting in the majority of GAN-produced images having white skin tones and masculine facial features [73]. They point out that GANs can increase data biases that are already in the dataset if GANs are used to generate facial data.

Before the publication of the work by Jain et al. [73], another team used a GAN to attempt to lower racial inequality with their focus on quantifying attractiveness to simulate equality of opportunity [74]. To accomplish this, they trained a network to take a subset of images, such as one gender, and be able to distinguish whether they are attractive or not. They then compared across the different subsets using publicly available datasets: CelebA [38], Soccer (many analysts, one dataset) [75], and Quick Draw! [76]. They designed their generator and discriminator network structures based on previous works [77–79] and used conditional batch normalization [80]. Overall, they improved on the simulated equality of opportunity with their GAN-based approach [74].

A larger example of a GAN demonstrating racial inequality is seen with a team that created a face-generating GAN [81]. The GAN was used to generate faces that would pass on multiple individuals when compared using top-performing face authentication systems such as DLib [82], FaceNet [83], and SphereFace [60]. They termed these faces "master faces" [81]. To generate face images, they use Dlib's embedding representation as the input to their network. Their network has a linear layer and four de-convolutional layers, based on the DC-GAN architecture [72]. They trained on DLib's embedding representations of the FFHQ dataset [68]. Upon inspection of the faces generated that are displayed in their paper, the highest proportion of any race of generated images is Caucasian [81]. Examples of generated images are shown in Figure 2.

Figure 2. Example Images of MasterFace: MasterFace is an adversarial approach to the facial recognition task where a high proportion of generated images pass for the majority of faces on many facial recognition models [81]. The (**a–i**) rows demonstrate 9 different sets of Masterfaces. We include this figure to demonstrate the highest proportion of any race generated is Caucasian faces, demonstrating the skew across race in many facial recognition models. Reprinted/adapted with permission from Ref. [81]. 2021, IEEE.

While there are various examples of GANs having large racial biases, there are also GANs that display the ability to decrease racial biases. One such work used a classical GAN-based approach to lower the racial bias in machine learning. Their approach consisted of training a network to identify race using California Census data, followed by an adversarial network to train against the identifying network. Their method increased race identification accuracy from 39% to 76% on their dataset [84]. This demonstrates the ability of GANs to greatly increase the ability of classification networks particularly with race. It also demonstrates that improvements continue to be made with GANs to decrease racial inequality.

4.2. Cross-Race Transformation

While using a racially balanced dataset to train a facial recognition model is beneficial, it often results in a tradeoff with decreasing the size of the datasets. To continue the use of large-scale facial recognition datasets, a beneficial method is race transformation. This method augments datasets to be racially balanced by transforming the race of images to other races.

Yucer et al. [22] overcomes the issues of racially unbalanced datasets using a racial transformation data augmentation approach. They used a four-race dataset: African, Asian, Caucasian, and Indian to compare more easily with the RFW (Racial Faces in the Wild) dataset. For the racial transformation, they trained six CycleGAN models [85] on the BUPT-Transferface dataset [15]. For facial recognition, they trained a common DCNN, Resnet [86], and used a ResNet100 [61] to obtain the final 512-D feature space representation. They experimented with various loss functions: Softmax [60], CosFace [87], and ArcFace [61]. They trained on a subset of 1200 images from VGGFace2 [43] with 300 images for each of their four races. Each of these 300 images was then transferred to the other 3 races using the CycleGANs for the augmented dataset. Their results not only improve accuracy on the RFW dataset but also the overall accuracy on the LFW (Labeled Faces in the Wild) dataset [22]. Example images of the transferred race images are available in Figure 3.

A similar approach was taken by Ge et al. [88] as they use a Fan-Shaped GAN (FGAN) to also transfer the race of an individual to another race. Their network structure is a combination of previous architectures [85,89] with the addition of spectral normalization [78]. For the dataset, they note that RFW is collected from MS-Celeb-1M. So, they collect their images from MS-Celeb-1M with 5000 images in each racial subset for their dataset. They compare their network against the StarGAN [89] and CycleGAN [85]. In doing so, they displayed that their approach was more accurate in all races for FID and received a better inception score on all races besides African [88].

One recent work in racial image generation transforms gender and age in the same system [90]. Their pipeline takes the input image, detects the faces and eyes, crops, normalizes, generates the face image by GRA-GAN, and estimates gender/race/age using a CNN. This pipeline creates a method to control for extra variation that is outside the scope of the GRA-GAN. They demonstrate that their GRA-GAN outperforms or has comparable results to top image-to-image GANs such as Pix2Pix [67], CycleGAN [85], Modified CycleGAN [91], and Enhanced CycleGAN [92]. They state that their network could be used to augment data to prevent training from overfitting to certain genders, races, or ages [90].

While many methods for balancing datasets through data generation have focused on training a new model for transferring race, the work by Jain et al. [93] uses an existing Style GAN to perform the generation. Previous methods identified the need to scale their method up with additional subjects and computational power, the work by Jain et al. [93] provides a method for transferring style to an image to transfer the race. Using this method, Jain et al. [93] pre-trained a facial recognition network on the augmented dataset, which outperforms corresponding models not pre-trained with their augmented dataset. Their approach demonstrates a solution to previous methods' need to scale up the transformation approaches.

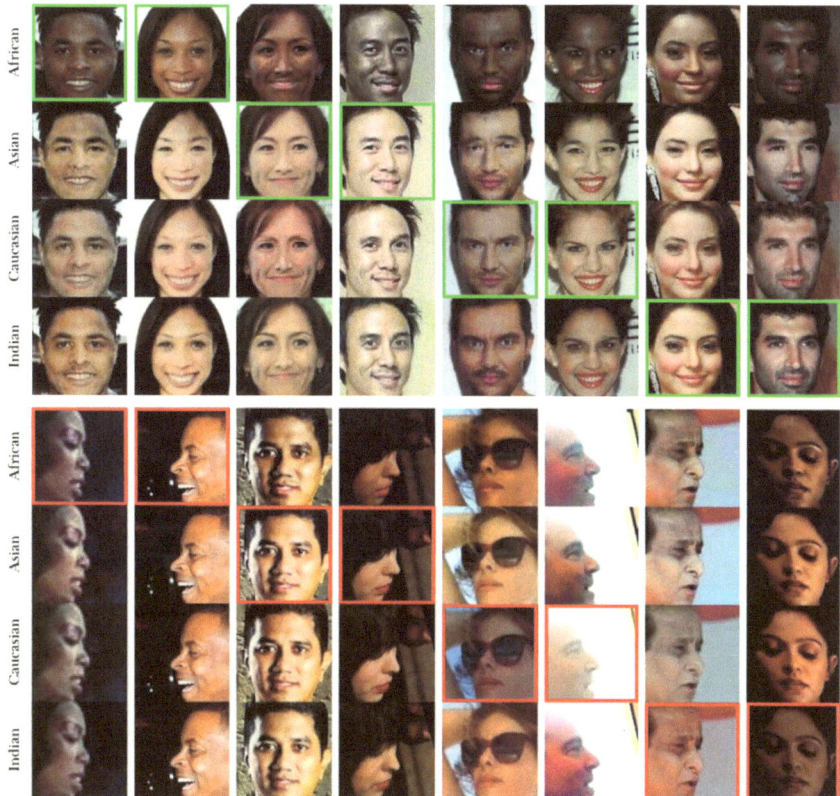

Figure 3. Example Images of Transferring Race: The top images demonstrate successful race transfers while the bottom images demonstrate failures. The green and red bounding boxes demonstrate the original image. As observed in the bottom images, the GAN struggles with extreme head poses and varying lighting [22].

While racial transformation sounds promising to balance a dataset, there remain many problems. Some of these problems include whether or not the images of a person that has been racially transformed to a new race should be considered as positive, negative, or not even considered to the original image or other images of that same person [94]. In contrast, the approach of limiting the dataset to only use an equal number of images from each race is a more defined approach to the solution. However, it does limit the size of the dataset instead of increasing the size. The benefits and the problems of each of these approaches are an open research question.

One of the most recent image generation methods has generated an entire dataset for the use of overcoming the skew across race in facial recognition. DigiFace 1M provides 1 million synthetically generated faces that are balanced across race and adds various accessories to make the datasets encompass a larger spread of data. Using only their dataset, they were able to achieve a 95.82% on the LFW dataset without using any of the LFW training images. As opposed to other methods of using GANs or stable diffusion, DigiFace 1M was created using a computer graphics pipeline [29]. Training on this racially balanced dataset resulted in a high accuracy on the LFW dataset, demonstrating promise for racially aware facial recognition systems. An example from the DigiFace 1M dataset is provided in Figure 4.

Figure 4. DigiFace 1M Example Image: DigiFace 1M [29], one of the most recent image generation datasets, generates the face and then changes lighting, background, and pose.

4.3. Intersection of Racial Dataset Balancing and Gender

As we discuss racially balancing datasets through data generation, we note that similar responses have also been proposed for balancing across gender. Previously, we discussed the GRA-GAN approach that uses the same network to generate gender, race, and age [90]. While other works had transferred across race and age [92], the GRA-GAN was the first approach to also transfer across gender. Previous related approaches classified gender for tasks such as face aging [95].

The results of the GRA-GAN demonstrate the improvement over multiple biases when training to overcome the biases in the same network. Their work shows the large interrelation between racial and gender bias.

4.4. Discussion on Balancing Datasets through Data Generation

Balancing datasets through data generation to minimize racial bias is relatively new to the field of image generation. Preliminary methods published in 2020 demonstrated the success on samples of larger datasets [22], while recent publications have scaled to full datasets by using pre-existing networks [93]. In addition, the benefit of training a network to not only transfer across race but also gender and age demonstrates an improvement over only transferring across race [90].

The field of racially balancing datasets through data generation has followed the progression of GANs using both CycleGANs and FanGANS. Other image networks mitigating racial bias in related tasks [96] have used diffusion to generate images while balancing datasets through data generation for facial recognition has turned to using computer graphic pipelines [29]. One of the next steps for balancing datasets through data generation for facial recognition is to use latent diffusion models as various other fields of image generation have.

5. Network Improvements across Human Race

Efforts to mitigate the performance disparities across different races in facial recognition systems continue to evolve with various innovative approaches. This work focuses on approaches that include refining loss functions, optimizing training methodologies, modifying datasets, and novel network architectures. In addition, as various methods rely on race recognition within the overarching solution, we include a discussion on identifying race. As gender bias is interrelated with racial bias, we discuss network improvements that decrease both racial and gender bias. We provide a brief discussion on related tasks' network improvements and an overall discussion on network improvements in facial recognition across human races.

5.1. Network Improvements on the RFW Dataset

This section focuses on improvements measured on the RFW dataset [15], a popular racially balanced test dataset. Table 5 compares various improvements discussed in this section. The SER (as defined in Section 3) is also reported in this table to facilitate straightforward comparison to methods trained on unbalanced datasets shown in Table 3.

Table 5. RFW Accuracies Across Network Improvements: This table presents the accuracies, in percentages, achieved by state-of-the-art (SOTA) methods on the RFW dataset. Each method is trained on the BUPT-Balancedface dataset and uses the ArcFace loss, except for IMAN and CosFace approaches. The highest accuracy in each column is bolded and enclosed in brackets. "STD" denotes the standard deviation and "SER" represents the skewed error ratio. "↓" describes that a smaller value is an improvement while "↑" demonstrates that a larger value is an improvement.

Method	Loss-ArcFace	White	Black	East Asian	South Asian	Average (↑)	STD (↓)	SER (↓)
IMAN [15]	✓	93.92	92.98	90.60	90.98	92.12	1.38	1.55
CosFace [87]	X	95.12	93.93	92.98	92.93	93.74	0.89	1.45
ArcFace [61]	✓	96.18	94.67	93.72	93.98	94.67	0.96	1.64
ACNN [97]	✓	96.12	94.00	93.67	94.55	94.59	0.94	1.63
PFE [98]	✓	96.38	95.17	94.27	94.60	95.10	0.80	1.58
DebFace [99]	✓	95.95	93.67	94.33	94.78	94.68	0.83	1.56
GAC [100]	✓	96.20	94.77	94.87	94.98	95.21	0.58	1.37
RL-RBN [10]	✓	96.27	94.68	94.82	95.00	95.19	0.63	1.43
MBN [101]	✓	96.25	95.38	95.32	94.85	95.45	0.51	1.37
Rethinking [102]	✓	89.1	85.5	71.8	75.8	80.55	7.01	2.59
PCT [103]	✓	97.00	[96.22]	95.73	96.38	96.33	0.52	1.42
Sensitive Loss [20]	X	[97.23]	95.82	[96.50]	[96.95]	[96.63]	0.53	1.51
GABN [104]	✓	95.78	94.71	94.51	95.21	95.05	[0.49]	[1.30]

Accompanying the RFW dataset, Wang et al. [15] provides an initial baseline method for the dataset. This baseline, the Information Maximization Adaptation Network (IMAN), has two main stages: pseudo-adaptation and a custom mutual information loss. The pseudo-adaptation focuses on pre-clustering to obtain initial improvement in the target domain. Then, the mutual information loss uses the distribution of the target classifier to obtain larger decision margins.

The CosFace solution presents a loss function that incorporates a cosine margin to the distances between intra-class and inter-class face representations [87]. This margin increases inter-class pair distances and decreases intra-class pair distances. Although CosFace was released prior to the RFW dataset, results are included from Gong et al. [100] in Table 5 that evaluated the CosFace loss with a ResNet34 architecture.

A pivotal improvement on the RFW task and facial recognition in general is the ArcFace (Additive Angular Margin) loss [61]. Instead of relying on direct distance measurements, the innovative ArcFace loss uses the angle of the arc between the two facial representations. This puts the facial representations along the exterior of the arc in multidimensional space. Inserting this defined embedding representation prior allows for a more robust facial representation. This has become widely adopted across facial recognition with the majority of the following methods within this section using the ArcFace loss as illustrated by the Loss-ArcFace column in Table 5. It is important to note that ArcFace is now a popular loss function used in various applications [105–108].

Along with updating loss functions, there is an additional focus on incorporating conventional methods with deep learning techniques, specifically hand-crafted features. Some of these hand-crafted features are crowd counting, camera angle, camera height, appearance, and scale of the individuals. The ACNN method applies these hand-crafted features to the neural network facial recognition approach [97]. This extra information outperforms a similar-sized CNN without the hand-crafted features. This approach was also released before the RFW dataset, Gong et al. [100] evaluated the ACNN method on the RFW dataset, and we include these results in Table 5.

The use of conventional methods to overcome racial bias in facial recognition shifted towards using probabilistic approaches. The Probabilistic Face Embeddings (PFE) approach learns a Gaussian latent space representation of the face [98]. While most facial recognition approaches use neural networks to separate the multi-dimensional representation of the face, the PFE uses a variational auto-encoder, similar to image generation methods such as latent diffusion models [66], to encode the face into a latent space representation with a mean and a variance. The latent space Gaussian representations are compared to determine whether the facial representations correspond to the same individual. Although this approach is not widely adopted, it remains competitive with other racially aware methods, as seen in Table 5.

Architectural advancements have been developed to further improve facial recognition across race. One such improvement, the debiasing adversarial network (DebFace), uses an image-to-feature encoder, four attribute classifiers, a distribution classifier, and a feature aggregation network [100]. The four classifiers—gender, age, race, and identity—turn potential biases into informed features, thus improving performance across underrepresented groups.

Continuing in architectural improvements, the Group Adaptive Classifier (GAC) method uses an adaptive classification within the network structure to obtain higher accuracies [100]. They use a group of adaptive classifiers that assign the individual to a demographic group. A demographic-specific kernel then performs the final classification. These demographic-specific kernels learn unique racial characteristics, thus improving accuracy.

Recent studies have explored significant enhancements in training methodologies. One notable approach, the Reinforcement Learning-based Race Balance Network (RL-RBN) [10], uses reinforcement learning as a novel method for training facial recognition. They deliberately pick the action, reward, and objective functions to ensure balanced learning across race. The action function permits three outcomes: keeping the margin between classes the same, shifting the margin to a larger value, and shifting the margin to a smaller value. The reward model aims to standardize distances and mitigate skew across racial groups. To achieve this the reward is calculated using the distance between the Caucasians and the race of the individual [10]. The objective function is a deep Q-Learning function [109,110] which learns the optimal policy for the agent [10]. While reinforcement learning is not frequently used in facial recognition tasks, this study underscores the importance of enhancing training methods beyond merely refining datasets, losses, and architectures.

Wang et al. [101] proposes another significant improvement in training methodology with the introduction of the Meta Balanced Network (MBN), a meta-learning method that improves fairness across skin tones. The MBN uses two loss functions: training loss and meta loss. The meta loss weights the training loss to ensure equal weight adjustment across all skin tones during backpropagation. While other studies emphasize the necessity of balanced training data, this approach is able to use skewed datasets without skewing the final result.

Coe and Atay [1] investigates the optimal network architecture to minimize racial bias in facial recognition systems. To demonstrate that each model learns different races in different proportions, they compare AlexNet [111], VGG16 [112], and ResNet50 [113]. Their results demonstrate that VGG16 outperforms both AlexNet and ReseNet50 in terms of accuracy across different races [1]. This indicates that the performance across race varies based on network architecture, despite being trained on the same data. As their approach did not report their results on the RFW dataset, the results are not included in Table 5.

A not-expected approach is seen as the researchers claim that training only on one race is not inherently disadvantageous [102]. They demonstrate that by training only using African faces, they achieved less skew across race than by training with a balanced dataset. They also found that they obtained higher accuracy across race by using additional images for an individual instead of adding more identities. To come to their findings they performed their testing on four recent top facial recognition models: VGGFace2 [43], CenterLoss [59], SphereFace [60], and ArcFace [61]. They note that training on one race decreases the overall size of the dataset and emphasize that having a larger dataset would result in even higher metrics [102]. Their experiments and findings result in a new and unique method for obtaining higher accuracies across race.

Serna et al. [20] proposed Sensitive Loss, a modification of a sensitive triplet generator and the triplet loss function [114]. Their approach emphasized how transfer learning a racially skewed facial recognition model can decrease the skew across race. To demonstrate the performance of the sensitive loss, they evaluated their loss function across three baseline models: VGG-Face [39], ResNet-50 [113], and ArcFace [61]. Their loss greatly improved the Equal Error Rate and decreased the standard deviation across the DiveFace dataset, RFW dataset, and the BUPT-Balancedface dataset.

An additional method returned to the architectural improvements in the Adversarial Information Network (AIN) approach. Here, they minimize the target classifier and maximize the feature extractor. Then, they use a graph neural network to find the likelihood of the target data [115]. As the AIN approach reported the RFW results in a non-conventional method, we do not include the AIN results in Table 5.

Research has shown that networks tend to focus on varying facial regions based on the individual's race. To address this issue, Li et al. [103] introduced the Progressive Cross Transformer (PCT). This innovative approach employs a dual transformer arrecognition process.

Introduced in 2023, the Gradient Attention Balance Network (GABN) is a facial recognition model designed to analyze the same facial regions regardless of the race of the individual [104]. They use attention masks to enforce structured regions of interest, effectively minimizing racial disparities, as illustrated by the results in Table 5.Introduced in 2023, the Gradient Attention Balance Network (GABN) is a facial recognition model designed to analyze the same facial regions regardless of the race of the individual [104]. They use attention masks to enforce structured regions of interest, effectively minimizing racial disparities, as illustrated by the results in Table 5.

5.2. Racial Classification

Various facial recognition approaches require racial classification methods, either directly [10,20,99,101,102,104,115] or indirectly [100,103]. Thus, discussing racial classification methods and their improvements is crucial. In 2014, a review article [54] cited the highest accuracy for identifying race as nearly 99% [116], misleading some to consider race classification as a solved problem. However, this impressive accuracy used 3D imaging techniques to identify race [117], whereas this work focuses exclusively on race identification with monocular images—a significantly more challenging task.

5.2.1. Two-Class Race Classification

Instead of focusing on classifying across many races, initial research focused on distinguishing between two races. One such group focused on distinguishing Black and White individuals in one network and in another network distinguishing Chinese and Non-Chinese [118]. Their network was based on the CIFAR-10 network [119]. For their datasets, they collected images from various sources. From the MORPH-II dataset [120], they used 43,130 face images of Black and White individuals, from the Casia-Webface dataset [37], they used 101,771 images of Black and White individuals, from the CASIA-PEAL dataset [121] they chose 5429 images of Asian individuals, from the FERET dataset [122] they used 3407 images of Black and White individuals [118]. The reported overall accuracy was 100% for identifying Black individuals and 99.4% for White individuals [118]. On the Chinese and non-Chinese classification task, they achieved 91.6% accuracy for identifying Chinese individuals, and 93.5% for non-Chinese individuals. These high accuracies demonstrate a strong ability to identify race in a narrow scope of Chinese and non-Chinese individuals or Black and White individuals.

Some may argue that identifying just a few races is oversimplifying a complex task. Within one race or demographic category, there may be significant racial variation. To explore intra-racial performance, one group of researchers developed a network to identify a face as either from northern India or from southern India. Upon collecting and labeling a custom dataset, the method achieved human-level accuracy but with different error patterns [123]. Their findings demonstrate the ability of neural networks to classify race at a more precise level, even within a specific race.

Vo et al. [124] based their racial recognition model on the VGG architecture [112]. They scraped individuals' profile pictures and race from Facebook. This was done to obtain images at different poses, lighting, accessories, and imaging conditions. They then used a Haar Cascade classifier [125] to crop, and label 6100 faces with 2892 Vietnamese and 3208 images in other races, creating their VNFaces dataset. They obtained an 88.87% overall accuracy using this model [124]. This dataset contains increased variation across lighting, accessories, and image conditions, resulting in a more difficult classification task.

5.2.2. Multiple-Class Race Classification

While various methods focus on differentiating between two races for race classification, many facial recognition models require multiple races for their approach. One method that identifies race across the four labeled races in the UTKFace dataset [42] based their network architecture on ResNet V1 [126] followed by L2 normalization and fully connected layers achieved an average race classification of 90.1% [127].

One set of researchers focused their neural network on identifying the race of individuals that are Chinese, Japanese, or Korean [128]. To collect a dataset to train on, they scrapped Twitter, specifically the followers of Asian celebrities. They used the username and the primary language of the profile description to label the race. Then, their approach predicted the correct race of 78.21% Chinese, 72.80% Japanese, and 73.80% Korean [128], demonstrating great success in race classification while also demonstrating that race classification remains unsolved.

As researchers published the FaceARG dataset, they also trained and compared four unique SOTA convolutional neural networks on the task of recognizing race [12]. They chose to include VGG19 [112], Inception ResNet v2 [126], SE-ResNet24 [129], and MobileNetV3 [130]. The results of each of these four networks are shown in Table 6. Their MobileNetV3 achieved their highest overall F1 score at 96.64 on the four-class human race classification [12]. To test the robustness of their system, they altered the images with experiments including eye blur, eye occlusion, nose blur, nose occlusion, mouth blur, mouth occlusion, grayscale, increasing brightness, decreasing brightness, and image blur. For overall accuracy in identifying race, all robustness experiments maintained over 90% accuracy, except for eye occlusion, which dropped to 80.74% accuracy [12]. All of this demonstrates the ability of CNNs to classify race at a fairly high accuracy, even with some important parts of the face occluded.

Table 6. Race Classification Results: This table presents the results of human race classification obtained by four networks on the FaceARG dataset [12]. The maximum value of each metric within its respective row is highlighted in bold and enclosed in brackets.

Race	Metric	VGG-19	Inception ResNet-v2	SeNet	MobileNetV3
Afro-American	P_r	96.68	96.88	95.27	[96.97]
Afro-American	R_e	97.96	98.20	98.32	[98.44]
Afro-American	F_1	97.32	97.54	96.77	[97.70]
Asian	P_r	98.27	98.43	97.94	[98.52]
Asian	R_e	97.76	97.92	96.96	[98.20]
Asian	F_1	97.32	98.18	97.45	[98.36]
Caucasian	P_r	94.91	95.61	95.43	[96.20]
Caucasian	R_e	94.00	[95.00]	94.28	94.12
Caucasian	F_1	94.45	[95.30]	94.85	95.15

Table 6. Cont.

Race	Metric	VGG-19	Inception ResNet-v2	SeNet	MobileNetV3
Indian	P_r	94.37	94.51	[94.95]	94.89
Indian	R_e	94.52	94.32	94.00	[95.80]
Indian	F_1	94.44	94.41	94.47	[95.34]
Overall	P_r	94.06	96.36	95.90	[96.64]
Overall	R_e	96.06	96.36	95.89	[96.64]
Overall	F_1	96.06	96.36	95.89	[96.64]

5.3. Related Tasks

While there are various network improvements that are being accomplished in facial recognition to decrease the variance across race, other tasks also benefit from focusing on race. One similar task is race, gender, and age classification. In the release of the FairFace dataset, Karkkainen and Joo [13] trained four different classification networks all with the same setup: DLib's face detector [131], a ResNet-34 [113], and the ADAM optimizer [132]. The difference between the four networks was what dataset they were trained on: UTKFace [42], LFWA+, CelebA [133], and their new racially aware dataset, FairFace. They took these four trained networks and evaluated them. The cross-dataset accuracy findings on the White race vs. Not White race are shown in Table 7a for race classification, Table 7b for gender classification, and Table 7c for age classification. They note that the model trained on the FairFace dataset outperforms all others. The results emphasize the benefit that comes from focusing on race while training not only facial recognition or race classification tasks but also gender and age classification. Their findings demonstrate the need for generalization across race on more tasks than facial recognition. We acknowledge that the White vs. Not White definitions are used although the definition of White or Not White will vary across which country the labeler resides in or cultural backgrounds that the labeler has.

Table 7. (a) Race Classification: Race classification accuracies are presented as percentages for White and Not White categories, emphasizing the differences across racial groups [13]. We note that the balanced dataset achieves the highest accuracies for most test datasets. The highest accuracy in each column is highlighted in bold and enclosed in brackets. (b) Gender Classification Across Race: Gender classification accuracies are presented as percentages for White and Not White categories, emphasizing that race has lower accuracies across various tasks [13]. We note that the balanced dataset achieves the highest accuracies for most datasets tested. The highest accuracy in each column is highlighted in bold and enclosed in brackets. (c) Age Classification Across Race: Age classification accuracies are presented as percentages for White and Not White categories, emphasizing that race has lower accuracies across various tasks [13]. The highest accuracy in each column is highlighted in bold and enclosed in brackets. Reprinted/adapted with permission from Ref. [13]. 2021, IEEE.

		(a)		
		Tested on (White Accuracy—Not White Accuracy):		
		FairFace (Balanced)	UTKFace (Unbalanced)	LFWA+ (Unbalanced)
Trained on:	FairFace (Balanced)	[93.7%]–[75.4%]	93.6–80.1%	[97.0%]–[96.0%]
	UTKFace (Unbalanced)	80.0–69.3%	91.8%–[83.9%]	92.5–88.7%
	LFWA+ (Unbalanced)	87.9–54.1%	[94.7%]–38.0%	96.1–86.6%

Table 7. Cont.

		(b)			
		Tested on (White Accuracy—Not White Accuracy):			
		FairFace (Balanced)	UTKFace (Unbalanced)	LFWA+ (Unbalanced)	CelebA (Unbalanced)
Trained on:	FairFace (Balanced)	[94.2%]–[94.4%]	[94.0%]–[93.9%]	92.0%–[93.0%]	[98.1%]–[98.1%]
	UTKFace (Unbalanced)	86.0–82.3%	93.5–92.5%	91.6–90.8%	96.2–96.2%
	LFWA+ (Unbalanced)	76.1–73.8%	84.2–83.3%	[93.0%]–89.4%	94.0%–94.0%
	CelebA (Unbalanced)	81.2–78.1%	88.0–88.6%	90.5–90.1%	97.1–92.1%
		(c)			
		Tested on (White Accuracy—Not White Accuracy):			
		FairFace (Balanced)	UTKFace (Unbalanced)		
Trained on:	FairFace (Balanced)	[59.7%]–[60.7%]	56.5–61.6%		
	UTKFace (Unbalanced)	41.3–41.8%	[57.6%]–[61.7%]		

Another example of benefiting performance based on race is seen with the Inclusive-FaceNet solution. Their model is used to detect face attributes. It does this by using the race and gender representations that are transfer-taught to the model. To transfer-learn race and gender, they train a FaceNet model [83] and extract features from the avgpool layer. This layer learns race and gender. Then, to further learn race, they obtained over 100,000 images from famous individuals [134–136]. Then, after combining these transfer learnings, they obtained higher results in face attribute detection across race and gender than the network without the transfer learnings [137].

Pastaltzidis et al. [138] explored the bias in the RWF-2000 dataset [139], a law enforcement project created for violent activity recognition. They note that certain demographics are over-represented in the training dataset. To counteract this bias, they implemented a unique data augmentation method that force-balances the dataset to be more representative of the population. They achieved this by modifying videos that over-represent minority groups, using body movement tracking to replace the individual with others from a different race. This resulted in a more balanced dataset, and their results show promise for using synthetically generative models to balance various datasets. These examples of network improvements across related tasks demonstrate the improvements that come from focusing on race during trainings.

These three studies demonstrate the benefit of a racially balanced dataset, race classification pre-training, and force balancing a dataset through augmentation are beneficial to more than only facial recognition. These improvements also transfer to other classification and detection tasks by decreasing the disproportionate accuracies between races. This improvement is critical for the integration of systems in real-world applications.

5.4. Intersection of Network Improvements across Race and Gender

Many of the network improvements across human races could also be applied to improving the bias across gender. Our work separates network improvements across race into four categories: loss/training, architecture, dataset modification, and the use of additional data. Each of these four categories not only decreases racial bias but also has been seen to decrease gender bias. The improvement in loss/training can be seen with Conti et al. [140] presenting the use of a von Mises–Fisher mixture model, which takes a trained facial recognition model and trains a shallow network with the fair von

Mises–Fisher loss. The improvement across architecture can be seen with the work of Gwyn and Roy [141], which focuses on analyzing different architectures to identify the optimal architecture for minimizing gender bias. They find that VGG-16 is one of the architectures with the least amount of gender bias. This is the same conclusion that Coe and Atay [1] concluded was optimal for reducing racial bias. From these two studies, we see the VGG-16 network minimizing not only racial bias but also gender bias.

Just as dataset modifications decrease the racial bias in facial recognition, Tian et al. [142] demonstrates that data augmentation affects gender bias as well. Similar results are seen with the use of additional data. The BFW dataset [17], demonstrating that having additional data to balance datasets benefits not only race bias but also gender bias. As the discussion around minimizing racial bias through network improvements begins to grow, the overlap between minimizing gender bias also grows. The decrease in racial bias and gender bias are connected, allowing improvements from one to be modified to benefit the other.

5.5. Discussion on Network Improvements

General trends emerge in the analysis of the varying network improvements for decreasing the skew across race in facial recognition. In Table 8, we classify each improvement into one or more of the following categories: loss/training improvements, architectural changes, dataset modification, and using additional data.

Table 8. Network Improvements Discussion: While there are various improvements that are made in overcoming racial bias in facial recognition, we classify these improvements into four categories: loss/training, architecture, dataset modification, and additional data. We also define which methods are improved from further race classification research. The table is sorted by publication year and then alphabetically by method. The checkmark (✓) defines when it is categorized into each column.

Method	Year	Loss/Training	Architecture	Dataset Modification	Additional Data	Benefits from Race Classification
ACNN [97]	2017				✓	
InclusiveFaceNet [137]	2017		✓		✓	✓
CosFace [87]	2018	✓				
ArcFace [61]	2019	✓				
IMAN [15]	2019	✓	✓			✓
PFE [98]	2019			✓		
DebFace [99]	2020		✓		✓	✓
RL-RBN [10]	2020	✓				✓
GAC [100]	2021		✓			✓
MBN [101]	2021	✓	✓			✓
PCT [103]	2021		✓			✓
Rethinking [102]	2021	✓		✓		✓
Using VGG16 [1]	2021		✓			
AIN [115]	2022		✓			✓
Fairness aware augmentation [138]	2022			✓		✓
Sensitive Loss [20]	2022	✓				✓
GABN [104]	2023	✓	✓			✓

The loss and training improvements began with the CosFace loss [87] and then was built on by the IMAN approach with its custom mutual information loss [15]. But the most commonly used loss for facial recognition, particularly for racially balanced facial recognition, is the ArcFace loss [61]. Other losses have been developed [104]; however, none have been as widely accepted as the ArcFace loss [61]. Along with adapting new loss functions, there was also a focus on improving training approaches such as new attempts to use reinforcement learning [10] or losses that force the network to focus on the same parts of the face regardless of race [104].

Most publications on improvements for mitigating the skew across race for facial recognition focus on improving the architecture of the neural network. Initial methods were built to learn the race and gender initially and then learn the facial recognition task [137]. These methods were followed by having multiple stages of the network to learn the race and the face separately [15] or within the same architecture [99]. Other methods learned a probabilistic latent space representation of the face [98] or compared different popular architectures on the task [1]. Most recently, the contributions have focused on architectures that can compare skin tone [101] and approaches that focus on maintaining the networks focus on the same parts of the face, regardless of race [104,115].

There have also been improvements in modifying the dataset with novel ideas such as only training on one race that improves cross-race results [102] or more common ideas of force balancing datasets [138]. Other approaches have attempted to include previous methodologies, such as using hand-picked features [97] and incorporating different tasks (gender, age, race, and identity) [99].

Overall, many of the methods are centered around inserting prior information within loss functions [15,61,87,104], modifying architectures to learn additional tasks [15,99,101,104,115], and modifying the dataset or incorporating additional data [97,99,102]. Each method contributes to mitigating the skew across race in facial recognition.

6. Future Work

The field of facial recognition focusing on substrata, such as the human race, is a growing field. There are many methods where future work could be created and added upon. As discussed previously, much work has been carried out to create racially balanced datasets. This approach offers multiple benefits. It primarily enhances the ability of a system to achieve high accuracy in realistic, generalized scenarios. This area of research is still lacking as the number and size of racially unbalanced datasets greatly dwarf those of racially balanced datasets. Future work could focus on making larger datasets with the intent to have equal sampling from the stratum of the human race.

Another future work was discussed previously in race transformation. This would be used to take an image of an individual in one race and transfer it to all other races that we are interested in. Then, doing that with all the images for that individual would create a new individual that could be used as an additional training sample. With high quality race transformation, one could take any racially unbalanced dataset and augment the dataset to have an equal distribution across all racial groups. This could be carried out by replacing GAN racial transformation networks with diffusion racial transformation networks. While GANs were originally used as the SOTA generative deep learning approach, diffusion has surpassed GANs in many categories and shows promise for the ability to create a race transformation network [143].

To better aid racially balanced performance across human races, race recognition using monocular images must be improved. With certain strata outperforming other strata in classification, it is difficult to scrap images for races with lower classification accuracies. To create the optimal racially balanced dataset, the race classification of human faces must also be improved.

As this work focuses on comparing racially unbalanced/balanced datasets, balancing datasets through data generation, and network improvements across the human race using monocular cameras there are limitations to our study. Some of these limitations include that bias across datasets is not limited to race, but rather also is connected or even interconnected with other biases such as gender or age. We recognize that gender [62,144,145] and age [146] are not covered in great detail within this survey. Future survey papers could center around the conjugation of race, gender, and age in facial recognition.

7. Conclusions

Understanding bias in deep learning is a widespread and evolving field, presenting complex challenges. We provide an analysis of race imbalance across many popular facial recognition datasets and the increasing trend of new facial recognition datasets to be racially balanced. We discuss the promising attempts to balance datasets through data generation accompanied by a discussion on the impact of data generation. We discuss various network improvements that aim to reduce racial bias in facial recognition systems. These include loss modifications, training methods, architecture improvements, data modification, and incorporating additional data. Finally, we provide a list of future work that researchers can follow. Overall, the skew across race in facial recognition is decreasing but requires further research to mitigate the problem fully.

Author Contributions: Conceptualization, A.S. and D.-J.L.; methodology, A.S.; software, A.S.; validation, A.S., and S.T.; formal analysis, A.S.; investigation, A.S.; resources, D.-J.L.; data curation, A.S.; writing—original draft preparation, A.S.; writing—review and editing, A.S., D.-J.L., S.T. and Z.S.; visualization, A.S.; supervision, D.-J.L.; project administration, D.-J.L.; funding acquisition, D.-J.L. All authors have read and agreed to the published version of the manuscript.

Funding: This research received no external funding.

Data Availability Statement: No new data were created or analyzed in this study. Data sharing is not applicable to this article.

Acknowledgments: During the preparation of this work, the authors used Grammarly, Word Tune, and ChatGPT to rephrase specific key sentences for clarity and grammar. After using these tools/services, the authors reviewed and edited the content as needed and take full responsibility for the content of the publication.

Conflicts of Interest: The authors declare no conflicts of interest.

References

1. Coe, J.; Atay, M. Evaluating impact of race in facial recognition across machine learning and deep learning algorithms. *Computers* **2021**, *10*, 113. [CrossRef]
2. Cavazos, J.G.; Phillips, P.J.; Castillo, C.D.; O'Toole, A.J. Accuracy comparison across face recognition algorithms: Where are we on measuring race bias? *IEEE Trans. Biom. Behav. Identity Sci.* **2020**, *3*, 101–111. [CrossRef] [PubMed]
3. Krishnapriya, K.; Albiero, V.; Vangara, K.; King, M.C.; Bowyer, K.W. Issues related to face recognition accuracy varying based on race and skin tone. *IEEE Trans. Technol. Soc.* **2020**, *1*, 8–20. [CrossRef]
4. Pagano, T.P.; Loureiro, R.B.; Araujo, M.M.; Lisboa, F.V.N.; Peixoto, R.M.; Guimaraes, G.A.d.S.; Santos, L.L.d.; Cruz, G.O.R.; de Oliveira, E.L.S.; Cruz, M.; et al. Bias and unfairness in machine learning models: A systematic literature review. *arXiv* **2022**, arXiv:2202.08176.
5. Parikh, R.B.; Teeple, S.; Navathe, A.S. Addressing bias in artificial intelligence in health care. *JAMA* **2019**, *322*, 2377–2378. [CrossRef] [PubMed]
6. Ntoutsi, E.; Fafalios, P.; Gadiraju, U.; Iosifidis, V.; Nejdl, W.; Vidal, M.E.; Ruggieri, S.; Turini, F.; Papadopoulos, S.; Krasanakis, E.; et al. Bias in data-driven artificial intelligence systems—An introductory survey. *Wiley Interdiscip. Rev. Data Min. Knowl. Discov.* **2020**, *10*, e1356. [CrossRef]
7. Fountain, J.E. The moon, the ghetto and artificial intelligence: Reducing systemic racism in computational algorithms. *Gov. Inf. Q.* **2022**, *39*, 101645. [CrossRef]
8. Abdurrahim, S.H.; Samad, S.A.; Huddin, A.B. Review on the effects of age, gender, and race demographics on automatic face recognition. *Vis. Comput.* **2018**, *34*, 1617–1630. [CrossRef]
9. Suresh, H.; Guttag, J.V. A framework for understanding unintended consequences of machine learning. *arXiv* **2019**, arXiv:1901.10002.
10. Wang, M.; Deng, W. Mitigating bias in face recognition using skewness-aware reinforcement learning. In Proceedings of the IEEE/CVF Conference on Computer Vision and Pattern Recognition, Virtual, 14–19 June 2020; pp. 9322–9331.
11. Morales, A.; Fierrez, J.; Vera-Rodriguez, R.; Tolosana, R. Sensitivenets: Learning agnostic representations with application to face images. *IEEE Trans. Pattern Anal. Mach. Intell.* **2020**, *43*, 2158–2164. [CrossRef]

12. Darabant, A.S.; Borza, D.; Danescu, R. Recognizing Human Races through Machine Learning—A Multi-Network, Multi-Features Study. *Mathematics* **2021**, *9*, 195. [CrossRef]
13. Karkkainen, K.; Joo, J. Fairface: Face attribute dataset for balanced race, gender, and age for bias measurement and mitigation. In Proceedings of the IEEE/CVF Winter Conference on Applications of Computer Vision, Virtual, 5–9 January 2021; pp. 1548–1558.
14. Hupont, I.; Fernández, C. Demogpairs: Quantifying the impact of demographic imbalance in deep face recognition. In Proceedings of the 2019 14th IEEE International Conference on Automatic Face & Gesture Recognition (FG 2019), Lille, France, 14–18 May 2019; pp. 1–7.
15. Wang, M.; Deng, W.; Hu, J.; Tao, X.; Huang, Y. Racial faces in the wild: Reducing racial bias by information maximization adaptation network. In Proceedings of the IEEE/CVF International Conference on Computer Vision, Seoul, Republic of Korea, 27 October–2 November 2019; pp. 692–702.
16. Li, A.; Tan, Z.; Li, X.; Wan, J.; Escalera, S.; Guo, G.; Li, S.Z. CASIA-SURF CeFA: A Benchmark for Multi-modal Cross-ethnicity Face Anti-spoofing. *arXiv* **2020**, arXiv:2003.05136.
17. Robinson, J.P.; Qin, C.; Henon, Y.; Timoner, S.; Fu, Y. Balancing biases and preserving privacy on balanced faces in the wild. *IEEE Trans. Image Process.* **2023**, *32*, 4365–4377. [CrossRef] [PubMed]
18. Ning, X.; Nan, F.; Xu, S.; Yu, L.; Zhang, L. Multi-view frontal face image generation: A survey. *Concurr. Comput. Pract. Exp.* **2023**, *35*, e6147. [CrossRef]
19. Page, M.J.; Moher, D.; Bossuyt, P.M.; Boutron, I.; Hoffmann, T.C.; Mulrow, C.D.; Shamseer, L.; Tetzlaff, J.M.; Akl, E.A.; Brennan, S.E.; et al. PRISMA 2020 explanation and elaboration: Updated guidance and exemplars for reporting systematic reviews. *bmj* **2021**, *372*, n160. [CrossRef] [PubMed]
20. Serna, I.; Morales, A.; Fierrez, J.; Obradovich, N. Sensitive loss: Improving accuracy and fairness of face representations with discrimination-aware deep learning. *Artif. Intell.* **2022**, *305*, 103682. [CrossRef]
21. Samaria, F.S.; Harter, A.C. Parameterisation of a stochastic model for human face identification. In Proceedings of the 1994 IEEE Workshop on Applications of Computer Vision, Sarasota, FL, USA, 5–7 December 1994; pp. 138–142.
22. Yucer, S.; Akçay, S.; Al-Moubayed, N.; Breckon, T.P. Exploring racial bias within face recognition via per-subject adversarially-enabled data augmentation. In Proceedings of the IEEE/CVF Conference on Computer Vision and Pattern Recognition Workshops, Virtual, 14–19 June 2020; pp. 18–19.
23. Merriam-Webster. Race. Available online: https://www.merriam-webster.com/dictionary/race (accessed on 24 May 2024).
24. Merriam-Webster. Ethnicity. Available online: https://www.merriam-webster.com/dictionary/ethnicity (accessed on 24 May 2024).
25. Merriam-Webster. Ethnic. Available online: https://www.merriam-webster.com/dictionary/ethnic (accessed on 24 May 2024).
26. Office of Management and Budget. *Revisions to OMB's Statistical Policy Directive No. 15: Standards for Maintaining, Collecting, and Presenting Federal Data on Race and Ethnicity*; Office of Information and Regulatory Affairs, Office of Management and Budget, Executive Office of the President: Washington, DC, USA, 2024.
27. Howell, A.J.; Buxton, H. Towards unconstrained face recognition from image sequences. In Proceedings of the Second International Conference on Automatic Face and Gesture Recognition, Killington, VT, USA, 14–16 October 1996; pp. 224–229.
28. Huang, G.B.; Mattar, M.; Berg, T.; Learned-Miller, E. Labeled faces in the wild: A database for studying face recognition in unconstrained environments. In Proceedings of the Workshop on faces in 'Real-Life' Images: Detection, Alignment, and Recognition, Marseille, France, 17–20 October 2008.
29. Bae, G.; de La Gorce, M.; Baltrušaitis, T.; Hewitt, C.; Chen, D.; Valentin, J.; Cipolla, R.; Shen, J. Digiface-1m: 1 million digital face images for face recognition. In Proceedings of the IEEE/CVF Winter Conference on Applications of Computer Vision, Waikoloa, HI, USA, 3–7 January 2023; pp. 3526–3535.
30. Shorten, C.; Khoshgoftaar, T.M. A survey on image data augmentation for deep learning. *J. Big Data* **2019**, *6*, 60. [CrossRef]
31. Mehrabi, N.; Morstatter, F.; Saxena, N.; Lerman, K.; Galstyan, A. A survey on bias and fairness in machine learning. *ACM Comput. Surv. (CSUR)* **2021**, *54*, 1–35. [CrossRef]
32. Fisher, R.A. Statistical methods for research workers. In *Breakthroughs in Statistics: Methodology and Distribution*; Springer: Berlin/Heidelberg, Germany; 1970; pp. 66–70.
33. Cowles, M.; Davis, C. On the origins of the .05 level of statistical significance. *Am. Psychol.* **1982**, *37*, 553. [CrossRef]
34. Ortega-Garcia, J.; Fierrez, J.; Alonso-Fernandez, F.; Galbally, J.; Freire, M.R.; Gonzalez-Rodriguez, J.; Garcia-Mateo, C.; Alba-Castro, J.L.; Gonzalez-Agulla, E.; Otero-Muras, E.; et al. The multiscenario multienvironment biosecure multimodal database (bmdb). *IEEE Trans. Pattern Anal. Mach. Intell.* **2009**, *32*, 1097–1111. [CrossRef]
35. Kumar, N.; Berg, A.; Belhumeur, P.N.; Nayar, S. Describable visual attributes for face verification and image search. *IEEE Trans. Pattern Anal. Mach. Intell.* **2011**, *33*, 1962–1977. [CrossRef] [PubMed]
36. Wolf, L.; Hassner, T.; Maoz, I. Face recognition in unconstrained videos with matched background similarity. In Proceedings of the CVPR 2011, Colorado Springs, CO, USA, 21–25 June 2011; pp. 529–534. [CrossRef]
37. Yi, D.; Lei, Z.; Liao, S.; Li, S.Z. Learning face representation from scratch. *arXiv* **2014**, arXiv:1411.7923.
38. Yang, S.; Luo, P.; Loy, C.C.; Tang, X. From facial parts responses to face detection: A deep learning approach. In Proceedings of the IEEE International Conference on Computer Vision, Santiago, Chile, 13–16 December 2015; pp. 3676–3684.
39. Parkhi, O.M.; Vedaldi, A.; Zisserman, A. Deep Face Recognition. In Proceedings of the BMVC 2015—British Machine Vision Conference 2015, British Machine Vision Association, Swansea, UK, 7–10 September 2015.

40. Kemelmacher-Shlizerman, I.; Seitz, S.M.; Miller, D.; Brossard, E. The megaface benchmark: 1 million faces for recognition at scale. In Proceedings of the IEEE Conference on Computer Vision and Pattern Recognition, Las Vegas, NV, USA, 26 June–1 July 2016; pp. 4873–4882.
41. Guo, Y.; Zhang, L.; Hu, Y.; He, X.; Gao, J. Ms-celeb-1m: A dataset and benchmark for large-scale face recognition. In Proceedings of the European Conference on Computer Vision, 2016, Amsterdam, The Netherlands, 11–14 October 2016; Springer: Berlin/Heidelberg, Germany 2016; pp. 87–102.
42. Zhang, Z.; Song, Y.; Qi, H. Age progression/regression by conditional adversarial autoencoder. In Proceedings of the IEEE Conference on Computer Vision and Pattern Recognition, Honolulu, HI, USA, 21–26 July 2017; pp. 5810–5818.
43. Cao, Q.; Shen, L.; Xie, W.; Parkhi, O.M.; Zisserman, A. Vggface2: A dataset for recognising faces across pose and age. In Proceedings of the 2018 13th IEEE International Conference on Automatic Face & Gesture Recognition (FG 2018), Xi'an, China, 15–19 May 2018; pp. 67–74.
44. Maze, B.; Adams, J.; Duncan, J.A.; Kalka, N.; Miller, T.; Otto, C.; Jain, A.K.; Niggel, W.T.; Anderson, J.; Cheney, J.; et al. Iarpa janus benchmark-c: Face dataset and protocol. In Proceedings of the 2018 International Conference on Biometrics (ICB), Gold Coast, QLD, Australia, 20–23 February 2018; pp. 158–165.
45. Grother, P.; Ngan, M.; Hanaoka, K. *Face Recognition Vendor Test (FVRT): Part 3, Demographic Effects*; National Institute of Standards and Technology: Gaithersburg, MD, USA, 2019.
46. Golzar, J.; Tajik, O.; Noor, S. Convenience Sampling. *IJELS* **2022**, *1*, 72–77. [CrossRef]
47. Thomee, B.; Shamma, D.A.; Friedland, G.; Elizalde, B.; Ni, K.; Poland, D.; Borth, D.; Li, L.J. YFCC100M: The new data in multimedia research. *Commun. ACM* **2016**, *59*, 64–73. [CrossRef]
48. Merler, M.; Ratha, N.; Feris, R.S.; Smith, J.R. Diversity in faces. *arXiv* **2019**, arXiv:1901.10436.
49. Birmajer, D.; Blount, B.; Boyd, S.; Einsohn, M.; Helmreich, J.; Kenyon, L.; Lee, S.; Taub, J. Introductory Statistics. 2021. Available online: https://touroscholar.touro.edu/oto/26/ (accessed on 5 April 2024).
50. s-celeb-1m Challenge 3: Face Feature Test/Trillion Pairs. Originally. Available online: http://trillionpairs.deepglint.com/overview (accessed on 14 June 2020).
51. Google. Freebase Data Dumps. Originally. Available online: https://developers.google.com/freebase/data (accessed on 24 May 2024).
52. Face++ Research Toolkit. Available online: https://www.faceplusplus.com/ (accessed on 24 May 2024).
53. Merriam-Webster. Nationality. Available online: https://www.merriam-webster.com/dictionary/nationality (accessed on 24 May 2024).
54. Fu, S.; He, H.; Hou, Z.G. Learning race from face: A survey. *IEEE Trans. Pattern Anal. Mach. Intell.* **2014**, *36*, 2483–2509. [CrossRef] [PubMed]
55. Microsoft Azure. Available online: https://www.azure.cn. (accessed on 24 May 2024).
56. Zhou, E.; Cao, Z.; Yin, Q. Naive-deep face recognition: Touching the limit of LFW benchmark or not? *arXiv* **2015**, arXiv:1501.04690.
57. Baidu Cloud Vision Api. Available online: http://ai.baidu.com/ (accessed on 24 May 2024).
58. Amazon's Rekognition Tool. Available online: https://aws.amazon.com/rekognition/ (accessed on 24 May 2024).
59. Wen, Y.; Zhang, K.; Li, Z.; Qiao, Y. A discriminative feature learning approach for deep face recognition. In Proceedings of the European Conference on Computer Vision, Amsterdam, The Netherlands, 11–14 October 2016; Springer: Berlin/Heidelberg, Germany, 2016; pp. 499–515.
60. Liu, W.; Wen, Y.; Yu, Z.; Li, M.; Raj, B.; Song, L. Sphereface: Deep hypersphere embedding for face recognition. In Proceedings of the IEEE Conference on Computer Vision and Pattern Recognition, Honolulu, HI, USA, 21–26 July 2017; pp. 212–220.
61. Deng, J.; Guo, J.; Xue, N.; Zafeiriou, S. Arcface: Additive angular margin loss for deep face recognition. In Proceedings of the IEEE/CVF Conference on Computer Vision and Pattern Recognition, Long Beach, CA, USA, 16–20 July 2019; pp. 4690–4699.
62. Acien, A.; Morales, A.; Vera-Rodriguez, R.; Bartolome, I.; Fierrez, J. Measuring the gender and ethnicity bias in deep models for face recognition. In Proceedings of the Progress in Pattern Recognition, Image Analysis, Computer Vision, and Applications: 23rd Iberoamerican Congress, CIARP 2018, Madrid, Spain, 19–22 November 2018; Proceedings 23; Springer: Berlin/Heidelberg, Germany, 2019; pp. 584–593.
63. Sarridis, I.; Koutlis, C.; Papadopoulos, S.; Diou, C. Towards Fair Face Verification: An In-depth Analysis of Demographic Biases. *arXiv* **2023**, arXiv:2307.10011.
64. Goodfellow, I.; Pouget-Abadie, J.; Mirza, M.; Xu, B.; Warde-Farley, D.; Ozair, S.; Courville, A.; Bengio, Y. Generative adversarial nets. In Proceedings of the Advances in Neural Information Processing Systems 27 (NIPS 2014), Montreal, QC, Canada, 8–13 December 2014.
65. Sohl-Dickstein, J.; Weiss, E.; Maheswaranathan, N.; Ganguli, S. Deep unsupervised learning using nonequilibrium thermodynamics. In Proceedings of the International Conference on Machine Learning, PMLR, Lille, France, 7–9 July 2015; pp. 2256–2265.
66. Rombach, R.; Blattmann, A.; Lorenz, D.; Esser, P.; Ommer, B. High-resolution image synthesis with latent diffusion models. In Proceedings of the IEEE/CVF Conference on Computer Vision and Pattern Recognition, New Orleans, LA, USA, 19–24 June 2022; pp. 10684–10695.
67. Isola, P.; Zhu, J.Y.; Zhou, T.; Efros, A.A. Image-to-image translation with conditional adversarial networks. In Proceedings of the IEEE Conference on Computer Vision and Pattern Recognition, Honolulu, HI, USA, 21–26 July 2017; pp. 1125–1134.

68. Karras, T.; Laine, S.; Aila, T. A Style-Based Generator Architecture for Generative Adversarial Networks. In Proceedings of the IEEE/CVF Conference on Computer Vision and Pattern Recognition (CVPR), Long Beach, CA, USA, 16–20 June 2019.
69. Jin, Y.; Zhang, J.; Li, M.; Tian, Y.; Zhu, H.; Fang, Z. Towards the automatic anime characters creation with generative adversarial networks. arXiv 2017, arXiv:1708.05509.
70. Croitoru, F.A.; Hondru, V.; Ionescu, R.T.; Shah, M. Diffusion models in vision: A survey. IEEE Trans. Pattern Anal. Mach. Intell. 2023, 45, 10850–10869. [CrossRef]
71. Peebles, W.; Xie, S. Scalable diffusion models with transformers. In Proceedings of the IEEE/CVF International Conference on Computer Vision, Paris, France, 2–6 October 2023; pp. 4195–4205.
72. Radford, A.; Metz, L.; Chintala, S. Unsupervised representation learning with deep convolutional generative adversarial networks. arXiv 2015, arXiv:1511.06434.
73. Jain, N.; Manikonda, L.; Hernandez, A.O.; Sengupta, S.; Kambhampati, S. Imagining an engineer: On GAN-based data augmentation perpetuating biases. arXiv 2018, arXiv:1811.03751.
74. Ting, D.S.W.; Cheung, C.Y.L.; Lim, G.; Tan, G.S.W.; Quang, N.D.; Gan, A.; Hamzah, H.; Garcia-Franco, R.; San Yeo, I.Y.; Lee, S.Y.; et al. Development and validation of a deep learning system for diabetic retinopathy and related eye diseases using retinal images from multiethnic populations with diabetes. JAMA 2017, 318, 2211–2223. [CrossRef] [PubMed]
75. Silberzahn, R.; Uhlmann, E.L.; Martin, D.P.; Anselmi, P.; Aust, F.; Awtrey, E.; Bahník, Š.; Bai, F.; Bannard, C.; Bonnier, E.; et al. Many analysts, one data set: Making transparent how variations in analytic choices affect results. Adv. Methods Pract. Psychol. Sci. 2018, 1, 337–356. [CrossRef]
76. Wheatley, G. Quick Draw; Mathematics Learning: Bethany Beach, DE, USA, 2007
77. Miyato, T.; Koyama, M. cGANs with projection discriminator. arXiv 2018, arXiv:1802.05637.
78. Miyato, T.; Kataoka, T.; Koyama, M.; Yoshida, Y. Spectral normalization for generative adversarial networks. arXiv 2018, arXiv:1802.05957.
79. Gulrajani, I.; Ahmed, F.; Arjovsky, M.; Dumoulin, V.; Courville, A.C. Improved training of wasserstein gans. In Proceedings of the Advances in Neural Information Processing Systems 30 (NIPS 2017), Long Beach, CA, USA, 4–9 December 2017.
80. Dumoulin, V.; Shlens, J.; Kudlur, M. A learned representation for artistic style. arXiv 2016, arXiv:1610.07629.
81. Shmelkin, R.; Wolf, L.; Friedlander, T. Generating master faces for dictionary attacks with a network-assisted latent space evolution. In Proceedings of the 2021 16th IEEE International Conference on Automatic Face and Gesture Recognition (FG 2021), Jodhpur, India, 15–18 December 2021; pp. 1–8.
82. King, D.E. Dlib-ml: A machine learning toolkit. J. Mach. Learn. Res. 2009, 10, 1755–1758.
83. Schroff, F.; Kalenichenko, D.; Philbin, J. Facenet: A unified embedding for face recognition and clustering. In Proceedings of the IEEE Conference on Computer Vision and Pattern Recognition, Boston, MA, USA, 7–12 June 2015; pp. 815–823.
84. Mandis, I.S. Reducing Racial and Gender Bias in Machine Learning and Natural Language Processing Tasks Using a GAN Approach. Int. J. High Sch. Res. 2021, 3, 17–24 [CrossRef]
85. Zhu, J.Y.; Park, T.; Isola, P.; Efros, A.A. Unpaired image-to-image translation using cycle-consistent adversarial networks. In Proceedings of the IEEE International Conference on Computer Vision, Venice, Italy, 22–29 October 2017; pp. 2223–2232.
86. He, L.; Wang, Z.; Li, Y.; Wang, S. Softmax dissection: Towards understanding intra-and inter-class objective for embedding learning. In Proceedings of the AAAI Conference on Artificial Intelligence, New York, NY, USA, 7–12 February 2020; Volume 34, pp. 10957–10964.
87. Wang, H.; Wang, Y.; Zhou, Z.; Ji, X.; Gong, D.; Zhou, J.; Li, Z.; Liu, W. Cosface: Large margin cosine loss for deep face recognition. In Proceedings of the IEEE Conference on Computer Vision and Pattern Recognition, Salt Lake City, UT, USA, 18–22 June 2018; pp. 5265–5274.
88. Ge, J.; Deng, W.; Wang, M.; Hu, J. FGAN: Fan-Shaped GAN for Racial Transformation. In Proceedings of the 2020 IEEE International Joint Conference on Biometrics (IJCB), Houston, TX, USA, 28 September–1 October 2020; pp. 1–7. [CrossRef]
89. Choi, Y.; Choi, M.; Kim, M.; Ha, J.W.; Kim, S.; Choo, J. Stargan: Unified generative adversarial networks for multi-domain image-to-image translation. In Proceedings of the IEEE Conference on Computer Vision and Pattern Recognition, Salt Lake City, UT, USA, 18–22 June 2018; pp. 8789–8797.
90. Kim, Y.H.; Nam, S.H.; Hong, S.B.; Park, K.R. GRA-GAN: Generative adversarial network for image style transfer of Gender, Race, and age. Expert Syst. Appl. 2022, 198, 116792. [CrossRef]
91. Kim, Y.H.; Lee, M.B.; Nam, S.H.; Park, K.R. Enhancing the accuracies of age estimation with heterogeneous databases using modified CycleGAN. IEEE Access 2019, 7, 163461–163477. [CrossRef]
92. Kim, Y.H.; Nam, S.H.; Park, K.R. Enhanced cycle generative adversarial network for generating face images of untrained races and ages for age estimation. IEEE Access 2020, 9, 6087–6112. [CrossRef]
93. Jain, A.; Memon, N.; Togelius, J. Zero-shot racially balanced dataset generation using an existing biased stylegan2. In Proceedings of the 2023 IEEE International Joint Conference on Biometrics (IJCB), Ljubljana, Slovenia, 25–28 September 2023; pp. 1–18.
94. Sumsion, A.; Torrie, S.; Sun, Z.; Lee, D.J. Overcoming deep learning subclass imbalances: Comparing the transfer of identity across a racial transformation. Electron. Imaging 2023, 35, 1–6. [CrossRef]
95. Yang, C.; Lv, Z. Gender based face aging with cycle-consistent adversarial networks. Image Vis. Comput. 2020, 100, 103945. [CrossRef]

96. Lui, N.; Chia, B.; Berrios, W.; Ross, C.; Kiela, D. Leveraging Diffusion Perturbations for Measuring Fairness in Computer Vision. In Proceedings of the AAAI Conference on Artificial Intelligence, Vancouver, BC, Canada, 20–27 February 2024; Volume 38, pp. 14220–14228.
97. Kang, D.; Dhar, D.; Chan, A. Incorporating side information by adaptive convolution. In Proceedings of the Advances in Neural Information Processing Systems 30 (NIPS 2017), Long Beach, CA, USA, 4–9 December 2017.
98. Shi, Y.; Jain, A.K. Probabilistic face embeddings. In Proceedings of the IEEE/CVF International Conference on Computer Vision, Seoul, Republic of Korea, 27 October–2 November 2019; pp. 6902–6911.
99. Gong, S.; Liu, X.; Jain, A.K. Jointly de-biasing face recognition and demographic attribute estimation. In Proceedings of the Computer Vision–ECCV 2020: 16th European Conference, Glasgow, UK, 23–28 August 2020; Proceedings, Part XXIX 16; Springer: Berlin/Heidelberg, Germany, 2020; pp. 330–347.
100. Gong, S.; Liu, X.; Jain, A.K. Mitigating face recognition bias via group adaptive classifier. In Proceedings of the IEEE/CVF Conference on Computer Vision and Pattern Recognition, Virtual, 19–25 June 2021; pp. 3414–3424.
101. Wang, M.; Zhang, Y.; Deng, W. Meta balanced network for fair face recognition. *IEEE Trans. Pattern Anal. Mach. Intell.* **2021**, *44*, 8433–8448. [CrossRef] [PubMed]
102. Gwilliam, M.; Hegde, S.; Tinubu, L.; Hanson, A. Rethinking common assumptions to mitigate racial bias in face recognition datasets. In Proceedings of the IEEE/CVF International Conference on Computer Vision, Virtual, 11–17 October 2021; pp. 4123–4132.
103. Li, Y.; Sun, Y.; Cui, Z.; Shan, S.; Yang, J. Learning fair face representation with progressive cross transformer. *arXiv* **2021**, arXiv:2108.04983.
104. Huang, L.; Wang, M.; Liang, J.; Deng, W.; Shi, H.; Wen, D.; Zhang, Y.; Zhao, J. Gradient attention balance network: Mitigating face recognition racial bias via gradient attention. In Proceedings of the IEEE/CVF Conference on Computer Vision and Pattern Recognition, Vancouver, BC, Canada, 18–22 June 2023; pp. 38–47.
105. Li, Z.; Liu, F.; Yang, W.; Peng, S.; Zhou, J. A survey of convolutional neural networks: Analysis, applications, and prospects. *IEEE Trans. Neural Netw. Learn. Syst.* **2021**, *33*, 6999–7019. [CrossRef] [PubMed]
106. Chan, E.R.; Lin, C.Z.; Chan, M.A.; Nagano, K.; Pan, B.; De Mello, S.; Gallo, O.; Guibas, L.J.; Tremblay, J.; Khamis, S.; et al. Efficient geometry-aware 3d generative adversarial networks. In Proceedings of the IEEE/CVF Conference on Computer Vision and Pattern Recognition, New Orleans, LA, USA, 19–24 June 2022; pp. 16123–16133.
107. Chen, S.; Wang, C.; Chen, Z.; Wu, Y.; Liu, S.; Chen, Z.; Li, J.; Kanda, N.; Yoshioka, T.; Xiao, X.; et al. Wavlm: Large-scale self-supervised pre-training for full stack speech processing. *IEEE J. Sel. Top. Signal Process.* **2022**, *16*, 1505–1518. [CrossRef]
108. Wang, M.; Deng, W. Deep face recognition: A survey. *Neurocomputing* **2021**, *429*, 215–244. [CrossRef]
109. Mnih, V.; Kavukcuoglu, K.; Silver, D.; Rusu, A.A.; Veness, J.; Bellemare, M.G.; Graves, A.; Riedmiller, M.; Fidjeland, A.K.; Ostrovski, G.; et al. Human-level control through deep reinforcement learning. *Nature* **2015**, *518*, 529–533. [CrossRef]
110. Watkins, C.J.; Dayan, P. Q-learning. *Mach. Learn.* **1992**, *8*, 279–292. [CrossRef]
111. Krizhevsky, A.; Sutskever, I.; Hinton, G.E. Imagenet classification with deep convolutional neural networks. In Proceedings of the Advances in Neural Information Processing Systems 25 (NIPS 2012), Lake Tahoe, NV, USA, 3–6 December 2012.
112. Simonyan, K.; Zisserman, A. Very deep convolutional networks for large-scale image recognition. *arXiv* **2014**, arXiv:1409.1556.
113. He, K.; Zhang, X.; Ren, S.; Sun, J. Deep residual learning for image recognition. In Proceedings of the IEEE Conference on Computer Vision and Pattern Recognition, Las Vegas, NV, USA, 26 June–1 July 2016; pp. 770–778.
114. Hoffer, E.; Ailon, N. Deep metric learning using triplet network. In Proceedings of the Similarity-Based Pattern Recognition: Third International Workshop, SIMBAD 2015, Copenhagen, Denmark, 12–14 October 2015; Proceedings 3; Springer: Berlin/Heidelberg, Germany, 2015; pp. 84–92.
115. Wang, M.; Deng, W. Adaptive Face Recognition Using Adversarial Information Network. *IEEE Trans. Image Process.* **2022**, *31*, 4909–4921. [CrossRef]
116. Manesh, F.S.; Ghahramani, M.; Tan, Y.P. Facial part displacement effect on template-based gender and ethnicity classification. In Proceedings of the 2010 11th International Conference on Control Automation Robotics & Vision, Singapore, 7–10 December 2010; pp. 1644–1649.
117. Toderici, G.; O'malley, S.M.; Passalis, G.; Theoharis, T.; Kakadiaris, I.A. Ethnicity-and gender-based subject retrieval using 3-D face-recognition techniques. *Int. J. Comput. Vis.* **2010**, *89*, 382–391. [CrossRef]
118. Wang, W.; He, F.; Zhao, Q. Facial ethnicity classification with deep convolutional neural networks. In Proceedings of the Chinese Conference on Biometric Recognition, Chengdu, China, 14–16 October 2016; pp. 176–185.
119. Krizhevsky, A.; Hinton, G. Convolutional deep belief networks on cifar-10. *Unpubl. Manuscr.* **2010**, *40*, 1–9.
120. Ricanek, K.; Tesafaye, T. Morph: A longitudinal image database of normal adult age-progression. In Proceedings of the 7th International Conference on Automatic Face and Gesture Recognition (FGR06), Southamtpon, UK, 10–12 April 2006; pp. 341–345.
121. Gao, W.; Cao, B.; Shan, S.; Chen, X.; Zhou, D.; Zhang, X.; Zhao, D. The CAS-PEAL large-scale Chinese face database and baseline evaluations. *IEEE Trans. Syst. Man Cybern.-Part A Syst. Hum.* **2007**, *38*, 149–161.
122. Phillips, P.J.; Moon, H.; Rizvi, S.A.; Rauss, P.J. The FERET evaluation methodology for face-recognition algorithms. *IEEE Trans. Pattern Anal. Mach. Intell.* **2000**, *22*, 1090–1104. [CrossRef]
123. Katti, H.; Arun, S. Can you tell where in India I am from? Comparing humans and computers on fine-grained race face classification. *arXiv* **2017**, arXiv:1703.07595.

124. Vo, T.; Nguyen, T.; Le, C. Race recognition using deep convolutional neural networks. *Symmetry* **2018**, *10*, 564. [CrossRef]
125. Lyons, M.; Akamatsu, S.; Kamachi, M.; Gyoba, J. Coding facial expressions with gabor wavelets. In Proceedings of the Proceedings Third IEEE International Conference on Automatic Face and Gesture Recognition, Nara, Japan, 14–16 April 1998; pp. 200–205.
126. Szegedy, C.; Ioffe, S.; Vanhoucke, V.; Alemi, A.A. Inception-v4, inception-resnet and the impact of residual connections on learning. In Proceedings of the Thirty-first AAAI Conference on Artificial Intelligence, San Francisco, CA, USA, 4–9 February 2017.
127. Das, A.; Dantcheva, A.; Bremond, F. Mitigating bias in gender, age and ethnicity classification: A multi-task convolution neural network approach. In Proceedings of the European Conference on Computer Vision (ECCV) Workshops, Munich, Germany, 8–14 September 2018.
128. Wang, Y.; Feng, Y.; Liao, H.; Luo, J.; Xu, X. Do they all look the same? Deciphering chinese, japanese and koreans by fine-grained deep learning. In Proceedings of the 2018 IEEE Conference on Multimedia Information Processing and Retrieval (MIPR), Miami, FL, USA, 10–12 April 2018; pp. 39–44.
129. Hu, J.; Shen, L.; Sun, G. Squeeze-and-excitation networks. In Proceedings of the IEEE Conference on Computer Vision and Pattern Recognition, Salt Lake City, UT, USA, 18–22 June 2018; pp. 7132–7141.
130. Howard, A.; Sandler, M.; Chu, G.; Chen, L.C.; Chen, B.; Tan, M.; Wang, W.; Zhu, Y.; Pang, R.; Vasudevan, V.; et al. Searching for mobilenetv3. In Proceedings of the IEEE/CVF International Conference on Computer Vision, Seoul, Republic of Korea, 27 October–2 November 2019; pp. 1314–1324.
131. King, D.E. Max-Margin Object Detection. *arXiv* **2015**, arXiv:1502.00046.
132. Kingma, D.P.; Ba, J. Adam: A method for stochastic optimization. *arXiv* **2014**, arXiv:1412.6980.
133. Liu, Z.; Luo, P.; Wang, X.; Tang, X. Deep learning face attributes in the wild. In Proceedings of the IEEE International Conference on Computer Vision, Santiago, Chile, 13–16 December 2015; pp. 3730–3738.
134. Vrandečić, D.; Krötzsch, M. Wikidata: A free collaborative knowledgebase. *Commun. ACM* **2014**, *57*, 78–85. [CrossRef]
135. Rothe, R.; Timofte, R.; Van Gool, L. Deep expectation of real and apparent age from a single image without facial landmarks. *Int. J. Comput. Vis.* **2018**, *126*, 144–157. [CrossRef]
136. Somandepalli, K. *Prediction Race from Face for Movie Data*; University of Southern California: Los Angeles, CA, USA, 2017.
137. Ryu, H.J.; Adam, H.; Mitchell, M. Inclusivefacenet: Improving face attribute detection with race and gender diversity. *arXiv* **2017**, arXiv:1712.00193.
138. Pastaltzidis, I.; Dimitriou, N.; Quezada-Tavarez, K.; Aidinlis, S.; Marquenie, T.; Gurzawska, A.; Tzovaras, D. Data augmentation for fairness-aware machine learning: Preventing algorithmic bias in law enforcement systems. In Proceedings of the 2022 ACM Conference on Fairness, Accountability, and Transparency, Seoul, Republic of Korea, 21–24 June 2022; pp. 2302–2314.
139. Cheng, M.; Cai, K.; Li, M. RWF-2000: An open large scale video database for violence detection. In Proceedings of the 2020 25th International Conference on Pattern Recognition (ICPR), Milan, Italy, 10–15 January 2021; pp. 4183–4190.
140. Conti, J.R.; Noiry, N.; Clemencon, S.; Despiegel, V.; Gentric, S. Mitigating gender bias in face recognition using the von mises-fisher mixture model. In Proceedings of the International Conference on Machine Learning, PMLR, Baltimore, MD, USA, 17–23 July 2022; pp. 4344–4369.
141. Gwyn, T.; Roy, K. Examining Gender Bias of Convolutional Neural Networks via Facial Recognition. *Future Internet* **2022**, *14*, 375. [CrossRef]
142. Tian, F.; Liu, W.; Zhao, S.; Liu, J. Face Recognition Fairness Assessment based on Data Augmentation: An Empirical Study. In Proceedings of the 2022 IEEE 22nd International Conference on Software Quality, Reliability, and Security Companion (QRS-C), Guangzhou, China, 5–9 December 2022; pp. 315–318.
143. Avrahami, O.; Fried, O.; Lischinski, D. Blended latent diffusion. *ACM Trans. Graph. (TOG)* **2023**, *42*, 1–11. [CrossRef]
144. Palmer, M.A.; Brewer, N.; Horry, R. Understanding gender bias in face recognition: Effects of divided attention at encoding. *Acta Psychol.* **2013**, *142*, 362–369. [CrossRef] [PubMed]
145. Ng, C.B.; Tay, Y.H.; Goi, B.M. A review of facial gender recognition. *Pattern Anal. Appl.* **2015**, *18*, 739–755. [CrossRef]
146. Terhörst, P.; Kolf, J.N.; Huber, M.; Kirchbuchner, F.; Damer, N.; Moreno, A.M.; Fierrez, J.; Kuijper, A. A comprehensive study on face recognition biases beyond demographics. *IEEE Trans. Technol. Soc.* **2021**, *3*, 16–30. [CrossRef]

Disclaimer/Publisher's Note: The statements, opinions and data contained in all publications are solely those of the individual author(s) and contributor(s) and not of MDPI and/or the editor(s). MDPI and/or the editor(s) disclaim responsibility for any injury to people or property resulting from any ideas, methods, instructions or products referred to in the content.

MDPI AG
Grosspeteranlage 5
4052 Basel
Switzerland
Tel.: +41 61 683 77 34

Electronics Editorial Office
E-mail: electronics@mdpi.com
www.mdpi.com/journal/electronics

Disclaimer/Publisher's Note: The title and front matter of this reprint are at the discretion of the Guest Editor. The publisher is not responsible for their content or any associated concerns. The statements, opinions and data contained in all individual articles are solely those of the individual Editor and contributors and not of MDPI. MDPI disclaims responsibility for any injury to people or property resulting from any ideas, methods, instructions or products referred to in the content.

www.ingramcontent.com/pod-product-compliance
Lightning Source LLC
LaVergne TN
LVHW072315090526
838202LV00019B/2287